2000

Legal Executions in New England

ALSO BY
DANIEL ALLEN HEARN

Legal Executions in New York State:
A Comprehensive Reference, 1639–1963
(McFarland, 1997)

LEGAL EXECUTIONS
IN NEW ENGLAND

A Comprehensive Reference,
1623–1960

by

Daniel Allen Hearn

McFarland & Company, Inc., Publishers
Jefferson, North Carolina, and London

British Library Cataloguing-in-Publication data are available

Library of Congress Cataloguing-in-Publication Data

Hearn, Daniel Allen, 1958–
    Legal executions in New England : a comprehensive reference,
1623–1960 / by Daniel Allen Hearn.
       p. cm.
    Includes bibliographical references and index.
    ISBN 0-7864-0670-4 (library binding : 50# alkaline paper) ∞
    1. Executions and executioners — New York (State) — History —
Chronology.   I. Title.
HV8699.U5H388   1999
364.66'0974 — dc21   98-49841
                                                    CIP

Manufactured in the United States of America

McFarland & Company, Inc., Publishers
  Box 611, Jefferson, North Carolina 28640

This book is dedicated to the innocent victims,
lest it be only the guilty who acquire a place in history

Contents

Preface

Capital punishment has been a transcendent feature of American jurisprudence for nearly 400 years. It has also been hotly debated by Americans for an equal length of time. New England is one region of the United States where that controversy has been especially acute. Since the U.S. Supreme Court allowed the resumption of the death penalty in 1976 (after a nine-year hiatus) all six of the New England states (Connecticut, Maine, Massachusetts, New Hampshire, Rhode Island and Vermont) have seen attempts to restore that form of punishment for certain serious crimes. The success and failure of those attempts at reinstatement have been varied. As of this writing only Connecticut and New Hampshire have actually passed laws for a limited resumption of capital punishment. In Massachusetts an effort at restoration recently failed by only one vote. Rhode Island enacted a narrowly defined statute after more than a century of total abolition only to have it invalidated by the State judiciary. Efforts to bring back the death penalty in Maine and Vermont have so far proven unsuccessful. As of this time (1999) only Connecticut has prisoners who are actually awaiting execution. However two generations have passed since the last time that State — and the New England region as a whole — took the life of a condemned person.

One aspect of this ongoing controversy has been a desire by both Abolitionists and Proponents of capital punishment to cite historical data to either support their respective positions or to belittle that of their opposition. This has resulted in the circulation of much misinformation — primarily because there has not been (until now) a reliable reference source for each of the hundreds of legal executions which were carried out in New England throughout that region's history. This book attempts to fill that void by providing a reliable and unbiased record of just exactly who was executed in New England and what those persons were said to have done to have such a fate thrust upon them. Each case has been written up on an individual basis and strives to include as much information as possible about its respective circumstances without being unduly prolix. Data regarding each defendant's name, age, gender, occupation and ethnicity are provided wherever the source materials for that case have contained such information. There are further data on the method and location of each execution and whether those events were carried out in public, private or semi-private surroundings.

In some cases it is also reported whether the facts thereof contributed to the ongoing debate over capital punishment.

Researching this book required more than ten years of careful study. Fortunately, original source materials have proven to be abundant in New England. Unlike the cases of some other regions of the United States, the court records and newspaper files of New England have come down to the present time fairly intact. There was also a thriving trade there in so-called "gallows literature"; from the 17th century on New England printers turned out numerous books and pamphlets on true crime topics, many of which survive in the archives of that region and beyond.

One thing which became apparent during the gathering of information for this book was the fact that the New England region (when compared to some other areas of the country) practiced unusual restraint in the imposition of capital punishment. Some offenses which were nominally capital crimes according to statute (such as blasphemy, idolatry, perjury and the non-fatal smiting of one's parents) never resulted in even one execution. Similarly, some crimes which were capital in other regions of the country (such as coining, forgery, kidnapping and horse theft) were never punished capitally in New England. Contrary to popular belief, those convicted of witchcraft were never *burned* in New England. Nor were pirates ever bound to tide stakes and drowned by rising water. There have indeed been cases where innocent persons were put to death but there have also been cases where purportedly innocent persons were undeniably guilty. Perhaps one of the most striking facts to be revealed by this compilation is that defendants of African ancestry were never singled out for capital punishment in New England. For instance, of the 160 persons legally executed in Connecticut, only 16 or exactly 10 percent were of African ethnicity — hardly a lopsided record with such persons as the predominant victims. Similarly, of the 65 persons executed in Massachusetts during the 20th century only *two* were African American. Such figures do not support the popular notion that persons of African heritage were disproportionately on the receiving end of capital punishment in New England.

Court records and contemporary news accounts have been my primary sources of information. For many of the earlier cases diaries and handwritten journals have also been of use. Second-hand sources such as published histories have been handled with extreme caution due to their varying degrees of accuracy. In some cases I have had to peel away centuries of folklore until only the naked facts remained. In other cases I have had to expose errors, censorship and revisionism.

My acknowledgments are few because I myself did all of the research for this book. I worked on my own time and at my own expense. However I would be remiss if I did not express my gratitude to those individuals and institutions whose cooperation were instrumental in bringing about the successful completion of my fact-finding mission. First, I must mention the American Antiquarian Society (located at Worcester, Massachusetts), whose incomparable holdings of early New England newspapers and other literature (such as books, pamphlets and broadsides) were a priceless source of information. I am especially indebted to Russell Martin, keeper and guardian of the Society's newspaper collection, who assiduously provided me with many rare and fragile volumes that are still in their original form and are yet to be microfilmed. In addition, Russell patiently endured my rather annoying insistence on repeated double-checking and cross-checking of contemporary news accounts.

Another gentleman to whom I am indebted is Stephen Grimes of the Supreme Court Judicial Records Center in Pawtucket, Rhode Island. He has not only been instrumental in rescuing most of that state's early court records from decades of neglect but also ferreted out for me many original documents which had not been touched by human hands for more than a century.

Lastly and unreservedly I must honorably mention my close friend and mentor, Major Watt Espy, Jr., of Headland, Alabama, a dedicated historian and lover of the truth who first aroused my interest in the subject of this book and who has ever been an inspiration to me. Widely regarded as America's foremost authority on executed persons, Espy has patiently endured my, at times, obtrusive manner even in spite of our differing views on the death penalty. Although I did not ask him to supply me with information for this book, I would have found the task of writing it impossible without Espy's example.

Lastly I must say that although I do have a personal opinion on the matter of capital punishment, I have *not* sought to use this book as a pulpit to further that opinion. It is my purpose to simply present the facts and let the record speak for itself. Readers may draw their own conclusions.

Persons Executed and Their Crimes

(*Listed Chronologically*)

1623

Unidentified Man, white, age unknown. *Larceny.* The crime was committed on an unknown date near Weymouth, Massachusetts. The first mention of a legal execution in the New England region dates from the winter of 1623. Some months earlier, an ill-fated colony was established at a place called *Wessaguscus*, now Weymouth, about 25 miles north of Plymouth. The settlement was the brainchild of a London merchant named Thomas Weston. Seeking to emulate the nearby Plymouth colony, Weston recruited about 60 rather low class men and outfitted them for his enterprise. Under the leadership of one Richard Greene (a brother-in-law to Weston), this company came ashore in the summer of 1622. Almost from the start, things began to go wrong. Worst of all, Richard Greene was a poor diplomat; he alienated the resident Native Americans with the result that they refused to trade with his people. By the time winter came around there was great scarcity among the newcomers. Low on ammunition, Greene and his men were unable to bring in enough game to feed themselves. Some of the men then began stealing from the

Native American corn cribs. The owners of the corn were upset by this and they demanded that the thieves be punished. Not daring to risk a war over the matter, Greene offered to surrender a man who he had identified as a corn thief. The reply of the Native Americans was a demand that Greene himself see justice done. Accordingly, as the highest authority in the tiny colony, Greene ordered that the thief be hanged. So it was done at Weymouth in January 1623.

1630

John Billington, white, age 40. *Murder.* The crime was committed on an unknown date near Plymouth, Massachusetts. This offender had been among the original passengers aboard the *Mayflower* when it made its initial landing in 1620. He was not a Pilgrim in good standing. Governor Bradford described Billington as the head of one of the "profanest families" in the colony. He was an outspoken malcontent who was frequently in trouble. After nine years of contentious coexistence with his neighbors, Billington finally went too far when he deliberately gunned down one of them. The victim was a "young man" named John Newcomen (white) one among many with whom Billington had quarreled. It so happened that Billington was out hunting one day when he caught sight of Newcomen. The latter saw Billington in his path armed with a blunderbuss. So he hid behind a tree. Billington took a shot at him, inflicting a nasty shoulder wound. Infection and poor medical attention combined to make the wound a fatal one. Since this was the first capital case to arise in the Plymouth colony the officials thereof sought the advice of their colleagues in Boston. The matter was duly considered and it was decided that the death penalty was appropriate under the circumstances. Billington was accordingly hanged at Plymouth on or about September 30, 1630.

1637

William Schooler, white, age unknown. *Murder.* The crime was committed on an unknown date in Essex County, Massachusetts. This man had once been a London wine merchant. Scandals in his personal life obliged him to leave England and he eventually made his way to the colony of Massachusetts. One day Schooler's attention was drawn to an advertisement posted by a young woman of Newbury. She was seeking a guide to take her through some unfamiliar terrain. Schooler answered the ad and it was agreed that he act as the woman's guide for a fixed sum of money. Accordingly Schooler and the woman set about their journey. It was the last the woman was ever seen alive. Schooler returned to his home sooner than expected and told his roommate that he had left the woman at a point near her destination. Suspicion being aroused, Schooler was closely questioned. When no further evidence was forthcoming Schooler was released. Several months later an Indian found the badly decom-

posed body of the woman. Her clothes were laying next to her in a pile and it was from them that she was identified as one Mary Sholy (white, age unknown), the same person who had hired William Schooler. This led to Schooler's rearrest. Then a chain of circumstantial evidence developed: the body was found in a place well off the route to Miss Sholy's known destination; it looked as if she had been deliberately led astray. It was also recalled that Schooler was flush with money when he returned home from the trip— more money than his stated fee. There were suspicious bloodstains on Schooler's clothes which he claimed to be pigeon blood. Scratches on Schooler's face had also drawn attention at the time. Then there was a dubitable story that Schooler had told about meeting a bear soon after he had parted company with the decedent. By his own admission, he had made no effort to assist the woman under such circumstances. Worst of all, Schooler broke jail while awaiting trial thus making a bad impression even worse. It was strongly suspected that Schooler had led Mary Sholy into the wilderness with an intention of doing harm to her. Few doubted that he had robbed and murdered the woman. The added fact that her body was found nude led many to suspect that Schooler had also raped the woman. A jury believed the worst when it was shown that Schooler had agreed to guide Miss Sholy through a region of which he himself had no prior experience. In addition to that, the victim had been found in a very remote place— hardly the kind of spot where a well-intentioned guide would leave a woman alone. Schooler admitted that his services as a guide were substandard. However he denied robbery, rape and murder. He was hanged at Boston on September 28, 1637.

John Williams, white, age unknown. *Murder.* The crime was committed on an unknown date near Salem, Massachusetts.

This man was a ship carpenter who got into trouble for stealing and was locked up in a loghouse which served as the Essex County jail. There he conspired with another prisoner named John Hoddy (white, age unknown) to escape. The two men accordingly broke their fetters and dug their way out of the loghouse. Then they fled into the wilderness. On the following night they made camp near a pond. It was there where Williams turned on his companion and struck him down with a rock. Then he took the decedent's clothes even though they were soaked with blood. Williams dried the bloody clothes and then put them on. Then he wandered into Ipswich where he immediately drew attention to himself. Suspicious locals arrested Williams and kept him in custody. A week later a herdsman found the body of John Hoddy. The fact that the dead man was naked established a link with the clothes worn by Williams. A short time later both men were identified as escapees. At that point Williams confessed. He was brought to Boston and there convicted of capital murder. The penalty was death by hanging. On September 28, 1637, that sentence was carried out.

1638

Arthur Peach, Thomas Jackson and **Richard Stinnings,** whites, ages about 22. *Murder.* The crime was committed on an unknown date in Bristol County, Massachusetts. Arthur Peach, described as "a lusty young man," was the catalyst of the crime which brought himself and two companions to the gallows. Originally an indentured servant, Peach had volunteered for military service during the Pequot War of 1637. He was duly enlisted and saw much action. Having traveled in the course of the Pequot War, he was loath to return to the mundane life of a servant. He made a plan to run away and seek a new life in the Dutch settlements far to the west. These plans took on added urgency when Peach ran up debts and got a girl pregnant. He accordingly got together with three other malcontents and set out on a westward trek. Indian paths brought the runaways deep into the territory of the Narragansett tribe. There they made camp one evening and encountered a Narragansett brave who was returning home from a visit to a trading post. The white men invited the Native American man to share their campfire. Unaware of evil intentions, the lone traveler accepted the offer. Then in an unguarded moment the man was run through the body with a rapier and left for dead. He was also robbed of his trade goods, consisting of three jackets and five belts of wampum. The victim of this crime lived long enough to reach a Narragansett village. There he told of his misfortune. The headman of the village sent warriors in pursuit of the murderers and all four were captured. They were not dealt with summarily because the Narragansetts were bound by treaty to turn over to English authority any renegade servants they caught. The four prisoners were accordingly brought to Plymouth and there charged with the murder of the Native American trader. Politics required that a special example be made of them. All four were sentenced to death and representatives of the Narragansett tribe were invited to witness the executions. Accordingly on September 4, 1638, the above-named trio were hanged at Plymouth. The fourth condemned man (one Daniel Cross by name), made a successful jailbreak and eluded capture. When the triple execution had been carried out the Narragansetts declared themselves satisfied with the white man's justice.

Dorothy Talbye, white, age unknown. *Murder.* The crime was committed on an unknown date at Salem, Massachusetts. This female offender lived at Salem with her husband, John Talbye, and four children. The family was one of the humblest in the community. Life was not easy for them. John Talbye, a man of slight build, was especially hard put to till his land and provide his family with the basic necessities of life. Church services provided the only diversion the Talbyes knew. Dorothy in particular sought solace through prayer. However when her prayers went unanswered, Dorothy grew disillusioned. Then a change came over her: she began breaking the sabbath and acting irrationally. She picked quarrels with neighbors and clergy alike. She even went to the extreme of naming an infant daughter "Difficult Talbye." Matters went from bad to worse in the Talbye household as Dorothy's depression deepened. The next to suffer was her husband. Dorothy took to physically attacking the man with her fists and also with household objects. She refused to cook, sew or clean her house, claiming that God had commanded her to eschew all domestic duties. All who sought to reason with Dorothy were contemptuously disregarded. Eventually Dorothy found herself arraigned in a court of law for assaulting her husband. She also got herself ex-communicated from the Salem church. Dorothy's condition continued to deteriorate. Barred from the church, despised by her neighbors and crushed by poverty, she assailed her husband even more fiercely than before. As a result, Dorothy was again brought to court and there censured for conduct unbecoming a wife and mother. Then she was sent to the whipping post. The lash had its desired effect and for a while Dorothy behaved in a civil manner. However as summer yielded to autumn she slipped into her former ways. The prospect of another hard winter was more than her fragile mind could bear. In November her mind snapped for good. She imagined that her daughter, Difficult Talbye, would be better off dead than alive. So she attacked the little girl and broke her

neck. The law promptly pounced on Dorothy Talbye. She was charged with "The unnatural and untimely death of her daughter." She freely admitted the crime and said that her motive sprang from a pathetic desire to save the child from a life of poverty. Oddly however, she refused to enter a plea to her indictment and it was only after an exasperated court threatened her with torture that she entered a plea of "guilty." A full trial was then deferred and sentence of death was pronounced. When asked if she had anything to say, Dorothy replied that she preferred to be executed by the ax instead of the rope. On December 10, 1638, this troubled woman was taken from the jail at Boston and brought to the gallows. She wore a veil over her face to spite the spectators. She paid no attention to clergymen. She had to be forcibly led to the noose and forcibly pinioned. All the while she remained silent but in a final gesture she snatched the veil from her face. Then she was hanged with her features exposed.

1639

Nepaupauck, Native American, age unknown. *Murder.* The crimes were committed in 1637 in Connecticut. This offender was captured by Indians who were allied with the English and brought as a prisoner to New Haven. There he was charged with committing atrocities during the Pequot War of 1637. In particular, it was alleged that Nepaupauck had gone along on a war party which raided the town of Wethersfield. During that raid Nepaupauck was alleged to have killed a white man named Abraham Finch. He was also said to have carried off a white child into captivity. Further charges were brought against Nepaupauck in relation to a triple murder that had been committed on the Connecticut river. Three men in a small boat had been attacked and slain on that occasion and it was charged that Nepaupauck had cut off their hands and presented them to a hostile chief as trophies. Nepaupauck admitted the charges against him and accepted a death sentence with stoic indifference. On October 30, 1639, he was beheaded by the marshal of New Haven and his head was put on a pole.

1641

William Hackett, white, age 19. *Bestiality*. The crime was committed on an unknown date at Salem, Massachusetts. This offender was a young farmhand described as a "very stupid, idle and ill-disposed boy." One Sunday morning a Salem matron looked out her window and got the surprise of her life: a clear view of William Hackett behaving indecently with a cow. The incident was reported to the authorities and Hackett was arrested. Questioned closely, he admitted that the charge against him was true. Hackett and the cow were both brought to Boston for further examination. The General Court of the colony considered the matter and opted for capital punishment. Doubts about executing someone on the testimony of only one witness were laid to rest when Hackett again confessed. On or about December 30, 1641, the condemned man and the cow he had abused were both brought to the Boston gallows. There Hackett was made to watch as the cow was killed. Moments later Hackett was hanged. Then he and the cow were buried together.

1642

George Spencer, white, age unknown. *Bestiality*. The crime was committed on an unknown date at New Haven, Connecticut. During the winter of 1642 a New Haven farmer named Henry Browning sold a pregnant sow to a neighbor named James Wakeman. In February the sow gave birth to a litter of piglets. In examining the newborns, Wakeman was appalled to find one which was badly deformed; the piglet had only one eye in the middle of its face along with other abnormalities. It so happened that the eye of the deformed piglet had a milky colored hue to it much like one of the eyes of farmer Browning's hired man, George Spencer. This led to a suspicion that the deformed piglet was the result of an illegal coupling of George Spencer and the mother sow. The fact that Spencer already had an unsavory reputation made belief in the paternity seem all the more plausible. Spencer initially denied the allegation. However when he was confronted with the deformed piglet a superstitious dread overtook him and he confessed that he had indeed had carnal knowledge of the sow. A court considered the evidence and decreed that Spencer should be put to death. Accordingly on April 8, 1642, the condemned man and the mother sow were both brought to the gallows at New Haven. There the man was forced to watch as the sow was killed with a sword. Spencer was hanged a few moments later. Then he was buried together with the sow.

Thomas Graunger, white, age 17. *Bestiality*. The crime was committed over a period of time at Duxbury, Massachusetts. This juvenile offender had lived with his parents at Scituate but was later apprenticed to a farmer at Duxbury. One day he was caught in the act of indecent behavior with a horse. When questioned about his sexual habits, Graunger said that he had acted in a similar manner with other animals. He then admitted having had carnal knowledge of the following creatures: a mare, a cow, two goats, five sheep, two calves and a turkey. All of that livestock was carefully rounded up and held as evidence. Graunger was convicted of capital felony largely on his own confession. A court also heard the testimonies of those who knew of him abusing animals. The penalty was death. On September 8, 1642, a large pit was dug next to the gallows at Plymouth. There Thomas Graunger was forced to watch as the animals he had been with were slaughtered one by one. All of the carcasses were then thrown into the pit. When the last of the animals had been killed, Graunger was hanged. Then his body was thrown among the animal carcasses and covered with earth. Thus were the objects of Graunger's concupiscence buried with him.

1644

Mary Latham, white, age 18. **James Britton,** white, age about 30. *Adultery.* The crime was committed on an unknown date at Weymouth, Massachusetts. In the year 1641 the colony of Massachusetts enacted a criminal code by which *adultery* was held to be a capital offense. Although this law remained in effect for many years the only known instance of its actual implementation occurred in the year 1644.

Teenage Mary Latham lived at Marshfield. She was an attractive girl, sociable, religious and well-to-do. She fell in love with a young man of her hometown only to be jilted by him. The experience left Mary distraught. She then declared that she would marry the first eligible man who came along. In such a way she wound up with a spouse who was nearly three times her age.

It did not take Mary Latham long to distance herself from her husband. She regretted her marriage and even menaced her mate with knives. She longed for a younger man. Finally she found one in the person of James Britton, a jaunty fellow of nearby Weymouth. Britton was despised by the prudish inhabitants of his town. He galled them with his easygoing lifestyle and contempt for Puritan propriety. He was also a known womanizer who scandalized the community by giving bawdy entertainments at his house. It was not long before the Britton-Latham symbiosis became the talk of the town. The climax came late one night during a party. James and Mary left their gay companions and went into some nearby woods where they had sex with each other. They did not go unobserved. The next day their doings were common gossip. Adultery was a serious crime and someone reported what had happened. The lovers were promptly arrested. Both contritely admitted that they were guilty as charged. However the authorities on the spot could not agree on what legal procedure to follow. Both prisoners were sent to Boston where they were tried for their lives before the Court of Assistants.

There was much disagreement among the judges about the legalities of this case. Controversy centered around whether the testimony of only one witness was sufficient to support a death sentence. The point was eventually carried in favor of the prosecution when the confessions were produced in evidence. Both defendants were then condemned.

Appeals were made in each case seeking reversals of the convictions and sentences. That spawned another round of debate by the judges. Some argued that the evidence was insufficient and some even dared to question the severity of the law itself. Others contended that since the statute was based on the Mosaic Law it was condoned by God Himself and was therefore infallible. Adultery was specified as a capital crime in Leviticus 20:10. Who then, it was asked, could dare to dispute the matter? Who could say that the punishment did not fit the crime? As for allegations of insufficient evidence, the confessions of both defendants were once again cited. The appeals were then dismissed.

On March 21, 1644, the two lovers were hanged on the Boston gallows. Mary Latham made a short speech in which she warned young women against the folly of sexual misconduct. James Britton spoke along the same lines in an address to young men of the audience.

William Franklin, white, age unknown. *Murder.* The crime was committed during the winter of 1643-1644 at Boston, Massachusetts. This offender lived at Roxbury, close to Boston. An apprentice boy named Nathaniel Sewall (white, age about 13) had been placed with him only to subjected to cruel mistreatment. Franklin apparently had a total disregard for the boy's health and well-being; he is reported to have beaten, starved and tortured the youngster. For instance, the boy was sick with scurvy and Franklin made no effort to relieve his condition. Franklin also left the boy in unheated quarters with nothing to cover him. Franklin hoisted the boy up into a chimney and left him suspended there for a long time. Franklin withheld food from the boy and beat him without mercy. Lastly, Franklin strapped the boy down across the back of a horse although he was in a dying condition and carried him like that through five miles of winter weather. Then Franklin had the nerve to complain before a magistrate that the boy was a useless servant. Nathaniel Sewall eventually died a victim of his hard usage. His master was held criminally responsible for his death. Franklin remained arrogant in the face of the charges which were brought against him. His attitude was enough to get him ex-communicated from his church. He was convicted of willful murder by the Massachusetts Court of Assistants and the guilty verdict was upheld on appeal. A warrant was then issued for Franklin's execution. He accordingly died on the Boston gallows (in June of 1644), unrepentant for his brutality.

Busheage, Native American, age unknown. *Murder.* The crime was committed in May of 1644 at Stamford, Connecticut. This offender entered the house of an unidentified "poor man" when only the wife and infant child of that homeowner were present. He then picked up a lathing hammer and severely battered the woman of the house with it. When the intruder thought that the woman was dead he helped himself to some clothing and fled. The woman lived long enough to identify her attacker as an Indian. Several weeks later the killer was caught by other Indians and turned over to the English. He was brought to New Haven where he admitted the crime. He also gave up the clothing which he had stolen. A New Haven court sentenced the guilty man to death by decapitation. The execution took place sometime in August of 1644. Busheage was tied to a chair and in that position had his head smitten off by a curved sword. The executioner bungled his job; no less than eight chops were required to carry out the death sentence.

Goodwife Cornish, white, age unknown. *Murder.* The crime was committed in the autumn of 1644 at York, Maine. The story of this woman begins in 1634 at the settlement of Weymouth, Massachusetts. There dwelled Goodman Richard Cornish and his unnamed wife. The Cornishes were a mismatched pair. Richard Cornish is described as a tireless worker while his wife is said to have been a woman of loose habits. Few missed her when she and her husband moved to York in 1636. Once settled in the new abode, Goodwife Cornish wasted no time in reestablishing her notoriety. For the next eight years she and her husband managed to survive in a state of mutual toleration. One day in 1644 however the battered body of Richard Cornish was found floating in the York river. He was impaled on a stake. His canoe was also found deliberately weighted down with stones. A cry of murder was raised. The sensational news swept the town and surrounding countryside. Had hostile

Indians killed Richard Cornish? Probably not. Although the man's skull had been crushed as if by a war club no one could imagine an Indian being so wasteful as to purposefully sink a good canoe. Such a craft would have been desirable plunder to an Indian. Moreover, what Indian, it was asked, would squander precious time by weighting down a canoe when he could be making good his escape? For these reasons it was determined that the murder of Richard Cornish was the work of some crafty white person. Suspicion fell upon the widow of the decedent. She had openly despised her husband. She was also rumored to have committed adultery. Her arrest soon followed. When questioned, the woman freely admitted to extramarital affairs. She even identified a man named Edward Johnson as one of her lovers. As for the murder, she stoutly denied all knowledge of it. The local authorities then decided to subject Goodwife Cornish and Edward Johnson to what was known as "Trial by Touch."

It was widely believed in those days that "murdered blood cried for vengeance" just as the blood of Abel was said to have "cried up from the ground." This formed the rationale for a further belief that if a murderer touched the corpse of his victim, that corpse would either bleed or have the "blood come fresh upon it." Goodwife Cornish and Edward Johnson were both confronted with the decomposed remains of Richard Cornish and compelled to put their hands thereon. As they did so, blood oozed from the dead man's wounds.

Both of the accused were next brought before a council of local officials. The ensuing "trial" was a farce. The prosecution's only evidence was the result of the "Trial by Touch" and hearsay about the woman's character. It was her reputation more than anything else that counted against Goodwife Cornish. She was declared guilty and condemned to death. Edward Johnson was acquitted.

During her "trial" Goodwife Cornish continued to deny all knowledge of the murder. She repeated her admissions of lewd conduct and even named a local official as one of her lovers. Few doubted the story because the man had a reputation of his own. Goodwife Cornish was hanged at York in December of 1644. There the matter ended.

1646

William Plaine, white, age about 45. *Blasphemy and pederasty.* The crimes were committed over a period of time at Guilford, Connecticut. This case is in a class by itself. William Plaine was one of the original settlers of the town of Guilford. He owned a large tract of land which he farmed. He was also appointed his town's first fire inspector. Although married, Plaine was undeniably bisexual. He felt a special attraction for teenage boys and if Winthrop can be believed, he organized a considerable number of them into a secret society of sorts. It was alleged that Plaine had sex with his young male intimates more than 100 times. When some of them questioned the propriety of what they were doing, Plaine is further alleged to have allayed their fears by denying the existence of God. It was only a matter of time before news of Plaine's doings reached the ears of authority. When the full extent of the scandal became known the governor of New Haven was too shocked to act on his own initiative. He wrote to the governor of Massachusetts for advice. The answer he received was fatal for William Plaine. The guilty man was hanged at New Haven in June of 1646. The boys who had cavorted with him went to the whipping post.

1647

Mary Martin, white, age 22. *Murder.* The crime was committed on December 13, 1646, at Boston, Massachusetts. This female offender lived at Casco Bay (Maine) with her father and a younger sister. Nothing is known of her mother. The elder Martin is described as a respectable merchant. One of Mary Martin's grandfathers is said to have been a Lord Mayor of the English port city of Plymouth.

Mary Martin was considered a promising young woman. However her situation began to deteriorate in the year 1645 when, for unknown reasons, her father returned to England and left his two daughters to fend for themselves in the New World. The girls hired themselves out as servants; Mary in the household of a certain Mr. Mitton. One thing led to another and before long Mary was sleeping with her employer.

After several months Mary tired of her situation and quit Mr. Mitton's employ. She then went to Boston and found a position there with a dowager named Mistress Bourne. Soon however Mary was mortified to find herself *enceinte*. In desperation she sought every means to hide her condition. She took to wearing oversized clothes and stayed indoors as much as possible. All that she succeeded in doing was to arouse the suspicions of the local goodwives, some of whom tattled to Mistress Bourne. Others openly taunted Mary with remarks like "Where is thy husband?" Regardless of the pressure, Mary denied all rumors of pregnancy. She was also defended by Mistress Bourne, who was either naive or sympathetic. This situation lasted for several months. On the above date Mary shut herself up in a darkened room and gave birth to a baby girl. She decided to kill the infant in order to conceal her shame. She attempted to smother the baby by kneeling on its face. Next, she scoured the room with soap to expunge traces of the birth. While thus engaged, the baby regained consciousness and started to cry. Mary then dashed its head against the floor so that it died. Then she stashed the little corpse in a chest and went to bed exhausted.

On January 1, 1647, Mistress Bourne sailed for England like Mary's father had done. This time however arrangements had been made for placing Mary with another employer. With the protecting hand of Mistress Bourne removed, Mary was subjected to renewed gossip. Worn down by her ordeal, she decided to tell the goodwives exactly what they wanted to hear. Yes, said Mary, she had given birth to an illegitimate child. However she added that the baby was stillborn and that she had cremated it. Mary hoped that such a disclosure would end her troubles. She was mistaken. One of the busybodies searched Mary's former home and found the murdered baby.

Caught in a lie, Mary Martin was arrested. A coroner's inquest was held. So was a "Trial by Touch." The findings were certified to a grand jury. At her trial Mary was confronted with the evidence against her. It was said that fresh blood had oozed from the face of the dead baby when Mary put her hands on it. Mary was then seized with a superstitious dread and confessed her guilt. She acknowledged all that was charged against her. The court then sentenced her to death.

Mary Martin was hanged from the Boston gallows on March 18, 1647. Her execution was a bungled affair. Writing in the year 1699, Cotton Mather reported that Mary Martin had to be hanged twice. The noose had been set wrong at the first drop, causing Mary to merely dangle in the air. Only after the same noose was properly reset did she strangle to death at the end of the rope. Mather reasoned that since Mary had murderously assaulted her baby twice (first by kneeling upon it and secondly by dashing it against the floor), a vengeful God had ordained that she be made to hang twice.

Alse Youngs, white, age unknown. *Witchcraft.* So far as is known the year 1647 marks the New England debut of judicial prosecutions and death penalties for so-called "witchcraft." This "offense," either real or imagined, was defined as the having of illicit dealings with the "devil." It was considered one of the most heinous crimes—if not the single most heinous crime—known to early American jurisprudence. It was certainly the most sensational crime and it evoked untold terror in the minds of the day. In a society which based itself on an unvarying diet of Calvinism and worship of the Christian God, the notion of any member of that society being in league with the devil, or "Satan, the Grand Enemy of God and Mankind" was intolerable under all circumstances. Such an offense not only hazarded the eternal ruin of the offender's immortal soul but struck at the very fundamentals of society. The Mosaic Law was explicit: "Thou shalt not suffer a witch to live" (Exodus 22:18). Since the higher canons of 17th century law were similarly based it is hardly surprising that such a flagitious crime was deemed capital by every one of the early colonies.

Unlike inquests into other high crimes, witchcraft prosecutions came in deadly spurts. The first (if it may be called such), terrorized the Connecticut river valley and western Connecticut shore from 1647 to 1654. It claimed the lives of seven women and one man by the time it ran its course. The second major outbreak occurred in the vicinity of Hartford and spanned a one year period from 1662 to 1663. Its net result was three women and one man put to death. By far the worst outbreak was that of 1692–1693 in Essex County, Massachusetts, where witch hunting had its grand finale and resulted in 20 executions.

The final toll of these upheavals cannot be appraised in terms of executions alone. A witchcraft accusation was never a minor thing. It could destabilize an entire community. For every convicted "witch" that went to the gallows there were many others who suffered varying degrees of shame and disgrace. Throughout the last half of the 17th century New England saw dozens of luckless people driven into exile, flight, financial ruin, ex-communication and even insanity through the relentlessness of "witch hunting." Where superstition and over-refined scruples of "righteousness" combined with the instinctive human fear of the unknown, resultant tension surged past its breaking point to produce panic in its most horrific form.

The colony of Connecticut was the first to experience a witch hunt followed very closely by Massachusetts. From contemporary sources we learn that on May 26, 1647, a woman named Alse Youngs was executed at Hartford for alleged witchcraft. She is an historical enigma. A partial answer can be offered to the question of her identity. However no details are known to survive concerning the manner and circumstances of her downfall. The very name of New England's first known "witch" is even muddled; it is variously given as "Alse," "Aschah" and "Alice." She was a resident of Windsor and may or may not have been related to one John Youngs who lived there from 1640 to 1649. How, when and why Alse Youngs aroused the antipathy which culminated in her death are unknown. The court records of her case are lost. But it is certain that she was hanged and significant that she opened a dark and tragic chapter in American history.

1648

Margaret Jones, white, age unknown. *Witchcraft.* Better documented than the case of Alse Youngs is the Massachusetts case of Margaret Jones. She lived at Charlestown with her husband, Thomas Jones. She was a skilled herbalist, a dispenser of home remedies and a rudimentary chiropractor. She also had a knack for correctly predicting the progression of illnesses. Those who scorned the advice of Margaret Jones earned her displeasure. When the conditions of such persons failed to improve, the cause was laid to Margaret's malice. Stung by such talk, Margaret Jones was not adverse to confronting her detractors. That sort of behavior intensified the feelings against her. Who but a witch, it was asked, could have such insight? When those same detractors suffered losses to their livestock through illness and accident suspicion mounted against Margaret Jones. She was thought to have put evil spells upon the smitten animals.

Animosity against Margaret Jones was further strengthened by another factor: a superstition of the time which held that a witch could be detected by burning part of a hexed object. If such an object was indeed hexed, it was believed that the witch responsible for that hex would be drawn to the scene of the fire. Parts were cut from the animals thought to have been hexed by Margaret Jones. Then those same animal parts were ritually burned. Margaret Jones confirmed suspicion against her by coming to the scene of the fire and demanding an explanation.

While this was enough to satisfy the credulous, convincing a court of law to hang Margaret Jones was an entirely different matter. A formal complaint was lodged and Margaret's husband got caught up in it as well. The couple was arrested and brought before the Court of Assistants, the highest court in the colony.

The court proceeded cautiously. It had not handled a witchcraft case before and it was determined to commit no error. The first concern was to collect evidence for a grand jury. After many depositions had been gathered it became apparent that further evidence was needed. The court then resorted to a thing called the Hopkins Method.

Before describing this so-called Hopkins method it must first be understood that witches were believed to be physically marked with so-called teats, a brand of sorts with which the devil marked his disciples and which were, upon detection, considered con-clusive proof of witchery. These witch teats were believed to be insensitive to pain; when pierced by needles known as witch prickers the suspect was thought to feel no pain thereby. It was also believed that the teats would not bleed when pricked. The teats were further believed, in most cases, to be secreted in the most private parts of the human body. They might be anywhere: in the armpits, around the genitals, under the tongue, etc. Hence great care had to be used when searching for them. It became a sordid routine of witchcraft inquiries for suspects to be strip-searched for these supposed marks of the devil. Matrons would examine female suspects and specially appointed men would examine male suspects. The most fantastic aspect of teats concerned a belief that in addition to being a diabolical mark they also served as a source of nourishment for evil spirits that were believed to attend witches. These attendant spirits were called imps or familiars and they might come in any shape or form such as a dog, cat, bird, frog, lizard, snake, mouse, etc. It was also believed that at least once in every 24 hour period a witch had to allow her imp or imps to suck sustenance from his or her teats—usually droplets of blood, lymph fluid or semen. Hence the demonic imps would appear at least once each day in order to be suckled, at which time they were said to be visible to the human eye. Such beliefs gave rise to the practice of watching—wherein a suspected witch would be confined in an enclosed room and put under a strict watch for 24 hours in the belief that if guilty, imps would appear during that time to be suckled. If any suspicious creatures appeared and were duly seen by the watchers during the time of the watch, the suspect was deemed guilty. This practice was perfected and widely used during the 1640s by the infamous English witch hunter Matthew Hopkins. Hence its cognomen of the Hopkins Method.

Such was the means by which the

Massachusetts Court of Assistants sought to ascertain the guilt or innocence of Margaret Jones and her husband. Both were strip-searched for teats. Warders examined every inch of their bodies for any suspicious looking mole, wart or fleshy protuberance that might be a mark of the devil. Then both were confined in close quarters and carefully watched.

In the case of Thomas Jones the results of these tests were negative. In the case of Margaret Jones however the matrons who examined her reported the presence of suspected teats on her person. It was further adduced that she was actually seen suckling an imp in the form of a "little child." When an officer chased after the apparition it vanished without a trace. More likely, the prolonged sleeplessness which the watcher imposed on himself during the course of his watch had caused him to imagine things.

At her trial Margaret Jones seemed more intent on vilifying her accusers than in defending herself. She defied the judges, insulted the jury and reviled all who testified against her. While her courtroom demeanor certainly did her more harm than good, it was the evidence of the imp which was especially damning. Margaret Jones was declared guilty and sentenced to die.

On June 15, 1648, the Boston gallows claimed another victim in the person of Margaret Jones. She died hard. In a long final speech she bitterly denounced all that she had been forced to endure and she bid damnation to all those who had brought her to such an end.

Alice Bishop, white, age unknown. *Murder.* The crime was committed on July 22, 1648, at Plymouth, Massachusetts. In the summer of 1648 there lived at Plymouth the bourgeoisie family Bishop. The patriarch was Goodman Richard Bishop and his wife was Good-

wife Alice Bishop. The couple had a four-year-old daughter named Martha Bishop. History has neglected to record what Goodman Bishop did for a living. He and his wife were of hearty stock, having endured all the hardships of life in early Plymouth. Industrious, religious and frugal, they persevered through the numbing winters, kept alert for hostile Indians and stayed on cordial terms with their neighbors.

On the above date Goodman Bishop was away on business. His wife and daughter remained at home. Rachel Ramsden, a neighbor and family friend, stopped by the Bishop house. After chatting with Alice Bishop for a while she went down the street to fetch some buttermilk. Upon returning from that errand, Rachel Ramsden was horrified to discover that Alice Bishop had taken a butcher knife to little Martha and cut her throat from ear to ear. Blood was everywhere.

Rachel Ramsden fled from the scene and blurted the news to her parents. Her father then hurried to the house of the governor and informed the authorities. A posse of 12 armed men was sent to the Bishop house. Alice Bishop was found disoriented and tearful. Blood was seen smeared on a ladder which led to an overhead chamber. Fearing the worst, some of the possemen climbed the ladder. They soon found the dead child. By then Alice Bishop had become hysterical.

On August 1, 1648, a formal inquest was held before the governor of the Plymouth colony and his council. The testimonies of Rachel Ramsden and the 12 possemen were carefully sifted. When Alice Bishop was called to tell her side of the story she frankly admitted the murder. She was then held for trial by the Plymouth Colony court.

The trial was a mere formality. Alice Bishop pled guilty and expressed regret for what she had done. She remained silent when asked why she had killed her daughter. Sentence of death was then decreed. Alice Bishop accordingly went to the Plymouth gallows on October 4, 1648. The motive for her crime was never explained.

Mary Johnson, white, age unknown. *Witchcraft.* This woman was a domestic servant in the town of Wethersfield, Connecticut. Nothing is known of her family. The earliest known mention of her dates from the summer of 1646 when she was sentenced to the whipping post for what may or may not have been a conviction for theft. She next appears on December 7, 1648, when the Connecticut General Court found her guilty of "familiarity with ye devil." She had confessed herself guilty of the charge.

The original trial record in this case is lost. However some details have been preserved through secondary sources. Writing 41 years after the events, Cotton Mather described the substance of Mary Johnson's confession in the following words:

> She said that a devil was wont to do her many services. Her master once blamed her for not carrying out the ashes and a devil did clear the hearth for her afterwards. Her master sending her into a field to drive out some swine that used to break into it, a devil would scurry them out and make her laugh to see how he feezed them. Her first familiarity with the devils came by discontent; wishing the devil to take that and the other thing and the devil to do this and that, a devil appeared unto her and asked what services he could do for her. She confessed that she was guilty of the murder of a child and that she had been guilty of uncleanliness with both men and devils.

From such a diatribe it is safe to conjecture that Mary Johnson was unhappy in her situation as a menial servant. Her joyless circumstances may have unbalanced her mind. The fact that her conviction was based on her own confession adds a bizarre twist to the case. Mather's recital hints at mental illness or at least an overheated imagination. At any rate, Mary Johnson's confession was accepted as literal truth by the Connecticut authorities. It was enough to bring the woman to the gallows. She was hanged at Hartford in December of 1648.

1650

Alice Lake and **Elizabeth Kendall,** whites, ages unknown. *Witchcraft.* These women, the next two victims of New England's preoccupation with witchery during this period, were residents of the greater Boston area. While the exact dates of their executions are unknown, surviving evidence would tend to place them sometime in the year 1650.

Alice Lake lived at Dorchester. Her maiden name was Alice Lee. When young she was bound as a domestic servant in the household of a certain Mr. John Philips. Following her manumission, she married a man named Henry Lake and bore at least four children. The details of her alleged witchcraft are almost entirely lost. The court records no longer exist. Whether or not she had previously bore the reputation of a witch cannot even be conjectured. Most of what is known of her comes from a letter written in 1684 by Nathaniel Mather to his brother, Increase Mather, following the publication of a book by the latter. Said Nathaniel Mather of Alice Lake:

> The devil drew in by appearing to her in the likeness of and acting the part of a child of hers then lately dead on whom her heart was much set.

Even this scrap of information is not entirely trustworthy. The Rev. Hale tells a pathetic story of her last day on earth: while going to her execution she disappointed the ministers who attended her by denying all matters of witchcraft. Yet she said that she considered her end as being justified anyway. When asked why she felt that way, she said that years earlier while still a single woman, she had become pregnant and had attempted to give herself an abortion. So while innocent of witchcraft, she still regarded herself as one who had had murder in her heart. Therefore, said Alice Lake, she deserved to be hanged.

While it can be argued that most of those executed for "witchcraft" were victims of credulous testimony, Elizabeth Kendall of Cambridge was a victim of deliberately false testimony. She was hanged for supposedly conjuring the death of a baby which had died of frostbite. We are completely dependent upon Hale for what details have survived of this affair. His account runs as follows:

A principal witness was a Watertown nurse who testified that she said Kendall did bewitch to death a child of Goodman Jennings of Watertown. For the said Kendall did make much of the child when it was well but which then quickly changed its color and died a few hours later. The court took this evidence among others; the said Jennings not knowing of it. But after Kendall was executed (who also denied her guilt to the death) Mr. Richard Brown, knowing and hoping better things of Kendall, asked the said family Jennings if they suspected her to bewitch their child. They answered "no." But they judged the true cause of the child's death to be thus: The nurse had the previous night carried the child out and kept it abroad in the cold for a long time until the red gum was come out upon it and the cold had stuck in the red gum. And that they judged to be the cause of the child's death. And though said Kendall had come in that day and made much of the child, they perceived no wrong to come from her. After this the said nurse was imprisoned for adultery and there delivered of her bastard. Mr. Brown went

to her and told her that it was just with God to leave her to such wickedness as a punishment for murdering Goody Kendall by her false witness bearing. But the nurse died in prison and so the matter was not further pursued.

Hale's account raises several important questions. First, where was Richard Brown throughout Kendall's detention when his good character reference might have saved her? Where was the family Jennings all the while? It is highly unlikely that both Brown and Jennings were unaware of the prosecution. Since they "perceived no wrong to come to the child" from Kendall, they might have spoken in her defense. Yet there is no indication of their having done so. What were the so-called "other evidences" which the trial court took into consideration? It would seem unlikely that Kendall was already a suspected witch given the stated opinions of Brown and Jennings. How was it that a death sentence was handed down by a court of law based principally upon the word of a mendacious nurse? The fact that the nurse was an adulteress says little for her character. Hence it would seem improbable that the court relied on her testimony alone. A logical theory might be that the "other evidences" were the testimonies of physicians concerning the post-mortem examination of the dead baby. Since doctors of that era were prone to attribute whatever they would not otherwise explain to witchcraft, it might have been that they failed to correctly diagnose the "cold stuck in the red gum" as hypothermia and therefore they tried to save face by corroborating the nurse's tale.

Thomas Newton, white, age about 50. *Adultery.* The crime was committed over a period of time at Fairfield, Connecticut. Peter and Elizabeth Johnson, a married couple, were among the first settlers of Fairfield in 1639. They had previously landed at Boston with an infant son. Two more boys were born to them after their arrival in Connecticut. Three houses away from the Johnsons dwelt a widower named Thomas Newton. There is direct evidence that Elizabeth Johnson had improper relations with him because she bore him a baby boy. Sometime in the year 1649 Peter Johnson died. Shortly afterward his widow was arrested along with Thomas Newton. Both were charged with adultery, a capital offense. They were jailed on December 30, 1649. A grand jury indicted both parties on February 26, 1650. A joint trial was held in May. Guilty verdicts were returned on May 15, 1650. Both defendants were sentenced to death. Thomas Newton was hanged at Fairfield on May 27, 1650. Elizabeth Johnson was reprieved for an unspecified reason. On June 6, 1650, she was set free. She then remarried and moved away. The queerly timed death of Peter Johnson cast a sinister shadow over what would otherwise have been a simple case of infidelity. The decision to deny clemency to Thomas Newton was probably influenced by the suspicious death of his paramour's husband.

1651

John Carrington, white, age 49. **Joan Carrington,** white, age unknown. *Witchcraft.* On March 6, 1651, a Hartford grand jury returned capital indictments against a poor carpenter named John Carrington and his wife, Joan Carrington. The charge in each case was "familiarity with Satan." A close study of the Carringtons is precluded by an acute lack of documentation. Virtually nothing is known about the specifics of the charges which they faced. Although both of their indictments have survived in the court records, they are worded in general terms. It is highly probable that both were executed on or about April 1, 1651, at Hartford, Connecticut.

Personal notes on the Carringtons are sparse though not completely lacking. It appears that John arrived at Boston in the summer of 1635 with a spouse named "Mary." By the summer of 1643 he had migrated to the Connecticut town of Wethersfield. There he remained in circumstances of poverty until being caught up in a witch hunt. His wife, Mary, apparently died prior to 1650 since John was married to another woman at the time of his arrest. Her name was Joan Carrington.

Only a conjectural guess can be made as to the identity of Joan Carrington. According to the records of the Connecticut court:

September 6, 1649: Thomas Stanton plaintiff contra Joan Sipperance in an action for slander to the utter undoing of his wife's good name and almost taking away her life, to the damage of £200. Awarded 30 shillings plus costs.

December 6, 1649: Joan Sipperance is adjudged to pay double for the lace she stole and threefold for the time she absented herself from her master's service.

It is quite possible that Joan Sipperance and Joan Carrington were one and the same person. Circumstantial evidence supports such a theory. First is the similarity in first names, "Joan" not being a common female cognomen in the records of the time. Secondly, the dates all fit; Joan Sipperance vanishes from the records barely a year before Joan Carrington appears.

Third is the matter of the slander suit. What kind of slander could have been so egregious as to "almost take away life"? Quite probably an allegation of witchcraft, the crime for which Joan Carrington was put to death. Had Joan Sipperance called Goodwife Stanton a witch only to have it backfire on her in the form of a slander suit? Fourthly, Joan Sipperance is described as having been a truant servant in December of 1649. Did she obtain her manumission shortly thereafter and marry—thus accounting for the disappearance of her name from the records around that time? Moreover, in the caste-conscious society of the 17th century who else but a wayward servant would marry a man of mean circumstances like John Carrington?

Mary Parsons, white, age unknown. *Murder.* The crime was alleged to have been committed in February of 1651 at Springfield, Massachusetts. The year 1651 was a time of sensational terror in the Connecticut river valley. There was mortal danger with which to contend. The threat, however, did not come in conventional form. There were no rampaging Indians nor extremes of weather. For the most part the peril was psychosomatic, an instinctive fear of the unknown which fed upon itself and only found relief when put in tangible form through the fabrication of scapegoats. It was a tragic by-product of the times, the sordid offscourings of superstition fomented by a repressive theocracy which sought to govern through mind control instead of through an ostensible Christian benevolence. Writing four decades afterward, Cotton Mather accurately described what was vexing New England in the early 1650s:

> A malefactor accused of witchcraft as well as murder and executed in this place more than forty years ago did then give notice of an horrible plot against the country by witchcraft then laid, which if it were not seasonably discovered would probably blow up and pull down all the churches in the country.

Hence it was the devil and his agents who were thought to be aprowl in New England. Their evil machinations (whether real or imagined), struck at the very foundations of Puritan society. It was the duty of every God-fearing citizen to be on the watch for witches and

to denounce them whenever detected or suspected.

It seemed as if the devil had truly cast his shadow over New England during the early 1650s. Already two "witches" had been executed at Boston. Then early in 1651 a married couple were arrested at Springfield on similar charges. At the same time another couple was charged with witchcraft a few miles down river at Wethersfield. Then before the year was even half over came news that the shoreline towns of Stratford and Fairfield were infested with the forces of evil. The perceived danger threatened to overwhelm society.

Trouble had been brewing at Springfield for some time before finally coming to a climax in 1651. To better understand the details as they unfolded, it is necessary to explain what gave rise to the problem.

There arrived at nearby Windsor in 1637 the family of one Thomas Marshfield. He and his wife (whose name is unknown) had at least two children, a daughter and a son named Samuel. The patriarch of the family died in 1643 and his estate, encumbered by debts, was impounded. The widow was left without assets and so went to live with her son who had previously gone off on his own to Springfield.

Coeval with the widow Marshfield's arrival at Springfield was the appearance there of a woman named Mary Lewis. This Mary Lewis was immediately stigmatized because her husband was a Roman Catholic. Equally as bad, in public opinion, was the fact that Mary Lewis had been estranged from her spouse for seven years. Social handicaps not withstanding, Mary Lewis fell in love with a morose laborer named Hugh Parsons and soon was affianced.

The desire of Mary and Hugh to marry posed a legal problem. The local magistrate, William Pynchon, could not sanction such a match until the matter of Mary's extant marriage had been settled by a higher authority. Pynchon therefore consulted the government in Boston. In reply, a favorable judgment was granted based on the premise that Mary's seven year separation from her Catholic spouse gave her legal status as a divorcee. So it came to pass that Hugh Parsons and Mary Lewis were married at Springfield on October 27, 1645. Three children would follow.

The irregular circumstances of this marriage, the stigma of Roman Catholicism in Mary's background and Hugh's dour disposition all combined to render the newlyweds unpopular in their community. They were the targets of incessant gossip. If not the actual catalyst of this hostility, the widow Marshfield certainly contributed to it. Not to be outdone, the new Goodwife Parsons went on the offensive. Said she of the widow Marshfield:

> She was suspected to be a witch at Windsor and it was publicly known that the devil followed her house at Windsor. And for all I know, he follows her here as well.

Mary Parsons also alleged that the widow Marshfield used witchcraft to cause eerie lights to appear at night and as a means of purloining wool. As a result, the widow Marshfield sued for slander.

The lawsuit went against Parsons and Magistrate Pynchon gave her a choice: either pay the plaintiff £3 damages or take 20 lashes at the whipping post. Mary Parsons opted to pay up. Lacking silver with which to make up the amount in question, it was agreed to settle the matter for 24 bushels of corn. Hugh Parsons (who was niggardly by nature) loathed the prospect of parting with bushels of corn. He tried to wheedle the widow Marshfield into accepting less than the full amount. Marshfield refused to budge. A confounded Hugh Parsons then said:

> The corn will be as lent. It will do you no good. It will be as wildfire in your house and as a moth in your clothes!

These ominous words capture the character of Hugh Parsons. He was a cryptic, choleric man who over a period of time managed to alienate most of his peers. His vague and menacing remarks, (such as that which he spoke to the widow Marshfield) were the bane of the community. He was the inspiration for and the target of many dark rumors. It was not long before people began associating personal misfortune with Hugh's remarks. For instance, a woodchopper claimed to have injured himself shortly after having words with Hugh Parsons. A woman claimed to have been annoyed by a strange light in her bedroom one night and to have suffered complications with a pregnancy. A toddler was said to have been frightened by a spectral dog. A woman who had refused to sell some milk to Hugh Parsons had her cow stricken ill. A piece of meat had inexplicably vanished from a stewpot. Even the local minister, George Moxon, joined in the gossip; he told of how his two daughters had fallen ill shortly after an argument with Hugh Parsons. According to popular consensus, the cause of all these troubles was witchcraft practiced by Hugh Parsons.

A public inquest was held to investigate the matter. Magistrate Pynchon spent weeks gathering "evidence" against Hugh Parsons. One after another the townsfolk trekked to Pynchon's house to tell their stories. Some of the testimonies were so puerile that Parsons himself would not condescend to rebut them. For the most part he maintained a taciturn demeanor throughout the proceedings. The most damaging allegations, however, came from an unexpected source: his own wife.

Mary Parsons had been going downhill for a long time. Ever since her arrival in Springfield things had gone wrong for her. She had had to endure the vituperation of her neighbors. Then her children died one by one. A frosty rapport with her husband also contributed to her decline; Hugh Parsons was a negligent and moody spouse. He made his wife miserable through what today would be called "mental and physical cruelty." Mary Parsons described this as follows:

He used to come home in a distempered frame. Sometimes he has pulled off the bedclothes and left me naked on the bed and quenched the fire. Sometimes he has thrown peas about the house and made me pick them up...

By the time of her husband's arrest early in 1651, Mary Parsons was an emotional and physical wreck. That she had lost her mind is the only plausible explanation for the bizarre charges she brought against her husband. The tales speak for themselves:

Mary Parsons, your wife, says that one reason why she suspects you to be a witch is because you cannot abide anything spoken against witches. She said to you "I hope that God will find out all such wicked persons and purge the land of all witches ere it be long." To this she says that you gave her a naughty look but never a word. But presently after, on a slight occasion, you took up a block and made as if you would throw it at her head. But yet in the end you did not do so but threw it down on the hearth of the chimney. This expression of your anger was because she wished the ruin of all witches.

Mary Parsons being asked what reasons she had to suspect her husband for a witch gave these reasons: Because when I say anything to anybody in secret to such a friend as I am sure would not speak of it, he would come to know it by what means I cannot tell. Secondly, because he used to be out at night till midnight and about half an hour before he comes home I shall hear some noise or another about the door or about the house. Because often in his sleep he makes a gabbling noise but I cannot understand one word he says. And when I asked what it was that he talked about in his sleep, he would say that he had strange dreams. One time he said that he dreamed that the devil and he were fighting and that the devil had almost overcome him but that at last he had gotten the mastery of the devil.

Benjamin Cooley says upon oath that Mary Parsons told him above a year since that she feared her husband was a witch and that she had so far suspected him that she has searched him when he has been asleep in bed and could not find anything by way of (witch marks) about him unless it be in his secret parts.

Francis Peppers says upon oath that when I came to see Mary Parsons ... as soon as she saw me she said to me "Your heifer is bewitched!" I asked her how she could tell. She said that her husband had bewitched it and that now he had bewitched me and he knows now what I say and he now terrifies me in this place, striking her hand upon her thigh.

John Matthews says upon oath that being in talk with Mary Parsons about witches, she said to me that her husband was a witch. I asked her how she knew it. She said that the devil came to him in the night and sucked him and made him cry out.

From the tenure of these testimonies it is obvious that Mary Parsons lived in terror of her husband. Such certainly contributed to driving her mad. Hugh Parsons was himself exasperated by his domestic situation. Although he probably didn't recognize his wife's condition as insanity, he once remarked:

She is the worst enemy that I have considering the relation that is between us. And if anyone speaks evil of me, she will speak as ill and as much as anyone else.

On another occasion he said:

If ever any trouble comes to me it will be by her means. She will be the means to hang me.

February of 1651 saw the Parsons tragedy poised on the brink of its worst stage. Mary's mind was hanging by a thread, her marriage was in a state of irretrievable breakdown and her husband was under inquiry for a capital crime. But the worst aspects of the case were yet to unfold. On March 4, 1651, little Joshua Parsons, the last surviving child of Hugh and Mary Parsons, succumbed to an infection of the genitals. Hugh received the news stoically but for Mary it was the last straw. She regarded her husband's stoicism as conduct antithetical to natural parental behavior and she accused the man of bewitching his own child to death.

At this point magistrate Pynchon reached the limit of his jurisdiction. No longer was he dealing with only one capital charge (witchcraft); he was now faced with two capital charges: witchcraft and murder by witchcraft. He could collect evidence but do no more. Under strong guard, Hugh Parsons was sent to Boston to stand trial before the Court of Assistants.

For a short time Mary Parsons remained in Springfield. Bereft of friends, family and means of support, the townspeople were assigned turns to provide her with the bare necessities of life. Only grudgingly did they comply. Soon the unbalanced woman went completely crazy and fancied herself a witch. On April 3, 1651, one of her neighbors went to magistrate Pynchon with the following tale:

Thomas Cooper says upon oath that being appointed to watch Mary Parsons about mid–March last, among other things she told me that she was now hampered from relating so much as she had done against her husband at Mr. Pynchon's. But, said she, could that dumb dog have spoken it would have been better with me than it is. But, said she, if I might speak with him before Mr. Pynchon face to face, I would make that dumb dog speak! I then said to her why do you speak so of your husband? Methinks that if he was a witch there would be some sign or mark of it upon his body. For they say that witches have teats upon some part or other of their bodies. But so far as I hear there is not any such apparent thing on his body. She answered that it is not always so. But said she: Why do I say so? I have no skill in witchery. Why may it not be with him as it was with me? That night that I was at Goodman Ashley's the devil came into his body only like a wind and so went forth again. For so the devil told me that night. Methinks I should have been a witch before now but that I was afraid to see the devil lest he should frighten me. But the devil told me that I should not fear. I will not come in any apparition but only come into your body like a wind and trouble you a little while and presently go forth again. And so I consented. And that night I was with my husband and Goodwife Merrick and Bessie Sewall in Goodman Stebbing's lot and we were sometimes like cats and sometimes in our own shapes and we were plotting for some good cheer. And they made me go barefoot and make the fires because I had declared so much to Mr. Pynchon.

As a result of this diatribe Mary Parsons was herself committed upon suspicion of witchcraft and sent to Boston for trial. Her delusions continued unabated and in addition to damning herself as a witch, she further astounded her listeners by declaring that it had been she and not her husband who had murdered little Joshua Parsons. Hence two indictments were framed against her: one for witchcraft and another for murder.

Mary's confession of infanticide effectively eviscerated the prosecution's case against her husband because the allegation that he had bewitched his own son to death was the principal charge against him. So the Boston authorities decided to defer his trial and proceed with the case against his wife instead. Moreover, Mary was gravely ill at the time and there is evidence that her case was deliberately expedited so that she would not die in the meantime and thereby cheat the law. Hugh was kept in prison for the time being.

The trial of Mary Parsons opened on May 9, 1651. The defendant pled not guilty to the charge of witchcraft. Regardless of her confession, she was acquitted of that charge. As for the charge of killing her child however, she reiterated her previous confession and pled guilty. The court sentenced her to die for infanticide and set the date of her execution at May 29, 1651.

There is considerable confusion among historians as to whether Mary Parsons was actually hanged on schedule or died in prison while awaiting execution. Careful scrutiny of the evidence supports a conclusion that she was indeed hanged. First, there is Mather's reference to her, already cited, in which he states implicitly that she was executed. Secondly, a contemporary newspaper mentions the case and confirms the execution.

Hugh Parsons remained in prison for an entire year before his case came up for trial. The hearings opened on May 12, 1652. The verdict of the jury was a legal oddity:

The jury of life and death finds against Hugh Parsons by the testimony of such as appeared in court so much as give them grounds not to clear him. But considered with the testimonies of others that are at Springfield whose testimonies were only sent in writing, as also the confession of Mary Parsons and the impeachment of some of the bewitched persons of the said Hugh Parsons, which if the General Court take the confession of Mary Parsons and the impeachment of the bewitched persons or other of them and the testimonies that are in writing but appeared not in person as authentic testimonies according to law, then the jury finds the said Hugh Parsons guilty of the sin of witchcraft.

From this muddled verdict it is plain to see that Hugh's jury was perplexed. While Mary's confession of child-murder had inhibited an outright conviction, the concept of "reasonable doubt" did not necessarily impel an acquittal in those days. In the minds of the jurors there was enough remaining evidence (even with Mary's confession duly considered) to preclude an outright acquittal. Hence the jury dared not decide either way. They opted instead to pass the matter onto the General Assembly, an even higher authority than the Court of Assistants. Hugh Parsons remained in prison pending further debate.

The General Assembly a.k.a. the General Court acted where the Court of Assistants vacillated. Hugh Parsons was decreed not guilty and released. Through an agent, he sold his property in Springfield and had the proceeds remitted to him in Boston. Then he sought a new life elsewhere. It is not known if he ever succeeded in rebuilding his shattered fortunes. Unlike his deranged wife however he at least escaped from Massachusetts with his life.

Goodwife Bassett, white, age unknown. *Witchcraft*. In May of 1651 a special tribunal was authorized to meet at Stratford, Connecticut, for the purpose of trying a certain Goodwife Bassett "for her life." The charge was witchcraft. The documents relating to Bassett's trial are lost. However it can be safely conjectured that the proceedings were momentous. A witch trial was never a minor event under any circumstances but the added element of a confession in this case rendered the affair all the more sensational. In addition, the simple fact that a *special* court was authorized attests to what must have been proceedings of great magnitude. There must have been a large number of witnesses to be heard, so many in fact that it precluded the expense of having them all travel to Hartford where the trial would ordinarily have been held.

Who was Goodwife Bassett? The question has troubled historians and the answer is open to speculation. Donald Lines Jacobus, one of Connecticut's foremost genealogists, suggests that she was the wife of one Thomas Bassett who settled at Windsor in 1635. This man fought in the Pequot War of 1637 and later moved to Stratford.

As for Goodwife Bassett's so-called "confession," the fact thereof is one of the few details of her case which is historically certain. Our only glimpse of the intimate details comes in two separate lines from a quasi-related lawsuit three years afterward.

Elizabeth bade her do as the witch at the other town did, that is, discover all she knew to be witches.

…because Goodwife Bassett when she was condemned said there was another witch at Fairfield that held her head full high…

Given the lack of additional information, all that can be further said of Goodwife Bassett is that she was hanged at Stratford probably during the month of June, 1651. Her death however did not calm any nerves. Even while she was being buried in an unmarked grave the minds of the witchhunters were turning toward Fairfield and the as of yet undetected witch that was said to be there.

1653

Goodwife Knapp, white, age unknown. *Witchcraft.* Following the execution of Goodwife Bassett at nearby Stratford, the people of Fairfield, Connecticut, lived in a state of anxiety for two years. They felt that evil was among them. Who was the unknown witch of whom Goodwife Bassett had spoken? Was it a friend? Was it a relative? Was it a neighbor? It never occurred to anyone that the whole matter was ambiguous. After two years suspicion finally attached itself to an impoverished woman named Goodwife Knapp. She was the spouse of a certain Roger Knapp and very probably had come with him ten years earlier as a destitute refugee from Delaware. Suspicion was also aimed at a feisty woman named Mary Staples, whose husband, Thomas Staples, had been penalized in 1650 for negligence in guarding the executed Thomas Newton.

Allegations against Goodwife Staples never got beyond the stage of simple gossip. However, Goodwife Knapp was less fortunate. She was arrested, imprisoned, indicted, strip-searched for witch marks, tried, convicted and hanged. Once again there is a paucity of documentation but enough has survived to show that the proceedings in this case were no small matter. As in the Bassett case, a quorum of judges was sent down from Hartford. As for the precise details of the charges against Goodwife Knapp, there are only oblique allusions to so-called "Indian Gods" and images of some kind that were traded between Native Americans and the accused witch. There were also blemishes on the defendant's body which were taken for marks of the devil.

The execution of Goodwife Knapp took place at Fairfield in November of 1653. The scene has been recorded in detail. Prior to going to the gallows the condemned woman was badgered by these busybodies. She had, however, a resolute mind; all efforts to wring incriminating statements from her failed.

An incident connected with Knapp's execution illustrates the superstition of the time: when her body was brought to the grave a crowd of curiosity seekers gathered around it. They wanted to see the marks of a witch. Led by the aforesaid Mary Staples, they stripped the clothing from the corpse and rudely pawed it over.

There seemed to be more motive than curiosity in Mary Staples, she who did "pull the teats that were found about Goodwife Knapp and was very earnest to know whether they were indeed witch teats." Staples was, it will be recalled, under suspicion herself. Said she: "Here are no more teats than I myself have or any other woman." Quite possibly Staples dreaded a similar examination and desperately tried to head off suspicion by belittling the marks on Knapp's body. Goodwife Knapp had earlier indicated that Mary Staples had also received "Indian Gods." The aggrieved husband of Mary Staples even sued Fairfield's leading citizen, Roger Ludlow, for defamatory remarks about his wife in relation to the case at hand. It would seem that the family Staples was frightened to the core and became frantic in its efforts to ward off the onus which had destroyed Goodwife Knapp.

Mary Staples was never completely successful in clearing her name. For the rest of her long life she was rumored to be a witch. The stigma struck with her to the bitter end. In 1692, a whole 39 years after the Knapp affair, Fairfield once again became embroiled in a witch hunt. Mary Staples, by then an elderly widow, got caught up in it. She was arraigned on a charge of witchery but escaped when a grand jury refused to indict her. She did not, however, escape the animus of her neighbors, as the following testimony shows:

At a court held at Fairfield ye 15th day of September 1692: the testimony of Hester Groment, aged 35 years or thereabout be that when she lay sick sometime in May last she saw about midnight the widow Staples, that is to say the shape of her person, sitting upon the floor in the inner room and the shape of Mrs. Staples dancing upon the foot of the bed with a white cup in her hand and so performed three times. Sworn in court.

1654

Lydia Gilbert, white, age unknown. *Murder and witchcraft.* The crime was allegedly committed on October 3, 1651, at Windsor, Connecticut. This luckless individual lived at Windsor and was probably a daughter of Thomas Gilbert, a resident there since 1644. Assuming that she was indeed such a daughter, she had five siblings, one of whom, Jonathan Gilbert, was marshall for the county of Hartford.

It is possible that civic duty compelled Jonathan Gilbert to arrest his own sister and officiate at her execution.

Boarding at the Gilbert household was a 58-year-old bachelor named Henry Stiles. He had had business dealings with Thomas Gilbert and was undoubtedly a friend of that man's family. He was also a member of the local militia. On October 3, 1651, tragedy overtook him. While engaged in a training exercise he was mortally wounded by the accidental discharge of a blunderbuss carried by a fellow militiaman named Thomas Allyn. An official inquest severely censured Allyn for "homicide by misadventure" but then let the matter rest.

Three years passed and then a remarkable thing happened: the case was reopened. Allyn was exonerated and the death of Henry Stiles was attributed "to homicide by means of witchcraft." Thomas Allyn had not been careless with his gun, it was concluded, rather he or his gun had been "bewitched" into fatally wounding Henry Stiles. Prime suspect: Lydia Gilbert of Windsor.

On November 28, 1654, a Hartford grand jury found a bill of indictment against Lydia Gilbert in the following words:

Lydia Gilbert, thou art here indicted by the name of Lydia Gilbert, that not having the fear of God before thine eyes, thou hast of late years or still do give entertainment to Satan, the great enemy of God and mankind, and by his help hath killed the body of Henry Stiles besides other witchcrafts, for which according to the law of God and the established law of this colony, thou deservist to die.

There remains another incredible fact to add to this already incredible series of events: a trial court actually found the defendant guilty as charged.

Sentence of death was mandatory (especially since the charge of witchcraft was aggravated by an additional charge of murder) and execution almost certainly followed at Hartford on or about December 15, 1654.

So much for the cold facts and reasonable probabilities. We must now take a closer look at what the surviving documentation tells us.

The indictment states that the main charge against Lydia Gilbert was the alleged murder of Henry Stiles by supernatural means. However, particular attention must be paid to the words "besides other witchcrafts."

What other witchcrafts?

It would seem that Lydia Gilbert had a reputation above and beyond the Stiles affair. And that reputation must have been bad indeed to support a guilty verdict based on such far-fetched charges.

A big unanswered question involves exactly what it was that was alleged to have kindled Lydia Gilbert's alleged malice against Henry Stiles in the first place. We know that both were residents of the same household, at least for a while. We know that Stiles was a bachelor and may reasonably conclude that Lydia Gilbert was likewise unmarried. Was Lydia a spinster daughter of the Gilbert family who cast longing eyes on an eligible bachelor only to be spurned and/or jilted by him? Was it her indignation at such a rejection that caused Lydia Gilbert to resent Henry Stiles to a point where she would inspire suspicion over what had at first seemed like an accidental death?

Even more sinister possibilities concern the part which may have been played by the Allyn family.

Thomas Allyn, the young man whose carelessness had killed Henry Stiles, was a son of Matthew Allyn, one of the most eminent men in Connecticut at that time. One cannot dismiss the possibility that the elder Allyn played a part in railroading Lydia Gilbert. We know that the Allyns, the Gilberts and Henry Stiles were all residents of Windsor. They certainly knew each other. The elder Allyn was one of the town's richest men and one of the largest landowners in Connecticut. He was a delegate to the General Court nearly every year from 1648 to 1658. He was also a magistrate of the colony from 1657 to 1667, a commissioner for the United Colonies of New England, etc. There can be no doubt that he was intimately acquainted with both the judges and the jury which condemned Lydia Gilbert. Moreover, there is direct evidence that Thomas Allyn was his father's favorite son. Matthew Allyn had passed over his eldest son, John Allyn, in favor of the younger son Thomas when he made bequests in his will. Matthew Allyn left his house and lands in Windsor (his home hearth) to his younger son Thomas while his eldest son was assigned a wilderness tract in far-off Killingworth. Matthew Allyn was undoubtedly cognizant of the stigma which his favorite son suffered due to his negligence in the death of Henry Stiles. The quintessential question then is just how far the father went or would have been willing to go in order to exculpate his favorite son. Since he wished to leave his homestead to Thomas, he was faced with the problem of that son's social position in Windsor, a position that had been sullied by the death of Henry Stiles. Hence the son's problem became the father's problem. Thomas could never have hoped to enjoy his inheritance in complete concord unless his stigma was removed. Hence the fabrication of a scapegoat in the person of Lydia Gilbert.

Did Matthew Allyn have a hand in instigating the preposterous charge against Lydia Gilbert? Did he use his influence to sway a court of law? Did he in fact orchestrate a judicial murder?

There is a dearth of hard evidence by which to substantiate such a charge against Matthew Allyn but circumstantial evidence is suggestive to a point which makes it impossible to ignore.

1655

Walter Robinson, white, age 15. *Bestiality.* The crime was committed on an unknown date at Milford, Connecticut. This juvenile offender was a shepherd boy employed by a Milford squire named John Fowler. On the day when young Robinson committed his capital crime he was tending a flock of sheep in a large pasture overlooking Long Island Sound. Unknown to Robinson, a fisherman happened to pass by the spot just as he was in the act of copulating with his female sheepdog. Scarcely able to believe his eyes, the fisherman reported what he had seen. Robinson was questioned and he admitted the truth of the fisherman's allegation. A New Haven court did not take Robinson's age as a mitigating factor. The boy was made to face the full penalty of the law. On March 4, 1655, he was brought to the New Haven gallows.

There Robinson was forced to watch as the sheepdog was killed with a sword. Then the boy was hanged. He and the dog were buried together.

John Knight, white, age unknown. *Pederasty.* The crime was committed over a period of time at New Haven, Connecticut. This man was a servant in the household of a New Haven squire named William Judson. He was also a compulsive child molester who was attracted to girls and boys alike. On one occasion Knight was made to sit upon a gallows with a rope around his neck because he had behaved indecently with young girls. The experience (which in those days was a mark of extreme disgrace) did little or nothing to reform him. Knight finally went too far when he seduced 14-year-old Peter Vinson, an apprentice lad of the same household. When it was determined that Knight had had carnal knowledge of the boy on more than one occasion he was sentenced to death. He was hanged at New Haven sometime in the month of June, 1655. When it was further determined that the boy had yielded to Knight's advances of his own free will, a public whipping was decreed for him. The same punishment was meted out to the girls with whom Knight had been intimate. Knight's employer, William Judson, was made to pay a stiff fine when it was determined that he had tried to conceal the scandal.

1656

Anne Hibbins, white, age unknown. *Witchcraft.* William and Anne Hibbins, a married couple, had arrived at Boston in the early 1630s. They were people of substance. Goodman Hibbins established himself as a successful merchant and further augmented his social position by serving as an elite magistrate on the Massachusetts Court of Assistants. His wife, Anne, may have been a sister of Lieutenant Governor Richard Bellingham.

Anne Hibbins presents a marked contrast to the popular notion of an accused witch usually being a despised member of the lower classes. She was a despised member of the *upper* class.

It would appear that Anne Hibbins and her husband were a mismatched pair. While William Hibbins pursued a career of distinction, his wife made herself one of the most unpopular women in Boston. She had a haughty, domineering, argumentative and abrasive way about her. As early as 1640 opinion was turned so decidedly against her that she was excommunicated from the Boston church. The charges were general contumacy and connubial insubordination. Business losses suffered by her husband are said to have driven her to the emotional brink.

It is not unreasonable to presume that the social eminence of William Hibbins kept his wife from being denounced as a witch long before such charges were actually brought against her. But William Hibbins died in 1654 and with his protecting hand removed, Anne Hibbins became vulnerable. Having seen some of her neighbors gossiping about her in the street and correctly guessing that she was the topic of their conversation, Anne Hibbins confronted them. Her manner was far from polite. Soon there was additional gossip: only a witch, it was said, could know the gist of a conversation when she was out of earshot.

A formal charge of witchcraft was not long in coming. Anne Hibbins was tried for her life before the Court of Assistants in the spring of 1655. Details of the trial are scanty. A more than natural astuteness in gossip was evident and there were also references to smitten livestock.

The verdict of the Court of Assistants called for a retrial. The matter was then brought before the highest tribunal in the colony: the General Court. It seems likely that the magistrates who comprised the Court of Assistants could not bring themselves to condemn the widow of one of their former colleagues. So Anne Hibbins remained in jail for another year. The General Court took up her case on May 14, 1656, and brought in a clear-cut verdict of guilty. The sentence was death and the unpopular widow went to the Boston gallows on June 19, 1656.

1659–1661

William Robinson, Marmaduke Stevenson, Mary Dyer and **William Leddra,** whites, ages unknown. *Violating terms of banishment.* These people were religious zealots who gave their lives for their cause. Some consider them martyrs while others regard them as fools. Before examining them as individuals it is first necessary to review antecedent events.

The founders of Massachusetts came to America in order to establish a realm where they could live and worship according to "their own particular creed." They were very definitive on that point. Unlike the framers of the United States Constitution a century and a half later, the Puritans had no grand ideas of religious freedom or religious tolerance. Their colony was designed to allow no sect but their own. They reasoned that the presence of others would invite sedition. So early on they strove against an influx of infidels.

Religious non-conformity began to vex the Bay Colony Puritans almost immediately after their arrival. Indeed, the germ came on board their very first ship in the person of Roger Williams, who was destined to earn a place in history as the founder of Rhode Island. In 1631 Williams caused a stir by declining a Boston ministry because the position would have precluded him from advocating complete renunciation of the Church of England. So he went instead to Plymouth where his views were more favorably received and he served as a minister there from 1632 to 1633. Williams became an early advocate of the separation of Church and State and he rankled Massachusetts orthodoxy by criticizing its theocratic principles of government. He openly despised the obtrusive manner in which the Puritans sought to impose their sectarian views on others and he castigated them for what he saw as the less than honorable ways in which they acquired Indian land.

By 1634 Williams had antagonized the Bay Colony establishment to a point where it refused to sanction his appointment to the church at Salem. He took the pulpit anyway, claiming that secular authority had no prerogative in ecclesiastical matters.

The theocrats were outraged by such defiance. In 1636 they retaliated by having Williams arrested, forcibly removed from the Salem pulpit and convicted on a trumped-up charge of sedition. He was condemned to banishment and abided that decree by sailing south with a band of followers and founding the settlement of Providence, Rhode Island.

The adventures of Roger Williams were a rare example of defiance with a happy ending. However, the fate of Anne Hutchinson, the next person to challenge the theocrats, was quite different.

Anne Hutchinson was an intelligent woman of spirit who arrived at Boston in 1634 with her husband and children. Possessed of an obliging demeanor, she made many friends. Social gatherings at her home became popular events. It did not take long for theology to enter conversation at the Hutchinson homestead. Anne had conceived a belief that faith alone was a sufficient ticket to salvation. Hence she found herself at odds with an established church which preached that faith must be augmented by good works. Heresy was brewing at Anne Hutchinson's house and the situation did not go unnoticed.

Even the theocrats themselves were of a divided opinion. The governor, Sir Henry Vane, and several influential ministers saw little threat in Anne Hutchinson. However, she was bitterly denounced by the deputy-governor, John Winthrop, and another brace of ministers. The tide finally turned against her in 1637 when Governor Vane returned to England. His successor, Winthrop, called a synod which condemned Anne Hutchinson as a heretic. Some of her followers took this as their cue to become reconciled to the establishment. Others were banished. Anne herself was among the latter and she wound up in Rhode Island. Six years later she and her entire family were massacred by hostile Indians in a tragedy which her enemies called divine retribution.

A short period of religious tranquility came to Massachusetts after the purge of Anne Hutchinson. The propaganda value of her fate was not without its effect. But it was to be only a matter of time before a new controversy arose.

In the year 1647 or thereabout an English shoemaker named George Fox conceived a notion that God could be directly approached without the use of ritualistic intermediaries such as a standing clergy, an organized church, sacraments, sermons, formal books of prayer, etc. He reasoned that divine inspiration, which he termed "the Inner Light," was a thing of spontaneity which could happen to anyone who Almighty God chose to favor. A formal creed was therefore deemed unnecessary. Fox believed that all human beings were created equal and remained so in the eyes of God. He also advocated scrupulous honesty, non-violence and simplicity in personal habits.

George Fox soon attracted a following whom he called "the Children of the Light." Soon they came to refer to themselves as "Friends" and "The Society of Friends." But they became most widely known by the cognomen of "Quakers," originally a scornful epithet given to them in mockery of an alleged trembling motion which was said to characterize their fervor.

That Fox's teachings were well-intended is beyond question. But his sect was still a sect. And throughout history all sects have had one thing in common: namely a conceited belief that their particular tenets — and theirs alone — are the one true path to salvation. Convinced of this in their turn, the Quakers conceived the usual missionary zeal and set out to convert the world.

A cold reception awaited them in Massachusetts. Notoriety having preceded them, their arrival was anticipated with alarm. Many of their beliefs were in direct conflict with those of the Puritans and were regarded as dangerous threats. For instance, Quaker disregard for conventional rank and social class structure clashed with a caste-conscious and regimented society like that of the Bay Colony. Quakers were odious to the theocracy for their disdain of an ordained clergy as well as for what was construed as deliberate disrespect for authority. Equally galling was Quaker refusal to take required oaths of fidelity, refusal to pay taxes and refusal to bear arms for the common defense.

Such nonconformity was intolerable, especially when it was noted how the Quakers actively sought converts. Magistrates, ministers and conscientious Puritans in general united in opposition to Quakerism. If they could not eradicate or at the very least contain the perceived threat, they were resolved to try.

Beginning in 1657 the Bay Colony sought to hinder Quakers through statutory means. Quakers were officially denied residence and barred from traveling in Massachusetts. Any shipmaster who knowingly gave them passage was subject to a crushing fine. Quaker writers were banned and Quakers themselves were brought to the whipping post and the pillory.

Quaker zeal intensified under persecution. While the less hearty of them sought refuge in Rhode Island, the more intensely devoted (and in many cases *fanatical*) reasoned that they were on a sacred mission and resolved to endure any extremity. Hence the severity of the Bay Colony's anti–Quaker campaign became a matter of degrees. When statutory measures failed to have their desired effect, physical mutilation and the threat thereof followed. Before long obstinate Quakers were not only being pilloried and whipped but were having their ears hacked off, their noses slit and their tongues pierced with hot needles. By the autumn of 1658 the authorities of Massachusetts had reached the final extreme: they enacted a law mandating perpetual banishment for all Quakers on pain of death.

With the passage of this law many Quakers finally got the message and moved out of Massachusetts. However, a handful of fanatics opted to defy the banishment act. They reasoned that martyrdom was more glorious than living to further the greater glory of God. Among such individuals were four people named William Robinson, Marmaduke Stevenson, Mary Dyer and William Leddra.

The best known of this foursome was Mary Dyer. She and her husband, William Dyer, were long-standing residents of Boston. Originally a member of the Boston church, Mary Dyer became a friend and follower of Anne Hutchinson. Shortly before the exile of the latter, Mary Dyer gave birth to a badly deformed child. Such a birth was viewed as a divine judgment of Mary's heretical rapport with Anne Hutchinson, an opinion which was further aggravated by the fact that the only witnesses to the birth were Anne Hutchinson herself and a midwife of dubious reputation.

It is quite possible that this irregular childbirth affected Mary Dyer's mind to a point where she as propelled toward religious zealotry. Such is the only known reason which might explain her subsequent conduct. Between the time of Anne Hutchinson's banishment in 1637 and the arrival of the Quakers in 1657 Mary Dyer had 20 years in which to search for greater harmony with God. She seems to have regarded the coming of the Quakers as the long sought object of a quest. Quaker beliefs answered her psychological needs and she embraced the new sect with unbounded enthusiasm.

As the severity of anti–Quaker measures increased, William Dyer opted to relocate to Rhode Island. He, his wife and children accordingly left Boston. However, Mary Dyer loathed passive conduct and decided to join other Quaker fanatics in defying the Banishment Act. The result was that she and two male companions (William Robinson and Marmaduke Stevenson) were seized and sentenced to death. On October 22, 1659, all three were drawn to the Boston gallows. The two men were hanged but Mary Dyer was reprieved at the last moment through the efforts of her family. She was granted her life on condition that she get out of Massachusetts and stay out. Then in order to strike terror into her, she was forced to watch the dying agonies of Robinson and Stevenson.

Mary Dyer was brought back to Rhode Island by her eldest son. However, she could not be restrained for long. Within a matter of weeks she was back in Boston. Her arrest was soon in coming and she was once again condemned. On June 1, 1660, she was drawn to the gallows for a second time. Still she might have lived; at the place of execution she was offered a final chance to abide by the decree of banishment. Mary Dyer refused the offer. So her execution was carried out.

Many historians have attempted to paint a romantic picture of Mary Dyer and the so-called "courageous martyrdom" which she suffered. She has been portrayed as a heroine of free conscience and a pioneer of religious liberty. However, the facts of her case speak for themselves: she had more than an ample opportunity to save her life *and* retain her faith. She merely had to stay out of a certain place in order to do so. The fact that she rashly sought martyrdom on her own initiative indicates that she either had *or may have had* a mental disorder. Whether deranged or not, she was still mentally competent to understand the law and the price to be paid for violating it. For these reasons some have said that her blood was on her own hands.

Massachusetts hanged another Quaker on March 14, 1661. His name was William Leddra. However, in a letter dated September 9, 1661, the King of England forbade the further use of capital punishment in such cases. Lesser penalties did, however, continue to be imposed for many years. The colonies of Plymouth, New Haven and Connecticut also adopted anti–Quaker measures but they never went to the extremes of Massachusetts. Gradually the climate changed, not only in Massachusetts but elsewhere. The influence of Puritan theocrats waned with the passing of time and Quakers became tolerated and even accepted. Bigotry was unable to withstand the fact that New England offered opportunities to more than just a select few.

1662

William Potter, white, age about 60. *Bestiality.* The crime was committed on numerous occasions at New Haven, Connecticut. This man had lived at New Haven since the time of its earliest settlement. He was a farmer by occupation, credibly educated, a churchgoer and a family man. Beneath that veneer a dark secret lurked within William Potter: since the age of 11 he had been addicted to an unnatural craving for non-human sexual partners. Throughout the course of his lifetime he had carnal knowledge of the following creatures: dogs, horses, cattle, sheep and swine. On one occasion his wife caught him with the family dog. Another time his son caught him with a sow. So appalled were those persons that they brought the matter to the attention of local authorities. When the full extent of Potter's transgressions became known (primarily through his own confession), a visibly sickened court had no qualms about sentencing the man to death. The penalty was pronounced by the governor of New Haven himself. On June 6, 1662, the last act in this tragedy took place. On that date William Potter was brought to the gallows. A large pit was dug there into which were thrown the carcasses of every animal known to have been abused by the condemned man. These consisted of a cow, two calves, three ewes and two pigs. Potter was forced to watch as the animals were killed and thrown into the pit. Then Potter himself was hanged and his body was thrown into the same pit. He was considered unfit for burial among humans.

1662–1663

Mary Sanford, Nathaniel Green-smith, Rebecca Greensmith and **Mary Barnes,** whites, ages unknown. *Witchcraft.* The second worst witch hunt in colonial America took place at Hartford, Connecticut, in 1662 and 1663. In all, 12 people were accused. Of that number four were executed, five fled for their lives, one was rescued through outside intervention, another escaped on a technicality and one got off with only a smeared reputation. The affair bore

tragic consequences not only for the parties involved but for their community in general. Before recounting those events however, it is first necessary to examine the personalities and events which combined to foment such an upheaval.

William and Judith Ayres, a married couple, had been notorious characters at Hartford since at least 1651. Low on the social scale (William was described as a "tinker"), they were frequently in court on misdemeanor charges, allegations of theft being recurrent against William Ayres.

Another unpopular pair were Andrew and Mary Sanford. Their legal trail is less extensive than that of the Ayreses but there is evidence that Andrew Sanford was resented in the community for bad faith in business dealings. Mary Sanford was a busybody with an uncanny knack for discovering personal secrets about her neighbors.

It was with these two families that the Hartford witch hunt of 1662–1663 began.

It will be recalled that Lydia Gilbert was almost certainly executed at Hartford in December of 1654. The Ayreses and Sanfords were probably among the spectators of that event. Whether subsequent events were actually connected remains uncertain but William Ayres seems to have made a snide remark of some kind at the time which offended the Sanfords because on December 7, 1654, Andrew Sanford sued William Ayres for slander. The exact details of this slander suit are not recorded but it is not at all unreasonable to speculate that Ayres, motivated by the prevalent news of witchery, made a derogatory reference to Mary Sanford's talent for ferreting out personal secrets. When the case came to trial, however, Sanford's low reputation belittled his position as a plaintiff; he was awarded only a derisory 12 pence damages.

Matters then assumed the proportions of a slow boil. Seven months after the slander suit, William and Judith Ayres were required to post personal bonds of £20 each for their good behavior. We are not informed of the exact reason for such a move by the Hartford authorities but the cause must have been egregious since a total of £40 was a ruinous amount to impose on a lowly tinker and his wife. It is particularly significant to note that Goodwife Ayres was placed under a bond of her own apart from that of her husband. The onus of a witch was probably mounting against her at the time as was undoubtedly the case with Goodwife Sanford.

Then in the summer of 1658 came the first serious omen to the events of 1662-1663. Andrew Sanford sued a man named William Edwards for "defamation in a high degree." He demanded damages of £50 and was awarded the small but tidy sum of £5. Soon afterwards William Ayres also sued Edwards and was awarded a handsome £9 plus 14 shillings and costs. The precise nature of the expensive "defamations" is unrecorded but there can be little doubt that Edwards had hurled the epithet of "witch" at both Sanford and Ayres. We may also presume that Edwards was left smarting from his pecuniary penalties and had a hand in stirring up popular antipathy against his foes.   -

This sort of tension persisted for another three years. The names *Sanford* and *Ayres* grew odious in Hartford. By the winter of 1662 William Ayres had become so piqued that he lashed back at one of his antagonists, a certain Christopher Crow by name. The result was that Crow slapped Ayres with a slander suit to the extraordinary tune of £100. The lawsuit was never acted upon. For three weeks later hell broke loose at Hartford.

On March 23, 1662, an eight-year-old girl named Elizabeth Kelly fell ill of a strange malady. Three days later she was dead. During the delirium which preceded her death she babbled and raved against Judith Ayres. Afterwards her frantic parents recounted the death-bed scene which is here reprinted *in extenso*:

Witnesses that our said daughter on the 23rd of March 1662 being ye Lord's day, was in good health as she was all for a long time before to our apprehension and had not any sign nor before done anything that we knew that might be providential to her health. And on ye said Lord's day dismissed from her grandmother's house and with her came to our house ye wife of William Ayres, who going to eat did take hot broth out of ye boiling pot and did immediately eat thereof and did require our said child to eat with her of ye same which we did forbid, telling her it was too hot for her. But ye child did eat with her out of ye same vessel whereupon she began to complain of pains at her stomach for which remedy I gave her a small dose of ye powder of angelica root which gave her some present ease. We did at that present wonder that ye child should take so for not having nourished so to do but we did not then suspect ye said Ayres. In ye afternoon of ye same day ye child went to ye meeting again and did not make complaint at her return home. But about three hours in ye night next following, ye said child being in ye bed with me and asleep, did suddenly start up out of her sleep and throwing up her hands, cried Father! Father! Help me! Help me! Goodwife Ayres is upon me! She shoves me, she kneels on my body, she will break my bowels, she pinches me, she will make me blast and blow! Oh father! Will you not help me?! with other such expressions of like nature to my great grief and astonishment. My reply was lay you down and be quiet. Do not disturb your mother. Upon which she was a little quiet but presently started up again and cried out with greater violence than before against Goodwife Ayres, using much ye same expressions aforesaid. Upon rising, I lifted a bundle and took her up and put her in ye bed with her mother from which time she was in great extremity of misery, crying still out against ye said Ayres and asking that we would give her a drink. On ye Monday she cried out against ye said Ayres saying Goody Ayres torments me! She pinches me with pins! She will kill me! Oh father, set on ye great furnace and scald her! Get ye broadaxe and cut off her head! If you haven't got a broadaxe get ye narrow axe and chop off her head! with many ye like expressions continually proceeding from her. We used what physical help we could obtain and that without delay. But we could not conceive nor others for us that her malady was natural. In that sad condition she continued till Tuesday, on which day I and Bethiah Kelly being in ye house and ye wife of Thomas Whaples and ye wife of Nathaniel Greensmith, ye child being in great misery, ye aforesaid Ayres came in whereupon ye said child said to her: Goodwife Ayres why do you torment me and pinch me? Goodwife Whaples said to ye child: You must not speak so against Goodwife Ayres. She comes in love to see you. While ye said Ayres was gone ye child seemed well and fell asleep. Ye said Ayres said: She will be well again, I hope. Ye same Tuesday night ye child told us both that when Goody Ayres was with her alone she said to ye child: Betty, why do you speak so much against me? I will be even with you for it before you die. If you will say no more of me, I will give you a fine lace for your dress. Bethiah Kelly, perceiving her whispering with ye child and telling her something. I asked her what it was she said. Ye said Ayres answered: A lace for a dress. Ye said Ayres departing, ye child was more quiet till midnight and then she broke out afresh as before against Goodwife Ayres. Moreover, on ye same Tuesday ye child said: Father, why do you not go to ye magistrates and get them to punish Goodwife Ayres? Pray father go to ye magistrates. If I could go myself I would complain to them of how she

misuses me. In ye same plight she continued till Wednesday night and then died. Ye last words she spoke were: Goodwife Ayres chokes me! Then she was speechless.

Elizabeth Kelly died on March 26, 1662. Since the circumstances of her death were deemed suspicious, a coroner's inquest was held and an autopsy was ordered. On March 31, 1662, a grisly scene was enacted in the local cemetery as the dead girl was cut open moments prior to burial. The body was already decomposing and the stench associated with it was almost unendurable. The coroner was unable to identify a specific cause of death. However, he did note several peculiarities which he could not readily explain by conventional means. Then like the typical 17th century physician that he was, the coroner had recourse to pronounce the death as being due to witchcraft.

This news threw the entire community into an uproar. The psychological impact alone was devastating. Soon a number of unstable persons became excited and imagined themselves beset by witches. Every bodily ache and pain was ascribed to assaults by disciples of the devil who were eager to destroy others just as they had little Elizabeth Kelly. Three young women were principally affected by this craze. One was the sister of a minister. The most conspicuous of them, however, was named Ann Cole. An eyewitness later described the scene around her:

> This Ann Cole was taken with strange fits wherein she or rather the devil as tis judged making use of her lips, held a discourse for a considerable time. The general purport of it was to this purpose: that a company of familiars of the Evil One, who were named in the discourse that passed from her, were contriving how to carry on their mischievous designs against some and especially against her, mentioning

sundry ways they would take to that end, as that they would afflict her body, spoil her name, hinder her marriage, etc. wherein the general answer made among them was "She runs to her rock." This method having been continued for some hours, the conclusion was: "Let us confound her language that she may tell no more tales." And then after some time of unintelligible muttering the discourse passed into a Dutch tone (a family of Dutch then living in the town), and therein an account was given of some afflictions that had befallen others, among the rest a young woman (next neighbor to the Dutch family), that could speak but very little (laboring of that infirmity from her youth), had met with great sorrow as pinchings of her arms in the dark, etc. whereof she had before informed her brother (one of the ministers of Hartford). In that Dutch toned discourse there were plain intimations given by whom and for what such a course had been taken with her. Judicious Mr. Stone (who is now with God), being bye when the latter discourse passed, declared it in his thoughts impossible that one not familiarly acquainted with the Dutch (which Ann Cole had not at all been), should so exactly imitate the Dutch tone in the pronunciation of English. Sundry times such kind of discourse was uttered by her which was very awful and amazing to the hearers. Mr. Samuel Hooker was present the first time and Mr. Joseph Haynes, who wrote what was said. So did the relator also when he came into the house sometime after the discourse began. Extremely violent bodily motions she many times had even to the hazard of her life in the apprehensions of those that saw them. And very often great disturbance was given in the public worship of God by her and two other women who had also strange fits. Once in special, on a day of prayer kept on that account, the motion and noise of the afflicted was so terrible that a godly person fainted under the appearance of it.

Horrifying to the 17th century mind as were the details of this account, by far the most nefarious aspects of Ann Cole's ordeal were the incriminating statements she made concerning "a company of familiars of the Evil One." In all, she denounced seven people. Judith Ayres was the first to be arrested. Shortly afterward, Andrew and Mary Sanford were taken into custody. Next came Judith Varlet (the Dutch neighbor), and Rebecca Greensmith, a next-door neighbor of Ann Cole. A feisty woman named Elizabeth Seager was also apprehended as was an ill-reputed weaver named James Wakeley. Still others would follow.

During the month of May a grand jury was impaneled to consider the masses of evidence which had accumulated. Judith Ayres was prosecuted first. Her case looked bad. She was accused of using witchcraft to murder Elizabeth Kelly and of having a hand in the molestation of Ann Cole. It may be presumed that Ayres was searched for witch marks (standard procedure), but she also seems to have been subjected to the infamous *Water Test.*

The *Water Test* was a superstitious method for the detection of witches. It had its origins in continental Europe but was brought to England early in the 17th century. Writing in the year 1597, the King of Scotland (who later became King James I of England), advocated this test. It consisted of tying suspected witches cross-limbed with a cord and setting them upon a body of water (usually a pond), to see whether they would float or sink. The rationale behind the test was that true witches, in renouncing baptism, incurred the enmity of the natural element of water. Hence that element would not accept them into its midst and not allow them to sink into it. So if an accused person sank when put upon the water, he or she was deemed innocent of witchcraft where if the accused floated, he or she was deemed guilty. There was never any shortage of skeptics to this method of witch detection. However the fact that it was advocated by no less a person than the King of England meant that it was accredited in English territories.

If Increase Mather can be believed, the following scene took place at Hartford in the spring of 1662:

> There were some who had a mind to try whether the stories of witches not being able to sink under the water were true. Accordingly a man and woman mentioned in Ann Cole's Dutch-toned discourse had their hands and feet tied and so were cast into the water and they both apparently swam after the manner of a buoy, part under, part above the water. A bystander imagining that any person bound in that posture would be so borne up, offered himself for trial. But being in like manner gently laid on the water, he immediately sank right down. This was no legal evidence against the suspected persons nor were they proceeded against on any such account. However doubting that a halter would choke them though the water would not, they very fairly took their flight, not having been seen in that part of the world since.

Special attention must be paid to the words "This was no legal evidence against the suspected persons not were they proceeded against on any such account." Mather was lying when he wrote that statement. Judith Ayres was almost certainly the "woman" mentioned in the account; therefore it is impossible to believe that she was taken out of prison and subjected to the *Water Test* without official sanction. Moreover, the *Water Test* is known to have been used in Connecticut as late as 1692 *with official sanction.* Mather was apparently trying to minimize the criticism suffered by his Hartford colleagues.

While a grand jury was hearing evidence in May of 1662 (the water or-

deal was only one segment of the evidence), Ann Cole continued her ravings unabated. She became the darling of the local religious community and was fussed over and mollycoddled. Fasts were proclaimed and prayer sessions held for her "deliverance." Four ministers named Samuel Stone, John Whiting, Samuel Hooker and Joseph Haynes were the principal ecclesiastics in attendance, preaching, prodding, probing and prying as they went. Haynes (who was only 21 years old), even went to the extent of appointing himself a sort of stenographer; he stayed by Ann Cole constantly, quill pen and parchment in hand, and assiduously wrote down every word she babbled. He also earned the contempt of the accused persons. Rebecca Greensmith said that she wanted to "tear him in pieces." Once when Ann Cole screamed that Elizabeth Seager was a witch, the latter shrugged it off and sarcastically said that Haynes "had written a great deal of hodge podge that Ann Cole had said," i.e., a great deal of *non-sense* that Ann Cole had said. [Seager actually used much coarser language.]

That month of May also saw Hartford surprised by a sensational jailbreak. Judith Ayres slipped her chains and got away — probably with outside help. She was secretly harbored for a short time by Elizabeth Seager. Then she got together with her husband and made an overland dash for Rhode Island. So anxious were the Ayreses to get out of Hartford that they even left their eight-year-old son abandoned there. All of the property they left behind was confiscated.

Extradition demands were promptly sent to the governor of Rhode Island — also known to some as *Rogues Island*— because that colony was a popular refuge for nonconformists. A warrant was issued there for the arrest of Judith Ayres but the woman gave her pursuers the slip. There were later nasty allegations that the governor of Rhode Island had personally seen to it that the fugitive was not found. At any rate, neither Judith Ayres nor her husband ever returned to Connecticut.

Meanwhile in Hartford, the escape of Judith Ayres was taken as an admission of guilt. This convinced the local authorities there that they were on to something enormous and opinions were thereby hardened against the next two docketed cases: those of Andrew and Mary Sanford.

The trial of Andrew Sanford opened on June 6, 1662. The exact nature of the charges against him are obscure since the records of his case are lost. However, it seems quite certain that at least part of the charges had to do with the alleged abuse of Ann Cole. Sanford was lucky; he got off with a hung jury.

Mary Sanford was not so fortunate. Her trial opened on June 13, 1662. Presumably, she was also charged with complicity in the Ann Cole affair although her indictment specifies that she was charged with having illegal clairvoyant powers bestowed on her by the devil. The testimonies in her case have also perished but the jury had no reservations about returning a guilty verdict. Mary Sanford was sentenced to death and was almost certainly hanged on or about June 25, 1662.

The conviction of Mary Sanford (and probably the sight of her body twitching at the end of a rope), greatly alarmed the other implicated persons. Andrew Sanford got out of town. James Wakeley fled to Rhode Island. So did a Wethersfield couple named Henry and Katherine Palmer.

Shortly after the close of the Sanford trials the court adjourned for the summer. Judith Varlet and Rebecca Greensmith were bound over to the December sessions. In October Varlet got a lucky break; her powerful brother-in-law, Peter Stuyvesant (who was the governor of New Amsterdam), intervened on her behalf. As a result thereof, Varlet was released and allowed to relocate to Stuyvesant's domain.

Rebecca Greensmith remained in jail. Squalid conditions, loathsome food and callous warders exasperated her plight through the long months of durance. Interrogations wore her down. She was baited and badgered by curiosity seekers and hounded incessantly by ecclesiastics. Eventually she was pushed beyond the limits of human frailty and, judging from what followed, her mind snapped.

One of the ministers of Hartford, John Whiting, described what happened next when Rebecca Greensmith faced a grand jury in December of 1662:

> ...the court sent for Mr. Haynes and myself to read what we had written [Ann Cole's prattle] which when Mr. Haynes had done (the prisoner being present), she forthwith and freely confessed those things to be true, that she and other persons named in the discourse had had familiarity with the devil. Being asked whether she had made an express covenant with him, she answered that she had not, only that she promised to go with him when he called, which she had accordingly done several times and that the devil told her at Christmas they would have a merry meeting at which time the covenant would be drawn and subscribed. A person at the same time being present desired the next day to more particularly inquire of her about her guilt, it was accordingly done, to which she acknowledged that though when Mr. Haynes began to read she could have torn him in pieces and was so much resolved as might be to deny her guilt (as she had done before), yet after he had read a while she was as if her flesh had been pulled from her bones (such was her expression) and so could not deny any longer. She also declared that the devil first appeared to her in the form of a deer or fawn skipping about her wherewith she was not much frightened but by degrees he contrived to talk with her and that their meetings were frequently at such a place near her own

house and that some of the company came in one shape and in particular one in the shape of a crow came flying to them. Amongst other things she owned that the devil had frequent use of her body with much seeming but indeed horrible, hellish delight to her.

Oblivious to the probability that Rebecca Greensmith was crazy, magistrates, ministers and the public at large accepted her story as a frank and candid account of true witchcraft. The woman was believed implicitly without regard to probability or even *possibility*. Nor was she content with merely ruining herself; she decided to drag her husband down with her by declaring him a witch as well. Consequently the grand jury wasted no time in handing down indictments against both of the Greensmiths for capital felony. The date was December 30, 1662.

Rebecca Greensmith appears to have pled guilty. Then on January 8, 1663, she testified against her husband as follows:

That my husband on Friday night last, when I came to prison, told me that now thou hast confessed against thyself, let me alone and say nothing of me and I will be good unto thy children. I do testify that formerly when my husband hath told me of his great travail and labor, I wondered at it how he did it. This he did before I was married and when I was married I asked him how he did it and he answered me that he had help that I knew not of. About three years ago as I think it, my husband and I were in the woods several miles from home looking for a sow that we lost and I saw a creature, a red creature, following my husband. When I came to him I asked him what it was with him and he told me it was a fox. Another time when he and I drove our hogs into the woods beyond the pound that was to keep young cattle several miles off, I went before the hogs to call them and looking back, I saw two creatures like

dogs, one a little blacker than the other. They came after my husband pretty close to him and one did seem to me to touch him. I asked him what they were. He told me he thought foxes. I was still afraid when I saw anything because I heard so much of him before I married him. I have seen logs that my husband hath brought home in his cart that I wondered at it that he could get them into the cart, he being a man of little body and weak to my apprehension. The logs were such that I thought two men such as he could not have done it. I speak all of this out of love to my husband's soul and it is much against my will that I am now necessitated to speak against my husband. I desire that the Lord would open his heart to own and speak the truth.

I also testify that I being in the woods at a meeting, there was with me Goody Seager, Goodwife Sanford and Goodwife Ayres. At another time there was a meeting under a tree in the green by our house and there was there James Wakeley, Peter Grant's wife, Goodwife Ayres and Henry Palmer's wife of Wethersfield and Goody Seager. There we danced and had a bottle of sack. It was in the night and something like a cat called me out of the meeting and I was in Maj. Varlet's orchard with Mrs. Judith Varlet and she told me that she was much troubled with the marshal, Jonathan Gilbert, and cried. She said if it lay in her power she would do him a mischief or what hurt she could. Taken upon oath in court.

This confession made Rebecca Greensmith a celebrity. Her story was widely circulated and it became a sensation. She was questioned and requestioned until every last ounce of information was extracted from her. She probably couldn't invent fantasies fast enough to satisfy her listeners. So appalled and enthralled was the Hartford court that any defense Nathaniel Greensmith might have attempted was swept aside. He and his wife were both convicted and sentenced to death. They were hanged at Hartford on or about January 25, 1663.

Meanwhile a grand jury handed down two further indictments against another pair of suspected witches: Elizabeth Seager and Mary Barnes. Seager had a fearsome reputation in her community. She was known to have fraternized with convicted witches. She had even helped the notorious Judith Ayres to escape. The hysterical Ann Cole had raved against her and she was frowned upon for the open contempt that she had for the entire witch hunt. She quarreled with ministers and neighbors alike. Her sarcastic remarks were the bane of her enemies. Stories circulated about her involvement with the forces of evil. The following example will stand for the rest:

Robert Stern testifieth as followeth: I saw this woman Goodwife Seager in ye woods with three more women and with them I saw two black creatures like two Indians but taller. I saw likewise a kettle there over a fire. I saw the women dance around those black creatures and while I looked upon them one of the women, Goody Greensmith, said look who is yonder. Then they ran away up the hill. I stood still and ye black things came towards me and then I turned to come away. He further said that he knew the persons by their clothes, having observed such clothes on them not long before.

Her reputation and tart tongue not withstanding, Elizabeth Seager had luck on her side. Her trial ended in an acquittal on technical grounds. She was tried again the following summer and again acquitted. In 1665 she was tried a third time, convicted but reprieved on a technicality. Other occasions found her charged with adultery and blasphemy. She managed to dodge the gallows at least five times. Then she deemed it prudent to get out of town.

Mary Barnes is the least known entity of the Hartford witch hunt. There is no known documentation linking her with any of the other defendants. Nor do we know under what circumstances she was brought to court. The precise details of her alleged witchery are likewise unknown. As an individual, she is known to have been a resident of Farmington. She was the daughter of one Thomas Andrus of that place and the wife of one Thomas Barnes, a veteran of the Pequot War. She was indicted along with Elizabeth Seager on January 6, 1663. She was found guilty and was almost certainly executed shortly thereafter, probably together with the Greensmiths.

An interesting detail which historians of the Hartford witch hunt have all overlooked is the fact that on the very same day of the Seager and Barnes indictments, a severe earthquake rumbled through New England. The following account of it has survived:

On January 6, 1663, a great earthquake was felt throughout New England. It began at about half past five o'clock PM. While the heavens were serene there was suddenly heard a roar like that of fire. The buildings were shaken with violence. The doors opened and shut by themselves. The bells rang without being touched. The walls split asunder. The floors separated and fell down. The fields put on the appearance of precipices and the mountains seemed moving out of their places. The first shock continued for nearly half an hour. Several violent shocks succeeded this the same evening and the next day. Nor did the earthquake cease until the following July. The effects of the first in January were remarkable: Many fountains and small streams were dried up. In others the water became sulfurous. Many trees were torn up and thrown to a considerable distance and some of the mountains appeared to be much moved and broken.

A seismic disturbance of such magnitude would certainly have been felt at

Hartford. Whether the event influenced the witch hunt then in progress is unknown.

1667

Peter Abbott, white, age about 28. *Murder.* The crime was committed on an unknown date at Fairfield, Connecticut. This offender was the eldest son of Robert and Mary Abbott, an English couple who settled at Watertown, Massachusetts, in 1634. Peter Abbott was born there about 1639, the second child of his parents. Seven more siblings would follow in the years to come. By the 1650s the Abbotts had relocated to Branford, Connecticut, where the patriarch of the family had a substantial farm. As Peter Abbott grew toward adulthood it became apparent that he was "afflicted with a lunacy." For that reason he was kept close to home, working in tandem with his father. Peter Abbott's mental problem was not a bar to marriage however. A wife was found for him in the person of Elizabeth Everts of Guilford. Robert Abbott died in 1658 and Peter Abbott, as the eldest son, received a handsome inheritance. He used those proceeds to establish himself in a new home at Fairfield. It was there where he turned on his wife and child one night and slit their throats as they slept. Elizabeth Abbott died but the child recovered. Peter Abbott was sent to Hartford for trial and there he was capitally convicted. His mental derangement was not accepted as a mitigating factor. He was hanged at Hartford on October 16, 1667. One chronicler reports that "he died stupidly and sottishly."

1668

Ruth Briggs, white, age about 30. *Murder.* The crime was committed on February 15, 1668, at New Haven, Connecticut. This female offender was reputed to be the most shameless woman of her time. Her story, which begins in a dysfunctional home and ends at the gallows, is a sordid tale of moral and physical breakdown through years of violence, deprivation, promiscuity and general turpitude. It is a tale of ruin by degrees.

Ruth Briggs was not a Connecticut native. She came from Massachusetts. Her parents, Nicholas and Elizabeth Pinion, had settled at the Essex County town of Lynn sometime in the 1640s. They were a discordant couple who were ill-suited for parenthood. Both were frequently in court. Nicholas Pinion was an irascible illiterate who regularly beat his wife. Elizabeth Pinion was no better; so bellicose was she that two separate occasions found her in court on assault charges. She was also arrested three times for fighting with her husband in violation of a peace-keeping bond. The worst documented flareups between Goodman and Goodwife Pinion occurred in 1647 and 1648 when Nicholas was again charged with spousal abuse. It was said that he had beaten his wife so badly that she had suffered four separate miscarriages. Elizabeth Pinion also accused her husband of killing one of their infant children. Nicholas Pinion retaliated by accusing his wife of adultery, then a capital crime. The woman was actually tried for such an offense before the Massachusetts Court of Assistants in the spring of 1648. She managed to win an acquittal on the capital charge but was convicted of "swearing and lewd behavior" and sentenced to be "severely whipped" once at Boston and again at Lynn.

Beatings, court battles, miscarriages and allegations of capital crimes not withstanding, Nicholas and Elizabeth Pinion somehow managed to stay together. They raised a brood of five children; at least that many survived their infancies. Ruth was the eldest survivor.

On December 28, 1657, young Ruth Pinion married a neighbor named James Moore. The newlyweds made their home at Lynn and brought a daughter into the world. Then tragedy struck: James Moore suddenly died in the summer of 1659 and Ruth became a young widow with a child on her hands. She settled her husband's estate and moved in with her parents. Then she started sleeping around. She became notorious and was scolded in a court of law for having "ensnared and deluded sundry young men upon pretense and promise of marriage only to countenance and cover unlawful familiarity with them." In short, Ruth Pinion Moore was a woman of ill repute even before she came to Connecticut.

Eventually Massachusetts became too hot for the pugnacious family Pinion. The entire household moved to New Haven. Once resettled, they all returned to their former ways. Ruth herself fell in with bad company at the local ironworks where a number of unprincipled males were employed. She became their boon companion and served them in the basest of ways.

Chief among Ruth's new acquaintances was a known lecher named Patrick Moran. He not only slept with Ruth on numerous occasions but made improper advances towards her two younger sisters as well, one of whom was only 15 years old. By the autumn of 1664 Moran's behavior had so outraged Ruth's mother (Elizabeth Pinion) that she filed a formal complaint.

Moran countered the charges by claiming that Mother Pinion's motives in filing the complaint were less than honorable. He said that the woman was pressing a false accusation and attempting to manipulate the court. It was alleged that the plaintiff sought to thus avenge herself upon the defendant for having denied her credit on merchandise.

Moran was a scoundrel by any description but his rebuttal had a ring of truth to it. First of all, Ruth (and possibly her sisters as well) was a willing object of Moran's concupiscence. Furthermore, Mother Pinion was entirely capable of fabricating or at least embellishing such a charge. Lastly, it is impossible to dismiss Mother Pinion as the aggrieved parent she claimed to be. No paragon of virtue herself, it is not beyond possibility that she had countenanced the scandal of her daughters and Moran for the sake of material gain (she might have even deliberately prostituted them), only to turn against Moran when he balked at her increasing demands. An independent witness testified on Moran's behalf that he had once seen Mother Pinion fly into a rage when Moran had refused her some linen. She had then threatened Moran, calling him insulting names and chased him from her house with an axe.

The New Haven court considered the bad reputations of Ruth and her mother and acquitted Moran — reluctantly — since he had a reputation of his own. Moran then sued his accusers for slander and managed to collar them for £5 damages plus costs. However, his victory was pyrrhic; in handing down its decision the court made it clear that it considered Moran a public rascal.

Ruth went back to the ironworks and resumed her relations with Moran and his co-workers. She was used as a concubine by them and she enjoyed it.

By the summer of 1665 Ruth decided to get married again. Her new husband was Peter Briggs of Killingworth. Within a matter of days, however, Ruth abandoned her spouse and returned to the ironworks. Then to make matters worse, a Massachusetts man who Ruth had previously deceived with a promise of marriage showed up at New Haven to claim his bride. He learned that she was already married and also reviled as the town tramp.

This state of affairs so scandalized

New Haven that Ruth was arrested. She was charged with abandonment, unlawful flight, perjury, fornication, adultery, contempt of court and conduct unbecoming a wife and mother. A disgusted court decreed banishment and Ruth was sent back to Massachusetts where she sat out the following year.

By the summer of 1667 Ruth's mother was found dead and Ruth herself was back in New Haven. She initially hid out at the ironworks but when months went by without any move by the authorities she made bold to move in with her father. In January of 1668 Nicholas Pinion was charged with harboring a public enemy: his own daughter. By then winter had set in and it was argued that the weather precluded sending Ruth away. The court required Nicholas Pinion to post a bond to ensure that he would turn his daughter out by the first day of spring.

Ruth was not fated to leave New Haven on her own recognizance. When she did leave, she was under arrest and charged with capital felony. Debauchery at the ironworks had caught up with her. She had become pregnant and had made away with her baby at birth. Suspected of so doing, Ruth was arrested and sent to Hartford for trial.

The story of Ruth's downfall and the circumstances which led up to it are quite racy. Many of the details are unfit for publication. Ruth was also a compulsive liar. Her testimony before a Court of Inquiry was a masterpiece of prevarication. Some of the tales she told were so preposterous that they eradicated any sympathy which might have otherwise come her way. Indeed, it seems to have been her inability to tell the truth more than anything else which sealed her fate.

What happened was this: On February 21, 1668, Ruth was arraigned before a New Haven magistrate on suspicion of handling stolen goods. She lied from the start by attempting to throw the blame on her dead mother. Then Ruth was accused of concealing a recent pregnancy. Her physical state had aroused suspicion and a sudden change in her condition seemed incredible. Ruth stoutly denied that she had been pregnant. The magistrate did not believe her; a panel of matrons was ordered to give Ruth a physical examination. Ruth resisted and had to be examined by force. The matrons reported that Ruth's breasts were full of milk. Ruth then swore that her breasts were in such a condition because she was in the habit of breast feeding her *nine-year-old daughter*.

The next day Ruth was confronted with a putrid petticoat which six women swore was in such a condition to leave no doubt that it had been used as a swaddling cloth. Ruth denied ownership of the petticoat even though her own sister-in-law testified to the contrary. Another family member told of how Ruth had risen from her bed during the wee hours of February 15, 1668, and stayed outdoors a considerable time. When she returned she was in a delicate condition. It was alleged that she had given birth during that time.

Ruth continued to deny everything. She was confronted with an herbal draught that she had prepared for the purpose of inducing a miscarriage. Ruth said that evidence was contrived.

An exasperated magistrate ordered Ruth confined to a dank dungeon. Three days later she changed her tune. She admitted that she had given birth as suspected but said that the baby was stillborn. She also admitted that she had buried the baby in a swamp. When asked about the circumstances of the child's conception, she told a tale of having wandered about late one night in a disoriented frame of mind. Weak and vulnerable, she had met a male neighbor and fainted in his arms. When she awoke, she said, the man was in the act of raping her.

By this time the New Haven court was unwilling to believe anything Ruth said — especially the story about her baby being stillborn. An order was given for the dead infant to be exhumed and Ruth led officers to the spot where she had buried it. The corpse was successfully retrieved and a coroner's inquest ruled it a case of willful homicide.

Before sending her off to Hartford for trial and final judgment, the New Haven authorities questioned Ruth about her sex life. When asked if she had "sinned" frequently with the father of her dead infant, Ruth declared "more times than I have fingers and toes." (She had previously claimed only one act of intimacy with the same man.) She also described her dalliance with other men — Patrick Moran especially — and she took relish in relating the details. Ruth also galled her Puritan listeners by saying that she had committed adultery "six times on ye Lord's day."

The New Havenites could take no more. Extremities of winter weather not withstanding, Ruth was sent to Hartford under a strong guard where she arrived on or about March 10, 1668. Her trial before the Court of Assistants opened on May 12, 1668.

The ultimate fate of Ruth Briggs was decided at Hartford. The records of the Court of Assistants for 1668 are lost but it is certain that Ruth was convicted and hanged on or about June 1, 1668. In a pathetic letter dated March 16, 1668, she apologized for her past conduct and begged her relatives to give testimony on her behalf. The delicately written words "my very life depending upon your witness" illustrate the gravity of her situation.

In the spring of 1676 Ruth's father died at New Haven. His last will and testament was probated according to law and while Ruth's siblings were all mentioned as survivors and heirs; Ruth herself (although she was the eldest child) was not mentioned at all. This omission from the list of Nicholas Pinion's survivors almost certainly means that Ruth was dead by the time the will was made. Further evidence of Ruth's execution is found in a journal for the years 1664 to 1683 kept by the Rev. Simon Bradstreet, a contemporary of Ruth Briggs. There is found a reference to "a woman hanged in Connecticut in 1668 for adultery and infanticide." The woman so mentioned can only be Ruth Briggs.

Unidentified Woman, white, age unknown. *Murder.* The crime was committed on an unknown date in Essex County, Massachusetts. *Bradstreet's Journal* reports the execution of a female offender at Boston in October of 1668. The woman was hanged for "murdering her child." Moreover, the woman's mother and a Salem physician named Dr. Emery were both named as accessories in the matter. They were made to sit on the gallows with ropes around their necks, each flanking the dangling form of the executed woman. The loss of court records for this period precludes further study of this case.

1670

Two Unidentified Men, one white and one Native American, ages unknown. *Grand Larceny & Murder.* The crimes were committed on unknown dates at Salem and Roxbury, Massachusetts, respectively. *Bradstreet's Journal* reports a double hanging at Boston in October of 1670. Both of the offenders were men. The first of them was condemned for "frequent and notorious theft" and was said to be "the first man ever hanged in this land upon any such account." The other offender was a Native American man who killed his wife. According to Bradstreet, the couple was lodging at the house of an "Englishman" in the Boston suburb of Roxbury. The husband threw his wife out of a "chamber window" so that she fell to the ground and broke her neck. The loss of court records for this period precludes further study of these cases.

Thomas Flounders, white, age unknown. *Murder.* The crime was committed on July 11, 1670, at Wickford, Rhode Island. This offender was a tradesman of moderate means. On the above date he was tending his shop when in walked a rival named Walter House (white, age unknown). This visitor picked an argument with Flounders over a lawsuit in which the two men figured. Flounders lost his temper and attacked House with a cudgel. The latter was severely beaten and succumbed to his wounds. Flounders was brought to Newport and charged with willful murder. He was hanged there on November 2, 1670.

1671

Young Matoonas, Native American, age unknown. *Murder.* The crime was committed on an unknown date near Dedham, Massachusetts. This offender was put to death for killing a white man named Zachary Smith. *Bradstreet's Journal* reports that the victim was shot down on the highway near Dedham. Five years later the father of this offender was also executed [see Old Matoonas, 1676], although for crimes of his own. The scene was the Boston gallows. Young Matoonas died there in June of 1671. His head was cut off and set atop the gallows as a macabre ornament. Five years later the head was still there. When Old Matoonas was executed in 1676 his head was also cut off. It was then stuck on a spike and put alongside the head of Young Matoonas. Thus were father and son reunited.

Unidentified Man, Native American, age unknown. *Murder.* The crime was

committed on an unknown date at Woburn, Massachusetts. This offender is said to have "knocked an English maid on the head with his hatchet in her master's house." He was hanged at Boston in June of 1671 and his body was afterwards exposed in a crow cage. *Bradstreet's Journal* reports that the treatment of the bodies of this offender and that of Young Matoonas caused resentment in their respective tribes and was a contributing factor to King Philip's War.

William Thomas, white, age unknown. *Burglary.* The crime was committed in April of 1671 at Newport, Rhode Island. This man was a crony of Matthew and Eleanor Boomer, a Newport couple who were reputed to be receivers of stolen goods. It so happened that a Bostonian goldsmith named Mr. Kimball had a retail outlet in Newport. The Boomers allegedly masterminded a burglary of that establishment and recruited William Thomas for that purpose. Thomas followed his instructions and broke into the goldsmith's shop. He carried off loot for a considerable value which he allegedly fenced through the Boomers. Somehow Thomas got caught before he was able to leave town. He was put on trial and convicted of capital felony. Clemency was refused by the Rhode Island general assembly. William Thomas was then ordered for execution. He was hanged at Newport on June 9, 1671.

1672

Unidentified Man, white, age unknown. *Murder.* The crime was committed in April of 1672 somewhere in Massachusetts. This offender was a servant in the house of a squire named Mr. Davy. A female servant of the same household reported him to their master for some infraction, thus causing the male servant to receive "two or three blows." Smarting from that experience, the male servant took a gun and shot the informer dead. This homicide brought the male servant to his death on the Boston gallows in May of 1672. Loss of the court records for this period precludes further study of this case.

Thomas Rood, white, age about 45. *Incest.* The crime was committed over a period of time from about 1670 to 1672 at Norwich, Connecticut. This man was condemned by the Connecticut Court of Assistants for having sexual intercourse with his daughter, Sarah Rood. So flagrant had his cavorting been that Rood did not even attempt to deny it. He pled guilty to his indictment and accepted a death sentence without protest. He was hanged at Hartford on October 18, 1672. It is quite possible that Rood was the only person in American history to be executed for consensual incest. His daughter got off with a lesser sentence. She was the eldest child of Thomas and Sarah Rood of Norwich. She was 23 years old at the time of her trial and she had eight younger siblings.

1673

William Forrest, John Smith and **Alexander Wilson,** whites, ages unknown. *Mutiny & Piracy.* The crime was committed early in the year 1673 on the high seas. The English brig *Antonio* sailed from the port of Lisbon with a valuable cargo. Unknown to the captain and other officers aboard, a conspiracy was hatched among the aforementioned crewmen to take over the ship and embezzle the cargo. When the *Antonio* was nearing the Bay of Biscay the plotters put their plan in motion. They overpowered the officers and forced them into a lifeboat. Then the officers were cast adrift while the mutineers sailed westward. Several weeks later the *Antonio* arrived at Boston. The pirates initially passed themselves off as respectable mariners and made arrangements to dispose of the cargo which they had hijacked on the local market. While this was going on another ship arrived at Boston bearing the captain and officers of the *Antonio*. It was by pure coincidence that the newly arrived vessel had come across the stranded officers while at sea and had rescued them. There was mutual astonishment when officers and mutineers encountered each other at Boston. The true facts of the *Antonio's* voyage were reported to the city fathers and the entire crew of that vessel was arrested. The above-named men were identified as the ringleaders of the piratical conspiracy to seize control of the *Antonio*. All three were charged with mutiny and piracy. All were capitally convicted. They were hanged at Boston on an unknown date in the year 1673.

Thomas Cornell, white, age about 50. *Murder.* The crime was committed on February 8, 1673, at Portsmouth, Rhode Island. Rebecca Cornell (white, age 73) was an aging widow who signed her estate over to her son and daughter-in-law with the understanding that the recipients provide her with dower quarters and suitable care in her old age. Once Thomas Cornell had the property safely in his possession, however, he subjected his mother to forms of neglect which bordered on abuse. The old lady was consigned to an unheated room. She was also denied blankets and adequate food. It soon became clear to her that she was regarded as an unwanted burden and she complained about her plight to anyone who would listen. On the above date the elder Mrs. Cornell was found dead on the floor of her parlor close to the fireplace. She was badly burned. Thomas Cornell said that his mother had fallen asleep in a rocking chair while smoking her pipe, thereby causing her clothes to ignite with fatal results. This story was taken at face value and a funeral was held for the decedent. Four days later a man named John Briggs (white, age 64, who was a brother of Mrs. Cornell) went to the authorities with a strange tale: He said that his sister's ghost had appeared to him and revealed that she had been killed by her son. The ghost also said that the story of her death had been contrived. A close examination of the remains turned up evidence of mistreatment. In particular, a "suspicious wound" was found on the dead woman's abdomen which made the coroner suspect foul play. When the case came to trial it was alleged that Thomas Cornell had kicked and stomped his mother to death before setting her clothes on fire. A jury concurred in that belief and Thomas Cornell was convicted of willful matricide. He was hanged on the Newport gallows on May 23, 1673.

Indian John, alias "Punneau," Native American, age unknown. *Murder.* The crime was committed on March 21, 1673, at Portsmouth, Rhode Island. This offender got drunk on the above date and forced his way into the house of a white man named Richard Bulgar. The only person home at the time was Mrs. Lottira Bulgar (white, age unknown), the homeowner's wife. The intruder raped Goodwife Bulgar with such fury that she succumbed to vaginal trauma. Further details of the crime are too obscene for publication. Indian John was captured shortly afterward and brought to Newport for trial. When he sobered up he claimed to have no memory of the crime. He was hanged on the Newport gallows on May 23, 1673.

Jankssick, Native American, age unknown. *Murder.* The crime was committed on an unknown date somewhere in Rhode Island. This offender killed a fellow tribesman named Ossawan (age unknown) with deliberate malice. The exact details of the crime are not re-

corded. A jury consisting of six Englishmen and an equal number of Native American men convicted Jankssick of capital murder. Sentence of death was then imposed. Jankssick accordingly met his doom on the Newport gallows on November 5, 1673.

1674

Benjamin Goad, white, age 17. *Bestiality.* The crime was committed on February 7, 1674, at Roxbury, Massachusetts. This juvenile offender was observed in an act of gross indecency with a horse. When brought to trial he was convicted not only by eyewitness testimony but also by his own confession. The precise details of those accounts are unfit for publication. Benjamin Goad was carried to the Boston gallows on April 2, 1674. There he was forced to watch as the horse was killed by the executioner. Then Goad himself was hanged by the neck until dead. His body was later thrown into a pit along with the carcass of the horse.

Quaoganit, alias "The Old Man," Native American, age uncertain. *Murder.* The crime was committed in March of 1674 somewhere in Rhode Island. Very little is known of this case. Quaoganit killed his Native American wife under unknown circumstances. On May 11, 1674, the Rhode Island Court of Trials sentenced him to death for his crime. Quaoganit was accordingly hanged at Newport on May 19, 1674.

Indian Tom, Native American, age unknown. *Rape.* The crime was committed on June 15, 1674, somewhere in Massachusetts. This offender had indecently assaulted the wife of a fellow tribesman named John Jempson. Her name was Sarah Jempson. When the case was brought to trial, six Native American men were evenly matched with six Englishmen to comprise the petit jury.

All twelve of the jurymen voted to convict. Indian Tom was accordingly sentenced to death. He was hanged at Boston on September 10, 1674.

1675

Robert Driver and **Nicholas Feavour,** whites, age about 20. *Murder.* The crime was committed on February 10, 1675, at Portsmouth, New Hampshire. These young men were servants and or apprentices in the service of a Portsmouth fish dealer named Robert Williams (white, age unknown). They did not like their assignments and are reported to have behaved in a "slothful" manner. When their master reprimanded them they decided to free themselves from his service. On the above date Mr. Williams was relaxing in his parlor; he was seated in a chair and smoking a pipe. The two servants snuck up behind him with axes in their hands and they struck him down from behind. Both of the killers fled from the scene but were captured after a short manhunt. They were then brought to Boston and tried at a special session of the Court of Assistants. Both were capitally convicted. They were hanged from the Boston gallows on March 18, 1675.

Henry Green and **Negro Cloyes,** a white man and a black man respectively, ages unknown. *Murder.* Their crimes were committed during the early months of 1675 at Farmington, Connecticut, and at Stamford, Connecticut, respectively. Henry Green lived at Farmington. For some unknown reason he attacked a "young child" named John Biggs (white) and hacked him to death with an axe. Cloyes was a free Negro who lived at Stamford. He too was an axe murderer, the victim being his wife (name and age unknown, presumably black). The motives for these crimes are not mentioned in the meager court records of the time.

Both men were brought to Hartford for trial. Both pled guilty to their indictments. They were hanged at Hartford on June 1, 1675.

Tobias, Mattashunnamo and **Wampapaquan,** Native Americans, ages unknown. *Murder.* The crime was committed on January 29, 1675, at Namasket, an Indian settlement in Plymouth County, Massachusetts. These men were high ranking members of the Wampanoag tribe of Native Americans. All were close advisors to Metacom, aka "Philip," the high chief of a confederation which included several powerful subgroups of the Algonquian Nation. Tobias and Wampapaquan were father and son respectively. They along with Mattashunnamo were alleged to have murdered a so-called "Christian Indian preacher" named John Sassamon (age unknown) on the above date at the behest of the chief, aka Philip. The victim was severely beaten and then killed by having his head twisted around clockwise until his neck broke. His body was thrown into an icy pond. The motive for the murder was said to be retaliation against the victim for having warned the governor of Plymouth about a conspiracy among certain Native American tribes—a conspiracy to make war against the English settlers from Cape Cod to the Connecticut River valley. Tobias, Mattashunnamo and Wampapaquan were all denounced by supposed eyewitnesses to the murder of John Sassamon. They were brought to Plymouth and there convicted of capital felony. On June 8, 1675, Tobias and Mattashunnamo were hanged at Plymouth. Wampapaquan was also brought to the gallows that day but in his case the rope broke. He was then reprieved for a month. On July 8, 1675, a firing squad carried out his death sentence. These executions set off a full scale Indian war which lasted for more than a year and which devastated the New England colonies, especially Massachusetts,

Plymouth and Rhode Island. Entire towns were destroyed in the course of this war and thousands of people were killed on both sides. Metacom, aka Philip, aka "King Philip," used the execution of his lieutenants as an excuse to go on the warpath. His tribe, the Wampanoags, was joined by the allied Narragansett and Nipmuck tribes. Some of the worst atrocities in American history were committed during the course of this conflict which is known by the cognomen of *King Philip's War*.

Unidentified Man, Native American, age unknown. *Espionage.* The crime was committed in June of 1675 in the vicinity of Plymouth, Massachusetts. The *London Gazette* No. 1017 printed a lengthy dispatch from New England about the outbreak of King Philip's War. Under the date of "June 31, 1675," is a report about the execution of an Indian spy at Plymouth. Nothing further is known of this case.

Little John, Native American, age unknown. *Murder and sedition.* The crimes were committed over a period of time from June to September, 1675, in southeast New England. This man came to Boston as a messenger during King Philip's War. There he was recognized as one who was "a murderer of the English." The precise details of those alleged murders are unknown. Little John was hanged from the Boston gallows on September 22, 1675.

Samuel Guile, white, age unknown. *Rape.* The crime was committed on December 25, 1674, at Amesbury, Massachusetts. This man was a Haverhill resident. On the above date, while in the woods, he did "violently and forcibly seize on and commit a rape on the body of Mary Ashe, the wife of John Ashe of Amesbury." The victim was a white woman. No further details of the crime are known. Guile was brought to Boston

and tried by the Court of Assistants. The verdict went against him. Death on the gallows was decreed in this case and Guile suffered accordingly on October 16, 1675.

1676

Two Unidentified Men, Native Americans, ages unknown. *Espionage and sedition.* Their crimes were committed over a period of time in 1675 and 1676 in southeastern New England. These men were hostile tribesmen who acted against the English during King Philip's War. One of them was found hiding in a barn and was brought to the English camp near Taunton, Massachusetts. There he was tortured in a vain effort to make him divulge his purpose. A drumhead court martial then condemned him as a spy. A firing squad put him to death on January 10, 1676. Four days later another hostile Indian was brought to the same camp as a prisoner. He was identified as a member of Philip's council. A firing squad then put him to death. The date was January 14, 1676.

Joshua Tift, white, age unknown. *Treason.* The crime was allegedly committed in December of 1675 in Rhode Island. This man was a Rhode Island farmer who was abducted by hostile Indians (in this case members of the Narragansett tribe) and forced to live among them as a slave. In January of 1676 he was found by English soldiers during a raid on a hostile Indian village. Tift was brought back to the English base of operations for that area (probably Newport, Rhode Island) and accused of willfully joining the enemy. He was even alleged to have taken part in the fighting against his own people. In his defense, Tift insisted that he had been kidnapped and forcibly led into captivity. His detractors retorted by saying that he had made no effort to escape and bore no signs of torture. Tift was charged with treason and convicted by a court martial. He was hanged and quartered on January 18, 1676.

Canonchet, Native American, age unknown. *Murder and sedition.* The crimes were committed over a period of time in 1675 and 1676 in southeastern New England. This offender was a ranking member of the Narragansett tribe. He had a longstanding grudge against the English because of an incident which occurred in 1637. During the Pequot War of that year Canonchet's father, Miantonimoh, had been captured by the English and turned over to a rival tribe as a political sacrifice. Canonchet then swore a vendetta against the English and for that reason he took an active part against them during King Philip's War. As a known hostile, Canonchet was outlawed by the English. A price was put on his head. On March 27, 1676, a Connecticut expedition set out in pursuit of Canonchet. He was captured by warriors of the Mohegan-Pequot Nation (allies of the English and sworn enemies of the Narragansetts) and brought to an English camp near Stonington, Connecticut. There Canonchet was put to death by firing squad on April 4, 1676. His head was cut off and brought to Hartford as a trophy. His arms and legs were hung from trees. The rest of his body was burned.

Captain Tom and **One Unidentified Man,** Native Americans, ages unknown. *Murder and sedition.* The crimes were committed over a period of time in 1675 and 1676 in southeastern New England. These men were Indian warriors who fought against the English during King Philip's War. They were captured and brought to Boston as prisoners. There they were determined to have taken active parts in the hostilities. They were also alleged to have committed atrocities upon English settlers. Both were hanged from the Boston gallows on June 22, 1676.

Unidentified Man, white, age about 26. *Offense unknown.* The crime was evidently committed in the vicinity of Northampton, Massachusetts. *Bradstreet's Journal* reports a military execution at Northampton in July of 1676. The condemned man is described as "a stranger in this country who was pressed into service against the Indians." His offense was probably desertion from the armed forces. A council of war ordered that he be hanged and the sentence was carried out.

Wotuchpo, alias "Tuckpoo," Native American, age unknown. *Murder and sedition.* His crimes were committed over a period of time in 1675 and 1676 in southeastern New England. This man was a warrior who took up arms against the English during King Philip's War. He was brought to Plymouth as a prisoner and was there identified as an active hostile who had taken part in raids against English civilians. He was also alleged to have been involved in atrocities. Wotuchpo died by the headsman's axe at Plymouth on July 6, 1676.

Woodcock, Quanapowhan, John Num and **Keeweenam,** Native Americans, ages unknown. *Murder and sedition.* The crimes were committed on March 12, 1676, near Plymouth, Massachusetts. These offenders were active participants in the Native American uprising known as King Philip's War. On the above date they joined a war party which attacked the house of a white man named William Clarke. A total of 11 civilians were massacred on that occasion. The crime caused panic in the capital of the Plymouth colony because it was committed very close thereto. John Num confessed that he had also murdered three other English settlers. Several months after the Clarke family slaughter four members of the war party were captured and identified as the above-named quartet. All were brought to Plymouth as prisoners. All were condemned by a Plymouth court. Woodcock, Quanapowhan and John Num were executed there on July 9, 1676. Keeweenam met the same fate on July 21, 1676. All were beheaded.

Old Matoonas, Native American, age unknown. *Murder and sedition.* The crimes were committed over a period of time in 1675 and 1676 in southeastern New England. This offender's son had been executed for killing a white man in 1671 [see Young Matoonas, 1671]. The loss embittered Old Matoonas against the English in general and it was for that reason that he took an active part in hostilities during King Philip's War. He is known to have led an attack on the town of Mendon, Massachusetts, on July 4, 1675. The massacre on that occasion was one of the worst atrocities of the war. On August 2, 1675, a war party led by Old Matoonas ambushed a body of English troops who were on the march in the neighborhood of Brookfield, Massachusetts. Numerous casualties were suffered by the English on that occasion. Many other acts of violence and rapine were attributed to this vindictive man. He was finally captured by allied Indians and brought to Boston as a prisoner. There he was put to death by firing squad on July 27, 1676. His head was cut off and put next to the head of his son atop the Boston gallows.

Sam Barrow, Native American, age unknown. *Murder and sedition.* The crimes were committed over a period of time in 1675 and 1676 in southeastern New England. This offender is described as "a noted rogue among the enemy" who was responsible for many "inhuman murders and barbarities" committed upon English settlers during King Philip's War. He was captured near Taunton, Massachusetts, and brought as a prisoner to the English army camp near there. A drumhead court martial condemned him to death with no period of grace allowed. He was, however, granted permission to smoke his pipe just before his execution. Then he was tied to a tree and tomahawked. The date was August 7, 1676.

Potock, Native American, age unknown. *Murder and sedition.* His crimes were committed over a period of time in 1675 and 1676 in southeastern New England. This offender is described as having been a "chief counselor of the Narragansetts" and as such a ringleader in the armed conflict known as King Philip's War. Potock was captured by Rhode Island troops and brought to Boston as a prisoner. There he was fully identified as one who had played a key part in planning the war against the English settlers. He was executed by firing squad at Boston on August 10, 1676.

Quanopan, Sunkoorunasuck, Wonanquabin and **John Woropoak,** Native Americans, ages unknown. *Murder and sedition.* Their crimes were committed over a period of time in 1675 and 1676 in southeastern New England. These men were warriors who fought against the English during King Philip's War. They were especially known to have taken part in an attack on the town of Warwick, Rhode Island, which had devastating consequences for that place. In addition to the Warwick raid, they were linked to the murders of English settlers elsewhere. All four were put to death by musketry at Newport, Rhode Island, on August 27, 1676.

Choos, Native American, age unknown. *Murder and sedition.* The crimes were committed over a period of time in 1675 and 1676 in southern New England. This offender was a warrior who had taken an active part against the English during King Philip's War. In the aftermath of Philip's death in August of 1676, many of his followers either surrendered or fled. Choos was one who took the latter option. He was eventually caught at Stratford, Connecticut, and sent as a prisoner to Hartford. There he was condemned as a hostile. He was executed in an undisclosed manner at Hartford in September of 1676.

Eight Unidentified Men, Native Americans, ages unknown. *Murder and sedition.* Their crimes were committed over a period of time in 1675 and 1676 in southeastern New England. These men were warriors who had fought against the English during King Philip's War. They were brought to Boston as prisoners during a roundup of hostile elements. While most Indian captives were sold into slavery as a matter of policy during this time, there were some who were deemed too dangerous for that. These eight men were so regarded. They were all put to death by firing squad at Boston on September 13, 1676.

Three Unidentified Men, Native Americans, ages unknown. *Murder and sedition.* Their crimes were committed over a period of time in 1675 and 1676 in southeastern New England. These offenders were warriors who actively engaged in hostilities against the English during King Philip's War. They were known to have killed civilians and to have committed atrocities. All three were hanged at Boston on September 21, 1676.

Stephen Goble and Daniel Goble, whites, ages unknown. *Murder.* The crime was committed on August 7, 1676, near Concord, Massachusetts. These men were residents of Concord, Middlesex County. They may or may not have been siblings. On the above date they joined a gang of armed white men who attacked a peaceful settlement of Native Americans not far from Concord.

Three unarmed women were killed in the attack along with three young children. Although it was then wartime, the Indians who suffered these casualties were officially at peace with the English. The attackers knew this beforehand. Fearful that the crime might alienate the Native American tribes that were allied with them, the English authorities promised speedy action against the killers. Four white men were arrested and put on trial. All four were sentenced to death. Stephen Goble was accordingly hanged at Boston on September 21, 1676. Daniel Goble met the same fate five days later. The other two defendants were reprieved.

Sagamore Sam, Netaump, alias "One Eyed John," **Maliompe** and **Old Jethro,** Native Americans, ages unknown. *Murder and sedition.* Their crimes were committed over a period of time in 1675 and 1676 in southeastern New England. These men were Indian warriors who fought against the English during King Philip's War. All were identified as active participants in that conflict who murdered civilians and committed atrocities. They also fought in several battles against armed English troops. In particular, Netaump was alleged to have killed an English officer named Captain Hutchinson. All four of these offenders were hanged from the Boston gallows on September 26, 1676.

Caleb and **Columbine,** Native Americans, ages unknown. *Murder and sedition.* Their crimes were committed over a period of time in 1675 and 1676 throughout southeast New England. These men were hostile warriors who had fought against the English during King Philip's War. They were taken in a general roundup during the waning days of that conflict and brought to Boston as prisoners. They were identified as "open and murderous enemies" who had killed civilians and committed wartime atrocities. Both were hanged from the Boston gallows on October 12, 1676.

Annawon and **Tispaquin,** Native Americans, ages unknown. *Murder and sedition.* Their crimes were committed over a period of time in 1675 and 1676 throughout southeast New England. These men were high ranking warriors who fought against the English during King Philip's War. They were captured during the closing days of that conflict and brought to Plymouth along with other prisoners. There it was determined that both had taken active parts in the late hostilities. Both were charged with committing atrocities. They were put to death by decapitation at Plymouth on November 1, 1676.

1677

Cornelius, Native American, age unknown. *Murder and sedition.* The crimes were committed over a period of time in 1675 and 1676 in southeastern New England. This offender appears to have been the last man executed for hostile activities during King Philip's War. The precise details of the charges brought against him are unknown but he was identified as one who had taken an active part against the English. A firing squad ended his days at Boston on February 15, 1677.

Benjamin Tuttle, white, age 42. *Murder.* The crime was committed on November 17, 1676, at Stamford, Connecticut. This man belonged to a prominent New Haven family. On the above date he was a guest in the house of his sister, Sarah Tuttle Slawson (white, age 31) at Stamford. Somehow brother and sister got into an argument over how to prepare a meal. The squabble escalated until Benjamin Tuttle lost his temper and attacked his sister with an axe. The woman was first struck down from behind. Then she was crammed head-

first into her own fireplace while her children looked on in horror. Goodman Slawson was away at the time. Tuttle was charged with sororicide and sent to Hartford for trial. He was hanged there on June 13, 1677.

1678

John Stoddard, white, age 16. *Murder.* The crime was committed on June 6, 1678, at New London, Connecticut. This juvenile offender is described as a "vagabond youth" and a "reckless lad." In reality he was a rebellious adolescent who became all of the following: mass murderer, baby killer, and committer of fratricide. Stoddard lived with his widowed mother and one younger sibling. At the age of 15 he considered himself the man of the house. It therefore came as a rude shock to him when his mother remarried. Stoddard hated his stepfather from the start. He regarded the man as an interloper and made no effort to hide his animosity. When his mother had a baby by her second husband, Stoddard was galled beyond endurance. He stomped out of the house in a foul temper and wandered about for many days. On the above date he approached the home of a neighbor named Thomas Bolles and knocked on the door. Stoddard knew that Mr. Bolles was out of town at the time. So as expected, he was met by the woman of the house: Zipporah Bolles (white, age 25) and her three small children: Mary Bolles (white, age five), Thomas Joseph Bolles (white, age three), and John Bolles (white, age one). The sun had just gone down and Stoddard asked Goodwife Bolles if he could stay for the night. He also made indecent proposals to the woman. Zipporah Bolles took offense at what Stoddard had to say. She slapped the impudent boy across his face and told him to get out of her house. This made Stoddard angry. He then picked up an axe that lay nearby and killed the woman with it. Then he attacked the terrified toddlers and hacked them to death as well. Only the one-year-old infant was spared. The triple murder remained a mystery for more than a month. During that time Stoddard returned to his mother's house. On July 24, 1678, he was left to babysit his seven-year-old brother and one-year-old half-brother. As the seven year old played at a distance from the house, Stoddard hacked the baby to death with a hatchet as it lay in its cradle. Then he joined his little brother at play and said that he saw an Indian running from the house. The name of the murdered baby was John Sampson (white). The killer repeated his story about an Indian when he ran to report the crime. However, the authorities became suspicious of Stoddard and they questioned him closely. There were inconsistencies in his story which developed into a chain of evidence against him. Stoddard finally broke down and admitted that he had killed the baby. When asked for his reason he said that he could not tolerate the baby's crying. The real reason, however, was his well-known hatred of his stepfather. When it had been definitely established that Stoddard had killed the baby it was then suspected that he might know something about the Bolles family slaughter. Additional questions were asked and before long Stoddard owned up to that crime as well. Sent to Hartford for trial, Stoddard was hanged there on October 9, 1678.

1679

Peter Pylatt, black, age unknown. *Rape.* The crime was committed on September 6, 1679, at Newport, Rhode Island. This offender was a slave in the house of a Newport merchant named Christopher Holder. On the above date he attacked his master's daughter, a minor named Elizabeth Holder, and beat her to within an inch of her life. Then he raped her repeatedly. Pylatt was brought before the highest court in Rhode Island and convicted of capital felony. He was hanged at Newport on November 10, 1679.

1681

William Cheney, white, age unknown. *Rape.* The crime was committed on August 2, 1681, at Dorchester, Massachusetts. This man was a sex addict who had little or no self-control. Not satisfied with being the father of 21 children, he cheated on his wife repeatedly and crowned all by forcing himself on his teenage maidservant, Experience Holdbrooke by name. That last offense earned him a conviction for capital felony. Cotton Mather reports that a reprieve had been approved for this man contingent on his evincing a contrite attitude. On the day set for his execution Cheney refused to listen to a sermon and thereby made a bad impression. Because of that the reprieve was withheld. Cheney then went to his death on the Boston gallows. The date was September 22, 1681.

Negro Jack, black, age unknown. *Arson.* The crime was committed on July 14, 1681, at Northampton, Massachusetts. This offender was a slave in the household of a Connecticut man named Samuel Wolcott. He lived along with his master in the town of Wethersfield. Somehow Jack wound up at Northampton on the above date, a full day's journey from his home. There he entered the house of a Lt. William Clark during the nighttime hours. Jack later said that he was looking for food. He took a burning stick from the kitchen fireplace in order to light his way. Somehow in the darkness there, the flame came into contact with a combustible substance. A blaze began either by accident or design and the house burned down. Jack was sent to Boston for trial by the Court of Assistants. A jury refused to believe his story of the fire being an accident. The verdict was guilty of capital felony and the sentence was death. Jack was accordingly hanged from the Boston gallows on September 22, 1681. His body was cremated.

Negress Maria, black, age unknown. *Arson and murder.* The crime was committed on July 12, 1681, at Roxbury, Massachusetts. This offender was a slave in the household of a squire named Joshua Lambe. Apparently disgruntled, she snuck out of her quarters shortly after midnight on the above date with an intention of creating havoc. She went first to the house of a neighbor named Thomas Swan and slipped into the place undiscerned. There she took a hot coal from the grate and used it to kindle a fire amid the wooden floorboards. As the blaze gained strength, Maria hurried back to her master's house where she set another fire with malicious intent. Both dwellings were either severely damaged or destroyed. In one of them a young child was killed. Maria was suspected and questioned closely. She admitted setting fire to her master's house but denied the crime against Thomas Swan. Two other neighborhood slaves, she said, were responsible for that fire. A grand jury considered charges against Maria plus the pair she implicated. In the case of the latter it was decided to waive indictments on condition that both parties be sold out of the colony. Maria herself was made to bear the full brunt of the law. She was convicted on her own confession and sentenced to death. Because her crime had caused loss of life in addition to loss of property, it was decided to make a special example of Maria. Hers would be no easy death on the gallows; instead she was ordered to be burned at the stake. She accordingly suffered that fate at Boston on September 22, 1681.

1682

Allumchoyse, Native American, age unknown. *Murder.* The crime was committed on June 5, 1682, at Wethersfield, Connecticut. This man got together with a fellow tribesman named Waquaheeg on the above date for the purpose of hunting deer. The two men left their home in Farmington and followed a path through the forest which brought them to an area which is now the town of Newington. There they killed a deer. After some discussion about what to do next, the hunters decided that they would barter the venison for liquor. They accordingly took the deer carcass upon their shoulders and went toward Wethersfield, the nearest habitation of white people. Coming to a road, the two men called at every house they passed. At one house they traded part of their kill for a pint of rum. At another house they made a deal for three quarts of hard cider. All the while they drank of their proceeds and by the time that most of the venison was traded both men were quite intoxicated. They still had a quarter of the deer by the time they reached Wethersfield Center. Seeking to be rid of it, they called at the house of William Randall and offered the meat for trade. The woman of the house, Elizabeth Randall (white, age unknown), examined the deer quarter and decided that she did not want it. This answer displeased the drunken Allumchoyse. He pulled a knife on Goodwife Randall and fatally stabbed her in the back. Allumchoyse admitted his guilt but blamed "firewater" for making him crazy. It was a useless argument. Allumchoyse was sentenced to death. He was hanged at Hartford on June 28, 1682.

1686

Squampam, Native American, age unknown. *Murder.* The crime was committed on January 7, 1686, at Wethersfield, Connecticut. Ensign Samuel Wright operated a trading post that was frequented by Native Americans of both sexes. On the above date a brave by the name of Squampam came there to barter for some goods that he needed. In so doing, he encountered several other Native Americans who had come to the trading post for the same purpose. Then something went terribly wrong. Squampam lost his temper for an unknown reason. He picked up a big broadaxe and ran wild with it. By the time his tantrum had subsided, Squampam had not only wrecked the trading post but had fatally injured two other Native Americans. The dead were identified as a brave named Nannoe and a woman called "The squaw of Wataquanaman." Both had suffered massive injuries. Squampam was first made to feel the derision of his own people. The fact that he had drawn a weapon in a trading place branded him with infamy in Native American eyes. The breach of protocol was regarded as an even graver offense than murder. Squampam was declared outcast and left to face the white man's law. He was soon put on trial. Not a single Native American would speak on Squampam's behalf. Such was the abhorrence felt for one who had drawn a weapon in a trading place. On March 2, 1686, the double murderer and taboo breaker was hanged at Hartford.

James Morgan, white, age about 30. *Murder.* The crime was committed on December 10, 1685, at Boston, Massachusetts. This man was a customer in a tippling house operated by a widow named Constante Worcester. There he drank to excess and started acting belligerently. Somehow another imbiber named Joseph Johnson (white, age unknown) ran afoul of Morgan. The latter then grabbed a metal spit from a utensil rack and brandished it like a sword. He attacked Johnson and ran the

man through the belly with the point of the spit. Johnson suffered a mortal wound and he died three days later. Morgan was contrite when he sobered up. A jury later convicted him of willful murder. The penalty was death by hanging. Morgan accordingly died on the Boston gallows on March 11, 1686.

Jonathan Neponet, Native American, age unknown. *Murder.* The crime was committed on an unknown date in Suffolk County, Massachusetts. Little is known of this case. The defendant was condemned for a double murder, the victims being a Native American couple known only as "Old Aquito and Squaw." The motive for the crime is unknown as is the manner in which the crime was committed. The killer was hanged from the Boston gallows on November 18, 1686.

1687

Unidentified Woman, white, age unknown. *Murder.* The crime was committed on an unknown date in Bristol County, Massachusetts. This obscure case is known only from a single sentence notation. On November 3, 1687, the Boston magistrate Samuel Sewall made the following entry in his diary: "Mrs. Anne Williams tells me that an English maid was executed last Thursday at Bristow for murdering her Indian child." Bristow is present-day Bristol, Rhode Island. In 1687 that town was the seat of Bristol County, then under the jurisdiction of the Plymouth colony. Five years later that same territory was merged into Massachusetts. At an even later date the town of Bristol itself was ceded to Rhode Island. It thus comes as no surprise that the court record of this case is lost. We may still deduce several things from the scanty notation in Sewall's diary: The defendant was a white woman and quite probably young.

She became pregnant out of wedlock by a Native American man. She then made away with the baby because she was ashamed of the way it was conceived. The infanticide did not go undetected. The high court of Bristol County condemned the defendant for capital felony and she was accordingly hanged on October 27, 1687.

1688

Ann Glover, white, age unknown. *Witchcraft.* The year 1688 was a time of great tension in New England. Roman Catholic King James II was in the third year of an unpopular reign and his brand of politics was eroding the quality of life for thousands of people in England itself as well as in the colonies. James was loathed for his religious beliefs and he knew it. He was also obsessively wary of rebellion against his rule. The result was a progressively severe despotism whose principal tools of government were the rope and the axe. Political killings and judicial murders were common throughout the realm.

Across the ocean in America the colonists watched nervously as James and his henchmen spread terror and death throughout the mother country. There was fear that the royal wrath would extend itself to New England. The fact that the sovereign was a papist galled the Protestant colonists to a point where it was almost more than they could bear. Such a fact could hardly hope to escape the royal paranoia and many felt that it was only a matter of time before repressive measures were taken against the colonists. These apprehensions were partially fulfilled in the year 1686 when a new royal governor arrived at Boston. He was the haughty and autocratic Sir Edmund Andros. His instructions from the home government were appalling to the colonists. All existing charters from Massachusetts to Maryland were offi-

cially annulled and all the territory therein was reorganized into a colossal jurisdiction called *The Dominion of New England.* Andros himself was vested with what amounted to dictatorial powers over that vast domain.

The colonies dearly cherished their individual charter rights and they were loath to relinquish them. Still they dared not defy the king. So all grudgingly submitted to Andros. From the beginning there was discontent. Andros clamped new restrictions on the press, on travel, on marriages and on the ownership of land. He also levied taxes in an arbitrary manner. Nor were sectarian matters immune from his tampering; the new governor encouraged the propagation of Episcopalianizm — a policy which antagonized Puritan theocrats. Many feared that a state-sanctioned tolerance for Roman Catholics would be next. Others feared that the home government was deliberately attempting (in a subtle way) to bait the colonies into revolt in order to furnish an excuse for imposing even harsher measures.

These were omens of 1776.

After two years of Sir Edmund Andros and his administration the political situation in New England was approaching a critical point. Talk of rebellion began to spread. However, during this same time at Boston — the epicenter of the trouble — people suddenly found themselves distracted by a different kind of threat. A scourge worse than Andros had suddenly burst upon the scene: witchcraft.

The widow Ann Glover, an elderly charwoman, was suspected of bewitching boys and girls. Long rumored to be a witch, she had in her old age actually come to think of herself as one. Those circumstances combined with the psychosomatic illnesses of four children sealed her fate. She would become a victim of misdiagnosed dementia.

Although the court records are lost, the Boston minister Cotton Mather (then a young man of 25), was an eye-witness to the whole affair. Fascinated, he made his observations of the case the subject of a book and in so doing left posterity with its first in-depth account of a New England witch case.

According to Mather, the trouble began in the summer of 1688 at the house of a stonecutter named John Goodwin. This man had six children: three boys and three girls aged six months to 15 years. Mather also stresses (in his characteristically righteous manner) that the children were respectable and scrupulously reared in the religion of the day.

Mather failed to note that dread of witches was an inherent part of 17th century rearing and that it was his own dogma that engendered the same. The Goodwin children were at a critical point in their lives: the age of character building. They were highly impressionable and easily overstrung. One day when 13-year-old Martha Goodwin accused an Irish laundress of purloining some of the family linen, she incurred the displeasure of the woman's mother, Ann Glover. The latter accosted the girl and spoke harshly to her. Martha Goodwin was frightened to the core.

It was not long before a fear of witches manifested itself in Martha Goodwin. First came mental agitation and then by degrees came physical agitation. Moreover, the same craze spread to three of the girl's siblings: 11-year-old John Goodwin, Jr., seven-year-old Mercy Goodwin and five-year-old Benjamin Goodwin. Mather described their ordeal as follows:

Sometimes they would be deaf, sometimes dumb, sometimes blind and often all this at once. One while their tongues would be drawn down their throats; another while they would be pulled out on their chins to a prodigious length. They would have their mouths opened to such a wideness that their jaws went out of joint and anon they would clap together with a force like that of a strong spring lock. The same would happen to their shoulder blades and their elbows and wrists and several of their joints. They would at times lay in a benumbed condition and be drawn together like those that are tied neck and heels. Then presently be stretched out, yea, drawn backwards to such a degree that it was feared the very skin of their bellies would have cracked.

The frantic parents summoned physicians but the symptoms baffled those professionals. They did not realize that the children were sick merely because they *thought* that they were sick. Instead, the physicians had recourse to the usual verdict of 17th century physicians when they were stumped: witchcraft.

The last thing that frazzled Bostonians needed in the summer of 1688 was a witch scare. The whole town was thrown into an uproar. It was then that the confrontation between Martha Goodwin and Ann Glover was remembered. At once the situation seemed to make sense; Glover was a reputed witch and she had threatened Martha Goodwin. She was also an Irish Catholic and for that reason alone was not considered a citizen in good standing. At a preliminary hearing before local magistrates Glover was evasive. When it was decided to put her to the test of reciting the Lord's Prayer she failed to impress her listeners. She was then remanded to prison.

Meanwhile several Boston ministers proclaimed fasts and prayer meetings. They preached sermons and hovered about the Goodwin children. Cotton Mather was at their forefront. Although he meant well, he used the situation as a learning experience and made an already edgy community tense in the extreme.

Ann Glover, hitherto one of Boston's humblest residents, reveled in the attention that was suddenly thrust upon her. In her senile mind she imagined herself to be exactly what she was accused of being: a witch. She played the part to perfection. Mather tells of one incident:

Order was given to search the old woman's house from whence there were brought into court several small images or poppets or babies made of rags and stuffed with goat hair and other such ingredients. When these were produced the vile woman acknowledged that the way to torment the objects of her malice was by wetting her finger with her spittle and stroking these little images. The abused children were then present and the woman still kept stooping and shrinking as one that was almost pressed to death with a mighty weight upon her. But one of the images being brought unto her, immediately she started up after an odd manner and took it in her hand. But she had no sooner taken it than one of the children fell into sad fits before the whole assembly.

Glover irked her inquisitors by speaking Gaelic instead of English, by constantly talking to herself and by acting suspiciously in general.

Continued Mather:

They asked her whether she had any to stand by her and she replied that she had. Looking very pertly in the air, she added, "no, he is gone." She then confessed that she had one who was her "Prince" with whom she maintained I know not what communion. For which cause the night after, she was heard expostulating with a devil for his thus deserting her, telling him that because he had served her so basely and falsely she had confessed all.

While it is doubtful that she was an actual witch, it is apparent that Glover deluded herself into believing that she was one. Bostonians were quick to believe the worst. However, the trial court was remarkable for the caution it employed. The defendant's irrational conduct had raised doubts about her sanity. The court ordered an experiment with the aforesaid rag dolls to see if the Goodwin children were shamming. A mental examination of the prisoner was also ordered.

Ann Glover proved to be her own worst enemy. She fooled six doctors into believing her mentally disturbed but essentially sane. Relieved of its qualms by the psychological report, the trial court sentenced Glover to death. Then for the first and only time, Sir Edmund Andros and the local religious community found something on which they could agree: no clemency for Ann Glover. On November 16, 1688, the Boston magistrate Samuel Sewall recorded the passing of the demented old woman with a one-line entry in his diary: "The widow Glover is drawn by to be hanged."

A few weeks later an insurrection broke out at Boston. Sir Edmund Andros was forcibly deposed and the political affairs of New England resumed their normal course.

1689

Pammatoock, Native American, age unknown. *Murder.* The crime was committed in 1664 at Tisbury, Massachusetts. This offender was one of the native inhabitants of Martha's Vineyard, a large island off the southern coast of Massachusetts. According to sources dating back from the time in question, Pammatoock had relations with a young woman named Sarah (Native American, age unknown) and got her pregnant contrary to tribal law. In order to hide the fact, he killed Sarah by undisclosed means. Suspected at the time, Pammatoock was not prosecuted because the evidence against him was insufficient. Twenty-five years later another Native

American woman was found slain on Martha's Vineyard. Pammatoock was questioned but denied all knowledge of the matter. However, he was requestioned about the 1664 murder and unexpectedly admitted that he was the guilty party in that case. Based on that confession, Pammatoock was tried for the 1664 crime 25 years after the fact. The court sentenced him to be hanged. On September 26, 1689, the sentence was carried out at Edgartown. As he was standing on the gallows Pammatoock was asked again if he was responsible for the more recent murder. He denied all involvement therein and was probably telling the truth.

1690

Hugh Stone, white, age unknown. *Murder.* The crime was committed on April 20, 1689, at Andover, Massachusetts. This man fatally slashed the throat of his pregnant wife, Hannah Stone (white, age unknown). The couple had a disagreement over selling a piece of land. On the above date they walked around the property in question to look it over and discuss the matter. No agreement could be reached whereupon Stone lost his temper and attacked his wife with a knife. Neighbors heard the victim's screams and ran to the scene. Stone was then disarmed and restrained. When the case came to trial Stone pled guilty. He was very contrite. On January 2, 1690, he was hanged from the Boston gallows.

Thomas Johnson, white, age unknown. *Murder and piracy.* The crime was committed on October 4, 1689, on the high seas. During the summer and early autumn of 1689 the coastal waters of Massachusetts were the hunting grounds of a pirate sloop commanded by a brigand named Thomas Pound. Among other criminal acts committed

by Pound and his crew were the following: On August 9, 1689, off the coast of Plymouth the fishing ketch *Mary* was overtaken and plundered of all its movable valuables. From there the pirate vessel made its way around Cape Cod. On August 27, 1689, it turned up in Martha's Vineyard Sound where it attacked and plundered the merchant brig *Merrimack*. In response to numerous complaints, the governor of Massachusetts sent an armed sloop in search of pirates. On October 4, 1689, battle was joined near the Elizabeth Islands. The commander of the pursuing vessel, Captain Samuel Pease (white, age unknown) was killed in the engagement. Still, the superior firepower of the warship humbled the pirates. All those who survived the battle were brought to Boston and put on trial for their lives. In all, 14 pirates were sentenced to death. Shortly before the day set for the mass execution, however, all but one were reprieved for reasons that have never been fully explained. The one who was singled out for execution was Thomas Johnson. He was denied clemency because he was said to be the one who had struck down Captain Pease. Death by hanging was his fate at Boston on January 27, 1690.

John Armung de la Forest, white, age unknown. *Murder.* The crime was committed on an unknown date in Bristol County, Massachusetts. This man was the last person to be executed under the laws of the old Plymouth colony. Little is known of him, however, because the record of his trial is lost. Reportedly a Frenchman, de la Forest killed one of his fellow countrymen under unknown circumstances. He was brought to trial at Bristol (now a part of Rhode Island) and sentenced to death. Shortly before the time set for his execution he broke out of jail and fled as far as New York. There he was caught. In July of 1690 the acting governor of New York sent the escapee to Plymouth under strong guard.

De La Forest arrived there on July 30, 1690, and was ordered to be hanged within 24 hours. The sentence was duly carried out by the sheriff of Plymouth.

1692
Preface to the
Salem Witch Trials

We now arrive at one of the most controversial episodes in American history: The Salem Witch Trials.

Over the years dozens of books have been written about this affair. For centuries it has been a *cause célèbre* among historians, sociologists, psychologists and occultists. The debate over reason, effect and repercussion will probably never end. Even the local tourist industry in present-day Salem has capitalized on a morbid fascination which persists in both the trials themselves and the blood that was shed.

It was in the winter of 1692 that the trouble began innocently enough in the household of the local minister, Samuel Parris. Unknown to him, several children in his parsonage were finding diversion from the winter doldrums in the company of Tituba, his West Indian slave woman. Tituba was an obliging sort. Being genuinely fond of the young girls who comprised her audience, she entertained them with tricks of palmistry and petty divination. She also gave them tasty confections and thrilled them with scary tales of voodoo.

Principal among Tituba's listeners were her master's daughter, Betty Parris (age 9) and niece, Abigail Williams (age 12). They were joined by several of their neighborhood friends: Ann Putnam (age 12), Mary Walcott (age 16), Elizabeth Hubbard (age 17), Elizabeth Booth and Susannah Sheldon (both age 18), Mercy Lewis (age 19) and Mary Warren (age 20). Still others would follow in the course of time.

As members of a society which considered most diversions sinful, it was not long before the girls felt guilt for their pastimes with Tituba. Next came fear of discovery and retribution. Their delicate natures could not withstand the strain and they found themselves beset with fear. Soon a disquieting change was noted in the girls. Beginning with Betty Parris and Abigail Williams, they grew moody and irrational. Then as the psychosis deepened they experienced symptoms of hysteria: hallucinations, screaming, and thrashing of the limbs. Observers were dismayed. William Griggs, the town physician, could find no conventional diagnosis. His inevitable verdict: *Witchcraft.*

Samuel Parris was initially reluctant to accept such findings. He vacillated in a vain hope that the trouble would pass. His neighbors, however, had no such reservations. They were eager to believe the worst. One of them, a notorious busybody named Mary Sibley, had the temerity to try an occult experiment with the stricken girls. She prepared a so-called *Witch Cake.* This was a concoction of raw meal that was mixed with urine taken from the ailing girls. The "cake" was then fed to the Parris family dog in the belief that it was really a demon assigned by the devil to keep an eye on the parsonage. In such a way it was believed that the girls would thus be enabled to identify the witches who were troubling them.

Incredibly, this unauthorized experiment yielded its desired result. The dog ate the "cake" and the girls denounced three people as the authors of their plight. At this point the situation began to get out of hand. Before long all of the girls who had known Tituba caught the same mental fever. Then as the news spread they were joined by others. Every borderline psychotic in Salem seemed to get in on the act. It was the beginning of a calamity that would convulse the entire countryside.

Despite the probability that all of the "afflicted persons" were mental cases, their allegations in the wake of the *Witch Cake* incident were taken seriously. Three people were arrested: Tituba and two white women named Sarah Good and Sarah Osburne. All were likely scapegoats.

According to popular opinion, Sarah Good was the antithesis of her surname. A slovenly woman who was well past her prime, she had long been regarded as a nuisance because she begged from door to door.

Sarah Osburne was an even older woman who had fallen out of standing with the local church. For years she had been a known sabbath-breaker and there were ugly rumors about her marriage. She was also terminally ill.

Good, Osburne and Tituba were arrested on February 29, 1692. The next day they were arraigned before two magistrates named Jonathan Corwin and John Hathorne. The two white women both denied the charges against them but they did so in a less than convincing manner. Sarah Good even went so far as to impugn the hapless Sarah Osburne. In the case of Tituba, however, there was no reticence; she was almost eager to tell her interrogators whatever they wanted to hear. She said that the devil had appeared to her four times, alternately in the form of a hog and as a large black dog. Each time he had attempted to entice her. Tituba said that each time she had resisted the devil's advances. Then five witches appeared to her, four women and a "tall man from Boston," who tempted her to torment the girls of the parsonage with invisible assaults. Tituba identified two of the female witches as Sarah Good and Sarah Osburne but claimed not to know the identities of the others. She further added that she had been loath to harm the girls at the bidding of the witches but had yielded when they threatened to "do worse to her." She also said that the witches had forced her — against her will — to ride through the air on sticks with them for evil purposes. Sarah Good was said to have an imp in the form of a yellow bird and Sarah Osburne was said to be the mistress of a sphinx-like creatures. Tituba stated implicitly that it was Good and Osburne rather than she who bore the responsibility for molesting the girls of the parsonage.

This nonsense merits several remarks: First, the whole of it was obviously contrived by a frightened slave. Tituba was clearly intimidated by the dour magistrates. Her sole concern was in saving her own neck. Therefore she fabricated a tale to the best of her uneducated ability. Throwing the blame on her fellow defendants was the best way she knew to exculpate herself. Furthermore, her husband and fellow slave, John Indian, also became involved. He made indiscriminate accusations of witchery. In his case, however, there was an insidious ring of method in his otherwise irrational actions. While Tituba seemed mainly concerned in self-preservation, John Indian was a sly opportunist; he recognized and readily seized a chance to antagonize his hated Anglo-Saxon subjugators by using their own fear as a tool against them.

Tituba's tale was accepted at face value by the examining magistrates. Lucid reasoning was unthinkable under such circumstances.

It must also be pointed out that Tituba's tale was double-edged: In one breath she impugned the wretched Sarah Good and Sarah Osburne while in another breath she inspired more questions in the minds of her listeners. The sick girls were present at her examination and they heard from her own mouth descriptions of familiar spirits and imps such as "yellow birds, red and black rats," etc. They heard Tituba talk of a "tall man from Boston" and tell of three yet to be identified witches in addition to Good and Osburne. Tituba had stimulated the imaginations of her audience. The result would prove devastating.

All three suspects — Tituba, Good and Osburne — were remanded to prison to await trial. For the latter, prison proved to be her final abode; she died there on May 10, 1692. Tituba was sold to a slave trader and the proceeds were used to defray court costs. Soon she was out of the country. Sarah Good was destined to end her days on the gallows.

On March 11, 1692, a "day of fasting and prayer" was observed at Salem. At the same time, a meeting of ministers was convened to discuss the current situation. Then on the same day trouble struck again: one of the ailing girls, Ann Putnam, imagined that she saw another witch. This time it was not a despised harridan but rather one Martha Corey, a respectable churchgoer quite unlike the previous suspects. Before long all of the parsonage girls were denouncing the new suspect and she was taken into custody.

Next came a preposterous accusation against a senior citizen named Rebecca Nurse. She had long been popular in the community for her benevolence and personal warmth. Nevertheless she was "cried out upon" for allegedly sending a spectral image of herself to torment several of the deranged girls. It was charged that her image had bitten them, pinched them, throttled them and otherwise abused them. It was also charged that her image had borne a book in its hands and demanded that the girls either sign their names or set their hands thereto. Dreadful tortures were threatened for refusal to comply. The book was said to be "the devil's book," a hellish roster that all witches had to sign.

Although the denunciation of Martha Corey had scandalized most citizens they had nonetheless countenanced her arrest. In the case of Rebecca Nurse, however, the charges were so farfetched that they raised doubts in many minds. A new idea began to circulate: could an evil spirit impersonate an innocent person? It seemed virtually impossible that so saintly a woman as Rebecca Nurse could be a witch. Perhaps, it was thought, her alleged spectral assaults upon the girls were satanic illusions. The devil was said to be the "Master of Lies"; perhaps that wily fiend was perpetrating a diabolical hoax in order to destroy an innocent person. It was a perplexing theory which was bound to become the foremost legal issue facing the witch hunt. As for Rebecca Nurse, however, the concept of the so-called "Spectral Evidence" being flawed had not yet advanced itself far enough in legal minds to save her.

No one suspected the real root of the problem: the fact that the afflicted girls were really misdiagnosed mental cases.

At the same time there occurred an event which proved beyond any doubt that absurdity knew no bounds. This was the denunciation and arrest of a *five-year-old child*: Dorcas Good, daughter of Sarah Good. She told interrogators that she was a witch and that her "mommy" had made her one. She also told a tale of how she had a familiar spirit in the form of a snake which sucked fluid from one of her fingers. Her mother, she said, had three familiar spirits or imps in the form of multi-colored birds.

Despite the near certainty that little Dorcas Good thought the whole thing a game, her story was taken as legal evidence against both she and her mother. Moreover, the five-year-old girl was put in chains and locked up in jail.

On April 3, 1692, the local minister, Samuel Parris, preached a shrewdly worded sermon which, more than anything else, was a veiled attack on Rebecca Nurse. The congregation noted that point. Among the listeners, however, was a sister of Rebecca Nurse, one Sarah Cloyse by name. She became upset by the smear against her sister's reputation and stomped out of the service. It was enough to set the deluded girls screeching against her just as they had against her sister.

From this point on accusations

began to multiply at an alarming rate. Mary Warren accused her employers, John and Elizabeth Proctor. On April 19, 1692, three more suspects were arraigned: Giles Corey, the elderly and rather stupid husband of Martha Corey, one Abigail Hobbes, who was probably more crazy than demonically possessed and one Bridget Bishop, an irascible woman who had been notorious throughout the countryside for more years than her neighbors cared to admit.

And so events wore on. By the beginning of May the pace of accusations became torrential. The examining magistrates could barely keep up with them. The jails became filled and then overcrowded. Ten grew to 20, then 20 grew to 40, then 40 grew to 80 and so on. When a new royal governor, Sir William Phipps, arrived at Boston on May 14 he found himself faced with a grave crisis. Nor could it have happened at a worse time; there was war on the frontiers and a political reorganization in the works. The new governor's answer was to set up a Special Court of Oyer & Terminer and assign it the exclusive task of handling the witchcraft cases. It was an astute move. However, the governor's astuteness foundered on his choice of chief judge for the new court. For that important position he selected the one man in Massachusetts who was perhaps *least* suited for the job: Deputy Governor William Stoughton, an inflexible bigot by any description. He considered prudence in the handling of witchcraft accusations an even worse crime than witchcraft itself. He was an icy and merciless man who believed in the validity of "spectral evidence" and who would allow compromise on no point whatsoever.

The special court of Oyer & Terminer was created on May 27, 1692, and it began its sessions at Salem on June 2. Governor Phipps himself preferred to do battle with corporeal enemies like Frenchmen and Indians. He soon departed for Canada with an army. Stoughton was left behind to rule in his absence.

We shall now proceed to a case by case examination of the 20 persons who were put to death by order of William Stoughton and his special court of Oyer & Terminer.

Bridget Bishop, white, age about 55. *Witchcraft.* When the Court of Oyer & Terminer met on June 2, 1692, the first defendant to be brought before it was Bridget Bishop. Why it was decided to begin with her is unclear. There are two *possible* reasons: she was a subject of especially vociferous denunciation and her reputation was abominable. Moreover, the court realized that it was faced with a difficult mission. It wished to traverse the legal morass as correctly as its credulity would allow. So it opted to first dispose of the most pressing case, assess its procedural aspects and use it as a model.

But who was this luckless person who earned the dubious distinction of becoming the witchcraft court's first victim? Who was Bridget Bishop?

Only a sketchy answer can be given. Professor Enders Robinson, in his excellent book, *The Devil Discovered*, identifies her by the maiden name of Bridget Playfer. In England she married one Samuel Wasslebee. Then she came to Massachusetts with that spouse in 1660 or thereabout. By 1664 she was a widow and it was from that time that her reputation went downhill. This was because when Samuel Wasslebee died it was rumored that his wife had cast a lethal spell on him.

Undaunted, Bridget Playfer Wasslebee married a prosperous widower named Thomas Oliver in the summer of 1666. Oliver was 65 years old at the time yet he fathered a daughter by his new wife. Hence it would seem that Bridget was substantially younger than her second husband. Their marriage proved to be a strained one and it is from the circumstances thereof that we obtain our first insight into Bridget's character. She was a pugnacious woman who quarreled bitterly with her mate. For instance, in 1669 both husband and wife were censured by the Essex County court for domestic violence. A neighbor testified to having been frequently called to the Oliver home to mediate disorders and break up physical altercations.

In 1677 Bridget and her then-76-year-old spouse were again censured by the County Court for similar offenses. This time they faced public humiliation. The court ordered that they "stand back to back on a lecture day in the public marketplace both gagged for about an hour with a paper fastened to each of their foreheads upon which their offense should be fairly written." One of Thomas Oliver's grown children managed to save her elderly father from this disgrace by substituting a fine. But Bridget endured the penalty as decreed.

A similar turbulence seems to have marked everything with which Bridget became involved. Indeed, years later at her last trial a recurring theme in the testimonies against her indicated that she was a downright nasty woman. In the 17th century it was only too easy for such a woman to acquire the sobriquet of "witch."

Thomas Oliver died in 1679. Late that same year his wife was arraigned before the Essex County Court on a charge of witchcraft. A slave had told of entering a barn and seeing Bridget perched on an overhead beam only to vanish when he swatted at her with a rake. The slave also alleged that Bridget had prowled his master's house in the shape of a black cat.

As Bridget stood appeached of a capital offense, the County Court could proceed no further than mere arraignment. She would have to travel to Boston to plead her case before the highest court in the colony: The Court of Assistants. So Bridget posted bail and waited for a summons. When her case came up a grand jury refused to accredit the stories of the slave. Bridget was allowed to go free because no indictment was found. She then returned to Salem and settled down with a third husband, 61-year-old Edward Bishop. He would survive her.

Bridget seems to have gotten along better with her third husband than with her second. At least no violent squabbles are mentioned in the county records. Her position in the community at large, however, was anything but tranquil. The onus of a witch stuck with her. Exoneration by a Boston grand jury meant nothing in the minds of her Salem neighbors. An incident which was brought out at her 1692 trial illustrates the antagonism Bridget endured following her 1680 court appearance:

Samuel and Sarah Shattuck, neighbors of Bridget, had an imbecile son who was prone to spasmodic motor contortions. Unable to correctly diagnose the boy's problem, his parents cared for him as best they could until one day when a visitor suggested that the boy was bewitched. At once it all seemed to make sense to the Shattucks. Bridget Bishop had previously been to their house to complain about another child of theirs (presumably for harassing her) and had departed from the premises grumbling minaciously. Now the Shattucks reasoned that she had cast an evil spell on their sick child in order to avenge herself on their entire household. But how to right the wrong? The visitor offered a solution: he and the sick boy would approach Bridget under false pretenses. They would obtain material goods from her and thereby break her spell. Goodman Shattuck, who was willing to try anything at that point, agreed to this proposal. He gave the visitor some money and told him to buy a jug of cider from Bridget Bishop. He also sent the sick boy along on the mission.

It took great courage for the man and boy to approach the witch's domain. They fortified themselves accordingly and knocked on Bridget's door. When Bridget asked them what they wanted they requested a drink of her. Bridget was not deceived. Seeing the Shattuck boy, she suspected mischief. Then she lost her temper. Bridget chased the man from her yard with a shovel. She also caught the boy and thrashed him without mercy. It was a sorry man and boy who returned to tell of their adventure with Bridget Bishop.

For some time previous to the Shattuck incident Bridget had also acquired a lurid reputation for annoying young men as they lay in their beds at night. In 1678 she was alleged to have come in ghostly form to the chambers of 22-year-old William Stacy and 28-year-old Samuel Gray. In 1684 two more men of similar age claimed to have received nocturnal visits from the specter of Bridget Bishop. One of them, 24-year-old Richard Coman, said that she had come to him on three successive nights, while the other, 26-year-old John Louder, said that her spirit had sat upon his mid-section, grabbed him by the throat and attempted to throttle him.

While a sexual undertone is impossible to ignore in the tales of these four young men, one of them, John Louder, took his narrative a step beyond mere bedroom pranks. He told what was perhaps one of the most fantastic tales — if not the single most fantastic tale — to be found in the annals of New England witchcraft cases. Cotton Mather, in his *Wonders of the Invisible World*, related Louder's story as follows:

John Louder testified that upon some little controversy with Bishop about her fowles, going well to bed, he did awaken in the night by moonlight and did clearly see the likeness of this woman grievously oppressing him which miserable condition she held

him, unable to help himself, till near day. He told Bishop of this but she denied it and threatened him very much. Quickly after this, being at home on a Lord's day, with the doors shut about him, he saw a black pig approach him, at which he going to kick, it vanished away. Immediately after, sitting down, he saw a black thing jump in at the window and come and stand before him. The body was like that of a monkey, the feet like a cock's but the face much like a man's. He being so extremely frightened that he could not speak, this monster spoke to him and said "I am a messenger unto you. I understand that you are in some trouble of mind and if you will be ruled by me, you shall want for nothing in this world." Whereupon he endeavored to clap his hands upon it but could feel no substance. Then it jumped out of the window again but immediately came in by the porch though the doors were shut and said "You had better take my counsel!" He then struck at it with a stick but struck only the groundsill and broke the stick. The arm with which he struck at it was presently disabled and it vanished away. He presently went out of the back door and saw this Bishop in her orchard going toward her house but he had not power to set one foot forward unto her. Whereupon returning into his house he was immediately accosted by the monster he had seen before, which goblin was now going to fly at him whereat he cried out "The whole armor of God be between me and thee!" So it sprang back and flew over the apple tree, shaking many apples off the tree in its flight. At its leap it flung dirt with its feet against the stomoch of the man whereupon he was struck dumb and so continued for three days together.

What is one to make of such testimony? Was Louder crazy? Was he drunk? Did he contrive his story? Or did he really encounter a demon? The question can be debated.

In 1685 truly solid evidence (or so it seemed) arose against Bridget Bishop. Workmen employed in dismantling the foundation of a house in which she had lived discovered secreted in niches "several poppets made of rags and hog bristles with headless pins in them." These were believed to be witch dolls and of course Bridget Bishop was thought to be responsible for them.

By far the most serious allegations against Bridget had to do with a number of foul murders that she was rumored to have perpetrated through means of witchcraft. The death of her first husband was attributed to her maledictions. William Stacey believed that she had slain his daughter Priscilla in 1690. Samuel Gray suspected her of having a hand in the untimely death of one of his children as well. Bridget was also accused of destroying an unidentified pair of twin infants.

With such credentials it is no small wonder that Bridget Bishop was denounced at Salem in 1692. Her notoriety earned her the distinction of being the first to face trial. She found herself appeached on April 18 when a girl named Susannah Sheldon reported a vision in which Bridget figured. According to the girl's account:

On the fourth day at night came Goody Oliver [Bishop] and Mrs. English and Goodman Corey and a black man with a high crowned hat with books in their hands. Goody Oliver bade me touch her book. I would not. I did not know her name but she told me that her name was Goody Oliver and she bade me touch her book. I asked her how long she had been a witch and she told me above 20 years. Then there came a snake creeping over her shoulder which crept into her bosom.... Then Goodman Corey and Goody Oliver kneeled down before the black man and went to prayer. Then the black man told me that Goody Oliver had been a witch for 20 years and a half. Then they all set to biting me and so went away.... On the sixth day at night came Goody Oliver and Mrs. English, Goodman Corey and his wife.... Then Goody Oliver told me that she had killed four women; two of them were the Foster wives and John Trask's wife and did not name the other.

It is obvious from the content of this diatribe that Susannah Sheldon was actively coached. Adults were constantly discussing witchcraft matters within earshot of her. Many of those same adults despised Bridget Bishop. The girl also heard the stories of Tituba. Acutely susceptible, she readily picked up what she heard and embellished it for her listeners. Within a very short time four other girls were also howling against Bridget Bishop.

The hapless woman was arraigned on April 19 amid an intimidating atmosphere. Facing her were dour magistrates, armed guards and hostile witnesses. The meetinghouse was tense. In the front row sat the so-called "afflicted maidens" dressed in their best clothes. Behind them stretched a capacity crowd which filled every seat, jammed the aisles and spilled outdoors. People craned their necks and jockeyed for position. Little children were placed astride sturdy shoulders to get a better view. Outside still others pressed their faces to the windows. Then a hush fell over the murmuring throng as the center of attention [Bishop] arrived and the sheriff bellowed a throaty cry of "Make way!" At long last the public was going to see the "wicked witch," the "mass murderess," the "horrible she-beast of Salem" whose name was the terror of the town. For years, all agreed, she had thwarted justice with her crafty stratagems but now she would answer for her crimes.

The crowd parted before the sheriff's procession and Bridget Bishop was brought to the front of the room. There she faced the judges. But before even one word could be said, pandemonium erupted in the courtroom. The girls who had a moment before been sitting serenely in the front row went berserk. With frantic screams they hurled themselves out of their seats, thrashed about on the floor, tore at things, clutched at things and had to be physically restrained from injuring themselves. A shrill of horror ran through the crowd. Most thought that the "witch" was trying to murder the girls before the very eyes of authority. Although Bridget Bishop was held fast by guards, her incorporeal specter was said to be assaulting the objects of her malice. Only the girls could see the phantom which attacked them and they pointed to it as it supposedly flitted about the room. The brother of Mary Walcott drew a sword and slashed at the air in an effort to strike the invisible fiend. Again and again he swung the sword until his sister finally shrieked that he had cut the phantom's throat. Bridget Bishop's coat was found to have a tear in it at precisely the same spot.

Only with the utmost difficulty was order restored. When the commotion subsided to a point where magistrate John Hathorne could make himself heard, he asked the girls if it was indeed Bridget Bishop who had abused them. Elizabeth Hubbard, Ann Putnam, Abigail Williams and Mercy Lewis all answered in the affirmative. Bridget Bishop denied everything. But as she shook her head in denial the girls were once again hurled into paroxysms of pain. The same thing happened whenever the accused woman made any bodily motion. If Bridget Bishop so much as rolled her eyes the girls reacted. If she nodded her head, the same. Likewise if she shifted her stance, tapped her foot, motioned with her fingers or even sighed. Another murmur ran through the crowd of spectators. It was thought that the "witch" had the impudence to practice her craft right there in the

courtroom. The crowning blow came when Bridget was asked whether or not she felt "troubled to see the afflicted persons so tormented." She replied with an expression of contempt.

Bridget Bishop was remanded back to prison while additional "evidence" was collected against her. It was swift in coming. A deranged woman named Abigail Hobbes astounded the public by confessing herself a witch and naming many others in the process, among them her own parents. Before long that woman's mother, Deliverance Hobbes, was tricked into self-incrimination; she said that because of her willingness to cooperate with authority, the wrath of Bridget Bishop had beset her. She said that Bridget came to her in spectral form as she lay in jail, castigated her and demanded that she resubmit to the devil. "She would have me set my hand to the book!" said Deliverance Hobbes. "But I would not. Neither did I consent to hurt them (the girls) again.... It was Goody Bishop that tempted me to deny all that I had confessed before." Hobbes also alleged that Bridget Bishop had come to her in ghostly form together with other witches and demanded that she partake of a diabolical sacrament of "roast and boiled meat."

It was decided to reexamine Bridget Bishop. Again the woman found herself paraded before a packed assembly. Again the meetinghouse became the scene of psychosomatic convulsions convincingly acted out. Again Bridget Bishop was denounced as the cause of it all. At that point the accused woman could take no more.

"Liars!" she screamed.

At that, the chaos was renewed. The girls shrieked and swooned.

"What contract has thou made with the devil?" demanded the examining magistrate.

"None!" hollered Bridget Bishop.

"She calls the devil her God!" wailed Ann Putnam.

Bridget continued to deny everything. Realizing that he was getting nowhere, the inquisitorial magistrate decided to change tactics.

"Do you not see how they are tormented?" asked magistrate Hathorne. "You are practicing witchcraft before us. What do you say to this? Why do you not have a heart to confess the truth?"

"I am innocent! I know nothing of it! I am no witch!" retorted Bridget Bishop.

At that point magistrate Hathorne sprung a wily snare:

"Have you not," he sneered, "given consent that some evil spirit should do this in your likeness?"

Hitherto unable to wring a confession from the accused woman, Hathorne attempted to trick her with an analogous argument. That also failed to break Bridget's resolve. She remained firm. Finally amid a continued uproar from the girls and the opprobrium of the adult audience, an exasperated magistrate ordered Bridget returned to prison. Then her case was submitted to a grand jury.

Four separate indictments were returned against Bridget Bishop. Then even further indignities were imposed on her: She was forced to endure the physical examination of her naked body for marks of the devil. A panel of matrons was employed for that purpose. Two separate "searches" were conducted and no spot or orifice escaped perusal. The matrons found what they were looking for (or thought that they did), and they filed an official report to that effect.

The trial of Bridget Bishop opened at Salem on June 2, 1692. It was a one-day affair. Seven judges headed by Deputy-Governor William Stoughton comprised the court. Bridget was allowed no counsel; at least no one is known to have risked their skin to defend her. The evidence produced was but a rehash of the scurrilous stories that had long circulated about her. The prevailing lunacy of the "afflicted girls" counted heavily against her as well. Cotton Mather, who later wrote of the trial, captured the quintessence of the proceedings when he remarked, "There was little occasion to prove the witchcraft, it being evident and notorious to all beholders." Bridget Bishop was predoomed by popular opinion and prejudice. On June 10, 1692, the sheriff of Essex County did his duty as ordered and did "cause Bridget Bishop to be hanged by the neck until she was dead."

Sarah Good, white, age 38. *Witchcraft.* After disposing of Bridget Bishop, the Special Court of Oyer & Terminer recessed until June 30, 1692. When the court reconvened the case of Sarah Good was one of five which formed its docket.

Sarah Good had been going downhill for many years. She was looked upon with disdain and had little self-respect. By 1692 she was prime material for a witchcraft accusation and was, not surprisingly, one of the very first to be denounced. She had been born at Wenham, one of nine children (seven girls and two boys) of John and Elizabeth Solart. Her father was French by nationality and a tavernkeeper by profession. When Sarah was aged 18 her father committed suicide. Then for ten years thereafter Sarah remained on the fringe of her family while her siblings haggled over the dead man's estate. In 1682 Sarah turned up at Salem and married a manumitted servant named Daniel Poole. Within a year's time she was widowed and forced to become a ward of the town. In 1685 she married another man of mean circumstances named William Good. He was a poor provider but did manage to keep Sarah in a perpetual state of pregnancy. For the next seven years the couple's home was wherever they found temporary shelter and their livelihood was drawn from whatever odd jobs William Good could find. Sarah Good supplemented their meager income by panhandling, and that, combined with poor personal hygiene, made her the bane of the town.

Sarah Good was initially arrested on February 29, 1692, and arraigned the following day on suspicion of being one of those responsible for the alleged molestation of the girls who had been taken ill at the Salem village parsonage. The slave woman Tituba had testified that four witches (one of whom she identified as Sarah Good) had inveigled her to torment the so-called "afflicted maidens." Sarah Good in particular, according to the slave, had a familiar spirit in the form of a yellow bird which sucked fluid from between her fingers. She was also alleged to have sent a demonic wolf to attack the girls.

Although it was highly irregular for magistrates to accept the word of a slave over that of a free white person, such a point of law was rendered academic by the courtroom antics of the "afflicted maidens." They were present at the arraignment of Sarah Good and were thrown into convulsions at the very sight of the woman. The reason for this, according to Tituba, was that Sarah Good was using witchcraft to maul the girls there and then. Moreover, the physical phenomena adduced by the girls was well acted. Few could doubt that their screams and contortions were genuine evidence of witchcraft. As for Sarah Good, so despised was she that her own family turned against her. The woman's husband even called her a witch. Her own daughter—five years old—said that she was a witch who had even corrupted her own offspring. Sarah Good herself, who was, as usual, pregnant at the time of her arrest, was tossed into a squalid dungeon together with her five-year-old daughter. She suffered many more indignities in the days that followed. She also had a miscarriage.

The prosecution collected "evidence" against Sarah Good throughout the spring of 1692. The woman seemed to have left a trail of blighted livestock wherever her begging had been rebuffed. However, when she faced the Court of Oyer & Terminer on June 30, 1692, she was charged specifically with bewitching three persons named Sarah Bibber, Elizabeth Hubbard and Ann Putnam.

The conviction of Sarah Good would have been a matter of routine were it not for an incident which arose during her trial that added to the infamy of Chief Justice Stoughton and the other bigots who comprised the witchcraft court. One of the "afflicted persons" screamed that Sarah's image had stabbed her with a spectral knife and broken the blade in so doing. A piece of knife blade was indeed found. However, a man in the audience stepped forward and told of how he had broken his own knife the previous day and tossed away the broken piece in the presence of the "afflicted person" in question. The broken piece was found to exactly fit the greater part of the knife's blade which the man had retained and it at once became clear that the "afflicted girl" had merely retrieved the broken piece for a purpose of mischief. However, Chief Justice Stoughton would not be deterred from his purpose even by the exposure of deliberate fraud in his courtroom. Instead of stopping the proceedings there and then, discharging the innocent prisoner and punishing the "afflicted girl" for perjury, he merely warned her to tell no more fibs. Then he let the trial continue.

It was on such evidence that Sarah Good was cast for death. She was hanged on July 19, 1692.

Rebecca Nurse, white, age 71. *Witchcraft.* This unfortunate woman was born at Yarmouth, England, on February 21, 1621, the eldest of eight children of William and Joanna Towne. Her entire family emigrated to Massachusetts in the summer of 1640 and shortly afterwards Rebecca was wed to one Francis Nurse. Both were 19 years old at the time of their marriage and during the course of the ensuing years they raised a brood of eight children, four boys and four girls.

From early in her life Rebecca Nurse was noted for an innocuous and benevolent disposition. She was a dutiful mother and obliging friend who performed numerous acts of kindness. She was also an assiduous churchgoer revered for sanctity and grace. Few who knew her failed to experience her charm and personal warmth.

Goodman Nurse had originally been a man of modest means. Through careful economy and sheer perseverance, however, he gradually aspired to a level of prosperity beyond what popular opinion thought fit for one of his caste. His big opportunity had come in the year 1678 when he accepted an option on a 300-acre farm. A deal was worked out with the seller wherein the purchase price would be paid in 20 annual installments and it thence became a collective effort of the Nurse family — parents, children and grandchildren — to make the property prosper in order to meet that financial obligation.

The Nurses were a perfect example of what is known as an extended family, that is, a household consisting of more than one nuclear family of two or more generations which operated under one roof as a single social and economic unit. In other words, the elderly Francis and Rebecca Nurse were the respective patriarch and matriarch of one large household consisting of their eight grown children with their respective spouses and offspring. Their collective long-range goal was to provide a place for the secure retirement of Francis and Rebecca while simultaneously creating a tangible investment that would form the second generation's legacies.

By working for many years as a close-knit unit on an exclusive homestead, the Nurse family gradually grew to resemble more of a community unto itself rather than merely a common neighbor in a larger community. There were some who formed an opinion that the Nurses held themselves aloof from the rest of their town. Not only were the Nurses successful but they had become self-sufficient. This gave rise to envy. An old grudge further aggravated the situation. James Allen, the man from whom the Nurses bought their farm, had originally acquired the property through marriage. The land had been set aside from an older and larger estate to serve as his wife's dowry. Allen's wife had died soon after her marriage and her family came to resent her husband as an opportunist who had done them out of a substantial piece of property. Everything about the matter was legal but it still bode ill. To make matters worse, Allen had sold out to a third party — Francis Nurse — without making a conciliatory gesture to his wife's kin. Hence the Nurses were in their turn resented as interlopers by a certain segment of their community.

By 1692 Rebecca Nurse had grown old. She was then 71 years of age and for the most part deaf. She did not allow her infirmities to preclude her from regular attendance at sabbath day services nor from making the most of her declining years in the bosom of a supportive and affectionate family. However, old age was not to be her final nemesis. The disaster which was destined to overtake Rebecca Nurse was a fomentation of jealousy. All the support and insulation of her family would prove ineffectual against such an enemy.

Rebecca Nurse was first denounced as a witch by 12-year-old Ann Putnam on March 13, 1692. On that date the girl reported a vision of an elderly woman abusing her and tempting her to sign the so-called "devil's book." The girl did not recognize the offensive specter at the time but could only say that it was the apparition of one who she had regularly seen at sabbath day services. Exactly how she came up with the name of

Rebecca Nurse is uncertain but it would seem quite probable that she was actively coached by some person or persons who envied the Nurses. Before long the girl's mother also joined in the denunciation and within a few days the whole pack of crazed girls was crying out against the woman. On March 23, 1692, a warrant was issued for the arrest of Rebecca Nurse.

It was at this point that the first open opposition to the witch hunt surfaced. Friends and family flew to the defense of Rebecca Nurse. An accusation against a person of her caliber was deemed so preposterous that for a moment doubt even crossed the minds of the over-zealous magistrates in charge of the arraignments. Rebecca's own reaction was meek and resigned. "If it be so, the will of the Lord be done," said she.

The old woman was brought before magistrate John Hathorne and his board of arraignment on March 24. Hathorne, for the first time unsure of himself, proceeded delicately.

"Have you seen this woman hurt you?" he asked the "afflicted maidens."

At once Abigail Williams and Ann Putnam went into their routine of convulsions and shrieks. "Yes! Yes!" they yelled.

"Goody Nurse," said Hathorne, "here are two who complain of you hurting them. What do you say to it?"

Rebecca answered with composed dignity. "I can say before my Eternal Father that I am innocent and God will clear my innocence."

At that point the court admitted several written testimonies as proxy evidence against the defendant. They were the accounts of persons who claimed to have seen the "afflicted persons" suffer seizures outside of the courtroom and heard them claim that Rebecca Nurse was responsible for them. She denied all culpability.

"Are you an innocent person relating to this witchcraft?" asked Hathorne

in a manner more tender than had been thought to be within his ability.

The case was drifting in Rebecca's favor. Perceiving the trend, the mother of Ann Putnam gave vent to a dramatic outburst: "Did you not bring the black man with you? Did you not bid me tempt God and die? How often have you ate and drank to your own damnation?" she screamed.

"Oh Lord, help me," signed Rebecca Nurse and she spread her hands in a gesture of supplication.

That was a cue for which the "afflicted girls" had been waiting. They threw themselves into paroxysms of agony which continued with every bodily movement made by the defendant. They screamed that evil spirits were issuing from Rebecca's body to torment them. They yelled that the devil, in the form of a Negro, was standing beside her and whispering instructions to her. They said that evil spirits in the form of invisible birds were fluttering about her. The scene was utter chaos.

Rebecca Nurse continued to deny everything. So magistrate Hathorne, whose opinion was once again drifting in favor of the accusers, tried to snare her with a clever question:

"Possibly you may apprehend that you are no witch. But have you not been led aside by temptations that way?"

"I have not!" stated Rebecca firmly.

At that point all Hathorne could think to say was: "What a sad thing it is that a church member here and now of Salem should be thus accused and charged."

"A sad thing sure enough!" shrieked Gertrude Pope, one of the "afflicted persons," at which they were all set to their antics once again. Cross-examination continued for a short time longer but soon the uproar became insurmountable and the session was discontinued. Rebecca Nurse was remanded to prison.

Additional depositions were added to the prosecution's dossier as the weeks wore on. The "afflicted persons" continued to cry out against Rebecca Nurse with unwavering vehemence. Abigail Williams even went to the extreme of saying that Rebecca's specter had molested her numerous times, alternately tempting her to sign the "devil's book" and threatening to throw her into the fire if she refused nefarious solicitations. She also reported visions of Rebecca sitting in council with the devil and other visions in which the woman's specter claimed to have committed three murders.

The mother of Ann Putnam, not to be outdone, told a tale of being bitten and beaten with chains by an apparition of Rebecca Nurse. She also reported that Rebecca's specter had come to her on a mission to torture her in revenge for her earlier testimony and that the same specter had also told her of three murders which it had committed. Moreover, it reported an additional murder: that of a young child of the Putnam family, recently deceased, out of revenge for defamatory remarks its parents had made about Rebecca Nurse, her sisters and her long dead mother. Even worse, Ann Putnam's mother told of a ghostly visitation by six children in their burial shrouds who she perceived to be six deceased children of a sister of hers who lived in Boston. Also the apparitions of yet another sister with her respective children — all dead and swathed in burial clothes — who pitifully implored justice for their murdered blood.

The woman's testimony was the product of a diseased mind. But it was taken seriously by authority and by a majority of the public.

The trial of Rebecca Nurse on June 30, 1692, was farcical in the extreme. So riddled with prejudice and procedural errors was it that it ranks with the worst of legal travesties. Initially, all the scurrilous accusations that had already been dredged up against the woman were rehashed in court. To that was added the continuous ravings of the "afflicted persons" and in at least one instance the outright fraud of an "afflicted person": Sarah Bibber had pulled pins from her clothing, jabbed herself with them and blamed Rebecca Nurse for making her do it. The elderly defendant was also strip-searched for marks of the devil. Conversely, the jury weighed the mitigating factors of the defendant's long years of Christian profession, a favorable array of character references and Rebecca's impressive courtroom demeanor. Hitherto the jury had been confronted only with defendants of base reputation: persons like Bridget Bishop and Sarah Good who were regarded as villains at best. Rebecca Nurse was different and that fact carried weight with the jury. When the jurymen filed back into court to give their verdict the foreman said, "*Not Guilty.*"

The uproar which followed was indescribable. The "afflicted persons" outdid themselves for dramatic effect. They screamed and raved and threw themselves about the courtroom. Their tantrums surpassed all previous outbursts. A scene of such intensity had not been seen up to that point and there were not a few who feared an imminent onslaught by all the demons in hell.

The judges were visibly displeased by the verdict. They did not resort to rabid manifestations themselves but they did disgrace themselves by uttering a number of unprofessional remarks. At least one judge openly voiced non-acceptance of the verdict and another said that he would demand a retrial. Chief Justice Stoughton, likewise displeased, addressed the jury when order was restored:

"I will not impose on the jury," said he, "but I must ask if you considered one statement made by the prisoner. When Deliverance Hobbes (a self-confessed witch) was brought into court to testify, the prisoner, turning her head to her said, 'What, do you bring her? She is one of us.' Has the jury weighed the implications of that statement?"

The jury was intimidated by the austere chief justice. They then withdrew to reconsider their verdict. What had Rebecca Nurse meant when she referred to the notorious Deliverance Hobbes as *"one of us"*? Did she mean a fellow witch? The truth was that she simply meant a fellow prisoner but that point was lost for the moment. Moreover, the jury was appalled by the devastating impact its verdict of acquittal had had upon the "afflicted persons" in the courtroom. Were the renewed sufferings of those persons a divine sign that the jury had erred? With such nagging questions newly implanted in their minds the jurymen decided to take no chances. They reversed themselves and voted for conviction. They would leave it to God to sort the innocent from the guilty. Then Rebecca Nurse, like so many other luckless individuals, was sentenced to death.

Even greater humiliations were in store for Rebecca Nurse. Having been torn from her family, falsely denounced, stripped naked and searched for witch marks, chained in a filthy dungeon and condemned to death was still not enough to satisfy her enemies. Before the ultimate disgrace of hanging was inflicted, one more degradation was added: Rebecca Nurse would be forced to undergo the ritual of excommunication from her church — the same church of which she had been so devoted a member for so many long decades. Accordingly on July 3, 1692, a sabbath day, a scene of shame took place. Rebecca Nurse, who by then had broken down from the trauma of her ordeal, was placed in a chair and carried before the assembled congregation. A stinging decree of banishment was pompously pronounced and the wretched woman was then ignominiously cast out. Only the gallows remained.

Even in these extremes, Rebecca's loyal family had not been idle. They were determined to somehow —*anyhow*— find a way to save their matriarch. When solicitations on her behalf failed with the authorities at Salem they hurried to Boston to implore the mercy of the governor. Somehow they gained access to Sir William Phipps and enumerated all the errors and inconsistencies of the case against Rebecca Nurse. A reprieve was granted. But it was not to prevail. Word of the reprieve reached Salem with incredible speed and at once the "afflicted persons" suffered relapses. Only the death of the "witch" as directed by law could deliver them from their plight. Hence the governor found himself besieged with counterarguments and the reprieve was rescinded. Rebecca Nurse went to the gallows on July 19, 1692.

Susannah Martin, white, age 67. *Witchcraft.* This ill-fated woman was English-born, the youngest daughter of one Richard North. When she was 13 years old her family migrated to New England where her father became one of the original settlers of Salisbury, Massachusetts. Her teenage years were spent in local domestic service. On August 11, 1646, she married a widower named George Martin, set up house with him at Amesbury and over the next 21 years raised a brood of five boys and three girls. She became a widow in 1686.

The reputation of Susannah North Martin was abominable. For more than half a century she was reviled for alleged misdeeds ranging from infanticide to witchcraft. Cotton Mather, who chronicled her 1692 trial, spoke for many when he called Susannah Martin "one of the most impudent, scurrilous, wicked creatures in the world." Yet while almost certainly exaggerated, her notoriety may have been partially self-earned; after allowing a generous discount for common antipathy there still remains enough of Susannah Martin in surviving accounts to reveal her as a spirited, contentious woman.

Susannah's troubles started before she was married. A rumor of the time alleged that she had been caught in the act of strangling an illegitimate child and that she had threatened the life of the person who had caught her. Proof was lacking but the gossip took root. At one point, in 1669, her husband sued on her behalf. But so unsavory had Susannah's name become by then that when a court ruled in her favor, it awarded damages that were more of an insult than a commiseration.

The epithet of "witch" is first known to have been flung at Susannah in the year 1660 when she was 35 years old. There dwelled in Salisbury at that time a man named William Browne who had a mentally unbalanced wife named Elizabeth. One day this Goodwife Browne encountered Susannah Martin on the road and imagined that the latter vanished into thin air. The hallucination unnerved Goodwife Browne and she fell into an agitated mental state. The condition continued to plague the woman intermittently for several months during which time she grew physically ill as well as mentally ill and raved about Susannah Martin when delirious. In the spring of 1661 a formal complaint was made against the suspected witch. A grand jury considered the matter but refused to find an indictment. Shortly afterward, an indignant Susannah Martin accosted Goodwife Browne and told her off as only she could. Goody Browne then had another mental breakdown. A story was told of an evil spell cast upon the woman by a vindictive Susannah Martin.

Worse trouble befell Susannah in 1669. That year she found herself again accused of witchcraft and again confronted with the old tale of infanticide. An extremely high bond of £100 which she was required to post attested to the seriousness of her predicament. As for the precise nature of the complaints which were lodged against her at that time, several retrospective testimonies from her 1692 trial provide details. For instance:

Twenty-nine-year-old John Pressy (who was probably drunk at the time) became disoriented while walking home one evening and took a wrong path three times. He wound up walking in circles. Then he set out a fourth time and came to a point near Susannah Martin's house. There he was alarmed to see a strange light paralleling him just off the road. The light seemed to match his progress step for step, and, growing apprehensive of it, Pressy struck at it with a stick. Then he tripped in the darkness and fell into a ditch. Next, when he got back up again and had walked a short way, he was astounded to see —or imagine that he saw— Susannah Martin standing by the side of the road. She extended to him no greeting but followed him with her eyes as he passed. Eventually Pressy reached his home but was terrified to think that he had tangled with a witch during his walk. According to his reasoning, Susannah Martin had caused him to become lost in the darkness and had followed him in the form of a ghostly light. Within hours Pressy's weird ordeal was the talk of the town. Rumor further embellished the details by alleging that Susannah Martin had that very day complained of body pains as a result of being swatted with a stick by Goodman Pressy while in supernatural form the previous night. No one stopped to consider the more probable explanation that Susannah Martin, lantern in hand, had been patrolling the perimeter of her property against foxes and raccoons at the time of Pressy's passage. She might have even set a lantern down on the ground to act as a night beacon only to have it bashed to bits by the befuddled Pressy.

Another tale of the time involved another drunk named John Kimball.

Wishing to obtain a dog for himself, this Kimball sought out Susannah Martin because she was known to be the owner of a bitch that had had puppies. Susannah and her visitor could not agree on pick of the litter so Kimball went elsewhere. Shortly thereafter Kimball encountered Susannah's husband who asked him if he was still interested in one of his wife's puppies. Kimball replied in the negative. When Susannah Martin heard of that she reportedly quipped, "If I live I'll give him puppies enough!" Mischief was not long in coming to John Kimball. While returning home one day from a house that he was building, Kimball kept stumbling over tree stumps despite his best efforts to the contrary. Then he encountered a small animal — "like a puppy" — which ran playfully about him in circles and even darted between his legs. Fearing the unknown creature, Kimball frantically swung at it with his woodchopper's axe and worked himself into a frenzy in the process. Then, according to his own account, "the puppy gave a little jump and seemed to go into the ground." Continuing along the way, Kimball was next accosted by a second creature "somewhat bigger than the first but as black as a coal." This second creature attacked Kimball; "it flew at his belly and then at his throat and over his shoulder." Kimball then claimed to have fought the animal off with his axe.

Soon the talk of the town was that an angry Susannah Martin had sent demonic puppies to harass Kimball. No one stopped to consider the fact that wolves were common in those days; the drunken man had more likely come upon a wolf pup near its den and then its protective mother.

It was drivel such as this which brought Susannah Martin to court in 1669. However, she again managed to emerge a free woman. Then she launched a counter attack. Through her husband, Susannah filed three separate lawsuits against her antagonists charging malicious slander. She recovered little by way of redress and was left to stew in her indignation. When one man was unable to resist the temptation to tease her about the situation, Susannah sarcastically retorted, "Beware lest some she-devil fetch thee away!" That very night a cat (which was probably a household pet) jumped onto the man's bed and scared him half to death. It was thereafter said that Susannah Martin had attacked the man in fervid, feline form.

This kind of controversy continued unabated for another 23 years. An entire generation of Amesbury-Salisbury residents grew up fearing Susannah Martin. Young and old alike regarded her with dread and most took care to avoid her. Few indeed were they who dared to risk her wrath.

One such individual was an army lieutenant named John Allen. He had once refused to haul some lumber for Susannah Martin. Displeased, Susannah grumbled some remark to which Allen retorted, "Dost threaten me, old witch? I'll throw thee into the brook!" and he made a motion to grab her. But Susannah outran the man and escaped. Soon afterward a strange series of events befell the rash lieutenant. He put his oxen to graze with other livestock on Salisbury Beach only to have the entire herd act irrationally for no discernible reason. Water formed no barrier to the beasts; they plunged into the Merrimack River and swam to an island. Then when drovers arrived at the scene the oxen suddenly stampeded. They jumped into the ocean and swam as far out as the eye could see. The majority of the oxen were later cast up drowned on Salisbury Beach and there was not a man among the drovers who did not believe that the animals had been bewitched by Susannah Martin.

For the last two years of her life Susannah had to contend with another enemy named Joseph Ring. This man owed a petty gambling debt (two shillings) to a third party. He persisted in welshing on the debt and was of such a character as to spread witchcraft allegations in an attempt to divert attention from his own shortcoming. He not only slandered the person to whom he owed the money but dragged Susannah Martin into his tales as well. He said that the fellow to whom he was indebted (one Thomas Hardy) was a wizard and that he had accosted him several times, each time using black magic to carry him to witch meetings where he witnessed forbidden revelry and was tempted to join the ranks of the damned. Susannah Martin, he alleged, was a regular at such affairs and on one occasion in particular he claimed to have watched as she turned herself into a black hog.

Susannah first became involved in the Salem imbroglio toward the end of April 1692, when two of the Parris parsonage girls cried out against her.

It is highly probable that the "afflicted girls" denounced Susannah Martin only because they were maneuvered into doing so by busybodies. Susannah was a resident of Amesbury whereas the girls resided in Salem Village. By 17th century standards the two towns were far distant from each other. Children such as the Salem girls, being young and of limited geographic range, could hardly be expected to have known and recognized a resident of far-off Amesbury without being coached. In short, Susannah Martin and the Salem girls were complete strangers to each other who were brought together through the machinations of a third party. This "third party" was the bunch of busybodies who hovered around the "bewitched" girls, determined to hang onto every word they babbled. "Do you not see a short old woman?" asked these hangers-on. "Is there not a short old woman among those who afflict ye?" It was loaded questions such as these

which induced the "afflicted girls" to denounce Susannah Martin. When the suggestion of a "short old woman" was answered in the affirmative, the next step for the busybodies was to put forward the name of the suspect they had in mind all along: Susannah Martin of Amesbury. The girls took their cue and picked right up on it; they immediately began screeching against yet another innocent but friendless person. An arrest warrant for Susannah Martin was promptly issued.

When Susannah was arraigned on May 2, 1692, the magistrates found her courtroom demeanor even more galling than the obstreperous antics of the "afflicted persons." She was flippant in her answers and made little or no effort to conceal her contempt. She even dared to laugh when confronted in court with the crazed individuals (by then eight in number) she was accused of bewitching. Such impudence was insufferable to the magistrates and it hardened their opinion. However, if the meekness of a Rebecca Nurse had been unavailing in such circumstances, a prejudiced bench was academic for Susannah Martin. She realized early that her position was hopeless and decided to at least afford herself the personal satisfaction of treating her accusers with derision.

When Susannah entered the courtroom it was the signal for the "afflicted persons" to demonstrate their well-practiced routine of swooning and raving. Three of the girls screamed against Susannah Martin for supposedly biting, pinching and otherwise tormenting them. An unimpressed Susannah Martin greeted the tirade with contemptuous laughter.

"What! Do you laugh at it?!" gasped magistrate John Hathorne, scarcely believing his ears.

"Well I might at such folly!" guffawed Susannah Martin.

"Is it folly to hurt these persons?" demanded Hathorne.

"I never hurt man, woman or child," said Susannah.

At that point one of the girls shrieked vociferously and the others joined in. Susannah Martin spat contempt at them again by laughing in their faces.

"What ails these people?" demanded the magistrate.

"I do not know," shrugged Susannah.

"But what do you think?" asked Hathorne.

"I do not desire to spend my judgment on it," huffed Susannah.

And so the duel continued.

"Have you no compassion for these afflicted?" asked Hathorne.

"No! I have none!" snapped Susannah Martin.

"Do you not see how God evidently discovers you?" quizzed Hathorne.

"No, not a bit for that," said Susannah.

"But all the congregation thinks so!" said Hathorne.

"Let them think what they will," shrugged Susannah.

The prisoner refused to budge. All the magistrates could do at that point was return her to prison. Then the courtroom degenerated into a madhouse. The slightest bodily movement on Susannah's part hurled the "afflicted persons" into spasms of agony. A glance, a finger movement, even the wetting of her lips was all it took. Some of the girls screamed that they were struck deaf. Others acted as if they were dumbfounded. Some displayed bites and welt marks. Others claimed that an astral projection of Susannah Martin was sitting on an overhead beam, gloating over the scene in the chamber below. Others said that the devil, in the form of a "black man," was standing beside Susannah Martin throughout the proceedings, whispering instructions to her. All of the "afflicted persons" were ordered to touch the prisoner in order that they be re-lieved from their fury but none could muster the strength to do so.

When Susannah Martin came to trial on June 29, 1692, her fate was a bygone conclusion. Every scurrilous tale of the previous 50 years that her detractors could recall was entered as evidence against her. Likewise did the continuous ravings of the "afflicted persons" count to her detriment. The jury did not hesitate to vote for conviction and Susannah Martin was sentenced to death. She was hanged on July 19, 1692.

Elizabeth How, white, age about 57.

Witchcraft. This woman was born in England and came to Massachusetts with her parents shortly afterward. She had a brother who was probably her senior and two sisters who were born at Rowley, Massachusetts, in 1639 and 1644. The names of her parents were William and Joan Jackson.

Virtually nothing is discernible of Elizabeth Jackson's childhood. However, on April 13, 1658, she married 23-year-old James How, Jr., of Ipswich and subsequently became the mother of two sons and three daughters.

The family How appears to have lived peaceably at Ipswich until the year 1682 when they became involved in a land dispute with the neighboring family of one Samuel Perley. That clan (which clearly appears to have been motivated by spite) openly disliked the Hows. When a ten-year-old girl of theirs, Hannah Perley, fell ill, they twisted the circumstances in order to malign Elizabeth How.

Testimony produced at Elizabeth's 1692 trial by a Rowley minister vividly illustrates the mendacity of the Perley family:

The testimony of Samuel Phillips, aged about 67 years, Minister of the word of God in Rowley, saith that Mr. Payson (minister of God's word also in Rowley) and myself went at the desire of

Samuel Perley of Ipswich to see his young daughter who was visited with strange fits. In those fits, as her father and mother affirmed, she mentioned Goodwife How as if she was in the house and did afflict her. When we were in the house the child had one of her fits but made no mention of Goodwife How. When the fit was over she came to herself. Then Goodwife How went to the child and took her by the hand and asked her if she had ever done her any hurt. And she answered, "No, never, and if I did complain of you in my fits I knew not that I did so." I can further affirm upon oath that young Samuel Perley, brother to ye afflicted girl, while looking out of a chamber window (I and the afflicted child being outdoors together) said to his sister, "Say Goodwife How is a witch! Say Goodwife How is a witch!" But the child spoke not a word that way. I looked up to the window where the youth stood and rebuked him for his boldness to stir up his sister to accuse Goodwife How when she had cleared her from doing any hurt to her. And I added, "No wonder that the child in her fits did mention Goodwife How when her nearest relations were so frequent in expressing their suspicions within earshot of the child when she was out of her fits that the said Goodwife How was the instrument of mischief to the child."

Had the authorities at Salem Village in 1692 been as rational as the Rowley minister in 1682 the outcome of the witch trials would have been quite different.

Irrespective of the Rev. Phillips recognizing Hannah Perley's problem as being more psychological than diabolical, the Perley kin naturally sided in with the girl's parents and added tales of their own to the detriment of Elizabeth How. Rumors spread through the countryside. There were tales of Elizabeth How entering little Hannah Perley's chamber through cracks in the walls. There were tales of Elizabeth How popping in and out of the oven, going up and down the chimney, leaping in and out of the windows, etc.

The allegations were preposterous in the extreme. Still there was no shortage of people who were willing to believe the worst. Elizabeth How was thereafter a butt for gossip and her reputation suffered irreversible damage.

There was more trouble two years later when Elizabeth How sought membership in the Ipswich church. Some of the more bumptious members of the congregation flew to arms. Rejection of the new applicant became a holy crusade and so great a fuss was raised that Elizabeth was denied admittance. Moreover, her enemies chided her by telling tales of evil things that supposedly befell all who had dared to speak against her.

An incident which took place in 1685 illustrates the flimsy basis upon which Elizabeth's enemies built their allegations. Her husband had hired a sawyer to hew a parcel of fence posts. The task was completed with the assistance of a member of the Perley family. When Elizabeth How learned that the sawyer had shared the job with one of her enemies, she refused delivery of the finished goods. This was because she suspected that the quality of the fence posts would be substandard by intentional design of the Perley worker. It turned out that Elizabeth's suspicions were well-founded; the fence posts were found to be flawed in such a way that they broke upon slight impulse. They had been sabotaged. Consequently the sawyer was obliged to hew a better batch. However, it was rumored thereafter that Elizabeth How had bewitched the original batch of fence posts. The Perley family member who had sabotaged the fence posts did not like the fact that Elizabeth How had caught him. So he spread rumors about her.

With such a reputation it was only a matter of course that Elizabeth attracted attention at Salem Village in 1692. She was denounced in the latter part of May, arrested on the 28th of that month and arraigned on the 31st. She faced the full fury of the witch hunters when first brought into court. Six young women accused her of abusing them and they demonstrated a full gamut of antics to support their claim. All screamed maniacally. Some writhed on the floor. One showed a pin stuck in her hand and another displayed welts on her arms. Still another swooned while two more shrieked that they saw the specter of Elizabeth How upon her. John Indian (the husband of Tituba) also got into the act. "Oh, she bites! She bites!" he wailed as he thrashed about on the floor in an act of deliberate fraud. Some bailiffs carried him over to Elizabeth How and she was ordered to touch him whereupon he came to his senses again as did one of the girls who acted in a like manner.

In addition to this courtroom farce the tales of the Perley family were produced in evidence against Elizabeth How. There were also stories about bewitched livestock and so on. But by far the cruelest jab came from Elizabeth's own brother-in-law. He had refused to accompany her to her arraignment and later testified that she had hexed some of his swine in retaliation.

It is significant to note that by the time of Elizabeth How's trial (which took place on June 30, 1692), several desperate individuals were endeavoring to save themselves by making false confessions. Some of them implicated Elizabeth How in their tales. It had been reasoned by the authorities that a contrite witch need not necessarily be damned; therefore any who confessed their guilt would be spared the death penalty in order that they be rehabilitated and thereby deny the devil an addition to his ranks. The Puritans saw it as their duty on the one hand to extirpate witches but to also keep souls from the devil wherever possible. Hence only obdurate non-

confessors would be executed and it became one of the greatest tragedies of the witch hunt that there were innocent persons under condemnation whose principles precluded them from falsely incriminating themselves. Elizabeth How was one such person. She bravely maintained her innocence under extreme duress. Even the imminent threat of the gallows failed to shake her resolve. Thus did she die, eschewing falsehood to the end on July 19, 1692.

Sarah Wildes, white, age 63. *Witchcraft.*

This woman was born in England, one of seven children of William and Abigail Averill. She came to Massachusetts with her parents at the age of eight and grew up at Ipswich in circumstances of penury. By the age of 20 she had been sent to the town whipping post at least one time for fornication. By age 26 she was bereaved of both parents and at the abnormally late age of 34 she married for her first and only time.

The nuptials of Sarah Averill and 44-year-old John Wildes of Topsfield were solemnized on November 23, 1663. The bridegroom was a widower with seven children and Sarah presented him with an eighth child, a boy named Ephraim, in December of 1665.

For reasons long forgotten the new Goody Wildes was loathed by the kin of her husband's first wife. She was especially repugnant to the dead woman's brother and sister, John Gould and Mary Gould Reddington by name. They may have frowned upon the fact that Sarah came from a poor family. There might have been hard feelings over what became of the first wife's possessions. The possibilities are numerous. Whatever the case, it was the Gould family that was chiefly responsible for branding Sarah Wildes with the infamy of a witch.

The allegations of witchcraft are traceable to around 1670 when one of Sarah's stepsons suffered an illness which could not be explained. The boy recovered but his maternal aunt, Mary Gould Reddington, so hated his stepmother, Sarah Wildes, that she used the event as an excuse to malign her. Within days the whole community was abuzz with gossip and as the years passed the poisonous seeds sowed by Mary Gould Reddington grew and mutated until the name of Sarah Wildes was anathema to God-fearing people.

For instance, one harvest day in 1674 two teenaged brothers named John and Joseph Andrews came to Sarah's house and asked her if they might borrow a scythe. The woman refused their request. However, as they were turning to leave a bystander noticed a scythe hanging nearby which belonged to one of Sarah's stepsons and bade the lads take it on condition that they obtain permission from its owner who was then at a place which they would pass. So the Andrews brothers took the scythe in direct disobedience of Sarah Wildes who became annoyed and sent her eight-year-old son after them with an order to return the scythe forthwith. The Andrews brothers ignored the little boy. Then they went to mowing hay. They did, however, properly obtain permission for use of the scythe from its owner. Three cartloads of hay were cut, the scythe was returned and one load of hay was safely transported to storage. However, bizarre trouble soon struck. Upon garnering the second load of hay, six strong oxen were suddenly and unaccountably disabled. For all their combined might they could not budge the haywagon. Then to make matters worse, one of the wagon wheels became mired despite the ground being firm. Accordingly, the Andrews brothers were required to jettison the load of hay for fear that a wrathful Sarah Wildes had bewitched their wagon. Not until the wagon was empty were the oxen able to free the wheel. Then with *terra firma* regained the Andrews boys reloaded the wagon and managed to proceed without

further difficulty to the top of a steep hill. There they paused and prepared for a delicate descent. However, right at that point a snake spooked the oxen and the result was a runaway haywagon careening down the hill at wild speed with John Andrews hanging on to it for dear life. Amazingly, the wagon remained upright for the entire length of the hill but it overturned at the bottom, scattering the hay and hurling John Andrews into a brook. The young man was dazed but essentially unhurt. Then he and his brother once again pitched the hay into the cart. No sooner did they finish that task than a new woe confronted them: try as they might, they could not properly fasten the ropes which secured the load. The bindings persisted in hanging loose thereon. In such a condition the Andrews boys staggered home. Night had fallen by then and they encountered concerned friends on the road who had set out in search of them. The would-be rescuers likewise strove to secure the hay ropes though without success and there was no man among them who did not fear the worst when Sarah Wildes was mentioned.

The gossip over this incident nettled Sarah Wildes. It also set off a feud between her and the Andrews family. One day in 1679 the mother and sister of the Andrews boys encountered Sarah Wildes on the road. The mother used the occasion to pick an argument with Wildes. She accused her of putting a hex on her boys. Sarah responded in a cocky manner which prompted Mother Andrews to call her daughter to her side. Then according to the daughter's account of the incident, Sarah Wildes gave her the "evil eye." "Immediately I did fall into such a trembling condition that I was as if all my joints did knock together so that I could hardly go along," recounted the daughter, whose name was Elizabeth Andrews Symonds. She also embellished her story further by saying that the spectral form of Sarah

Wildes had come to her bedroom in the night for no good purpose.

A week later Elizabeth Andrews Symonds encountered Sarah Wildes in the local meetinghouse and once again claimed to feel the malignant effects of the evil eye. "As I was sitting in my seat," said Elizabeth Andrews Symonds, "Goodwife Wildes came by and I was immediately taken with such a pain in my back that I was not able to bear it and fell down in the seat. I did not know where I was and some people carried me out of the meetinghouse. But I knew nothing of it until afterwards when I came to myself. A great many people came about me to ask what was the matter with me. Goodwife Wildes came and stood at the end of the table and I replied and said, 'There she is!' and my mother bade me go and scratch her but I could not stir."

Naturally the Andrews family fell right in with the Goulds when it came to detesting Sarah Wildes.

Mary Gould Reddington had ever maintained that Sarah Wildes had hexed her nephew Jonathan Wildes in 1670 or thereabout. But while she seems to have initially acted out of malice she also seems to have grown to believe her own nonsense. By 1677 she was in failing health and attributed her condition to witchcraft. In desperation she sought out the Rev. John Hale of Beverly, a much esteemed minister, and spilled her heart out to him with one story after another about Sarah Wildes and how "that witch" had plagued her for years, ruining her health and property.

When Sarah's husband heard of the Hale interview he threatened to sue the Reddingtons for slander. But Goodman Reddington managed to dissuade John Wildes with an argument that his calumnious wife had little time left to live and that the problem would therefore solve itself. Nevertheless John Wildes insisted upon confronting Mary Gould Reddington and when the time

came, he brought one of Sarah's brothers along with him as witness. Mary Gould Reddington blanched before the two men and denied having ever impugned Sarah Wildes. "She replied that she knew no harm my wife had done her," reported the pacified husband.

Mary Gould Reddington was not only a liar and a hypocrite but a coward as well.

The slandered Sarah Wildes was less indulgent than her husband. She went on the warpath and determined to settle accounts with Mary Gould Reddington once and for all. One day she caught up with her quarry on the road to Salem and went into battle. Fully enraged, Sarah Wildes pulled her foe right off of a horse, threw her on the ground and probably would have beaten her to death had two other riders not come along and intervened. Needless to say, the two women remained bitter, remorseless enemies and Mary Gould Reddington vilified Sarah Wildes even on her deathbed.

Sarah Wildes probably felt some personal satisfaction by outliving Mary Gould Reddington. However, she was not destined to have peace in her life. Another foe arose in the person of the aforementioned Elizabeth Andrews Symonds. This woman was quite capable of antagonizing Sarah Wildes; she had long been in cahoots with Mary Gould Reddington and she was every bit as mendacious, hypocritical and cowardly. She was also inordinately sly.

Sensing that the strategy of traducing Sarah Wildes from a witchcraft angle was pretty well played out, Elizabeth Andrews Symonds sought to irk her in a way that was as novel as it was cutting. Why not, she thought, direct a carefully aimed jab at Sarah Wildes by snaring her beloved only son?

So Elizabeth Andrews Symonds prepared a punic ruse for young Ephraim Wildes. What she did precisely was allow the 23-year-old bachelor to pay court to one of her daughters. A romance blossomed and marriage was discussed. Then came trouble. The old story of Sarah Wildes casting the evil eye on Elizabeth Andrews Symonds resurfaced and it boded friction between the two prospective mothers-in-law. Ephraim Wildes sought to clear up the matter. He went to his sweetheart's mother and asked for an explanation. Elizabeth Andrews Symonds lied to the young man, saying that she bore no ill will toward his mother and she even attempted to throw the blame for past problems on the long-dead Mary Gould Reddington.

Ephraim Wildes was not deceived. He became disgusted and stomped out of the house. The marriage was canceled. The skillfully baited trap had worked to perfection; it certainly hurt Sarah Wildes to see her only son heartbroken.

How it was that Sarah Wildes came to the attention of the witch hunters in 1692 is easily explained. The family of her arch enemy, Mary Gould Reddington, was related to the prime catalysts of the Salem imbroglio, the Putnams. Hence it was a matter of course that Sarah Wildes be implicated. Indeed, she was near the very top of the Putnam family hit list, 12-year-old Ann Putnam having denounced Sarah Wildes at the instigation of her parents during the early stages of the witch panic in March of 1692.

All of this was bad enough but there was even worse in store for Sarah Wildes. In that year of 1692 her son, Ephraim Wildes, was constable for the town of Topsfield and on April 21 he was ordered to execute an arrest warrant which included the name of his own mother. At a late hour another officer was allowed to take his place.

Sarah Wildes was arraigned on April 22, 1692, amid the usual scenes of courtroom pandemonium. The so-called "Crown Witnesses" accused her of sitting on an overhead beam in spectral form throughout the proceedings, urging her victims to sign the devil's book and casting the evil eye upon all who beheld her. This performance was accompanied by screams and convulsions for added effect.

Sarah Wildes had her trial on July 2, 1692, and she was promptly convicted. Sentenced to death, she maintained her innocence to the end. On July 19, 1692, she was hanged along with four others.

John Proctor, white, age about 60. *Witchcraft.* This man was born in England, the namesake of his father. He had at least two brothers and one sister. The entire family emigrated to Massachusetts about 1645 and settled at Ipswich. In the years that followed, John Proctor married three times (he was widowed twice) and fathered 11 children. Over a period of time he amassed considerable land holdings which he farmed in unison with his brothers and adult sons. Proctor was also a licensed innkeeper but it was his third wife, Elizabeth Bassett Proctor (white, age about 39) who presided over that enterprise. John Proctor was openly contemptuous of the Salem witch hunt and of the so-called "afflicted girls" in particular. He saw no reason for them to be fussed over and prayed over; what they needed, said he, was a good beating and then they would be restored to normalcy. When Proctor heard that one of his servant girls, Mary Warren, was involved in the witchcraft inquest he fetched her home in a hurry and put her to work. He may have also given her a beating because he made no secret of an intention to "thrash the devil out of her." On April 4, 1692, several of the "afflicted girls" denounced Elizabeth Proctor. She was arrested at her place of business. When it came her turn to be arraigned John Proctor made it a point to be present. Because he was a threat to the celebrity status of the "afflicted persons" he too was denounced as a witch. Abigail Williams claimed that Proctor was every bit as malevolent as his wife.

Soon the whole pack was crying out against him, saying that his specter was pinching, beating and otherwise abusing them. One person even said that Proctor's evil spirit was sitting in the judge's lap. Sarah Bibber testified that Proctor tried to make her drink from a goblet filled with blood. Mary Warren said that he had tried to make her sign the devil's book. She also said that her employer's specter had sat on her stomach and tortured her until blood had run out of her mouth. There was a further charge that Proctor's evil apparition had tried to make Mary Warren eat unholy bread. Similar testimonies were given by Elizabeth Hubbard, Ann Putnam and Elizabeth Booth. The latter also accused the Proctors of using witchcraft to murder three people. On June 2, 1692, both of the Proctors — husband and wife — were strip-searched for marks of the devil. Nothing suspicious was found but a report to that effect did not save them. Neither did a petition signed by many persons who knew the Proctors as honest, industrious citizens. On August 5, 1692, sham trials were held. Guilty verdicts were returned against both husband and wife. Both were sentenced to death. John Proctor managed to save his wife by getting her pregnant. She was accordingly reprieved pending the birth of their child. Her death sentence was eventually commuted. John Proctor was not so fortunate. He was hanged on August 19, 1692.

John Willard, white, age about 30. *Witchcraft.* This man was the youngest person to be put to death during the Salem witch hunt of 1692. He was a successful farmer and a married father of three. For some reason Willard did not get along with his wife's side of the family. Even worse, those people became convinced that Willard was using black magic to get back at them. They blamed all of their bodily ills on Willard's alleged maledictions. On May 10, 1692, a formal complaint was filed against Willard charging him with witchcraft. A warrant was then issued for his arrest. Learning of these developments, Willard fled as far as Lancaster where he was taken by hue and cry. Meanwhile, one of his wife's relatives, 17-year-old Daniel Wilkins, lay dying of a mysterious illness. The boy lapsed into a coma on May 14, 1692, and a doctor declared witchcraft to be the cause of his malady. Desperate to prove their suspicions against Willard, the dying boy's family called in two of the so-called "afflicted persons," i.e., Mercy Lewis and Mary Walcott, because they were said to be able to see witches in their spirit forms. The girls told their listeners exactly what they wanted to hear: that the specter of John Willard was attacking Daniel Wilkins. Four days later — on May 18, 1692 — John Willard was arraigned on suspicion of witchcraft. The scene in the courtroom was out of control. Elizabeth Hubbard, Mary Warren and Ann Putnam all went into convulsions when Willard was brought in. John Indian (the husband of Tituba) could not resist the chance to incriminate a white man; he outdid himself by thrashing about in feigned agony. Susannah Sheldon screamed that she saw the devil whispering into Willard's ears. Mary Warren went into a swoon when Willard looked at her. Bailiffs carried her inert form over to where Willard was standing. Ordered to grasp the girl's arm, Willard did so whereupon she recovered her senses. Others claimed to see spirits of the dead rise up out of the floor and point accusing fingers at Willard. Order was only restored when Willard was carried off to jail. On June 2, 1692, a strip-search was conducted on the person of John Willard. Every inch of his body was examined for marks of the devil. None were found. Then followed two months of solitary confinement in a fetid prison cell. On August 5 the doomed man was brought to trial. There he was accused of 13 murders and numerous lesser acts of sorcery. Seven separate indictments were brought against him. Susannah Sheldon testified that four dead people stained with blood had appeared to her along with an apparition of Willard. The four ghosts accused Willard of killing them. Then they turned to the girl and became pale corpses before her eyes, each one telling her to report Willard to the law. It was further said that the image of Willard pulled a knife on Susannah Sheldon and threatened her with death. Willard was said to have two attendant demons in the form of two black pigs which sucked at his breasts. Willard's specter was also said to have knelt down before the devil in adoration. Willard was said to have tempted Susannah Sheldon to sign the devil's book.

It was testimony such as this that resulted in a death sentence for John Willard. He was hanged at Salem on August 19, 1692.

George Burroughs, white, age about 41. *Witchcraft*.

This man has been called the most socially prominent victim of the Salem witch hunt. Burroughs was the son of a Virginia couple named Nathaniel and Rebecca Burroughs. As a young man he enrolled at Harvard College. A seminarian, he graduated in 1670 and took up residence at Roxbury, Massachusetts. In 1674 he accepted an appointment to the First Church of Christ in Portland, Maine. Two years later he relocated his family to Salisbury, Massachusetts, in order to be safe from the Indian raids. In 1681 the ministry at Salem fell vacant and Burroughs was named to the position. Two years of internecine strife followed. The new minister had disagreements with his Salem parishioners which resulted in a stoppage of his pay. Not being one to tolerate such a situation, Burroughs resigned the Salem pulpit in 1683. He then returned to Maine where he remained for the next nine years. He initially took up his former position at Portland and later moved on to the town of Wells. On the domestic side, Burroughs had three wives and eight children. He was widowed twice.

Burroughs had left some bitter enemies behind when he left Salem. They were not the type to let the passage of time soften their resentment. When the witchcraft scare of 1692 was in full swing there were some who decided that it was time to bring down the Rev. George Burroughs. It so happened that Ann Putnam, one of the most malleable of the "bewitched persons," became the willing tool of the former minister's enemies. She was carefully plied with information about George Burroughs and induced to believe that he was one of her supernatural tormentors. As expected, Ann Putnam responded in a way which pleased those around her. On April 20, 1692, she reported a terrible vision: A diminutive man dressed in the habit of a minister urged her to sign the devil's book. He tortured her when she refused his solicitation. His name, he said, was George Burroughs. Then he gloatingly told of how he had fatally hexed his first two wives, two of his own children plus the wife and child of Deodat Lawson, his successor in the Salem ministry. Continuing her tale, Ann Putnam told of how the ghosts of the wizard's victims had risen up out of their graves and appeared before her. All said that they had been slain by George Burroughs and his black magic. Soon two more of the "bewitched girls" joined in the denunciation of Burroughs. Susannah Sheldon said that the ghosts of his victims had appeared to her as well. Mercy Lewis told of how Burroughs was a ringleader of the witches and how he had tried to entice her. He had even ridden through the air with her to the top of a mountain and subjected her to the third temptation of Christ.

Officers were sent to Maine with orders to arrest George Burroughs. On

May 4, 1692, he was taken into custody. Five days later he was arraigned at Salem. Nothing he could say or do had any credibility in the eyes of the witch hunters. He was presumed guilty from the start. Because of his status, Burroughs was first questioned in private. There the inquisitors wrung from him an admission that several of his children were not baptized. He was also accused of irregular Sabbath observance and spousal cruelty. Then he was subjected to a public arraignment where all of the "afflicted girls" acted out their usual routine of seizures and hysterical behavior.

Burroughs was tried for his life on August 5, 1692. In addition to the testimonies of the "afflicted girls," affidavits from several of his neighbors in Maine were entered as evidence against him. Stories were told of amazing feats of strength that Burroughs had performed; he had lifted heavy barrels of cider and molasses without any visible assistance. It stood to reason, said the deponents, that evil spirits were the source of his strength. Worst of all, some of the less resolute victims of the witch hunt had by this time learned that they could save themselves by turning Crown Evidence. As a result, some accused persons made false confessions in which they named imaginary accomplices. One self-confessed "witch" named Deliverance Hobbes, implicated George Burroughs in her revelations. The minister was said to be in high standing with the devil. He was said to be an organizer of witch meetings and an active recruiter.

Such was the evidence against George Burroughs. It wound up costing him his life. He was hanged at Salem on August 19, 1692.

George Jacobs, white, age about 77. *Witchcraft.* This man was probably the oldest victim of the Salem witch hunt. Bent with age, he could not walk without assistance. Jacobs had lived in Salem for 33 years during which time he amassed a considerable estate. In 1692 he was comfortably retired living in a large farmhouse with his second wife, a teenage granddaughter and a domestic intern named Sarah Churchill. The latter seems to have been the principal source of agitation against Jacobs. Her motives are not certain but her animosity was definitely aroused against her employer. Sarah Churchill accused the elderly George Jacobs of approaching her in spirit form and tempting her to sign the devil's book. On May 10, 1692, the man was arrested. Arraigned the next day, he scoffed at the scene which confronted him. Then Abigail Williams, Ann Putnam, Mercy Lewis, Elizabeth Hubbard, Mary Walcott and Sarah Churchill all went crazy in the courtroom. They were soon joined by Mary Warren and Sarah Bibber — the latter of whom was a crackpot by any description. Jacobs said that he was falsely accused. The so-called "afflicted persons" then put on a display of hysterics which disrupted the courtroom. Two of them, Ann Putnam and Abigail Williams, even ran about the room with pins stuck in their hands, crying that Jacobs had caused their injuries. The examining magistrate ordered Jacobs to recite the Lord's Prayer. When the old man stammered he was thrown into jail. Several days later George Jacobs was stripped naked and searched for marks of the devil. Three suspicious protuberances were found on him: one was near his right shoulder, one on his right hip and one inside his mouth. Each of these blemishes were pierced with pins by the examiners. Two of them were found to be insensitive to pain — considered proof that they were witch teats. The trial of George Jacobs took place on August 5, 1692. Mary Warren testified that the defendant came to her in spectral form and beat her with his cane. Mercy Lewis reported a similar experience in which Jacobs allegedly beat her with a stick because she had refused his offer of money to sign the devil's book. A teenage boy named John Doritch reported a vision in which a deceased couple named John and Anne Small had appeared to him and told of how Jacobs had hexed them to death. This was enough to secure a guilty verdict against the elderly George Jacobs. The hapless man was hanged on August 19, 1692.

Martha Carrier, white, age about 40. *Witchcraft.* This "Rampant Hag" as Mather called her, was considered by many to be one of the most satanic of all those who came before the Salem witchcraft court of 1692. "Queen of Hell" was another of her sobriquets. However, it was actually a lack of caste and a cantankerous disposition more than anything else that brought this woman to the gallows.

Martha was one of six children (four boys and two girls) of Andrew and Faith Ingolls Allen, original settlers of Andover, Massachusetts. It was probably there where Martha was born circa 1652. Of her girlhood no details survive. On May 7, 1674, she married one Thomas Carrier alias Morgan, an indigent laborer at least 20 years her senior who had gotten her pregnant.

Thomas Carrier came from Billerica and it was there where he and Martha made their first connubial home. Their child, a boy, was born two months after the marriage and the ensuing decade brought four more babies, two boys and two girls. Their economic lot was ever desperate and they were barely able to eke out an existence among the lowest of the low. By the winter of 1685 their situation had become so squalid that starvation was imminent and they had no other recourse but to go to Andover and move in with Martha's parents.

The Carriers were regarded as *canaille* by the citizens of Andover. The Board of Selectmen there passed a resolution declaring them *personae non gratis.* Moreover, the family did not help

its own situation; they caused ill will by ignoring a formal request that they leave town and they even had the temerity to thereafter solicit alms from the local Poor Fund. What truly outraged Andover, however, was a deadly epidemic of smallpox for which the Carriers were responsible. The dreaded contagion had appeared among their family members in the summer of 1690 and as a direct result of their violating quarantine, the disease spread throughout the town. The final toll was 13 people dead and dozens more scarred for life.

Martha Carrier and her family were lucky not to have gotten lynched. The reason why they were not so handled was because no one dared to approach them for fear of catching the pox. Afterward there were rumors of witchcraft. People recalled their sinister suspicions about the Carriers at Billerica and while reeling from the disfiguring scourge (smallpox) for which they were responsible, began to wonder if those same suspicions were not without foundation. The Carriers were churlish, destitute, ill-bred, ragged, unwashed and malevolent looking. They were likely candidates for witchhood in the public eye. Had these unwanted pariahs deliberately conjured up a pestilence? Had they requitted the town's animus with a diabolical disease? These were the questions that Andover asked itself.

During the two years that followed the smallpox epidemic Andover watched the Carriers with wary eyes. Yet no one dared to run them out of town. The selectmen did execute a shrewd move aimed at minimizing the family's social intercourse, however, by voting them a parcel of land well distant from the community hub.

Meanwhile popular animosity festered. It was whispered that Martha Carrier had murdered her own father and two of her brothers with the smallpox.

A man being granted land near the Carrier property, a boundary dispute arose and Martha mouthed some minacious remarks. Shortly afterward the man fell ill of a loathsome disease and it was believed that Martha had hexed him with the plague.

Another incident involved a brawl between Martha's teenage son, Richard, and his cousin, Allen Toothaker, in which the latter got the worst of it and retaliated by alleging that Richard Carrier had had supernatural assistance in the fight from an astral projection of his mother. Toothaker also told tales of Martha Carrier having cursed him.

The precise means by which Martha Carrier came to the attention of the Salem inquisitors in 1692 has never been specified with certainty. It is known that she was "cried out upon" during the month of May by Mary Walcott and Abigail Williams, two of the so-called "afflicted girls," probably as a result of auto-suggestion by those around them. Martha was arrested on May 28 and arraigned on May 31.

The arraignment proceedings were an obstreperous farce. When Martha entered the courtroom three of the "stricken girls" immediately accused her of abusing them in spectral form. "She bites me! She pinches me! She tells me she will cut my throat if I do not sign her book!" yelled the deranged Susannah Sheldon. Then the rest of the pack joined in with a gamut of antics. Some claimed to be stuck with pins. Some claimed to see an evil spirit hovering above the defendant. Others claimed to see the ghosts of those who had died in the smallpox epidemic of 1690. All went berserk when Martha Carrier looked at them.

Despite the pandemonium of the moment, Martha made some cool observations and gave some rational answers when questioned.

When the magistrates demanded to know whether she could strike down the "afflicted girls" with a glance, Martha replied, "They will dissemble if I look upon them!"

When the girls screeched that ghosts were flitting about the room, Martha upbraided the credulous magistrates by saying, "It is a shameful thing that you should mind these folks that are out of their wits." She even dared to call the girls "liars" in open court.

Needless to say, the girls were unaccustomed to such resolution in the face of their performances and they redoubled their clamor. At length the uproar grew so intense that the arraignment was discontinued.

It is significant to note that Martha Carrier — that "Rampant Hag" as she was called — had more common sense than the authorities who presumed to judge her. It was rage and frustration that drove her to waste her breath on a fool like magistrate John Hathorne.

Martha Carrier came up for trial on August 2, 1692. However, in the interval between that time and when she had been arraigned, there occurred some other developments in her case. The authorities arrested Martha's children on witchcraft charges and literally tortured two of them into incriminating their mother. According to a contemporary letter:

> Carrier's sons would not confess anything till they tied them neck and heels and the blood was ready to come out of their noses. Tis credibly believed and reported that this was the occasion of making them confess that one of them had been a witch for a month and the other for five weeks and that it was their mother who had made them so.

There were also other "confessions" entered as evidence at the same time which were detrimental to Martha's cause. For instance, a woman named Ann Foster (herself under condemnation and desperate to escape the gallows) testified that she and Martha Carrier had once resolved to attend a conclave of witches and were borne along thereto on a flying pole. However, she added, the pole had broken while airborne and caused both women to fall to earth.

Most preposterous of all was the "testimony" of Martha's seven-year-old daughter, Sarah, which was produced in court on August 11, 1692. It is here reproduced verbatim and it was actually accredited in a court of law.

> INTERROGATOR: "How long has thou been a witch?"
>
> SARAH CARRIER: "Ever since I was six years old."
>
> INTERROGATOR: "How old are you now?"
>
> SARAH CARRIER: "Near eight years old. Brother Richard says I shall be eight years old in November."
>
> INTERROGATOR: "Who made you a witch?"
>
> SARAH CARRIER: "My mother. She made me set my hand to a book."
>
> INTERROGATOR: "How did you set your hand to it?"
>
> SARAH CARRIER: "I touched it with my fingers. The book was red and the paper of it was white."
>
> INTERROGATOR: "You said you saw a cat once. What did this cat say to you?"
>
> SARAH CARRIER: "It said it would tear me in pieces if I did not set my hand to the book."
>
> INTERROGATOR: "How did you know the cat was your mother?"
>
> SARAH CARRIER: "The cat told me that she was my mother."

It was "evidence" such as this (and a generous helping of prejudice) that secured a verdict of guilty in the case of Martha Carrier. Sentenced to death, she remained resolute to the last in maintaining her innocence. She was hanged on August 19, 1692.

Giles Corey, white, age 75. Martha Corey, white, age about 65. *Witchcraft.*

It will be remembered that the Salem witch hunt produced only three initial suspects: Sarah Good, Sarah Osburne and the slave woman Tituba. It also bears remembering that the evil did not spread until the so-called "confession" of the latter. Tituba had alluded to additional witches who were yet to be identified and her amorphous diatribe had been fervently believed. The credulity of her listeners was limitless. Young and old alike dreaded the revelation of a satanic organization in their midst and rooting out that bad element was deemed imperative.

Thus did irrational fear drive Salem Village to devour itself in the year 1692.

There was, however, one redeeming characteristic of the situation: even under such volatile circumstances the populace was not unanimous in believing the tales of Tituba. There was, indeed, a minority of skeptics. Goodwife Martha Corey was one such person. She dared to conjecture that Tituba had a florid imagination. However, she also underestimated the peril of such an opinion.

Martha Corey's husband, 75-year-old Giles Corey, was less sophisticated than his wife. In fact, he was a bumpkin who from early on had been among the thrillseekers at the meetinghouse. Martha had tried to reason with him by pointing out that his domestic responsibilities were more important than sensationalism. But Giles Corey would not listen. He blundered on and even told of how his wife had hidden his saddle in an effort to hinder his attendance around the celebrated seeresses.

It is highly probable that this befuddled old man announced the incident of the saddle by way of conversation as he entered the sick-chamber of Ann Putnam and was heard by the girl herself as well as by others present. Such conduct on the part of his wife coupled with her already notorious skepticism held grave implications in some minds. Who else but a witch or at least one in sympathy with witches would act so suspiciously? No one yet dared to openly accuse but there were insinuations aplenty and young Ann Putnam, who was under pressure to name additional witches, saw her cue. She started belching anathema against Martha Corey.

Thus did the good people of Salem Village succeed in psychologically maneuvering a neurotic child into doing that which they themselves did not dare to do: denounce Martha Corey. The actual outburst seemed shocking to them. It was a thing at which their genteel hypocrisy blanched. Of course no one stopped to consider the fact that the true fault lay with those who mollycoddled the "afflicted persons" in open disregard of common sense. All that mattered was that seeresses were providing miraculous insights into the machinations of the forces of evil.

From the moment that Ann Putnam first uttered her name, Martha Corey was doomed.

Still, matters were yet to reach a point where hysteria transcended protocol. The matter of Martha Corey's caste had to be addressed. This woman, the inquisitors suddenly remembered, was not a lowly slave like Tituba or a friendless harridan like Good or Osburne. She was a respectable matron long established in the community. Even more importantly, she was an assiduous member of the Salem church. Accordingly on March 12, 1692, two men named Edward Putnam and Ezekiel Cheever took it upon themselves to pay Martha Corey a courtesy call. They wanted to personally investigate Ann Putnam's allegations while simultaneously paying deference to the suspect's social status.

As Ann Putnam had complained of being assaulted by Martha Corey's so-called "spectral image," the two men prior to their departure asked the girl how the offending phantom was clothed. It was their intention to seek corrobora-tion through whether Martha Corey's garments matched those supposedly worn by her specter. Of course the girl had not the faintest idea what clothes Martha Corey was wearing that day but she craftily said that the woman had witched away her "spectral sight" in anticipation of the men's visit. The men set out to see Martha Corey anyhow.

The woman was at home and alone when they arrived. Even before greetings could be exchanged Martha Corey astounded her guests by surmising their purpose. "I know what ye are come for," said she. "Ye are come to talk with me about being a witch." Her tone was annoyingly smug.

Rather abashed, the men admitted that such was so. Then they spoke of what Ann Putnam had said that day. Then Martha Corey delivered another bombshell: "But does she tell you what clothes I have on?" This time her tone was an intolerable blend of smugness, contempt and mockery.

As far as Putnam and Cheever were concerned, this incident clinched the case against Martha Corey. Not only was she guilty in their eyes but impudent as well. Before that day was out the details of the interview were upon every tongue and few were they who dissented from Putnam and Cheever's opinion. No one stopped to consider that Martha had been tipped off in advance about what had gone before. The only explanation that seemed reasonable was that the woman had come to such knowledge by illegal and supernatural means.

Popular animosity mounted against Martha Corey during the week that followed the notorious interview. Next, the animus festered beyond a point of no return. Martha's cocksure flippancy had offended everyone and reinforced the credibility of Ann Putnam. Furthermore, since the girl had encountered no rebuke for a risky appeachment of a church member, she was emboldened to expand her performance. Then the whole pack of "afflicted persons" joined in so that by week's end Martha Corey was considered public enemy number one.

Martha herself scoffed at the situation. She announced that she would not be intimidated. On March 19, 1692, she was afforded a chance to prove her point. Late on that day an arrest warrant was issued against her which could not be immediately executed. It so happened that the 19th was a Saturday and insufficient time remained in the day to apprehend her before the advent of the Sabbath. The following day was out of the question since it was illegal to serve warrants on a Sunday. Thus the law could not touch Martha until Monday. Martha was not one to let such an opportunity slip; she decided to deliberately scandalize the community by taking her usual place at Sabbath day services.

Salem would long remember the events of Sunday, March 20, 1692. On that day the townsfolk gawked in disbelief as they entered the meetinghouse and there saw Martha Corey—the reputed witch—seated among the pious. Such effrontery was unparalleled. There was the nemesis of the community dressed in her Sunday best, taking part in divine worship. And there was nothing anyone could do about it. Martha was still a de facto member of the church and fully entitled to all of its privileges as long as her arrest warrant went unserved. Neither parishioners, minister nor the governor himself could legally eject her under such circumstances. Martha knew that and she used the occasion to publicly defy her enemies.

It would have been bad enough had Martha Corey come to meeting that day merely to spite her detractors. But her presence was construed as a deliberate insult to God himself. Therefore her attendance at meeting that day was considered not only socially unacceptable but downright blasphemous. Many

could not bear the scandal. Moreover, the so-called "afflicted persons" (who were present) saw in the tense atmosphere an opportunity to resume their dramatics.

"Look where Goodwife Corey sits on the beam suckling her yellow bird betwixt her fingers!" shrieked 12-year-old Abigail Williams. At once the services were disrupted. All of the "afflicted persons" immediately fancied that an astral projection of Martha Corey was perched on an overhead beam and that an evil spirit in the form of a "yellow bird" was there along with her right in the very House of God. The "afflicted persons" also claimed to see the avian demon flying around the chamber. It was only with difficulty that the services were concluded.

On the next day Martha Corey's immunity expired and the sheriff pounced on her. The woman was then brought to the meetinghouse amid a panoply of execration. It was the same meetinghouse wherein she had outraged the congregation the day before. The minister of Salem opened the proceedings with a prayer. Martha Corey then created a stir by asking that she be allowed to pray as well. The presiding magistrates were in no mood to grant favors. Martha Corey had had her moment in the sun already and that was thought to be more than enough.

"We are here to examine you!" snapped magistrate John Hathorne. "We are not here to hear you pray!" and with that he launched his attack.

"Why do you afflict those children?" he demanded.

It was characteristic of Hathorne, most inept of magistrates, to presume guilt from the start.

Martha denied the charge against her.

"Then who does afflict them?" asked Hathorne.

"How should I know?" scoffed Martha Corey.

At once the uproar began. The "afflicted persons" fell into convulsions. They screamed that they were being assaulted by a ghostly image of Martha Corey and they waved their arms about as if they were warding off invisible blows. They claimed to see a familiar spirit in the form of a yellow bird flying about. They said that an image of Martha Corey — right there in the courtroom — was importuning them to sign a hellish covenant, threatening them with torture if they refused.

A rational Martha Corey remained undaunted. She denied the accusations with dignity and even dared to rebuke the magistrates, saying that they were mistaking madness for witchcraft. It was no use. Under the prevailing circumstances it would have been easier for Corey, as a sensible person, to act like a fool than it would have been for the magistrates, as fools, to act like sensible persons. Even the most eloquent defense would avail nothing in such an atmosphere. Like the stalwart woman that she was, Martha Corey tried anyway. She said that her long record as a church member was evidence in her favor.

"I am a gospel woman!" she protested.

"She is a gospel witch!" rejoined her accusers. The scene that followed rocked the meetinghouse to its foundations. It was said that the devil himself had come into the room. He was said to be standing next to Martha Corey in the form of an invisible Negro, coaching her with her answers. More verbal exchange followed between the defendant and the magistrates. Then followed more dramatics by the "afflicted persons." They fixed their eyes on Martha Corey and followed her every motion, using her movements as their cue for fresh outbursts of ranting and raving. If Martha moistened her lips the girls screamed that they were bitten. If she moved her fingers they screamed that they were pinched. When Martha brushed against the banister of the witness box one of the lunatics screamed "as if her bowels had been torn out" and hurled a shoe at Martha, striking her on the head. Within seconds the turmoil became insurmountable. There were cries that Martha was stabbing her victims with invisible bodkins. There were cries from the girls that Martha was stomping on them. There were cries that the beat of an infernal drum was heard and that such was signaling the forces of evil to mass for an attack. If any semblance of order remained it was chance alone that made it. Wild, ungovernable terror reigned. Women fainted and strong men shuddered at the invisible horrors unfolding around them. It was said that all the demons in hell were rearing up for a concerted effort to carry the town by storm.

Martha Corey's reaction to this display of paranoia was derisive. To the indignation of the assembly, she burst out laughing. "Ye are all against me and I cannot help it!" yelled Martha Corey as the guards hustled her off to jail.

For reasons that can be debated, Martha Corey was kept incarcerated for six months before she came to trial. While the Special Court of Oyer & Terminer disposed of one case after another, it oddly procrastinated with this early one. The judges were probably wary of Martha Corey's propensity for elocution; they may have sought to break her spirit with a long term of durance. The Salem church used similar caution when it ex-communicated Martha Corey. The minister did not dare to summon her before the assembled congregation as he had Rebecca Nurse. Instead, a decree of banishment was merely posted on the town bulletin board. It was not until September 9, 1692, that Martha Corey was brought to trial.

In the meantime Martha's doddering husband, Giles Corey, got himself into trouble. He had started by naively believing the tales against his wife. He even swore the following testimony before a court of law:

The evidence of Giles Corey testifieth and saith that last Saturday in the evening, sitting by the fire, my wife asked me to go to bed. I told her I would go to prayer and when I went to prayer I could not utter my desires with any sense and could not open my mouth to speak. My wife did perceive it and came towards me and said that she was coming to me. After this in a little space I did according to my measure attend the duty. Sometime last week I fetched an ox well out of the woods and he layed down in the yard. I went to raise him to yoke him but he could not rise and dragged his hind parts as if he had been slipshod and after did rise. I also had a cat sometime last week strangely taken on the sudden and did make me think she would have died presently. My wife bade me knock her in the head but I did not and since she is well. Another time going to duties I was interrupted for a space but afterward I was helped according to my poor measure. My wife has been wont to sit up after I went to bed and I have perceived her to kneel down on the hearth as if she was at prayer but heard nothing.

This puerile testimony was too ridiculous even for the Salem Board of Arraignment to bear. No one, it was thought, could truly be so stupid as to see a correlation between what Giles Corey had to say and the crimes of which his wife stood accused. Instead, Giles Corey was regarded as a prevaricator. For that reason he presently joined his wife among those accused of witchcraft.

It was only then that the truth dawned on Giles Corey. He knew well enough that he himself was not in league with the devil. So by the same token it dawned on him that his wife must be innocent as well. However, while Martha Corey spat reproaches at those who hounded and harangued her, Giles Corey became sullen and withdrawn. From that time on he resolved to be silent.

Martha Corey had her "trial" on September 9 and she was sentenced to death. She was hanged on September 22. Her husband met an even worse end. He spurned every admonition to acknowledge his trial court. Instead, he "Stood Mute," i.e., gave no answer when put to the plea. Again and again it was demanded of Giles Corey that he plead either guilty or not guilty to his indictment. Each time the old peasant stood silent, thereby balking the progress of his trial. Whether it was pride, contempt or sheer stubbornness which motivated such behavior is uncertain. Some historians have conjectured that Corey remained silent to save his estate from confiscation because the property of anyone convicted of capital felony was declared forfeit. So enraged did the judges become at Corey for this conduct that they cited him for contempt of court. Then they ordered that he be put to the torture of *peine forte et dure* until he either entered a plea to his indictment or until he died.

Peine forte et dure was a rarely invoked but notorious punishment reserved for those who refused to enter a plea to their indictments. This was the only time it was ever used in New England. On September 16, 1692, the elderly Giles Corey was led to an open field next to the Salem jail. As a gloating crowd watched he was laid flat on his back spread-eagle with his ankles and wrists tied to stakes. Then a rough wooden board the size of a door was laid atop his naked breast so that only his head and extremities remained exposed. Next, the sheriff and his deputies slowly piled heavy rocks atop the board so that the weight grew increasingly oppressive upon the prisoner. As each stone was added to the pile on top of him, Giles Corey was asked whether he would agree to enter a plea to his indictment and thereby allow his trial to proceed. The stubborn old man remained silent. Finally the accumulation of weight reached a point that was more than human frailty could bear. Ribs cracked and Giles Corey was crushed to death.

If any felt pity for Giles Corey they dared not say so. The sheriff, however, reserved the final indignity for himself. Seeing the tongue protruding from the dead man's mouth, he contemptuously used the point of his walking stick to force it back in.

Mary Parker, white, age about 40.

Witchcraft. The precise identity of this woman has been a matter of confusion among historians of the Salem witch hunt. She was, it seems, a full daughter of the tragical Giles Corey by his first wife, Margaret. It would thereby appear that Mary Parker was hanged side by side with her step-mother, Martha Corey, and her kinswoman, Alice Parker.

While the precise date of her birth cannot be ascertained, Mary Parker was probably born at Salem sometime in the early– to mid–1650s. She was therefore aged 40 or very close thereto at the time of her death. On May 29, 1673, she married one John Parker, the scion of a prominent Andover family who was then barely 17 years old.

John Parker looked to the sea for his livelihood although it is uncertain whether in the capacity of a fisherman, sailor or merchantman. He also seems to have made it a point to have kept his wife housebound and pregnant most of the time. Mary Parker, for her part, acquiesced to such circumstances since they were inherent in the frontier environment that was her world. She is known to have cherished the few moments that she had together with her youthful husband and she bitterly resented anything that came between them. One thing that did come between the couple was the local tavern. When

John Parker began to prefer that place to his own home, Mary Parker bristled. An incident which took place in 1684 illustrates the plight of this 17th century alcoholic's wife:

> John Westgate aged about 40 years testifieth that about eight years since, he being at the house of Samuel Beadle in the company of John Parker and several others, the wife of said John Parker came into the company and scolded and called her husband all to nought, whereupon I took her husband's part and told her it was an unbecoming thing for her to come after him to the tavern and rail in that manner. With that she came up to me and called me a rogue and bade me mind my own business and told me it was better that I had said nothing.

As circumstances would have it, this confrontation turned out to be only the beginning of what would be a memorable night for John Westgate. He remained in company with his fellow tipplers until a late hour and then set out for home on foot in a drunken condition. It was then that disaster struck. As Westgate swaggered down a darkened lane he fancied himself beset by a goblin. Westgate latter described the occasion as follows:

> Sometime afterward I was going from the house and heard a great noise when there appeared a black hog running towards me with its mouth open as though it would devour me. At that instant I fell down upon my hip and my knife ran into my hip up to the haft. But when I came home the knife was in its sheath. When I drew it out of the sheath the sheath immediately fell to pieces. Furthermore, when I got up from my fall, my stocking and shoe were full of blood and I was forced to crawl along by the fence all the way home. The hog followed me and did not leave until I got home. I also had a stout dog with me but it ran away, leap-

ing over the fence and crying much when as per usual it was used to worry any hog well. It was then that I apprehended the hog to be not a real hog but rather the devil or some evil thing and did further determine in my mind that it was either Goody Parker or through her means so that I do fear that she is a witch.

Before proceeding further it bears repeating that Westgate was almost certainly drunk throughout the porcine assault and that he embellished his tale accordingly. However, popular opinion was not interested in rational explanations. As far as the citizens of Salem were concerned there was witchcraft aprowl and Mary Parker was the prime suspect.

Thus did Mary Parker acquire a bad reputation a full eight years before the time of her final crisis.

Samuel Shattuck was one of many to whom Westgate blurted the tale of the demonic hog — the same Samuel Shattuck who had thrilled the community five years earlier with a tale of how Bridget Bishop had bewitched his imbecile son. Since that time Shattuck had developed a phobia and he frantically associated every indisposition of his son with infernal malice. Five years after tangling with Bridget Bishop this anxious father once again fancied that his boy was bewitched. The years had not improved the lad's condition and when Shattuck recalled that Mary Parker had once visited his home, he drew the inevitable conclusions:

Samuel Shattuck aged 41 years testifieth that in the year 1685 Goodwife Parker came to my house and went into the room where my wife and children were and she fawned upon my wife with very smooth words. A short time after that the child that was supposed to have been under an evil hand several years before was taken in a strange and unusual manner as if his vitals would have burst out through his breast bone, being drawn up together to the upper part of his breast and his neck and eyes drawn so much aside as if they would never come right again. He laid in so strange a manner that the doctor and others did believe he was bewitched. Some days after some of the visitors cut some of his hair to boil which they said that although they did with great tenderness, the child would shriek out as if he had been tormented. They put his hair in a skillet over the fire which stood plain on the hearth and as soon as they were gone out of the room it was thrown down. I came immediately into the room and could see no creature in the room. They then put the skillet on again and after it had boiled sometime Goodwife Parker came in and asked if I would buy some chickens. I told her nay. Then the women that were above in the chamber said to me it was a pity that I did not ask to see her chickens for they did not believe that she had any to sell. They advised me to send to her house to buy some, which I did, and a messenger brought me word that she said that she had none. He also told me that a woman who lived in the same house as Parker said that Parker had not any chickens for three weeks. Some days later Parker, her husband and two men came to my house to demand satisfaction of me. They asked me if I had said that Parker had bewitched my child and I said that I did believe it was so. She then said to me, "You are a wicked man! The Lord avenge me of you! The Lord bring vengeance upon you for this wrong!" One of the men asked her what had made her come to my house last Saturday. She said to sell chickens. Then she was asked why she had not let me have any after I had sent for some. She said because she had sold them. Then she was asked to whom she sold them and she said to so and so. So we presently sent to that party and his answer was that he had never bought anything of her. Well you see, said they, you have told us that which is not true. What then did you do with them? She was at a stand but at last said that her son had carried them to sea with him. But then her own husband told her that that was not true for that her son went to sea last Friday and if he had indeed carried the chickens to sea, she could not have brought them here the following Saturday. She could not give any true account of what she had done with the chickens but went into the room where the child was and told my wife that she was a wicked woman for saying so of her and told my wife that she hoped that she would see the downfall of her and so went away in great anger. This is all true and real to the utmost of my memory. After this threatening the child was continued in a very sad condition followed with very solemn fits which took away his understanding.

The tenure of Shattuck's story was to allege that Mary Parker had been responsible for his son's lunacy and that she had been found out through the ancient practice of burning part of a hexed object — in this case the hair of the presumed victim. Such an experiment (which recurs throughout New England witch lore) was believed to draw a guilty witch to the scene of the fire and thereby expose her. The appearance of Mary Parker that day at the Shattuck homestead was regarded as incriminating evidence against her. Moreover, the fact that she had been caught in a lie made a bad situation worse.

So it came as no surprise when Mary Parker was fingered as a suspected witch in 1692. Her initial appeachment that year probably occurred sometimes in April or May, shortly after that of her step-mother, Martha Corey. Evidence was accepted against her in June but it was not until September that she was formally charged. By then the overall crisis had attained new and unprecedented proportions. The original pack of accusing girls had been joined (and in some cases replaced by) other mental cases. Also, by September the sensationalism

of the witch hunt had inspired many false confessions. It seems to have been this latter feature more than anything else which brought about the downfall of Mary Parker.

Why did some people make false confessions? There were three reasons. First, some individuals were simply psychotic. Secondly, some saw confession as a shrewd means by which to avoid the gallows; it being by then recognized that the authorities would spare all who confessed in hopes of rehabilitating them. The judges saw no point in augmenting the devil's legions by executing admitted witches when they could be saved alive and reformed for the greater glory of God. Thirdly, and perhaps most pernicious of all, was a bizarre personal conclusion some reached after careful soul-searching: it was reasoned by this latter group that although they might not be consciously aware of it, there might nevertheless have been an unguarded moment in their lives when their faith had lapsed and thereby left them vulnerable to the devil. Hence there were some who were led to the utmost depth of self-delusion by doubting even their own inner consciences.

Mary Parker was implicated in the tales of three such "confessors" and it was that which appears to have finally prompted a grand jury to indict her. She was officially charged with bewitching two girls named Martha Sprague and Sarah Phelps. She was also accused (though not formally charged) of having a hand in the untimely death of one Timothy Swan, a man who was thought to have been killed by enchantment.

Mary Parker's arraignment, which took place on September 2, 1692, was a cursory farce. The mere mention of her name was enough to throw five so-called "afflicted persons" into convulsions from which they could only be delivered by the touch of the woman's hand. Magistrate John Hathorne, bigot that he was, assumed guilt from the start.

"How long hast though been in the snare of the devil?" were the first words out of his mouth.

Mary Parker could scarcely stammer a denial before the courtroom became a madhouse. Martha Sprague screamed in anguish. Mary Lacey and Mercy Wardwell did the same. A man named William Barker (one of the pseudo-confessors who turned Crown Evidence) yelled that not only was he himself a witch but that Mary Parker was one of his coven. Worst of all was the lunatic Mary Warren; she thrashed about in a frenzy, vomited blood all over the floor and came "near to having a pin run through her hand." The judges could take no more. They hastily closed the arraignment and had Mary Parker hustled off to jail after asking only one question of her.

A "trial" was held on September 17, 1692, at which Mary Parker received sentence of death. She refused to shame herself with a false confession and was therefore ordered for execution. She was hanged on September 22, 1692.

Alice Parker, white, age unknown. *Witchcraft.* Historians have generally paid scant attention to this victim of the Salem witch hunt. This is not surprising given the extreme dearth of documentation in her case. Even from a genealogical prospectus Alice Parker is an obscure entity. She is known to have been a resident of Salem and the wife of a man named John Parker. (The fact that her husband bore the same name as the husband of Mary Parker has resulted in much confusion.) It is there where concrete knowledge of her personal details ends. It would, however, seem to be reasonably probable that Alice Parker was somehow related through marriage to the aforesaid Mary Corey Parker. Genealogical investigation in her case is inconclusive.

It does appear that Alice Parker had a reputation for clairvoyance that at least partially underscored her downfall. A deposition from the scanty remains of her trial record attests thereto:

> Martha Dutch aged about 36 years testifieth that about two years ago John Jarman of Salem was coming in from sea and that I and Alice Parker of Salem were standing together and I said unto her, "What a great mercy it is to see them come home well. And through mercy," said I, "my husband had gone and come home well many times." And this I did say unto ye said Parker that I did hope that he would come home well from this voyage also. And Parker said, "No, nevermore in this world." And it came to pass as she then told me for he died abroad as I certainly hear.

As for the immediate charges that brought about her ruin, Alice Parker stood accused of bewitching Mary Walcott and the crazed Mary Warren. The case against her was based almost entirely on the notorious "Spectral Evidence," that is, the allegation that an incorporeal projection of her consciousness stalked victims in spirit form or that an evil spirit in her image wrought mischief by her consent. The mere sight of Alice Parker was enough to affect those who fancied themselves thus beset and when those same persons duly demonstrated in court that the touch of Alice Parker's hand was enough to restore them to their senses, it was enough to convince both judges and jury that the defendant was guilty.

Alice Parker was arraigned on September 6, 1692. She was tried and convicted three days later. On September 22, 1692, she was hanged at Salem.

Margaret Scott, white, age 75. *Witchcraft.* The next victim of the Salem witch hunt was septuagenarian Margaret Scott of Rowley. Her first recorded appearance was in 1642 as one Margaret Stevenson, a 17-year-old petitioner before the Massachusetts court of Assistants in a motion praying for permission to marry one Benjamin Scott. The petition was granted and the wedding took place. Six children followed between the years 1644 and 1656 but only three survived the death of their father in 1671.

The fatal denunciation of the elderly Margaret Scott in 1692 was at least partially predicated by an attack on her reputation some years previously. According to a deposition found in the meager remains of her trial record, the calumny involved the following:

> Philip Nelson and Sarah his wife do testify that for two or three years before the death of Robert Shilletto, we often heard him complain of Margaret Scott for hurting him. He often said that she was a witch and so he continued to complain, saying that he would never be well as long as she lived. And so he complained of her at times till he died.

This proves the existence of a simmering animus against Margaret Scott. Any resident of Essex County with such credentials was fair game for the witch hunters in 1692. An unstable woman named Frances Wycomb provided the final spark against Margaret Scott as follows:

> The deposition of Frances Wycomb who testifieth that soon after the first witchcraft court at Salem, this Margaret Scott or her appearance, who I know well, did come to me and grievously torment me by choking and almost pressing me to death. So she did continue afflicting me betimes till the 5th of August, being the day of her examination, as also several times since so that I believe in my heart that Margaret Scott is a witch.

There were probably other testimonies presented against Margaret Scott that were similar in nature but they have not survived. Still, they were enough to procure her arrest and arraignment. A trial was held in her case on September 17, 1692. The verdict was guilty and the sentence was death. Margaret Scott refused to save herself by means of a false confession. She died on the gallows at Salem on September 22, 1692.

Wilmot Redd, white, age about 55.

Witchcraft. This petulant woman was the wife of a Marblehead fisherman named Samuel Redd. Such comprises all that is known of her family and her origin. That she was one of that class of individuals who invariably incur the displeasure of her neighbors was attested clearly at her trial.

For instance, a woman of the surname "Sims" had once demanded satisfaction of Wilmott Redd for some purloined linen. The suspect replied with the testy oath "Would that ye nevermore shit nor piss!" And so it came to pass. Sims was soon afterward taken with "the disorder of the dry bellyache," as it was called, and remained constipated for a long time. She naturally blamed her "disorder" on Wilmot Redd.

There were undoubtedly many other tales in circulation at the time about Wilmot Redd but they have not been preserved.

From a rational prospectus, one might stop just short of calling this woman's ordeal a judicial murder. This is because it seems apparent that her adolescent accusers were prodded into denouncing her. Consider the testimony of Mary Walcott.

> I was for a considerable time afflicted by a woman who told me that her name was Redd and that she came from Marblehead. On the 31st day of May 1692, being the day of the examination of Wilmot Redd, I then saw that she was the very same woman that told me that her name was Redd and she did most dreadfully afflict and torment me during the time of her examination. For if she did but look upon me, she would

strike me down and almost choke me. Also on the day of her examination I saw Wilmot Redd or her appearance most grievously afflict and torment Mercy Lewis, Elizabeth Hubbard and Ann Putnam. And I believe in my heart that Wilmot Redd is a witch and that she has often afflicted and tormented me and the aforesaid persons by act of witchcraft.

The very format of this deposition is redundant. It recurs often and seems to have been an early "form letter" of sorts. Secondly, special attention must be paid to the words "I was afflicted by a woman who told me that her name was Redd and that she came from Marblehead." Common sense alone discredits this. Was the alleged specter of Wilmot Redd really so stupid as to blatantly incriminate itself? Or was this a more probable example of how a psychologically malleable person (Mary Walcott) was actively coached by others and turned into a vicarious accuser. It must be remembered that Mary Walcott was young and of limited acquaintance. How then did she know a woman from another town? She was surrounded by adults who openly discussed their own versions of events within her hearing. Those adults committed a cardinal error by making unguarded remarks because the so-called "afflicted girls" picked up on what was said. The results were devastating. The suspicions of others were thereby implanted in the "afflicted girls." This was the true tragedy of the Salem witch hunt. It was all a conglomeration of irrational fear and superstition compounded with misdiagnosed insanity and unrestrained auto suggestion.

Wilmot Redd was arraigned amid the usual courtroom uproar on May 31, 1692. Her trial did not take place until September 17 and when it was over she stood convicted on two indictments. The charges alleged "sundry acts of witchcraft" perpetrated by her upon two Salem girls named Elizabeth Booth and Elizabeth Hubbard. The defendant was hanged on September 22, 1692. Her husband, Samuel Redd, shrugged off his loss by remarrying six weeks later.

Ann Pudeater, white, age 70. *Witchcraft.* One of the most flagrant examples of how the Salem witch hunt was used to destroy an unpopular individual may be found in the case of Ann Pudeater, an aging widow who had scandalized her community.

Originally Ann hailed from parts unknown. Her first traceable appearance is at Salem in 1673 as a matron named Ann Greenslitt. She also had five grown children by then. Within a year of her arrival at Salem, her husband, Thomas Greenslitt, was dead and she was left to her own resources. Consequently Ann took to hiring herself out as a nurse.

About eight years before the Greenslitts came to Salem there appeared at that town a 24-year-old blacksmith named Jacob Pudeater. In the autumn of 1666 this young man married an alcoholic named Isabelle Mossier and went downhill from there. By 1673 he was miserable and his wife was well on her way to drinking herself to death, finally succeeding four years later.

Ann Greenslitt by that time, 1677, was well established in her capacity of a nurse for hire and it was she who attended the deathbed of Isabelle Mossier Pudeater. No sooner had the dying woman breathed her last than Ann Greenslitt and Jacob Pudeater announced their intention to marry. At once there were rumors of improprieties. It was said that the newly engaged couple had been carrying on adulterously. Some of the more vicious gossips even said that the couple had hurried the demise of the dead woman by plying her with poisoned rum. The fact that Ann Greenslitt Pudeater was old enough to be her new husband's mother did not look good either. In fact, so critical did public opinion become that a formal inquest was held on the death of Isabelle Mossier Pudeater three years after the fact. By then, however, Jacob and Ann were happily married — much to the disgust of their neighbors.

The couple survived the Court of Inquiry — again to the disgust of their neighbors. By then, however, Jacob Pudeater was living on borrowed time. He died in the autumn of 1681 at the age of 39, leaving Ann and her children as his principal heirs. His untimely death also added to the luridness of his wife's reputation. Ann was reviled as an opportunist who had slyly made away with her husband's first wife, then inveigled the man into naming her as his heir and then rid herself of him as well.

Although the precise means through which Ann Greenslitt was alleged to have murdered her way into the Pudeater estate is not known to have been specified at the time, it would seem likely that poison was thought to be her weapon. This is because a certain line of questioning at her 1692 arraignment attempted to zero in on certain "ointments and oils" she was known to possess — nearly 20 separate vials of suspicious substances. In her defense, Ann claimed that those items were merely lards which she used for making soap. She was not believed.

It must also be borne in mind that in the 17th century poisoning was regarded as a close cousin to witchcraft. Hence it is not surprising to find allegations of black magic in the case of Ann Greenslitt Pudeater.

A militiaman named Jeremiah Neal told of how his wife had been ill with the smallpox at a time when he had let Ann Pudeater borrow a mortar. Soon regretting his generosity, he asked for the mortar's return. As a result, said he, the smallpox proved fatal to his wife.

There was also a report that Ann Pudeater caused the death of a Goodwife Best through infernal means. There were tales of her spectral image flitting by men in the street. She was said to have tempted a recalcitrant witch with images of prospective victims and to have stuck thorns into those same images. She was even accused of using witchcraft to make a man fall out of a cherry tree.

Ann Pudeater fought back with remarkable acumen, especially after she had been condemned. She prepared a petition in which she raised a substantial point that one of her accusers was a convicted perjurer. How then, she asked, could that person's word be taken as evidence to deprive her of her life? No answer was given to her petition. Ann Pudeater was hanged at Salem on September 22, 1692.

Samuel Wardwell, white, age 46. *Witchcraft.* This man was a carpenter from the town of Andover. He seems to have attracted suspicion of witchery because of his reputation as a fortune teller. The fact that his prophecies were accurate wound up doing him more harm than good. The earliest mention of Wardwell dates from August 15, 1692. That was the day on which he was alleged to have used witchcraft to cause a young woman to be thrown from her horse. The victim in this case was one Martha Sprague, a resident of Boxford. One of the so-called "afflicted girls" (Mary Walcott) later testified that she had seen a spectral image of Wardwell pull Martha Sprague from her saddle. The lunatic Mary Warren also claimed that Wardwell had tortured her for refusing to sign the devil's book. Wardwell was arraigned at Salem on September 1, 1692. He quickly confessed that he was in league with the devil. When pressed for details he said that he had made a pact with the devil 20 years earlier. It was agreed between the devil and Wardwell that the latter should live to the age of 60 with no bodily infirmities. Wardwell further embellished his tale by saying that he had renounced his Christian baptism and accepted a rechristening by the devil. He said that he had signed the devil's book and consorted with demons in the shape of cats. One evil spirit in particular, he said, had come to him in the guise of a Negro. This confession earned Wardwell a conviction for capital felony. He was not, however, sentenced to death on the spot. Because he had confessed there was hope that he could be rehabilitated. That changed two weeks later when Wardwell retracted his confession. For so doing, he was included in the next batch of prisoners ordered for execution. He was accordingly hanged at Salem on September 22, 1692.

Mary Easty, white, age 58. *Witchcraft.* The last person to be put to death during the Salem witch hunt was Mary Easty, a full sister of the tragic Rebecca Nurse. She was born at Yarmouth in Norfolkshire, England, on August 24, 1634, and came to America six years later with her family. While still quite young she married Isaac Easty of Topsfield. In the years that followed she bore seven children and led the otherwise mundane life of a homemaker.

There is no recorded evidence that Mary Easty bore a sullied reputation prior to her final tragedy. Such sets her apart from most of her fellow sufferers. Instead, she seems to have been a victim of circumstances who was unwillingly drawn into the vortex through the implication of her being related to persons who were previously accused. She was first arrested on April 21, 1692, at which time she was charged with molesting certain individuals in the usual manner; that is to say by appearing to them in ghostly form and tempting them to sign the devil's book. Her arraignment took place on April 22 and she defended herself with dignity. So impressive was her courtroom demeanor that she succeeded in securing a release into her own recognizance on May 18.

Then the tide turned against Mary Easty. Whereas she had based her defense on the fact that accusations against her were uncorroborated and whereas certain of the "afflicted persons" had waned in their charges against her, one of them, the invidious Mercy Lewis, remained adamant. No amount of reasoning could deter the girl from the fantasy that Mary Easty was tormenting her. Consequently a new warrant was issued for the woman's arrest and 48 hours after her release Mary Easty found herself once again roused from her home and brought to jail.

The evidence produced against this woman consisted almost exclusively of the ravings of the so-called "afflicted girls." Mercy Lewis continued her denunciation unabated and one by one the other girls fell in with her. The Lewis girl claimed that a specter of Easty had threatened her with death for refusing to sign the devil's book. Another girl who relapsed into her delusions claimed to see Easty astride Mercy Lewis strangling her with a ghostly chain. It was enough to secure a guilty verdict against Mary Easty. The woman went to the gallows on September 22, 1692. She was the last to suffer the death penalty on such an account in colonial America. However, at the time few expected that such would be the case. For the next four months convictions continued unabated and there were death sentences aplenty. Only the intervention of Governor Phipps prevented additional executions.

What was it that suddenly caused wiser counsels to bring an end to the Salem terror? The question has been debated by historians at great length. One contributing factor was Mary Easty herself. Shortly after her death a young woman named Mary Herrick reported that Easty had appeared to her in a dream and spoke the following words:

I am going on the gallows to be hanged for a witch. But I am innocent. And ere a year be past thou shalt know it!

Several nights later the vision returned to Mary Herrick. This time Mary Easty brought another spirit with her, none other than the image of Madam Sarah Hale, the unimpeachable wife of the Rev. John Hale, a prime proponent of the witch hunt.

"Dost thou think that I am a witch?" asked the new specter.

"No! No! Thou art the devil!" shrieked the terrified girl.

It was then that the ghost of Mary Easty seemed appeased. Mary Herrick later said that the apparition went on to speak of its innocence. While Mistress Hale was plainly guiltless of witchcraft, her specter could still be discerned in a false light. So had it been with Mary Easty.

Mary Herrick made haste to report her vision. Soon the news reached the Rev. John Hale. He was appalled. He knew that his wife was blameless and at once he grasped the portent of the situation. Spectral evidence was not to be trusted. The innocent were being denounced because evil spirits had impersonated them. It was that rationale that spelled an end of the Salem witch hunt. From that time on people grew increasingly skeptical of the so-called "Spectral Evidence." Logic began to take the place of panic. The cost was 20 executions and a grievous social upheaval.

This concludes our account of the Salem witch trials.

1693

Elizabeth Emerson, white, age 27. *Murder.* The crime was committed on May 7, 1691, at Haverhill, Massachusetts. This female offender was the unmarried daughter of an Essex County couple named Mitchell and Hannah Emerson. According to her own account, Elizabeth Emerson had an affair with a married man named Samuel Ladd and committed adultery with him on seven separate occasions. She became pregnant and on the above date gave birth to twin girls. When the ordeal of childbirth was passed, the new mother put the infants into a pillow case. This she stashed in her hope chest with the result that both of the newborns were suffocated. Three days later Elizabeth sewed up the pillow case and buried it in her backyard. Meanwhile suspicion was aroused. Although Elizabeth had tried to conceal her pregnancy she was not entirely successful. On May 10, 1691, a committee of matrons came to her house accompanied by officers of the law. Many pointed questions were asked and Elizabeth admitted her maternity. A search of the property turned up evidence of fresh digging in the backyard. Soon the pillow case and its contents were recovered. The matrons examined the tiny corpses and gave it as their opinion that both had been carried to full term and were born alive. It was noted that one infant was grasping its umbilical cord in its hands while the other's cord was wrapped around its throat. This was taken as evidence that both had squirmed in desperation as they suffocated; hence incontrovertible proof that they were not stillborn. No marks of violence were found upon the bodies but the matrons were unanimous in declaring that both babies would have survived had they received proper care. Elizabeth Emerson insisted that the infants were stillborns. She also said that she had given birth while both of her parents slept in the same room. Both of the elder Emersons were questioned and both denied any knowledge of what had happened. A grand jury concluded that all of the Emersons were liars. It was impossible to believe that the babies were stillborn based on the testimony of the experienced matrons. It was also impossible to believe that Elizabeth's parents could not have known of their daughter's pregnancy, especially since she was carrying twins. Nor did the grand jury believe that both parents slept through the double childbirth in the same room where those births occurred. Indictments were therefore found against all three Emersons. Elizabeth Emerson was charged as principal in two counts of capital felony and her parents were charged as willful accessories. The Court of Assistants tried the case at Boston in September of 1691. A petit jury reached the same conclusions as had the grand jury and all three defendants were found guilty. All three were sentenced to death. Then the matter took an unexpected turn. The Governor in Council refused to issue death warrants because its members were (presumably) split in their opinions. Some members of the council (again presumably) wanted to give the Emersons the benefit of the doubt. The matter was held in abeyance for well over a year. Then Elizabeth Emerson confessed that she had known that at least one of the babies was born alive. She was unsure about the other. She also exonerated her parents of all complicity in the crime. In April of 1693 the newly established Superior Court of Judicature met to reconsider the case of Elizabeth Emerson. She was then called down to her original sentence of death. Her parents were not condemned a second time. Then they were apparently freed. The final act in this tragedy took place on June 8, 1693, when Elizabeth Emerson was hanged on the Boston gallows.

Negress Grace, black, age unknown. *Murder.* The crime was committed on December 25, 1692, at Boston, Massachusetts. This female offender was a slave in the household of a Boston merchant named James Taylor. On the above date she went into her master's garden and locked herself in an outhouse that was there. Then she gave birth to a baby boy in secret and made away with the infant by dumping it down the latrine. Suspicion was aroused when Grace returned to her master's house. Her movements were traced and the crime was discovered. Grace was then brought before the next Assize held for Suffolk County. There she was tried for willful and deliberate infanticide. A verdict of guilty was recorded in her case. Sentence of death was then pronounced. Grace was hanged from the Boston gallows on June 8, 1693.

1694

Jacob, Native American, age unknown. *Murder.* The crime was committed on November 2, 1693, at Natick, Massachusetts. This is an obscure case of a Native American man who fatally stabbed one of his fellow tribesmen. The victim was identified as "Indian Tom." The motive for the crime is unknown. Jacob was arrested within a short time and brought to Charlestown. There he was put on trial by the Superior Court of Judicature for Middlesex County. A jury convicted Jacob of willful murder and he was ordered for execution. He was almost certainly hanged at Charlestown on or about February 10, 1694.

Zachalenaco, alias "Zachary," Native American, age unknown. *Murder.* The crime was committed on December 24, 1693, in Suffolk County, Massachusetts. This offender lived at a place called "Kycomocho," an Indian settlement somewhere within the limits of Suffolk County. On the above date he got into a brawl there with a fellow tribesman named Wahanonaw (age unknown) and fatally slashed him across the throat. For this homicide Zachalenaco was brought to Boston and put on trial for his life. A jury convicted him of capital murder and a warrant was issued for his execution. Zachalenaco was accordingly hanged at Boston on or about May 15, 1694.

Daniel Matthews, white, age unknown. *Rape.* The crimes were committed on April 15, 1693, at Fairfield, Connecticut, and on June 20, 1693, at Wethersfield, Connecticut. This offender was an itinerant tailor by profession and a pervert by habit. Prepubescent girls were the objects of his concupiscence. On April 15, 1693, he was at Fairfield. There he enticed a ten-year-old girl named Elizabeth Cooley into s salt marsh and forced himself on her. A drover by the name of Robert Rumsey heard the girl's cries and hurried to the scene of the crime. There he found Matthews in the very act of raping the girl. His shirt was smeared with blood and he was in a state of full arousal. Rumsey rescued the victim from further assault but by then Matthews had already accomplished his purpose. Two matrons examined the victim and confirmed that she had been deflowered. Matthews was thrown into Fairfield jail and charged with capital felony. A few days later he broke out of his cell and disappeared. Two months later Matthews turned up at Wethersfield. There he stalked a 12-year-old girl named Mary Goodrich and overtook her in an apple orchard. What happened next is unprintable. Matthews was nabbed shortly thereafter by angry townspeople. He was very lucky to survive the encounter. Sent to Hartford, he was charged with a second capital crime and tried before the Court of Assistants. The evidence was conclusive and Matthews stood convicted. Sentence of death was passed upon him. Matthews somehow managed to wrangle a reprieve which kept him alive long enough to break out of jail again. He was caught a few days later. This time the Connecticut General Assembly got involved and Matthews had his reprieve revoked. He was almost certainly hanged at Hartford on or about November 1, 1694.

1695

Joseph Hyde, Native American, age unknown. *Murder.* The crime was committed on January 4, 1695, at Dedham, Massachusetts. This is a little known case of an Indian man who got into a row with another Indian man and killed him. The name of the victim was John Merchant and he was fatally bludgeoned with a rock. The killer, Joseph Hyde, was condemned at the next Assize held for Suffolk County. He was almost certainly hanged at Boston on or about May 15, 1695.

1696

John Andrews, white, age 51. **Esther Andrews,** white, age about 45. **Susannah Andrews,** white, age about 20. *Murder.* The crime was committed in September of 1694 at Carver, Massachusetts. John and Esther Andrews were a husband and wife. Susannah Andrews was their unmarried daughter. All lived together in the same house at Lakenham, the present-day town of Carver, Massachusetts. According to a capital indictment that was filed against all three of them, Susannah Andrews became pregnant out of wedlock. Her parents were aware of the situation but all three conspired to keep the matter secret. On the night specified in the indictment (the exact date is uncertain), Susannah Andrews arose from a bed that she shared with her mother and went outdoors. She made her way to a field near her house where she then gave birth to twins, a boy and a girl, both of which were healthy babies. As soon as the new mother was able to muster her strength she killed the infants by undisclosed means. She then returned to her house where her parents were alleged to have "countenanced, relieved, comforted and succored" her. In addition to that, both parents allegedly retrieved the bodies of the slain infants and buried them in secret. It is not known how this crime came to light after a year and a half. All three defendants were convicted of capital felony, Susannah Andrews as a principal and her parents as willful accessories. All three were sentenced to death at the Plymouth Assizes held in March of 1696. Since the mother and daughter (Esther and Susannah Andrews) both vanish from the records of Plymouth County at this time it is highly probable that they were hanged at Plymouth on or about April 5, 1696. The fate of John Andrews is an open question. He may have been executed and he may have been reprieved. There is no way to tell for sure. The records of Plymouth County mention him as late as 1699 when the Board of County Commissioners allowed him the payment of £10 to the county jailer for keeping him. This was a hefty sum of money in those days and it probably represents a lengthy term of incarceration, perhaps as long as two years. It is therefore apparent that John Andrews did not go to the gallows together with his wife and daughter. He may have been executed at a later date but this is not certain.

Mowenas and **Moquolas,** Native Americans, ages unknown. *Murder.* The crime was committed on October 5, 1696, in Hampshire County, Massachusetts. Described as "Albany Indians," these offenders were alleged to have ambushed a hunting party consisting of one white man and two so-called "friendly Indians," killing them all. The white man was identified as one Richard Church (age unknown), a resident of Hadley. The two Native American victims were not identified by name. The governor of Massachusetts issued a special commission for the swift trial of the alleged killers. This formality was held at Northhampton and ended in a dual conviction. How the two above-named men were apprehended is not known. On October 23, 1696, they were each bound to a tree and shot to death by the sheriff of Hampshire County. It was later said that this incident turned the Albany

Indians against the English settlers of the Connecticut River valley and was a contributing factor to the sanguinary raid on Deerfield there in 1704.

1698

Sarah Smith, white, age about 30. *Murder.* The crime was committed on January 11, 1698, at Deerfield, Massachusetts. This female offender spent the early part of her life in New Jersey. About the year 1690 she and her second husband, Martin Smith, relocated to Deerfield, Massachusetts, then a dangerously exposed frontier settlement in the Connecticut River valley. In 1695 a war party of French and Indians swooped down on the town. Martin Smith was carried off into captivity never to be seen again. Left alone, Sarah Smith pined for her missing husband. As the months passed with no word of him, however, she became increasingly vulnerable to the overtures of other men. One such individual was named Joseph Colson; he and Sarah Smith gravitated to each other and gradually a relationship developed between them. By the autumn of 1697 Sarah Smith was pregnant. Such boded ill for her. Although Martin Smith was absent and unaccounted for (he was probably dead), he was still considered Sarah's lawful husband. There had been no marriage annulment nor certification of widowhood since the time of Martin Smith's abduction. Therefore Sarah Smith was not legally free to pursue another relationship. Hence the liaison with Joseph Colson was more than simple fornication; it was considered adultery — a serious crime in those days — and to make matters worse, the child which Sarah was carrying was a bastard in the eyes of the law. Sarah could not face the world under such circumstances. She concealed her pregnancy to the best of her ability. On January 11, 1698, the situation came to a climax. Sarah locked herself in her bedroom on that day and gave birth to a baby girl. Then she choked the infant to death, wrapped it up in an apron and stashed it under her bed. The women of the neighborhood had been suspicious of Sarah for some time. When one of them came to nurse Sarah for a supposed illness (Sarah had told the concerned neighbor she was sick), she had occasion to see the bed in which Sarah lay. The condition of the sheets left no doubt in the visitor's mind that a baby had been born. This was reported to the other women of the vicinity and soon Sarah was besieged by inquisitive goodwives. One of them found the dead baby under the bed. As soon as the secret was out Sarah said that the baby had been stillborn — the usual dodge for women caught in such circumstances. A coroner's inquest disagreed. Marks of strangulation were found on the baby and its mother was charged with murder. A trial was held at Springfield on August 18, 1698. The verdict was guilty as charged. Seven days later — on August 25, 1698 — Sarah Smith was executed by hanging at Springfield. In commenting on this case, the Rev. Cotton Mather found Sarah Smith a disappointment. She had fallen asleep during her execution sermon and to Mather that was even worse than murder.

Sarah Threeneedles, white, age 19. *Murder.* The crime was committed on September 26, 1698, at Boston, Massachusetts. This female offender was the daughter of Bartholomew Threeneedles, a Boston laborer. Her mother's name was Damaris Threeneedles. According to a contemporary commentator, Sarah was a precocious girl who liked to sleep around. On one occasion she scandalized her family by giving birth to an illegitimate child. Punished for so doing, she went out and got pregnant again. On the above date she arose before dawn and made her way to an open pasture. There she gave birth to her second ille-

gitimate child, a boy. Sarah made no effort to preserve the baby's life. She simply left it laying on the ground so that it soon died of exposure. When Sarah returned home she was suspected of improper conduct. A search turned up the dead infant. Sarah then admitted her maternity but denied treating the decedent in a violent manner. However, bruises on the baby's person suggested otherwise. On October 29, 1698, this young woman was brought to trial. There was a dramatic scene when she saw a shopkeeper named Thomas Savage among the spectators. Screaming at the top of her lungs, Sarah accused the man of paternity. She also said that he had abandoned her when she told him that she was pregnant. It was his apathy, said she, which had brought about her ruin. Savage was visibly embarrassed by the public denunciation. However, he denied everything. The court convicted Sarah Threeneedles of capital felony and ordered her execution. Several days later she was caught in the act of sexual intercourse with another prisoner. This created yet another scandal. On November 17, 1698, the young woman was hanged from the Boston gallows.

1700

Three Unidentified Men, Native Americans, ages unknown. *Murder.* The crime was committed on an unknown date at East Haven, Connecticut. Writing in the year 1811, the late Dr. Timothy Dwight (then the president of Yale University) stated that three Indians had been executed at New Haven sometime during the year 1700 for the murder of a "colonist" at present-day East Haven. Dr. Dwight further adds that all three of the condemned men were members of the Quinnipiac tribe. No source is cited for this account and repeated searching has failed to locate any record of such an event. Assuming that Dr. Dwight's account is true (and this author has no cause to think otherwise), it would then be reasonable to suppose that the three murderers were condemned by a Special Court of Oyer & Terminer, the record of which is now lost.

1701

Esther Rodgers, white, age 21. *Murder.* The crime was committed on November 12, 1700, at Newbury, Massachusetts. This female offender was born at Kittery, Maine, in the spring of 1680. At the age of 13 she was sent to Newbury and was placed in the house of a prosperous squire named Joseph Woodbridge. There she was groomed in the ways of experienced homemakers. It so happened that Esther's employer included slaves among his assets. The free servants of the estate (such as Esther) had regular contact with the slaves and so it was that opportunities for illicit relationships arose. At the age of 17 Esther Rodgers found herself in such a relationship. According to her own account, she became involved with a slave boy of the same house and yielded her virginity to him. Finding herself *enceinte*, she kept the matter secret from both her lover and her employer. One day in the autumn of 1697 she locked herself in Mr. Woodbridge's attic and there gave birth to a child of mixed race. Esther then deliberately smothered the infant and stashed it amid the clutter of the attic. Later she brought the tiny body outdoors under cover of night and buried it in a vegetable garden. Esther got away with this crime. However, three years later she found herself in a similar situation. During the evening hours of the above date, Esther went out into a distant field where she gave birth to another baby of mixed race. She made no effort to preserve the life of the infant. Instead, she covered it with dirt and snow so that it suffocated. Then she returned to her residence. This time suspicion was aroused; Esther's physical condition had not gone unobserved by everyone. She was questioned but gave evasive answers. On the following day a search was made. Footprints in the snow led to the spot where Esther had given birth. Further searching located the dead baby. Eight months later Esther Rodgers was brought to trial before the Essex County Assizes. She confessed the crime with which she was charged and also admitted that she had been guilty of miscegenation. Details of her 1697 infanticide were also divulged. The court had no reservations about sentencing Esther Rodgers to death. On July 31, 1701, she walked to the gallows at Ipswich. There she was hanged by the neck until dead. Her body was *not* set in an iron gibbet after her death.

1704

John Quelch, white, age about 38. **John Lambert,** white, age about 49. **John Miller,** white, age about 40. **Erasmus Peterson,** white, age about 25. **Peter Roach,** white, age about 30. **Christopher Scudamore,** white, age about 28. *Piracy and murder.* Their crimes were committed over a period of time between July of 1703 and May of 1704 on the high seas. On July 13, 1703, the brigantine *Charles*, then stationed at Marblehead, Massachusetts, was commissioned by the governor of that colony to seek out and capture French ships off the coast of Canada. Command of this privateer was conferred upon Capt. Daniel Plowman, an experienced shipmaster. Shortly before his scheduled date of departure, Capt. Plowman was taken ill and forced to postpone sailing. He informed his financial backers of that fact in a carefully worded letter which contained another disquieting piece of news: the crew that had been taken aboard the *Charles* was not trustworthy. A conspiracy was suspected to exist among those men. Capt. Plowman did not elaborate further but he warned that speed was essential if the privateer's owners wished to preserve their investment. It would seem that the suspected conspiracy was even more advanced than the ailing skipper imagined because matters moved swiftly from then on. Before the owners could act on Plowman's recommendation the crew of the *Charles* seized control of the vessel. They locked Capt. Plowman in his cabin and set a course for the open sea. John Quelch, formerly first mate of the *Charles*, was then recognized as captain by the other 42 members of the crew. When the ship was well beyond the sight of land the deposed skipper was thrown overboard. He may have succumbed to his illness but it is more likely that he was murdered. Quelch then hoisted a pirate flag from his topmast and steered a course for the south Atlantic. By November the *Charles* was in Brazilian waters where it captured and looted at least nine ships. In May of the following year the *Charles* returned to Marblehead loaded with plunder. The crew dispersed and it soon became known that Quelch had attacked Portuguese ships knowing that they were of such nationality. Since Portugal was a recognized ally of England, attacks upon her shipping by an English vessel were in violation of treaty. Quelch and his crew were then declared pirates and orders were given for their arrest. Their ship and cargo were also seized by the government of Massachusetts. Of the 43 crewmen who had come ashore from the *Charles* only 25 were found and arrested. That number included Quelch himself. All monies found in the possession of the captured crewmen were confiscated. On June 13, 1704, a High Court of Admiralty was opened at Boston for the trials of John Quelch and his 24 co-defendants. Of this number, four were allowed to save their lives by turning Queen's Evidence against their comrades. One died in

prison. The remaining defendants, including Quelch himself, were all sentenced to death. Reprieves were granted to all but six of the condemned men. Those so spared eventually had their death sentences commuted to unspecified terms of military service. The six above-named men were ordered for execution because they were determined to have treated allied seamen with violence. Scudamore in particular was alleged to have murdered the captain of one Portuguese ship. On June 30, 1704, the six men to whom clemency had been denied were brought to a small island in the Boston harbor. There they were hanged upon a gallows specially built for the occasion. Of the confiscated pirate loot, none is known to have been returned to its rightful owners. Handsome shares of it were apportioned to all those who had played a part in the capture and trials of Quelch and his men. Eventually 788 ounces of gold were sent to England and deposited in the Royal treasury. The amount was barely half of what had been seized from the pirates.

Finch, Native American, age unknown. *Murder.* The crime was committed on May 30, 1704, on the Isle of Nantucket. This is an obscure case that was handled by a court which was specially convened for the occasion. Although the record of the trial is lost, we have been able to discern several details from other sources. Finch was a Nantucket Indian who murdered his squaw. He attempted to escape by swimming to another island but was caught and brought to Sherburne. He was hanged there a few weeks later, probably in August 1704.

1705

Negro Rochester, black, age unknown. *Arson.* The crime was committed on September 27, 1705, at Boston, Massachusetts. This offender was a slave in the custody of a Boston sailmaker named Adino Bullfinch. For some reason that has never been specified he took umbrage at a white woman known as the "widow Rebeckah Savage" and thought about ways to antagonize her. On the above date Rochester saw his chance. He broke into the widow's house and set the place on fire. The result was a total loss for the homeowner. Rochester was nabbed within a short time and charged with capital felony. He was hanged from the Boston gallows on November 23, 1705.

1708

Abigail Thompson, white, age about 37. *Murder.* The crime was committed on December 14, 1705, at Farmington, Connecticut. This female offender was the second wife of Mr. Thomas Thompson (white, age about 50), a widowed tailor who lived and worked at Farmington. A strong, masculine woman, she dominated her spouse and ordered him about at will. She also possessed an irascible disposition which she made no effort to control. Her step-children openly disliked her and there is evidence that Mr. Thompson himself regretted his second marriage. This alienation of affection only served to make Abigail Thompson grumpy and resentful. She became openly hostile toward her husband and even physically abusive. She constantly screamed and swore at the man. She threw stones and household items at him. She threatened to kill him and sometimes she would chase him out of their house with a knife. On one occasion Abigail Thompson even broke a chair over her husband's head. Thomas Thompson (who was a diminutive and rather docile man) had neither the strength nor the forcefulness of character to stand up to his wife. Abigail Thompson could not and would not respect such a spouse. Scorn and con-

tempt were all that she felt for him. Indeed, Mrs. Thompson's conduct even scandalized her neighbors; they regarded her as a termagant and kept their distance from her. It was on the above date that the discord within the Thompson home finally reached a climax. Abigail Thompson was berating her husband as usual when she suddenly picked up a pair of scissors and flung them at the man. A pointed tip of the scissors struck Mr. Thompson in the head with such force that his skull received a puncture wound. Neighbors were appalled as they saw the man stagger from his house. He was soaked with blood from head to foot and clutching at the wound on his head. When asked what had happened he said that his wife had thrown a pair of scissors at him. Abigail Thompson tried to lie her way out of the bad situation from the beginning. She said that she had merely tossed the scissors to her husband expecting him to catch them. Then when the dying man denied that account, Mrs. Thompson changed her story. She next said that she had thrown the scissors in her husband's direction but not with malicious intent. Then she said that her husband had struck her with a broom and had thereby brought about an angry reaction on her part. Thomas Thompson lingered for 19 days before succumbing to his wound. His wife was then charged with capital murder. When the case came to trial Abigail Thompson could not find a single person to testify in her behalf. Instead, one witness after another told of her brutal nature, her acts of violence, her hatred for her husband and her threats against his life. A disgusted jury brought her in guilty of willful murder without a recommendation for mercy. The chief justice then sentenced her to be hanged on June 19, 1706. Abigail Thompson, however, was not one to go to the gallows submissively. She immediately "pleaded her belly" (to use the vernacular of the time), thereby claiming pregnancy as a reason why her execution should be stayed. When this delaying tactic had run its course she began to bombard the Connecticut General Assembly with petitions and appeals. She claimed that the verdict against her was disproportionate because her crime amounted to negligent homicide and nothing more. For two whole years the General Assembly dickered over the case of Abigail Thompson. In May of 1707 the lawmakers lifted the stay of execution. Then they abruptly reversed themselves and put the matter off until the following year. On May 26, 1708, the General Assembly cited "great difficulty" in resolving the matter and voted for another lengthy stay. However, for reasons that remain unclear the lawmakers suddenly reversed themselves the very same day and ordered that the execution be carried out within 24 hours. Accordingly, on May 27, 1708, the condemned woman was brought to the gallows at Hartford and there put to death. On the following day the governor in council ordered that the sheriff of Hartford be compensated out of the public treasury for his "trouble and charge in order to the execution of Abigail Thompson the prisoner."

1709

Josias, Native American, age unknown. *Murder.* The crime was committed on December 1, 1708, at Dartmouth, Massachusetts. This offender was an alcoholic who attacked his wife, Margaret (Native American, age unknown), in their home on the above date and killed her in a drunken frenzy. The victim was beaten, stomped and bludgeoned with a burning stick. She was also forcibly thrust into her own fireplace where she suffered massive burns. Her husband was charged with capital murder and brought before the Bristol County Assizes. He was convicted there and sentenced to be hanged. Execution of the death sentence took place at Bristol (now a part of Rhode Island) on October 12, 1709.

Joseph Tanqua, Native American, age unknown. *Murder.* The crime was committed on June 4, 1709, at Dartmouth, Massachusetts. This offender and another Native American man named Isaac George (age unknown) were working in a potato field on the above date when they got into an argument. Joseph Tanqua whacked the other man over the head with a hoe, inflicting a wound which proved fatal 13 days later. The killer was subsequently brought before the Bristol County Assizes and convicted of willful murder. He was hanged at Bristol (now a part of Rhode Island) on October 12, 1709.

1710

Hannah Degoe, black, age 14. *Murder.* The crime was committed on or about April 12, 1710, at Rehoboth, Massachusetts. Prosecutions for infanticide posed a serious problem because the defendant could usually save her neck by claiming that the victim was stillborn. If no marks of violence were found to refute such a claim the prosecution faced an impasse which allowed defendants to go free for lack of evidence. Many accused baby killers saved their own lives in this way. Eventually a law was passed to close this loophole. In 1696 there was legislated "An Act to Prevent the Destroying and Murder of Bastard Children," a law that mandated the death penalty for any mother who concealed the birth, death or disposal of a child born out of wedlock regardless of whether the child was born dead or alive. As Fate would have it, the first known victim of this law in New England was a child herself.

On April 18, 1710, a grisly discovery was made in the house of Joseph Barney, Jr., at Rehoboth, Massachusetts. While cleaning out some rubbish that had accumulated behind a chimney, the body of a dead baby was found. Mr. Barney brought the matter to the attention of some local midwives who declared that the decedent had been a newborn and that the body had been concealed with deliberate intent. Suspicion fell upon a young servant girl who lived in the house. Her name was Hannah Degoe. When confronted with the situation she admitted her maternity as well as the act of concealment. These revelations were reported to the authorities. Hannah Degoe was arrested and taken to the county jail at Bristol. In September her case came up before the regularly scheduled session of the Bristol County Assizes. There the 14-year-old mother was convicted of capital felony and sentenced to death. She was subsequently hanged at Bristol (now a part of Rhode Island) on November 29, 1710.

1711

Waisoiusksquaw, Native American, age unknown. *Murder.* The crime was committed on April 12, 1711, at Stonington, Connecticut. This female offender belonged to the Mohegan-Pequot tribe of Native Americans. She lived in an Indian settlement near Groton along with her husband, one Wawisungonot by name. On the above date Waisoiusksquaw became angry with her husband and attacked him with a butcher knife. The man was disemboweled. When a grand jury met to consider indicting the killer six of her fellow tribesmen took part in the deliberations. The trial opened at Hartford on May 8, 1711, and resulted in a guilty verdict. Three days later sentence of death was imposed. All of the trial proceedings were carefully translated into the defendant's native language by two sworn interpreters. Waisoiusksquaw was hanged at Hartford on May 15, 1711. Only four days passed between sentence and execution.

Young Squamp, Native American. *Murder.* The crime was committed on December 1, 1710, at Hartford, Connecticut. Little is known of this case. On the above date Young Squamp had come to Hartford to barter for some hardware. While in town he encountered another Native American man named Mantoshoes and got into an argument with him. Young Squamp lost his temper and pulled a knife on the other man. In the brawl that followed Mantoshoes was stabbed. He died eight days later. Young Squamp was arrested at the scene and charged with aggravated assault. The charge was later upgraded to willful murder. The Connecticut Court of Assistants convicted Young Squamp of capital felony and ordered that he be put to death. Young Squamp was accordingly hanged at Hartford on May 15, 1711.

1712

Negro Mingo, black, age unknown. *Forcible sodomy.* The crime was committed on July 23, 1711, at Medford, Massachusetts. This offender was a slave in the household of a Charlestown mariner named Jonathan Dowse. On the above date he attacked a young girl named Abigail Hughes (white, age 14) and forced her to have sex with him in an unnatural way. According to the words of the indictment in this case, Mingo "entered her body not after the natural use of a woman but in a detestable and abominable way of sodomy, a sin among Christians not to be named." We forbear further details of the crime. When the case came to trial not a single word was spoken in Mingo's defense. He was speedily sentenced to death. On February 15, 1712, the condemned man was hanged on Cambridge Common.

Negress Betty, black, age unknown. *Murder.* The crime was committed on or about October 1, 1711, at Marshfield, Massachusetts. This female offender was a slave in the household of a Marshfield squire named Isaac Winslow. According to the record of her trial she was "found guilty of feloniously concealing the death of a bastard child born of her" and "privately burying and disposing of the said child." Such a crime was considered capital murder because the mother was furtive in the matter of not reporting the infant death and in attempting to keep the matter secret. Such behavior implied foul play on the mother's part, presumably willful infanticide. Betty was detected in such a scenario and was made to pay the full penalty of the law. She was hanged at Plymouth on May 7, 1712. At the same court a slave girl named Hittee was convicted of willfully burning down her master's house. This too was capital felony. However, in this case the court opted to spare the defendant. Reason: Her master had already suffered a substantial loss when his house burned down. The slave girl was a valuable asset worth a lot of money; to hang her would be to cause even further loss to her master. Therefore the man was allowed to sell Hittee on condition that she be shipped out of the colony.

Job the Indian, Native American, age unknown. *Murder.* The crime was committed on June 27, 1712, on Sakonnet Bay, Rhode Island. This offender was a slave in the household of one Giles Slocum, a squire who resided at Portsmouth, Rhode Island. Mr. Slocum had two young sons named Giles Slocum, Jr., and Matthew Slocum (white, aged ten and nine respectively). For some reason the above-named slave resented the boys and hatched a plan to destroy them. On the above date the weather was pleasant and Job offered to take the boys canoeing on Sakonnet Bay. Since Job was a family servant neither the boys nor their parents had any reason to distrust him. The boys were especially eager to go because their sense of adventure was aroused. So it was that Job set out upon the water with his master's sons. When the canoe reached a point that was well offshore Job dropped all pretense. He bludgeoned the elder boy with the wooden paddle that he was holding in his hands and then deliberately upset the canoe. When questioned about this calamity Job did not try to pass it off as an accident. Instead, he frankly confessed what he had done. He even told of how the younger boy was crying when he overturned the canoe. Job was brought before the Rhode Island Court of Trials and condemned to be hung in a crow cage. His execution took place at Newport on September 12, 1712. First he was hanged by the neck until dead. Then his body was dipped in tar (to slow decomposition) and set in an iron framework specially made for the occasion. This was then brought to a place called Wanamatoming Hill and hung from the top of a sturdy pole called a gibbet post. Denied burial, the remains of Job the Indian were thus left to swing in the breeze for many years.

1713

David Wallis, white, age about 24. *Murder.* The crime was committed in August of 1713 at Boston, Massachusetts. David Wallis and Benjamin Stolwood (white, age unknown) were seamen aboard a ship called the *Unity* which had arrived at the Port of Boston in August 1713. One day that month the two men got into a row as they were unloading cargo from their vessel. Wallis pulled a knife on Stolwood and stabbed him to death. A special court was called to adjudicate this killing. Wallis was convicted of capital murder and sentenced to death. He swung from the Boston gallows on September 24, 1713.

1715

Jeremiah Meachum, white, age about 40. *Murder.* The crime was committed on March 22, 1715, at Newport, Rhode Island. This man was a weaver by trade and quite probably crazy. On the above date he went berserk and attacked his wife, Patience Meachum (white, age unknown) with an axe. When his sister-in-law, Content Garsey (white, age unknown), tried to interfere she was also attacked. Both women were knocked senseless by blows to the head. Then the frenzied man slit their throats with a knife. Meachum's next act was to fling hot coals all over his house. By so doing he set the place on fire. Then he went to an upstairs room where he attempted to cut his own throat. In the meantime a crowd had gathered around the house, attracted by the screams of the two dying women. Meachum then appeared at a second floor window, wild-eyed and soaked with blood. He brandished his axe at the crowd and then suddenly leapt from the window, screaming as he did so. The crowd then pounced on Meachum but one man was severely injured before the killer was subdued. Several hearty men forced their way into the burning house and retrieved the bodies of the two victims. From then on justice moved swiftly. Within a matter of days Meachum was brought to trial. An outraged court ordered that he be hung in a crow cage. On April 12, 1715 — barely three weeks after his crime — Jeremiah Meachum died on the Newport gallows. His body was then set in irons and put alongside Job the Indian, whose remains were still drying in the wind after nearly three years.

Margaret Callogharne, white, age unknown. *Murder.* The crime was committed on January 29, 1715, at Boston, Massachusetts. This female offender was a servant in the household of a Boston tailor named John Cotta. On the above date she secretly gave birth to a baby out of wedlock and put an end to its short life by leaving it exposed to the winter elements. Unable to bury the infant because of the frozen ground, Margaret then wrapped the tiny corpse in a bundle of linen and stashed it under her bed. She probably would have gotten away with this crime had not her subsequent actions aroused suspicion. She took to her bed with complications from childbirth and told the other members of the household that she had twisted her leg in a fall. When some visitors came to bring her some broth they found her strangely absent. The mistress of the house was then informed and she made it a point to question Margaret. At first Margaret denied all suspicion of impropriety. Then the incriminating bundle was found under her bed. Margaret changed her tune at that point but clung to the common line that the baby was stillborn. A coroner's inquest (experienced in such matters) readily recognized the signs of hypothermia on the dead baby and discounted the claim of stillbirth. Margaret had been caught in one lie already and the inquest was therefore especially wary of what she said. A verdict of "willful murder" was returned and Margaret Callogharne was arrested. When the case came to trial a jury had no difficulty voting for conviction. Sentence of death was then imposed. The defendant requested an extra month in order to put her spiritual affairs in order. The favor was granted. Then on June 9, 1715, she was hanged from the Boston gallows.

1716

Negro Welcome, black, age unknown. *Burglary.* The crime was committed on February 11, 1715, at Boston, Massachusetts. This offender was a slave in the household of a Boston merchant named John Small. On the above date he broke into the house of a Bostonian named Jonas Clark and stole monies totaling £17 in value. Flush with that loot, Welcome made the rounds of the taverns. His free spending aroused suspicion and he was arrested. Twelve pounds was found in his pockets, quite a sum in those days for a humble slave. Welcome was spared the full penalty of the law on this occasion because his master made restitution to the injured party. A year later, however, Welcome was linked to a second burglary. He broke into the house of a widow named Ruth Preston on Hanover Street and stole a £5 bill of credit. This time there was no easy way out. Welcome was put on trial for capital felony and convicted. He was hanged from the Boston gallows on May 18, 1716.

1717

Jeremiah Phoenix, white, age unknown. *Murder.* The crime was committed on August 7, 1716, at Boston, Massachusetts. This man was a "victualer" by profession. On the above date a customer of his named Ralph Moxtershead (white, age unknown) partook of Phoenix's "victuals" and found them not to his liking. He then let Phoenix know how he felt in no uncertain terms. Phoenix was insulted by Moxtershead's remarks and he made a sarcastic reply. Then a fight broke out. Phoenix picked up a hatchet and flung it at Moxtershead. The weapon struck the latter on the head and fractured his skull. Moxtershead (who was a ropemaker by trade) lingered for 97 days before succumbing to his wound. Phoenix was then charged with willful murder. He was convicted without extenuating circumstances and ordered for execution. On June 13, 1717, he was hanged from the Boston gallows.

Thomas Baker, white, age 29. **John Brown,** white, age 25. **Peter Cornelius Hooff,** white, age 34. **Hendrick Quintor,** white, age 25. **John Shuan,** white, age 24. **Simon Van Vorst,** white, age 24. *Piracy.* The crime was committed on April 26, 1717, on the high seas. These offenders were crewmen serving under the command of a noted pirate named Samuel Bellamy. On the above date Bellamy was sailing off the coast of Cape Cod in his flagship the *Whydah* when he intercepted a smaller vessel called the *Mary Anne* which was bound from Boston to New York with a cargo of wine. The six above-named men were put aboard the *Mary Anne* as a prize crew while the original ship's company were taken aboard the pirate ship as prisoners. That night a terrible storm arose. The *Mary Anne* became separated from the rest of the pirate vessels (numbering three in all) and was driven ashore by the force of the tempest at Orleans. Instead of being smashed to pieces by the surf, the *Mary Anne* was cast onto the beach intact. Thus was her prize crew captured alive. The *Whydah* fared much worse. Driven farther north by the fury of the storm, she ran aground at Wellfleet and was pounded to splinters by the breakers. Of the 144 men aboard her only two survived. The bodies of drowned men continued to come ashore for weeks thereafter. In addition to the loss of life (which no one regretted), the *Whydah* carried a fortune in pirate treasure which became a total loss. It was that loss more than anything else which caused official consternation. Two hundred seventy-five years would pass before the treasure was salvaged. The six survivors of the *Mary Anne* were brought to Boston where they were charged with piratically seizing that vessel. All were tried by a High Court of Admiralty and all were found guilty. All six were sentenced to death. They were hanged at Boston on November 15, 1717.

1719

William Dyer, white, age unknown. *Murder.* The crime was committed on

February 13, 1719, at Newport, Rhode Island. This man was a carpenter by trade. He was also an abusive husband. His wife, Hannah Dyer (white, age unknown) refused to have sex with him during her pregnancies and it was that which made William Dyer grumpy. He threatened his pregnant wife with a knife, saying that he would rip her open. He also menaced the woman with an axe, slapped her around and pulled her hair. On one occasion he broke a stick over her head. The situation reached a climax on the above date when Dyer grabbed his wife by the throat and shook her violently. Suddenly the woman's body went limp in his hands. Dyer then panicked. He ran to the house of a neighbor shouting, "Come quickly! My wife is dying!" By then it was too late; Hannah Dyer was laying on the floor with bloody froth coming out of her nose and mouth. At first foul play was not suspected. The decedent was buried and William Dyer received the condolences of the town. Then several days later rumors started to circulate. Dyer's history of spousal abuse was reported to the coroner and an order was given for the exhumation of Hannah Dyer. An autopsy revealed that her neck was broken. William Dyer was charged with uxoricide and put on trial for his life. A jury brought him in guilty of capital murder. He was sentenced to death and on April 21, 1719, he was hanged at Newport.

1720

Negro Coffee, black, age unknown. *Murder.* The crime was committed on January 7, 1720, at Monroe, Connecticut. This offender was a slave in the household of a Durham, Connecticut, squire named Hezekiah Talcott. On or about January 3, 1720, he murdered a slave woman of the same household, one Negress Mary by name (age unknown), and fled in the direction of New Haven. Soon there was a hue and cry for him but Coffee raced ahead of the dragnet. He made his way westward along the Boston Post Road and crossed the Housatonic River into Fairfield County. When the ferryman returned to the New Haven County side of the river he was met by a crier who was circulating the alarm. Realizing that he had just brought the fugitive over to the opposite shore, the ferryman reported the matter to the authorities. A posse was then organized at Stratford and the pursuit continued. Coffee, however, was shrewd; instead of continuing west as everyone expected, he turned north at Stratford and proceeded up the Housatonic River valley. When he reached the fork in the river at present-day Shelton, he bore left and entered the hunting grounds of the Paugusset Indians. Meanwhile back in Stratford the posse lost a lot of time by heading in the wrong direction. It was not until many precious hours had been lost that Coffee's correct path was ascertained. Then the posse followed his trail to the border of Indian territory. At that point the posse had to change its tactics. A delegation went to the Paugusset chief and told him that a dangerous fugitive had come onto his land. The chief then ordered his three best trackers to hunt down the wanted man. The Native American trackers picked up Coffee's trail and followed it to a wilderness area known as the Ripton Woods, now the town of Monroe. The one thing that neither posse nor trackers knew was that Coffee had stolen a gun from his master. As the latter closed in on him, Coffee opened fire, killing an Indian man named Nascrow. Before he could reload his weapon, Coffee was seized by the other two trackers. Then he was turned over to the white men. Brought to Fairfield, the killer was locked up in the county jail and charged with capital felony. It was decided to try Coffee on the Fairfield County charges first for diplomatic reasons. A jury brought him in guilty and he was sentenced to death. Many Indians were on hand to witness his execution by hanging which took place at Fairfield on March 15, 1720.

Joseph Pease, Native American, age unknown. *Burglary*. The crime was committed on April 12, 1720, at Yarmouth, Massachusetts. This offender was a Cape Cod Indian who was put aboard a convict ship for some unknown reason. On the above date he escaped from his place of confinement and swam ashore. Making his way to Yarmouth, he stole two lambs from a Mr. Otis and hid them in the woods. Then he went to a farm owned by a man named Josiah Miller and rustled a sheep and two more lambs. Late the same evening Pease furtively approached a tavern that was run by a widow named Rebeckah Sturges. He then made an entry to the place by burrowing under the cellar door. He stole a bottle of rum, a batch of sweetcakes and a cashbox containing ten silver coins. All of that loot he carried off to his hideout in the woods. When he was discovered, Pease confessed what he had done. He was brought before the Barnstable Assizes and charged with nocturnal burglary—a hanging offense. He was convicted principally on his own confession and ordered for execution. The gallows claimed him at Barnstable on May 18, 1720.

Reuben Hull, white, age unknown. *Murder*. The crime was committed on April 25, 1720, at Westerly, Rhode Island. This case grew out of a lovers' quarrel. Reuben Hull was a Westerly yeoman who had been courting a young woman named Freelove Dolliver (white, age unknown) for a number of months. When Miss Dolliver sought to end their relationship Hull became angry and shot her dead. Further details are lacking except for the fact that Hull was sent to Newport for trial. He was hanged there on June 22, 1720.

Elizabeth Atwood, white, age unknown. *Murder*. The crime was committed on February 21, 1720, at Ipswich, Massachusetts. This female offender was the unmarried stepdaughter of an Ipswich squire named John West. Pregnant out of wedlock, she gave birth to a baby boy on the above date while alone in her bedroom. She then stuffed the infant into a pillow case and concealed the resultant bundle in the folds of her bedclothes. There the baby died by suffocation. Weak from her ordeal, Elizabeth remained in bed that day. Her mother, Elizabeth Atwood West, became concerned for her health and summoned a nurse in an effort to determine what was ailing her daughter. The nurse took one look at Elizabeth Atwood and declared that she had given birth not long before. Mother and daughter both became indignant at that point and denied the allegation. The nurse was then told to get out of the house but she soon returned with officers of the law. A search of Elizabeth Atwood's bedroom turned up incontrovertible evidence of childbirth: bloody swabs and a placenta stuffed in a chamberpot. Elizabeth and her mother then grudgingly changed their story. They admitted that a child had been born and they yielded up the dead baby that had been hidden in the bedclothes. Elizabeth then attempted to explain the situation by saying that she had given birth while in a standing position and that the newborn baby had thereby fallen to the floor with such force that it was taken up dead. Elizabeth also said that the umbilical cord had broken by itself and that she was uncertain whether or not the baby had been stillborn. When the case came to trial Elizabeth was forced to admit that she had made no effort to preserve the baby's life. It was also proven that she had attempted to conceal not only the birth itself but the disposal of the dead infant as well. This last fact was a capital crime in itself because it implied foul play. A jury convicted Elizabeth Atwood on the capital count and a warrant was issued for her execution. Her mother was tried as an accessory but was acquitted. On August 25, 1720, this young woman was brought to the gallows in her hometown of Ipswich. She dressed herself in soiled rags for the occasion and when asked why she took so little pride in her appearance, she said that she did not want to give the hangman a reason to strip her corpse.

1721

Joseph Hanno, black, age about 55. *Murder.* The crime was committed on November 10, 1720, at Boston, Massachusetts. As a child this man had been brought from Africa as a slave. In 1707 he was awarded his freedom and he settled down at Boston with a wife who is known only as "Negress Nanny." It is not known how Joseph earned his living. On the above date he killed his spouse by undisclosed means. Convicted of willful murder, Joseph was hanged from the Boston gallows on May 25, 1721. At the same time a white woman did public penance at the same gallows. Her crime: giving birth to a child of mixed race. This being considered the lowest depth of female self-degradation (especially if the father was Negro), the woman was made to sit on the gallows with a noose around her neck — a sign of extreme disgrace. Then she was whipped through the streets until her back was raw.

1723

Joseph Ewitt, Native American, age unknown. *Murder.* The crime was committed on August 12, 1722, at Barnstable, Massachusetts. Another obscure case, this one concerns a Native American man who killed a woman of his own race. Her name was Hosea Pilate. Nothing is known of the crime's motive or the manner in which it was perpetrated. The scene was an Indian community locally known as *Santuit.* Convicted of willful murder, Joseph Ewitt was hanged at Barnstable on June 13, 1723.

Negro Diego, black, age unknown. *Arson.* The crime was committed on April 2, 1723, at Boston, Massachusetts. This offender was a slave in the custody of a Boston blacksmith named John Harody. For some reason Diego had a grudge against a shopkeeper named John Powell. During the early morning hours of the above date Diego snuck over to Powell's residence and set the place on fire. He also kindled a blaze in the man's barn. The extent of the damage is uncertain but it was enough to result in a capital charge being brought against Diego. A jury voted to convict and the sentence of death was imposed. Diego was hanged from the Boston gallows on July 6, 1723.

William Blades, white, age 28. **John Bright,** white, age 25. **John Brown,** white, age 29. **Charles Church,** white, age 21. **Peter Cues,** white, age 32. **Edward Eaton,** white, age 38. **John Fitzgerald,** white, age 21. **Charles Harris,** white, age 25. **Thomas Hazel,** white, age 50. **Thomas Huggett,** white, age 24. **Daniel Hyde,** white, age 23. **William Jones,** white, age 28. **Abraham Lacy,** white, age 21. **Francis Laughton,** white, age 39. **Edward Lawson,** white, age 20. **Joseph Libbey,** white, age 21. **Thomas Linniear,** white, age 21. **Stephen Mundon,** white, age 29. **Thomas Powell,** white, age 21. **William Read,** white, age 35. **Owen Rice,** white, age 27. **Joseph Sound,** white, age 28. **James Sprinkly,** white, age 28. **William Studfield,** white, age 40. **John Tompkins,** white, age 23. **John Waters,** white, age 35. *Piracy.* The crime was committed on June 10, 1723, on the high seas. These men comprised the greater part of the crew of an eight-gun pirate ship called the *Ranger*. Charles Harris was the skipper. John Waters was the quartermaster and Thomas Powell was the gunnery officer. On the morning of the above date the *Ranger* was cruising the waters off Montauk Point, Long Island, in company with a second pirate ship of ten guns. Lookouts reported a large vessel on the horizon and the pirates supposed it to be a fat merchantman. Chase was given and the pirate ships gradually gained on their quarry. By the time they realized their mistake it was too late for the pirates to change their minds. The supposed merchant ship turned out to be *H.M.S. Greyhound*, a fully armed warship that was patrolling those same waters. At precisely eight o'clock in the morning both pirate ships opened fire on the man-o'-war. Fire was returned and for the next eight hours the three armed ships engaged in a running battle. Each tried to outdistance the other in order to stay out of cannon range but the *Greyhound* had the advantage in maneuverability. She raked her adversaries from stem to stern with a lethal bombardment which left many of the pirates dead and dying on their own decks. At four o'clock in the afternoon the smaller of the pirate ships struck her colors and called for quarter. It was the *Ranger*. She was badly mauled. After securing the beaten pirate ship with a force of marines, the *Greyhound* gave pursuit to the other outlaw vessel. By then however, night was falling and the wounded pirate ship escaped into the gloom near Block Island. The *Greyhound* then returned to the captured *Ranger* and escorted it into the harbor at Newport, Rhode Island. There the pirate crew was put in jail. Three weeks later a High Court of Admiralty was convened at Newport. All of the captured men were charged with capital felony. All of them sought to excuse themselves by saying that they had been forced to serve aboard the pirate ship against their will. The Admiralty Court then busied itself with sorting out the truth of the matter. Some of the defendants were able to produce satisfactory evidence to support their claims of being forced. Others were shown to be liars. Of the original ship's company of 48 there were found to be 26 with no extenuating circumstances for their presence aboard the pirate vessel. Of the remaining number, five had been killed in action and one had committed suicide. The rest were either acquitted or recommended to clemency. The mass execution of the 26 above-named men took place at Newport on July 19, 1723. All were hanged from a specially constructed gallows while their confiscated pirate flag fluttered overhead. Then their bodies were thrown into a trench on Goat Island.

1724

John Archer, white, age 27. **William White,** white, age 22. *Piracy.* Their crimes were committed over a period of time from August 29, 1723, till April 14, 1724, on the high seas. These men belonged to the crew of the *Revenge*, a pirate ship commanded by a notorious buccaneer named John Phillips. During the course of a cruise lasting from August 29, 1723, until April 14, 1724, the *Revenge* ranged all the way from Canada to Venezuela, capturing a total of 34 ships. All of these vessels were plundered. Many of them also lost crewmen because Phillips often forced able seamen to join him. Gradually the number of forced men aboard the *Revenge* grew to outnumber her original company of pirates. A conspiracy was hatched among the former to wrest control of the vessel from the latter. On April 14, 1724, the forced men rose upon their captors and a bloody battle ensued. The pirate captain Phillips had his skull pierced by an adze. The boatswain was decapitated with a broadaxe. Others were overpowered and thrown into the sea. The only reason why the above-named John Archer and William White were spared was because the forced men did not want to be mistaken for pirates themselves; some pirates had to be brought to trial so that the honest men could be officially cleared. Since all of the victors of the uprising were experienced sailors they had no difficulty bringing the pirate ship into the nearest port: Gloucester, Massachusetts. They also chopped off the head of the pirate captain and hung it from the bowsprit of the *Revenge*. When they came ashore they had the head preserved in a jar in order to use it as evidence at the upcoming trial. All parties were sent to Boston where the forced men were exonerated by a High Court of Admiralty. Four pirates were sentenced to death but only Archer and White were ordered for execution. They were hanged at Boston on June 2, 1724. An additional mark of disgrace was reserved for Archer because he had been quartermaster aboard the pirate ship. His body was brought to a small island in Boston harbor where it was set in an iron gibbet and left to rot.

1725

Peter Westcott, Native American, age unknown. *Murder.* The crime was committed on March 28, 1725, at Warwick, Rhode Island. Little information exists about this case. Peter Westcott for some unknown reason attacked a Negro man named Philip (age unknown) and stabbed him to death. From then on justice moved swiftly. Westcott was brought to Newport and tried before the General Court of Trials on a charge of willful murder. Less than four weeks after his crime he was hanged from the Newport gallows. Westcott met his doom on April 23, 1725. He was buried at the site of his execution.

Josiah Challenge, Native American, age unknown. *Murder.* The crime was committed on June 12, 1724, at Chilmark, Massachusetts. Josiah Challenge and Isaac Monoquit were Native American fishermen who lived on Martha's Vineyard. They worked on a sloop which regularly sailed out of Chilmark harbor. On the above date both men were preparing for yet another voyage and they set to work tidying up their vessel. Somehow an argument erupted. Josiah Challenge grabbed an axe and used it to strike down Isaac Monoquit. The wounds were fatal to the latter man. Josiah Challenge was then arrested and charged with capital murder. He was convicted of the crime and sentenced to death. His execution by hanging took place at Edgartown on May 25, 1725.

1726

Joseph Quasson, Native American, age unknown. *Murder.* The crime was committed on August 20, 1725, in York County, Maine. Joseph Quasson and Jonathan Boler (age unknown) were both Native American men from Cape Cod. They joined an auxiliary regiment of the Massachusetts infantry and were assigned to a cantonment in York County, Maine. On the above date both men were sharing a campfire in front of their tents. Somehow an argument began. Quasson then thrust the barrel of a loaded shotgun into Boler's groin and pulled the trigger. The results were fatal for Jonathan Boler. He died in agony three days later. Quasson was seized by fellow soldiers and turned over to local authority. He was convicted of willful murder at the next Assize held for York County. Then sentence of death was imposed. Quasson was accordingly hanged at York on May 12, 1726.

Samuel Cole, white, age 37. **William Flye,** white, age 27. **Henry Greenville,** white, age about 40. *Piracy.* Their crimes were committed during the spring of 1726 on the high seas. The slave ship *Elizabeth* sailed from the Isle of Jamaica in May of 1726 bound for the coast of Africa. In command was the captain, John Green by name. Among the crew were the three above-named men. All were malcontents. While at sea, William Flye (who was boatswain aboard the *Elizabeth*) hatched a conspiracy to take over the ship. He was joined by Samuel Cole, Henry Greenville and several other crewmen. On May 27 the mutineers struck. Shortly after one o'clock in the morning William Flye invaded the captain's cabin at the head of an armed gang. Captain Green was rudely roused from his bunk and forced to go up on deck. There he was given a choice: either jump overboard of his own accord or be forcibly thrown into the sea. The mutineers then gave the captain one minute to say his prayers. After that they picked the man up and hurled him over the side of the ship. Captain Green managed to grab ahold of a railing with one hand and he held onto it for dear life. However, one of the mutineers (named Thomas Winthrop) took up an axe and chopped off the captain's hand. The doomed man then fell into the sea where he either drowned or was eaten by sharks or both. Other mutineers then went after the first mate, one Thomas Jenkins by name. He was wounded with an axe before meeting the same fate as the captain. When both of the officers were out of the way William Flye was acclaimed the new skipper. His first order was that the ship's carpenter, doctor and gunner (indispensable members of the crew who had refused to join the mutiny) be clapped into irons and confined in the slave racks until they agreed to submit to the new regime. Then the mutineers declared themselves "Gentlemen of Fortune" and made

merry for a while. They also rechristened their ship the *Fame's Revenge* in honor of their new calling. When the sun came up a new course was ordered. The slaving voyage was abandoned and the ship turned around. By the third day of June the new pirate ship was prowling the coast of North Carolina. There it found a merchant sloop laying in the shelter of the Hatteras inlet. Slyly, the pirate ship approached the other vessel in a friendly manner and dropped anchor nearby. Then an invitation was sent to the sloop's officers to come aboard the *Fame's Revenge* for a visit and a cordial repast. The invitation was accepted and the unsuspecting seamen fell into the trap. Once aboard the pirate vessel they were told the true state of affairs. Flye also told the other skipper in a matter-of-fact tone that he wanted to trade ships. The sloop was faster than the slaver and Flye desired a swift ship. On pain of death the captain of the sloop was then told to bring his vessel alongside the pirate ship. Hostages were kept to assure the man's compliance. Honest efforts were then made to bring the sloop alongside the former slaver. However, wind, tide and current were all against the endeavor. The captain of the sloop then returned to Flye's vessel in a small boat to report that he could not comply with his order because of insurmountable nautical conditions. Flye was angered by this and he had his underlings give the other captain a severe beating. Then Flye sent some of his own men over to the sloop with orders to bring her about. More hours passed during which the pirates aboard the sloop neglected to pump out the bilge water therefrom. The result was a useless sloop lying at the bottom of the Hatteras inlet. Flye then made the officers of the sloop prisoners aboard the pirate ship and returned to the open sea. On June 7 the pirates overtook a Virginia-bound vessel and ransacked it from stem to stern. They found little of value, however, and had to settle for impressing six members of the ship's crew into piratical service. Then the plundered ship was allowed to continue on its way. Flye continued sailing in a northerly direction. Near Cape May he overtook a New York–to–Philadelphia passenger vessel which had more than 50 people aboard. The pirates picked the other ship clean of valuables, robbing both passengers and crew. They also impressed one man into their service before allowing the plundered vessel to continue its journey. After this the pirates set a course for Martha's Vineyard where they intended to go ashore for fresh water. However, they overshot their target and wound up in the Bay of Nantucket. There they attacked a fishing schooner and forced it to heave to. As the pirates were examining their prize another fishing vessel came into sight. Flye then ordered some of his ablest crewmen to pursue the newcomer in the ship that they had just captured. This was a fatal mistake for Flye. He thus left his own vessel undermanned and thereby found himself with more prisoners and forced crewmen than others who he could trust. The honest men now saw their opportunity and they overwhelmed the pirates by sheer force of numbers. Flye and his cronies were then taken below decks and chained to the slave racks, prisoners aboard their own pirate ship. A course was set for Boston and soon all were in the hands of the law. A High Court of Admiralty was convened on July 4, 1726, and the case of the slaver turned pirate was sorted out. All of the men who had been forced to serve under Flye were set at liberty. Flye himself along with three others were sentenced to death. Of those, one was reprieved when extenuating circumstances were found in his favor. On July 12, 1726, three of the pirates were hanged at Boston. They were William Flye, Samuel Cole and Henry Greenville. The bodies of all three were afterward brought to a small island in Boston harbor. There the latter two were buried. William Flye was singled out for special treatment. Denied burial, his body was set in an iron cage and left to dry in the wind. There it remained for many years, a warning to errant sailors.

Jean Baptiste Jeddre, alias Laverduze, and **Jean Baptiste Jeddre the Younger,** whites (father and son), ages unknown. **James Muse, Philip Muse,** and **John Michael,** Native Americans, ages unknown. *Piracy.* Their crime was committed in August of 1726 along the Maine coast. These men were renegades from the French and Indian forces that had fought along the northern frontier during the time when New England and New France were at war. Following the declaration of peace which marked the end of armed conflict (for the time being), during the summer of 1726 these men headed southward on their own to see what luck would bring them. They were originally a company of 11, consisting of the two above-named Frenchmen and six Native American braves that had been allied with New France, plus a Native American woman with her two young children, being the family of one of the allied Indians. Together this company made its way to the coastal region of Maine where they spotted a fishing schooner moored in a cove. The men determined to seize the vessel and use it to seek their livelihoods as pirates. Approaching the schooner in a friendly manner, the two Frenchmen and six Indians said that they wanted to barter for fish. Under such a pretense they were allowed to come aboard. Once all were on deck they pulled weapons on the crew and announced that they were hijacking the vessel. They ordered sail to be spread and a course set for the open sea. When the commandeered schooner reached a point several miles offshore it came in contact with a larger ship. The pirates then decided to give chase to the other ship, overtake her, murder her crew and transfer themselves thither in order to make use of a more commodious vessel. They also promised to let the fishermen go in peace once they had acquired the other ship. As they drew near that vessel, however, they saw that she was French and so they abandoned the pursuit. Then the pirates sat around for a while trying to decide what to do next. It was not long before one of the Indians discovered the schooner's supply of liquor. Within minutes all six of the Indians were besotted. The Frenchmen knew better than to interfere with drunken Indians. Therefore they stood guard by the arms locker so neither Indians nor fishermen could have access to guns. This was the chance for which the schooner's crew had been waiting. When the Indians became so drunk that they were incapable of giving assistance, the fishermen rushed the two Frenchmen and overpowered them. Then the fishermen broke into the arms locker, seizing guns and ammunition. They loaded muskets as fast as they could and opened fire on the six Indians. Taken by surprise, the drunken men panicked. Three of them jumped overboard to their deaths and the others were overpowered. When the skipper of the fishing schooner had regained control of his vessel he counted his prisoners and found that they consisted of the two Frenchmen plus three surviving Indians. The Native American woman and her two children had taken no part in the fighting and were therefore given the status of noncombatants. The schooner then set a course for Boston and arrived there without further incident. The fates of the woman and children are unknown; they may have been sold into slavery. The five male prisoners were charged with piracy and made to stand trial by an Admiralty Court. All five were capitally convicted and ordered for execution. All five were hanged at Boston on November 2, 1726.

1727

Elizabeth Colson, black, age unknown. *Murder.* The crime was committed on May 28, 1726, at Scituate, Massachusetts. Very little is known of this case, the trial record being incomplete and poorly preserved. Elizabeth Colson became pregnant out of wedlock and gave birth on the above date. She then made away with the baby by unspecified means. She was caught and charged with capital felony. An indictment was handed up against her and she pled guilty thereto. She was then ordered for execution and on May 25, 1727, she was hanged at Plymouth.

1730

Joseph Fuller, white, age unknown. *Murder.* The crime was committed on November 27, 1729, at Falmouth, Massachusetts. A scion of the *Mayflower* family Fuller, this offender operated a ferryboat between Martha's Vineyard and the mainland. He was also said to be mentally ill. On the above date Fuller turned on his wife, Martha Fuller (white, age unknown), and killed her with an axe. Then he chopped her body into little pieces for no apparent reason. Charged with capital murder, Fuller's alleged insanity was not enough to save him. He was convicted without a recommendation of mercy. On May 20, 1730, he was hanged at Barnstable.

1731

Negro Tom, black, age unknown. *Arson.* The crime was committed on August 9, 1730, at Malden, Massachusetts. This offender had been a slave in the household of a Maldenite named John Hutchinson. Sometime during the winter of 1730 he was sold to a new master: the town blacksmith in Marblehead, one Ebenezer Hawkes by name. This situation displeased Tom. He resented being uprooted against his will. He then decided to pay back his former master in kind. On the above date Tom made his way back to Malden. He deliberately chose a Sunday became he knew that the Hutchinsons were churchgoers. Sure enough, there was nobody at home when Tom arrived at his former abode. Entering the house, Tom used his prior knowledge of the place to locate Mr. Hutchinson's cashbox. He stole a handsome sum of money and then set the house on fire. When the Hutchinsons came home from church they found charred ruins where their house once stood. Negro Tom was reported to have been seen in the neighborhood at the time in question. A hue and cry caught up with him at Lynn. A search of his person turned up £50 in cash — an enormous sum for a slave to be carrying. Tom was then returned to Middlesex County and charged with capital felony. A trial court brought him in guilty and sentence of death was imposed. On February 10, 1731, Negro Tom was hanged on Cambridge Common.

Negress Hannah, black, age unknown. *Murder.* The crime was committed on July 3, 1731, at Wallingford, Connecticut. This offender was a slave in the household of a Wallingford squire named Moses Atwater. For some reason she conceived a homicidal hatred for two teenaged white girls that resided in the same house. Their names were Jemima Beecher and Hannah Merriman. The former was a maid in the employ of Mr. Atwater and the latter was a niece of that gentleman. Both shared a bedroom in the Atwater house where they slept in a large double bed. Shortly after midnight on the above date the slave woman crept into the aforesaid bedroom with a large butcher knife. There she attacked the sleeping girls. Jemima Beecher was stabbed in the throat and died almost instantly. Hannah Merriman fared bet-

ter; one of her ribs deflected a fatal thrust when the killer stabbed her in the chest. She then awoke and struggled with her assailant. Her screams then awoke the other members of the household and they subdued the murderess. Hannah was sent to New Haven and charged with capital felony. There the Superior Court made short work of her. On September 8, 1731, a guilty verdict was returned in Hannah's case. Then the court pronounced sentence: death within seven days. On September 15, 1731, this female offender was drawn through the streets of New Haven in a tumbrel. A large crowd awaited her arrival at the place of execution. There she was hanged and buried beneath the gallows. For that day's work the sheriff was paid £2. The executioner fared somewhat better; for his services the county paid £6 plus 10 shillings.

1732

Richard Wilson, white, age unknown. *Burglary.* The crime was committed on an unknown date at Boston, Massachusetts. The court records in this case being lost, we know of it only from the cursory lines of colonial newspapers. Richard Wilson was an Irish alcoholic. He broke into the house of a well-to-do Bostonian named Abiel Walley, Esq., and helped himself to the contents thereof. For that offense Wilson was sentenced to death. He was hanged from the Boston gallows on October 19, 1732.

Negro Jack, black, age unknown. *Rape.* The crime was committed on March 24, 1732, at Suffield, Connecticut. This offender was a slave in the household of a Windsor resident named Giles Ellsworth. On the above date he was walking along a road in nearby Suffield when he encountered an 18-year-old white girl named Abigail Austin. At first the two pedestrians exchanged greetings with each other. Then Jack pulled a knife on Miss Austin and forced her into the woods. What happened next is unprintable. Court records say that Jack perpetrated "great and grievous enormities" upon the person of Abigail Austin. The victim was left alive, however, and she reported what had happened. Since Suffield was then under Massachusetts jurisdiction Jack was brought to Springfield (then the seat of Hampshire County) and charged with capital felony. He was subsequently hanged there on November 2, 1732.

1733

Julian, Native American, age unknown. *Murder.* The crime was committed on September 12, 1732, at Braintree, Massachusetts. This offender was a slave in the household of a Bridgewater squire named Thomas Howard. He also was a malcontent. In the year 1730 he got in big trouble for barn burning but was eventually returned to his master by the courts. In September of 1733 he decided to run away. Julian was then advertised as a fugitive and a reward was offered to anyone who would catch him and return him to his owner. A bounty hunter named John Rogers (white, age 43) decided to go after this reward. He successfully tracked down Julian and made him a prisoner. Then he began the journey to Bridgewater with the intention of delivering Julian to the aforesaid Mr. Howard. Along the way, Rogers and his captive passed through the town of Braintree in present-day Norfolk County. There they stopped at a roadside inn to take some food and drink. Slaves not being allowed to dine in such places, Julian stood outside while his captor went inside. Julian then saw a chance to slip away and he found the urge to do so irresistible. The landlord of the inn happened to glance out a window just as Julian began to run. He saw

Julian heading for a cornfield and told Mr. Rogers. The bounty hunter then ran in pursuit of Julian. He knew that if Julian reached the cornfield he would easily lose himself therein. However, Julian saw Rogers coming and he decided to stand his ground. He pulled out a knife and fatally stabbed his pursuer. Seeing this, the innkeeper and his Negro man ran to the scene and tackled Julian. After a desperate struggle they disarmed and restrained the killer. Julian was then held until officers of the law arrived at the scene. Then he was sent to Boston and charged with capital murder. A conviction followed at the next Assize held for Suffolk County. On March 22, 1733, the runaway slave turned killer was hanged on the Boston gallows. His body was given to medical students.

Rebeckah Chamblitt, white, age 27. *Murder.* The crime was committed on May 8, 1733, at Boston, Massachusetts. This woman was a servant in the household of an unidentified Bostonian. She had occupied such a position since the age of 12. By the age of 27 she had not done much to improve her circumstances. Even worse, she then found herself unmarried and pregnant. On the above date Rebeckah was going about her chores when she was suddenly seized with labor pains. She hurried into the privy closet where she secretly gave birth to a baby boy. Then she threw the infant down into the feculent depths of the privy. Two days later the tiny body was discovered by other members of the household. Rebeckah was appeached because there had previously been rumors about her physical condition. Denials did her no good. A panel of matrons examined the suspect and confirmed that she had recently given birth. At that point Rebeckah changed her story and admitted her maternity. When asked why she had thrown the baby down the latrine she said that it had been a case of stillbirth. A coroner's inquest decided that Rebeckah was criminally responsible for the death of her child because she had made no effort to preserve its life. She had also attempted to conceal the entire matter and such conduct implied foul play. When the case came to trial the question of stillbirth was ruled immaterial. The mere facts of secret birth and disposal constituted capital felony in themselves. Rebeckah Chamblitt was convicted and sentenced to death. On September 27, 1733, she died on the Boston gallows amid an evangelical fanfare.

1734

John Stoicks, white, age 19. *Burglary.* The crime was committed on October 20, 1733, at Dracut, Massachusetts. There is probably more to this case than meets the eye. John Stoicks lived in the Middlesex County town of Dracut. He was only a teenager. On the above date he broke into the house of a neighbor named John Varnum and snooped around for valuables. He took a silver spoon and a handful of silver coins totaling £3 in value. For that crime a court sentenced him to be hanged and dissected. There was no clemency. On March 21, 1734, the young man was executed on Cambridge Common. His body was then turned over to some "skillful surgeons."

Amaziah Harding, white, age unknown. *Murder.* The crime was committed on July 18, 1733, at Eastham, Massachusetts. Amaziah Harding and his wife, Hannah Rogers Harding (white, age unknown), had been locked in an abusive marriage for more than 20 years. The situation finally reached a climax on the above date when Mr. Harding beat his spouse to death. He then laid her body down upon their bed and carefully tucked it in with blankets because he wanted to make it look like she had died

of natural causes. When Harding was satisfied that the scene looked convincing, he summoned a neighbor woman and told her that his wife had died. He also asked the woman to prepare the body for burial according to local custom. When the woman removed the bedclothes preparatory to washing the body she saw numerous cuts and bruises on the decedent. This led the mortician woman to suspect foul play; she knew that Harding had been an abusive husband and she flatly refused to dress the body for burial until the coroner had been summoned. Harding scoffed at this and declared himself "well satisfied" that his wife was dead. When asked why he felt that way, he said that his wife "had been a plague to him." The coroner concurred in the suspicion of foul play and a verdict was rendered accordingly. Amaziah Harding was then charged with capital murder. A grand jury first indicted him and then a petit jury convicted him. A circuit judge sentenced him to death. Amaziah Harding went to his doom reviled as an uxoricide. He swung from the gallows at Barnstable on June 5, 1734.

John Ormsby, white, age unknown. *Murder.* The crime was committed on December 22, 1733, at Boston, Massachusetts. This man was a barber by trade. He was also said to be mentally ill. One day during the autumn of 1733 he suddenly went loco. For no apparent reason Ormsby ran through the streets attacking pedestrians with a fork. He jabbed an unknown number of people before he was arrested and put in the Boston city jail. There Ormsby brooded until the above date. Then he went crazy again. Picking up a pewter chamberpot, he attacked his cellmates with frenzied determination. Two were severely beaten. One man named Thomas Bell (white, age unknown) was bludgeoned so badly about the face and head that he died three days later. Ormsby was then charged with capital murder. When his case came to trial his alleged insanity failed to save him. Ormsby was convicted of willful murder without extenuating circumstances. Such a verdict meant death on the gallows. Ormsby was accordingly executed at Boston on October 17, 1734.

Matthew Cushing, white, age 22. *Burglary.* The crime was committed on October 2, 1733, at Boston, Massachusetts. This young man was a Boston mariner. On the above date he teamed up with a crony named Edward Bushnell and prowled the neighborhood along Water Street. There this pair scouted around for likely places to rob. They finally examined the exterior of a house owned by one Joseph Cook and decided that the place was vulnerable. Shortly after midnight they returned to the vicinity and broke into Mr. Cook's house. They made off therefrom with a broadcloth jacket, a pair of leather breeches, a pair of shoes, a beaverskin hat, two guns and a set of brass buckles totaling £20 in value. Both were traced to their waterfront haunts and arrested on suspicion of burglary. Bushnell decided to save his neck by turning King's Evidence against his partner. Cushing was thereby convicted of nocturnal burglary, a hanging offense. He was executed at Boston on October 17, 1734. Had he not "behaved himself in a very unbecoming manner" during his trial he probably would have been pardoned.

Negro London, black, age unknown. *Rape.* The crime was committed on August 12, 1734, at Dedham, Massachusetts. This offender was a slave in the custody of a Boston merchant named Peter Lucee. On the above date London's master gave him an assignment: bring two mares to Dedham and deliver them to a certain horse-monger there. London set about his task riding one of the animals and keeping the other one in tow. As he passed through Roxbury he was hailed by a 16-year-old white girl named Sarah Clark. She asked London where he was going and when he answered Dedham, she asked if he would give her a ride to that place. London agreed and the white girl got on the second horse. In this way the two traveled side by side for several miles. When they were well along the road to Dedham they paused to let the horses drink from a brook. It was then that London made indecent proposals to the white girl. When the girl refused to go along with those proposals, London pulled a knife on her and declared that he would not take no for an answer. Then he forced the girl to have sex with him. When the time came to continue the journey London gave the girl a choice: she could either stay marooned in the woods or she could promise secrecy and go with him to Dedham. Sarah Clark took the latter option. She then climbed back upon one of the horses and rode with London for a while. As they passed the next house on the road, however, Sarah Clark jumped from the horse and ran screaming for help. This roused the occupants of the house and they came to the girl's rescue. Then the men of the place seized the rapist. London was brought back to Boston and charged with capital felony. Two days later he set the jail on fire and escaped. A manhunt soon brought him to bay. London was then declared an escape risk and slated for trial by a Special Court. All the while he asseverated his innocence to anyone who would listen. A jury disbelieved him, however, and a guilty verdict was returned. London was then sentenced to death. On November 11, 1734, he was brought to the Boston gallows. When asked if he had any last words he changed his story and admitted that he was guilty as charged. Moments later he was dead.

1735

Patience Boston, Native American, age 23. *Murder.* The crime was committed on July 9, 1734, at Falmouth, Maine. This female offender had been abandoned at an early age and forced to fend for herself on the streets of Barnstable, Massachusetts, where theft, charity and prostitution became the means of her survival. Late in her teens she managed to find a home under the roof of a Cape Cod squire named Elisha Thatcher. There she was "mated" with a Negro man named Boston, himself a slave in the same household. In the year 1732 a baby boy was born of this union. However, when the infant was seven weeks old it died under mysterious circumstances. Patience was accused of infanticide and put on trial for her life. A jury decided to give her the benefit of the doubt, however, and a verdict of acquittal was returned. (In view of subsequent events it is quite probable that Patience was really guilty.) Despite being freed by the courts, Patience next found herself in trouble on the home front. Her employer was furious at the loss of a valuable asset (the dead slave-baby), and he turned Patience out of his service. Once again she found herself homeless and unemployed. Notorious at Barnstable, she tramped her way to Maine in search of a new beginning. At Falmouth she was taken in by a merchant named Benjamin Skilling and given a servant's job. What happened next has never been fully explained. On the above date (July 9, 1734), Patience was walking down a Falmouth street when she came upon a young boy named Benjamin Trott (white, age 8). For no apparent reason Patience picked the boy up in her arms and threw him head-first down a well. The victim drowned and Patience was charged with willful murder. Eleven months passed ere the next Assize. Then Patience was once again put on trial for her life. She pled guilty with an air of ambivalence and was sentenced to death. On July 24, 1735, a large crowd gathered at York to see this woman hanged. Patience was drawn to the gallows in a wooden cart, seated on her coffin. The cart was driven under the gallows and Patience stood up in it with a noose around her neck. When asked if she had any last words, she said that she was sorry for what she had done. Then she walked off the cart-tail of her own accord and swung to her doom.

1736

Robin Nasson, Native American, age unknown. *Murder.* The crime was committed on March 7, 1736, at Sherburne, Massachusetts. Little is known of this case. Robin Nasson was a Nantucket Indian brave who became angry with his wife, Deborah Nasson (Native American, age unknown), and beat her to death with a stick. Then to make sure that the woman was dead he obliterated her face with a hatchet. Speedily tried and condemned, Robin Nasson faced death with stoic indifference. He was hanged at his hometown of Sherburne on July 14, 1736.

1737

Abiah Comfort, Native American, age unknown. *Murder.* The crime was committed on March 16, 1737, at Sherburne, Massachusetts. This offender was a Nantucket Indian squaw. She lived alone in a dreary hovel on the fringe of Sherburne that she had formerly shared with her deceased husband, Isaac Comfort. Shortly after midnight on the above date Abiah went out into an open field where, buffeted by the March wind, she gave birth to a baby girl. Then she strangled the infant and hid it in the sand. Twelve days later Abiah was betrayed by another member of her tribe. Local authorities then recovered the body of the dead baby and determined that it had come to its end by violence. A jury of matrons (which included seven Indian women) also subjected Abiah to a physical examination which confirmed that she had recently given birth. At the ensuing Assize held for the Isle of Nantucket, an indictment for capital felony was presented against Abiah Comfort. A complete confession guaranteed a guilty verdict. The sentence was death by hanging. Abiah Comfort was accordingly executed at Sherburne on August 31, 1737.

Ann, alias "Mulatto Nanny," black, age about 16. *Murder.* The crime was committed on March 28, 1737, at Newport, Rhode Island. Ann, alias "Mulatto Nanny," and Alice Allen (white, age 11) were apprentice domestics in the house of a Newport squire named John Easton. On the above date the two girls were left alone in the house while their employer went to visit his in-laws across town. During Mr. Easton's absence the boyfriend of the aforesaid Ann came to the house. He asked for a drink of rum which Ann poured for him out of Mr. Easton's private stock. Alice Allen saw this unauthorized tippling and said that she would report it to Mr. Easton. This irritated Ann to a point where she smacked the younger girl across the face and locked her in a closet. Then she had some private moments with her beau. The romantic interlude proved to be brief, however, because Alice Allen kicked open the closet door and ran out of the house screaming. Ann then lost her temper. That "brat" Alice had annoyed her once too often. Ann chased after Alice and caught her. A struggle then ensued during which Alice bit Ann. The latter then got the younger girl in a headlock and started to forcibly drag her back into the house. As she was doing this, however, Alice squirmed in such a way that she fatally twisted her neck. When Ann saw that Alice had suddenly

gone limp, she dragged the body into the backyard where she threw it down a well. The body was discovered when another servant went to draw water. A coroner's inquest was held and it was decided that the decedent had accidentally fallen into the well. A funeral accordingly took place and Alice Allen was buried. Several days later Mr. Easton decided to question Ann in private. Ann (who was either extremely stupid or extremely intimidated) then made the fatal mistake of changing her story. She told Mr. Easton that Alice had been knocked off balance by a swinging garden gate and thereby stumbled into the well. This story did not have the ring of truth to it and Mr. Easton let it be known that he suspected foul play. The body of Alice Allen was then exhumed and reexamined by the coroner. This time a broken neck was found. Ann was brought before the coroner and a cadre of hatchet-faced magistrates. She was also made to look upon the putrefying remains of Alice Allen. Badly frightened, Ann then changed her story again; yes, she said, she had deliberately put Alice in the well after breaking her neck in a struggle. When asked what occasioned the struggle, she said that Alice had threatened to tattle on her for giving rum to her boyfriend. When asked why she had lied, Ann said that she was afraid lest it be thought that she had killed Alice on purpose. This was exactly what the coroner concluded. Ann was then charged with willful murder. When the case came to trial Ann was not allowed counsel. She naively pled guilty to a capital charge that any attorney could have whittled down. Sentenced to death, Ann was hanged at Newport on November 4, 1737.

Hugh Henderson, alias John Hamilton, white, age 30. *Burglary.* His crimes were committed over a three-day period during September of 1737 in Worcester County, Massachusetts. This man is described as a "notorious offender" and a "transient person" from Newport, Rhode Island. On September 13, 1737, he turned up at Sutton, Massachusetts, where he broke into the house of a man named Perez Rice and absconded therefrom with a pair of shoes, a pair of stockings and a keg of rum. On the following day Henderson went to Shrewsbury. There he snatched a pocketbook containing a £3 note and a knife valued at four shillings. Then he went to Grafton and snuck into a house there. He was scared off on that occasion, however, and fled the scene, leaving his coat and the stolen knife behind him. On the very next day he went to Westborough and broke into the house of a squire named Abner Newton. There he stole a silver cup, a pair of stockings, a shirt, a silk handkerchief, an ivory comb, a pair of shoe buckles and two sets of metal buttons. He also raided Mr. Newton's kitchen and carried off an entire platter of corned beef and cabbage. Then he brought his loot to some nearby woods and sat down for a leisurely meal. Desiring something to drink, Henderson remembered seeing a cask of liquor in the squire's house. He then went back to the scene of the crime in order to swipe that beverage. It was a fatal mistake; Henderson was caught by the outraged homeowner and held for the sheriff. At the ensuing session of the Worcester Assizes three counts of burglary were lodged against Henderson. He was convicted on all three counts and sentenced to death. On November 24, 1737, he was hanged on Worcester Common.

1738

Katharine Garrett, alias "Indian Kate," Native American, age 27. *Murder.* The crime was committed on January 4, 1737, at Old Saybrook, Connecticut. This offender was a maid in the household of the Rev. William Worthington, minister of the local church in Old Saybrook. On the morning of the above date she complained of not feeling well and asked to be excused from her duties. Then she went to her room where she climbed into bed and got under the covers. The minister's wife offered her some medicine but Kate declined it and asked that she be allowed to sleep for a while. This request was granted. However, while the minister and his wife thought that Kate was asleep, she snuck out of the house and made her way to the barn. There she gave birth to a baby boy in secret. When the infant cried the noise made Kate panic. She grabbed a piece of wood and beat the baby over the head with it in order to silence its crying. After that Kate covered up the infant with hay and returned to her bedroom. Later that day Kate was invited to come into the minister's parlor and warm herself by the fire. She accepted the offer and soon fell asleep in a chair. When she arose from her seat an hour or so later she left a stain on the cushion where she had been sitting. This was noticed by the minister's wife who at once suspected that Kate had either given birth or was very close to doing so. Kate was then questioned but she denied the allegation. A short time later one of the neighborhood children reported that he had heard a baby crying in the minister's barn. The Rev. Worthington then went to the barn and looked around. He found the baby still alive but covered with secretions and rotten straw. The minister's wife was then called to the scene because she was an experienced midwife. She did her utmost to rescue the baby. However, when she placed a hand under the baby's head to support it she could feel that the skull was broken in several places. The baby died a short time later. Kate was then confronted with these developments and she admitted her maternity. She also admitted that she had bludgeoned the newborn. Legal wrangling continued for more than a year in this case. A Special Court was finally called to adjudicate the matter. Kate was then convicted of capital felony and sentenced to die. She was hanged at New London on May 3, 1738.

Philip Kennison, white, age unknown. *Burglary.* The crime was committed on April 20, 1738, at Charlestown, Massachusetts. This offender is described as a "transient person" from Greenland, New Hampshire. He was also a turner by trade. On June 8, 1735, he came to the borough of Brookhaven in Suffolk County where he broke into a shop kept by one Thomas Goodwin and carried off merchandise to the value of £250. Kennison was apprehended for that crime but escaped the extreme penalty of the law. On the above date he turned up at Charlestown where he broke into the shop of a merchant named James Hayes. Among the items which he stole on that occasion were a set of glass buttons, a pewter porriger filled with pins and needles, six pieces of ribbon, four women's girdles and two odd pieces of linen totaling £20 in value. Because it was his second offense, Kennison was denied clemency. He was hanged on Cambridge Common on September 15, 1738.

Thomas Davis, Peter LeGrand, Peter Jeffeau and **Francis Bowdoin,** whites, ages unknown. *Murder & Piracy.* The crime was committed on September 17, 1738, on the high seas. The sloop *Dolphin* sailed from Cape Francois, Haiti, on September 3, 1738, bound for Boston, Massachusetts. The crew consisted of the captain, one Adam Dechezeau by name (a Frenchman), and the first mate, whose name was Edward Towle (an Englishman). Also aboard were the following: four seamen named Thomas Davis (English), Peter LeGrand, Peter Jeffeau and Francis Bowdoin (all French) and a young cabin boy named Stephen Dechezeau, who was a nephew of the skipper. For some reason the four

above-named seamen conspired to murder their officers and take over the sloop. Two weeks into their voyage the Isle of Bermuda was sighted. This was the signal that the conspirators had agreed upon. Peter LeGrand struck the captain down from behind with an axe while the other three battered the first mate to death with hammers. Both victims were then thrown overboard. The cabin boy was spared for the time being, probably for immoral purposes. The sloop then continued in a northerly direction until it reached the waters near Block Island. There it was decided to throw the cabin boy overboard so that all outside witnesses to the crime would be eliminated. A short time later the sloop came too close to Block Island and it ran aground there. The four mutineers came ashore where they were met by the locals. When asked the whereabouts of the captain and mate they told an improbable story of them being lost at sea. A swinging jib boom had knocked the officers overboard in a storm, said they. This tale aroused suspicion and Rhode Island authorities were notified. The four mutineers were brought to Newport and kept separated. There they were bluffed into revealing the truth. A High Court of Admiralty was convened to adjudicate the matter. The result was four capital convictions. Appeals were disallowed. The sheriff of Newport oversaw the erection of a quadruple gallows on Bull's Point. The site was deliberately chosen to allow maximum vantage from both land and sea. On November 3, 1738, the three French prisoners were hanged while thousands of people watched. The one English prisoner, Thomas Davis, was found dead in his cell that same day. He had taken his own life. In spite of that, the sentence of hanging remained inexorable in his case; the dead body of Thomas Davis was carried to the place of execution and strung up along with the other condemned men. This was so no one could say that he had cheated the gallows.

1739

John Comfort, Native American, age unknown. *Murder.* The crime was committed on October 27, 1738, at Sherburne, Massachusetts. This man was a Nantucket Indian who earned his living as a whaler. On the above date he got together with a fellow tribesman named Joel Elisha (age unknown) and went out drinking. After several hours thus spent the two men went their separate ways. Both were in a moderate state of intoxication. John Comfort walked to his home where he continued drinking. At around sundown Joel Elisha unexpectedly came to Comfort's house for some reason. He approached the place by way of a footpath that led through Comfort's rather large vegetable garden. What happened next is known only from Comfort's version of the story: Comfort heard the sound of someone in his garden and supposed that a thief was raiding the place. He then picked up a piece of firewood and ran out into the garden where he attacked the supposed thief. Joel Elisha was beaten over the head with the piece of firewood and suffered a fractured skull. He died three days later. In his defense, Comfort said that he had been too drunk to be able to distinguish friend from foe in the darkness. A jury duly considered the matter but opted to convict John Comfort of capital murder. Drunk or not, he had acted out of malicious intent and that in itself was enough to negate his defense. A lesser verdict of manslaughter was disallowed. John Comfort was sentenced to death. He was accordingly hanged at Sherburne on August 22, 1739.

Sarah Simpson and **Penelope Kenny,** whites, ages unknown. *Murder.* Their crimes committed in August of 1739 at Portsmouth, New Hampshire. Both of these women gave birth out of wedlock. Both had concealed their pregnancies and both had secretly disposed of their dead infants. In the eyes of the law they were murderesses because their acts implied foul play. Trouble began on August 17, 1739, when a dead baby was found in a Portsmouth well. A search for suspicious persons led to a young widow named Sarah Simpson. She had for some time been rumored to be pregnant. When questioned, Simpson denied all knowledge of the child in the well but admitted that she had recently given birth. She then led officers to a shallow grave wherein was found a dead infant. Simpson was then charged with capital felony in her own right while inquiry began anew for the mother of the child in the well. On the following day the investigation focused on the house of one Joseph Franklin. That well-to-do citizen employed an Irish maid who had also been rumored to be pregnant. This was Penelope Kenny and she initially denied the allegation. A physical examination of her person was then proposed. Penelope Kenny refused to cooperate and was examined by force. A panel of experienced midwives reported that she had indeed given birth within the past few days. Confronted with the verdict of the midwives, Penelope Kenny remained evasive. She was then locked up in a squalid dungeon and told that she would stay there until she showed a better spirit of cooperation. One night of misery was enough to get Penelope Kenny to change her story. She said that she had given birth in her employer's cellar. There she had put a newborn baby into a tub, supposing it to be dead. When asked what had become of the baby she said that she had thrown it into a nearby river. It then being mid–August, the water level in the river was low. This made for an easy search but no dead baby was found there. Even though there was no direct evidence linking Penelope Kenny to the baby in the well, she shrewdly explained away the result of her physical examination by admitting that she had been pregnant and fabricating the story about a baby in the river. She knew that a search of the river would be fruitless and pinned her hopes on the King's Attorney dropping the case against her for want of a corpus delicti. A jury, however, felt satisfied that Kenny was guilty of capital felony anyway (even if she was not the mother of the child in the well) because she had admitted to willfully concealing the birth and death of an infant when she claimed to have dumped a baby in the river. Sarah Simpson and Penelope Kenny were both convicted of the charges against them and both were sentenced to death. They were hanged at Portsmouth on December 27, 1739.

1740

George Necho, Native American, age unknown. *Carnal knowledge of a minor.* The crime was committed on September 24, 1738, at Wells, Maine. The details of this case are mostly unprintable. On the above date George Necho abducted a young child named Susannah Kimball (white, age 3) and brought her to a secluded area. There he attempted to rape his captive. When it became apparent to Necho that his objective was physically impossible, he performed other lewd acts with the toddler instead. It is not known how Necho was caught. Outraged authorities were at first unsure what to do with him. While his crime was indeed of a sexual nature, Necho could not be charged with outright *rape* because there had been no actual penetration of the victim's private parts. It was finally decided to bring Necho up on charges of gross indecency, later amended to specify carnal knowledge of a minor. A jury convicted Necho of capital felony but that was not the end of the case. When the chief justice asked Necho the formal question of whether he knew of any reason why sentence of death should not be passed upon him, a

court-appointed defense counsel instructed Necho to claim the Benefit of Clergy. This threw the court into a quandary. While it was already established that outright rape was a felony without Benefit of Clergy, the judges were unsure about lesser sexual offenses and whether or not the Benefit of Clergy could be applied to them. Such a point of law required further deliberation and it was ordered that Necho be held in jail until the matter was decided. The judges probably hoped that Necho would die of exposure in his unheated cell and thereby solve the problem for them. Even so, it took well over a year for a decision to be reached. The judges then declared that the details of Necho's crime were too reprehensible to warrant mercy. Benefit of Clergy was therefore disallowed. A sentence of death was then pronounced and the governor issued a warrant for Necho's execution. On August 7, 1740, a large crowd gathered at York to witness the end of George Necho. The hangman did his job to everyone's satisfaction and the sheriff made a note of that fact on the death warrant.

Edmund Browne, white, age unknown. *Murder.* The crime was committed on August 22, 1739, at Townsend, Maine. This man was entertaining guests in his home on the above date. There was liquor in abundance there and Browne was one of several men who had too much to drink. This led to a nasty confrontation between Browne and a partygoer named David Bryant (white, age unknown). The more the two men argued the more heated became their respective moods. When Browne ordered Bryant to get out of his house the latter refused. It was then that Browne lost his temper. He ran outside to his woodpile and picked up an axe that lay there. Then Browne ran back into his house with the axe and attacked Bryant. Too drunk to realize his peril, Bryant was an easy target. He was killed instantly by massive axe wounds to his head and neck. Other guests disarmed Browne and held him for the sheriff. The man was subsequently convicted of capital murder. He was hanged at York on September 4, 1740.

1742

Harry Jude, Native American, age unknown. *Murder.* The crime was committed on June 18, 1742, at Nantucket, Massachusetts. Little is known of this case because of missing records. Harry Jude was a Nantucket Indian who killed a woman named Mercy Moab (Native American, age unknown) by unknown means for an unknown reason. The crime was considered aggravated enough to warrant a Special Court of Oyer & Terminer. The record of the trial is lost but Harry Jude is known to have been capitally convicted. He was hanged at Sherburne on or about September 1, 1742.

Jabez Green, white, age unknown. *Murder.* The crime was committed on September 28, 1741, at Brookfield, Massachusetts. This is a very obscure case. All that is known of it is as follows: Jabez Green, a man of unknown circumstances, quarreled with a similarly obscure individual named Thomas McClure (white, age unknown) and stabbed him to death. A jury adjudged Green to be guilty of capital felony and the man was sentenced to death. He was hanged on Worcester Common on October 21, 1742.

1743

Margaret Fennison, white, age unknown. *Murder.* The crime was committed on or about May 15, 1742, at Malden, Massachusetts. Described as a "poor woman," this female offender was the wife of a Boston butcher named Bartholomew Fennison. Sometime in the year 1740 her husband went to sea for an extended voyage. He was not gone for long before his wife cheated on him with another man. Margaret Fennison became pregnant and in June of 1741 she gave birth to a healthy baby boy. For the next 11 months the child was kept by its mother. Margaret Fennison managed to fool her neighbors into believing that the baby had been conceived on the eve of her husband's departure. However, as the months went by she began to worry more and more about her husband's return and how she would explain the presence of the child to him. Finally she became desperate. On or about the above date she bundled up the baby in a blanket and went to a deserted area in Malden. There she bludgeoned the baby with a rock. Then she stuffed the murder weapon into the folds of the blanket so it could act as a weight. When that was done she sank the bundle containing the baby and the rock in a flooded quarry. Several days later the bundle floated to the surface and was discovered by some passersby. The authorities were notified and an investigation traced the blanket to Margaret Fennison. An indictment was handed up against her in August of 1742 but she did not come to trial until the following January. The verdict was guilty of capital felony. When the judge asked Margaret Fennison if she had anything to say why the sentence of death should not be passed upon her, the answer she gave caused a sensation: she claimed to be pregnant. This was the usual dodge for female offenders in those days when they were facing execution. In Fennison's case the claim of pregnancy added even more scandal to an already scandalous affair. The defendant had been incarcerated for the better part of a year and if she was indeed pregnant there would be some fancy explaining to do by the jailer. It was then ordered that 12 experienced matrons be sworn in to make a physical examination of the prisoner. The exam was duly carried out and on February 7, 1743, a formal report was submitted to the court signed by all 12 matrons in which they dismissed the claim of pregnancy. The court then passed sentence of death on Margaret Fennison. The governor hesitated to issue a warrant for her execution because he was unconvinced by the report of the matrons. Better to let a little more time go by, he thought, in order to make absolutely sure that the matrons were correct in their verdict. On March 10 a death warrant was issued. Then a reprieve was given until April 14, 1743. By then it was sufficiently clear that the prisoner was not with child as she claimed. Thus there were to be no further reprieves. On the aforesaid date Margaret Fennison was brought to the gallows on Cambridge Common and there she was put to death. Her case has a strange sequel: Several months after the hanging news arrived at Boston concerning Margaret Fennison's absent husband. It was reported that on the exact same day and in the very same hour when Margaret Fennison was hanged, Bartholomew Fennison (although thousands of miles away), while still at sea, was knocked overboard by a swinging jib boom and drowned.

Simon Hew, alias "Simeon Howse," Native American, age unknown. *Murder.* The crime was committed sometime during the spring of 1743 at Nantucket, Massachusetts. This offender was a recidivist killer. On January 29, 1732, he got into a fight with another Native American man named Jethro Quanset and beat him to death with a stick. Brought to trial on a capital charge, Hew was convicted of manslaughter. His life was spared when he pled the Benefit of Clergy. Consequently on June 16, 1732, he was branded on his right hand with a hot iron in the shape of the letter "M."

Nine years later he killed again. The record of his second offense is lost but the crime was considered grievous enough to warrant the convening of a Special Court of Oyer & Terminer in August of 1743. The verdict was guilty of either murder or manslaughter with a sentence of death. The next news of Simon Hew, alias Simeon Howse, concerns his execution by hanging which took place at Sherburne on or about September 1, 1743.

Negro Jack, black, age unknown. *Rape.* The crime was committed on June 7, 1743, near Middletown, Connecticut. This offender was a slave belonging to a New York City merchant named Thomas Thomas. For a day or two previous to the above date, he had worked at unloading a cargo in the Port of Middletown, then a busy shipping point on the Connecticut River. Before making the return voyage to New York, the workmen of Jack's crew were given a day off. Most of them dallied around Middletown but Jack himself went to Haddam for some reason. Later that day Jack began the return trip to Middletown and walked along the highway thereto, present-day Route 9-A. There he encountered a lone female traveler on horseback and acted violently toward her. Jack grabbed the bridle of the woman's horse and made her come to a halt. Then he pulled the woman off the horse and beat her up in the middle of the road. After that he slung the breathless woman over the back of the horse and rode off with her into the woods. When he reached a spot that was suitably remote he pulled the woman off the horse and raped her. Then when he had had his fill of sex he slapped the victim across the face and taunted her by saying "Now you will have a black bastard!" When the woman begged for mercy he kicked her in the head. Then he picked up a tree branch that lay nearby and beat the woman with it until he thought that she was dead. He escaped from the scene by riding away on the victim's horse. Several hours later the bruised and battered woman managed to crawl out of the woods. A drover found her lying in the road near Higganum. She managed to gasp out an account of what had happened. There followed a hue and cry that overtook Jack as he was about to board a ship in Middletown. He was then brought before the injured woman and fully identified as her attacker. She was identified as a married white woman named Hannah Andros (age unknown), the wife of Mr. Ephraim Andros of New Hartford, who had been visiting friends in Haddam on the above date. Jack was convicted of capital felony at the next Superior Court for Hartford County. He was hanged at Hartford on November 16, 1743.

Negress Kate, black, age unknown. *Murder.* The crime was committed on April 28, 1743, at Wethersfield, Connecticut. This female offender was a slave in the household of a Wethersfield squire named Thomas Belding. On the above date she gave birth to a healthy male infant and strangled it to death with a curtain sash. Mrs. Belding testified that she had observed Kate late on the evening of April 27 and that she seemed to be in "very great distress as of a woman in travail." The white woman told Kate's master of her suspicions and advised that he send for a "granny" (i.e., elderly Negress midwife) to help Kate get through her ordeal. Kate denied that she was pregnant. Then she went into hiding. It was during that time that she gave birth. The next morning Mrs. Belding looked closely at Kate. She later reported that Kate showed "the lines of a woman newly delivered of a child." She also examined Kate's breasts and found them to be "full of milk." Kate resisted this examination to the best of her ability. A subsequent search of the house turned up the dead baby with a curtain

sash tightly knotted around its throat. The identity of the baby's father was not made a part of the official record. Kate was subsequently brought to trial for capital murder. She was convicted and sentenced to death. On November 16, 1743, she was hanged at Hartford.

1744

Negro Barney, black, age 16. *Malicious maiming.* The crime was committed on May 12, 1743, at Middletown, Connecticut. This case is in a class by itself. It has no parallel elsewhere in New England. So unique was it that a special legislative act was required in order for it to be adjudicated. Negro Barney, a juvenile offender, was a slave in the household of a Middletown squire named Jonathan Alling, aka Allyn. For some reason that was never disclosed, Barney conceived a virulent hatred for his master's six-year-old son, Thomas Alling. On the above date he brought the little boy into a secluded pasture where he stripped him naked. Then he attacked the boy's genitals with a knife. The victim was completely emasculated and left to die. Eight hours later Thomas Alling was found unconscious and awash in blood. He was still alive, though just barely. Seasoned physicians were horrified at the nature of his wounds. Somehow the victim was patched up enough to identify his assailant. Barney was arrested and admitted the crime with an air of nonchalance. He had to be held in a secret location to prevent him from being torn apart by outraged townspeople. When the case was brought before the Superior Court the judges were at a loss. There was no statute on the books that covered such a crime and the court doubted that it had enough authority to act on the matter. The Connecticut General Assembly then stepped in and passed a Special Act empowering the Superior Court to proceed as it saw fit. The results were devastating for Negro Barney. He pled guilty to a charge of willful castration (the exact words of the indictment are too obscene for publication) and underwent the following regimen of punishment: On November 16, 1743, he was brought to the Hartford gallows along with two other condemned prisoners. There he was made to watch as the other two were hanged by their necks until they were dead. Then Barney was himself set upon the gallows and made to sit there for the space of one hour with a rope around his neck and his hands tied behind his back (a mark of extreme disgrace in those days) while irate spectators pelted him with rocks, sticks and all kinds of garbage. He could not ward off the objects that were thrown at him because his hands were securely tied and he could not run away because any attempt to do so would have caused the rope to tighten around his neck with fatal results. When the hour was up, what remained of Barney was brought, still living, to the whipping post where 39 hard lashes were inflicted on him. After that the executioner applied a red hot branding iron to Barney's forehead and thereby marked him with a large letter "C" so that he would be ever after known as a "Castrator." When this torture was finished Barney was remanded to jail where he was chained down in a dank cell for 28 days. During that time he was fed on bread and water. At the end of 28 days (by which time his wounds were half-healed) he was again brought to the whipping post and given another 39 lashes. In such a way his wounds were all torn open. There followed another 28 days in an unheated cell with nothing but bread and water to sustain him. On January 11, 1744, what remained of Barney was again brought to the gallows. This time the executioner awaited him with a pair of red hot iron pincers. There the teenage prisoner had his sexual organs torn out by the roots. It is highly unlikely that he survived.

Edward Fitzpatrick, white, age unknown. *Murder.* The crime was committed on March 8, 1744, at Rutland, Massachusetts. For many years Daniel Campbell (white, age unknown) had worked as a tender of horses and mules in Boston. He was a frugal man who saved his money until he had enough to make a down payment on a farm in the Worcester County town of Rutland. There he hired a farmhand named Edward Fitzpatrick and went into business for himself. For some reason relations between the new farmer and his employee went rapidly downhill. All that Fitzpatrick would later divulge was that in his opinion Campbell was a "little dirty nasty fellow." In any case, Fitzgerald decided to do away with Campbell and help himself to the man's possessions. On the above date he decoyed Campbell into his barn and overpowered him there. Fitzgerald strangled Campbell to death with his bare hands and buried him in a shallow grave. Then he went into the farmhouse where he stole every article of value he could find. Fitzgerald even took the buttons from the dead man's clothing. Several days later Campbell was noticeably absent and his neighbors became alarmed. Fitzgerald gave evasive answers when he was asked about Campbell and in so doing he aroused suspicion of foul play. A search of the farm turned up the body of the missing man. Fitzgerald was arrested and a short time later confessed his guilt. He then led officers to the places where he had hidden items taken from the decedent. Among those items were a snuffbox, a skein of muslin and a pair of shoes with silver buckles. Fitzpatrick was convicted of capital murder at the next Assize for Worcester County. Thousands of people thronged Worcester Common to see him hanged on October 18, 1744.

1745

Negro Jeffrey, black, age unknown. *Murder.* The crime was committed on September 13, 1745, at Mendon, Massachusetts. This offender was a slave in the household of one Thomas Sandford, a deacon in the First Church of Christ at Mendon. For some time there had been ill feelings between Jeffrey and his master's wife, the exact particulars of which are unknown. The situation reached a climax on the above date when Jeffrey attacked Mrs. Sandford (white, age about 70) with a hatchet. The woman was hacked to a point where her own husband was unable to readily identify her. When Deacon Sandford heard a commotion in his kitchen he came to the scene just in time to see the killer decapitating his wife. Jeffrey then threatened his master with death if he dared to intervene. Then he ran out of the house and took to the woods. A posse was organized to hunt down the fugitive. However, while the possemen scoured the woods their quarry slipped back into town—the last place where anyone expected him to go. Jeffrey broke into a house where he found a keg of rum. He began drinking the rum and was soon so drunk that he was easily disarmed and taken into custody. He was subsequently hanged on Worcester Common on October 21, 1745. Then his body was dissected.

Elizabeth Shaw, white, age about 22. *Murder.* The crime was committed on June 29, 1745, at Windham, Connecticut. This offender was the unmarried daughter of William and Elizabeth Shaw of Windham. Pregnant out of wedlock, she concealed her condition by wearing padded garments. On the above date she went into the woods near her home where she gave birth to a healthy baby boy. Then she placed the infant in a rock crevasse and covered it up with leaves. This caused the baby to either smother or die of exposure. When Elizabeth returned home she was confronted by her own father and admitted what she had done. The scandal was reported to the authorities and Elizabeth Shaw was arrested. A committee of matrons gave her a physical examination which confirmed that she had given birth. Elizabeth then led officers to the spot where she had hidden the baby. The Superior Court of Windham County convicted this young woman on a charge of capital felony and issued a warrant for her execution. She was hanged at her hometown of Windham on December 18, 1745. A local tradition there (which is not generally credited) says that a last-minute reprieve was granted in this case but that the messenger bearing the news was delayed by inclement weather and arrived in Windham too late to save Elizabeth Shaw. Such tales are not uncommon in New England but in this case there might be some truth in it; the original death warrant for Elizabeth Shaw (which is on file in the Connecticut State Archives and which the sheriff would have held in his hands and read aloud at the time of her execution) clearly bears the scars of raindrops upon it. Bad weather notwithstanding, Sheriff Jabez Huntington was later paid £5 for his "perplexity in that day's performance."

1746

James Cattee, Peter Ferry and **Thomas Rigby,** whites, ages unknown. *Piracy and treason.* The crime was discovered on October 22, 1744, aboard a ship at sea. These men were natural born subjects of the King of England who were found to have traitorously served aboard a French warship. There being a declared war between England and France at this time, the conflict spread to North America where the respective colonies of those two countries took up hostilities against each other., On the above date an English warship, *H.M.S. Comet*, engaged a French privateer off the coast of Maine and forced it to surrender. Among the prisoners taken on that occasion were ten mariners who spoke English as their primary language. They were all brought to Boston where they remained in jail for more than a year while evidence of their true nationality was investigated. When the prosecution announced that it was ready to proceed to trial a Special Court of Admiralty was convened. The governor of Massachusetts presided in person. Of the ten defendants, seven of them were capitally convicted and ordered for execution. Then in the days preceding their date with death, four of the men were reprieved for various reasons. The above-named trio, however, were not so fortunate. They were hanged from the Boston gallows on July 24, 1746.

1747

Elizabeth Wakefield, white, age unknown. *Murder.* The crime was committed on May 28, 1747, at Cambridge, Massachusetts. This is an obscure case of infanticide. Elizabeth Wakefield was a young widow who lived at Cambridge. She became pregnant out of wedlock and was too ashamed to let the matter become generally known. On the above date she secretly gave birth to a living male infant which she killed by unspecified means and hid in a private place. The dead baby was discovered and a coroner's inquest concluded that it had died by violence. A panel of matrons also examined the suspected mother and confirmed that she had recently given birth. Elizabeth Wakefield's reaction to all this is unknown. However, the tone of a clemency petition that she wrote suggests that she confessed her guilt. A Middlesex County jury convicted this woman of capital felony and she was

ordered for execution. On October 8, 1747, she was hanged on Cambridge Common.

Mulatto William, black, age 17. *Murder.* The crime was committed on March 23, 1747, at Boston, Massachusetts. This juvenile offender was a slave belonging to a pair of Boston brothers named Benjamin and John Walker. On the above date William (who is described as having had a "mischievous disposition") somehow got his hands on a loaded musket and went swaggering down a street with it, waving it menacingly at passersby. When a woman called down scolding words to him from a second story window, William took a shot at her which barely missed. Then he reloaded his weapon and bid defiance to any who would try to disarm him. At that point everybody ran for cover. Moments later another young slave named Cato (black, age about 16), the bondsman of one John Dennie, came walking around a corner, oblivious to danger. William regarded this as an act of provocation. He then opened fire on Cato with fatal effect. Angry pedestrians pounced on William before he could again reload. Brought to trial for his crime, William was convicted of willful murder. On October 15, 1747, he was hanged on Boston Common.

1749

Negro Cuff, black, age about 16. *Rape.* The crime was committed on October 2, 1748, at East Haven, Connecticut. This juvenile offender was a slave in the household of a Capt. Joseph Tuttle. He made his home with the family of his master at East Haven. On the above date Cuff happened to spot a young white girl named Diana Parrish (age 15, daughter of Mr. Ephraim Parrish of Stamford) walking along a road not far from where he was working. Cuff later confessed that the sight of the girl filled him with an urge that he could not control. When he saw that there was no one else nearby, he grabbed the girl and dragged her into the woods. There he forced her to have sex with him. The victim went straight to the authorities and reported what had happened. Cuff was arrested and he admitted that the charge against him was true. When the case came to trial Cuff was assigned two lawyers to defend him. On their advice he pled not guilty. His prior confession, however, was entered as evidence against him. The verdict was guilty and the sentence was death. Cuff's defense counsels did not give up. They wrote an eloquent appeal to the Connecticut General Assembly using biblical references in an effort to get the death sentence commuted. Cuff even offered to submit himself to castration in exchange for clemency. In addition to that, he also requested that he be flogged, branded with a hot iron and sold out of the colony as a eunuch. The General Assembly received the appeal but voted it down. Cuff was then left to his fate. He was hanged at New Haven on or about May 15, 1749.

1751

Thomas Carter, white, age unknown. *Murder.* The crime was committed on January 1, 1751, at South Kingston, Rhode Island. This man was originally a mariner from Virginia. One of his voyages brought him to Newport, Rhode Island, where he met a woman and began a relationship with her. Carter wound up getting married and he decided to settle at Newport with his bride. He remained in that situation for 18 months before committing his capital crime. New Year's Day of 1751 saw Carter in a roadside inn at South Kingston. There he made the acquaintance of one William Jackson (white, age unknown), an itinerant merchant who dealt in fine leather goods. When it

became known that both men were from Virginia they had a cordial time together. Carter learned that Jackson was on a business trip to the area and that he was carrying merchandise of considerable value. Carter also learned that Jackson was traveling alone. On the following day Jackson resumed his journey. He took to the Boston Post Road where he was overtaken by Carter. Both men rode side by side until they reached a remote stretch of road. Then Carter struck Jackson down from behind and dragged him into the woods. There he stripped the unconscious man naked. He next took a rapier from among the victim's personal effects and ran him through the heart with it three times. Carter rolled the body into a brook and rode off with Jackson's clothing, horse and entire stock of merchandise. The total value of the stolen items was later set at £1000 — a fabulous sum in those days. Because the slain man was a stranger in Rhode Island he was not missed. Then eight weeks after the crime his frozen body was found. The cold weather had prevented decomposition from setting in and Jackson was therefore recognized by the innkeeper who had given him lodging on the last night of his life. The innkeeper also remembered that the decedent had been chummy with another customer who he identified as Thomas Carter of Newport. Further investigation found Carter flush with money in the days following Jackson's disappearance. It was later revealed that Carter had found a large amount of cash in Jackson's saddlebags and that he had also sold clothing, horse and leather goods for a handsome price. The Superior Court of Washington County (then known as Kings County) sentenced Thomas Carter to be hung in a crow cage. On May 10, 1751, more than 10,000 people came to South Kingston to watch the grisly ritual. Carter was first hanged from a gallows until he was dead. Then his body was dipped in tar and placed in a close-fitting iron cage. This was hung from the top of a tall pole at the scene of the crime. There it remained on public display for many years, a warning to evildoers.

Negress Phillis, black, age 17. *Murder.* The crime was committed on January 15, 1751, at Boston, Massachusetts. This juvenile offender was a slave in the household of a Boston apothecary named John Greenleaf. She chafed under the task of caring for her master's infant son, John Greenleaf, Jr. (white, age 1), and decided that murder would leave her free to spend her time as she pleased. Phillis stole arsenic from her master's apothecary shop and stirred it into some warm milk which she fed to the baby boy. The results were fatal for three people: John Greenleaf, Jr., Phillis herself and the mother of Phillis. The tiny victim of the poisoning died after two days in agony. When a court condemned Phillis to the gallows her mother collapsed from a nervous breakdown and died. Phillis herself lived until May 16, 1751. On that date she was hanged on Boston Common.

1753

Sarah Bramble, white, age unknown. *Murder.* The crime was committed on March 21, 1752, at New London, Connecticut. According to her indictment, on the above date Sarah Bramble, a "singlewoman of New London did privately and secretly" give birth to a living female infant which "by law was a bastard." Immediately thereafter she "did throw" the infant "down upon a certain bed" and "did entirely neglect to cherish, nourish and feed" it so that it did "then and there instantly die." She also hid the dead baby so that the fact of its birth would remain unknown. Nine days later the body was found and Sarah Bramble

was exposed. In September of 1752 a jury deadlocked over whether or not to convict this woman of capital felony. Some of the jurors thought that the baby may have been stillborn. Other jurors thought that the baby died because its mother had made no effort to keep it alive. Still others thought that the defendant had deliberately murdered the baby by forcibly throwing it down upon a bed until it died. A mistrial was declared and Sarah Bramble remained in jail for another year before her case was reheard. At the second trial the jury was less divided. Those jurors who wavered were won over by the prosecution when emphasis was placed on the fact that the defendant had deliberately hidden the dead baby. Such an act implied foul play and it was enough to swing the jury to a guilty verdict. Sarah Bramble was then convicted of capital felony and ordered for execution. On November 21, 1753, more than 10,000 people stood in a cold autumn rain to watch this woman die. Sarah Bramble refused to listen to a sermon that had been written for her and she went to the gallows without religious solace. The scene was a large field near New London.

1754

William Welch, white, age 23. *Murder.* The crime was committed on November 19, 1753, at Boston, Massachusetts. This man was an Irish mariner. According to his own words, Welch was raised by an unprincipled stepmother who encouraged him to steal. Not daring to displease the woman, young Welch became a skilled shoplifter by the age of ten. He was also trained to be a pickpocket and was quite adroit at that practice as well. For the rest of his life he had no qualms about stealing. When some of Welch's more law-abiding relatives learned of his stepmother's bad influence, they made arrangements to send the boy to sea. It was hoped that such an experience (and especially the harsh discipline thereof) would serve to reform young Welch. The boy crossed the Atlantic at the age of 16 but jumped ship when he reached Canada. He got a job with a saloonkeeper and promptly became addicted to alcohol. Prostitutes were another of his passions. To support his bad habits, Welch made full use of his thieving skills. In the years that followed, he roamed the length and breadth of New England, supporting himself by pilfering, shoplifting and picking pockets. Whenever the law came too close for comfort he would join the crew of a ship and go to sea for a while. On the above date Welch happened to be in Boston. There he was seen in the act of shoplifting but escaped into the crowds. The aggrieved merchant then called in a brawny fellow named Darby O'Brian (white, age unknown) and promised him a gold coin if he would hunt down the thief. Armed with a good description of his quarry, O'Brian set about his quest. He found Welch down by the waterfront and attempted to restrain him. Welch then pulled out a knife and slashed O'Brian across the abdomen so that "his bowels came out." The wound proved fatal. Welch was quickly taken into custody and charged with capital murder. He pleaded self-defense to no avail. Clemency was also denied. The end came on April 11, 1754, when Welch was hanged on the Boston gallows.

William Wier, white, age unknown. *Murder.* The crime was committed on April 6, 1754, at Boston, Massachusetts. William Wier and William Chisholm (white, age unknown) were dock workers along the Boston waterfront. On the above date both men were engaged in a job which entailed the stacking of firewood. Somehow an argument broke out between them. Wier lost his temper and struck Chisholm over the head with a piece of wood. The injured man suc-

cumbed within a short time. In his defense, Wier insisted that he had not struck the decedent with malicious intent; the altercation had gotten out of hand because of a sudden burst of anger. Wier's trial jury dismissed this defense and brought in a capital conviction. In the weeks that followed, Wier pleaded for clemency on the ground that he should have been indicted for nothing more than simple manslaughter or homicide by misadventure. The governor carefully examined the facts of the case and was at first inclined to agree with Wier. However, when Wier was found to have smuggled tools in his cell the governor became miffed and decided to let the law take its course. William Wier was accordingly hanged at Boston on November 21, 1754. Had he not tried to escape from prison he would probably have been pardoned.

1755

Eliphaz Dow, white, age unknown. *Murder.* The crime was committed on December 12, 1754, at Hampton Falls, New Hampshire. This man was a sharecropper who had a running feud with a neighbor named Peter Clough (white, age unknown) because it was alleged that he had killed one of the other man's cows as a deliberate act of malice. On the above date Eliphaz Dow was at the house of his brother, Noah Dow, when Clough came by and picked an argument with him. Noah Dow warned both men that he would allow no fighting in his house. Eliphaz Dow and Peter Clough then went outside and prepared to do battle. Clough said to Eliphaz Dow, "God damn you!" whereupon Eliphaz Dow warned Clough to watch his saucy mouth. Clough then told Eliphaz Dow to go to hell. At that point Eliphaz Dow picked up a hoe and smacked Clough on the head with it. The iron point of the tool pierced Clough's skull, killing him on the spot. Eliphaz Dow was then arrested and charged with capital murder. At his trial he tried to claim that Clough had provoked him to violence. However, the jury decided that such was no excuse; Eliphaz Dow should have watched his temper. The verdict was guilty and the sentence was death. Eliphaz Dow was accordingly hanged at Portsmouth on May 8, 1755.

John Seymour, white, age unknown. *Murder.* The crime was committed on July 7, 1754, at York, Maine. This man was probably crazy. A blacksmith by profession, Seymour had a history of aberrant behavior. In 1745 he attacked his wife for no apparent reason and attempted to cut her head off with a dull knife. The result was a nasty wound to the woman's throat. Seymour was convicted of attempted murder on that occasion and was made to sit upon the York gallows with a rope around his neck as a sign of disgrace. Nine years and nine children later Seymour and his wife were still together. On July 3, 1754, Christiana Seymour gave birth to a baby girl. Her husband used the happy event as an excuse to go on a drinking binge. For four days and four nights he remained in a state of extreme intoxication. On the morning of the fourth day — July 7, 1754 — Seymour awoke in a maniacal frame of mind. Wearing nothing but a loose-fitting shirt, he jumped out of bed and ran into the parlor where his wife was nursing the new baby. Glassy-eyed and disheveled, Seymour demanded that he be given the baby. Christiana Seymour refused to part with the infant because she mistrusted its father's mental state. Seymour then snatched the baby from its mother's breast and ran out of the house naked except for his unbuttoned shirt. Holding the terrified screaming baby in his hands, the crazed father ran through the streets until he reached a bridge that spanned the York River. Then he ran out onto the bridge and flung the baby into the river at midstream. The baby's mother garnered her strength and ran after him. All the while she shouted for help. When she saw her husband throw the baby off the bridge she ran into the river as far as she could go in an effort to save her child. It was no use. The baby was carried away by the current and drowned. Mrs. Seymour had to be treated for immersion and hysteria. She also became "dangerously ill" with complications from her recent childbirth. When John Seymour was visited in jail by his 13-year-old son, he told the boy that he expected to be hanged. When asked why he had killed his newborn child he said that the devil had told him to do it. Then he admonished his eldest boy to serve God with equal fervor. Seymour remained in jail for an entire year before he was brought to trial. Then he was convicted of capital felony and ordered for execution. He was hanged at York on August 11, 1755.

Negro Mark and **Negress Phillis,** blacks, ages unknown. *Murder and petty treason.* The crime was committed on June 30, 1755, at Charlestown, Massachusetts. These offenders were slaves in the household of a wealthy merchant named Capt. John Codman. They had been purchased by their master during their childhoods and raised amid conditions that were far from benevolent. Capt. Codman (white, age unknown) was not an easygoing man. He worked his slaves long hours and allowed them little free time. He also was a strict disciplinarian with a low tolerance level for any kind of levity. On one occasion Codman's slaves conspired to effect their deliverance from his ownership; they burned down the man's storehouse in a hope that the resultant loss would bring about their sale to a kinder master. This plan failed when Codman made up his loss through other means. Matters finally reached a critical point when Codman caught Mark in a dramshop and severely punished him. Angry and hurt, Mark began to contemplate murder. He then solicited the aid of some fellow slaves, one of whom was the aforementioned Phillis. All of them hated Codman for reasons of their own and they agreed to go along with the plot against his life. Mark had a hard time deciding how to kill his master. He knew that murder was a serious matter and he feared the judgment of an angry God. Because of this, Mark studied the bible with extreme care. He read and reread every chapter hoping to find some passage that would justify the homicide that he had planned. He finally located a biblical verse which he interpreted to mean that murder could be excused in the eyes of God if no blood was spilled. This narrowed Mark's choice of weapons down to one: poison. He accordingly instructed his fellow plotters to find and deliver to him a suitable amount of deadly poison. One slave with access to an apothecary's shop purloined a packet of arsenic and gave it to Mark, who in turn gave it to Phillis with instructions to mix it into their master's food. Phillis did as she was told; she prepared oatmeal and cocoa for Capt. Codman and laced his servings with enough arsenic to kill a dozen grown men. Codman ate the tainted food and was dead within 24 hours. A coroner's inquest confirmed that he had been poisoned. The household slaves were questioned closely when one of the decedent's daughters remembered seeing a suspicious-looking residue in a cooking vessel. One of the slaves, a man named Quaco, broke down and confessed what he knew. Mark and Phillis were arrested. Also charged were Quaco's wife, Phoebe, and a Bostonian bondsman named Robin, the latter of whom was named as the source of the poison. When the case came to trial Quaco and Phoebe were allowed to save their lives by testifying for the prosecution. Robin was lucky enough to be acquitted. Mark and Phillis were capitally convicted. Both were sentenced to death. On September 18, 1755, they were executed on Cambridge Common. In accordance with the penalty for petit treason (in this case the willful murder of a master by his bondsmen), Mark and Phillis were dragged to the place of execution on hurdles. There Mark was hanged from the gallows until he was dead. Phillis was chained to a stake and burned to ashes. Afterward the body of Mark was placed in an iron gibbet and set up at a crossroads. There it remained on display for 20 years.

1756

Negro Toney, black, age unknown. *Murder.* The crime was committed on an unknown date at Kittery, Maine. This offender was a mentally unbalanced slave in the household of a squire named Samuel Johnson. He claimed to be a victim of mistreatment so severe that it made him lose his will to live. Toney said that he contemplated suicide but was deterred from taking his own life when told that doing so would make him answerable to God for a mortal sin. He then determined that others could be maneuvered into taking his life for him; he would commit a capital crime and thereby incur the death penalty. It was then that Toney thought about killing his master. He reasoned that such an act would surely result in his execution. However, he could not get up the nerve to attack Mr. Johnson. His thoughts then turned to his master's five-year-old daughter, Mary Johnson, and he decided that she would make a suitable alternate. The child had far fewer sins against her, reasoned Toney, and therefore she would obtain easy admittance into heaven. Moreover, God would like it more if the girl was slain instead of her father, according to Toney's rationale. Convinced that such logic would excuse him in the eyes of God, Toney picked up little Mary Johnson and threw her down a well. Then he gave himself up to the authorities and explained his actions as aforesaid. Toney's death wish was soon fulfilled. The Superior Court of York County condemned him to the gallows for capital murder. He was accordingly hanged at York on July 29, 1756.

Joseph Hughes, white, age unknown. *Murder.* The crime was committed on March 14, 1756, on the high seas. This man had been captain of the schooner *Dove,* an ocean-going merchant vessel which put in at Rhode Island in the spring of 1756. It was reported that Captain Hughes had killed one of his crewmen with deliberate malice and a Special Court of Admiralty was called to adjudicate the matter. The homicide victim was identified as one Michael Clark (white, age unknown), a professional cooper who had signed aboard the *Dove* as a member of the crew. The motive for the crime and the manner in which it was perpetrated are not specified in the surviving records; the trial transcript is lost and only a short newspaper article speaks of the case. However, the circumstances of the murder were judged to be sufficiently aggravated to engender a capital conviction and a death sentence for the defendant. The last known fact is that a warrant was issued for the execution of Joseph Hughes at Providence, Rhode Island. The murderous skipper was probably hanged there in November of 1756. Nothing more is known of him.

1757

John Harrington, white, age unknown. *Murder.* The crime was committed on September 1, 1756, at Watertown, Massachusetts. Little is known of this case. John Harrington was a cordwainer who lived at Waltham. On the above date he went to Watertown to look at a shipment of leather. While there he somehow got into an argument with another man named Paul Learned (white, age unknown) and came to blows with him. The confrontation escalated until Harrington pounced on his antagonist and ran him through the back with a currying knife. Learned died of his wound and Harrington was charged with capital murder. A conviction and death sentence followed at the Middlesex County Assizes. John Harrington was subsequently hanged on Cambridge Common on March 17, 1757.

John Absalom, Native American, age about 62. *Murder.* The crime was committed on October 8, 1757, at Scituate, Rhode Island. On the above date this man attended a husking bee at the house of a farmer named Nathaniel Phillips. There he got into an argument with a younger man named Thomas King (white, aged about 30) and felt himself ill-used. Absalom left the house of his own accord but lay in wait nearby. As Thomas King exited the house later that evening Absalom sprang upon him with a knife and stabbed him in the stomach. The wound proved to be a moral one when King succumbed three days later. Absalom was arrested on the spot. He was brought before the Superior Court without delay and charged with capital murder. A conviction and death sentence were passed on him within a month of his crime. He was hanged at Providence on November 18, 1757.

1760

Samuel Parks and **Benjamin Hawkins,** whites, ages unknown. *Piracy.* The crime was committed on February 24, 1760, on the high seas. On February 21, 1760, the merchant schooner *Frances* sailed from the Isle of St. Christopher bound for Savannah, Georgia, with a cargo of liquor and slaves. The crew consisted of the captain, John Honey by name, along with a first mate named Samuel Parks, a supercargo named Francis Goffe and several professional seamen among whom were Benjamin Hawkins, William Devine, John Carter and John Gibbs. Unknown to the captain and the supercargo, a conspiracy had been hatched among the rest of the crew to seize control of the ship and embezzle the cargo. When the vessel was three days into its journey the plotters struck. The captain and the supercargo were overpowered. Then they were put into a lifeboat and set adrift on the open sea. Parks assumed command of the *Frances* from that point on. A change of course was ordered and on April 2, 1760, the schooner put into port at Newport, Rhode Island. There the acting captain impersonated the real captain and began negotiations to sell both ship and cargo on the local market. Four days later the mail brought a New York newspaper containing a legal notice about the *Frances* and a warning that said ship had been piratically hijacked. Evidently the captain and supercargo had survived their ordeal and raised an alarm. Rhode Island authorities promptly arrested the false captain (Parks) and three other members of the crew. All were charged with piracy. A Special Court of Admiralty was called to adjudicate the matter. Parks and Hawkins pled guilty and were sentenced to death. The other two crewmen were spared; one had turned King's Evidence and the other was acquitted when it could not be proved that he was a willing party to the crime. Both of the condemned men were ordered for execution. They were accordingly hanged at Newport on August 21, 1760.

1762

Fortune Price, black, age unknown. *Arson.* The crime was committed on February 19, 1762, at Newport, Rhode Island. Shortly after sundown on the above date church bells blared the fire alarm in the old city of Newport. A fearsome blaze had broken out in a warehouse owned by one Thomas Hazzard, a merchant who dealt in lamp oil, ammunition and other flammable goods. All along the main wharf buildings shuddered as barrel after barrel of combustible fluid exploded. Soon the night sky was filled with fireballs which rained down all over the city. Strong men raced to the scene with firefighting apparatus but were driven back by the intense heat. Then the inferno spread until four other warehouses were similarly engulfed. Frantically, sailors aboard ships in the harbor hacked away their rigging so the fireballs would not ignite their vessels. Elsewhere in the town the aroused population gave thanks to God that a heavy layer of snow was upon their roofs; otherwise the entire business and residential districts would have fallen prey to the flames. Those who lived near the Long Wharf had little time to save themselves; snatching up what personal effects they could, young and old fled into the cold winter night and were hard put to dodge the deadly fireballs which continued to rain down from above. There was only one way to fight the conflagration: the evacuated houses which stood nearest to the burning buildings would have to be blown up and hauled away. Then the fire would be left to burn itself out. In some houses kegs of gunpowder were used to hasten demolition. Other dwellings were hewn down by axemen. Then everybody who could carry a piece of wood was pressed into service to clear away the debris. Master and slave worked side by side long into the night. By dawn the crisis was past. In the days that followed it became apparent that this calamity was no accident. Then came a quintessential question: who would do such a thing? The answer was not long in coming. Negro Fortune was the culprit. Negro

Fortune, the disgruntled slave of Simon Price the blacksmith. Despite the popular indignation there was no mob action. The suspect was arrested and held for trial. Whether he confessed or was convicted on other evidence is uncertain but Negro Fortune was legally sentenced to death for his crime. Nearly everybody in Newport turned out to see him hanged there on May 14, 1762.

1763

Negro Bristol, black, age 16. *Murder.* The crime was committed on June 6, 1763, at Taunton, Massachusetts. This juvenile offender was a slave in the household of a physician named William McKinstry. Up until the time of his capital crime he had never shown an inclination to violence. His master had a spinster sister named Elizabeth McKinstry (white, age about 35) who came to Taunton for an extended visit. For some reason young Bristol conceived a deadly hatred for her. On the above date Bristol attacked Elizabeth McKinstry in the kitchen of his master's house. The woman was struck down from behind with a hot flatiron and had the flesh of her face deliberately seared with that instrument. Then she was flung down the cellar stairs where the killer finished her off with an axe. This happened early in the morning before the rest of the family had risen for the day. When the crime was discovered Bristol was gone. He had ridden off on one of his master's horses. A hue and cry was raised and the alarm reached Newport, Rhode Island, where the fugitive was caught. At the next Assize held at Taunton the teenage killer pled guilty to an indictment for capital murder. He was sentenced to death with little ado and hanged on December 1, 1763. The reason why Bristol killed Elizabeth McKinstry was never divulged to the public. Court records are also silent about the killer's motive.

1764

John Shearman, white, age unknown. *Burglary.* The crime was committed on October 7, 1761, at Newport, Rhode Island. This man was a professional mariner who liked to prowl around the back alleys of Newport in search of mischief. Shortly after midnight on the above date he broke into the house of a female shopkeeper named Sarah Kumroil and carried off a batch of loot which consisted of the following: £80 worth of Rhode Island paper currency plus 16 shillings worth of scrip. Also two shillings and nine pence worth of Connecticut paper currency, one pocketbook, one tortoise-shell snuffbox set with silver and pearls, one china snuffbox with a brass ring, a pair of silver shoe buckles, a pair of stone cufflinks set in silver, a pair of gold cufflinks and a silk purse containing more than 20 silver coins of different denominations. Because this crime was committed upon an inhabited dwelling during the nighttime hours it was considered capital felony. Shearman was caught with the goods shortly afterward and held for trial by the next Superior Court for Newport County. The evidence being conclusive against him, Shearman was sentenced to death. Then began a lengthy process of appeals. The Rhode Island General Assembly voted to grant Shearman a 14-month reprieve so his case could be brought before the King-in-Council. This was tantamount to a commutation of the death sentence because cases so appealed were routinely decided in favor of the defendant. While awaiting official word of the King's decision, Shearman got impatient and made a fatal blunder: he broke jail. A manhunt resulted in his capture and the matter was reported to the General Assembly. There the lawmakers turned against Shearman. They felt that their clemency had been abused and they voted to revoke Shearman's reprieve. This cleared the way for the issuance of a death warrant and the Newport County Superior Court acted accordingly. Shearman was then ordered for execution. He went to the Newport gallows on November 16, 1764.

1765

Joseph Lightly, white, age unknown. *Murder.* The crime was committed on January 8, 1765, at Waltham, Massachusetts. Little is known of this case. Lightly was a man of unknown occupation who lived at the town of Ware in Hampshire County. He cohabited there with a woman named Elizabeth Post (white, age unknown) and was reputed to be her common-law husband. On the above date the couple was staying at a Waltham inn. There they got into a spat and there Lightly struck his female companion over the head with a piece of firewood. Elizabeth Post succumbed to a skull fracture five days later. Charged with capital murder, Lightly was convicted at the next Assize held for Middlesex County. On November 21, 1765, he was hanged on Cambridge Common. He persisted in denying his guilt right to the last moment.

1768

Nathan Quibby, Native American, age unknown. *Murder.* The crime was committed on October 4, 1767, at Sherburne, Massachusetts. This offender was a Nantucket Indian by ethnicity and a whaling man by profession. While inward bound from a whaling voyage a quarrel erupted among the Native American crewmen of the ship to which Quibby was assigned. The captain of the ship would allow no brawling on his decks so it was agreed that the respective factions would have a showdown when they reached port. On the above date the whaler put in at Sherburne. The duelists then armed themselves with cutlery from the ship's hardware and went ashore. On one side was Nathan Quibby and another Native American man named John Charles. Opposing them were two other Native Americans named Peleg Titus and Isaac Jeffrey. Terrible was the battle which followed. When it was over Peleg Titus and Isaac Jeffrey lay dead on the beach. The former had been run through the body with a whale lance and the latter had been fatally gaffed with a boat hook. Quibby and Charles were arrested on the spot and charged with capital murder. On December 25, 1767, while still in jail awaiting trial, Quibby turned against his co-defendant (John Charles) and killed him with a smuggled knife. Thus when Quibby came to trial he faced three indictments for three murders. He confessed the crimes rather proudly and he was unperturbed when sentence of death was passed upon him. Virtually the entire population of Nantucket turned out to see him hanged there on May 26, 1768.

Isaac Frasier, white, age 28. *Habitual criminal.* His crimes were committed over a period of time from 1765 to 1768 mainly in Connecticut. This offender was born at North Kingston, Rhode Island, on February 9, 1740. His parents were poor and as a result their son was brought up disadvantaged. When Isaac was five years old his father died while on active service with the army. His mother, left destitute, was hard put to fend off starvation. When Isaac was eight years old his mother hoped to better his circumstances by putting him apprentice to a cobbler. There Isaac remained until the age of 16 amid conditions little or no better than those from whence he came. His master was a niggardly man who kept the apprentice on such short rations that theft alone kept Isaac from dying of hunger. During those same years Isaac's education was neglected so that he grew up illiterate. When Isaac reached the minimum age for military service he made haste to join the army. From 1756 to 1760 he remained on active campaign. But falling ill during the latter year, he was obliged to remain at a convalescent facility in Connecticut. When he recovered his health young Frasier made his way to Newtown in Fairfield County where he worked for two years as a farmhand. During that time he became an inveterate thief and when his reputation became insufferable he deemed it prudent to remove himself to Litchfield County. On July 14, 1765, Frasier broke into a store at Woodbury and carried off goods to considerable value. From there he beat a retreat to Orange County, New York, where he was taken up for a similar offense but broke jail. Heading eastward once again, Frasier crossed the border at Sharon, Connecticut, where he robbed another store. Arrested and sent to Litchfield jail, he broke out and returned to Newtown where he stole money from a woman. Nabbed shortly thereafter, Frasier was then sent to the Fairfield County jail from whence he made another successful escape. Back to Woodbury went Frasier where he robbed another store. Then he moved on to Waterbury where a goldsmith became his next target. Loaded down with items of precious metal, Frasier was pursued to Rhode Island and there arrested. He was then brought to New Haven and made to stand trial for burglary. Convicted, he was branded with a hot iron, severely whipped and also had his earlobes cut off. A short time later Frasier set a course for Boston but left a string of thefts in his wake. He broke into another store at Somers, Connecticut, shoplifted clothing at Pomfret and then went to Middlesex County in Massachusetts where he robbed two merchants in the same night. Then he headed westward. At Fishkill, New York, he added the crime of horse stealing to his record. Knowing

that he would incur the death penalty if he was caught in New York, Frasier rode the stolen horse all the way back to Boston. There he broke into another store. His next stop was Worcester where he was arrested for robbing a hatter. The Worcester County court sent Frasier to the whipping post. Then smarting from such treatment, Frasier broke out of jail before his sentence could be completed. He made his way back to Connecticut and robbed another store in Waterbury. Then he returned to Newtown where he did the same thing to the same woman who he had victimized there on a prior occasion. Not satisfied, he broke into a Newtown store on or about August 20, 1766. This time he was caught. Back to the Fairfield County jail went Frasier. He was brought before the Superior Court of that county and there convicted of burglary for a second time. As punishment he had the rest of his ears hacked off and was again branded with a hot iron. He was also whipped until his back was raw. After several days in agony Frasier again broke out of the Fairfield jail. He headed eastward. When he reached Boston he committed three burglaries in the same night. Taken up on a fugitive warrant, he broke out of jail and dared to return to Worcester where he committed three more burglaries. Then Frasier stole a horse but was pursued and taken into custody. Locked up at Worcester, he remained in irons for several months before he found a way to escape. The next stop for Frasier was Middletown, Connecticut, where he committed four burglaries in one night. After that he turned up at Norwalk where he ransacked another store. On March 28, 1768, it came the turn of another merchant at Fairfield. Frasier stole another horse there but a posse tracked him down. He was then returned to the Fairfield jail and charged with capital felony. Resenting the bad experiences he had had at Fairfield, Frasier found a way to set the jail on fire.

The blaze spread out of control and by the time it ran its course the jail, the courthouse and the guard quarters were completely destroyed. The Connecticut authorities could take no more. Frasier was sent to New Haven under heavy guard while the Fairfield officials pondered their loss. It was finally decided to convene a Special Court just to handle the case of Isaac Frasier. Back to Fairfield went Frasier and there he was sentenced to death as an incorrigible. Then Frasier managed to escape again. It seemed as if no jail could hold him. He made his way to Middletown where he broke into three stores and carried off all kinds of loot. His next stop was Charlestown, Massachusetts, where he was picked up for yet another burglary. Unaware of his record elsewhere, a Charlestown magistrate let Frasier go on bail. The wanted man then went to Shrewsbury and robbed a tavern there. Frasier was pursued and brought to Worcester where he was whipped as a common thief. It was there where Frasier was found by agents from Connecticut. He was then carried back to New Haven under heavy guard and kept under 24-hour surveillance. A warrant was then issued for the prompt execution of Isaac Frasier. Back to Fairfield went the condemned man and there he was finally hanged on September 7, 1768.

Negro Arthur, black, age 21. *Rape.* The crime was committed on January 1, 1767, at Rutland, Massachusetts. This offender was born at Taunton on January 15, 1747, as a slave in the house of one Richard Godfrey, Esq. According to his own account, Arthur spent the first 14 years of his life in the house where he was born. There he was well treated and even taught to read and write. A restless lad, Arthur ran away and went in search of adventure. He made his way to Cape Cod where he found refuge in a Native American settlement. It was there where the young runaway was introduced to his two ruling vices: liquor and sex. When he wore out his welcome on Cape Cod, Arthur set a course for Nantucket. There he was caught stealing and sent to the whipping post. Then he signed aboard a whaler and remained at sea for eight months. Upon returning, Arthur went to Taunton where he was cordially reunited with his master. For the next three years Arthur had liberty to sign aboard oceangoing ships and he accordingly made two or three voyages to the West Indies. In the autumn of 1764 he returned to Taunton once again but this time got into big trouble. He made indecent proposals to white women and was severely punished for that indiscretion. Once again Arthur went to the whipping post — this time to the tune of 39 hard lashes — and he was chained down for a while in the Taunton jail. When he was finally released he found that his master had turned against him; while that slaveowner had been willing to forgive a 14-year-old runaway, he could not find it in his heart to excuse Arthur's latest offense. The propositioning of white women was an entirely different matter; this time Arthur had broken a cardinal taboo and his master felt obliged to sell him. So off to the slave market went Arthur with a price tag around his neck. He was bought by a Rutland man named Captain Edward Clark and he remained the chattel of that person for the rest of his life. Captain Clark was a kind master but that did not stop Arthur from running away. He roamed as far as Middletown, Connecticut, committing numerous thefts. By the time he reached his former hideout on Cape Cod he had added six separate acts of horse stealing to his record. On the above date (January 19, 1767), Arthur was in the mood for female companionship; he went in search of an Indian woman with whom he was acquainted but found that she was out of town. Not one to be denied, Arthur then went to the house of a widow named Deborah Metcalf (white, age unknown) where he allegedly forced himself on the lone occupant. On the next day the victim went to Arthur's master and attempted to extort money from him. She said that she would forbear pressing a capital charge against Arthur if he was sold out of the colony. In addition to that, the woman demanded "suitable compensation" in the form of cash. Arthur's master opted to comply with this shakedown. He accordingly paid off the widow Metcalf and set out for New York with Arthur, intending to sell him there. In the meantime news of the alleged "rape" had reached the ears of authority and a warrant was issued for Arthur's arrest. He was overtaken on the road to New York and brought back to the Worcester County jail. When the case came to trial Arthur was convicted of capital felony. However, the court hesitated to pass sentence of death on him because the character of the alleged "victim" was reported to be less than honorable. Arthur then remained in jail for an entire year while the judges deliberated whether or not to grant him the Benefit of Clergy. During that time, however, the news of Arthur's many thefts trickled in. When the judges had a full report of them they took it as evidence that Arthur was an habitual criminal. This resulted in Arthur being denied the Benefit of Clergy for his sexual offense. A warrant was then issued for his execution. On October 20, 1768, thousands of people thronged Worcester Common to see Arthur hanged from the county gallows. The scene was long remembered by those in attendance.

Richard Ames, white, age unknown. *Army desertion.* The crime was committed in October of 1768 at Boston, Massachusetts. This man was a member of the 14th British regiment. In October of 1768 that body of troops arrived at Boston to do garrison duty there. Ames used the occasion to desert but he was caught before he got too far away. A court-martial decided that a special example was needed in order to overawe the other troops. For that reason Ames was sentenced to death. On October 31, 1768, the 14th Regiment was paraded on Boston Common and there obliged to witness the execution. Richard Ames was accordingly shot to death by a firing squad and buried where he fell.

John Jacob, Native American, age unknown. *Murder.* The crime was committed on February 15, 1768, at Litchfield, Connecticut. A resident of Farmington, this man and his wife decided to visit a Native American settlement near Litchfield for personal reasons. They reached their destination without incident and lodged in the wigwam of another Native American couple named James Chokerer and squaw. Apparently the two couples came from different tribes. The origin of John Jacob and wife is unknown but James Chokerer and his wife were reportedly members of the Schatacook tribe from nearby Kent. On the evening of the above date John Jacob suddenly picked up an axe and used it to strike James Chokerer a fatal blow on the head. The wives of both men were present at this time and they ran screaming through the neighborhood. This brought the local authorities to the scene where they had a hard time understanding the Indian language. When the situation was finally sorted out John Jacob admitted the murder. When asked why he did it he said because Chokerer was a "damned Schatacook." Jacob was charged with capital murder and convicted on his own confession. The female witnesses also gave their accounts of the crime to the local coroner but they were not called to testify at the trial. John Jacob was sentenced to death when the court found no mitigating factors to justify a lesser penalty. He was accordingly hanged at Litchfield on November 2, 1768.

Ruth Blay, white, age 25. *Murder.* The crime was committed on June 10, 1768, at South Hampton, New Hampshire. This celebrated case has long been rife with misinformation. A subject of folklore, it has had its facts twisted and romanticized by generations of storytellers to create a popular myth about innocence, wrongful execution and official misconduct. The truth, however, is quite different: Ruth Blay was undeniably guilty and the sheriff who officiated at her execution acted in strict accordance to his orders.

Ruth Blay was a seamstress who got pregnant out of wedlock. On the above date she went into a barn where she gave birth to a baby girl. She killed the infant by unspecified means and hid it in the barn. The remains were found there and four days later a coroner's inquest reported that the baby had "come to its death by violence."

Ruth Blay was brought to Portsmouth and tried before the August 1768 session of the Superior Court of Judicature on a charge of "private burial and concealment of her bastard child." The prosecution did not attempt to prove outright murder but instead limited itself to proving the fact of illegal concealment of a dead body—a capital crime in its own right because it implied murder. Ruth Blay was convicted by a jury and legally sentenced to death. A warrant was then issued for her execution to take place on November 24, 1768, between the hours of 12 o'clock noon and two o'clock in the afternoon. On November 23 the governor of New Hampshire issued a stay of execution which redirected the hanging to take place on December 9, 1768, "between the hours of ten o'clock in the morning and two o'clock in the afternoon." The hour of execution was moved up by two hours by order of the governor. On December 8 another stay was granted which reassigned the time of execution to December 23, 1768, without any change in hours. Hence the specified time of between ten o'clock in the morning and two o'clock in the afternoon remained in effect. On December 21 a third stay was issued which specifically fixed the time of execution at December 30, 1768, between the hours of ten o'clock in the morning and two o'clock in the afternoon — not an hour or two later as legend has it. The sheriff of Portsmouth accordingly carried out his orders in strict compliance with the letter of the death warrant and successive reprieves by hanging Ruth Blay shortly after ten o'clock in the morning of December 30, 1768, and he endorsed the back of the death warrant to that effect.

All of the aforesaid specifications as to dates and hours are clearly noted in the original documents of the Blay case located in the New Hampshire state archives. A popular fable which accuses the sheriff of acting improperly by moving up the time of the execution to suit his own schedule is apocryphal. On January 6, 1769, the *New Hampshire Gazette* reported the execution without any mention of irregular circumstances. It also reported that Ruth Blay signed a confession in the presence of three witnesses and that she met her end in a "very penitent" manner. If Ruth Blay was indeed innocent as legend says, she would not have signed a confession in front of three witnesses. Stories about her shrieking and screaming all the way to the gallows also ring false because hysterical behavior cannot be equated with the "very penitent manner" noted by the contemporary news account.

1770

William Lindsay, white, age unknown. *Burglary.* The crime was committed on September 8, 1770, at Lunenburg, Massachusetts. Little is known of this man aside from the fact that he was a roving thief. On June 18, 1770, he committed an act of grand larceny at Leominster and was accordingly sent to the whipping post. On the above date he went to Lunenburg and broke into the house of a citizen named Joseph Bellows. On that occasion Lindsay carried off loot consisting of the following: one beaverskin hat, one pair of leather breeches, two shirts, one pair of leather padded chaps, one pair of blue yarn stockings, one pair of men's shoes, one pair of metal shoe buckles, a set of garters, a set of knee buckles and several assorted pieces of linen. In addition, Lindsay went into the homeowner's larder and stole all his meats, being 30 lbs. of salted pork and 10 lbs. of salted beef. Since this robbery was made upon an inhabited dwelling during the nighttime hours Lindsay was charged with capital felony. He was convicted in short order and on October 25, 1770, he was hanged on Worcester Common.

William Shaw, white, age unknown. *Murder.* The crime was committed on September 14, 1770, at Springfield, Massachusetts. This man came from the town of Palmer. On the above date he was incarcerated in the county jail at Springfield on a misdemeanor charge. For some reason he turned against his cellmate, one Edward East by name (white, age unknown), and beat him to death with a piece of firewood. The charges pending against Shaw were upgraded to capital felony and he was condemned to be hanged. On the eve of his execution he was allowed some time alone with his wife. During that time the two changed into each other's clothes and Shaw walked past the guards undiscerned. Minutes later the trick was discovered and Shaw was hunted down before he could get out of town. He was executed the next morning on schedule. The place was Springfield, Massachusetts, and the date was December 13, 1770.

1771

Caesar Hazard, black, age about 16. *Aggravated assault.* The crime was committed on May 23, 1771, at North Kingston, Rhode Island. This case was a legal anomaly. Caesar was a slave belonging to Messrs. Robert and Gideon Hazard of North Kingston. He brooded when a young white boy named Benjamin Dealing (age about 12) accused him of stealing a rooster. On the above date Caesar armed himself with a wooden hedge stake and lay in wait for the boy who had gotten him in trouble. Benjamin Dealing was caught unawares and beaten without mercy. He remained in a coma for several days thereafter. What happened next was highly irregular. The prosecuting attorney decided that Caesar deserved the death penalty irrespective of the fact that Rhode Island law provided no such punishment for non-fatal assault. The right of eminent domain was then invoked in order to charge Caesar under an obscure *English* statute which had been passed in 1682 that permitted capital punishment for certain kinds of assault with intent to kill. This is possibly the only case in which an American colony superceded its own laws in order to secure the execution of a criminal defendant. Caesar was accordingly hanged at South Kingston on November 15, 1771. As he died he actually managed to repeat his crime. The force of his body jerking against the noose made the heavy ladder fall off the gallows. The falling ladder struck one of the spectators on the head, inflicting a life-threatening injury.

1772

Bryan Sheehan, white, age about 39. *Rape.* The crime was committed on September 15, 1771, at Marblehead, Massachusetts. This offender was born in Ireland and raised amid circumstances that were considered quite unorthodox: His father was a Roman Catholic and his mother a Protestant. The boys of the family were raised in their father's religion and the girls in that of their mother. This arrangement resulted in such discord that Bryan decided to leave Ireland altogether. At the age of 20 he signed aboard a fishing boat and went to Newfoundland. He then made his way southward to Boston where he entered the employ of a shipbuilder. There he found himself beset by religious problems once again; his employer required him to attend Protestant services and Sheehan, fearing the loss of his job, deemed it prudent to comply. Eventually the situation filled Sheehan with self-loathing and he resolved to go elsewhere. Maine was his destination of choice and it was there where he settled down and got married. The outbreak of the French and Indian War saw Sheehan enlisted in the army and he served for the duration of that conflict. He was not good about keeping in touch with his wife, however, and she was at length led to believe that he had died while on active service. There was mutual shock when Sheehan came home after six years only to find his wife remarried. He then gave his wife an ultimatum: choose which of her two husbands she would have on a permanent basis. The woman chose Sheehan but this did not end her marital problems. Sheehan could not reconcile himself to the fact that his wife had borne another man's child during his absence. He then walked out on the woman and made his way back to Massachusetts. It was at the town of Marblehead that Sheehan decided to make a fresh start. He took a room in a boarding house there and got a job in the local fishery. After a while Sheehan began to desire female company. He turned his sights on another lodger at his boarding house: a married woman named Abiel Hallowell (white, age unknown). Sheehan began to importune Mrs. Hallowell, first using flattery

and then offering her money. The woman indignantly refused the unwanted advances but Sheehan was determined. On the above date he forced his way into Mrs. Hallowell's room and beat the woman to within an inch of her life. Then he raped her repeatedly. Other residents of the boarding house finally tired of the victim's screams and came to her belated rescue. By then, however, the crime had already been committed. Sheehan was arrested and charged with capital felony. In his defense he admitted having sex with the victim but insisted that it was all consensual. A jury then considered the matter of the severe injuries suffered by the victim and refused to believe that those were also consensual. The verdict was guilty and the sentence was death. Nearly 12,000 people watched as Bryan Sheehan was hanged for his crime. The place was Salem, Massachusetts, and the date was January 16, 1772.

Moses Paul, Native American, age unknown. *Murder.* The crime was committed on December 7, 1771, at Bethany, Connecticut. This man was among the customers of a roadside tavern on the above date. He had too much to drink and was behaving obnoxiously. Because of this Paul was refused further service and told that he had better go home. Such an admonishment only made Paul more unruly. He demanded drink and made an ugly scene in doing so. The landlord then ejected him from the tavern for being drunk and disorderly. Paul felt that he had been ill-used. He swore that he would be avenged for such treatment and decided that he would kill the first person to step outside the tavern. He then armed himself with a heavy flatiron and lay in wait. Eventually one of the other tavern patrons prepared to go home for the night. It was a Waterbury man named Moses Cook (white, age unknown). When he stepped outside and began to untether his horse from the hitching post, Paul let out a war whoop and attacked him. Cook was caught by surprise and struck over the head with the heavy flatiron. The blow shattered his skull and he died shortly thereafter. The other customers ran out of the tavern and disarmed the killer. Paul was then brought to New Haven and charged with capital murder. He was convicted at the next session of the Superior Court. On September 2, 1772, thousands of people came to New Haven to see Moses Paul hanged. While thunder rumbled overhead the condemned man gave a speech in his native language (many of his tribesmen were present) denouncing the evils of alcoholism and vindictiveness and warning his fellow Native Americans to steer clear of those vices. Then he was put to death in the manner prescribed by law.

Solomon Goodwin, white, age unknown. *Murder.* The crime was committed on May 25, 1772, in Lincoln County, Maine. This man was a trapper who lived in the town of Bowdoinham, close to the Kennebec River. On the above date he was in a canoe with two other men proceeding up that waterway. One of the other men named David Wilson (white, age unknown) had a difference of opinion with Goodwin which escalated into an argument. Goodwin lost his temper and struck Wilson over the head with an oar. The blow knocked Wilson out of the canoe and into the water where he drowned. Goodwin did not make any effort to save him. The third member of the canoeing party reported Goodwin to the authorities. The result was a charge of capital murder. Goodwin was convicted when his case came to trial. He was hanged at Falmouth on November 12, 1772.

1773

Levi Aimes, white, age 21. *Burglary.* The crime was committed on August 27,

1773, at Boston, Massachusetts. This offender was the wayward scion of an otherwise respectable family in the Massachusetts town of Groton. As a teenager he was apprenticed to a tradesman but ran away and resolved to thereafter live by his wits. Eschewing honest work, young Aimes became a professional thief. His favorite targets were the shops of small merchants and he broke into dozens of them. In many cases the booty that he reaped was paltry: a few coppers, a hat, a handkerchief, a pair of shoes and so on. However, there were other times when the pickings were rich enough to support him for months on end. Aimes also stole horses which he used to extend his range. Sometimes he went as far as Connecticut and Rhode Island in his search for loot. One day while loaded down with stolen goods Aimes happened to pass by a gallows. The sight disturbed him and, according to his own words, he was seized with a premonition of his fate. Aimes saw himself hanging on that same gallows and the vision frightened him so badly that he decided to reform. He accordingly went looking for a job but was disappointed when no one would hire him. His lack of personal references counted against him as did his unsavory reputation. Discouraged and low on money once again, Aimes returned to the only occupation that he knew: professional thievery. He stole from gardens to feed himself and he stole from clotheslines to keep himself dressed. Aimes snatched pies from window sills and he raided fruit orchards at night. One day he went to Lexington and added sacrilege to his record; there he broke into the house of the local minister and stole some sacred vessels along with the family silver. Public indignation ran high when his theft became known. Aimes headed for Boston where he lost himself in the crowds. On the above date he teamed up with another ne'er-do-well named Joseph Atwood and broke into the house of a rich merchant named Martin Becker. There they found a cache of gold and silver coins totaling more than £60 in value. In the days that followed this heist Aimes thought that he had made a successful haul. Never before had he been so flush with money. Atwood, however, was careless; when he tried to change some of the stolen gold he aroused suspicion. When questioned as to how it was that an urchin had such wealth, he sheepishly admitted the burglary and named Levi Aimes as his accomplice. When Aimes was arrested he found that Atwood had already made a deal to testify against him. A conviction for capital felony was thereby assured. On October 21, 1773, a bound and shackled Levi Aimes was put into a tumbrel and drawn to the same gallows that had so badly frightened him several weeks earlier. There he was hanged by the neck until dead, his premonition fulfilled. Thousands of Bostonians were on hand to see him die.

1774

Daniel Wilson, white, age 24. *Rape.* The crime was committed on December 6, 1773, at Smithfield, Rhode Island. This offender was born at Bellingham, Massachusetts, on June 25, 1749. He lived with his parents till the age of 17 when he was apprenticed to a carpenter. By the age of 21 he was an independent housebuilder in his own right. It was not until the age of 23 that Wilson came into conflict with the law. At that point in his life he became acquainted with some men of poor character. The result was several incidents of burglary and horse theft. Wilson was caught more often than not but escaped the full penalty of the law each time by settling the matters in private. One of his cronies was an unprincipled young man named Joseph White. Together Wilson and White conspired to entice a young woman named

Dorcas Arnold (white, age 18). When cajolery failed to have its desired effect on Miss Arnold, the two men decided to entrap her. On the above date White went to Miss Arnold's home and said that he had an urgent message: an old woman who she usually nursed was very ill and needed her help. Dorcas Arnold was fooled by this and she agreed to follow White to a local ferry landing because such was the way to the old woman's house. When they reached the ferry landing they found that the keeper of the ferry boat had closed down for the night. White was previously aware of this and he directed Dorcas Arnold to a nearby house, saying that the ferry keeper lived there and that he would certainly agree to take her across the water given the nature of her situation. When Dorcas Arnold knocked on the door a voice bade her to enter the house. When she did so she found no ferry keeper but rather Daniel Wilson waiting there. At once the young woman surmised the true situation. She turned to leave but the two men barred her way. White and Wilson then overpowered Miss Arnold and stripped her naked. Then they dragged her into a bedroom where Wilson forced himself on her. The rape continued for half an hour while White stood watch outside the house. White also hammered on the house all the while (pretending he was mending it) in order to drown out the sound of the victim's protestations. When Wilson had finally had his fill he left the victim where she lay and threatened her with death if she dared to report what had happened. Then Wilson told White that it was his turn. As the other man was preparing to pick up where Wilson had left off, Dorcas Arnold saw a chance to escape. She jumped out a window and ran as fast as she could. Her screams aroused the entire neighborhood. The men of the place chased down the culprits when they heard the young woman's story. Once in custody, White admitted the part he had played in the crime. Wilson eventually confessed as well. When the case came to trial Wilson was convicted of capital felony and sentenced to death. White was convicted as an accessory but was spared the death penalty because he had not had sexual intercourse with the victim. Wilson managed to break jail no less than three times while he was awaiting execution. On two of those occasions he got as far as Connecticut before he was taken by hue and cry. On April 29, 1774, more than 12,000 people watched as Wilson was hanged at Providence, Rhode Island.

Valentine Duckett, white, age unknown. *Army desertion.* The crime was committed sometime during the year 1772 in or near Boston, Massachusetts. This man had been a soldier in the British 59th Regiment when it was stationed in eastern Massachusetts. He deserted and remained at large for two years before being caught at Boston in August of 1774. A court-martial condemned him to be shot to death by musketry. The sentence was carried out on Boston Common on September 9, 1774.

William Ferguson, white, age 28. *Army desertion.* The crime was committed during the autumn of 1774 at Boston, Massachusetts. This man was a soldier in the British 10th Regiment. Formerly stationed in Quebec, that regiment had been reassigned to Boston late in 1774. It was there and then that this William Ferguson deserted. He was caught and sentenced to death by a court-martial. A firing squad executed him on Boston Common on December 24, 1774.

1777

Moses Dunbar, white, age about 40. *Treason.* The crime was committed throughout the course of the year 1776 in Connecticut. This offender was a British sympathizer who lived at Waterbury. When the Revolutionary War broke out he refused to espouse the American cause. Instead, he went over to the enemy and offered his services thereto. Dunbar was then authorized to act as a recruiting agent for the British and he returned to Connecticut for that purpose. He was caught behind the American lines and initially charged with espionage and sedition. When it was discovered that he was a Connecticut man the charge was upgraded to treason against his homeland. Dunbar was tried and condemned by the Hartford County Superior Court. He was accordingly hanged at Hartford on March 19, 1777.

Daniel Griswold, white, age unknown. *Espionage and treason.* The crime was committed in the spring of 1777 in the vicinity of New Haven, Connecticut. This man was a British sympathizer who agreed to act as a secret agent behind enemy lines during the Revolutionary War. He was detected near New Haven and found to be a Connecticut man who had previously gone over to the enemy. A court-martial was called to hear his case and decided that he was guilty of espionage and treason, both of which were hanging offenses, especially in wartime. Daniel Griswold was accordingly executed at New Haven on May 5, 1777.

John Hart, white, age unknown. *Espionage, treason and sedition.* The crimes were committed in the spring of 1777 in and around Rhode Island. This man had once been a resident of Otter Creek, a settlement in Rhode Island. He was a British sympathizer who agreed to act as a secret agent against the American cause early in the Revolutionary War. He made his way to New York City after that place had been occupied by the British. There he was trained for the dangerous assignment of spreading counterfeit money behind the American lines. He was eventually nabbed at Exeter, Rhode Island, and found to be carrying a batch of bogus currency. A court-martial met at Providence to hear his case. The verdict was swift and thorough: death within 24 hours. John Hart was accordingly hanged at Providence on May 17, 1777.

William Stone, white, age unknown. *Espionage, treason and sedition.* The crimes were committed during the spring of 1777 in the vicinity of Hartford, Connecticut. This man was a British sympathizer who came to Connecticut in the capacity of an enemy agent. He doubled as a spy and recruiting officer. When it was learned that he had been a Connecticut resident he was also charged with treason. A court-martial condemned him to death. He was accordingly executed by hanging at Hartford on May 28, 1777.

Robert Thompson, white, age unknown. *Espionage, treason and sedition.* The crimes were committed during the spring of 1777 in the vicinity of Danbury, Connecticut. This man was a British sympathizer who came from Newtown, Connecticut. He was condemned by a court-martial for going over to the enemy and coming forth therefrom in the capacities of a spy and recruiting agent. General Samuel Parsons presided over the tribunal which heard this case. Since Newtown was then regarded as a hotbed of loyalist sentiment, it was decided that Thompson should be executed there as a warning. He was accordingly hanged at his hometown on June 9, 1777.

John Dennis, white, age unknown. *Murder.* The crime was committed on December 31, 1776, at New London, Connecticut. This man was a petulant mariner who lived in the seaport town of New London. On the above date he got

into a squabble with a colleague named William Garrick (white, age unknown) and knocked him over the head with a hoe. The sharp-edged tool fractured Garrick's skull and the man died after 18 days in a coma. Dennis was then charged with capital murder. It being wartime, the trial of Dennis was moved inland to Norwich. There the New London County Superior Court felt safe from enemy attack. It was there where he was hanged on August 6, 1777. A wife and five small children were left destitute by his execution.

Thomas Lake, white, age unknown. *Army desertion.* The crime was committed in September of 1777 at or near Boston, Massachusetts. Little is known of this case except that it is a rare instance wherein an American army deserter was executed by hanging instead of by firing squad. Since hanging was considered far more shameful than the other mode of execution, we may presume that the crime(s) of Thomas Lake were of an aggravated nature. He met his end on Boston Common on October 6, 1777.

1778

John Fretter, white, age unknown. *Army desertion and bounty jumping.* The crimes were committed in the spring of 1778 at or near Providence, Rhode Island. This man was a three-time recidivist who had been spared from two previous death sentences through official clemency. On at least three known occasions he enlisted in the American army for the sake of bounty money only to desert and reenlist elsewhere under a false name for additional money. On the third occasion Fretter conspired with a sentry named Jotham Sayer to desert from the American camp at Providence, Rhode Island. Both men were apprehended while making their way towards the enemy lines. A court-martial sentenced Fretter to death. Sayer was given 100 lashes at the whipping post and forced to watch as a firing squad executed Fretter. The scene was a parade ground near Providence. The date was May 28, 1778.

David Redding, white, age unknown. *Treason and sedition.* The crime was committed over a period of time from 1776 to 1778 mostly in Vermont. This is a poorly documented case of a British sympathizer (i.e., "Tory" or "Loyalist"), who was executed for engaging in activities inimical to the cause of American independence. The exact details of what Redding did are unknown but they probably involved offenses such as spying, acting as a guide for the enemy, marauding and disseminating counterfeit money — the usual crimes of people so accused. David Redding was hanged at Bennington on June 11, 1778.

William Brooks, white, age 37. **James Buchanan,** white, age 30. **Ezra Ross,** white, age 16. **Bathsheba Spooner,** white, age 32. *Murder.* The crime was committed on March 1, 1778, at Brookfield, Massachusetts. A lot of misinformation exists about this celebrated case. Of the hundreds of female defendants who have been legally put to death throughout the course of American history, Bathsheba Spooner was probably the most socially prominent. As the daughter of a general and the granddaughter of a minister, she enjoyed privileges and opportunities beyond those available to most other women of her time. She was pedigreed, beautiful, educated and wealthy. She was also a schemer, a catalyst, a liar, an adulteress and a child-seducer.

Bathsheba was born at Sandwich, Massachusetts, on February 13, 1746, the daughter of Timothy Ruggles, Esq., and Madam Bershaba Ruggles. Her father was an esteemed jurist who also held the rank of brigadier general in the British army. When Bathsheba was eight years old her parents relocated to the town of Hardwick where her father gained further laurels by becoming chief justice of the Worcester County Court of Common Pleas.

Timothy Ruggles was a worldly and autocratic man. He arrogated to himself the choice of who his daughter could marry. It was thus at the age of 19 that Bathsheba Ruggles found herself unwillingly paired with a man she loathed: 56-year-old Joshua Spooner of Brookfield. It mattered nothing to Timothy Ruggles that his son-in-law was nearly three times his daughter's age. The question of Bathsheba's happiness was of little concern to him. What did matter was the fact that Joshua Spooner was loaded with money.

Early in the year 1766 the marriage took place. Bathsheba Ruggles became Bathsheba Spooner and moved to her husband's house in Brookfield. There she forced herself to act the part of a dutiful, loving wife. She also forced herself to bear four children by her aging spouse. It was only after ten unhappy years that the scene suddenly changed; the American Revolution had begun and politics took a hand in Bathsheba's life. Joshua Spooner embraced the American cause but Timothy Ruggles did not. The result was that Bathsheba's father was banished for being a loyalist. With his restraining influence gone, his daughter was left free to manifest her true feelings for her husband.

As Joshua Spooner was by this time too old to join the American army (he was in his late sixties), he aided the Patriot cause as best he could by entertaining Continental soldiers as they passed through Brookfield. One such visitor was a 16-year-old boy from Ipswich named Ezra Ross.

This Ezra Ross had been born at Ipswich on July 20, 1761, to a respectable couple named Jabez and Joanna Ross. He was the 14th out of a brood of 15 children. He was also extremely handsome. Bathsheba Spooner noticed this physical aspect of Ezra Ross and felt herself drawn to him. The fact that she was twice his age did not deter her. She saw to it that her young visitor received the best of hospitality and Ezra Ross thereafter made it a point to return to the Spooner home whenever he had a furlough. January of 1778 found him there again. At the invitation of both Bathsheba and Joshua Spooner (the latter was genuinely fond of Ross) the young soldier wound up staying longer than usual. This was what Bathsheba Spooner had been awaiting. She worked her charms on Ezra Ross and seduced him. Then when the two had become regular lovers she turned her mind to thoughts of mariticide.

As Bathsheba Spooner and Ezra Ross were frequently seen in public together some gossips brought the matter to Joshua Spooner's attention. He scoffed at any suggestions of impropriety. Mr. Spooner naively reasoned that neither his wife nor his guest were capable of what the gossips said. Bathsheba was a seasoned woman of 32 and Ross was only a young lad of 16, he thought. Joshua Spooner seemed to have forgotten that he himself had been aged 56 when he married a young woman of 19.

Meanwhile the two lovers grew closer to each other. Then one day Bathsheba Spooner got up the nerve to broach the subject of eliminating her husband. Ezra Ross flinched at such a suggestion. He refused to commit himself. So Mrs. Spooner made a plan: she declared an open house to travelers (regardless of their political persuasion) in the hope of finding some mercenary hands to do her bidding.

Her patience was rewarded in February of 1778 when two British deserters came to her house. Their names were William Brooks and James Buchanan and it did not take long for their hostess to recognize them as being the type to

suit her purpose. Mrs. Spooner considered them to be perfect pawns; both were enemy aliens who she could easily blame for what she had in mind. She also surmised that they would hastily leave the area after they had killed the intended victim. So Mrs. Spooner lodged Brooks and Buchanan for an entire fortnight at her own expense. (She had to put them up at an inn when her husband ordered them out of his house.) Then by degrees she worked her powers of persuasion on them until she succeeded in igniting their avarice. She told them that her husband had a strongbox full of money which they could have if they did away with the owner.

By March 1, 1778, all was in readiness. That night Joshua Spooner stayed late at the local tavern while the conspirators positioned themselves around his house. Shortly before midnight he came walking home. As he crossed his front yard Brooks sprang from a concealed position and knocked him down. Then Brooks throttled Mr. Spooner with his bare hands while Buchanan and Ezra Ross (who had by then overcome his qualms) stripped the valuables from the victim's person. Then all three of the male conspirators picked up the unconscious man and heaved him head-first down a well. The assassins next went into the house where Mrs. Spooner gave them her husband's cashbox. The contents thereof were immediately divided. Then just as the female catalyst had anticipated, Brooks and Buchanan made haste to get out of town.

On the following day Joshua Spooner was conspicuous by his absence. A search was made for him and his body was found in the well. Brooks and Buchanan were suspected because of their flight and also because they were known to have been disliked by the decedent. A hue and cry was raised throughout the countryside. Brooks and Buchanan were detained at Worcester. They had difficulty explaining who they were and why they were in the area. They also had a hard time explaining the presence of nearly a thousand silver coins in their backpacks together with a watch and a set of shoe buckles bearing Joshua Spooner's monogram. Both suspects made contradictory statements which also incriminated Bathsheba Spooner and her teenage lover. All four were arrested and charged with capital murder.

On April 3, 1778, a grand jury handed up a quadruple indictment. The trial opened three weeks later. Mrs. Spooner, Brooks and Ezra Ross at first stood firm in their denials but Buchanan unexpectedly broke down and confessed everything. Faced with that development, the other two male defendants also admitted their guilt. Only Bathsheba Spooner remained unshaken.

Three confessions wrapped up the case for the prosecution. All four defendants were found guilty. In the case of Ezra Ross his age and service record were offered as mitigating factors but they failed to sway the jury in his favor. Subsequent petitions for mercy in his case were likewise rejected. Bathsheba Spooner pleaded pregnancy by Ezra Ross. With the gallows as her only alternative she felt no shame in declaring herself the paramour of a 16-year-old boy. Two separate physical examinations failed to confirm the pregnancy, however (although an autopsy would later reveal a different story), and a warrant for the execution of Mrs. Spooner was issued along with those of her confederates. On July 2, 1778, a throng of many thousands jammed Worcester Common to witness the rare sight of a quadruple hanging. Thunder rumbled ominously overhead as all four prisoners swung to their doom.

Thomas Steele, white, age unknown. *Army desertion and bounty jumping.* The crimes were committed over a period of time between 1776 and 1778. The true

name of this man is unknown; he was condemned under a pseudonym. He was said to have an extensive criminal record above and beyond that which brought about his execution. The immediate charges against him were repeated desertion from the American army and fraudulent reenlistment therein for the sake of monetary inducements. He is known to have pulled such a trick at least five times before his final apprehension. Among his many aliases were Steele, Williams, Harrison and Thomas Winthrop. As he walked to his execution he divulged that the initials of his true name were "R.I." A firing squad ended this man's career on July 7, 1778. The scene was Boston Common.

Elisha Smith, white, age unknown. *Army desertion and treason.* The crimes were committed during the summer of 1778 along the Connecticut–New York border. This man came from Litchfield, Connecticut. He had served in the American army but deserted and went over to the enemy in New York City. There he joined the British forces and bore arms against his fellow countrymen. For some unknown reason Smith deserted from the British ranks in October of 1778 and came back over to the American side. There he was recognized by members of his former regiment who were stationed at Greenwich, Connecticut. A court-martial was called to handle the matter. Smith was then convicted of willful desertion and treasonable misconduct. He was hanged in the American camp near Greenwich sometime during the last week of October, 1778.

John Blair and **David Farnsworth,** whites, ages unknown. *Espionage and sedition.* Their crimes were committed in October of 1778 near Danbury, Connecticut. These men were British sympathizers who took part in a mission to ruin the American economy by flooding it with counterfeit money. Nothing is known of Blair's antecedents but Farnsworth is said to have come from Lunenburg, Massachusetts. Both men had gone to the British in New York City shortly after the occupation of that place in 1776. There they were trained to act as secret agents behind enemy lines. Both of them were arrested by American sentries and brought to the regional headquarters at Danbury. In their saddlebags were found more than 700 coins of various gold denominations which upon closer examination turned out to be cast from an alloy of copper and zinc. A court-martial was called to try both men on capital charges. Both were convicted and sent to Hartford under heavy guard. They were hanged there on November 3, 1778.

John Bushby, white, age unknown. *Army desertion.* The crime was committed in the autumn of 1778 near Providence, Rhode Island. This offender was a three-time recidivist who had been spared from two previous death sentences. His last known assignment was that of a private in Colonel Vose's Rhode Island regiment. Twice before Bushby had been condemned by court-martials for willful desertion. A third offense committed on the heels of the previous two was one time too many. Bushby was again condemned and this time the sentence stuck. He was executed by firing squad at Providence on November 23, 1778.

1779

Edward Jones, white, age unknown. *Espionage.* **John Smith,** white, age unknown. *Army desertion.* Their crimes were committed in January of 1779 in Fairfield County, Connecticut. During the winter of 1779 an American army under General Israel Putnam lay encamped near the village of Redding, Connecticut. It was well known that this particular general had a low tolerance level for spies and deserters. On February 4 he convened a special court-martial to adjudicate several cases of military crime that had arisen in the preceding weeks. On the docket were two capital cases: those of the above-named Edward Jones and John Smith. The first of these men was a known loyalist (Tory) who came from the nearby town of Ridgefield. He had been found within the American lines under circumstances that were regarded as suspicious. Jones did not deny that he was a loyalist. He said that since he was a butcher by trade he had accepted an assignment from the British to go out into the countryside for the purpose of buying cattle. He claimed to be a mere provisioner who was going about his business. The court-martial did not believe this story. Jones was convicted of willfully going over to the enemy and coming forth therefrom as a spy. The penalty was death by hanging.

John Smith had been a private in the 1st Connecticut regiment. He was convicted of willful and deliberate desertion with intent to go over to the enemy. The penalty was death by firing squad. On the morning of February 8, 1779, the American forces under General Putnam were mustered forth to witness the executions. Both were carried out near Redding with no hitches.

Robert Young, white, age 29. *Rape.* The crime was committed on September 6, 1779, at Brookfield, Massachusetts. This man was a sex addict who was hanged for forcing himself on an 11-year-old girl. Born in Ireland, Young was the son of a respectable merchant. His father groomed him to follow in the family business and for that reason saw to it that the boy was credibly educated. The elder Young also arranged for his son to gain practical experience by placing him with a large wholesaler in Dublin. It was at the age of 15 that Robert Young made his transition to the big city and it was shortly thereafter that he discovered his carnal obsession. Dublin teemed with prostitutes and the teenage clerk was drawn to their company. He became their steady customer. It was during this same period that Young seduced one of his employer's female domestics. Then fearing discovery by his boss, the up and coming cad arranged for the woman to be fired from her job. After several months in Dublin it became impossible for Young to conceal his lifestyle. Such was his notoriety. When his employer learned of the situation he was scandalized. Young was severely reprimanded and threatened with dismissal unless he reformed. His answer was to quit his job and join the army. For the better part of a year Young remained assigned to the Dublin garrison. He was therefore able to continue his bad habits in the local haunts of vice. Still a teenager, Young next had to deal with the inevitable: he caught a venereal infection which plagued him for the rest of his life. At the age of 16 he was transferred to the Isle of Man and remained there for three years. During that time he continued to squander his pay in dens of ill repute. He also promised marriage to at least three local girls while on the Isle of Man. However, he deserted each of them in turn, leaving them pregnant and diseased. Young's next assignment was with the garrison of Gibraltar where he remained for several years and — to use his own words — "gave up to all manner of debauchery." The precise details are redundant. In the spring of 1777 the New World beckoned Young; he joined an expedition under General John Burgoyne and was sent to Canada. There he wooed a comely widow and left her in the same condition as he had many other gullible women. He also decamped with the widow's money when his regiment marched southward. Young went along with General Burgoyne on the ill-fated Saratoga campaign. He saw hard fighting

in the course thereof but did not become a casualty. In the wake of that expedition's defeat Young deserted and made his way to Massachusetts. There he concealed the fact of his British army service and passed himself off as an itinerant schoolteacher. He went from town to town leaving a trail of ruined women behind him. The fact that he carried and knowingly spread an infectious disease did not scruple Young in the least. After several months he settled at the town of Brookfield in the capacity of a schoolmaster. It was also there where he became affianced to a young woman named Anne Green. She soon found herself in the same condition as had many other females of Young's acquaintance. Then when Anne Green went to seek a cure, Young turned his attention to her little sister, Jane Green (white, age 11), and did the same thing to her. This time Young went too far. Jane Green told her outraged parents all that had happened between her and the schoolmaster. Young was arrested and confessed that he had "basely used" the 11-year-old girl. It was enough to bring him to court on a charge of capital felony. The verdict was guilty and the sentence was death by hanging. Robert Young was accordingly executed on Worcester Common. The date was November 11, 1779.

1780

Barnett Davenport, white, age 19. *Murder.* The crime was committed on February 4, 1780, at Washington, Connecticut. This teenage offender was born at New Milford on October 25, 1760, and raised amid conditions which may or may not have contributed to his delinquency. He never went to school. He never learned to read or write. He never received any religious instruction and he was never taught to respect the rights and property of others. Davenport was amoral. He had little sense of right and wrong and absolutely no sense of decency. The most salient of his features, however, was an innate malevolence; he was *evil* by nature and the story of his life (as told by himself) provides ample proof of that fact.

Davenport was turned out by his parents at the age of nine. He then began residencies in a series of foster homes. He never stayed long at one location because he either ran away or was told to go elsewhere. The foster families were unable to endure (and unwilling to tolerate) the boy's coarse, ill-bred ways. He was disrespectful, irascible, lewd, profane, dissolute and completely ungovernable. He was also an habitual thief, a shirker of his duty, a liar, a cheat and a schemer. Thoughts of murder first entered Davenport's mind at the age of 14 (according to his own account), and for the rest of his life he nursed a fascination for bloodshed and carnage. The outbreak of the American Revolution provided an opportunity for the young man to glut such fantasies and it was with such in mind that he made haste to join the army.

The autumn of 1776 saw the 16-year-old Davenport enlisted in a Massachusetts regiment. He went on the march to Fort Ticonderoga. He took part in the battles of Hobartown and Monmouth. He also served under George Washington at Valley Forge. And then there was the dark side: insubordination, looting, robbing the dead, theft of military stores, vandalism, marauding, stealing from his fellow soldiers and abusing civilians. He also deserted on more than one occasion. It was while a fugitive from his regiment (in November of 1779) that Davenport stole a horse and headed for his home territory of Litchfield County, Connecticut. There he appeared at the newly named town of Washington and sought shelter at the house of an aging squire named Caleb Mallory. According to Davenport's confession, he was taken into the Mallory home "out of pity and compassion" and provided with good clothing, good food, a comfortable place to stay and a job as the squire's hired man. How Davenport repaid his benefactor is remembered in the town of Washington to this day.

Caleb Mallory and his wife, Jane Mallory (whites, aged about 60), lived in what is known as the Romford Valley, a small but fertile tract which yielded rich crops. The place was secluded and naturally attractive. The native peoples had regarded the valley as holy ground, calling it "The land where the sweet waters join" (being the confluence of the Bantam and Shepaug rivers), and for centuries they had held their powwows there and used it as a trading place. It was also a center for the manufacture of arrowheads. A posh private school called "Rumsey Hall" now occupies the site. During the American Revolution, however, this valley was the domain of Caleb Mallory. There it was that the renegade Barnett Davenport found refuge.

According to Davenport's own words, he soon "determined upon the murder of Mr. Mallory and his family merely for the sake of plundering their house." He waited for a day when the Mallorys were at home with only their three young granddaughters — none of whom were capable of much physical resistance.

Shortly after midnight on the above date Davenport stealthily entered the master bedroom with a large wooden club. He then attacked the elder Mallorys as they lay in their bed. The couple were severely bludgeoned. Davenport kept hitting the victims until his weapon literally splintered into pieces. A seven-year-old granddaughter (Anne Mallory) was treated in the same way when Davenport found her sleeping in the same room. When he thought that the victims were dead (they were beaten beyond recognition), the killer began a thorough ransacking of the house. In another room he found two other grandchildren

(Elizabeth and Rachel Mallory, ages six and four), who were frightened and crying. Davenport tucked them into their bed and told them to go to sleep. Then he picked up an iron corn pestle (a formidable weapon when misused) and returned to the master bedroom where he once again battered the bodies of the three decedents, making absolutely sure that they were not only dead but thoroughly mangled. Finding himself soaked with blood and other gore, Davenport paused to bathe. Then he dressed himself in Mr. Mallory's finest clothes and set the house on fire before absconding with his loot. The house burned to the ground and the two other grandchildren who he had not slain outright perished in the blaze. It is said that their screams can still be heard on certain nights. In all, five people had been murdered.

From the scene of the crime Davenport went to New Milford where he looked up his younger brother, Nicholas Davenport (age 17), and entrusted him with some of the valuables that he had stolen from the Mallorys. Then he made his way to Cornwall where he hid out in the caves. Soon there was a hue and cry throughout the countryside. Barnett Davenport, the hired man of the murdered Mallorys, was suspected of the crime. He was soon reported at Cornwall and a posse pounced on him when he tried to leave the area. Nicholas Davenport was also arrested and charged with complicity.

A special court was called to try the Davenport brothers. Barnett the killer pled guilty to five counts of capital murder. Nicholas was convicted in a lesser degree. On May 8, 1780, Barnett Davenport was brought to the gallows at Litchfield. There he was hanged. His brother was forced to watch him die. Then the younger Davenport was given 39 lashes and made to sit upon the gallows with a rope around his neck for the space of one hour—a mark of extreme shame in those days. This was followed by ten years of hard labor in the mines.

Jeremiah Braun, white, age unknown. *Treason.* The crime was committed in the summer of 1780 along the Maine frontier. This man is described as having been a "Tory"—that is to say, an American who did not support the cause of independence during the Revolutionary War. Some Tories actively aided the British and Jeremiah Braun was one such person. He acted as a scout for a British raiding party which devastated the countryside in what is now the state of Maine. Eventually Braun was captured. He was brought to the camp of an American general named Peleg Wadsworth and there identified as an active Tory. The general convened a court-martial to try Braun for his crimes. The verdict was guilty and the sentence was death. Braun was accordingly hanged at Thomaston on August 28, 1780.

James Duncan, white, age unknown. *Army desertion.* The crime was committed in the summer of 1780 near Newport, Rhode Island. This man is said to have been a "soldier" (probably a private) in an American army regiment commanded by a Colonel Greene and stationed near Newport. A court-martial condemned him to be shot to death by musketry for willfully deserting his regiment in wartime. The execution was carried out at Newport on September 19, 1780.

1781

Alexander McDowell, white, age unknown. *Army desertion.* The crime was committed on an unknown date in the vicinity of Hartford, Connecticut. This is an extremely rare case in which an *officer* of the American army was put to death for violating military law. McDowell is described as having held the rank of lieutenant. He is also reported

to have filled the position of adjutant in a regiment commanded by a Colonel Wells. For some unknown reason McDowell deserted from the American forces and went over to the enemy. He was eventually captured and brought before a court-martial. Sentence of death was passed on him. On March 21, 1781, he was executed at Hartford. The precise method of his execution is unspecified in the contemporary accounts of the case. However, he was probably hanged due to the fact that his offense was treasonous.

Unidentified Man, white, age unknown. *Mutiny and insubordination.* The crime was committed on an unknown date at Newport, Rhode Island. This offender is described as having been a sergeant in the French army. He was attached to an artillery company which was stationed at Newport. A court-martial condemned him to death for attempting to murder a superior officer. No other details are known. The execution took place at Newport on June 1, 1781, and was probably done by firing squad.

Michael Lobidal, white, age unknown. *Murder.* The crime was committed on June 13, 1781, at Springfield, Massachusetts. This offender is described as a "Frenchman." He was playing cards in a Springfield tavern on the day that he committed his capital crime. Trying his luck against Lobidal was an Irish fellow named James McMullen (white, age unknown). Somehow the two men got into an argument over their card game and they squared off for a fight. The landlord then warned them that they had better take their troubles outside. Accordingly, Lobidal and McMullen stepped out into the street where they went to fisticuffs. In the heat of the battle Lobidal is said to have pulled out a "long knife" and to have given his adversary a "cowardly thrust in the breast" with it, thus bringing about McMullen's

untimely demise. Lobidal was then arrested and charged with capital murder. He was hanged at Springfield on November 8, 1781.

1783

William Huggins, white, age 23. **John Mansfield,** white, age 22. *Burglary.* The crime was committed on October 3, 1782, at Harvard, Massachusetts. These young men came from New York and Maine respectively. Huggins served credibly with the American army during the Revolutionary War. He was honorably discharged in the summer of 1782 and went to Stockbridge, Massachusetts, where he got a job on a farm. It was there where he met John Mansfield, who had wandered that far in a destitute state after escaping from a British prison ship. Huggins and Mansfield gravitated toward each other and soon became friendly. When the former said that he hated farm work the latter suggested that they go to Salem and sign aboard a privateer. Huggins agreed to accompany Mansfield on such a quest. But how? Both were penniless and could not afford to make the journey. They then decided to "finance their venture with the resources of other people" which was their polite way of saying that they would rely on the proceeds of thievery. Setting out from Stockbridge, the young adventurers set an eastward course. They begged for food along the way and stole from gardens when they were rebuffed. Eventually they came to a place called "Pelham" (a long defunct settlement in Hampshire County) and invaded the house of a Mr. and Mrs. Gray. After tying the man to his bed and locking the woman in a root cellar, the intruders ransacked the house for valuables. They found only a watch and some clothes with which they hurriedly decamped. Continuing eastward, Huggins and Mansfield entered Worcester

County and came to the town of Harvard. There they put up at an inn which was operated by one Silas Parkhurst. During the course of their stay, they noted the place where the innkeeper kept his money. Late on the following night they returned to the inn unobserved. Mansfield forced a window and slipped into the place while Huggins remained on watch outside. He entered the personal living quarters of the innkeeper while that man and his family lay sleeping. Then he took a cashbox containing a silver watch and coins to the amount of £4. Both of the burglars escaped from the scene as deftly as they had come. However, on the following day there was a hue and cry following discovery of the theft. Huggins and Mansfield were arrested at Concord and found to have the stolen goods in their possession. Both were charged with capital felony — in this case burglary in the first degree — which was defined as the forcible entry of an inhabited dwelling during the nighttime hours for the purpose of theft. A dual conviction followed. Huggins and Mansfield both admitted their guilt and were genuinely contrite. Both also said that their names were pseudonyms which they went by in order to spare their families the disgrace which they would have otherwise brought upon them had they divulged their real names. On June 19, 1783, both of these young men were hanged on Worcester Common.

1784

Cassumo Garcelli, white, age 23. *Murder.* The crime was committed on November 6, 1783, at Boston, Massachusetts. This man was an Italian sailor who killed another man in a tavern brawl. On the above date Garcelli was enjoying a shore leave with several of his fellow crewmen. They found their way to a public house operated by a Mr. Vose

and went inside. There the sailors called for a drink and joined in a round of dancing. As the time passed and the liquor continued to flow, Garcelli and his friends became quite jolly. Then one of the sailors tried to get fresh with a woman of the place. She shouted for help and from that moment on chaos reigned in the tavern. Some local men sought to defend the woman and they fought with the group of sailors. Garcelli and his companions pulled knives on their antagonists and leapt to the attack. A local man named John Johnson (white, age unknown) was fatally stabbed. The sailors then fled from the scene and most of them made good their escape. Garcelli was not so fortunate; he was arrested the following day and identified by multiple witnesses as one of the men who had stabbed John Johnson. Following his conviction for capital felony, Garcelli made a confession in which he revealed that he was guilty of two other murders, one in Puerto Rico and another aboard a ship at sea. He was hanged on Boston Common on January 15, 1784.

Francis Coven, white, age 22. *Burglary.* The crime was committed on June 4, 1784, at Boston, Massachusetts. This young man was born and raised in the south of France. He came to Boston in 1782 probably as a member of the French expeditionary forces which were then aiding the cause of American independence. In November of that same year he was brought up on charges of robbing a house in Roxbury and for mugging a Bostonian named James Parke. In addition to that, Coven broke jail twice but was caught each time before he got far. He wound up enduring a term of imprisonment plus 30 lashes at the common whipping post. On the above date he broke into the house of a Mr. John Justin and carried off several items of silverware. He also entered the establishment of a shopkeeper named Samuel Sellon and stole some articles of general merchandise. The crimes constituted burglary in the first degree and Coven was convicted thereof without recommendation of mercy. He was hanged on Boston Common on October 28, 1784.

Dereck Grout, white, age 36. *Burglary*. The crime was committed on March 25, 1784, at Boston, Massachusetts. This offender was born at Schenectady, New York, to an old-line Dutch family. During the Revolutionary War he served credibly with the American forces and prior to then he had been a bricklayer by trade. When peace was declared in 1783 Grout returned to Schenectady but soon quarreled with his father because he had served in the army contrary to the wishes of his parents. Disgusted with the situation, Grout boarded the Albany stagecoach and came eastward to Boston. There he was unable to find work at his chosen trade. He consequently turned to some acquaintances in the local Dutch community (who were of rather low caliber) and was induced by them to try his hand at criminal activity. The immediate result was two convictions for larceny and 30 lashes at the public whipping post. By then, however, there was no turning back for Dereck Grout. On October 25, 1783, he broke into the house of Nathaniel Wheeler at Boston and was arrested the next day. Thrown into jail, he remained there until the following year. Released in March of 1784, Grout then went on a spree: On March 24 he broke into the house of Gilbert Warner and carried off a set of silver spoons, an overcoat and nine pairs of stockings. On the following day he broke into the house of Elizabeth Elliott and took a silver spoon, a silver watch, a clock and 20 lbs. of salted pork. On April 2 he went to Roxbury and broke into the establishments of two shopkeepers named Seth Whitney and Lemuel Billing. The latter was a hatter by trade and Grout used the occasion to carry off

new headwear for all of his underworld acquaintances. He was finally linked to the Elliott burglary and charged with capital felony. Eventually he dictated a detailed confession. Dereck Grout was hanged on Boston Common on October 28, 1784.

John Dixon, white, age unknown. *Burglary*. The crime was committed on July 19, 1784, at Rehoboth, Massachusetts. Little is known of this man aside from the fact that he was a resident of Rehoboth. He happened to have a neighbor named James Daggett who operated a general store. Dixon cast covetous eyes on that establishment and he finally yielded to a temptation to rob the place. He broke in shortly after midnight on the above date and carried off the following items: a brass barreled pistol, eleven silk handkerchiefs, one pair of winter gloves, two pairs of winter stockings, four pillows, a hat, a powderhorn, half a pound of tea, a cheese, a box of crackers and other assorted edibles. Because Mr. Daggett made his home under the same roof as his place of business, Dixon was charged with the nocturnal burglary of an inhabited dwelling. Such constituted capital felony according to the law which then prevailed in Massachusetts. Caught with the goods, Dixon was easily convicted at the Bristol County Assizes. He was hanged at Taunton on November 11, 1784.

Richard Barrick, white, age 21. **John Sullivan,** white, age 18. *Highway robbery*. Their crime was committed on July 20, 1784, at Medford, Massachusetts. Both of these young men were homeless drifters. Both were Irish born. Barrick spent his childhood in an orphanage and was impressed into the British navy while still in his teens. Sullivan ran away from home at the age of 11 and joined the British army as a drummer boy. In the months that followed their respective inductions into the armed forces, both became adept at desertion and bounty jumping. During the Revolutionary War both came to New York aboard British warships from which they promptly deserted. From then on they lived life on the run. Both made their way to Connecticut where they put in with American guerrilla fighters who were really little more than armed freebooters. For the rest of the war they survived on the proceeds of nocturnal raids into enemy territory; their favorite targets being the Loyalists of Long Island. Both were captured on occasion but they always managed to find a way to rejoin their cronies. When peace was declared in 1783 they took to the roads and lived in much the same manner as they had during the war, robbing and stealing wherever they saw an opportunity. Both disdained honest work because they found theft to be more lucrative. In the spring of 1784 they met by chance at Boston. Joining forces, they mugged pedestrians and stole from shops all throughout the greater Boston area. On the above date they lay in wait for travelers along the Medford Turnpike. There they pounced on a man named Cyrus Baldwin (white, age unknown), severely beat him and stripped him of valuables. The loot consisted of a silver watch, a silk handkerchief, an enameled penknife and 14 silver shillings. This time the young bandits had gone too far. The robbery of Mr. Baldwin was routine by their standards but it produced a hue and cry which spread for miles in every direction. Barrick and Sullivan were taken up as suspicious persons and could not satisfactorily explain their movements. Then they were identified by Mr. Baldwin. Both were subsequently condemned as highwaymen. Both made detailed confessions while awaiting execution. Both were hanged on Cambridge Common on November 18, 1784.

Alexander White, white, age 22. *Mutiny and murder.* The crime was committed on August 7, 1784, on the high seas. This offender was born and raised in Ireland. While in his teens he went out to sea and he remained in that capacity for the rest of his life. One voyage brought him to Philadelphia where he became romantically involved with a young woman. By then, however, White was low on funds. He wanted to get married but was unable to afford suitable gifts for his bride-to-be. Humiliated by the situation, White decided to make another ocean voyage. He hoped that such a course of action would enable him to put his troubles behind him. He accordingly signed aboard a coastal schooner commanded by a Capt. Warren White (white, age unknown) and set out for Halifax, Nova Scotia. The schooner put in at New York where it took on cargo and passengers. Then it sailed eastward through Long Island Sound. All the while Alexander White could not get his mind off the woman he had left behind. He brooded over the fact that lack of money had ruined his marriage prospects. Finally he made a reckless decision: if it was money that was needed then money he would obtain regardless of all hazards. He would kill the captain and crew of the schooner and go ashore with their money. Then he would make his way back to Philadelphia and get married in style. On the above date the schooner lay becalmed in the waters off Cape Cod. As the captain was walking the deck White came up behind him with an axe, struck him down therewith and threw his body overboard. Then White attacked one of the passengers. Screams were heard and the rest of the crew overpowered the killer. White was then sent ashore where it was determined that the murder had occurred within the territorial waters of Massachusetts. Therefore the prisoner (White) was ordered to appear before the next session of the Supreme Judicial Court which was due to convene at Cambridge. White confessed his guilt and was capitally convicted. On November 18, 1784, he was hanged on Cambridge Common.

1785

William Scott and **Thomas Archibald,** whites, ages unknown. *Burglary.* The crime was committed on November 23, 1784, at Boston, Massachusetts. These men thought that it would be a good idea to rob the federal tax collector for the district of Massachusetts. On the above date they went to the house of that official — James Lovell, Esq., by name — and broke in. After rummaging around for a while they found a large metal strongbox which they surmised to be the repository of tax monies. This they seized and carried away to their hideout. When they broke open the box they found it to contain more than $25,000 in negotiable notes, gold and silver coins, paper currency and tax records. The hue and cry which followed this heist resulted in the close examination of anyone attempting to pass a negotiable draft drawn upon the banking houses of Boston. As long as the robbers spent only the cash portion of their loot they were safe. However, when they tried to pass some of the negotiable notes, they were caught. Both were charged with burglary in the first degree, a capital crime. Both were convicted in short order. Clemency was declared out of the question because the sternest kind of warning was deemed necessary to deter other potential offenders of this kind. The crime was not only regarded as a brazen act of larceny but an affront to the United States of America. National security required that the culprits pay the full penalty of the law. Both were accordingly hanged on Boston Common on May 5, 1785.

Hannah Peggin, Native American, age unknown. *Murder.* The crime was committed on November 10, 1784, at Belchertown, Massachusetts. This is an obscure case of a female offender who made away with her illegitimate baby. On the above date Hannah Peggin gave birth to a healthy male infant which she did not want. She then took a length of flax from a nearby loom and knotted it tightly around the baby's throat. The result was a fatal strangulation. Detected in the matter, Hannah Peggin was charged with capital felony. She pled not guilty but was unable to satisfactorily explain the evidence against her. Neither could she claim that the baby was stillborn because the flaxen noose was still around its neck when it was found. A jury convicted Hannah Peggin of willful infanticide and she was sentenced to death. She was accordingly hanged at Northampton on July 21, 1785.

Thomas Goss, white, age 52. *Murder.* The crime was committed on February 17, 1785, at Barkhamsted, Connecticut. This man was an innkeeper by profession and quite probably insane. He was born at Brookfield, Massachusetts, in the year 1733 and lost both of his parents by the age of 14. The next eight years he spent in foster homes. Goss joined the army at the age of 22 and served credibly for the duration of the French and Indian War (1755–1763). Upon receiving an honorable discharge at the conclusion of that conflict, Goss returned to the foster home where he formerly dwelled. In 1765 he set out on his own and came to Barkhamsted, Connecticut, where for the next 20 years he operated a successful inn. It is reported that Goss began to exhibit symptoms of insanity in the autumn of 1784. He fancied himself beset by minions of the spirit world and used to speak of goblins harassing him. He believed that fairies had hidden a treasure in the cellar of his house and he severely weakened the foundation of that structure by using a crowbar to pull stones therefrom while searching for the imaginary hoard. Goss also turned against his wife, Sarah Goss (white, age about 35), because he thought she was a witch. He refused to sleep in the same bed with the woman because he thought that the devil had supplanted him as her lover. Goss also evinced religious mania, calling himself the "Second Lamb of God" and the "Brother of Jesus Christ," among other such cognomens. Matters reached a climax on the above date when Goss killed his wife. The woman was sleeping in a large bed along with her three small children when Goss entered the room with an axe. There he hacked his wife to death and deliberately smeared her gore all over the bodies of the three children. Then he walked to a neighbor's house and nonchalantly told what he had done. When asked why he had killed his wife, Goss said that he had acted in order to prevent the woman from casting a spell on him. He also justified his crime by drawing a correlation between it and the slaying of the Egyptian taskmaster by Moses. When Goss was brought to trial his defense was based on his alleged mental derangement. The matter was duly considered but the jury was not impressed. This made the death penalty mandatory. Goss forbade any efforts to get his sentence commuted. He was duly hanged at Litchfield on November 7, 1785.

1786

Johnson Green, black, age 29. *Burglary.* The crimes were committed on April 14, 1786, at Shrewsbury, Massachusetts. This man is reported to have been an habitual criminal residing at Pomfret, Connecticut. On the above date he set out on a thieving expedition with the Massachusetts town of Shrewsbury as his objective. Once there, he broke into the house of a Mr. Henry Baldwin and carried off the following items: a pair of shoes, a set of silver shoe buckles, three jackets, a shirt, a set of buttons, a bottle of rum and

four shillings in loose change. Later the same evening Green broke into the house of Ross Wyman (also in Shrewsbury) and stole a piggy bank containing 16 shillings. From there he went to the house of John Farrar (also in Shrewsbury) and forced his way in. This time he took a pair of boots, a pair of shoes, a set of silver buckles, a pair of scissors, a spool of thread, a handkerchief, two bottles of liquor and copper coins totaling a shilling and eight pence in value. All of this loot he stashed in the woods and later retrieved at his leisure. When he was caught, Green remained sardonic. The Supreme Judicial Court for Worcester County sentenced him to death. While awaiting execution Green broke out of jail and headed for Rhode Island. There he committed another string of robberies while actually under sentence of death. Captured once again, Green was given up by the Rhode Island authorities on condition that his death sentence be carried out with no further delay. Back to Worcester went the condemned man under heavy guard. On August 17, 1786, he was hanged on Worcester Common.

Hannah Occuish, Native American, age 12. *Murder.* The crime was committed on July 20, 1786, at New London, Connecticut. This child was one of the youngest people in American history to be legally put to death as a capital felon. Little is known about her life aside from the fact that she was the result of a miscegenous union between a white man and a Native American woman. Her mother gave her up at an early age but did see to it that Hannah was placed with a respectable foster family. One day during the summer of 1786 Hannah went berry picking with a little girl half her age. When the two paused to take a rest Hannah allegedly took some of the younger girls' berries. When the younger girl, Eunice Bolles (white, age 6), objected to this, Hannah became angry and stomped all the way home. For the next shell comb and two skeins of linen. By then the entire area around Stockbridge was up in arms so the bandits made their way back to Alfredtown. There they attacked the house of Ebenezer French and beat up the occupants before carrying off the following items: a gun, a pair of boots, a silk handkerchief and a whole churn full of buttermilk. Four home invasions in the same night aroused the countryside and special companies of militia were called out to patrol the roads. The bandits meanwhile hid in the woods. Then on May 26 they struck again. They turned up at the town of Becket and burst into the house of Nathaniel Kingsley, Esq. There they found a silver watch and 13 gold coins which they seized and split among themselves. For the next two weeks the bandits lay low. Then on June 14 they struck again. Armed with the guns that they had previously stolen, they lay in wait for travelers near Lanesborough. When a coach-and-six came by at a rapid pace they shot the two leading horses, causing the coach to crash. In the passenger compartment they found a wealthy squire named Jonathan Brooks and they picked him clean of valuables. Then they went to the nearby house of Elijah Phelps and broke down the door. They roughed up the occupants of the house and ransacked every room. Here they found no money but made off with the following: a beaverskin hat, two overcoats, a pair of stockings, two sets of knee buckles, a saddle, a pair of velvet breeches and a fur covered toilet seat. Four days later they went to Egremont and broke into the house of Mr. Nehemiah Kellogg. There they helped themselves to three jackets, an overcoat, a pair of pants, two shirts, a silk handkerchief and a pocketbook. They also insulted the women of the house. By this time every gun in the county had been pressed into service by possemen eager to catch the bandits. Absolutely no one was allowed to go about unchallenged. Eventually the above-named pair and a third man

named Potter Allen were apprehended. All three were fully identified by the people they had robbed. All three were convicted of capital felony and ordered for execution. On December 6, 1787, thousands of Berkshire County residents descended on the little town of Lenox to witness the executions. Potter Allen was reprieved but Bly and Rose were left to their fates. They walked to the gallows surrounded by more than a hundred men-at-arms. When they reached the spot where they were to die a hush fell over the crowd. Bly then read an account of his life (which is now lost), while Rose said only his prayers. Then both men were hanged by their necks until they were dead.

1788

Archibald Taylor, white, age 31. **Joseph Taylor,** white, age 21. *Highway robbery.* The crime was committed on November 6, 1787, at Boston, Massachusetts. Little is known about these men aside from the fact that they were two out of a gang of muggers that was troubling the greater Boston area. They do not appear to have been related to each other, having come from Philadelphia and Ireland respectively. Archibald Taylor in particular is said to have had an extensive criminal record. Late in the evening of the above date a man named Nathaniel Cunningham (white, age unknown) was walking from Boston to his home in Cambridge when he was jumped by four armed robbers. The pedestrian was knocked to the ground and told that he would be killed if he did not surrender his valuables. Two of the assailants menaced the man with pistols while a third pressed a knife to his throat. Cunningham then gave up his money. He was also slapped around a little bit before the muggers let him go. As the thugs ran from the scene Cunningham screamed for help. He was heard by members of the night-watch, some of whom ran in pursuit of the muggers. Two of them were nabbed near the city gates and identified as Archibald and Joseph Taylor. The other two got away and the Taylors refused to divulge their identities. The law came down hard on the Taylors. Since they had attacked their victim in a public roadway they were charged with the capital crime of highway robbery. Both were condemned to death. On May 8, 1788, a gallows was erected on the spot where Nathaniel Cunningham was mugged. Then Archibald and Joseph Taylor were both put to death at the scene of their crime.

Elisha Thomas, white, age 42. *Murder.* The crime was committed on February 4, 1788, at New Durham, New Hampshire. This man was a Revolutionary War pensioner who got into a tavern brawl on the above date. All parties, including Thomas, fought dirty; kicking, tripping and other ungentlemanly tactics were involved. Thomas in particular is known to have held rocks in his fists. When matters got out of hand, a friend of Thomas named Capt. Peter Drowne (white, age about 40) intervened. He took Thomas aside and told him that enough was enough. Thomas, however, was too angry and too drunk to listen. Instead, he turned his wrath upon his friend. Dropping the rocks from his hands, Thomas pulled out a knife and fatally stabbed Drowne. When Thomas sobered up he was mortified by what he had done. However, by then it was too late. He was charged with capital felony and had nearly a dozen eyewitnesses testify against him. On June 3, 1788, more than 6000 people gathered at the little town of Dover to see Elisha Thomas pay the death penalty. It is reported that the hangman treated Thomas with uncommon civility and that Thomas died a sincere penitent.

Abiah Converse, white, age about 23. *Murder.* The crime was committed on March 30, 1788, at Chester, Massachusetts. This young woman was the unmarried daughter of one Benjamin Converse, a respectable citizen in the town of Chester. She was employed as a live-in domestic by a prosperous family of the same town. Becoming pregnant out of wedlock, Abiah did her best to conceal the fact. She was suspected by several people but dared not admit the truth. The matter came to a climax on the above date when Abiah secretly gave birth to a baby boy. She strangled the infant within minutes of its birth and attempted to conceal the tiny body by rolling it up in a ball of spinning wheel tow. Then she attempted to go about her business as usual. Try as she might, Abiah could not hide the physical symptoms of her ordeal. She swooned with post-natal complications and thereby drew attention to herself. The female members of Abiah's household were particularly suspicious of her. They searched around and finally found the dead baby. Upon being confronted with the evidence, Abiah immediately made use of the usual dodge for women in such circumstances: she said that the baby had been stillborn. However, a coroner's inquest reached a different conclusion. Abiah then confessed that she was guilty of infanticide. A trial court condemned her for capital felony. She was subsequently hanged at Northampton on July 17, 1788.

John O'Neil, white, age unknown. *Murder.* The crime was committed on February 13, 1788, at Bristol, Maine. This man was one of a group of English felons who had been sentenced to be "transported beyond the seas" for an indefinite term of years. He was put aboard a so-called "convict ship" with others of his kind (known colloquially as "Newgate Birds") and sent on his way. The ship which carried O'Neil was originally bound for Labrador but bad weather forced it to put in at Machias,

Maine, instead. When the weather cleared the ship was unable to resume its journey because its hull had been weakened. Therefore its human cargo was sent ashore in Maine. While arrangements were being made to send the convicts along the final leg of their journey by land at least one of them — namely John O'Neil — managed to escape. He wandered about the countryside as a fugitive for several days. Then he appeared at the farm of one Michael McCleary (white, age unknown) where he begged for food and shelter. McCleary saw the wretched condition of the man and took pity on him. Accordingly he gave O'Neil the things he sought and even allowed him to stay on as a farmhand. Soon, however, McCleary realized that he had made a mistake. The newcomer bore a bad character that he made little effort to conceal. Soon McCleary was afraid to sleep in his own house. He went to stay with a neighbor and expressed to that person the reason for his fears. McCleary did, however, continue to tend his farm during the daylight hours. On the above date the farmer presumably told O'Neil that he must find another home. O'Neil then beat McCleary to death with a coal shovel. On the same day the killer rode into town on the victim's horse and reported that the farmer was gravely ill. Then he returned to the farmhouse where he carefully cleaned the blood from the crime scene and lay the decedent in his bed in a posture of peaceful repose. On the following day O'Neil rode into town again where he reported that McCleary had succumbed to an illness. He also produced a forged deed in which the farmer had supposedly signed his property over to his hired man. This made the neighbors suspicious. A coroner's inquest was then assigned to investigate the untimely death of McCleary. In examining the body, it was found that the neck was broken and the skull fractured in five different places. Defensive wounds were also found on the hands and arms. When O'Neil was found to have the dead man's cash and jewelry in his pockets he was charged with capital murder. He was subsequently hanged at Wiscasset on September 11, 1788.

1789

William Smith and **William Denoffee,** alias "Donogan," whites, ages unknown. *Highway robbery.* Their crimes were committed on August 22, 1789, at Boston, Massachusetts. These men were muggers who attacked three unarmed pedestrians on the evening of the above date. First they stopped a Mr. Peter Forra (white) and menaced him with knives. They forced the man to give up his jacket, a silk handkerchief and his silver shoe buckles. Next they accosted a Mr. Samuel Brock (white) and took the silver-plated buckles from his shoes. Then they went after a Mr. Augustus Rallion (white) and did the same thing to him. Because all of the victims had been attacked in public roadways the crimes were considered highway robbery — a capital felony. At the same time public outcry had grown loud about the unsafe conditions that had then sprung up around Boston after dark. People had become afraid to walk the streets during the evening hours because of the seemingly large number of muggers which infested the metropolis. For this reason the governor decided that it was time to make an example of somebody. Smith and Denoffee were so selected. On October 8, 1789, both were hanged on Boston Common.

Rachel Wall, white, age 29. *Highway robbery.* The crime was committed on March 27, 1789, at Boston, Massachusetts. This female offender was the last woman to be executed in Massachusetts. She was, contrary to popular belief, neither a murderess nor a witch but merely a common thief. According to her own account, Rachel Wall was born at Carlisle, Pennsylvania, and brought up on a farm. As a teenager she ran away from home and became a wandering vagabond. Eventually she fell in with a kindred spirit named George Wall and married him. Together the newlyweds went to Philadelphia where they spent several months on the fringe of society. Then they made their way to New York where they fared no better. Eventually the couple got as far as Boston. There Rachel was abandoned by her spouse. Alone and destitute, the young woman took up residence in a bawdy-house where she earned her keep as a prostitute. Odd jobs and theft also supplemented her income. In the summer of 1785 Rachel was convicted of grand larceny by a Boston court of law. She was given 15 lashes at a public whipping post and sold into indentured servitude for a term of three years. In the summer of 1788 she was nabbed for breaking and entering and given another 15 lashes. It was also during this time (as she herself declared) that Rachel became a rather adept cat burglar. She specialized in robbing ships that were moored in Boston harbor. It was her practice to prowl the wharves at night looking for vulnerable ships. Then she would deftly slip into the sleeping quarters thereof and help herself to loose valuables. On one occasion she even snuck into a captain's cabin while both master and mate were asleep therein and made off unobserved with a sockful of coins. So practiced was she that she took the loot out from under a pillow as the sleeping captain reclined thereon. It was on the above date that Rachel finally went too far; she attacked a female pedestrian as she was walking along a public street. The victim, Margaret Bender (white), was knocked to the ground and had a handkerchief stuffed into her mouth to prevent her from screaming. Then Rachel tore the woman's bonnet from her head and also took both of her shoes. Running from the scene with said

loot, she was grabbed by other pedestrians and turned over to the authorities. The charge brought against her was highway robbery — a hanging offense. At her trial Rachel claimed to be a victim of mistaken identity. However, her extant notoriety proved to be an aggravating factor of insurmountable dimension. There were also multiple witnesses against Rachel. The verdict was guilty and the sentence was death. In reviewing the record of Rachel's conviction, Governor John Hancock (of Declaration of Independence fame) decided that the time was right to send a stern message of warning to the Boston underworld: female offenders would be held equally as liable as their male counterparts. For this reason Rachel Wall's application for clemency was rejected. She was accordingly hanged along with two male offenders on Boston Common. The date was October 8, 1789.

1790

Thomas Bird, white, age about 30. *Mutiny and murder.* The crime was committed in December of 1788 on the high seas. This was a federal case. The British sloop *Mary* sailed from Plymouth, England, in September of 1787 bound for the African coast. Aboard the sloop was the captain, John Connor (white, age unknown), and seven crewmen. After a voyage of nine weeks the *Mary* reached the Salos Islands where it joined a factory ship for the purpose of transporting whale oil to various ports of call. After several months spent in such a capacity the *Mary* set out for the Guinea coast where it took on a valuable cargo of ivory and spices. Captain Conner was said to have been a tyrant who worked his crew long and hard. He had even beaten his first mate to death in a fit of anger. When the captain ordered the rest of the crew to prepare the body of the dead mate for burial at sea he was met with a flat refusal. The crew declared that the captain was guilty of malfeasance and abuse of power and it was demanded that the *Mary* be put into the nearest port so that a legal inquest could be held on the body of the first mate. This was regarded as mutiny by the captain and it served to increase his foul mood. Captain Connor then singled out one of the crewmen and ordered him to sew up the body of the mate in his bedding. When the crewman refused to obey this order he was severely beaten by the captain and forced to jump overboard. The rest of the crew was cowed by this incident and they complied with the captain's orders. Thus the first mate was buried at sea. For several weeks thereafter the crew continued in its duty. However, plans for a mutiny were discussed.

By December of 1788 the vessel had come to the waters off Cape Lahu and the crew decided that the time for action had come. The above-named Thomas Bird (who was a native of Bristol, England) was either chosen to act on behalf of the crew or decided to act on his own. He took a gun from the sloop's weapons locker and crawled through an aft scuttle which offered a means of entry into the captain's cabin. From that position Bird fatally shot the captain. When the rest of the crew heard the shot they burst into the cabin and heaved the captain overboard. At that point the second mate took command of the sloop. Additional seamen were soon taken aboard to make up for those who had died and the course was set for New England. After a voyage of more than four months' duration (in the course of which yet another crewman died under mysterious circumstances), the sloop reached its destination. An anchorage was found at Cape Elizabeth on the Maine coast and a party of men went ashore to procure food and fresh water. When it became known that the *Mary* was carrying a rich cargo, its presence was reported to the customs authorities in Portland. They in turn suspected that a smuggling operation was in progress and armed ships were sent to intercept the *Mary*. The pursuing ships overtook the suspect vessel inside the territorial waters of the United States and compelled it to surrender. The *Mary* was then brought to Portland where both ship and crew were interned. In questioning the crew, the details of the mutiny became known. Then the American authorities made a controversial decision about how to proceed with the matter: instead of turning both ship and crew over to British authority, it was decided to charge the crew of the *Mary* with piracy and try them before an American court. Thus was the case of a foreign ship and a foreign crime taken up by a federal court. The ostensible reason for this decision was that the acting skipper of the *Mary* (formerly its second mate) was an American citizen. However, the *real* reason for the decision was because the American customs authorities could not resist the temptation to seize the rich cargo of ivory and spices which the *Mary* bore. When the case came to trial all crewmen except Thomas Bird were acquitted. It was then ordered that he be put to death by the federal marshal for the district of Maine. The condemned man was accordingly hanged at Portland on June 25, 1790.

John Bailey, black, age 19. *Burglary.* The crime was committed on April 25, 1790, at Boston, Massachusetts. This offender was a free Negro. He was born at New York City on March 6, 1771, to parents who were also free. As a young teenager Bailey went to sea. He spent four years aboard both warships and merchant vessels and became quite well traveled for a person of his age. One voyage brought him to Boston where he decided to test his mettle ashore. Not being the lazy type, Bailey got a job with a coachman and remained there for a year. He next applied to a candlestick maker and was taken on as an apprentice thereto. On the above date, according to his own account, Bailey was spending some time off with some other young fellows. Their conversation turned to bragging of their esoteric exploits. These included tales of sexual escapades and acts of criminal daring. Bailey had no tale of the latter to match those told by his comrades. So he acted on a dare and broke into the house of a Mr. Hugh Cargill. The loot he took on that occasion consisted of a handkerchief, a silver napkin ring, a silver spoon and a pair of shoe buckles. For that offense John Bailey was hanged on Boston Common on October 14, 1790.

Edward Vail Brown, white, age unknown. *Burglary.* The crime was committed on July 1, 1790, at Boston, Massachusetts. This man had once been a prosperous baker. However, a series of business reversals ruined him and he began stealing to support his needs. On the above date he broke into the house of a Mr. John Coffin Whitney and carried off the following items: a featherbed, two blankets, a tin kettle, a pair of pajamas, a warming pan, an iron pot, a coffee grinder, two salt shakers, a quilt, six knives, three forks and a set of earthenware dishes. For this crime the erstwhile baker was hanged on Boston Common on October 14, 1790.

Joseph Mountain, black, age 31. *Rape.* The crime was committed on May 26, 1790, at West Haven, Connecticut. This offender was born at Philadelphia on July 7, 1758. His parents were an emancipated Negro couple who lived with and were employed by the aristocratic Mifflin family. At the age of 17 young Joseph Mountain went to sea. He wound up in London, England, where he jumped ship and set out to see the sights of the town. Soon he fell in with a fraternity of bandits and it did not take him long to find ready acceptance in

such circles. The teenage newcomer was daring and shrewd. He went on numerous thieving expeditions in and around London and reaped a considerable harvest in stolen goods. By degrees he went from mugger to burglar to full-fledged highwayman. He preyed primarily on the well-to-do and was able to live quite comfortably on the proceeds of his depredations. He even managed to woo and marry a young white woman who was possessed of a handsome dowry. Mountain remained in England for the greater part of 12 years. He pulled one lucrative heist after another and was never caught. In 1780 he participated in the Lord Gordon riots (which devastated the city of London) and reaped more by looting than he might have earned in a lifetime of honest labor. Following the suppression of the Lord Gordon riots, Mountain deemed it prudent to leave London for a while. Mass executions of the rioters had become common and Mountain feared the consequences of what he had done during the time of civil upheaval. He accordingly went to sea again and made several trans–Atlantic voyages before returning to his London haunts. As a highwayman he then roamed the length and breadth of England. Once again his luck held and he escaped capture. However, the sight of some of his cronies swinging in gibbets induced him to move on. He accordingly crossed over to the continent and ranged all the way from Holland to Spain as a successful brigand. Finally after nearly 15 years of adventure Mountain decided to return to the land of his youth. He accordingly took passage on a ship to Boston and arrived there on May 2, 1790. There he found that times had changed. The United States of America had come into being. Fascinated by the transformation that had taken place, Mountain decided to make a journey from Boston to New York as a pedestrian. At Hartford, Connecticut, however, he met with a rude surprise; having run short of money he resorted to his habit of stealing to suit his needs. He was caught and given ten lashes on his bare back. It was the first time in Mountain's life that he had had to face justice and the experience left him more astonished than physically hurt. Still, he suddenly realized that he no longer enjoyed the same underworld esteem to which he had become accustomed. In Connecticut he was regarded as a "nigger" and nothing more. According to Mountain's own account, the resultant blow to his ego almost undid him. Scraping together the tattered remains of his dignity, Mountain got out of Hartford as fast as he could and moved on to New Haven. There he made the worst blunder of his life, one that was to have fatal results for him. While walking along the Boston Post Road (in what is now the town of West Haven), Mountain encountered two young white girls coming in the opposite direction. Desire crossed his mind when he saw the two girls. Forgetting that miscegenation was frowned upon in New England (unlike in Old England), Mountain made indecent proposals to the girls. Shocked by the Negro's impudence, the girls indignantly refused his solicitation. Mountain, however, was used to having his way with white women and he was not about to take "no" for an answer. He then assaulted the elder of the girls but she managed to break free and outrun him. Then he turned his attention to the younger girl, who was later determined to be 14 years old. Mountain dragged her screaming and struggling into a field where he raped her repeatedly. Shortly afterward a wagon train came upon the scene of the crime and its menfolk rescued the victim of the rape. By then, however, she had been severely injured in a female way. The women of the wagon train did their best to comfort the girl while the men pursued the rapist. Mountain was caught and brought back to New Haven. There he was charged with capital felony and held for trial. A capital conviction followed in due course. The end came at New Haven on October 20, 1790, when Joseph Mountain was hanged by the neck until dead. More than 10,000 people watched him die.

Samuel Hadlock, white, age about 50. *Murder.* The crime was committed on October 26, 1789, in Lincoln County, Maine. This man was an ill-tempered farmer who killed a neighbor for the sake of two shillings. Hadlock had had a business transaction with a fellow townsman named Elias Littlefield Gott (white, age unknown) and believed that he had been deliberately shortchanged by two shillings. Failing to obtain satisfaction from the other man, Hadlock armed himself with a wooden club and went looking for him. He burst into the house where Gott lodged and demanded his money. When the landlady said that Gott was not there, Hadlock started swinging his club. He wrecked the interior of the house and chased the occupants into the street. Then he happened to catch sight of Gott approaching the house from a different direction. Hadlock immediately went in pursuit of Gott. However, Gott saw Hadlock coming and he turned to flee. It was no use. Gott was weighed down by a pair of heavy boots and was swiftly overtaken. As Hadlock began beating him with the club, Gott cried out, "God have mercy on me!" Hadlock then shouted, "Pray! God damn you! This is the last time you shall have the opportunity!" and he continued the beating. Gott succumbed to his injuries two days later. Hadlock was subsequently convicted of capital murder. While awaiting execution he made a daring jailbreak and remained at large for many weeks. He was finally recaptured after an exciting sea chase. The end came at Wiscasset on October 28, 1790, when Hadlock was publicly hanged.

1791

David Comstock, white, age unknown. *Murder.* The crime was committed on December 27, 1790, at Gloucester, Rhode Island. Described as a "yeoman," this offender was chopping wood on the above date when he got into a heated dispute. It seems that Comstock had been hired by one Ephraim Bacon (white, age unknown) to hew several cords of firewood. When Bacon came to inspect the goods something displeased him. Words were exchanged and Comstock lost his temper. As Bacon turned to leave, the angry Comstock struck him down from behind with his axe. Then he repeated the blows until Bacon was hacked beyond recognition. The decedent suffered 14 axe wounds in all, nine of them on his face and head. Comstock fled from the scene but was found hiding in a haystack. Charged with capital murder, he was found guilty without mitigating circumstances. He was hanged before "a prodigious concourse of spectators" at Providence, Rhode Island, on May 27, 1791.

Thomas Mount, white, age 27. *Burglary.* The crime was committed on December 10, 1790, at Westerly, Rhode Island. This man was a professional thief who ranged from Maine to Virginia in his search for plunder. He never held a regular job; instead he spent his entire adult life either in jail or doing things that would land him there. According to a detailed confession that he made shortly before his execution, Mount was born in New Jersey. He ran away from home at the age of 11 and from then on lived as a vagabond. While still a young teenager he enlisted in the army of the United States but was quickly seduced by the ready availability of bounty money. He deserted and reenlisted several times (a capital offense) for the sake of such lucre and even went over to the enemy and played the same trick on

them. By the time he was 16 years old, Mount had been charged with more than a dozen capital felonies, both military and civil. However, each time he was either excused on account of his age or sentenced to the whipping post. By the age of 21 his criminal record included the following: desertion from the armed forces, bounty jumping, fraternizing with the enemy, highway robbery, burglary, armed robbery, breaking and entering, mugging, rape, embezzlement, grand larceny, jail breaking, shoplifting, storehouse robbery, trafficking in stolen goods, pocket picking, theft of military stores, defrauding his creditors, horse stealing, forgery, highjacking, contempt of court and in many cases multiple counts of the aforesaid. Mount broke jail more than a dozen times and bore the scars of hundreds of legally imposed lashes on his back. He was set in the stocks, pilloried and made to sit upon more than one gallows with a noose around his neck. Nothing reformed him and he matter-of-factly admitted that he was incorrigible. It was in Rhode Island that he finally overplayed his hand; on the above date he broke into the house of a Westerly merchant named Joseph Potter and helped himself to all kinds of valuables. Nabbed with the loot, Mount was charged with burglary in the first degree. When the extent of his criminal record became known the trial court had no qualms about imposing the death penalty. This time Mount was chained down in jail and watched around the clock by multiple guards to make sure that he did not escape. He was finally hanged at South Kingston on May 27, 1791.

1793

Samuel Frost, white, age 28. *Murder.* The crime was committed on July 16, 1793, at Princeton, Massachusetts. This man was a recidivist killer of unsound mind. Physically he is described as short and swarthy with closely cropped hair. The most noticeable of his physical characteristics, however, were his uncontrollable nervous tics; Frost used to incessantly shrug his shoulders, shake his head and stretch his arms in all directions. On September 24, 1783 (when he was 18 years old), Frost was helping his father with an excavation project. For no discernible reason he struck his father down from behind with an iron lever and did not leave off until the man's head was literally mashed beyond recognition. Charged with capital murder, the teenage defendant was acquitted when he was certified to be insane. Whether Frost was institutionalized following this verdict is unknown. The next definite information that surfaces regarding him is that he was taken in by a prosperous neighbor named Capt. Elisha Allen (white, age unknown) and retained as a member of that man's household for "several years." On July 16, 1793, Frost and his benefactor were working in the fields. Captain Allen busied himself with planting vegetables and he sent Frost to the barn to fetch a hoe. Several minutes later Frost came up behind Captain Allen with the hoe and used it to strike the man a lethal blow on the head. Once again Frost did not leave off his attack until the victim's head was battered beyond recognition. When his fury was spent the killer took to the woods. Every able-bodied man in the town joined forces to track him down. When he was cornered, Frost chose not to resist. When brought to trial he pled guilty to a capital charge. The court offered Frost a chance to retract his plea but he declined to do so. Then the court put off pronouncing sentence until a parade of witnesses were heard; the judges wanted to see if there were any mitigating factors that they could report to the governor to justify a commutation of the mandatory death sentence. This time the insanity defense was unavailing. The judges re-

jected all efforts to that effect as "frivolous pretense." Their rationale was that crazy or not, Frost was too dangerous to live. It was subsequently reported to the governor that no mitigating factors existed. Consequently a warrant was issued for the execution of Samuel Frost. The deranged defendant was accordingly hanged at Worcester on October 31, 1793.

1794

John Baptist Collins, Emanuel Furtado and Augustus Palacha,

whites, ages unknown. *Murder, mutiny and piracy.* The crime was committed on December 19, 1793, on the high seas. This was a federal case. On November 3, 1793, the American brig *Betsy* sailed from a Spanish port bound for Boston. The vessel was commanded by Captain Joseph Saunders. There was one passenger aboard plus a first mate and five regular seamen. The latter consisted of two Americans plus the above-named trio whose nationalities were Belgian, Portuguese and Italian respectively. When the brig was about halfway across the ocean it ran into rough weather. For nearly a week the sea remained angry. At first Capt. Saunders tried to ride out the storm. However, when the ballast shifted in the brig's hold, a change of course was ordered. The captain decided to make a run for the nearest land which was in the West Indies. This displeased the crew and the three foreign seamen (those above-named) decided to kill the officers and commandeer the ship. On the above date they forced their way into the captain's cabin and attacked the persons therein. The captain and first mate were both slashed repeatedly but managed to fight off their assailants. The lone passenger, Enoch Wood (white, age unknown), was killed. After that the captain and mate barricaded themselves in the aft part of the ship where they had access to food and water. The mutineers controlled the decks and the hold. They changed the vessel's course but soon began to feel the pinch of hunger and thirst. Demanding provisions from the besieged officers, they were at first refused. Then they turned on the two American crewmen who had not taken part in the mutiny. Those men were tied to the masts with rope and an ultimatum was given to the officers: either send out food and water or the two hostages would be tortured to death and eaten. Then if that did not work the mutineers would chop holes in the bottom of the ship so that all on board would die together. When the captain heard the screams of the hostages, he relented. Food and water were then given to the mutineers. The next four days produced a stalemated situation in which the officers remained holed up in their refuge. Then toward nightfall on the fourth day another ship was sighted. The mutineers turned course to avoid it but the captain and the mate hung a distress beacon in the cabin window which attracted the other ship. It proved to be a warship. The brig was accordingly boarded and the full situation became known. All parties were brought to Barbados where the American consul was given charge of the matter. The three prisoners were put in irons and sent to the Port of Boston for trial by a federal court. There they were sentenced to death. On July 30, 1794, all three were hanged on Boston Common.

Edmund Fortis, black, age about 35. *Murder.* The crime was committed on May 18, 1794, in Lincoln County, Maine. This offender was a runaway slave from Virginia. An habitual thief, he was considered troublesome by his owners and was consequently sold and resold several times. It was also a practice of his to run away and assume false identities in which he was detected more than once and severely punished. Moreover, Fortis was a self-admitted sex addict who left a trail of illegitimate children wherever he went. When Virginia became too hot for him, Fortis passed himself off as a freedman and joined the crew of an English merchant ship. He then made a voyage to Liverpool and a return trip to New England. At Wiscasset, Maine, he jumped ship and escaped into the forests. For several months thereafter he lived as a vagabond, stealing from gardens and chicken coops in order to survive. Eventually Fortis wandered into the town of Hallowell where there was a small Negro community. He found shelter there and even settled down with a woman of his own race. After about a year he moved to a place called Vassalborough where he became notorious as a drunkard, thief, gambler and satyr. On the above date he spotted a young white girl named Pamela Tilton (age 14) walking down a country lane. Fortis accosted the girl and made indecent proposals to her. When the girl refused to consent to such things Fortis dragged her into the woods and raped her. When the victim asked to be shown the way out of the woods Fortis raped her again. Then he choked her to death with his bare hands and covered up the body with forest debris. Two days later a search party found the victim. Fortis was suspected because of his unsavory reputation. He finally admitted every detail of the crime. When brought to court he pled guilty to a charge of capital murder. The sentence was death by hanging. Thousands of people thronged the little town of Dresden to see the sentence carried out on September 25, 1794.

1795

Negro Pomp, black, age about 20. *Murder.* The crime was committed on February 11, 1795, at Andover, Massachusetts. This offender was imported from Africa when he was three months old. Both of his parents made the journey with him as did all six of his siblings. The family does not appear to have been enslaved because when Pomp's father died soon after his arrival, the widow and mother parceled out her children among various households completely of her own accord. Pomp was sent to the town of Andover and there became indentured to a prosperous white man named Captain Charles Furbush. Conflict arose as Pomp entered his teenage years. He did not fully comprehend the terms of his indenture and he thought that he was free to wander about as he pleased. When told that he must wait until he reached the age of majority before he became his own master, Pomp rebelled. He ran away several times only to be caught and severely whipped each time. This further increased his resentment. As Pomp's 21st birthday approached he was told by Captain Furbush that he could remain in his household for as long as he liked thereafter; he would not be coldly ejected and left to fend for himself. Then Furbush made another remark to the effect that "he would not live forever." Pomp somehow interpreted this all to mean that he (Pomp) would become master of the Furbush estate upon the death of Captain Furbush. Therefore he decided to bring about the death of that person with the full expectation of taking his place. Shortly after midnight on the above date Pomp snuck into his master's bedroom with an axe. He then hacked Captain Furbush to death as he lay beside his wife. Mrs. Furbush was awakened and she ran from the house screaming. When she returned with reinforcements, it was found that Pomp had inflicted even further violence to the body of his master. Captain Furbush was found laying on his bedroom floor naked with his skull crushed and his throat cut. The entire chamber was awash with blood and brain matter. Pomp was quickly taken into custody but could not

at first understand why he was put in jail. He regarded himself as the new master of the Furbush estate. A trial was held before the Supreme Judicial Court for Essex County and Pomp was sentenced to death. He was hanged at Ipswich on August 6, 1795.

1796

Henry Blackburn, white, age unknown. *Murder.* The crime was committed on August 14, 1795, at Salem, Massachusetts. This man was a chimney sweeper who lived at the lower end of St. Peters Street in Salem. On the evening of the above date a sailor named George Wilkinson (white, age 24) came to Blackburn's house in order to visit a lady friend who lodged there. The visitor had just drawn his pay and he made it a point not to come calling empty-handed; he brought food and liquor with him which he shared with the entire household. Blackburn either knew or surmised that Wilkinson had money in his pockets. So he asked to borrow some. Wilkinson tried to evade what he regarded as a rather tacky request. Then he made an excuse to leave. As he headed for the door Blackburn barred his way and said that he would not let him go until he agreed to lend some money. Wilkinson saw that Blackburn had had too much to drink and he tried to step around the man. Blackburn then became angry. He picked up a sword and fatally stabbed Wilkinson with it. Although Blackburn said that he had not meant to actually kill the decedent, a coroner pronounced the incident a case of willful murder. Blackburn was consequently put on trial for his life. The fact that the crime had been committed in front of several witnesses made any defense futile. Blackburn was capitally convicted. He was subsequently hanged at Salem on January 14, 1796.

Thomas Powers, black, age 19. *Rape.* The crime was committed on December 7, 1795, at Lebanon, New Hampshire. This man was a free Negro. He was born at Wallingford, Connecticut, on September 15, 1776. According to his own account, Powers lost his virginity at the age of 12 and remained a sex addict for the rest of his life. On the above date he accosted a so-called "spinster" named Sally Messer (white, age unknown) as she was riding a palfrey down a lonely lane. He pulled the woman out of her saddle and raped her right in the middle of the road. Angry citizens hunted him down shortly thereafter and he was put in the Grafton County jail. Powers managed to escape twice but was caught each time. When his case came to trial, he was found guilty and sentenced to death. He was publicly hanged at Haverhill on July 28, 1796. It is said that shortly before his execution Powers sold his body to an anatomist. The purchaser later brought the corpse to a tanner who removed the skin and treated it with a preservative. Then the skin was made into a pair of boots.

1797

John Stewart, white, age 19. *Burglary.* The crime was committed on March 9, 1797, at Boston, Massachusetts. This young man was of Irish origin. As a teenager he was declared refractory by the ruling patriarch of his family. It was then decided to send young Stewart to America in the hope that the experience would prove beneficial. At the age of 16 he was packed aboard an immigrant ship with nothing more than a change of clothes and a small monetary stipend. Coming ashore at Wilmington, Delaware, the new arrival remained idle at first. Only when his money ran out did he start to look for a job. Stewart accordingly made his way to Pennsylvania and became a Lancaster County woodcutter.

He remained in that situation for two years and then set out for the big city. Arriving in Philadelphia, he got a job in a brickyard where he worked for several months. Then a virulent epidemic struck that city and Stewart decided to flee for his health. He made his way to New York where he found lodging and worked a series of low-paying jobs. Dissatisfied, he then took passage to Boston. There he went to work for a carpenter but soon fell into bad company. Introduced to parlous pastimes (such as drinking, gambling and whoring), young Stewart soon found himself short of cash. He then began stealing and wound up in jail. When he was released, Stewart found his cronies waiting for him. He then resumed his risky lifestyle. On the above date he ganged up with two others of his ilk and broke into the house of a Captain Enoch Rust, located on Prince Street in Boston. There the three intruders terrorized the occupants of the house. However, Stewart got a rude surprise when he burst into the bedroom of the homeowner's son. He was tackled by the stalwart tenant, disarmed and overpowered. Alarmed by the unexpected resistance, Stewart's accomplices fled. They were never caught. Stewart himself was held for the police. From there the wheels of justice turned quickly. Since the Suffolk Assizes were then in session Stewart's case was added to the docket. Within five days of his crime he was put on trial. A conviction for capital felony was handed down and Stewart was sentenced to death. His refusal to name his accomplices probably figured in the subsequent decision to deny him clemency. On April 7, 1797 — less than a month after his crime — John Stewart was hanged on Boston Common.

Richard Doane, white, age unknown. *Murder.* The crime was committed on July 4, 1796, at East Windsor, Connecticut. Described as a "transient person," this man was among a group of Independence Day revelers when he committed his capital crime. The scene was the Barrett Tavern near Warehouse Point, a roadside inn which catered to those involved in the tobacco trade. The above date was a holiday and the tavern was crowded. The landlord's "liquid assets" had been flowing freely all day. Among those who had had too much to drink were Richard Doane and a local man named Daniel McIver (white, age unknown). The latter somehow offended the former and a fight broke out. Doane threw McIver to the floor and stomped him. Then he grabbed McIver by the collar and repeatedly banged his head against the basin of the stone fireplace. As a result, McIver suffered a fatal skull fracture. Doane was then arrested and charged with capital murder. He was convicted and sentenced to death. A stay was granted when the condemned man appealed to the state legislature for clemency. Doane argued that he should not get the death penalty because there was no evidence of premeditation on his part. He admitted killing McIver in a drunken brawl but further stated that he did not mean to inflict a fatal injury on the man. The legislature considered the clemency petition and voted it down. Doane was told that he had brought his situation on himself and that he should have first considered the consequences of his actions. It is said that more than 6000 people watched as this man was hanged at Hartford on June 10, 1797.

Thomas Starr, white, age about 25. *Murder.* The crime was committed on August 2, 1796, at Middletown, Connecticut. This is a rather obscure case. Thomas Starr was a man of unknown occupation who lived at Middletown. On the above date he attacked a neighbor named Samuel Cornwell (white, age 25) and stabbed him seven times with what was described as a "penknife." The

victim succumbed after 11 days of agony. Although court records and newspapers mention this case both are silent as to the killer's motive. The Connecticut state legislature reviewed the record of Starr's conviction for capital murder. A clemency bill failed to attract support. Thomas Starr was then left to his fate. He was hanged in front of a large hometown crowd at Middletown on June 14, 1797.

Stephen Smith, black, age 28. *Aggravated burglary.* The crimes were committed in the spring of 1797 at Boston, Massachusetts. This offender was born a slave in Sussex County, Virginia. His entire childhood was spent on the plantation of a Mr. William Allen. When he was about 20 years old, "Negro Stephen" as he was then known, broke into his master's tannery and carried off a valuable parcel of leather. For Mr. Allen it was the final straw; the young slave had been a chronic source of mischief and it was decided to sell him. Consequently, Stephen was remanded to a slave trader and shipped to the West Indies. Somehow he managed to escape. Then he actually stowed away on the same vessel that had transported him and he made the return trip to Virginia. His luck held throughout the voyage and Stephen was not detected. When the ship dropped anchor at Norfolk the stowaway swiped a lifeboat late at night and rowed ashore. Stephen then stole food and clothing before seeking refuge in the woods. Eventually he was taken up as a runaway and returned to Mr. Allen. Once again he was shipped to the Indies and once again he escaped. He stowed away on a ship bound for Canada and made the entire voyage thereto without being discovered. He came ashore at Nova Scotia and there got into trouble; he was charged with assault plus breaking and entering. However, he managed to wrangle a pardon on condition that he leave the province. By then a free Negro,

Stephen changed his name to Stephen Smith and took a boat to Boston. There he found shelter in a succession of households, earning his keep through manual labor. Two of his employers were a Mr. Turner and a Mr. Goldsbury. It was subsequently proven (and confessed to by Stephen himself) that Stephen later returned to the houses of both those men after he had left their employ. In each case he broke in by night and stole whatever he could lay his hands on. He also set fire to each house in order to cover his tracks. Both of the aggrieved homeowners realized that they had something in common: Stephen Smith. In such a way was the culprit identified. Charged with capital felony, Stephen was convicted. He eventually confessed that he was guilty as charged. On October 12, 1797, he was hanged on Boston Common.

1798

Hopkins Hudson, white, age unknown. *Murder.* The crime was committed on September 8, 1798, at Cranston, Rhode Island. This man was a carpenter who quarreled with a blacksmith named Rufus Randall (white, age unknown) because he did not like the price of some metalwork which the latter had performed. The two men had a confrontation over the matter which escalated into a brawl. Hudson then pulled a knife on the blacksmith and stabbed him to death. Little time was wasted in adjudicating this case. Hudson was put on trial the same month and condemned to be hanged the next month. There was no appeal. He was accordingly executed at Providence on October 26, 1798.

Negro Anthony, black, age unknown. *Rape.* The crime was committed on March 7, 1798, at Greenwich, Connecticut. The trial papers in this case are lost. Therefore we must rely on second-hand accounts which did use the missing records as their source. Anthony was a free Negro who had come to Connecticut from Long Island. On the above date he accosted a teenage white girl named Mary Knapp and forced himself on her. Apprehended shortly thereafter, Anthony was charged with capital felony. He was convicted at the regular session of the Fairfield County Superior Court and ordered for execution. In a subsequent petition for clemency, Anthony admitted his guilt but asked that the death sentence be changed to perpetual servitude in the mines. He also contended that capital punishment for the crime of rape was disproportionate because several other states had discontinued it. Moreover, said he, the fact that Connecticut punished such an offense with death was unknown to him because he had spent most of his life in New York. The Connecticut state legislature considered the question of clemency and voted it down. Ignorance of the law, replied the lawmakers, was no excuse for breaking it. Anthony was publicly hanged at Danbury on November 8, 1798.

1799

Samuel Smith, white, age 54. *Burglary.* The crime was committed on June 22, 1799, at Sherborn, Massachusetts. This man was an habitual criminal who became the last person to be executed in New England for the crime of burglary. According to a lengthy confession that he made while under sentence of death, Smith was born at Middletown, Connecticut, on January 18, 1745. He had a normal upbringing and remained on the right side of the law throughout his early years. It was at the age of 27 that his life took a turn for the worse. Smith was jilted by a fiancée who decamped with all his savings. He tried to drink away his grief but could not escape the fact that he had been left destitute. Unwilling or unable to find a regular job, Smith took to stealing. He was nabbed at Litchfield and given a public whipping. By the age of 30 Smith was still down on his luck. With no place else to turn, he decided to join the army. He enlisted in the Continental forces for a term of three years. At first he found the soldier's life to be better than what he had left behind. However, a dispute over bounty money soured him on the service and he deserted. For the remainder of the Revolutionary War he wandered about New England living on the proceeds of theft. He finally settled down at Lancaster, Massachusetts, where he took up farm work. There he married and fathered five children. In 1787 Smith abandoned his family and went to New Hampshire. There he resumed a roving existence. When he ran short of money he had recourse to a new source of income: coining. He became adept at that racket and found it more lucrative than honest work. On November 17, 1787, he was arrested for sheep stealing and locked up at Concord, Massachusetts. There he had a parcel of bogus money traced to him. Faced with severe punishment, Smith then broke jail. He was caught and wound up sitting in the pillory. He also had his ears cut off. In the summer of 1791 he was arrested for stealing silverware with intent to make counterfeit coins. The result was a 15-year prison sentence. Sent to Castle Island (an infamous hellhole in Boston harbor), Smith remained there for 28 months. Then he made another jailbreak. This time he got as far as Pennsylvania where he bided his time for a while. Becoming homesick, Smith slipped back into Massachusetts where he found that his family had dispersed. Once again he took up the roving life. On June 15, 1799, he turned up at the town of Sherborn. There he broke into the house of a Mr. Joseph Richards and stole food and clothing. Five days later he went to Natick where he broke

into another house. On June 22, 1799, this vagabond returned to Sherborn where he set his sights on a storehouse owned by a Deacon Tucker. Forcing his way in under cover of night, Smith took a mixed bag of loot which he carried to Sudbury and stashed in the woods. There an honest hunter found the hoard by accident and recognized it as stolen goods. The local authorities were then informed and a watch was placed on the area. When Smith returned to retrieve his booty he fell into the trap. Brought before the Supreme Judicial Court for Middlesex County, he was charged with burglary in the first degree — a hanging offense. He was then found guilty without mitigating circumstances. When the governor reviewed the case he had only to look at the defendant's prior record to decide that clemency was not warranted. An order was then issued for Smith's execution. On December 26, 1799, thousands of people gathered on Concord Common where they saw that order carried out.

1801

Jason Fairbanks, white, age 20. *Murder.* The crime was committed on May 18, 1801, at Dedham, Massachusetts. Jason Fairbanks and Elizabeth Fales (white, age 18) were young lovers who came from upper-class families. They talked about getting married. The parents of Miss Fales, however, would not give their consent to such a union because they perceived a personality disorder in their daughter's suitor. Consequently the young couple took to meeting in secret. Their favorite trysting spot was a birch grove not far from the house of Miss Fales. On the above date Fairbanks decided that he must force the issue of marriage one way or the other. He accordingly met his sweetheart at the usual spot and insisted that she elope with him. When Miss Fales hesitated

Fairbanks lost control of himself. He then attempted to rape the young woman. His manner was rough and Miss Fales began to scream. Infuriated by the unexpected resistance, Fairbanks pulled out a knife and started slashing at Miss Fales. He did not stop until he had inflicted nearly a hundred wounds. When Fairbanks saw that the victim was disemboweled and nearly decapitated, he started slashing at himself. Then when he was completely awash in blood he went walking toward the decedent's house, shouting for her parents. All the while he brandished the gory knife and harangued the other members of the Fales family, bidding them to come and see what he had done and blaming them for having driven him to such an extreme. The male members of the Fales family disarmed Fairbanks and then went running to the scene of the crime. There they found the victim beyond all earthly aid. The killer was patched up and made to face a charge of capital murder. He was convicted on incontrovertible evidence. On September 10, 1801, a gallows was erected on Dedham Common. The weather was pleasant and thousands of people flocked to the scene. It is said that more than 700 wagons and carriages — all crammed with spectators — came out from Boston for the occasion. Hundreds more streamed into Dedham from other directions. Fairbanks walked from the jail to the gallows dressed in his burial shroud. When asked if he had any last words, he shook his head negatively. Then he told the executioner that he was ready. After hanging for half an hour Fairbanks was pronounced dead. The crowd was satisfied and it dispersed in an orderly manner.

1802

Ebenezer Mason, white, age unknown. *Murder.* The crime was committed on May 18, 1802, at Medfield, Massachusetts. Ebenezer Mason and William Pitt Allen (white, age unknown) were farm laborers who didn't have any love for each other. The fact that Allen had married Mason's sister only made matters worse. It so happened that Mason's father had died without making a will. His property wound up in probate and was ordered split between Ebenezer Mason and his sister. This settlement infuriated Mason because he felt that the money would thereby fall to the despised William Pitt Allen simply because he was married to the female beneficiary. Mason threatened Allen over the matter and said that he would make sure that he never saw a penny of the disputed money. He accordingly appealed the judgment of the Probate Court and thereby stalled the final settlement. After more than a year of litigation, however, it was ordered that the estate be settled according to the original decree. Ebenezer Mason would not stand for it. On the above date he and his adversary (Allen) were working in the fields. Mason stood in the back of a manure cart shoveling out its contents while Allen followed behind with a hoe, spreading the manure around the crops. Mason waited for a moment when Allen's back was turned and then bludgeoned the man with his shovel. He then repeated the blows until Allen's head was "nearly chopped to pieces." The ferocity of the attack evinced a lot of pent-up hatred in the killer. As a result of this act neither Allen nor Mason got the money. It all went to the widowed sister. On October 7, 1802, a gallows was erected on Dedham Common and Ebenezer Mason was hanged therefrom.

1803

Caleb Adams, white, age 19. *Murder.* The crime was committed on September 13, 1803, at Pomfret, Connecticut.

This young man had been orphaned at an early age. Consequently he was raised by an uncle in the town of Brooklyn. When Caleb was aged 16 it was decided to place him with a wealthy squire in the Abingdon section of Pomfret. There the boy was engaged to learn about agriculture. For the next three years Caleb went about his business diligently for the most part. There was only one area of concern: Caleb seemed to have a natural cruel streak in him and he had to be reprimanded several times for mistreating farm animals. It so happened that Caleb's employer had a young foster son named Oliver Woodward (white, age 6). This little boy nettled Caleb by following him everywhere and getting in his way. Finally Caleb decided that he would rid himself of the nuisance. He lured the younger boy into the woods under the pretense of cutting a flute for him. When they reached a spot that was lonely and remote, Caleb turned on the little boy. He crushed his skull with an axe and slit his throat from ear to ear. Two days later Caleb's employer went looking for him because he was absent without leave. He was found at the house of his uncle in Brooklyn. When asked the whereabouts of little Oliver, he nonchalantly replied that he had "left him in the woods." This answer alarmed Caleb's employer. Caleb was then brought back to Pomfret and subjected to an interrogation. Soon he confessed that he had killed Oliver Woodward. Then he led authorities to the body. When the case came to trial there was a concerted effort to get Caleb declared insane. In support thereof it was shown that Caleb's father was a lunatic and that Caleb himself was subject to "strange moods" that no one could explain. The jury did not go for it. Caleb was pronounced guilty of capital murder and he was ordered for execution. On November 29, 1803, nearly 10,000 people saw him hanged at Windham.

1804

John Battus, black, age 19. *Murder.* The crime was committed on June 28, 1804, at Canton, Massachusetts. This offender was born at Boston on April 4, 1785. His father abandoned him when he was five years old and his mother, left destitute, was forced to enter an almshouse. Two years later a prosperous white man came to that place of refuge in order to find a suitable houseboy. John Battus was selected from a pool of several dozen. So it was that he left Boston at the age of seven and went to the Norfolk County town of Canton where his new employer lived. There he would spend the rest of his life. As the boy grew it became apparent that he was ill-suited for housework. Therefore he was given duties as a farmhand with the understanding that he would be free to go his own way when he reached the age of majority. During these same years Battus may or may not have been kept on short rations, however, because as he later confessed, he became an inveterate thief with edibles as his favorite loot. On the above date Battus was working in a cornfield when he happened to see a young girl walking down the lane. Her name was Salome Talbot (white, age 13) and she was returning home from a day spent picking berries. Battus stalked her until they reached a stretch of road that ran through a patch of evergreens. Then he made his move. He pounced on the girl and dragged her into the woods. He beat her until she could no longer put up any resistance. That done, he tore her clothes off and raped her. The girl cried out that she would tell her parents whereupon Battus decided to kill her. Ht took up a stone (which was later found to have weighed 16 pounds) and used it to batter her about the head. When that mistreatment failed to kill the girl outright, Battus dragged her to a nearby pond and held her face beneath the water until she drowned. Two days later searchers found the body. Then on the following day Battus took fright and fled. By so doing he gave himself away. He was captured at Attleborough on July 6 and soon confessed his guilt. He was held for a court of law and duly condemned in strict accordance with legal procedure. Battus was hanged on Dedham Common on November 8, 1804.

1805

Samuel Freeman, black, age 25. *Murder.* The crime was committed on May 12, 1805, at Ashford, Connecticut. This is a little known case of a young black man who was involved in an abusive relationship with a Native American woman. The victim's name was Hannah Simons. She was slain by undisclosed means. Samuel Freeman admitted beating her up on the day before her death but he stubbornly denied killing her. As he stood on the gallows he declared that he was guilty of other crimes deserving death but not guilty of the crime for which he was condemned. He was hanged at Windham on November 6, 1805.

1806

Ephraim Wheeler, white, age about 35. *Incestuous rape.* The crime was committed on June 8, 1805, at Windsor, Massachusetts. This man's marriage had been going downhill for a long time. The final straw came on the above date when Wheeler attacked his wife with a bayonet. He was prevented from injuring the woman when a male boarder restrained him. Wheeler then declared that he was clearing out of the house and leaving his wife to fend for herself. He also said that he was taking his two eldest children with him, a 13-year-old girl named Betsy Wheeler and a 9-year-old boy named Ephraim Wheeler, Jr. The girl put up a tearful pleading to the contrary when

told that she must go with her father. It soon became apparent why. Her protests notwithstanding, Betsy Wheeler was put upon a horse with her little brother. Then her father took hold of the bridle and led the animal down the road. After a mile or so, Mr. Wheeler and the children passed through an area of dense woods. The father stopped the horse there and told his children to dismount. When they had done so, he instructed the boy to tend the horse while he and the girl went to look for herbs. Once again the girl put up a tearful resistance but she finally obeyed her father. The two then went into the woods while the boy remained in the road with the horse. What happened next is unprintable. Half an hour later the father and daughter came out of the woods. The girl was in tears and also in considerable pain. She also bore many cuts and scrapes. Wheeler then allowed the children to return to their mother but he threatened the girl with death if she ever dared to tell what happened in the woods. When Betsy Wheeler got home she was very distressed indeed. Thinking that she "might as well die one way as another" (to use her own words), she told her mother everything. She also said that it was not the first time that such a thing had happened. Mrs. Wheeler promptly called an officer of the law. Some matrons also examined the girl and confirmed that she had been raped. Betsy Wheeler repeated her story to a local magistrate, then to a grand jury and then to a petit jury. As a result her father was convicted of capital felony. He denied the charges to no avail. Thousands of people signed petitions asking that the death sentence be commuted to life at hard labor but the governor in council voted against clemency. Ephraim Wheeler was accordingly hanged at Lenox on February 20, 1806.

Dominic Dailey and **James Halligan,** whites, ages unknown. *Murder.*

The crime was committed on November 9, 1805, at Wilbraham, Massachusetts. It is possible that these men were innocent of the crime for which they were executed. The evidence against them was flimsy at best and both denied the matter to the death. Halligan is described as a "young man" of fair reputation. Dailey is said to have been a "subtle" man of "riper years." Both were recent arrivals from Ireland. On November 2, 1805, they set out together on an overland journey from Boston to New York City. Too poor to go by stagecoach, they resolved to walk the distance and by the seventh day they had reached the town of Wilbraham. It was there where — guilty or not — they made their rendezvous with destiny. Coming along the highway in the opposite direction was a lone traveler named Marcus Lyon (white, age 23) mounted atop a handsome horse. It is alleged that Dailey and Halligan (by then tired of walking) shot Lyon in his saddle, pulled him off the horse, pistol-whipped him to death, robbed him of his money and dumped his body in the Chicopee River. A 13-year-old boy later testified that he saw both men leading the murdered man's horse away from the spot where the crime was committed. (A hat identified as belonging to Marcus Lyon was found there shortly afterward.) The men soon realized that they had been seen and they abandoned the horse. Several hours later the horse was taken up as a stray and recognized as the property of the missing Marcus Lyon. Suspicion of foul play arose and a search party scoured the area. In addition to Lyon's hat, the search turned up the man's body face down in the shallow river. Also found were two broken pistols, the handles of which were matted with blood and hair. A path in the underbrush clearly showed that Lyon had been dragged from the road to the riverbank. There followed a hue and cry for the men who had been seen with the decedent's horse. Based on the boy's description, a suspicious pair were reported to have been seen in Springfield where they crossed the Connecticut River. From there they had turned south and crossed the state line. Innkeepers in Suffield, Windsor and Hartford all reported their presence as well as the facts that they paid with silver and seemed to be in a hurry. From Hartford the trail led to New Haven and then westward along the Boston Post Road. A posse finally caught up with the men at Rye, New York. Both surrendered peaceably and agreed to return to Massachusetts. There they were identified by the 13-year-old boy who had seen two men near the scene of the crime with the dead man's horse. Upon searching the suspects they were found to have enough money on them to pay for an easier mode of transport to New York. Why had they chosen to walk? Both were also found to have pistol holders sewn into the insides of their coats which showed evidence of being used but which were then empty of weapons. Was that because they had discarded those damaged and bloody weapons near the scene of the crime? Furthermore, Halligan had had some pay due him at Hartford. Why did he fly through the town in such haste without bothering to collect his money? A canister of beer was also found in their possession which was traced to a store near the scene of the crime. While it is possible that Dailey and Halligan had happened along the crime scene in time to merely discover the unattended horse, neither of them said so. Instead they chose to deny almost everything. They did acknowledge setting out from Boston on foot seven days before the date of the crime, thereby averaging 20 miles per day. However, they could not satisfactorily explain why they had suddenly accelerated their pace so that they made it all the way from Wilbraham to Rye — a distance of 130 miles — in less than half as much time thereby averaging 50 miles per day. The second leg of their journey looked more like a precipitous flight than anything else. When Dailey and Halligan were brought to trial the prosecution knew that it had a weak case. However, the state's attorney skillfully made the most of the 13-year-old boy's identification of the defendants as the same men who he had seen with the decedent's horse. Anti-Irish and anti–Catholic prejudice may or may not have done the rest. Dailey and Halligan were convicted and the governor of Massachusetts signed a warrant for their execution. Both were hanged at Northampton on June 5, 1806.

Josiah Burnham, white, age 62. *Murder.* The crime was committed on December 18, 1805, at Haverhill, New Hampshire. This man was born at Kensington, Connecticut, on August 12, 1743. Throughout the course of his life he earned a living as a blacksmith, a schoolmaster, a surveyor, a realtor and as an investor in securities. Contentious by nature, Burnham was frequently in court, either suing someone or threatening to do so. Sometimes he even found himself in court as a defendant; he is known to have served at least one prison term for welshing on his debts. On the above date Burnham was locked up in Haverhill jail. He had somehow gotten himself involved in a messy divorce battle and he was being held in connection therewith. Sharing the same cell with him were two other white men named Russell Freeman and Joseph Starkweather. Burnham had no better luck getting along with his cellmates than he did with the rest of society. He became enraged when the other men belittled his latest legal problem. For days the three men bickered, Freeman and Starkweather taking sides against the mercurial Burnham. Then somehow the latter got his hands on a rusty old scythe blade. He waited for the other two men to fall asleep and then attacked them with that weapon. Both were fatally stabbed.

Burnham next found himself charged with capital felony. He retained a young lawyer named Daniel Webster to defend him. This lawyer was destined to become a famous statesman but he failed to save Josiah Burnham. A conviction for double murder resulted in a sentence of death by hanging. Appeals were disallowed. The final act came on August 12, 1806, when more than 10,000 people came to Haverhill to witness the execution of the aging killer. It was Burnham's 63rd birthday.

1807

Harry Niles, Native American, age unknown. *Murder.* The crime was committed on March 22, 1807, at Lisbon, Connecticut. Little is known of this offender. He is described as a "transient person" whose last known address was in the town of Lisbon. On the above date he attacked his wife, Mary Niles (Native American, age unknown), with homicidal fury. The woman was beaten with a tree limb, punched, kicked and stomped. She died the following day. No motive was ever cited for this crime. Harry Niles was subsequently convicted of capital murder and ordered for execution. Thousands of people watched as he was hanged at New London on November 4, 1807.

1808

Joseph Drew, white, age 24. *Murder.* The crime was committed on January 11, 1808, at Falmouth, Maine. This man was born in York County, Maine, on October 9, 1783. At the age of 18 he was apprenticed to a blacksmith and spent the next three years learning the trade. When young Drew reached the age of majority he moved to Falmouth where he set up a smithy of his own. It was there where he ran afoul of the law. What happened was this: Sometime in December of 1807 a deputy sheriff named Ebenezer Parker (white, age unknown) arrested a Falmouth resident named Levi Quinby for failure to pay his bills. Quinby was then placed in the charge of the local jailer. Within a short time Quinby convinced the jailer that he was not a flight risk. He also asked to be allowed to return to his home, promising that he would surrender peaceably whenever required to do so. The jailer knew Quinby personally and also knew that he was not a violent offender. Therefore the request was granted. However, in the days that followed, Quinby armed himself with a club and carried that weapon around with him wherever he went. He said that he would not hesitate to "defend himself" if and when deputy Parker came to rearrest him. On the above date Parker went after Quinby. The latter sought to escape and he engaged the deputy in a pursuit. Parker wound up chasing Quinby through the streets of Falmouth. It was during this chase that Quinby suddenly ducked into Joseph Drew's place of business. He then bolted the door behind him and begged Drew for refuge. Drew took pity on the harried man. He then told him to go hide in the back room. Seconds later the deputy started pounding on the door. Drew asked him what he wanted and was told that the fugitive was seen entering his shop. Drew denied the presence of any such person and told the deputy to get lost. This answer annoyed Parker to a point that he broke down the door. That, in turn, made Drew angry. The blacksmith took red hot horseshoes from his forge and flung them at the deputy. Dodging the barrage, Parker said that he would have his prisoner. He also threatened to arrest Drew for harboring a fugitive. The furious Drew would not listen; instead he ordered the deputy to get off his property. Then the two men went at fisticuffs with each other. Levi Quinby saw all of this from his place of concealment. He then tossed his club to Joseph Drew. The blacksmith caught the club and beat up the deputy with it. Parker was then disabled by numerous blows to the head. Seven days later he died of a skull fracture and the charge against Drew was upgraded to capital murder. Quinby was likewise charged. When the case came to trial Drew was convicted and sentenced to death. Quinby was acquitted because no witness had actually seen him furnish Drew with the murder weapon. The irascible blacksmith was hanged at Portland on July 21, 1808.

Cyrus Dean, white, age unknown. *Murder.* The crime was committed on August 3, 1808, near Burlington, Vermont. This man was one of a gang of smugglers who were operating on the Winooski River. Ordinarily he belonged to the town of Swanton, Vermont. On the above date Dean and his cronies were going about their illicit business. There were seven of them in all. Customs agents planned to intercept them at a point along the aforesaid river. Two agents named Jonathan Ormsby and Asa Marsh (whites, ages unknown) took up positions on the Burlington side of the river while a third agent named Ellis Drake (white, age unknown) manned a small boat on the river itself. All were heavily armed. As the smugglers came down the river in their own vessel they observed the customs men. Suspecting an ambush, they decided to shoot first and ask questions later. One of the smugglers, Samuel Mott by name, was an expert marksman. He opened fire on Ormsby and Marsh with the result that both were killed. Cyrus Dean and the other smugglers opened fire on the boat containing Ellis Drake and several other customs men. Gunfire raked the boat from stem to stern. The fusillade killed Ellis Drake and forced his companions to dive into the water. The toll of this clash was three customs agents dead and some others injured. Such an affront to the law could not go unanswered. The militia was called out to deal with the situation. All of the smugglers were then rounded up and charged with capital murder. Samuel Mott and Cyrus Dean drew death sentences. The others got off with lesser verdicts. Due to a flaw in the indictment, Mott was granted an arrest of judgment. A retrial was ordered and a verdict of manslaughter was rendered. Thus it was that Mott escaped execution. He had to sit in the pillory, endure 50 lashes and serve ten years at hard labor. Cyrus Dean fared worse; his conviction was upheld on appeal and he was ordered for execution. He was accordingly hanged at Burlington on November 11, 1808.

1811

Ebenezer Ball, white, age unknown. *Murder.* The crime was committed on January 28, 1811, at Robbinston, Maine. This man was a lumberjack who worked the densely wooded area between Eastport and Calais. He came under suspicion of coining and on January 26, 1811, a warrant was issued for his arrest. Since the area where Ball dwelled was sparsely populated there was no sheriff or deputy on hand to execute the arrest warrant. Therefore responsibility for the same was assigned to a posse of yeomen. Heading this posse was a man named John Tileston Downes (white, age unknown) who, on the same day that the warrant was issued, went after the wanted man. Ball submitted to arrest in a peaceable manner and was brought before a magistrate. There it was decided that the evidence was insufficient to justify detaining Ball. The man was then released with a warning that any further evidence would result in his rearrest. Two days later that further evidence was forthcoming. Once again John Tileston

Downs led a posse to the house of Ebenezer Ball. This time the wanted man was in a combative mood. When he saw the possemen approaching he took up a shotgun. Then he went walking down a logging trail. There the posse overtook him and demanded his surrender. Ball then started shooting. A full charge struck Downes in the stomach, fatally wounding him. The rest of the posse then retreated and Ball took to the woods. Two days later he was captured by a heavily armed search party. The nearest court was at Castine, a hundred miles to the west. Ball was taken there and put on trial for his life. A jury convicted him and the trial judge certified that there were no mitigating factors. The governor then issued a warrant for Ball's execution. The otherwise sleepy town of Castine saw its population more than triple as the "hanging day" drew near. Spectators filled every inn and boarding house to capacity. Those who could find no accommodations bivouacked in the fields and along the roadsides. Ball himself retained an obdurate demeanor all the while. He annoyed the local religious community by spurning all offers of religious solace. He also refused to evince any contrition for his crime. On October 31, 1811, he walked to the gallows unassisted.

1812

Samuel Tully, white, age 42. *Murder and piracy.* The crime was committed on January 9, 1812, on the high seas. This was a federal case. The American schooner *George Washington* sailed from Philadelphia on October 17, 1811, bound for Tenerife with a cargo of corn. The crew consisted of the captain, Uriah Levy by name; the first mate, Samuel Tully, and five able seamen named John Dalton, Joseph Neal, Daniel Hopkins, George Cummings and John Owen, the last of whom was a Negro cook. On

December 13, 1811, the vessel reached its destination without incident. The cargo was unloaded and sold for $2500 cash. Ten days later the schooner left Tenerife and went to the Isle of May — located in the Cape Verde group — which it reached on January 4, 1812. There the captain went ashore to negotiate for a return cargo. In his absence, first mate Samuel Tully assumed command of the schooner. After five days Capt. Levy was still unable to strike a deal with the merchants ashore. The first mate meanwhile cast covetous eyes on the money that had been taken aboard at Tenerife. He then conspired with Seaman Dalton to run off with the schooner and embezzle the money. On the above date Capt. Levy was still ashore. The conspirators decided to leave him there. They then cut the anchor cables and told the other crewmen that the schooner was adrift. Tully ordered them to spread sail and make for the open sea. Two of the crew — Neal and Hopkins — noticed the sabotage of the anchor cables and protested loudly. They surmised what Tully was doing and refused to be party to it. Tully then allowed them to get into a lifeboat and row themselves ashore. However, he would not allow Cummings and Owen to join them. For the next two weeks the stolen schooner maintained a westerly course. Then one night Seaman Cummings tried to single-handedly wrest control of the vessel from Tully and Dalton. In the struggle that ensued Cummings was overpowered by the pirates and thrown overboard. The next day land was sighted. It was the Isle of St. Lucia in the Lesser Antilles. Tully and Dalton put all of the stolen money in the one remaining lifeboat. Then they scuttled the schooner before setting out for shore. They also allowed John Owen, the cook, to join them in the lifeboat instead of leaving him to go down with the ship. When the lifeboat reached shore, Tully and Dalton said that they were the only survivors of

a wreck. Owen, however, took the first opportunity to report the entire matter to the authorities. He was then arrested on suspicion of piracy as were Tully and Dalton. An American ship subsequently brought all three to the Port of Boston where they were indicted by a federal grand jury. John Owen was allowed to turn government witness against the two white men. He thereby earned immunity from prosecution. Tully and Dalton were capitally convicted. On December 10, 1812, both men were drawn to a gallows on the Boston waterfront. There Samuel Tully was hanged while Dalton was forced to watch. Only then was it announced that Dalton had been reprieved.

1813

John Cummings and David Lord,

whites, ages unknown. *Army desertion.* Their crimes were committed in June and July of 1813 at Burlington, Vermont. Very little is known about these men. Their court-martial files have not survived. The one newspaper account which mentions them is short on details. Cummings was a private in the American army. He deserted from the Burlington cantonment sometime in June 1813, and was caught shortly thereafter. A court-martial convicted him of willful desertion and ordered that he be shot to death by musketry. The sentence was carried out at Burlington on July 12, 1813. On that same day a second soldier named David Lord deserted from the Burlington cantonment. He had witnessed the execution of Cummings but did not feel deterred by the experience. This David Lord was also a private in rank. He is further known to have been a resident of Thetford, Vermont. Within a short time he too was caught and condemned by a court-martial, probably the same one that had handled the case of Pvt. Cummings. The sentence meted out to him was no different. Another firing squad was formed and once again the soldiers of the Burlington cantonment were made to witness the execution of one of their own. The date was July 28, 1813.

Henry Pyner, black, age unknown. *Rape.* The crime was committed sometime in the spring of 1813 in Hampshire County, Massachusetts. Henry Pyner was a free Negro. He makes his first appearance in the records of the Hampshire County Supreme Judicial Court on April 25, 1809, when he pled guilty to a charge of grand larceny and was sentenced to three years in the Massachusetts State Prison. He appears to have completed his term on schedule and to have returned to his home territory. His next known offense was a capital one: namely the forcible rape of a white woman. The record of his trial for that crime is missing. Such is not surprising since the only newspaper to mention the case says that the details were too obscene to be published. A conviction and death sentence were meted out to Pyner at the September 1813 term of the Hampshire County Supreme Court. The next we hear of Pyner — and the last we hear of him — is on November 4, 1813, when he is drawn to a public gallows at Northampton. There he is reported to have confessed his guilt and to have been legally hanged without further incident.

Ezra Hutchinson, white, age unknown. *Rape.* The crime was committed sometime in the spring of 1813 in Berkshire County, Massachusetts. This is another case that suffers from a dearth of information. All that is known of Ezra Hutchinson is that he was a low class white man who lived on the fringe of society. He was said to dwell in a remote corner of the town of Stockbridge. According to the only surviving newspaper to mention the case, Hutchinson forced himself on an unmarried white woman named Sally Bates. It was enough to earn him a conviction for capital felony. He was hanged at Lenox on November 18, 1813.

1814

James Anthony, white, age unknown. *Murder.* The crime was committed on February 15, 1814, at Rutland, Vermont. This man was a hatter who had his own workshop in the business district of Rutland. For reasons that were never made clear he lured a merchant named Joseph Green (white, age unknown) to his shop on the evening of the above date and murdered him there. The victim was beaten over the head with an iron, strangled and then stashed beneath a woodpile. Three days later some concerned citizens began a search for the missing man. James Anthony came under suspicion when he was seen with a bruised face and spots of blood upon his clothes. When asked for an explanation he told an improbable story. Then to make matters worse, he told conflicting stories. It was decided to make a thorough search of Anthony's workshop. More bloodstained clothes turned up there which Anthony tried to explain away by saying that he had used them to sop up a nosebleed. Then a pair of bloodstained hats turned up concealed beneath a furnace; Anthony said that he had put them there to dry. After that a wallet containing the sum of $47.75 in cash was found hidden in the same furnace and some of the searchers claimed to recognize it as being the property of the missing man. The clincher came when one of the searchers poked his cane into an aperture in Anthony's woodpile and felt something soft. It was the body of the slain man. Anthony merely shrugged his shoulders and said that he did not know how the body came to be there. He also told a vague story of having loaned his workshop to some gamblers on the night that Green had disappeared. A jury took exactly seven minutes to convict James Anthony of capital murder. On the morning of the day set for his execution — April 14, 1814 — the condemned man tricked his deathwatch guard into averting his attention from him for several minutes. Then he ripped the lining out of his coast and made it into a crude noose. Breaking a piece of wood from a chair, Anthony inserted it crosswise between some stones in the ceiling of his cell and knotted the free end of the coat lining around the wood. Then he stood upon his bed, put his head into the loop of the makeshift noose and hanged himself. All efforts to revive him were futile. There are conflicting reports about what happened next. Some say that the sheriff was afraid to disappoint the thousands of people who had come to Rutland to witness the execution and so caused the dead body of James Anthony to be carried to the gallows and strung up there a second time. Other accounts are silent as to the fate of Anthony's body.

Adam Wilson and **John Goodenough,** whites, ages unknown. *Army desertion and bounty jumping.* Their crimes were committed in October of 1814. On November 4, 1814, a wartime court-martial convened at Fort Independence (near Boston) for the purpose of deciding the fates of five American soldiers who had been adjudged guilty of willful desertion. All five were sentenced to be shot to death by musketry. In reviewing the sentences, the commanding general decided that clemency was appropriate for three of the defendants. One was spared because he appeared to be contrite. Another was spared because he had no record for previous misconduct. The third was pardoned because he was only a teenager. In two cases, however, there were no mitigating factors. These were the cases of privates Adam Wilson and John Goodenough. The first of these men had

belonged to the 40th Massachusetts Infantry and had failed to return from a furlough that had been granted him on October 14, 1814. The second man, Goodenough, had not only deserted his regiment but had aggravated the offense by bounty jumping. To be precise, he was found to have enlisted in the 30th Massachusetts Infantry early in October 1814, and to have collected an enlistment premium on that occasion. Days later he deserted and made his way to Providence, Rhode Island, where he fraudulently reenlisted under another name for the sake of another monetary inducement. The commanding officer at Boston decided to make examples of Wilson and Goodenough. On November 10, 1814, both men were stood before a firing squad and executed pursuant to their sentences. Boston newspapers chose not to report the matter because it was considered inimical to the American cause.

1816

Miner Babcock, black, age 19. *Murder.* The crime was committed on June 21, 1815, at Preston, Connecticut. This young man was a free Negro. He was born at Voluntown on February 4, 1796, to a married couple who were also free. At the age of nine young Babcock's parents hired him out as a houseboy. However, it soon became apparent that the lad was not suited for such a role. In the years that followed, Babcock found himself in a wide variety of jobs ranging from farmhand to keeper of a tollgate to cook aboard a Long Island Sound schooner. When Babcock was 18 years old his father died. His mother then began a relationship with another black man named London. She also invited her new beau to share her home. Miner Babcock did not like that turn of events. He had always felt close to his mother and he resented the stepfather-to-be as an interloper. On the above date Miner

Babcock was an overnight guest at his mother's house. A tiff took place on that occasion between Babcock's mother and her lover. Babcock took his mother's side in the matter and had harsh words with London. Then a fight broke out. The two men tussled with each other. In the heat of the moment Miner Babcock picked up a butcher knife and stabbed his adversary in the abdomen. Then seeing that the thrust did not have its desired effect of disabling the other man, Babcock followed it up with five more thrusts. London was literally disemboweled by the wounds. He died soon afterwards. Miner Babcock was then taken for murder. He had two trials and was capitally convicted each time. On June 6, 1816, thousands of people braved gale force winds to flock into the little city of Norwich so they could witness the end of Miner Babcock. After an impressive religious service the condemned man was put in the back of a wagon together with the coffin that was soon to receive his body. Then a splendidly attired company of mounted grenadiers escorted him to the gallows. Few were able to hear Babcock's final speech because of the howling wind. However, all could plainly see him as he swung to his doom.

Peter Lung, white, age 49. *Murder.* The crime was committed on July 31, 1815, at Middletown, Connecticut. Peter Lung and his wife, Lucy Kelley Lung (white, age about 47), were a discordant couple who owed their misfortunes to alcoholism. Drunken quarrels had induced each of their four children to move out as soon as they were old enough to do so. Unwilling to admit his own shortcomings, Peter Lung was exasperated by the fact that his wife shared them. He railed against her drinking habit without making any effort to clean up his own act. To him it was all fine and well for a man to drink to excess but he regarded similar conduct in a woman as slovenly, unladylike and inexcusable. On the above date Peter Lung came home at a late hour. As he neared his house he was puzzled to see the door wide open and all the lamps lit. Entering the front room, he found his three grandchildren sleeping on a bed fully clothed. In the kitchen there was no meal prepared. In the bedroom lay Mrs. Lung passed out drunk. Her person stank of liquor. Peter Lung then lost his temper. He booted his wife off the bed with a powerful kick and ordered her to wash and feed the grandchildren. Mrs. Lung then sassed her husband, saying that if he wanted a meal prepared he could fix one for himself. The argument then escalated until Peter Lung slapped his wife several backhands and kicked her in the rump. Then he went outside to the garden and dug up some potatoes with which to feed the family. Two days later Mrs. Lung began to complain about a pain in her side. She went to sleep in a rocking chair that night and did not awaken the next morning. An autopsy showed that she had succumbed to internal injuries. Evidently the kicks the woman had received had ruptured something inside her. Peter Lung was then charged with capital murder. At his trial several people testified that Lung had been habitually abusive toward his wife. In addition to that, his elderly mother-in-law told of how she had witnessed such scenes time and again. The death of Lucy Lung was said to be directly attributable to spousal mistreatment. In his defense, Peter Lung admitted striking and kicking his wife but denied any homicidal intent. A jury was not impressed. The state legislature considered an application for clemency and voted it down. The law was then left to take its course. The end came on June 20, 1816, when Peter Lung was hanged at Middletown.

1817

Henry Phillips, white, age 25. *Murder.* The crime was committed on December 1, 1816, at Boston, Massachusetts. This individual was a Welsh merchant seaman. He made his first ocean voyage as a nine-year-old cabin boy and in the years that followed he became remarkably well traveled. Sailing in British and American vessels, young Phillips crossed the Atlantic a dozen times. He visited nearly every port in the Mediterranean, spent time in equatorial Africa and went on trading expeditions to the Indian Ocean. In all that time he was never known to have broken the law. The above date found Phillips at the Roe Buck Tavern in Boston. There he was lodging while awaiting the departure date for yet another ship on which he was to sail. It so happened that on the evening of the same date a young couple was seated in the parlor of the Roe Buck Tavern where they were reading a bible by candlelight. Also present was an Italian sailor named Gaspare Denegri (white, age 25), who had had a little too much to drink. Denegri saw the couple reading their bible and decided that it would be fun to tease them. He then playfully blew out the candle that they were using thus depriving them of their reading light. The candle was relit only to be blown out again. This was repeated several times. Phillips saw what was going on and he came to the defense of the bible readers. He warned Denegri that enough was enough and bade him to tease the readers no more. Denegri disregarded this warning and Phillips became increasingly annoyed. Finally Phillips lit the candle himself and told Denegri that if he blew it out again he would do so at his peril. Denegri was too drunk to realize that Phillips was serious. So he blew out the candle again. Then a fight broke out. Phillips and Denegri tangled with each other. The landlord of the tavern intervened and succeeded in separating the two men before matters got out of hand. He then declared in a stern tone of voice that the Roe Buck Tavern was a respectable place and that no brawling would be tolerated there. Then the landlord announced that it was closing time and told Denegri that he must leave. Denegri and his drinking buddies obeyed the landlord but murmured among themselves as they walked out the door. An hour or so later Denegri came stomping back to the tavern and began pounding on the door. He made a loud scene, calling Phillips by name and saying that he had unfinished business with him. It was also obvious that Denegri was excessively drunk. The landlord feared to let Denegri in because he thought that he had a knife. Phillips was both angry and embarrassed. He picked up an iron tool called a loggerhead (used for broaching casks of ale) and made ready to confront his antagonist. When he opened the front door of the tavern Denegri was not there; he had by then gone around to the back door. Phillips followed him behind the tavern where he knocked him over the head with his improvised weapon. Denegri was felled and later found to have suffered a fatal skull fracture. He died a week after being injured. Phillips insisted that he had not meant to kill Denegri but only to disable him until he sobered up. A jury, however, saw things differently. A capital conviction was returned and Phillips was sentenced to death. More than 20,000 people watched as he was hanged at Boston on March 13, 1817. Most of the spectators felt sympathy for him.

Amos Adams, black, age 28. *Rape.* The crime was committed on August 29, 1817, at Weston, Connecticut. Although history books and contemporary newspapers both mention this case, neither say very much about it. All that is known of Amos Adams the person is that he was a free Negro. Where he dwelled and how he made his living are unanswered questions. The record of his trial is missing as well and what remains to be told is rather sketchy. Adams is said to have set his sights on a married white woman named Lelia Thorp. He waited for a time when her husband was away before he dared to act. On the above date Adams saw his chance. He went to the unguarded house of Lelia Thorp and forced his way in. After terrorizing the lone occupant he forced himself on her. Then he fled into the night. Several hours later he was taken by hue and cry. It was not until a court of law condemned him that Adams finally admitted his guilt. He also acknowledged responsibility for several other sex crimes that had occurred in the Weston area. In consequence of these things, November 13, 1817, was proclaimed a "hanging day" at the little city of Danbury. On that day Amos Adams was led from the jail to the meetinghouse with a white cap on his head and a noose around his neck. There he was forced to listen to a lengthy sermon. After that came mandatory prayers. When the religious service finally ended the condemned man walked from the meetinghouse to the gallows. More than 15,000 people watched his every move. When the fatal spot was reached there were more prayers and benedictions. Then Amos Adams was hanged by the neck until he was dead.

1818

Samuel Godfrey, white, age 32. *Murder.* The crime was committed on November 5, 1814, at Windsor, Vermont. This man was born at Chatham, Massachusetts, on March 22, 1782. When he was eight years old his parents relocated to Hudson, New York. There young Samuel Godfrey was apprenticed to a hatter and for the rest of his life he had frequent recourse to that trade. As a teenager Godfrey formed a desire to go to sea. He accordingly took the necessary steps to pursue that ambition but found the same to be ill-fated; over the course of the next several years he was impressed into the British navy on three separate occasions. Those experiences left their mark on him both physically and psychologically; he developed a nervous disorder from a flogging that he received aboard one British ship and he was also left embittered to a high degree. Between his involuntary stints in the Royal Navy Godfrey attempted to settle in Nova Scotia on a permanent basis. There he followed his hatting trade in a credible manner but had to be constantly on his guard. The naval press gangs were very active there and Godfrey was determined not to be snared a fourth time. Finally the pressure became too great and he was forced to close up shop. With his savings he purchased a schooner with an objective of entering into the coasting business. This too proved to be an ill-starred venture for Godfrey. The schooner was wrecked in a storm. Wiped out financially, Godfrey then headed west with nothing but his clothes and three silver coins. He made it as far as Quebec where once again his experience as a hatter served him well. For the next three years Godfrey plied his trade between Quebec and Montreal, earning a modest but satisfactory living. In 1811 he decided to leave Canada altogether. Godfrey then set a course for Vermont where he went from town to town as a transient hatter. In Rutland he even teamed up with a kindred tradesman named James Anthony for a while — the same James Anthony who was condemned for murder in 1814 [see Anthony, 1814]. In September of 1812 Godfrey joined the American army. It then being wartime, he saw action along the northern frontier. Shortly thereafter he decided that the life of a soldier did not suit him. He later claimed that unfair treatment had caused him to think about deserting his regiment. Not daring to risk a firing squad for such an offense, Godfrey then hit upon another way of shortening his enlistment: he stole goods from a civilian with a deliberate intention of being caught and charged with grand larceny in a civilian court of law. Pleading guilty, he was then sentenced to a term in the Vermont State Prison and thereby effected his discharge from the army. The next step in Godfrey's plan was to petition the governor of Vermont for a pardon and thereby regain his complete liberty. However, before his petition was acted upon Godfrey became involved in another set of circumstances which ultimately had fatal results for him; he quarreled with the overseer of the prison workshop and was thrown into solitary confinement. There he brooded over what he once again regarded as unfair treatment. When he was eventually returned to the general prison population he was angry and short-tempered. On the above date — November 5, 1814 — Godfrey was once again employed in the prison workshop. This time he was operating a weaver's loom. When tally time came Godfrey found that he had completed more work than his quota for that day. He then declared that he would make up for the surplus the next day by slackening his pace. This the overseer did not like to hear. Godfrey wound up getting put on report. When the warden of the prison, Thomas Hewlett (white, age unknown), made his rounds that day he was told of Godfrey's situation. Desiring to hear Godfrey's side of the story, Hewlett went over to the man's work station in order to question him. Godfrey said that he was being ill-used and he poured out a torrent of complaints. The warden listened patiently but the more Godfrey spoke the more upset he became. Finally the warden told him to take the rest of the day off. Orders were then given to the workshop overseer to have Godfrey escorted back to his cell. By then, however, Godfrey was in an explosive mood. He yelled defiance at the overseer who had put him on report "for no good reason," as he said. Then he smashed a

wooden chair on the concrete floor and grabbed one of the chair legs to use as a weapon. He also grabbed a knife from a nearby cobbler's bench. Advancing on the overseer with the chair leg in one hand and the knife in the other, Godfrey leapt to the attack. The overseer defended himself with a sword whereupon the warden attempted to restrain Godfrey. In the struggle that followed, Godfrey jabbed the warden in the side with the cobbler's knife before finally being subdued. At first the warden's wound was not thought to be serious. However, gangrene set in and the man succumbed four weeks later. Godfrey was then charged with capital murder. He had three trials in which he was capitally convicted each time. A lengthy series of reprieves also figured in the situation during the course of which it was argued that the evidence against Godfrey could not support a capital verdict. At most, it was said, the crime amounted to simple manslaughter because there was no premeditation. The state legislature also considered the case but voted against clemency. The prevailing rationale was that the killer of a prison warden could not be spared for any reason. A gallows was finally erected on the Woodstock town green and on January 13, 1818, thousands of people watched as Samuel Godfrey was hanged from it.

1819

Francis Frederick, white, age 32; **John Rogg,** white, age 27; **Peter Peterson,** white, age 17; and **John Williams,** white, age 27. *Murder & Piracy.* The crime was committed on July 22, 1816, on the high seas. This was a federal case. It is also an extremely rare instance of a juvenile offender being put to death by order of a federal court. The story begins on July 1, 1816, when the American schooner *Plattsburg* sailed from the Port of Baltimore. The vessel was bound for Bremen with a cargo of coffee. Also on board were gold and silver coins (totaling $42,000) with which a return cargo was to be purchased when the schooner reached Germany. Commanding the *Plattsburg* was Capt. William Hackett (white, age unknown), who was assisted by a first mate named Frederick Yeizer (white, age unknown) and a second mate named Stephen Onion. Also present aboard ship was a supercargo named Thomas Baynard (white, age unknown). The rest of the crew consisted of nine able seamen, among whom were the four above-named. It so happened that Capt. Hackett ran a tight ship. He allowed no liquor aboard his vessel and he took means to confiscate an illicit supply which the crew had smuggled in their seachests. This was deeply resented by the crewmen. In addition, the captain and first mate had struck several members of the crew for what they perceived to be insolent behavior. These incidents were small in themselves but they combined to inspire the crew with thoughts of mutiny. After three rigorous weeks at sea it was decided that the officers should be slain and the schooner commandeered. On the above date the captain, first mate and supercargo were all seized by mutineers. Then they were thrown overboard. The second mate was spared when he agreed to join the uprising. The money which the schooner was carrying (in all probability the *real* object of the mutiny) was divided among the crew. Alterations were next made to the ship's papers and a new course was plotted. On August 13, 1816, the *Plattsburg* entered a port on the coast of Norway. There the ship's cargo was sold on the black market. The crew scattered at that point. Shortly afterward the truth became known and an alarm was circulated for the missing crewmen, six of whom were eventually caught over a two-year period. All were sent to Boston for trial by a federal circuit court. The second

mate, Stephen Onion, became a government witness and it was principally through his testimony that the above-named quartet were declared murderers, mutineers and pirates. A fifth defendant escaped with a lesser verdict. The fact that Frederick, Rogg and Peterson were foreign nationals (they were from Minorca, Denmark and Sweden respectively) did not hinder their extraditions to the United States nor their accountability to American law. They along with the other convict, John Williams (who was himself a New Yorker), were all hanged at Boston on February 18, 1819.

Peter Johnson, black, age unknown. *Rape.* The crime was committed on May 20, 1819, at Sheffield, Massachusetts. Nothing is known of this offender's personal history. He appears to have been a free Negro and a resident of the town where he committed his capital crime. According to his confession, Johnson had his eye on a married white woman named Charity Booth. On the above date he became aware of the fact that Mr. Booth had been called out of town on business. That night Johnson went to the Booth residence and forced his way in. Then he proceeded to terrorize the occupants, being Mrs. Booth and her two young children. Johnson beat up the woman and raped her while the toddlers looked on helplessly. After effecting his purpose, the assailant took to the woods. Two days later he was taken by hue and cry. On November 25, 1819, a reportedly contrite Peter Johnson was taken from the Lenox jail and brought to the local meetinghouse where he was made the subject of a lengthy religious service. After being preached to for several hours he was carried to a gallows and hanged.

1820

Luther Virginia, black, age unknown. *Murder.* The crime was committed on November 14, 1819, at High-gate, Vermont. This offender is described as a "youngerly colored man of intemperate and dishonest habits." He once worked for a Highgate Falls inn-keeper but lost that job when he was caught stealing from the till. A conviction for grand larceny followed and Luther was sent to the Vermont State Prison. On October 15, 1818, he was granted a pardon. Free once more, he returned to the greater Highgate area. On the above date Luther boldly strode into his former place of employment and demanded liquor. Instead of being served he was told to get off the property. Luther then became belligerent. A fight broke out and Luther had to be forcibly restrained. Then a white man named Rufus Jackson (age unknown) joined the innkeeper in showing Luther to the door. This incensed Luther even further. He then resolved to get even with Rufus Jackson. Several hours later Jackson left the inn and set out for his home on horseback. Luther lay in wait for him on the far side of the Missisquoi River. He was armed with a piece of wood that he had taken from a fence. As Jackson rode along unsuspectingly, Luther used his weapon to knock the man from his horse. Then he beat him to death with it. The riderless horse found its way back to the inn and was recognized as the property of Rufus Jackson. A search party found the man's badly beaten body. Luther Virginia was traced to his home just over the Canadian border. A search of the place turned up Jackson's watch concealed in a bed. Luther Virginia was brought to St. Albans and tried by a court which was specially called for the occasion. On December 13, 1819, he was convicted and ordered for execution. One month later thousands of people thronged St. Albans to see Luther Virginia hanged. Bitterly cold weather did not deter them. The death sentence was carried out with impressive solemnities and Luther Virginia

found his place in the town's history. The date was January 14, 1820.

Michael Powers, white, age 51. *Murder.*

The crime was committed on March 2, 1820, at Boston, Massachusetts. This man was born and raised in County Wexford, Ireland. There he was a farmer by profession. In 1798 he participated in a civil upheaval in the aftermath of which he was obliged to flee his native country. After spending the next four years in England he took passage on an immigrant ship to Boston. There he went to work as a hod carrier and a bricklayer. The next 15 years of Powers's life were generally uneventful. He lived frugally, saved his money and kept up a regular correspondence with his relatives in the old country. Eventually five cousins of Powers decided that they would like to follow him to America. They accordingly made a deal in which Powers would advance each of them money to pay for their passage across the Atlantic Ocean. It was further agreed that the money would be repaid to Powers as soon as the new arrivals established themselves in their new homes. Each cousin received a loan of £9-5-0 which aggregated to $25 at the prevailing rate of exchange. Then they made the trans-Atlantic voyage and settled at Boston. After allowing a reasonable amount of time to pass, Powers asked his cousins to settle their debts with him. Only one of them did so in an honorable manner. The others either pled poverty or avoided Powers altogether. Faced with such a situation, Powers started to become annoyed. Most irksome to him was a cousin named Timothy Kennedy. This man flatly refused to pay up and even antagonized Powers by making no secret of the fact that he could easily afford to part with the amount in question. Powers finally took Kennedy to small claims court in an attempt to recover his money. There he was bitterly disappointed to have a judgment recorded against him because he had nothing in writing with which to prove Kennedy's indebtedness. As a result, Kennedy walked out of court unscathed. Then as an added indignity, Powers was ordered to pay costs. This was more than Powers could bear. It was bad enough that Kennedy had dodged his debt for more than two years; the loss of the lawsuit made Powers angry beyond the point of self-control. On the above date Powers caught Kennedy alone in his boardinghouse (located on South Russell Street in Boston) and beat him beyond recognition. Then he chopped off the man's head with a broadaxe and buried him in the cellar. A search for the missing man resulted in the discovery of his remains. Powers heard the news and fled as fast as he could. Two weeks later he was nabbed in Pennsylvania. When the case came to trial Powers garnered a fair amount of sympathy on the grounds that the victim had been guilty of provocative conduct. This, however, was insufficient in itself to eschew a guilty verdict. The facts of the homicide were plain and the evidence against Powers was incontrovertible. Although the trial court could find no legal grounds to spare Powers from the mandatory death sentence, he was granted the indulgence of burial without autopsy — in those days a sign of special favor. Powers then declared himself content and he asked that his execution not be delayed. He was hanged at Boston on May 25, 1820. As an added favor, Powers was put to death without public notice and at a deliberately early hour. In that way the crowd of spectators was kept to a minimum.

Edward Roswaine, William Holmes and Thomas Warrington,

whites, aged about 25. *Murder and piracy.* Their crime was committed on July 4, 1818, on the high seas. This was a federal case. The schooners *Buenos Aires* and *Tucuman* were privateer vessels that had been outfitted in and had sailed from a port in Argentina. They were really little more than pirate ships which preyed upon unarmed commerce vessels. On May 28, 1818, both schooners were cruising together in the waters off Cadiz, Spain. There they fell in with a Spanish merchant ship and seized it by force of arms. A prize crew was then put aboard the captured vessel and told to sail it back to their home port in Argentina where it would be liquidated and the proceeds credited to the privateers. Command of the prize crew was assigned to one "Reed" by name. He in turn was assigned a first mate named "Joseph" and three seamen named Edward Roswaine, William Holmes and Thomas Warrington. These latter three were adventurers from England, Scotland and Connecticut respectively. At first the prize voyage went according to plan. The original Spanish crew of the captured vessel was put ashore in the Cape Verde Islands unharmed. Then the privateers continued on their way to Argentina. At some point in the subsequent voyage the above-named trio formed a conspiracy to murder their officers (Reed and Joseph) and seize control of the prize vessel. They would then bring the ship to an American port, dispose of it there and embezzle the proceeds. It was on the above date that the plot was set in motion. As the mate, Joseph, was taking a nap on deck he was pounced upon by the conspirators and thrown overboard. The prize master, Reed, heard a voice calling for help and when he looked out his cabin window he saw Joseph bobbing up and down helplessly in the ship's wake. Reed immediately ran onto the deck only to be similarly overpowered and thrown into the sea. The doomed man managed to catch ahold of a rope and cling to it for dear life. Holmes then slashed at him with a knife in an attempt to break his grip on the rope. When that failed, Holmes simply cut the rope and Reed fell into the ocean where he was left to his fate. With the officers out of the way the conspirators changed the vessel's course and headed north. On August 30, 1818, they put in at Scituate, Massachusetts, where they unaccountably abandoned the prize vessel and fled ashore. All three were rounded up by local officials and sent to Boston. A subsequent investigation determined the true particulars of how the three men had come to be in their situation. The added fact that the United States was then at peace with Spain led to the trio being branded as pirates. All three were tried by a federal court in Boston and all were sentenced to death. The United States Supreme Court took the case on appeal due to the questions of jurisdiction but the final decision went against the defendants. All three were hanged at Boston on June 15, 1820. Their bodies were given to a medical school.

1821

Stephen Merrill Clark, white, age 16. *Arson.* The crime was committed on August 17, 1820, at Newburyport, Massachusetts. This juvenile offender lost his life because he could not resist the blandishments of a female catalyst. Stephen Merrill Clark was the scion of an otherwise respectable family. Born at Newburyport on August 20, 1804, he was raised in a loving and supportive home. His nature, however, was an impressionable one and once he fell in with bad company there was no redeeming him. In Clark's case the "bad company" took the form of a cadre of female prostitutes. Clark allowed himself to be enticed into a relationship with at least one and possibly more of the inmates of a so-called "disorderly house" which was notorious in his hometown. He soon became smitten by what he mistakenly perceived as "love." In reality the so-called "abandoned women" were only too aware of Clark's susceptibility. Using sex as their bait, they soon had the infatuated teenager completely in their power. Clark was willing to risk anything for them and thus he became a deluded tool in their hands. It so happened that these unscrupulous women harbored a grudge against some of the more law-abiding of Newburyport's residents. They had had aspersions cast upon them and they resented it deeply. They decided to make the willing Stephen Merrill Clark the instrument of their revenge. But how? The answer was simple: have the smitten boy set fire to the property of their enemies. They began with a scowling moralist named Elihu Brown. He owned a barn on Green Street that was packed with provender and valuable farm equipment. Acting at the women's behest, Clark fired the barn with the result that it was a total loss. Arson was suspected from the start but the culprit escaped detection. Emboldened by this success, Clark struck again on the very next night. He snuck into a stable owned by a goodwife named Phoebe Cross and set it ablaze. The result was a spectacular conflagration which destroyed an entire block of stables and warehouses located between Charter and Temple streets. In addition to that, the fire spread out of control and consumed three large dwelling houses. No one was killed but the loss of property was substantial. Some valuable horses perished and five families were left homeless. The occupants of the burned houses were also left destitute because they lost all of their possessions as well. Clark was eventually found out due to his inability to keep his mouth shut. Some imprudent remarks he made were overheard and they did not go unreported. When he was confronted, Clark quickly confessed and said that the "harlots" had put him up to it. Faced with this, the female catalysts abandoned Clark; they said that Clark had confessed his guilt to *them* and that they felt it to be their civic duty to report the matter. The women escaped prosecution because no one could be found to corroborate Clark's allegations against them. Clark himself was charged with arson in the first degree — a capital offense. He was convicted on evidence consisting primarily of his own confession. Because the instigators of Clark's crime had gone free and because Clark was only 16 years of age, a movement arose in his favor. The governor's council was inundated with appeals for clemency — all to no avail. The council considered the matter and denied clemency by a unanimous vote. In a statement released after the announcement of its decision, the council justified itself by saying that clemency in such a case would set a pernicious example. When Clark set the fires he was fully cognizant of the fact that he was committing a capital crime. He also knew that his actions were deliberately wrong. Sparing him would be tantamount to encouraging other prospective incendiaries. On May 10, 1821, this youthful offender was hanged at Salem, Massachusetts.

Michael Martin, alias "Captain Lightfoot," white, age 26. *Highway robbery.* The crime was committed on August 13, 1821, at Medford, Massachusetts. This celebrated felon has been the subject of much misinformation. His exploits have been over-embellished and over-romanticized by generations of storytellers. In reality, Martin was far from the dashing highwayman of legend. He was, at best, a thief — and not a very gallant one at that. When the apocrypha is removed from his story we are left with this: Michael Martin was born in the parish of Connehy, about seven miles from Kilkenny, Ireland, on April 9, 1795. He was the youngest of five children born to a farm couple named Joseph and Maria O'Hanlon Martin. At the age of 14 he was apprenticed to a brewer. At age 17 he stole money from his father and ran away to Dublin where he got a job in a distillery. Two years later he decided to

return home. Along the way he stopped at a tavern where he made the acquaintance of one John Doherty. This man was a professional criminal who went by the sobriquet of "Captain Thunderbolt." He took a liking to young Martin and induced him to join up with him. This was in the summer of 1816. For the next two years this symbiosis haunted the roads of Ireland, robbing peddlers and lone travelers. When Ireland became too hot for them they took a boat to Scotland. After a month or two there they became discouraged and slipped back into Ireland. Soon they were forced to separate in order to hinder pursuit. They would never see each other again. Martin donned a disguise and went to Waterford. There he booked passage on a ship to New York. On June 17, 1819, the vessel was forced to put in at Salem, Massachusetts, because it had run out of fresh water. Martin went ashore there. For the next 14 months he worked on a farm in Essex County. At the end of that time he received an inheritance which tempted him to go into business for himself. He leased a brewery which he was forced to close in May of 1821 due to poor management. Martin then made his way to Quebec and survived by mugging people. When the pickings grew slim in Canada he stole a horse and slipped across the American border. Then he moved in an easterly direction, committing several holdups along the way. On the above date he finally overplayed his hand; he forcibly stopped a buggy in which were a well-dressed couple named Major and Mrs. John Bray. The incident occurred along the Medford Turnpike as the Brays were returning home from a reception given by the governor of Massachusetts. Martin rode his stolen horse up to the passenger compartment of the buggy. Then he threatened Major Bray with a pistol and uttered the classic line, "Your money or your life!" Major Bray handed over his wallet whereupon the robber said, "I now demand your watch, sir!" Bray then relinquished a gold watch. Mrs. Bray was not molested. Before galloping away Martin looked in the wallet and was disappointed to find only nine dollars. Bray read his thoughts and said, "Upon the honor of a gentleman, that is all the money I have about me." Martin then sarcastically replied, "I rob none but gentlemen, sir." Then he fled into the night. Soon there was a hue and cry throughout the countryside. The governor of Massachusetts was furious when he heard that one of his guests had been robbed. Martin ditched his horse and stole another one. Then he fled westward to Springfield where the owners of the horse caught up with him. Martin's captors did not hang him from the nearest tree. Instead, they brought him back to Middlesex County to face a non-capital charge of horse theft. It was only when a gold watch found on Martin matched one advertised as having been stolen from Major Bray that the aggrieved horse owner realized that he had snared a highwayman. This development resulted in the charge against Martin being upgraded. He now faced an indictment for capital felony. Major Bray and his wife both identified Martin as the man who had accosted them. Following his conviction in a court of law, the governor of Massachusetts was only too happy to sign a warrant for Martin's execution. The highway robber was then hanged at Cambridge on December 20, 1821.

Daniel Davis Farmer, white, age 28. *Murder.* The crime was committed on April 4, 1821, at Goffstown, New Hampshire. This offender was born at Manchester, New Hampshire, on March 28, 1793. As a teenager he worked for a Goffstown farmer named Joshua Ayer and in so doing became acquainted with Mrs. Anna Ayer (white, age unknown), the wife of his employer. This Anna Ayer was a woman of poor reputation. When

her husband died she went from bad to worse. Becoming pregnant, she applied to her local Board of Selectmen for assistance. The answer she received was either identify the father of the child or go hungry. Anna Ayer then denounced Daniel Davis Farmer, who was by then a married man. Farmer was accordingly arrested on a charge of siring an illegitimate child. Whether the charge was true or not is far from certain. However, the allegation was enough to send Farmer into a rage. On the above date he drank heavily and stomped over to the widow Ayer's house. There he forced the woman to drink rum before matter-of-factly telling her that she must die. Then he began beating her with a club. Mrs. Ayer's adolescent daughter ran screaming from the house only to be chased down by the intruder. Farmer severely beat the girl before bludgeoning her with a rock. Thinking her dead, he dragged the girl back into her house by the ankles and threw her under a bed. Then he focused his anger on the mother again. Taking a set of metal tongs from the fireplace, he literally broke them over the woman's head. Then he continued the assault with a shovel. Farmer did not stop beating Anna Ayer until brain matter flowed from her wounds. When he finally thought that both of the victims were dead he set the house on fire and fled into the woods. The girl crawled out from under the bed and knocked over a barrel of beer. By so doing she put out the fire that Farmer had set. Later she dragged herself to a neighbor's house where she gave the alarm. The killer was quickly captured. On December 27, 1821, thousands of people descended upon the little town of Amherst to witness the execution of Daniel Farmer. When the time came, two horse-drawn sleighs emerged from the gates of the county jail; in one sat the condemned man and in the other was his coffin. Mounted troops escorted the procession. At the gallows religious services were performed. All was speeded up when the prisoner began to lose his nerve. He was then hanged without further ado.

1822

Gilbert Close and Samuel Clisby,

whites, both aged 23. *Highway robbery.* Their crime was committed on August 13, 1821, at Boston, Massachusetts. Gilbert Close was a New Yorker by nativity. Samuel Clisby came from New Hampshire. Nothing is known about the early lives of either man because both of them refused to divulge any information to that effect. They got to know each other as convicts in the Massachusetts State Prison where each had been sent for unspecified offenses. Both were released from their durance in the summer of 1821. They opted to stick together but were either unable or unwilling to find honest livelihoods. On the evening of the above date both men were loitering in the vicinity of the West Boston bridge. There they spotted a well-dressed pedestrian named Ezra Haynes (white) walking down Cambridge Street. The man had a look of prosperity about him so Close and Clisby reasoned that he must have a handsome sum of money on his person. Both decided then and there to rob Mr. Haynes. They walked by an outdoor hardware display and deftly made off therefrom with a long-handled gardening tool, the head of which was made of cast iron. They then stalked Mr. Haynes. When they reached a spot that was well away from the street lamps they pounced on the unwary pedestrian. Knocking the man to the ground, Close gave him a severe beating with his blunt instrument. The weapon drew blood which spattered on both attackers. Clisby used a knife to rip open the pockets of the victim's clothes and thereby get at his money. Once the loot was secured the muggers left Mr. Haynes battered and bloodied in the middle of the street.

The next day there was a roundup of suspicious characters. Close and Clisby were reported as having been seen with bloodstained clothes the previous night. Both were fully identified by Mr. Haynes. In addition to that, the victim was doubly sure of the identification because he knew Clisby from a previous encounter. When the suspects were questioned about their bloody garments they gave evasive answers. Because the crime was committed in a public thoroughfare with dangerous weapons both were charged with highway robbery — a hanging offense. A jury convicted both of them and both were ordered for execution. As their date with the gallows drew near both men made confessions. Close admitted cutting the man's pockets open but denied striking him with a dangerous weapon. Both offenders were publicly hanged at Boston on March 7, 1822.

Samuel Greene, white, age 24. *Murder.* The crime was committed on November 8, 1821, at Charlestown, Massachusetts. This is the second of only two cases in New England wherein a white person was executed for victimizing a Negro. Samuel Greene was a drifter from Meredith, New Hampshire. He lived on the proceeds of burglaries and other thefts. According to his own account, he was responsible for the fatal robbery of a peddler in Maine. He also admitted to a highway robbery near Middleton, Vermont, in which an unarmed Frenchman was slain. On July 3, 1818, Greene was committed to the Massachusetts State Prison following a conviction for grand larceny. Toward the end of his four-year term he became involved in a plot to escape. The situation went awry, however, due to a jailhouse informer named Billy Williams. From that time on, Williams (black, age unknown) was a marked man. On the above date Greene caught up with Williams in the prison workshop. He attacked the man with an

iron bar and beat him without mercy. Williams had all four of his limbs broken plus all of his ribs. In addition to that, he had most of his teeth knocked out and his skull fractured. He succumbed to his injuries after a week in agony. Samuel Greene was identified as the assailant. He was charged with capital murder and convicted. On April 25, 1822, he was publicly hanged at Boston.

1824

George Henry Washington, Native American, age unknown. *Murder.* The crime was committed on March 20, 1824, at Hebron, Connecticut. The record of this case contains few details. George Henry Washington is described as a "transient person" who earned his livelihood by unknown means. On the above date he killed his wife, Margery Washington (Native American, age unknown), by bludgeoning her with a stick. No motive for the crime was ever disclosed. The Connecticut state legislature was willing to commute the death sentence in this case but Washington spurned an appeal, saying that he wanted no favors from the white man. On June 1, 1824, more than 10,000 people jammed the little town of Tolland to see this offender hanged. An entire company of cavalry joined a like number of infantry in escorting Washington to the gallows. There the prisoner met his end with an air of stoical indifference.

Perez Anthony, black, age unknown. *Murder.* The crime was committed on January 24, 1824, on the high seas. This was a federal case. Even so, little is known of it. Perez Anthony was a crewman aboard an unidentified American ship. On the above date that vessel was in the Bay of Honduras. Anthony quarreled with a fellow crewman named Theodore Stodder (white, age unknown)

and the two had to be forcibly separated. Anthony is described as having endured a "slight provocation" and as having brooded over the matter for the next several hours. Then he let his indignation get the better of him. Anthony broke into a weapons locker and got his hands on a double-barreled shotgun. He loaded the weapon and went looking for Stodder with it. When Anthony found the object of his search he opened fire with both barrels. Theodore Stodder was killed instantly. Anthony was quickly disarmed by other members of the crew and placed under arrest. The captain of the ship ordered that he be confined in a secure area. He was then brought to the Port of Boston where a federal circuit court convicted him of willful murder. Defense arguments alleging insanity on the part of the defendant were disallowed. So was an attempt to say that the shotgun had been discharged accidentally. Perez Anthony was hanged before a large crowd of Bostonians on December 22, 1824.

1825

Seth Elliott, white, age 36. *Murder.* The crime was committed on July 25, 1824, at Knox, Maine. This man was an alcoholic farmer who wound up becoming a filicide. He is described as having been a credible member of his community when sober. Conversely, he was the exact opposite whenever he was drinking. Alcohol made Elliott surly and it was his wife and youngest child who became the objects of his ire on such occasions. Elliott is reported to have slandered his wife in obscene terms, calling their youngest child "the fruit of her infidelity" and saying that he would put both mother and child on the street. On the above date Elliott awoke with a hangover. He refused to get out of bed and he remained there all morning with the very child that he disliked, a son named John Wilson Elliott (white, age 3). When Elliott's eldest son (a boy of 13) came in from the fields at midday he found his inebriated father and little brother still in bed but awash with blood. Seth Elliott had fatally slashed the throat of his youngest child and made an ineffectual attempt to do the same thing to himself. The elder boy immediately ran from the house screaming. The neighborhood was aroused and some grown men hurried to the scene. There they found Seth Elliott in a state of extreme intoxication. A bloody razor lay nearby. When Elliott was aroused from his stupor all he did was shout obscenities and threaten those who had come in contact with him. When questioned about the homicide he said that his wife had attacked him and the child. Later the same day Elliott attempted to justify his actions by saying that he was within his rights "to do what he pleased" with the dead child because as its sire he felt that he had the power of life and death over it. When the case came to trial Elliott used an insanity defense. A disgusted jury, however, took less than an hour to convict him of capital murder. The penalty was death by hanging. On February 3, 1825, thousands of sightseers thronged the town of Castine in expectation of a rare treat: the public infliction of capital punishment. Seth Elliott rode to the gallows in a wagon seated atop his coffin. Then for nearly an hour he addressed the crowd in a clear voice, reciting the story of his life and warning all to consider the woeful effects of "intemperance." Prayers were said and while still in the midst of them Seth Elliott was swung to his doom.

Horace Carter, white, age 26. *Rape.* The crime was committed on February 23, 1825, at Brookfield, Massachusetts. This offender was born at Sturbridge in the year 1799. He never went to school. At the age of nine his parents put him out to board and he remained in such

circumstances for the rest of his life. At the age of 14 Carter was taken on as a farmhand by a Mr. Daniel Hodges of Weston. He wound up staying there for seven years. When he reached the age of majority he became his own master and wandered about the countryside in search of odd jobs. By then he had grown into a tall brawny fellow and as such had little difficulty finding work. On the above date Carter went to Brookfield where he spent some hours drinking with his buddies. When the time grew late he set out for his home on foot. Along the way he was overtaken by one Brutus Hodges who offered him a ride in his covered wagon. The weather then being damp and raw, Carter was glad to accept the ride. He wound up at the wagon owner's house where the two men finished off a jug of cider. Shortly before midnight Carter announced his intention of going to Brimfield. He accordingly set out for that place on foot. By then he was intoxicated to excess. After walking a couple of miles in the rain and fog Carter came in sight of the local poorhouse. Discouraged by the bad weather, he decided that the poorhouse would be a good place to seek shelter. He then approached the building and knocked on one of its doors. A voice called out to him asking to know who was there whereupon Carter said that he was an overseer of the poor who had come to check on the place. The inmates of the poorhouse did not believe him. Carter was denied admittance and told to come back at a decent hour. Undaunted, Carter then broke down the door and forced his way in. He found himself in a spartan chamber occupied by three elderly women and a crippled boy. Carter went to the fireplace and warmed himself for a while. He saw that the paupers were too physically infirm to resist his intrusion. After several minutes he called upon one of the elderly women to put more wood on the fire. The only one who had strength enough to do so was Ruth Ainsworth (white, age 78), and she was too frightened to move. Without any warning, Carter suddenly pounced on her and tore off all her clothes. Then he raped her in front of her helpless roommates. The next day there was a roundup of suspicious persons. The four paupers all identified Carter amid a group of 20 men. Charged with capital felony, Carter eventually confessed. On December 7, 1825, a gallows was erected on Worcester Common. Thousands of people gawked as the condemned man was slowly drawn to the place of execution in a coach-and-six. Alongside him marched a company of Light Infantry while ahead of him a military band led the way. All kept tune while drummers played a death march. All were dressed in black, including the horses. Carter himself was indifferent to the scene. He met his end without saying a word.

1826

John O'Halloran, alias "John Holland," white, age unknown. *Murder.* The crime was committed on December 11, 1825, at Boston, Massachusetts. Jonathan Houghton (white) is described as an "elderly" watchman who used to patrol the streets of Boston at night. On the above date he encountered John O'Halloran, an Irish immigrant, swaggering about drunk. The man was armed with an axe and he was swinging the thing about in a reckless manner. When Houghton attempted to restrain the obnoxious carouser he became the next target for O'Halloran's axe. The watchman had his side split open and he died eight days later. The killer was quickly seized and charged with capital murder. He was hanged in front of Boston's Leveret Street jail on March 3, 1826.

Samuel Charles, Native American, age unknown. *Murder.* The crime was

committed on October 25, 1825, at Richmond, Massachusetts. This is an obscure case that stemmed from a drinking bout that got out of hand. On the above date a group of native tribesmen had gathered for a social occasion. Among them was Samuel Charles. Liquor flowed freely and by the evening hours many of the guests, including Charles, were either drunk or well on the way to becoming so. Also present was a Negro man named Joel Freeman. He was an emancipated slave. Samuel Charles did not care for Freeman's presence at the party. Sometime after midnight Charles picked up a loaded shotgun, jabbed the end of it into Freeman's ribs and pulled the trigger. Freeman was fatally wounded. Charles then resumed his drinking as if nothing had happened. Eleven months passed before Charles was brought to trial. He and several other partygoers were charged with capital murder. Charles was the only one convicted. On November 22, 1826, thousands of people poured into the little town of Lenox to witness the end of Samuel Charles. A military parade escorted the condemned man to the gallows. When he was asked if he had any last words, Charles answered in the affirmative. He then made a short speech in which he denied the killing of Joel Freeman. He did, however, admit to being an accomplice in the matter. Then he was hanged by the neck until dead.

1827

John Duncan White, alias "Charles Marchant," white, age 23. **Winslow Curtis,** alias "Sylvester Colson," white, age 22. *Murder and piracy.* Their crime was committed on August 28, 1826, on the high seas. This was a federal case. The schooner *Fairy* sailed from the Port of Boston on August 20, 1826, bound for Gottenburg with a cargo of coffee, rice, sugar and tobacco. The crew consisted of a youthful captain named Edward Selfridge (white, age 23) and a first mate named Thomas Jenkins (white, age 25), along with four seamen named John Murray (white, age 19), John Hughes (white, age 24) and the above-named Curtis and White. The last of these men was a moody malcontent who had argued with the first mate even before the schooner sailed. Matters went from bad to worse as the voyage got underway. White chafed under shipboard conditions; he hated his officers, he was insubordinate and he resented having to do lookout duty. When the first mate slapped him across the face one day it was enough to drive him to mutiny. He approached Winslow Curtis and asked him if he would join in murdering the officers and taking over the ship. Curtis, it turned out, had his own reasons for disliking service aboard the *Fairy*; the captain had caught him sleeping on watch one night and had awakened him by throwing a bucket of salt water on him. Curtis therefore agreed to join in White's conspiracy. Shortly after midnight on the above date White attacked the first mate with an axe as the man lay sleeping on deck. The murder was effected without rousing the rest of the crew. Curtis then helped White in throwing the slain man overboard. Then both of the mutineers burst into the captain's cabin where the occupant was taken by surprise. They beat the captain severely before dragging him up onto the deck and throwing him alive into the sea. Curtis later told of how they could hear the captain crying for help as the ship sailed on. After disposing of the officers, White and Curtis confronted the two remaining crewmen. Both were threatened with death unless they did as they were told. The killers next plundered the captain's cabin but were bitterly disappointed not to find any money therein. They then took out their frustration by vandalizing the ship. They cut away the anchors, smashed the water casks and heaved the cargo overboard.

Then they changed the ship's course and headed north. When they came to a point near Cape Breton Island they scuttled the *Fairy* and came ashore in a lifeboat. Crewmen Murray and Hughes accompanied them. When questioned by Canadian officials the killers said that their ship had gone down after springing a leak. Murray and Hughes, however, told a different tale. All four were arrested and sent to Boston for trial by a federal court. Murray and Hughes were not prosecuted because their story was believed. Both were used as government witnesses against Curtis and White. After being capitally convicted, Curtis made a confession in which he corroborated most of the prosecution's testimony. Neither he nor White were very forthcoming with personal information about themselves, however. All they would divulge to that effect was that they came from Buxport, Maine, and Dover, England, respectively. On the morning of the day appointed for their execution, John Duncan White was found hanging in his cell. Winslow Curtis wound up going to the gallows alone. Both men did, however, share the same grave. The place was Boston, Massachusetts. The date was February 1, 1827.

1829

John Boies, white, age unknown. *Murder.* The crime was committed on February 9, 1829, at Milton, Massachusetts. This man was an alcoholic wife abuser. The fact that he had a drinking problem was of little consequence to Boies. However, the fact that his wife, Jane Boies (white, age unknown), shared that weakness was something that he refused to abide. Boies would severely beat the woman whenever he smelled liquor on her person. On one occasion he blackened both of her eyes and broke two of her ribs. On another occasion he broke both of her arms. Whenever Mrs.

Boies appeared bruised and beaten she would tell gratuitous fibs like "I fell out of a wagon" or "I was injured by a well-sweep," etc. Few believed her because there was ample evidence in the community that John Boies was by nature a brutal man. On the above date the man came home and found no supper prepared for him. Surmising the reason why, Boies looked in the bedroom. There he found his answer: Jane Boies passed out on her bed drunk and naked. This time John Boies lost his temper like he never had before. He dragged his naked wife off the bed and beat her without mercy. Then he grabbed an axe from the woodpile and hacked her to death. Investigators later counted 15 axe wounds on the woman's body. John Boies stubbornly refused to admit the crime even though there was incontrovertible evidence of his guilt. On July 7, 1829, thousands of people gathered on Dedham Common to see this man hanged for the murder of his wife. None were deterred by the excessively hot weather.

1830

John Francis Knapp, white, age 20. **Joseph Jenkins Knapp, Jr.,** white, age 27. *Murder.* Their crime was committed on April 6, 1830, at Salem, Massachusetts. Capt. Joseph White (white, age 82) was one of the most socially prominent men in Massachusetts. A retired merchant and shipping magnate, he had amassed a considerable fortune. He lived in an opulent mansion which still stands on Essex Street in Salem. For years Capt. White had been secretive about how he planned to dispose of his estate and his advancing age only served to heighten speculation. Among his potential heirs was the aforesaid Joseph Jenkins Knapp, Jr., who was married to a grand-niece of the elderly tycoon. This relative-by-marriage was anxious lest Capt. White's estate not fall to the

grand-niece to whom he (Knapp) was married and thereby come under his own control. Unable to bear the suspense any longer, Knapp went rummaging around until he found Capt. White's will. When he read the document Knapp was chagrined to learn that White had other plans for the bulk of his estate. Faced with this, Knapp decided to take preventive measures; he destroyed the will and conspired to bring about White's demise. In such a way, reasoned Knapp, the probate court would award the major portion of White's estate to the man's most direct descendent (the wife of Joseph Knapp) because White would have supposedly died intestate. Joseph Knapp then approached his younger brother, John Francis Knapp, and acquainted him with what he had in mind. He also offered him $1000 in gold if he would kill Capt. White. After thinking the matter over, John Francis Knapp came to a split decision: he declined to commit the murder himself but did agree to recruit a pair of hitmen. Those so selected were another pair of brothers: Richard and George Crowninshield, reputed to be malcontents who would do anything for money. On the above date Joseph Knapp unlocked a rear window in Capt. White's house. Late that same evening the hired assassins climbed into the house by that route. Then as George Crowninshield allegedly stood watch, Richard Crowninshield snuck into Capt. White's bedroom. The victim was slain in his bed by being hit over the head and stabbed 13 times in the heart. Several weeks passed before there was a break in the case. By then the truth had been leaked to the underworld and an attempt was made to blackmail the Knapps. An extortion letter naming all four conspirators fell into the hands of the authorities. Then all four were arrested. Joseph Knapp — the catalyst of the entire matter — was the first one to flinch; he offered to turn state's evidence against the Crowninshields if he was granted immunity from prosecution. The offer was accepted. However, Richard Crowninshield preempted the prosecution by committing suicide in his cell. This unexpected development left the state's case in a difficult position; under Massachusetts law accessories could not be tried as such unless the principal defendant was convicted first. With Richard Crowninshield dead, the cause of the prosecution was thrown off course. It was then decided to try John Francis Knapp as principal. The noted statesman Daniel Webster was appointed lead prosecutor. Faced with the prospect of testifying against his little brother, Joseph Knapp reneged on his plea bargain. Without his testimony it took two separate trials to convict the younger Knapp. The first trial ended in a hung jury. Then a retrial ended in a capital conviction for willfully aiding and abetting the crime of premeditated murder. Next came the turn of Joseph Jenkins Knapp. With his immunity revoked, the prosecution came down hard on him. He was also capitally convicted. The last defendant, George Crowninshield, was acquitted when two women provided him with an alibi. On September 28, 1830, a well-behaved crowd estimated at 5000 people gathered at Salem to witness the execution of John Francis Knapp. Then on December 31, 1830, the process was repeated as Joseph Jenkins Knapp was hanged from the same gallows.

1831

Joseph Gadett and **Thomas Collinett,** blacks, ages unknown. *Murder and piracy.* Their crimes were committed on August 18, 1830, on the high seas. This was a federal case. The American brig *Orbit* had sailed from the Port of New York on what was intended to be a trading expedition to South America and Africa. The vessel left its home port sometime in the summer of 1828 and reached Brazil without incident. There the captain and crew spent more than a year going about their business. On January 17, 1830, the *Orbit* sailed out of the Brazilian port of Bahia loaded with trade goods. A course was then set for the African coast where the brig arrived after a voyage of about 40 days. For the next several months the *Orbit* carried on a lucrative trade there. Her South American goods were exchanged for a fortune in ivory, palm oil and precious metals. At two calling points along the way, the captain of the *Orbit*, one Samuel Woodbury (white, age unknown) by name, discharged the majority of this crew so they could return to their homes aboard other ships. In their place another crew was recruited. Of the original crew only two men (named William Strike and Charles Bowen) opted to remain for the duration of the voyage. The new crew consisted primarily of Portuguese and Negro seamen, among the latter of whom were the above-named Joseph Gadett and Thomas Collinett. It did not take long for the valuable cargo to excite the cupidity of the new crewmen. A plot was hatched among them to murder the captain, take over the ship and embezzle the cargo. The ringleaders were Gadett, Collinett and an unnamed Portuguese. On the evening of the above date Capt. Woodbury decided to enjoy the tropical climate by sleeping on the ship's deck instead of in his cabin. He was then attacked in his sleep by the Portuguese conspirator while Gadett and Collinett stood lookout. Capt. Woodbury was hacked to death with an axe and thrown overboard. Gadett and Collinett stood by with harpoons during the course of the murder, ready to cut down anyone who might try to interfere. They also confronted the original two crewmen, Strike and Bowen, and gave them a choice: either join in the conspiracy or die like the captain. Both men knew better than to refuse. The mutineers next concerned themselves with dividing the cargo among the crew. Then for the next several days the *Orbit* was the scene of non-stop revelry, gambling and rapine. Gaddett, Collinett and the Portuguese killer all made themselves at home in the captain's cabin. On September 11, 1830, the *Orbit* encountered another American brig called the *Mentor*. A small boat (in which were the aforementioned William Strike and Charles Bowen) was sent alongside the *Mentor* in order to exchange nautical information. Strike and Bowen had not had their hearts in the mutiny and they saw this as a way out. When they got aboard the *Mentor* they told of what had happened aboard the *Orbit*. Soon the pirates realized that all was not well. They quickly spread sail and fled, leaving Strike and Bowen aboard the other brig. All of the pirates were fully identified and had "wanted" posters bearing their names and descriptions circulated throughout every Atlantic and Caribbean port. The ultimate fate of the *Orbit* is unknown because the vessel was never seen again. Nor were the majority of the mutineers. Gadett and Collinett, however, turned up on the Isle of St. Vincent and were taken into custody. From there they were sent to Cuba and put aboard an American warship which brought them to the Port of Boston. A federal district court tried them there on charges of piracy. Both confessed their guilt when the personal papers and belongings of the murdered Capt. Woodbury were produced in evidence against them. The incriminating materials had been found with the defendants at the time of their arrest. In addition to that, William Strike and Charles Bowen were on hand to testify for the prosecution. Both prisoners were condemned by the court which tried them. Both were publicly hanged at Boston on July 1, 1831.

Oliver Watkins, white, age 35. *Murder.*
The crime was committed on March 22,

1829, at Sterling, Connecticut. This man was born at Ashford, Connecticut, in October of 1793. When he was ten years old his father decided to relocate his entire household to Pennsylvania. Young Oliver Watkins made the move and there spent the remainder of his childhood. A brawny fellow, Oliver devoted his teenage years to hard labor; he worked as a roustabout clearing land, building roads, digging wells and chopping wood. He was careful to save his money and by the age of 20 he had enough to buy his own farm. In 1816 he married a young woman named Roxanna Adams. Two years later the couple journeyed to the town of Sterling, Connecticut, where they were the guests of relatives. There Oliver Watkins met a brother-in-law with whom he had corresponded. The two men got to talking and they agreed to swap their respective farms. Hence Watkins and his family became permanent residents of Sterling. (The fact that Watkins left a lot of unpaid bills in Pennsylvania was later cited as the true reason for his willingness to relocate.) Once settled in Connecticut, Watkins augmented his farm by opening a sawmill. He also hired himself out as a teamster. For personal diversion he began an adulterous relationship with one Waity Burgess by name. She was reputed to be one of the most unsavory women in the area. She had been banished on one occasion for running a house of prostitution. Watkins fell passionately in love with her and was none too secretive about it. Soon the affair was the scandal of the district. When Roxanna Adams Watkins found out about it she begged her husband to desist. He angrily refused and from that time on grew increasingly surly toward his wife. On the above date Watkins approached his spouse as she lay sleeping in bed. Notwithstanding the fact that the woman had a baby next to her, Watkins grabbed a bead necklace she was wearing and twisted it tightly around her neck.

He did not let go until his wife was strangled to death. The next morning a report was made to the effect that the decedent had succumbed to a seizure. However, the matrons who prepared the body for burial were puzzled by the indentation marks of the bead necklace on the dead woman's throat. They were also puzzled at finding the necklace broken and beads scattered about the bedclothes. A report was made to the authorities. Two days later the state's attorney for Windham County appeared at the local cemetery and halted the funeral of Roxanna Adams Watkins. There would be no burial, said he, without an autopsy. Oliver Watkins did not like the idea but he was in no position to prevent it. Surgeons later declared that the decedent had died of a crushed larynx. Suspicion of foul play was thereby confirmed. Oliver Watkins had two trials and was twice convicted. On August 2, 1831, he was hanged before a large crowd. The scene was the little town of Brooklyn, located in the northeast corner of Connecticut. It was the last public execution in that state.

1832

Amasa Walmsley, Native American, age 25. *Murder.* The crime was committed on September 18, 1831, at Burrillville, Rhode Island. This offender was a scion of the Naragansett tribe of Native Americans. He was born at Burrillville, Rhode Island, on August 24, 1806, and spent his entire life in that general area. At the time of his capital crime he was living in Smithfield and was without regular employment. It so happened that Amasa Walmsley had a brother named Thomas Walmsley who lived at Burrillville, the place of their birth. On the above date Amasa went to visit his brother and the two men wound up at the local tavern. When they had eaten and drunk their fill they returned to Thomas Walmsley's home. There they met with a rude surprise: some of the lowest vagabonds of the vicinity were having a party there. Most objectionable of all was the presence of two tramps named John Burke (white, age unknown) and Hannah Frank (black, age unknown) who were reputed to be of extremely poor character. The couple lived in the woods, they were openly miscegenous and they survived by raiding vegetable gardens. In addition to that, their physical condition bespoke their circumstances: they were drunk, disheveled, half naked and unwashed. Thomas Walmsley let them continue to drink and dance for a while because he was half-drunk himself. Then when he could endure their presence no longer he ordered them to get out of his house. John Burke and Hannah Frank did as they were told. However, they were only gone a few minutes when one of the female partygoers said that they had stolen some of her clothes. She then requested the Walmsley brothers to follow after them and give them a good thrashing. Since the Walmsleys were both well-primed with liquor they needed little coaxing. They immediately set out after John Burke and Hannah Frank. Overtaking the couple on the road, Thomas Walmsley stood by while Amasa Walmsley attacked the pair with a stick. The man and woman were too drunk to resist. Both were beaten senseless by Amasa Walmsley and left lying in the road. Their assailant then spat on them and returned to his brother's house. Shortly afterward he came back to the scene of the beating with an axe and found John Burke still lying there. Amasa Walmsley then chopped the man's head off. The next day Hannah Frank was also found dead. She had succumbed to a skull fracture. Both of the Walmsleys were arrested and charged with two counts of capital murder. Both were convicted and sentenced to death. Both petitioned for clemency but only Thomas Walmsley was spared. Amasa

Walmsley was left for execution. On June 1, 1832, more than 10,000 people watched as he was hanged at Providence, Rhode Island.

1833

William Teller, white, age 28. **Caesar Reynolds,** black, age 29. *Murder.* The crime was committed on April 30, 1833, at Wethersfield, Connecticut. These men were convicts who killed a guard while attempting to escape from the Connecticut State Prison. William Teller was a native of New Jersey. He had served prison sentences both there and in New York before coming to Connecticut where he was caught in the act of passing bad money. At the time of his capital offense he was serving a 15-year sentence. Caesar Reynolds came from Rhode Island. He was declared incorrigible following a third conviction for burglary and was serving a mandatory life sentence when he committed his capital crime. He had previously served two separate terms in the Connecticut State Prison. It so happened that Teller discovered a way in which to pick the lock on his cell. Feeling that the advantage thus gained was too good to leave unexploited, he confided the fact to Caesar Reynolds, one of his jailhouse cronies. For his own part, Reynolds had been hard at work for some time fashioning a skeleton key which would open every lock in their cellblock. However, he was unable to put the key to use because he could not reach the lock on the door of his own cell. It was therefore agreed that Teller would first pick the lock on his cell and then come over to Reynolds who would in turn pass the skeleton key out to him through the grate on his cell door. Teller would then use the key to liberate Reynolds and together they would make a break for it. Late on the above date the two conspirators put their plan in motion. The lone

guard on duty, Ezra Hoskins (white, age 67), was not only past retirement age but deaf as well. Consequently he did not hear Teller tampering with the locks. Reynolds was let out of his cell according to plan and together both prisoners made their way along the tier of cells unseen and unheard by the guard. It was their plan to next get into the women's quarters and slip out of the prison through a garbage chute that was there. The female prisoners were not party to the escape plan and when one of them saw Teller and Reynolds trying to gain admittance to their quarters she called for the matron. In the meantime the skeleton key broke off inside the lock on the gate of the women's quarters. An alarm was raised. Soon there was all the noise and confusion associated with a call to general quarters. Ezra Hoskins, the duped guard, came running and he encountered Teller and Reynolds. A struggle ensued during which Hoskins was fatally bludgeoned with an iron bar. Teller then tried to make the best of a bad situation; he undressed the murdered guard and put on his uniform. Then he tried to bluff his way out of the cellblock. In this, however, he was not successful. Teller and Reynolds were both subdued by other guards. They were subsequently charged with capital murder. Both were condemned. They were hanged at the Hartford County jail on September 6, 1833.

Amos Miner, white, age 46. *Murder.* The crime was committed on June 21, 1832, at Foster, Rhode Island. This man was born at Stonington, Connecticut, on September 23, 1785. He received a credible education there and entered the business world as a schoolmaster. After several years spent in that occupation Miner discovered that he could make more money by working in the textile mills. He accordingly gave up the teaching profession and became a factory hand. For the next 20 years Miner drifted from mill to mill. He married and fathered six children. The reason why he did not tarry long in any one location was because he was a credit abuser; he liked to run up bills and then move on without paying up. His last residence was in the town of Killingly, Connecticut. There he repeated his modus operandi and packed up his belongings when the dunning notices became more than he could bear. On the above date Miner rose before dawn and set a course eastward with his wife and children. The family walked along the old Hartford to Providence stagecoach route (present-day Route 6) and soon crossed the Rhode Island border. That same day one of Miner's creditors heard of his flight. Determined not to let the debtor escape, the aggrieved party set out in pursuit. Late in the day he caught up with his quarry. Miner and his family were resting beneath a roadside shade tree in the town of Foster. It so happened that Miner had already secured employment at a nearby mill. When the creditor saw Miner he told him that he had brought the town constable of Killingly along with him to enforce his claim. Then the constable stepped forward and demanded that Miner settle his account with the creditor. In reply, Miner told both men to go to hell. Neither had any legal ground to accost him, taunted Miner, because they were no longer in the state of Connecticut. Then Miner picked up an axe that he had been carrying and menaced both men with it, saying that if they dared to come any closer to him they would do so at their peril. The creditor and the constable both had to admit that they could not legally enforce a Connecticut claim in Rhode Island. They then backed off and went in search of local authorities with Miner's mocking laughter ringing in their ears. The rebuffed men proceeded to make a complaint before the local justice of the peace, who in turn issued a writ for Miner's arrest on a charge of

threatening with a dangerous weapon. The writ was then placed in the hands of one John Smith (white, age 81), the elderly but feisty sergeant for the town of Foster. Together with the two complainants both the justice of the peace and the town sergeant (who was also a deputy sheriff) set out to arrest Miner. They found him not far from where the first confrontation had occurred. When the men came within earshot of Miner they called out to him an order to halt. Miner asked them what they wanted whereupon John Smith said words to the following effect: "We are the law! As such we do require that you surrender to us!" Amos Miner then said in a cocky manner, "Come and get me! You sons of bitches!" He also brandished his axe again and bade defiance to any who would dare approach him. Since John Smith the sergeant did not carry firearms he picked up a sturdy stick and prepared to square off with Miner. Both men exchanged threats once again and then they came to blows. Smith parried the axe with his stick, knocking Miner off balance. However, as he moved in to tackle his man, Miner recovered enough to swing the axe. The sharp edge of the axe caught Smith between the shoulder blades and split his spine open. Smith then fell to the ground whereupon Miner swung the axe again and decapitated the sergeant with one chop. After that, Miner chased after the other three men, saying that he would serve them in the same way. The unarmed men ran for dear life and managed to avoid their attacker. Later that same day a posse was organized and Miner was seized through sheer force of numbers. Charged with the willful murder of a lawman, Miner had little chance of avoiding the gallows. Still, he took his case to trial, hoping to escape with a manslaughter verdict. A jury did not oblige him. Amos Miner was publicly hanged at Providence, Rhode Island, on December 27, 1833.

Charles Brown, black, age unknown. *Highway robbery.* The crime was committed on February 11, 1833, at Providence, Rhode Island. Colonel Richard Smith (white) owned a successful produce store at the corner of North Main and Thomas streets in Providence. At ten o'clock in the evening of the above date Smith closed his business and proceeded to walk home. He carried the day's receipts with him in a leather valise. While walking along Meeting Street this retailer was suddenly set upon by two muggers. One of them (later identified as Charles Brown) struck Smith across the back of the neck with a heavy club. Smith fell to the ground whereupon the other mugger (Moses Simmons by name) snatched the valise and went running down the street. Smith recovered quickly from the blow he had received. He wrested the club from Charles Brown and struck him a disabling blow with it. Then he started to chase Simmons, who seeing himself closely pursued, threw the valise into a churchyard. Smith then paused to recover his property. In the meantime many neighborhood residents came to the scene in response to the victim's shouts. They gave chase to the muggers but lost them in the darkness. On the following day there was a roundup of suspicious persons. Charles Brown and Moses Simmons were among them. Both were identified by Colonel Smith. Both were charged with capital felony — in this case highway robbery — because they had assaulted and robbed their victim in a public thoroughfare. A dual conviction followed at the March term of the Supreme Judicial Court of Rhode Island. Both defendants were sentenced to death. Because Simmons (who was also a Negro) cooperated with the authorities and had not actually struck the victim it was decided to spare his life. The state legislature voted to commute his death sentence. No mercy was shown to Charles Brown. He was granted two stays of execution during which time there failed to surface any news of a mitigating nature. Brown was described as a "bad character" in and around Providence and the label stuck. He was publicly hanged there on December 27, 1833.

1834

David Sherman, Native American, age 36. *Murder.* The crime was committed on June 7, 1833, at Norwich, Connecticut. This man was an alcoholic who chopped his wife and baby to death with an axe. On the above date Sherman announced his intention to cut some wood. He set about the task but returned to his home a short time later, saying that he had changed his mind and wanted to enjoy himself instead. He then spent the remainder of the daylight hours slurping from a cider barrel. When supper time came Sherman was too drunk to eat anything. His wife, Hannah Sherman (Native American, age unknown), became annoyed at his deportment. She threatened to leave him unless he cleaned up his act. She also refused his demand for some money because she knew that he would squander it on liquor. A little while later Mrs. Sherman sat down in a chair and began to nurse her youngest child, a baby named Edward Sherman, age 16 months. Her angry husband then came up behind her with an axe in his hands. He swung the axe at the woman with such force that both hers and the baby's heads were split open with one blow. Sherman's other children then ran screaming into the street where they caught the attention of passersby. Some men then went to the scene of the crime where they found the victims thrown into a corner and covered with a rug. When Sherman was arrested he said that his only regret was in having killed the baby. When asked why he had done such a thing he said that he resented his wife for keeping a tight rein on the family's finances. She had taken the wages of their children, said he, without giving any of the proceeds to him. The reason for the woman's parsimony was obvious; David Sherman had long proven himself to be irresponsible with money because he spent every penny on liquor. However, Sherman found such reasoning inconceivable because he was unwilling to admit that he had a drinking problem. Instead, he found it easier to resent his wife. Sherman found no sympathy in court. On June 17, 1834, he was hanged at the New London County jail.

Henry Joseph, black, age unknown. *Mutiny and murder.* The crimes were committed on August 14, 1834, on the high seas. This was a federal case. The American brig *Juniper* sailed from the Port of Boston on August 2, 1834, bound for Surinam with a cargo of lumber and foodstuffs. The crew consisted of nine men including the captain, one James Crosby (white, age unknown) by name and a Negro cook named Henry Joseph. When the vessel was 11 days out of port the cook committed some kind of disciplinary infraction which incurred the displeasure of both the captain and the first mate. As a result, Joseph was ordered flogged while the rest of the ship's company witnessed the punishment. Since the vessel could not do without its cook, the captain allowed Joseph to return to duty without spending any additional time in irons. On the following day Joseph prepared meals for the crew as usual. Dinner was served to the officers in the captain's cabin. Afterward the captain and mate turned in to their bunks for the night while Joseph cleared away the remains of their meal. When he completed his task, Joseph bid the officers a good night and snuffed the lamp which hung in their cabin. It was then that Joseph sought revenge for the flogging of the previous day. As soon as the lamp was out, he drew a butcher

knife from the folds of his clothes and attacked the two officers. Captain Crosby was stabbed to death in his berth and the mate (one William Eldred by name) was severely wounded. The other members of the crew were roused by the screams of the victims. They burst into the captain's cabin and overpowered the killer. Several hours later the *Juniper* signaled to a northbound vessel that it had trouble aboard. The other ship then came alongside and sent a boarding party to see what was wrong. By mutual agreement Joseph was put aboard the northbound vessel as were witnesses from among the crew of the *Juniper*. The other vessel then exchanged an equal number of its own crewmen so the *Juniper* could complete its voyage to Surinam. On September 2, 1834, the northbound vessel arrived at Boston where Joseph was turned over to federal authorities. His trial opened there on October 28, 1834. A conviction followed quickly as did an order for Joseph's execution. A second defendant named Amos Otis was also convicted but he was granted a full pardon when it was determined that Joseph had acted on his own. Henry Joseph met his end on December 2, 1834, when he was publicly hanged before a large crowd of Bostonians.

1835

Joseph Sager, white, age 36. *Murder.* The crime was committed on October 5, 1834, at Gardiner, Maine. This is the case of a philandering husband who poisoned his wife. It so happened that Joseph Sager had married a woman who was 12 years his senior. As time went by he came to regard his spouse as physically repellent. Sager wanted a younger woman and he also wanted to be free to look for one. He began a series of illicit amours but dared not pursue them openly while his wife was alive. He then resolved to solve that problem by eliminating the unwanted woman. Arsenic became his instrument. Starting slowly, Sager mixed small doses of the poison in his wife's food. It was his hope to make her physical decline appear natural. The victim, Phoebe Sager (white, age 48), soon fell ill. She became bedridden, vomited continuously and had to be tended by a live-in nurse as her condition worsened. One day Joseph Sager prepared a draught for his wife made of wine and beaten eggs. As the woman drank the concoction she noticed a gritty white substance in the dregs of the drink. She also felt a sensation of fine sand in her mouth. Furthermore, the nurse once saw Sager mix a "white powder" into milk which he served with the sick woman's tea. When asked about it he said it was medicine. Despite being deathly ill, Phoebe Sager still had the presence of mind to suspect the truth. When a doctor came to visit she confided those suspicions in him. After that her symptoms grew worse until she died in agony. The physician refused to sign a death certificate without an autopsy. When the decedent was opened there was found to be severe inflammation throughout the entire length of the digestive tract. In addition to that, a foreign substance resembling "white sand" was found in the viscera. Further analysis confirmed the presence of arsenic in a quantity more than sufficient to cause death. Joseph Sager was then arrested on suspicion of murder. He denied all wrongdoing and said that the dead woman must have taken the foreign substance as a stimulant. When a jury heard the testimonies of Mrs. Sager's doctor and nurse, however, there was nothing her husband could say that would save him. The verdict was guilty and the sentence was death. On January 2, 1835, thousands of people braved bitterly cold weather to see Joseph Sager pay for his crime. The city of Augusta was thronged that day as it hosted its first and only legal hanging.

Pedro Gilbert, Latino, age 38. **Manuel Costello,** Latino, age 30. **Manuel Boyga,** Latino, age 44. **Angelo Garcia,** Latino, age 28. **Juan Montenegro,** Latino, age 31. **Francisco Ruiz,** Latino, age 34. *Piracy.* Their crime was committed on September 20, 1832, on the high seas. This was a federal case. The American brig *Mexican* sailed from the Port of Salem, Massachusetts, in the summer of 1832 bound for Rio de Janeiro. The voyage was uneventful until the vessel came within sight of the Brazilian coast. There she fell in with a schooner called the *Pinda* which was flying a Brazilian flag. In reality the *Pinda* was a Cuban pirate ship commanded by the above-named Pedro Gilbert. The American vessel obeyed a signal to halt because it was in the territorial waters of Brazil. In such a way the pirate ship gained the element of surprise. The pirates came aboard the *Mexican* and disarmed the crew. Then they plundered the vessel of every article of value that they could find. Among the booty was $20,000 in gold and silver with which the American skipper had intended to purchase a cargo when he reached Argentina. When the pirates finished looting the *Mexican* they herded the crew into the vessel's hold where they tied up everyone from captain to cabin boy. Then they set the ship on fire and cast her adrift. It was intended that the crew of the *Mexican* go down with their ship. After the pirates went on their way several of the American crew managed to free themselves from their restraints. They put out the fire and saved both themselves, their ship and their fellow crewmen. Then they sailed back to Massachusetts where the piracy was reported to American authorities. A warship was sent in pursuit of the *Pinda* but it failed to locate her. A year and a half later the pirate ship turned up on the African coast where it had gone to fetch an illicit cargo of slaves. A British warship had been alerted and the *Pinda* was brought to bay. It so happened that the pirate ship was found at anchor in a cove. Knowing their position to be hopeless, Gilbert and his crew rowed ashore and fled into the jungle. British marines pursued them and captured a few. Then a war broke out. Because the native chiefs were in league with the slave traders they gave refuge to the fleeing pirates. This incensed the British commander who retaliated by burning more than a dozen villages. When the hostilities finally simmered down, 16 of the pirates were in custody including their captain and first mate. A prize crew was put aboard their ship. A search thereof turned up incontrovertible proof of piracy: armaments, flags of different nations and items stolen from ships which the *Pinda* had victimized. A manifest belonging to the *Mexican* was among the incriminating evidence. All of the prisoners were clapped into irons and taken to England. There they were examined by a Court of Admiralty and ordered to be extradited to the United States for trial. On July 23, 1834, the British sloop of war *Savage* set sail from England with the prisoners. The vessel reached the Port of Salem, Massachusetts, on August 13. Her presence there created a sensation at first but when it was learned that the British had done the Americans a favor, the visiting ship was hospitably received. The 16 prisoners were then sent to Boston for trial before a federal court. Seven of them were capitally convicted. The rest fared differently; at least one committed suicide and two were acquitted when it was proven that they were not aboard the *Pinda* when it overtook the *Mexican*. Others were sent to prison for indefinite terms and one was excused on account of his age. On June 11, 1835, the captain of the pirate ship and four of his crew (Pedro Gilbert, Manuel Costello, Manuel Boyga, Angelo Garcia and Juan Montenegro) were publicly hanged at Boston. The first mate, one Bernardo de Soto by name, was reprieved when it was learned that he had tried to spare the crew of the American ship. The last pirate, Francisco Ruiz (who had been carpenter aboard the *Pinda*) managed to secure several stays of execution by feigning insanity. The ploy eventually failed and he was hanged from the same gallows as his mates on September 12, 1835.

1836

Abraham Prescott, white, age 18. *Murder.* The crime was committed on June 23, 1833, at Pembroke, New Hampshire. This teenage killer may or may not have been crazy. At the very least, he was of substandard intellect. Prescott had been taken in by a gentleman farmer named Chauncey Cochrane. Knowing that the lad lacked the mental acumen to survive on his own, Cochrane provided him with a home in return for his feeding the livestock and doing other chores around the farm. Such was the kind of work for which young Prescott was suited. He went about his tasks diligently and eventually came to be regarded by the Cochranes as a member of their family. Such boded ill because in Prescott's puerile mind was formed an idea that the situation also meant that he was heir to all that the Cochranes owned. He then figured that he would inherit the farm if his benefactors died. During the early morning hours of January 6, 1833, young Prescott arose from his bed and took an axe from a nearby woodpile. Gripping the axe tightly, he entered Mr. Cochrane's bedroom and attacked the man as he slept. Chauncey Cochrane suffered a glancing blow to the head which awoke him. Perceiving his peril, the man jumped out of the bed and disarmed the attacker. Prescott appeared to be in some kind of trance. Because of that he was able to talk his way out of the situation by saying that he had been sleepwalking. He also claimed that he was unaware of what he had done because he was not awake when he made the assault. Cochrane decided to give Prescott the benefit of the doubt. Several months then passed without further incident. On the above date — June 23, 1833 — Cochrane's wife, Sally Cochrane (white, age 28) decided to go berry picking in the woods. Abraham Prescott went with her. Several hours later he returned home alone in a visibly agitated state. When asked what was wrong he told Mr. Cochrane that he had struck Mrs. Cochrane over the head with a piece of wood and that he thought he had killed her. Chauncey Cochrane went running to the scene only to find his wife beyond all earthly aid. She had been fatally bludgeoned. Cochrane then confronted Prescott and demanded an explanation. Prescott said that he had had a toothache come upon him and sat down under a tree to rest. He had fallen asleep there but remembered nothing else until he woke up. By then Sally Cochrane was dead. Prescott said that he feared that he had killed the woman in his sleep. This was too much for Chauncey Cochrane. He reasoned that mentally cognizant or not, Prescott was dangerous. He had no choice but to turn him over to the law. A sensational court battle followed. The defense based its case on a new concept called "somnambulism"; i.e., the unconscious performing of physical acts while in one's sleep. The jury didn't buy it. The prosecution offered a more persuasive case — especially when it got Prescott to admit that he considered himself the Cochrane family heir. Allegations that the defendant had intended to rape Mrs. Cochrane were unsubstantiated. Still, the prosecution had found a motive. This in itself successfully countered the mental illness defense. Abraham Prescott was capitally convicted. A long series of reprieves followed while the issue of Prescott's sanity (or lack thereof) was argued and reargued. In the end the governor-in-council concluded that there was indeed method in Prescott's alleged madness. Clemency was therefore refused. The end came at the town of Hopkinton on January 6, 1836, when the troubled young man was hanged before a large crowd of people.

Simeon Crockett, white, age 26. Stephen Russell, white, age 27. Arson.

Their crime was committed on October 22, 1835, at Boston, Massachusetts. Simeon Crockett was born and raised in Maine. He was a wheelwright by trade. In May of 1835 he experienced difficulties with his wife and resolved to seek a better life elsewhere. He accordingly got on a ship in Bangor and sailed away to Boston. There he signed aboard a mackerel boat and tried his hand at fishing. A voyage of several weeks was enough to convince him that he was not suited to such an occupation. When the boat returned to port Crockett wandered about the wharves pondering his next move. He made the acquaintance of a drifter named Stephen Russell and set out with him in search of work. A newspaper ad served as their guide. Carpenters were wanted by a slumlord named Joshua Benson in order to patch up a tenement building he owned on South Street Place. The structure was a large ramshackle affair made entirely of wood. It was home to more than a hundred people, mostly poor Irish immigrants. It was also in need of many repairs. Crockett and Russell accordingly offered their services to the slumlord and were given the job. Both set to work but were appalled by the squalid conditions that prevailed in the tenement. Crockett was heard to say that he wished the place would burn down. On the evening of the above date Crockett and Russell made the rounds of the neighborhood saloons. Both got drunk. Sometime during the course of the evening their conversation turned toward Joshua Benson and his low-class tenement building. Both thought that it would be a jolly thing to set the place on fire. They accordingly made their way to the aforesaid premises and went down into the rat-infested cellar. There they found piles of wood shavings, shingles, crates and other combustibles. They splashed kerosene all over the place and then tossed a lighted match down the cellar stairs. The fact that more than a hundred people were asleep in the rooms above them did not matter in their minds. All at once the building burst into flames. With no time to save their possessions and no time to clothe themselves, panic-stricken people started jumping out of windows. In the smoke-filled hallways men, women and children trampled each other to escape the inferno. Within 20 minutes the building was a total loss. More than 20 families were made homeless and destitute. The fact that no one was killed was hailed as a miracle but many physical injuries had been sustained. That same night it was reported that the "carpenters" had been seen in the tenement. It was considered odd that they were there after hours — especially since they had completed their assignment the previous day. Why had they been there? Had it not been Crockett who was heard to say that he wished the place would burn? These were the questions that the burned-out residents asked themselves. Police traced Crockett and Russell to their lodgings and pounced on them. Both confessed what they had done. An angry crowd almost succeeded in meting out its own brand of justice to the suspects but both were whisked away to a secret location. It was left to a court of law to consider the matter. A double conviction followed on the charge of arson in the first degree, by law a capital crime. Both defendants were sentenced to death. They were hanged at the Suffolk County jail on March 16, 1836.

1839

Archibald Bates, white, age unknown. *Murder.* The crime was committed on October 2, 1838, at North Bennington, Vermont. The official record of this case was lost in a courthouse fire many years ago. Consequently little information remains. We can only present a sketchy account based on a distant newspaper of the time. Archibald Bates lived at Shaftsbury. His age and occupation are unknown. He had a brother named Philemon Bates who lived at North Bennington. For some reason Archibald Bates hated his brother's wife. On the above date he was heard to mutter threats against the woman, whose name is not recorded. Archibald's father heard the threats and became alarmed. The elder Bates went to Philemon's house to warn him. While speaking of the matter, the two men left the threatened woman in another room because they did not wish to upset her. Suddenly a shot rang out. Father and son hurried into the adjoining room only to find Mrs. Bates dead in a chair. She was still in the act of nursing her infant child. She had been shot through the head. Archibald Bates was seen running out of the yard with a rifle in his hands. Some men chased him down and found live ammunition in his pockets. Nevertheless he denied the shooting. Only after being convicted of capital murder did Archibald Bates confess his guilt. He was publicly hanged at Bennington on February 6, 1839.

Benjamin Cummings, white, age about 45. *Murder.* The crime was committed on October 23, 1838, near New Bedford, Massachusetts. This man is described as having been a "boisterous, dissipated fellow" in and around the settlement of Freetown, then a suburb of New Bedford. Another account refers to him as a "drunken vagabond" who was "unfortunately a husband and father." He had served time in the Massachusetts

State Prison for the crime of malicious wounding. During the summer of 1838 a warrant was issued for the arrest of Cummings on a charge of public intoxication. Cummings was told of the matter and regarded it with contempt. He insulted the local constable, one Asa Clark by name, and dared him to serve the warrant. On the above date Cummings was more drunk than usual. He declared that if the constable had not the courage to arrest him, he would give the man further cause to do so. Then he beat up his wife and forced her to run out of their house all nude. Mrs. Cummings managed to grab some of her garments from a clothesline. Then she went to Asa Clark and told him what had happened. She also said that her husband intended to harass Asa Clark by vandalizing his house. Clark then decided that he would like to catch Cummings in the act. He accordingly called his son, Asa Clark, Jr. (white, age 23), and several other men to help him. All lay in wait near the house of the elder Asa Clark. Sure enough, Benjamin Cummings came along in the night and started throwing rocks at the house. Several windows were broken. Asa Clark, Jr., then emerged from his place of concealment and tackled Cummings. In the struggle that followed Cummings pulled out a knife and fatally stabbed the younger Asa Clark. He was then arrested at the scene. Despite being caught in the very act of the homicide by multiple witnesses, Cummings emphatically denied his guilt. He continued to scream his innocence throughout his trial and right up to the very moment of his execution. He was hanged at the Bristol County jail (in Taunton) on August 7, 1839.

1844

Lucian Hall, white, age 26. *Murder.* The crime was committed on September 24, 1843, at Middletown, Connecticut. This offender was a native of the town which witnessed both his crime and his execution. His mother had died when he was a toddler so he was raised by an apathetic father and a less than loving step-mother. As a boy Lucian Hall never attended school nor had any religious training. So neglectful were his guardians that he was forced to steal just to feed and clothe himself. Disgusted with his situation, he ran away from home at the age of 16 and hired himself out as a farmhand. Being taken in by a gentleman planter at Farmington, the lad was offered a chance to go to school for the first time in his life. He decided that he would make the attempt but he was soon expelled from the local academy for insulting a Negro student. That was the end of Lucian Hall's schooling. From that time on he developed a progressive penchant for crime, especially theft. He wound up doing two years in the state prison for robbery in a dwelling house. Upon being released he got a job in Meriden working for a wealthy planter named Levi Yale. There he remained without incident for five years, his salary being sufficient to negate the need to steal. Then Hall got married and all went downhill from there. His wife induced him to leave Mr. Yale's employ and soon he was feeling the pinch of poverty. Hall found himself impelled to start stealing again. On the above date he approached the house of a Mr. Ebenezer Bacon in the Westfield section of Middletown. Believing all of the occupants of the house to be away at church, Hall surmised the place to be vulnerable. He climbed into the house through an open window and started looking around for valuables. It so happened that the lady of the house, Lavinia Bacon (white, age unknown), had remained at home that day. She caught Hall in the act of rifling a desk. She also recognized the intruder and called out his name. Hall then panicked. He picked up a chair and attacked Mrs. Bacon with it. When he had beaten her senseless with the thing he next went into the kitchen and fetched a butcher knife. It was with the latter weapon that he finished off the victim. When he was sure that Mrs. Bacon was dead, Hall scooped up some coins from the rifled desk and fled. He buried his loot in the woods. Then he got washed up and went to church where he asked God to forgive him for what he had done. When the crime was discovered Hall was reported as having been seen in the area. When he was questioned he tried to lie his way out of the situation without success. He finally wound up making a full confession. On June 20, 1844, he was hanged at the Middlesex County jail.

1845

Thomas Barrett, white, age 33. *Murder.* The crime was committed on February 18, 1844, at Lunenburg, Massachusetts. This man was an Irish immigrant. He left a wife and four children in the old country and set out for America to seek his fortune. On May 21, 1841, his ship landed at Boston. Barrett then proceeded to hire himself out as a farmhand and experienced cattleman. Eventually he worked his way to the town of Lunenburg where he was hired by a rancher named Oliver Whitney. The new man also made extra money by carrying provisions to a nearby railroad cantonment. On the above date Barrett got drunk and decided that he must have a woman. He then set his sights on an isolated cabin where dwelled an aging widow named Ruth Taylor Houghton (white, age 70). Knowing that the woman lived alone, Barrett expected little difficulty in accomplishing his purpose. He accordingly forced his way into Mrs. Houghton's home and demanded that the occupant submit to his desires. Despite her age, the woman was a feisty sort. She slapped Barrett across his face and told him to get out of her house. Then a fight broke out. Mrs. Houghton

defended herself to the best of her ability but was eventually overpowered. Barrett beat her to within an inch of her life (breaking all of her ribs in the process) and raped her. Then he strangled her with his bare hands. The crime was discovered when well-wishers came to congratulate Mrs. Houghton on the occasion of her birthday. The interior of the house was a complete shambles; furniture and broken dishes lying strewn about. Barrett came home the same day with a black eye and a scratched face. He also came home without his gloves; only then did he realize that he had left them at the scene of the crime. Lawmen found the gloves and traced them to Barrett. He tried to explain away the evidence by saying that he had sold his gloves that day to a workman at the railroad cantonment. No such person could be found there so Barrett was charged with capital murder. He was hanged at the Worcester County jail on January 3, 1845.

John Gordon, white, age 29. *Murder.* The crime was committed on December 31, 1843, at Johnston, Rhode Island. Nicholas Gordon was an Irish immigrant who had settled at Cranston, Rhode Island. There he came to own and operate a general store. Business was good and Nicholas Gordon was thus enabled to pay for his mother's subsequent passage to Rhode Island from the old country. During the summer of 1843 he also sent for his two brothers, John and William Gordon. Reunited once again, the three Gordon brothers considered ways in which they could pursue their livelihoods. Since William was a tailor by trade he was able to find employment with no difficulty. Nicholas had his store and was thereby self-supporting. John Gordon, however, posed a problem; he had no ready skill. It was Nicholas who thought of a solution: he would open a tippling house next to his store and make his brother the manager thereof. All of the Gordons agreed to this proposal so Nicholas went ahead and applied for a liquor license. Then came trouble. It so happened that the Gordons had a powerful neighbor in the person of one Amasa Sprague (white, age 45), a wealthy textile magnate. Besides having a lot of money, this man also had political connections; his brother had been governor of Rhode Island and his son a United States senator. What proved inimical to the Gordons, however, was the additional fact that Amasa Sprague was a bumptious teetotaler who would allow no tippling house near his home. He opposed Nicholas Gordon's liquor license application and he used his influence to secure its rejection. Nicholas and William Gordon were disappointed but John Gordon was fully enraged. He determined to get revenge on Amasa Sprague. Knowing that Sprague used a footpath which led through a certain wooded area, John Gordon armed himself with a rifle and lay in wait there. Sure enough, Sprague came walking along the path oblivious to danger. When the sniper saw the object of his wrath he decided that the man was not worth a bullet. So he pounced on Sprague and knocked him down. Then he beat him in a maniacal manner and also battered him about the head with the butt end of the rifle. So vicious was the assault that Sprague was beaten beyond recognition. When the rifle was later found discarded in the woods, its wooden stock was shattered and its barrel was bent, further evidence of the assailant's ferocity. The gun was identified as the property of Nicholas Gordon. However, that man and his brother William both had alibis for their whereabouts at the time in question. That left John Gordon. Lawmen knew he had a motive for murder. In addition, his boots fit perfectly with the killer's tracks in the snow. John Gordon had also been seen carrying a rifle near the scene of the crime. Lastly, a bloody jacket was found not far from the murder scene; it being a very cold day it was therefore reasoned that the killer could not have gone far. He must have headed for the nearby house of Nicholas Gordon, especially since the footprints led in that direction. All three of the Gordon brothers were arrested on suspicion of murder. When the case came to trial Nicholas and William were saved by their alibis; both were acquitted. John Gordon, however, was found guilty and sentenced to death. He vehemently maintained his innocence despite the evidence against him. He also claimed to be a victim of anti–Irish bigotry. On February 14, 1845, he was hanged at the Rhode Island State Prison, still asseverating his innocence. Lingering doubts led the state of Rhode Island to abolish capital punishment seven years later.

1846

Andrew Howard, white, age 22. *Murder.* The crime was committed on September 19, 1843, at Rochester, New Hampshire. This offender was an illiterate farmhand who dreamed of escaping from his humdrum environment. Having heard that passenger ships sailed from the New England ports on a regular basis, he decided that he would like to leave the area by such a route. He finally set his heart on a voyage to New Orleans. There was only one problem: he had no money. Howard then thought of a simple solution: armed robbery. On the Meaderborough Road there lived an unmarried brother and sister named Jacob and Phoebe Hanson (whites, ages unknown). They were frugal Quakers who were rumored to have a stash of money in their house. On the above date Howard armed himself with a rifle and set a course for the Hanson homestead. Jacob Hanson happened to be away at the time so it was Phoebe Hanson who answered the door. Howard stuck the muzzle of his weapon in her face and demanded money. The woman gave him all that she had, about five dollars. Not satisfied, Howard demanded more. When Phoebe Hanson told him that she had no more money, she was shot dead. Howard then proceeded to ransack the house. During the course thereof he broke open a storage trunk and found $29 in silver. That was the extent of his loot. A neighbor discovered the crime when he came to see the victim about some cider. Andrew Howard was nabbed a short time later. Silver coins found in his possession corresponded with what Jacob Hanson reported to be stolen. Two trials followed. Then came a long series of reprieves while New Hampshire legislators dickered over the issue of capital punishment. In the end, efforts to abolish the death penalty in that state were voted down. Andrew Howard was then ordered for execution. On July 8, 1846, thousands of people descended upon the town of Dover to see Andrew Howard hanged. They did not go home disappointed.

Andrew Potter, white, age 23. Murder. The crime was committed on February 9, 1845, at New Haven, Connecticut. This young man was born at Hamden, Connecticut, on December 22, 1821. He was the son of Jabez and Almira Potter, a respectable couple. When Andrew Potter came of age he moved to the university town of New Haven where he went to work as a railroad section hand. He also found occasional employment on an oyster boat. It so happened that an acquaintance of his, one Lucius Osborn (white, age 27), owned an expensive pocket watch that he used to use to impress the girls. One time Potter asked to borrow the watch for a similar purpose. His request was granted after which the watch was duly returned to its owner. However, Potter coveted the watch. He finally decided that he must have it at all costs. Knowing that Osborn would never willingly part with the watch on a permanent basis by any peaceable means, Potter hatched a ruse

to lure the man to his doom. He told Osborn that he knew of some girls who would be willing to have sex with them. Then he made a date to meet Osborn at a point along the railroad tracks. Osborn did not suspect any danger so he came to the rendezvous. Sure enough, he was wearing his prized pocket watch. When he reached the railroad tracks he saw Potter approaching from the opposite direction. Potter was carrying an iron-tipped pike pole in his hands. When the two men met, Osborn pointed to the pike pole and jokingly said to Potter, "What are you doing with that thing? Are you planning to kill somebody?" Little did Osborn suspect that that was exactly what Potter had in mind. Potter (who later said that he had been astonished by that question) told Osborn that he had found the pike pole along the railroad tracks and was using it as a walking stick. Then he bade Osborn to come along with him because the "girls" were waiting. Both men then walked along the railroad tracks for a while. When they reached a point near the Quinnipiac River bridge Potter let Osborn get a couple of steps ahead of him. Then he struck him down from behind with the pike pole. Osborn fell to the ground whereupon Potter continued to jab him about the head and neck. The sharp iron barb on the end of the pike pole pierced Osborn's skull in six different places. When Osborn was finally dead Potter took his pocket watch. Then he threw the murder weapon into the Quinnipiac River so it would look like Osborn had been hit by a train. The victim was found the next day frozen into a pool of his own blood and brain matter. The coroner had to use an axe to hack the body free from its frozen gore. Then the killer overplayed his hand: he forged a promissory note purportedly signed by Osborn in which the pocket watch was pledged to himself (Potter) as security for a loan. Then he went to the coroner's inquest and entered the forged note as evidence in case he was questioned about why he had Osborn's watch. Suspicion turned against Potter when other witnesses at the inquest said that Osborn had been wearing the watch when he left home on the day of his death. Charged with the crime, Potter eventually confessed his guilt. He was hanged at the New Haven county jail on July 20, 1846.

1849

Enos Dudley, white, age 40. *Murder.* The crime was committed on March 5, 1848, at Grafton, New Hampshire. This man was a Methodist minister who did away with his wife, Mary Dudley (white, age unknown), so he could be free to pursue another woman. On the evening of the above date the Dudleys were returning home from a prayer meeting when their sleigh overturned. Mary Dudley was reported to have been fatally injured in the alleged incident. Her husband received the condolences of the community while the decedent was laid to rest with all due solemnities. Within a matter of days, however, Enos Dudley's conduct aroused unfavorable comments. His dalliance with another woman was done with unseemly haste. In addition to that, his grief did not appear to be genuine. Several people voiced their suspicions to the authorities. A magistrate considered the matter and issued an exhumation order. A postmortem examination was then conducted on the remains of Mary Dudley over the vociferous objections of her widower. The result was a revelation that the woman had been strangled. Enos Dudley was arrested on April 3, 1848, and charged with the willful murder of his wife. At his trial the prosecution contended that Dudley had first beat and choked his wife along a snowy country road and then overturned his sleigh with deliberate intent to fake an accident. He almost got away with it. Dudley denied

the charge to no avail. A jury considered the matter and became disgusted with what it considered to be rank perfidy in a supposed man of the cloth. The verdict was guilty without recommendation of mercy. On May 23, 1849, thousands of country folk poured into the town of Haverhill to witness the end of the mendacious minister. Nor were they disappointed; the Rev. Enos Dudley was hanged on schedule.

Washington Goode, black, age 31. *Murder.* The crime was committed on June 28, 1848, at Boston, Massachusetts. This man was the cook aboard the *Nacoochee,* a seagoing bark which was docked in the Port of Boston on the above date. Each evening when the crew was given shore leave Goode headed for a neighborhood called the "Black Sea," located along Richmond Street. The locale was a disreputable one replete with saloons, brothels and other dens of infamy. There Goode made the acquaintance of a prostitute named Mary Ann Williams and consorted with her for several successive nights. On the above date Goode noticed that his doxy had a new handkerchief. When he asked her where it had come from, the woman rather matter-of-factly named another of her male suitors. That answer made Goode jealous. He snatched the handkerchief and angrily tore it to shreds. Then he demanded to know the identity of the giver. Seeing Goode's ire, Mary Ann Williams did not dare to withhold the information. The man was one Thomas Harding (black, age 33), another mariner. Armed with this name plus a description, Goode went looking for his rival. He finally caught up with him on Richmond Street. Harding was hit over the head with a blackjack and run through the back with a butcher knife. He died at the scene. The local nightwatch traced Goode to a Negro boarding house that same night. There he was arrested without incident. When the case came to trial there was clear evidence of premeditation. The jury took 35 minutes to return a capital verdict. On the morning of his execution Goode made a desperate attempt at suicide. He swallowed a large quantity of tobacco and stuffed a blanket in his mouth so he could drown in his own vomit. In addition to that, he got ahold of a piece of glass and slashed his arms severely. He was bleeding profusely when the guards found him. Without any further ado Goode was placed in a chair and carried to the gallows awash in his own blood. Then he was hanged by the neck until he was dead. The scene was the Suffolk County jail. The date was May 25, 1849.

1850

Daniel Pearson, white, age 41. *Murder.* The crime was committed on April 11, 1849, at Wilmington, Massachusetts. Originally a devoted family man, this offender lost everything because he had a drinking problem. He had lived at Wilmington for many years only to be turned out of his house by an impending divorce decree. He relinquished control of his property there and went to Boston where he hired himself out as a manservant. His wife and twin daughters continued to dwell in his former residence. After three years of brooding and self-pity Pearson became mentally unstable. On the above date he started drinking heavily. Then he hatched an evil scheme. Purchasing a knife, a pen, paper and a bottle of laudanum, he put the items in a bag and set out for Wilmington. All the while he continued to drink his gin. By the time he got off the train in his former hometown he was too drunk to even know his whereabouts. He wandered about aimlessly for the better part of the night. Then at about four o'clock in the morning he stumbled upon his former home. He tapped on a window and awoke his estranged wife.

She let him in and gave him something to eat. Then the woman returned to her bedroom and lay back down beside her young children. She fell asleep there while Daniel Pearson remained in the kitchen warming himself by the stove. Sometime during the hour before dawn he ran into the bedroom with a drawn knife and attacked his sleeping family. In the commotion that followed, Pearson's wife, Martha Pearson (white, age 38), was slashed to death. So were the couple's twin daughters, Sarah and Lydia Pearson (white, age 4). When the mother and children were dead the killer arranged their bodies in such a way as to make it look like a case of double murder and suicide. The two children — who had their throats cut — were placed upon the bed. Martha Pearson was left where she fell but had the murder weapon put in her right hand. She also had laudanum splashed on her. Lastly, the killer forged a suicide note which he left at the scene. Then he caught a morning train to Boston. When the crime was discovered the ostensible murder-suicide was almost immediately discounted. The scene was an obvious contrivance. When Daniel Pearson was reported to have been seen in the area an all-points bulletin was issued for him. Boston police arrested him the same day. The fact that Pearson had previously purchased the implements of the crime was taken as evidence of premeditation. A jury took little time to return a capital verdict. All doubts were removed when the defendant wrote out a detailed confession shortly before the time set for his execution. On July 26, 1850, he was hanged at the Middlesex County jail.

John Webster, white, age 58. *Murder.* The crime was committed on November 23, 1849, at Boston, Massachusetts. This celebrated killer was the scion of a prominent Boston family. His father, Redfield Webster, had been a gentleman of substance well known in patrician circles. As a young man, John Webster attended Harvard University from whence he graduated with honors in 1811. After completing post-graduate studies there he was appointed an Erving Professor of Chemistry and Mineralogy at the prestigious Massachusetts College of Medicine. In addition to that, Dr. Webster maintained an office on Tremont Street in Boston where he served as a physician to society's elite. In 1825 he moved to Cambridge where he carried on a close association with his alma mater as a visiting professor and deliverer of guest lectures. As a pedigreed academician Dr. Webster was accepted in high places. Such a lifestyle, however, was expensive and for the rest of his life Webster had to juggle his finances. He frequently found himself in debt but strove to maintain a veneer of solvency. Sometimes he was forced to borrow money and it was such a practice which ultimately led to his undoing. Among the lenders to whom Webster applied was an eccentric bachelor named George Parkman (white, age 54), himself a man of higher learning. He had matriculated at the University of Aberdeen, and, like Webster, had pursued a career in medicine and the teaching thereof. As he grew older, however, he left those pursuits for what were then the more profitable practices of real estate speculation and money-lending. He was every inch a character out of a Charles Dickens novel: tall, thin and high-strung with a frock coat, a stovepipe hat and an icy, rigid demeanor. Such was the man to whom John Webster applied for a loan of $400. The money was granted only after Webster pledged his valuable collection of minerals as collateral. Then came trouble. Parkman learned that Webster had already pledged his mineral collection to other creditors. Furious, he marched into Webster's office and announced that he was calling in the loan. Payment in full was demanded. Webster protested in vain; he told Parkman that

he could not make full payment. Parkman would not hear of it and he began to pester Webster. His methods were relentless: he bombarded Webster with dunning notices and made it a point to embarrass him in front of other people. He told other lenders that Webster was a bad risk. He even attended Webster's lectures in order to antagonize him with catcalls. Webster tried to avoid Parkman but the latter warned that unless the money was paid he would continue to badger him. On the above date Parkman finally overdid it; he stomped into Webster's laboratory and started to harangue the harried debtor. As the conversation grew more heated so did Webster's frame of mind. When Parkman threatened to use his considerable influence to have Webster turned out of his job the man finally snapped. He grabbed a piece of firewood and used it to strike Parkman a resounding blow on the head. Parkman died within seconds from a fractured skull. Webster was chagrined by what he had done but did not panic. He first tried to revive Parkman. When that failed he decided to secretly dispose of the body. Webster locked the doors of his laboratory and went to work on the decedent. He stripped Parkman naked and burned his clothes in his assay furnace. Then he butchered the body with cutlery; Parkman was dismembered and eviscerated. After that Webster began to gradually dispose of the remains by burning them in his furnace. Two days later missing person notices went up all over the Boston area. A handsome reward was promised to anyone who could clear up the sudden disappearance of George Parkman. Inspired by this, the janitor of the Massachusetts College of Medicine began to snoop around. The man had seen some testy confrontations between Webster and the missing man. He had also seen Parkman enter Webster's laboratory on the above date but had not seen him leave. Finding the doors and windows of Webster's laboratory securely locked, the janitor put his ears to the outside walls thereof in an effort to hear any sounds therein. When he came to the brick backing of Webster's assay furnace he found it too hot to touch. Someone was apparently burning something in the furnace. The janitor suspected the truth and resolved to find out for sure. During the day he kept a sharp eye out for anything amiss while he swept the floor and tidied up inside the laboratory. After hours, however, he worked at tunneling into Professor Webster's inner sanctum: a walk-in vault where he kept his organic specimens and dangerous chemicals. When the janitor finally succeeded in his quest to break into the vault he was horrified to have his suspicions confirmed. Freshly butchered human remains were found there. When the authorities were informed of this a more thorough search of Webster's laboratory was ordered. Additional human remains turned up hidden in a chest. Most telling of all, however, was a set a human dentures found in the furnace which were positively identified as those of George Parkman. A contrite Dr. Webster eventually confessed to having committed the murder. He also claimed mitigating circumstances on the ground that there had been no premeditation on his part. A trial jury, however, became annoyed with the fact that Webster had tried to conceal the crime. For that reason there was no recommendation of mercy. John White Webster — Ivy League alumnus and tenured professor of chemistry — was ordered for execution. He spent his final days in the same cell that had held the lowly Negro Washington Goode a year earlier. On August 30, 1850, he was hanged at the Suffolk County jail.

Henry Leander Foote, white, age 37. *Murder.* The crime was committed on September 14, 1849, at Northford, Connecticut. This man was a painter by trade and a wanderer by habit. After roaming the country for many years he returned to the place of his birth (Northford) with nothing to show for his time away but a collection of tall tales and a worn-out set of clothes. His widowed mother, Mrs. Olive Foote (white, age 60), took him into her home and gave him a place to stay. There the prodigal son became acquainted with his young niece, Emily Cooper (white, age 14), whom he had not seen since she was born. As time went by, Henry Foote's proximity to his niece inspired him with salacious fantasies about her. Obsession soon followed. Still, Foote did not dare to proposition the girl outright. Instead, he had recourse to guile. He prepared a basket of ripe tomatoes (of which he knew the girl to be fond) and laced them with knockout drops. Then on the above date he intercepted the girl on her way to school and invited her to partake of his fruit. Emily Cooper ate one of the loaded tomatoes and promptly passed out unconscious. Henry Foote then dragged her into some bushes and raped her. Fearing that she would expose him, Foote then went a step further: he took a knife to the unconscious girl and cut out her gullet. After that he went home and started to drink heavily. When his mother objected to his conduct he flew into a rage and attacked her with a hammer. The woman was beaten into a coma. Foote than made an unsuccessful attempt at suicide. Neighbors found him bleeding from self-inflicted cuts. They patched him up and called police. Efforts to save Mrs. Olive Foote were unavailing; she died 12 days later. The remains of Emily Cooper were located when carrion birds were seen. It so happened that the grand jury for New Haven County was then in session. The case of Henry Foote was reported to it and an indictment came quickly. When Foote's mother succumbed to her injuries a second indictment was returned. Henry Foote faced two counts of capital murder. When put to trial Foote admitted his guilt and threw himself on the mercy of the court. A jury refused to accept his alcoholism as a mitigating factor. The penalty was death by hanging. On October 2, 1850, that penalty was carried out at the New Haven County jail.

James McCaffrey, white, age 36. *Murder.* The crime was committed on October 29, 1849, at Hamden, Connecticut. East Rock is a large natural escarpment which overlooks the city of New Haven. It has been a popular excursion spot for centuries. During the 1840s the summit of East Rock was the site of a tippling house, an elderly couple named Charles and Ann Smith (whites, aged about 80) being the proprietors thereof. For many years the Smiths had made their living by selling food and drink to the sightseers who came to East Rock. By the autumn of 1849, however, they had had enough. They were getting on in years and they let it be known that they were willing to sell out. One fine October day a transient person named James McCaffrey came to town. Since no tour of New Haven was considered complete without a visit to East Rock, this individual found his way there and in so doing made the acquaintance of Mr. and Mrs. Smith. He listened with interest when he heard that the site was for sale. Telling the Smiths that he desired to buy them out, McCaffrey made a date to come back later and talk things over. All the while, however, his mind was turning in a sinister direction; he surmised that the Smiths had saved up a considerable sum of money and that those funds were hidden in their house. McCaffrey used the ensuing time to go rummaging around New Haven; he picked up a cheap handgun and an axe. As he approached the Smith residence later that day he concealed the axe along a footpath. When he knocked on the door he was received cordially. Mrs. Smith said that dinner was not yet ready. Then McCaffrey, by design, asked Mr. Smith to take a walk around the property with him while they talked business. The two men went to the scenic rim of East Rock and beheld the magnificent view which makes the place famous. A few minutes later Mrs. Smith rang the dinner bell and both men started on their way back to the house. As they passed the spot where the axe lay concealed, McCaffrey took that weapon in his hands and used it to strike down Mr. Smith from behind. As he fell, the victim emitted a loud groan which was heard by his wife. She came running to the scene only to see McCaffrey standing over her dying husband with a bloody axe in his hands. The woman screamed. Then as she turned to flee, McCaffrey pulled out his handgun and shot her in the back. He also finished her off with the axe. When both of the Smiths were dead the killer ran into the tippling house and began a frenzied search for valuables. What, if anything, he found was never determined for certain. Early the next morning some sightseers came upon the mutilated bodies of the victims. A check of their establishment revealed evidence of robbery. In addition to that, the dinner table was found to be set for three people and food was found in the pots just as Mrs. Smith had left it. There followed a hue and cry which reached all the way to Canada. It was there where McCaffrey was found on February 23, 1850. Speedily returned to New Haven, the killer denied the crime to the day of his death. No one believed him. On October 2, 1850, he was hanged at the New Haven County jail.

1854

James Clough, white, age 29. *Murder.* The crime was committed on July 16, 1852, at Fall River, Massachusetts. This man was a drifter from Maine. During the early morning hours of the above date he was burglarizing houses in Fall River. When he entered one house on

Rock Street his movements were observed. A crowd gathered but Clough gave it the slip. Then a hue and cry was raised throughout the city. Armed parties of citizens blocked the roads in an effort to hem in the suspect. Sometime after dawn a constable named Gideon Manchester (white, age unknown) spotted a suspicious-looking stranger near the railroad station. It was James Clough. The constable followed the man up Central Street and then onto Green Street. Soon the suspect realized that he was being followed. He started to run, whereupon the constable did the same. Then suddenly Clough spun about with a gun in his hand and opened fire on his pursuer. Manchester was shot through the body and died three days later. Clough fled from the scene of the shooting but could not get out of town because the roads were blocked. He hid in a small shed near the corner of Durfee and Pine streets. A short time later some children saw him and told their parents. The shed was surrounded and Clough was ordered to surrender on pain of death. He was found with the murder weapon on his person. Also seized from him were burglary tools and a large sum of money. Clough was sent to Taunton for trial by the Bristol County Supreme Judicial Court. There he was sentenced to death. Another man who had killed his wife with sulfuric acid was also condemned by that court. However, when the day of execution came only James Clough faced the hangman. The other killer had managed to wrangle a commutation of his sentence. The scene was the Bristol County jail. The date was April 28, 1854.

Michael Jennings, white, age 17. *Murder.* The crime was committed on July 24, 1853, at North Haven, Connecticut. This juvenile offender had come from Ireland with his parents. While the elder members of his family settled at Brooklyn, New York, young Michael Jennings set out on his own for Connecticut. In the vicinity of New Haven he found work with a tanner and became engaged to learn that trade. However, the lure of better pay was too much for him to resist and he ran off to seek a better opportunity in a brickyard. There he was hired by a Mr. Brazillai Bradley and for the next three weeks he boarded with that man and his wife in their home at North Haven. At the end of that time Jennings once again felt the lure of better opportunity and he absconded from the Bradley residence. In the days that followed things did not work out as Jennings had anticipated. He decided to return to his parents in Brooklyn but first thought that he would ask Brazillai Bradley for some pay that he felt was his due. Bradley declined to part with any money. Instead, the man told Jennings that he had a nerve to ask when he had run off and left his board unpaid. At best, said Bradley, he would call the matter even by letting the amount in question cancel out the unpaid board. Jennings did not like that answer and he went away muttering. On the above date Mr. Bradley went to church. His wife, Esther Eaton Bradley (white, age 38), remained at home because she did not feel well. When the man returned to his residence that afternoon he found his wife lying on the kitchen floor slashed to death. The house was ransacked. Suspicion turned to Michael Jennings when neighbors reported his presence in the area at the time in question. On the following day the suspect was found walking along the railroad tracks in New Haven. His clothes were newly washed yet unmistakably bloodstained. Spots of blood were also found on his boots and those boots were found to match tracks left at the scene of the crime. The coins in his pockets, including a gold piece, were found to correspond with money missing from the Bradley home. In addition, Jennings was found to have passed paper currency that was smeared with blood.

Most damning of all, however, was a knife that the suspect carried on his person; its point was broken off and the same missing point was found embedded in one of the decedent's ribs. The knife point fit perfectly when matched with the broken weapon which Jennings carried. There was no doubt that the young man had gone to the Bradley home determined to get the money he felt was due him and that he had killed Mrs. Bradley in the process. Jennings denied the charge to no avail. He was indicted for the crime, tried and convicted. A movement to have the state legislature commute the death sentence fizzled when it was reported that the victim had been stabbed more than 100 times. Clemency was refused and on July 11, 1854, the teenaged Michael Jennings died on the gallows. The scene was the New Haven County jail. There was no confession.

Thomas Casey, white, age 20. *Murder.* The crime was committed on September 17, 1852, at Natick, Massachusetts. This is a rather obscure case of double homicide. Thomas Casey had been apprenticed to a shoemaker named Israel Taylor, aka Ouvra Taylor. He had run away from his master but came back on the above date with murderous intentions. Mr. Taylor and his wife, Angelina Taylor (whites, aged about 40), were attacked in their home and hacked to death with an axe. The motive for the crime is unknown. Casey fled from the scene but was overtaken by irate citizens on the road to Framingham. It was at first proposed to lynch him but wiser counsels prevailed. Duly convicted by a court of law, Thomas Casey was ordered for execution. He was hanged at the Middlesex County jail on September 29, 1854.

1858

James McGee, white, age 27. *Murder.* The crime was committed on Decem-

ber 15, 1856, at Charlestown, Massachusetts. A Canadian by birth and a brickmaker by trade, James McGee came to the town of Somerville when he reached the age of majority. There he got married and settled into a new home. However, his plans for the future were cut short when he caught his wife in bed with another man; an outraged McGee made a "murderous assault" on the trysters and wound up drawing a 12-year term in the state penitentiary. There he brooded for five years. Sometime during the course of his incarceration McGee developed an intense dislike for the deputy-warden, one Galen C. Walker (white, age 42) by name. The precise reason for the animus is unknown. At any rate, McGee made a plan to assassinate Walker. He somehow got hold of a knife and concealed it in his cell. Then on the above date McGee attended services in the prison chapel. Knowing that the deputy-warden would be there, McGee carried the knife on his person. When the services ended McGee approached Walker and said that he had a note for him. He next pulled a piece of paper from his pocket and made to hand it over. As Walker reached out to take the paper, McGee reached into the folds of his clothes with his other hand, unsheathed the knife, and began slashing at his target. Within seconds Walker was stabbed in the neck, chest and groin. The prison chaplain then ran to the scene and disabled McGee by smacking him on the head with a bible. Guards found the chaplain holding onto the dazed assassin by the hair. They were too late to save Walker however; the man was already dead. McGee was capitally convicted for this killing and ordered for execution. He was hanged at the Suffolk County jail on June 25, 1858.

Abraham Cox, black, age about 60. **Peter Williams,** white, age 28. *Mutiny and murder.* The crimes were committed on August 29, 1857, on the high seas.

This was a federal case. On July 27, 1857, the brig *Albion Cooper* left Portland, Maine, bound for Cuba. On board her was a seven-man crew consisting of the following: Captain Daniel R. Humphrey, First Mate Collingwood P. Smith, Second Mate Quinton D. Smith and Able Seamen Thomas Fahey, Charles King, Peter Williams (all whites), and a Negro cook named Abraham Cox. When the brig was a week out of port Peter Williams quarreled with the first mate. Tempers flared and the seaman pulled a knife on the mate. For this the captain ordered that Williams be put in irons and placed on short rations. Cox the cook fed Williams while he was chained in the ship's hold and somehow the prisoner managed to talk the cook into going partners with him in a mutiny. By the last week of August Williams had managed to euchre his way out of durance. He pretended to be contrite and asked to be returned to duty. The captain was moved to grant the request primarily because the vessel was left short-handed by the confinement of Seaman Williams. On the above date the *Albion Cooper* anchored in the Stirrup Keys in order to ride out heavy weather. It was then that the conspirators struck. Late at night they armed themselves with axes and went on a rampage. The captain was murdered in his cabin. The first and second mates were chased down and hacked to death. Seaman King was similarly slain in the forecastle. The last remaining member of the crew, Seaman Fahey, fared somewhat better; he was confronted by the mutineers and given a choice: either join them or die. Fahey (who is described as a "young Irish lad") knew better than to refuse such an offer. The reason why he was spared was because the mutineers needed an extra pair of hands to manage the ship. However, it soon became apparent that three men were insufficient to handle the vessel, let alone two. A decision was then made to abandon ship. The mutineers stripped the vessel of food, valuables and fresh water and provisioned one of the lifeboats accordingly. Then they set out for shore. The *Albion Cooper* was set afire and scuttled. By September 2, 1857—five days after the mutiny—the ocean currents had carried the lifeboat into the shipping lanes. There it was found by another American ship that was en route to Cuba. When the rescue vessel reached port, Seaman Fahey disclosed the truth about what had happened. Cox and Williams were arrested and turned over to the American consulate. Then a strange thing happened: Williams claimed to have seen the ghosts of the murdered men. So frightened was he that he confessed every detail of the mutiny. Cox also admitted his guilt. The prisoners were put on the next vessel bound for their home port of Portland, Maine, with certified transcripts of their confessions as well as the testimony of Seaman Fahey. Then another strange thing happened: Fahey died of some undisclosed cause before the homebound ship reached Portland. He was buried at sea. When Cox and Williams learned that the principal witness against them was dead they retracted their confessions. The maneuver availed them nothing. A federal district court tried them when they reached Maine and the confessions were admitted as evidence. So was the written testimony of the deceased Thomas Fahey. The verdict was guilty for each defendant and for each the sentence was death. On August 27, 1858, thousands of people poured into the town of Auburn to witness the double execution of the *Albion Cooper* mutineers. Each man spoke from the gallows: Williams to say that he had indeed committed the murders and Cox to say that he had merely been present at the time. When both men finished speaking they were hanged by their necks until they were dead.

1861

Alexander Desmarteau, white, age 22. *Murder.* The crime was committed on November 5, 1858, at Chicopee, Massachusetts. This offender was a Quebecois by birth. Upon reaching the age of majority he became an itinerant peddler and headed southward to ply his trade among the French-speaking settlements in the Connecticut River valley. The real reason why he chose such a route was because he was a known sexual offender in his homeland and deemed it prudent to go elsewhere. By the autumn of 1858 Desmarteau had made his way to Chicopee, Massachusetts, where there was a sizable contingent of Quebecois. He accordingly made that locale his base of operations. Soon he noticed the comings and goings of a young orphan girl named Augustina Lucas (white, age eight) and made it a point to watch her closely. He learned that the child was of a trusting nature and that she lived with a foster family that sometimes left her at home unattended. On the above date Desmarteau saw the child's foster parents leave their home. Lights continued to burn in the house so Desmarteau surmised that the girl was still there. He then drove his wagon to the address in question and knocked on the door. Augustina Lucas answered the knock whereupon Desmarteau enticed her with a warm invitation to go for a ride with him. In this way the trusting child was lured out of the house. She got into the wagon with the "nice young man" and the two rode off into the gathering dusk. Desmarteau headed for a remote area along the bank of the Connecticut River. There he choked the little girl into submission and raped her repeatedly. When he was finally sated he bludgeoned the child to death with a rock and threw her body into the river. Then he went home and proceeded to get drunk. By that time the girl's foster parents had reported her missing. Desmarteau was arrested the same night when neighbors told of seeing him with the victim. Charged with abduction, he soon confessed to rape and murder as well. The river was dragged with grappling irons for several days before the child's body was recovered. By then it was also revealed that the suspect had committed molestations in the area around Hartford, Connecticut. Legal maneuvering kept Desmarteau alive much longer than was ordinarily the case in those days. However, the end was never in doubt. On April 26, 1861, this child-killer was hanged at the Hampden County jail. His own family despised him for what he did and they refused to claim his body.

1862

George Hersey, white, age 29. *Murder.* The crime was committed on May 3, 1860, at Weymouth, Massachusetts. This celebrated defendant was a machinist in a shoe factory. In 1857 his life's plans were drastically altered when his young wife, Hannah Hersey, succumbed to an undisclosed illness. Single once again, George Hersey sold off the contents of his home and became a boarder with a family that lived near his place of employment. In 1859 he began to court an estimable young woman named Mary Tirrell and eventually became engaged to her. Then in December of that same year Mary Tirrell became seriously ill. She died on January 2, 1860. George Hersey was emotionally shattered by the loss and he slipped into depression. Miss Tirrell's surviving family members felt sorry for the bereaved widower who had lost both a wife and a fiancée. Seeking to ameliorate George's anguish, the Tirrells invited him to come live with them. George accepted and so became a member of the Tirrell household. He continued to brood, however, and wound up losing a lot of time from work. Mary Tirrell's elder sister, Betsy Frances Tirrell (white, age 25), lived in the same house and felt herself drawn to the rather handsome George Hersey. She did her best to cheer him up and took pleasure in doing him favors like sewing and pressing his clothes. As subsequent events would show, she also took it upon herself to satisfy George's sexual needs. After two or three months of this scenario George began to distance himself from Betsy Frances Tirrell; his roving eye had latched onto a 16-year-old girl named Loretta Loud. George considered this new entity more desirable than the plain-looking Betsy Frances but he carried on the courtship in secret lest the Tirrells (who were his landlords and benefactors) think him immodest. Then in April of 1860 George Hersey received two rather rude surprises: Betsy Frances Tirrell informed him that she was pregnant and Loretta Loud told him to get out of her life. It so happened that George had attempted to circumvent Loretta's reservations about pre-marital sex. Loretta would not hear of it and she told George to seek his satisfaction elsewhere. This left the matter of Betsy Frances Tirrell. George regarded her as a convenient concubine and nothing more. He did not love her and he certainly did not want to marry her, pregnant or not. Therefore he decided that both she and her unborn child had to be eliminated. Since Betsy Frances's condition was not yet apparent, George filled her mind with visions of disgrace. In such a way he got her to consent to an abortion. But how to go about it? So-called "illegal operations" were both risky and expensive. George then solved the problem by telling Betsy Frances that he would furnish her with a "medicine" that would "set her right." Betsy Frances agreed to cooperate. George Hersey then went to Boston and bought a packet of crystallized strychnine — a poison which is deadly to humans. On the above date

George mixed the lethal drug into a jar of jam and gave the same to Betsy Frances with instructions to swallow a spoonful of it before she went to bed at night. The trusting Betsy Frances did as she was bidden and died in agony. Her family was perplexed by such an untimely death so soon after that of their other daughter. An autopsy was proposed but George objected vociferously; he professed horror at the mutilation of a loved one but his true motive soon became apparent. The patriarch of the Tirrell family overruled George and the autopsy went forward. Two days later a grisly scene unfolded in the parlor of the Tirrell house as a team of surgeons cut open the body of Betsy Frances. To the surprise of all, George Hersey asked if he might be allowed to observe the proceedings. The request was considered unorthodox but none could think of a reason to deny it. George was therefore present as the surgeons eviscerated the late Betsy Frances. At first all appeared normal. However, when the probers removed the decedent's intestines and uncovered her womb they found a 12-week fetus therein. It was then that the surgeons suspected mischief. They asked George to leave the room and they finished the autopsy in private. Various internal organs were removed and carefully preserved for toxicological analysis. As the head surgeon was walking to his carriage afterward George approached him and anxiously asked if they found anything during the autopsy. The surgeon looked George straight in the eye and said, "What did you expect us to find?" Then the man shattered whatever illusions George still retained by saying that poison was suspected. This turned out to be only the beginning of the killer's troubles. When the parents of Betsy Frances learned that she had been pregnant they ordered George to quit their home forthwith. Then came the results of the toxicological exam: death from ingesting the alkaloid of *Strychnos nux vomica*, i.e., strychnine poisoning. A further investigation soon established that George Hersey had purchased the lethal substance shortly before the death of Betsy Frances Tirrell. He also made inquiries about it in several places. In addition to that, he had a clear motive for murder. A grand jury agreed and George was so charged. When the case came to trial a petit jury was no more sympathetic. After listening carefully to the arguments both for and against George Hersey a conviction for capital murder resulted. The penalty was death by hanging. On the morning of his execution Hersey removed all doubts by confessing that he was guilty as charged. However, he insisted that there had been no foul play by him in the deaths of his wife, Hannah Hersey, or of his fiancée, Mary Tirrell. On August 8, 1862, the gallows claimed George Hersey at the Norfolk County jail. The condemned man walked the distance from his cell to the rope with his eyes closed because he did not want to see the manner of his death.

Gerald Toole, white, age 24. *Murder.* The crime was committed on March 27, 1862, at Wethersfield, Connecticut. This offender came to the United States in 1858. He settled at New Haven, Connecticut, where he soon made himself notorious as a brawler. For his livelihood, Toole opened a low-class saloon which became a magnet for local riffraff. Police were happy when the place burned down in 1860. Two families were left homeless by the blaze and a subsequent investigation determined that Toole himself was responsible; he had set the fire in an effort to defraud his insurance company. A charge of first degree arson followed and Toole was sentenced to life behind bars at the Connecticut State Prison. No sooner did he begin serving his sentence than he became a chronic disciplinary problem. On the above date Toole began misbehaving in the prison shoe shop. He refused to work and dared

the guards to do something about it. The warden of the prison, Daniel Webster (white, age 50), was then called to the scene. He then proceeded to give the unruly prisoner a "slight reprimand" as a newspaper quaintly described it. In reality, the warden beat Toole with a nightstick. This had its desired effect and Toole resumed his work. However, he determined to get revenge on the warden. Toole used the next several hours to gradually sharpen a shoe knife at his work station. Then he secreted the knife on his person and began to antagonize the guards again. The guards shoved Toole into a closet and called the warden a second time. It was exactly what Toole wanted them to do. When the warden reached the scene he was told that Toole had been acting up again. Peeved by the situation, Warden Webster made for the closet with his nightstick at the ready. However, when he opened the closet door, Gerald Toole was ready for him. The prisoner rushed out of the closet and tackled the warden. Taking the man by surprise, Toole then stabbed him three times with his concealed knife before bystanders were able to intervene. Toole was subdued and the warden walked away from the scene. His wounds were initially believed to be minor. Within a matter of hours, however, the warden's condition took an abrupt turn for the worse. After a night of agony the man felt that his end was near. He remained coherent long enough to dictate a last will and testament. Then he died. Gerald Toole later said that he was subjected to harsh retaliation by the prison guards. The exact details were never revealed. A conviction for capital murder was not long in coming. On September 19, 1862, Gerald Toole was hanged at the Hartford County jail. More than 300 people were allowed to attend his supposedly "private" execution.

1863

William Lynch, white, age 26. *Mutiny.* The crime was committed on April 9, 1863, at Boston, Massachusetts. This man was a private in the 2nd Massachusetts cavalry. On the above date he incited a riot among the Union troops stationed at Camp Quincy, Boston. The motive for the disturbance is not known but during the course of the same a Sergeant Burlingham and a Corporal Balcolm were put in fear of their lives. When order was restored Private Lynch was identified as the ringleader of the mutineers. A court-martial duly considered the matter and ordered that Private Lynch be shot to death by musketry. The execution took place at Fort Independence (a military installation located on an island in Boston harbor) on June 16, 1863. As the condemned man faced the firing squad he shouted, "Shoot me in the breast! Don't mark my face!" The firing squad obliged him.

William Laird, white, age 27. *Army desertion.* The crime was committed on October 11, 1862, somewhere in Maryland. A resident of Berwick, this man enlisted in the 17th Maine infantry on August 18, 1862. By the time of the above date his regiment had arrived at Fort Ricketts, Maryland, preparatory to going into action. Private Laird deserted on that date and made his way back to Maine. There he was caught. He was then brought to Fort Preble, a military installation near Portland, and arraigned before a court-martial. Convicted of willful desertion, Private Laird was condemned to be shot to death by musketry. A Fort Preble firing squad carried out the sentence on July 15, 1863.

James Callender, black, age 20. *Murder.* The crime was committed on September 7, 1862, at Otis, Massachusetts. This offender was the son of a transient couple who bore a bad reputation in and around Berkshire County. Society looked askance at Callender because he was a product of miscegenation; his mother was a white woman and his father a black man. To make matters worse, young James Callender was a lazy type who refused to get a job. He had no sense of decency and felt that he could do as he pleased. On April 1, 1862, he got together with a half-brother of similar credentials and went to Sandisfield. There he knew of a white woman whose husband had gone off to war. Her name was Mrs. Peasley and she had only herself and a small child at home. Callender and his half-brother forced their way into the woman's house. They terrorized the two occupants before announcing the purpose of their visit: they wanted Mrs. Peasley to service them sexually. The woman tried to resist but she was overpowered. Then the intruders took turns raping her in front of her young child. In the days that followed this attack there was a roundup of suspicious characters. Both of the rapists were among those apprehended. However, Mrs. Peasley was only able to identify one of them with certainty. As a result, Callender's half-brother was sentenced to life in prison. James Callender himself escaped unscathed. Then on the above date there occurred a crime which had few equals in terms of brutality. In the town of Otis there dwelled a young couple named George and Emily Jones (whites, age 26). They in turn had two young children named George Jones, Jr. (white, age four), and Sarah Jones (white, age two). On the above date — September 7, 1862 — Mr. Jones went to church while his wife and children remained at home. After a while Mrs. Jones decided that she would pick some berries a short distance yonder. She then set about that task and brought her children with her. James Callender observed this family grouping and noted well the fact that there was no man to be seen. He then pounced on

Mrs. Jones and beat her severely. Then he tore all of her clothes off and raped her right in front of the children. When Callender finally had enough sex he fatally bludgeoned Mrs. Jones with a rock. Annoyed by the crying of the woman's terrified children, he next went after them. Both of the toddlers were picked up and swung around by their ankles so that their heads were dashed against a large boulder. When all three victims were dead Callender covered them with forest debris and went his merry way. A couple of hours later George Jones came home from church and was puzzled by the absence of his wife and children. Then as more hours passed he began to get worried. He finally organized a search which was soon halted on account of darkness. On the following day there was still no word of the missing persons. Then many townspeople became involved. One party of searchers passed by the berry patch where they found children's baskets and articles of feminine attire. Then they came upon rocks that were smeared with blood and brain matter. A swarm of flies finally revealed the spot where the bodies lay concealed. The sight was enough to make strong men swoon. We shall forbear further details of the crime scene. There followed a roundup of all known criminals — especially those who were sex offenders. James Callender was among those so apprehended. In the days that followed the number of suspects steadily shrank as one by one the prisoners accounted for their whereabouts. After nearly three weeks of nonstop investigation James Callender was still being detained. Then he suddenly made a surprise confession. He said that he and his father, Thomas Callender (black, age 55), had resented the Jones family ever since George Jones had accused them of surreptitiously milking his cows at night. On the day of the murders, according to James Callender, he and his father had come upon the woman and children in the berry patch. They then took turns raping Mrs. Jones, each of them alternately holding her down for the better leverage of the other. James Callender concluded his story by saying that he had killed the woman while his father killed the children. The elder Callender was struck dumb when told of what his son had declared. He finally recovered enough to deny all involvement with the crime. He was also able to provide enough evidence to convince a grand jury that he was innocent. For that reason no indictment was found against Thomas Callender. He was eventually freed but he *was* forced to witness the execution of his son at the Berkshire County jail on November 6, 1863. The reason why James Callender impugned his father has never been explained. He was the last criminal to be hanged at Lenox.

1864

William Barnett, white, age 57. *Murder.* The crime was committed on August 27, 1862, at Burlington, Vermont. This offender was an English immigrant who lived together with his wife, Anne Barnett (white, age 35), in a slum district known as Skinner's Lane. Both were alcoholics who quarreled frequently. William Barnett earned a meager living as a cattle doctor and a privy cleaner. Late on the evening of the above date he drank himself into a temper and turned on his wife. He beat the woman severely and threw her onto a bed where he finished her off with a butcher knife. Then the killer faked a scene to make it look as if the decedent had committed suicide. William Barnett was charged with capital murder when a coroner determined that the victim's wounds could not possibly have been self-inflicted. A conviction followed in a court of law. On January 20, 1864, the man was hanged at the Vermont State Prison.

Sandy Kavanaugh, white, age 59.

Murder. The crime was committed on January 8, 1862, at Burlington, Vermont. This is an obscure case in which an aging drunkard killed his equally besotted wife. Sandy and Catherine Kavanaugh lived together in a rundown house at the bottom of College Street. They became notorious thereabouts for loud quarrels. On the above date Sandy Kavanaugh beat his wife over the head with a rum bottle and cut her throat with a pocketknife. The killer tried to explain away the homicide by saying that the victim was drunk when she slipped and struck her head against a stove. However, he could not satisfactorily explain why her throat was cut and why her hands bore defensive wounds. On January 20, 1864, this uxoricide was put to death by hanging at the Vermont State Prison.

Charles Carpenter and Matthew Riley, whites, both aged 21. *Army desertion and bounty jumping.* Their crimes

were committed in December of 1863 in Vermont and Massachusetts. These young men were believed to have originally come from Cohoes, New York. They had long criminal records and were described as being of "the worst character." They were also suspected of belonging to a gang which made a regular business of bounty jumping the armed forces during the Civil War. Both used pseudonyms during the course of their misadventures but their real names were believed to be James McCarty and John Roach respectively. On December 4, 1863, both of them appeared at Sunderland, Vermont. There they enlisted with Company E of the 5th Vermont volunteers. They collected an enlistment bounty and deserted two days later. Deciding to stick together, both fugitives made their way to Springfield, Massachusetts, where they repeated the same trick. They enlisted with a Massachusetts regiment, collected the enlistment bounty and promptly deserted. Following this second offense, both men donned disguises and set a course for New Hampshire. They meant to repeat their fraud in the Granite State. However, both were seized by alert railroad detectives before they reached their destination. Then they were brought to Boston where a court-martial awaited them. Along the way they attempted to escape by jumping from a moving train but both were soon recaptured. On April 22, 1864, the entire company of Fort Warren (a military installation located on an island in Boston harbor) stood at attention while a firing squad dispatched the two bounty jumpers. Afterward all marched past the execution ground to view the riddled corpses as they were lowered into their unmarked graves.

Francis Couillard Spencer, white, age 34. *Murder.* The crime was committed on May 14, 1863, at Thomaston, Maine. This man was an habitual criminal who spent more than half his life in jail. On January 17, 1860, he was committed to the Maine State Prison from Cumberland County under a five-year sentence for attempted rape. While in the state prison he developed a deadly hatred for the warden of that institution, Richard Tinker (white, age about 60), because he had several times put him in solitary confinement. On the above date Spencer was working in the prison wheelwright shop when warden Tinker came there to observe things. Seeing his chance, Spencer sprang upon the warden with a knife and stabbed him in the neck. The victim bled to death within seconds. As soon as the killer struck the fatal blow he shouted, "I'll let 'em know there's one man in this prison that ain't afraid to die! God damn 'em!" It was a mocking reference to the state of Maine's practice of routinely commuting death sentences to terms of imprisonment. This killer *dared* the state of Maine to hang him and on June 24, 1864, the state of Maine obliged. A gallows was erected

on the site of the crime and Francis Spencer was swung to his doom.

1866

Edward Green, white, age 32. *Murder.* The crime was committed on December 15, 1863, at Malden, Massachusetts. This man was the postmaster of the aforesaid town. He was also deep in debt. On the above date Green needed change for a $20 bill. So he stepped out of the post office and went next door to the local bank. There he found the place almost empty of people. Only one clerk was on duty. Green accordingly got his change. However, as he stood at the teller window counting his coins his eyes were drawn to a large batch of currency nearby. As he returned to the post office with his change, Green became tempted by the other money that he had seen. Without further ado, he took a pistol from his desk drawer and went back to the bank. He then walked up to the lone cashier and shot him point-blank in the forehead. Then Green grabbed all the money from the teller station ($5000) and fled from the scene. No one saw him. The crime was discovered several minutes later when a customer walked into the bank. The victim was subsequently identified as one Frank Converse (white, age 17), the son of the bank president. In the aftermath of this murder and robbery investigators were at a loss. For an entire month no one suspected that the culprit was right next door to the bank. Then suddenly Edward Green began paying off his numerous debts. His creditors were delighted to receive payment but one or two of them wondered how the hitherto impecunious Green was able to clear his accounts so sweepingly. When asked about it Green became sullen and evasive. His demeanor gave the impression that he was hiding something. Local officials then decided to take their chances and ask Green directly if he knew anything about the bank job. Green astounded his listeners by admitting that he was the guilty party. When the case came to trial, Green pled guilty to a charge of capital murder. He was accordingly sentenced to death. For the next two years the governor of Massachusetts vacillated on whether to issue a warrant for Green's execution. It finally took a new governor to decide the matter. On April 13, 1866, the former postmaster was hanged at the Middlesex County jail.

Albert Starkweather, white, age 24. *Murder.* The crime was committed on August 1, 1865, at Manchester, Connecticut. This ill-fated young man was born at Hartford on March 2, 1841. His father, Benjamin Starkweather, was a prosperous wholesaler of meats and provisions. The elder Starkweather and his wife, Harriet Starkweather, are described as having been devoted parents who saw that their son was well bred and credibly educated. Matters took a turn for the worse in 1854 when Benjamin Starkweather fell ill and died. His widow liquidated his business and used some of the proceeds to purchase a 70-acre farm in the then-rural town of Manchester. Thirteen-year-old Albert Starkweather was left to be raised in a home devoid of a fatherly presence. He had only his mother and one sister who was ten years his junior. For companionship he turned to the local farmhands and became familiar with their ways. This proved to be a mixed blessing for the growing boy. Country living had unique advantages but it also had drawbacks; while young Albert was spared the more sordid temptations of the city, he was also exposed to influences that were pernicious in their own sort of way. Those with whom Albert associated were not of the highest caliber and by the time young Starkweather came of age their influence upon him was clearly evident. The result was a cavalier womanizer whose reputation left nothing to the imagination.

It was the compulsive pursuit of women that made Albert Starkweather turn to murder. After summarily using and discarding several bachelorettes the young rake met one who dared to set conditions on him. Albert was curtly dismissed with a warning not to come back until he had established himself as an independent man of means. This rebuke made Albert crave the elusive female more than ever. But how to acquire wealth and thereby satisfy her? The answer was simple: *murder*. Albert had a maternal uncle who had previously indicated that he planned to bequeath a handsome sum to his nephew. The man was a farmer with a sizable workforce who all took their meals together. During an unguarded moment Albert snuck into the kitchen and there made use of a packet of arsenic that he had deliberately brought for that purpose. He mixed the poison into a batch of dough which the cook then unwittingly baked into bread. The members of the household ate the tainted bread and became dangerously ill. Several were not expected to live, including Albert's uncle. However, diligent medical attention saved all except one unidentified farmhand. The cook who baked the bread was initially blamed for what had happened. Charged with murder, that hapless person was forced to endure a harrowing ordeal before she was finally exonerated by Albert Starkweather's confession.

Failing to kill his rich uncle, Albert next turned his attention to the members of his immediate family. By then he was utterly obsessed with the elusive young woman and he determined that he must — at any cost — obtain the wealth to satisfy her. He then reasoned that if his mother and sister were dead he would inherit the family property. On the above date Albert put his plan into motion. At four o'clock in the morning he burst into the room where his mother and sister lay sleeping and attacked them with an axe. Harriet Starkweather (white, age 46) and Ella Starkweather (white, age 14) were hacked to death in their beds. So frenzied was the assault that both of the victims were mutilated beyond recognition. Then to make doubly sure that they were dead, the killer stabbed each of them a dozen times with a butcher knife. After that, Albert Starkweather inflicted some superficial wounds on himself and set the house on fire. He then ran to the nearest neighbor's and gasped out an improbable story about being attacked by armed intruders. Lawmen were suspicious of Albert from the start. They arrested him the same day.

It did not take Albert Starkweather long to confess what he had done and why. When a newspaper reporter interviewed him in his cell he made the following statement: "I don't believe they will hang me. Public opinion is all against me now but it will die out. When Jeff Davis was first caught everybody said Hang him! But they don't have that feeling now. So it will be with me. They blame me too more than they would if I had killed somebody else besides my mother. They are down on me because I killed her but I don't see why it is any worse to kill your mother than any other person. I suppose when a man kills another man he does it to get rid of a nuisance. Thats all I killed my mother for — to get rid of a nuisance!"

Albert Starkweather was hanged at the Hartford County jail on August 17, 1866. Although his family owned a large plot in the Hartford cemetery he was denied burial there. It is said that he was thrown among the nameless dead in a place reserved for paupers.

1868

John Ward, alias "Jerome Levigne," white, age 25. *Murder*. The crime was committed on August 28, 1865, at Williston, Vermont. This man was a New York City roughneck who took part in an alleged murder-for-hire plot. At Williston, Vermont, there lived a feisty woman named Sally Griswold (white, age 57). She had made a fortune during the California gold rush of 1849 (as an innkeeper) and was able to live comfortably thereafter. Together in the same house with Mrs. Griswold there dwelled her husband, Ephraim Griswold, as well as her foster daughter, Adelia Potter, and that woman's husband, Charles Potter, plus a 12-year-old houseboy named Edward Call. When it became known that Mrs. Griswold had made a will in which she bequeathed all of her property to her foster daughter, Charles Potter allegedly became obsessed with greed. He reasoned that if his mother-in-law was eliminated (so the story goes), her estate would come under his control. Accordingly, he is said to have made a trip to New York City for the purpose of finding a suitable assassin. After prowling the worst haunts of the Manhattan underworld he allegedly found a recently discharged soldier-of-fortune named John Ward, alias "Jerome Levigne." According to the subsequent confession of that man, he (Ward) listened to Potter's proposal and agreed to kill Mrs. Griswold for $500 plus whatever valuables he might find in her house. Potter is alleged to have agreed to those terms and to have set a date on which he would take the rest of the family away on an excursion. So it transpired on the above date that Ward took a train to Vermont and found Mrs. Griswold at home with only the houseboy for company. Ward waited for nightfall and then broke into the house. Mrs. Griswold was attacked in her kitchen and beaten with a blackjack. She put up a fight, however, and the struggle was carried on from room to room before Ward finally prevailed. He knocked Mrs. Griswold unconscious. Then he caught the houseboy and locked him in a closet. After that he returned to the woman and cut her throat from ear to ear. The body was then wrapped in a quilt and hidden in an adjoining barn. Ward then rifled the house for valuables and fled into the night. Early the next morning passersby were alerted by the houseboy's screams. Thus was the crime discovered. A special detective was hired to find the killer. It was then reported that the conductor on a southbound train had taken note of a suspicious person that night. The suspect had drawn attention because he was wearing a heavy overcoat (it then being summer) to conceal blood-stained clothes. Blood was also visible on the man's shoes. An alert was posted and several days later the same man was seen on a northbound train. He was evidently on his way to collect his $500 fee from the person who had hired him. From there the detective picked up his trail and followed him back to New York. In such a way was the suspect's identity ascertained. Ward and Potter were both charged with the crime. The former was convicted and the latter was acquitted. Shortly before the time set for his execution, Ward wrote a lengthy confession in which he implicated Potter and the victim's foster daughter. He also said that others were in on the crime and that he (Ward) was merely present at the time. He claimed that the actual murder was committed by a man named Walter Moore. When asked why his clothes had been bloodstained, Ward said that he had been in a brawl. Walter Moore was never located and it is doubtful that he ever existed. John Ward was sent to the Vermont State Prison under sentence of death. On March 20, 1868, he died on the gallows there.

Samuel Mills, white, age 28. *Murder.* The crime was committed on December 8, 1866, at Franconia, New Hampshire. This man was an English immigrant who worked at the Grafton County copper mines in Lisbon, New Hampshire. Desiring to make a new life for himself in the American west, he committed robbery and murder to finance that goal. On the above date Mills went to the miners' dormitory in Lisbon while the other men were at work. He then broke open the storage trunk of a fellow employee and made off with the valuables he found therein. Wanting more loot, Mills then set a course for the nearby town of Franconia where he had formerly resided. There he called on his erstwhile landlord, one George Maxwell (white, age 65) by name. Mills was given a cordial reception and invited to stay for dinner. The two men then chatted while Maxwell set an extra place at the table. Then when Maxwell went to his pantry to fetch some edibles Mills made his move. He struck Maxwell down from behind with a piece of firewood and stabbed him 11 times. There was a struggle but Mills prevailed. After that he beat the victim beyond recognition with the chunk of firewood and split his head open with an axe. Despite the fact that he was drenched in blood, the killer then sat down and ate the meal that Maxwell had prepared for him. It was later shown that he did not even wash his hands because half-eaten biscuits were found on the table smeared with blood. Mills followed up his sanguine repast by searching the dead man's house from top to bottom. He stole every item of value that he could find. Then he jumped aboard a freight train that was headed north. Crossing the Canadian border without incident, Mills turned westward. He eventually reentered the United States by way of Lake Superior and made his way to Wisconsin. Meanwhile back in New Hampshire the copper miners were angered by the theft in their dormitory. When they heard the news of the Franconia homicide they told about their missing colleague who had formerly boarded there. A special detective was then assigned to the case.

That individual reasoned that since the prime suspect was a miner he would be likely to pursue that line of work elsewhere. Hence detailed descriptions of the wanted man were sent to every mining camp in the United States and Canada. Several weeks later police in Illinois arrested a man who matched the description of the fugitive. It was Samuel Mills himself. He had applied for work at a mine there and came under suspicion. Upon being returned to the scene of the crime, Mills broke down and admitted his guilt. Then for the better part of a year he confounded his jailers by escaping three times and attempting to do the same right up to the very day of his execution. On May 6, 1868, thousands of people poured into the town of Haverhill to see Samuel Mills pay the death penalty. It was the last public hanging in the New England states.

Charles James, white, age 23. **Silas James,** white, age 32. *Murder.* Their crime was committed on February 28, 1868, at Worcester, Massachusetts. These men were the wayward scions of a prominent Rhode Island family. Their grandfather had been a United States senator from that state. Although frequently reported to be brothers, they were in fact first cousins. Silas was the more intelligent of the two while Charles is described as a lackey who idolized Silas. Together they sought a livelihood through chicanery. Gambling was their special interest and they were well known in gaming circles as men who were less than honorable. In one noted scandal they were rumored to have poisoned an expensive race horse. When asked about the matter shortly before their execution, they admitted that the rumor was true. Among their many dens of resort was a glitzy casino located in the Union block of downtown Worcester. The place was run by a professional gambler named Joseph Clark, alias "Big Joe Clark" (white, age unknown), who was noted for his ostentatious personal habits. On the above date the James cousins used their personal acquaintance with Clark to gain admittance to his living quarters located above his place of business. Once inside they threw off all pretense and attacked their host. Charles James split Clark's head open with a hatchet while Silas James aided and abetted. Then the killers robbed the victim of $12,000 in cash plus expensive jewelry. After that they knotted a rope tightly around the dead man's neck and hung him from one of his own bedposts. Seeking to cover up the crime, the Jameses next proceeded to splash kerosene all over the room and set it on fire. One of Clark's lady friends saw the killers as they fled from the premises. She summoned casino personnel who managed to extinguish the blaze. Clark was found badly burned with his brain protruding from the wound on his head. Silas James was subsequently nabbed at the Worcester train station. Charles James got away to Rhode Island but was soon after chased down and caught by a crowd that had recognized him from a wanted poster. As he as fleeing from the crowd, Charles James was seen to throw away a bundle. It was found to contain a large sum of money plus the slain man's gold watch and diamond stickpin. When confronted with the evidence, Charles James confessed the whole affair. A double conviction followed on a dual indictment for capital murder. Some effort was made to have the sentence of Charles James commuted on the ground that he had merely been a tool of his crafty cousin. As for Silas James, his cause was not even espoused by opponents of capital punishment. Such was the scorn that he had incurred. On September 25, 1868, both cousins were simultaneously hanged at the Worcester County jail.

1869

Clifton Harris, black, age 19. *Murder.* The crime was committed on January 17, 1867, at Auburn, Maine. This individual had come north as a refugee at the close of the Civil War. After wandering about for several months he stopped at Auburn and there took a servant's job. Deciding to remain in that position, Harris soon acquired a local reputation for rowdyism and lewdness. On the above date a blizzard of unprecedented severity blew down out of the north woods. Auburn was caught in the thick of it and all business was suspended. Clifton Harris took advantage of the situation to approach the house of two aging ladies named Susannah Kinsley and Polly Caswell (whites, ages 64 and 67 respectively). He knocked on their door and implored shelter from the storm. Polly Caswell took the matter at face value and let Harris in. It was a fatal mistake. No sooner did Harris enter the house than he picked up a chair and attacked the woman with it. Polly Caswell was beaten to death. Harris then went into a bedroom where the other woman, Susannah Kinsley, lay ill. He beat and raped the second woman in her own bed before slashing her to death with a knife. Still not satisfied, he took a hatchet to the faces of both victims and hacked them until they were unrecognizable. For the next two days the blizzard continued to rage. When it was over some neighbors of the two women became concerned for their well-being. Upon going to their house, they found the door ajar. When they went inside they found the mutilated bodies of both women frozen solid in their own gore. The body of Susannah Kinsley bore unmistakable signs of rape in addition to other traumatic injuries. The authorities immediately ordered a roundup of all suspicious characters. Clifton Harris was held for questioning and he soon admitted his guilt. He implicated a certain white man as an accomplice but later retracted that part of his confession. When the case came to trial Harris and the white man were both convicted. When Harris changed his story, however, the white man (whose name was Verrill) was granted a new trial. He finally went free because the prosecution had no case against him without the testimony of Harris. After Harris was sentenced to die he again changed his story in an attempt to reimplicate the white man. However, by then even the prosecution dismissed him as an unreliable perjurer. Thus Harris was left to face the gallows alone. He was executed at the Maine State Prison on March 12, 1869.

Hiram Miller, alias "Henry Wilson," white, age 32. *Murder.* The crime was committed on July 23, 1867, at Weathersfield, Vermont. Joshua and Abigail Gowing (whites, aged 55) were a prosperous farm couple who lived near Ascutneyville, a scenic enclave within the town of Weathersfield. Among their hired hands was the above-named Hiram Miller. He came from an established family in the town of Richford, close to the Canadian border. Desiring to conceal that fact for some reason, Miller went by the alias "Henry Wilson" and such was the cognomen by which he was known at Ascutneyville. At some time during the course of his employment there, Miller or "Wilson" became aware of the fact that Mr. and Mrs. Gowing had a cache of easily negotiable bearer bonds. His cupidity aroused, Miller or "Wilson" determined to take the bonds for himself. In order to play it safe (according to his rationale), Miller alias "Wilson" quit his job. He then bade farewell to Mr. and Mrs. Gowing and returned to his hometown. Feeling that he was then a safe distance from Ascutneyville, the killer-to-be reasoned that he would thus have no difficulty proving an alibi for his whereabouts. On the above date then, Miller boarded a late-night train and headed southward. Arriving at Claremont, New Hampshire, he surreptitiously made his way across the long covered bridge which spanned the river there. That route brought him into the territory of Weathersfield, Vermont, and from there it was but a short trek across the fields to Ascutneyville. At four o'clock in the morning, Miller alias "Wilson" approached the house of Joshua Gowing. He entered the yard without a sound and took an axe from the woodshed. Then he pounded on the door of the farmhouse and called upon Gowing to get up quickly. He impersonated a neighbor and hollered out that the cows had broken into the cornfield. Gowing hurriedly threw on some clothes and said that he was coming. No sooner did he open the door, however, than he was instantly slain by a tremendous axe blow. Then the killer burst into the house and attacked Mrs. Gowing. The woman was hacked to death in her own bed. With both of the homeowners dead, Miller began a thorough ransacking of the farmhouse. The intruder soon came upon a mentally retarded son of the victims but spared him in the belief that it was bad luck to kill an imbecile. However, with only moonlight to guide him, Miller failed to see a 12-year-old daughter of the decedents who was also there. Too frightened to move, the girl huddled where she was long after the killer had gone. She was found at dawn by neighbors who were engaged to work with Mr. Gowing that day. When questioned about the carnage in the house the girl identified "our farmhand Henry Wilson" as the culprit. There followed a fearsome hue and cry which spread across the countryside. A short time later Miller alias "Wilson" was seen in Windsor nonchalantly walking down the main street. When it was demanded of him that he explain his presence there he said that he had arrived on the morning train with an intention of looking for work. Arrested and brought to the scene of the crime, Miller remained impassive. When the news of his whereabouts spread, a lynch mob quickly formed. It was only with difficulty that Miller was whisked away from the scene. He was taken to Rutland and held there for nearly a year in the worst possible conditions. When he was finally brought to trial he was unfazed by the existence of an eyewitness to his crime. Miller insisted that he was innocent and he continued to make that claim right up to the moment of his execution. He was hanged at the Vermont State Prison on June 25, 1869.

Josiah Pike, white, age 30. *Murder.* The crime was committed on May 7, 1868, at Hampton Falls, New Hampshire. This man was an alcoholic roustabout who worked for an elderly farm couple named Mr. and Mrs. Thomas Brown (whites, ages 77 and 78). So severe was Pike's drinking problem that he even imbibed the alcohol-based embalming fluid used at his wife's funeral. In April of 1868 this Pike abruptly quit his job. He then set a course for Massachusetts and what was then the wide-open town of Newburyport. There he squandered all of his severance pay. Needing more money, Pike then decided to rob his former employers. On the above date he drank himself into a frenzy and headed for Hampton Falls. By the time he arrived there he was ready to dare anything. Late at night he approached the house of Thomas Brown. He paused to take an axe from the woodpile and then pounded on the door. When Mrs. Brown came to see who was there she was immediately cut down by blows from the axe. Hearing the woman's screams, Mr. Brown ran to her aid only to be dealt with in the same way. Believing both of the Browns to be dead, Pike proceeded to ransack their house. He used the lethal axe to smash open a desk which contained about $500

in cash and jewelry. Seizing that loot, the killer hastened back to Newburyport where he resumed his revelry. As things turned out, the Browns were not killed outright. Although terribly wounded, they were still alive when the crime was discovered. Mrs. Brown succumbed to her injuries two days later. Mr. Brown managed to hang on for five days during which time he gasped out the name of the killer. At once the manhunt began. Pike was reported to be in Newburyport and he was arrested there the following day. Thomas Brown's wallet was found in his possession. Returned to New Hampshire, Pike pled guilty to two counts of capital murder. He was soon ordered for execution. During the mandatory one-year period between his sentencing date and punishment date, efforts were made to get the death sentence commuted. It was argued that Pike suffered from a newly recognized illness called dipsomania, a form of madness brought on by a morbid craving for alcohol. The plea failed to win the governor's sympathy. Accordingly, on November 9, 1869, Josiah Pike was hanged at the New Hampshire State Prison.

1871

Henry Welcome, white, age 17. *Murder.* The crime was committed on October 3, 1868, at Hinesburg, Vermont. This juvenile offender belonged to a respectable family in the small town of Hinesburg. According to his own confession, he ran away from home at the age of 16. Winding up in Boston, he fell in with some street-wise types and was soon exposed to every kind of vice. When he returned home a year later he had changed for the worse. Believing an elderly neighbor named Perry Russell (white, age 76) to have a hoard of negotiable bonds in his house, Welcome determined to seize them. On the above date he armed himself with a heavy metal door hinge and went to the Russell homestead. It was after midnight when he pounded on the door. Perry Russell got out of bed and called for the visitor to identify himself. Welcome then shouted the name of one of Mr. Russell's farmhands. Recognizing the name, Russell unbolted the door. He was immediately attacked by Henry Welcome and beaten to death. The victim's wife ran from the house unseen by the attacker. She headed for the closest neighbor. In the meantime, Welcome ransacked the Russell residence in a frenzied search for the bonds. He found them not. When he heard the approach of a rescue party he fled into the night. Recognized by the decedent's wife, Welcome was advertised as a fugitive. Two days later he was caught at Waterbury. Following the trial and capital conviction of this young man, great efforts were made to get his sentence commuted on account of his age. A bill to spare Welcome's life passed the State House of Representatives but was voted down by the senate. The youthful killer was then left to his fate. On January 20, 1871, he went to the gallows at the Vermont State Prison.

James Wilson, white, age 46. *Murder.* The crime was committed on August 14, 1870, at Wethersfield, Connecticut. This man was an habitual criminal who had served jail time in Ohio, Michigan, New Jersey, New York and Connecticut. The product of a Manhattan street gang, Wilson never bothered to learn a trade other than that of professional burglary. At the time of his capital crime he was an inmate of the Connecticut State Prison where he had been sent for breaking into a department store and stealing a valuable cache of silk. When he was brought to court to answer for that charge, Wilson was confronted by one William Willard (white, age 52), the warden of the Connecticut State Prison. Willard attested to the fact that Wilson was a recidivist burglar, having previously served a six-year term in state's prison under a different name. Because of this Wilson received a harsher sentence for the silk heist than he might have otherwise received. He then formed a deadly hatred for Warden Willard and determined to get even with him. For two years Wilson bided his time. He studied the warden's movements and carefully watched for any sign of vulnerability. When Wilson learned that Willard made personal visits to prisoners in their cells he knew that the time for action had come. He purloined a knife from the prison shoe shop and smuggled it to his cell. Then he spent long nights honing the knife to razor-sharp proportions. When he felt that all was ready, Wilson inserted the haft of the knife into the end of a cane that he was allowed to have. He fit the knife securely in place so that he had a formidable weapon. Then he wrote a fabricated message on a writing tablet and requested that the warden come to his cell while in the course of his nightly rounds. Wilson passed the writing tablet through the bars to him. As Willard began to read the message, Wilson jabbed his improvised sword through the bars, stabbing the man in the belly. Warden Willard was caught unawares and took the full force of the thrust. He had to be carried from the scene with his intestines protruding from the wound. He died within a short time. Wilson later tried to justify his crime by alleging that the decedent had singled him out for abuse. He also said that he had been beaten, starved, fed on garbage and otherwise mistreated. Whether or not Wilson exaggerated his claims is open to speculation. It *is* known, however, that he had been an obnoxious prisoner who had incurred disciplinary action on numerous occasions. James Wilson was subsequently hanged at the Hartford County jail on October, 13, 1871.

1873

James McElhaney, white, age 30. *Murder.* The crime was committed on August 17, 1872, at Boston, Massachusetts. This man came from Ireland when just a small child. His parents settled at Cambridge, Massachusetts, and it was there where they raised their son. At the age of ten James McElhaney was apprenticed to a glassblower and he remained in that line of work for the rest of his life. He subsequently married a girl named Emma Roberts (white) and began to raise a family. At the time of their wedding husband and wife were aged 28 and 17 respectively. When the novelty of marriage wore off, the teenaged Mrs. McElhaney realized that she had made a mistake. Her husband had an ungovernable temper which he made no effort to restrain. He did not aggravate the problem with drinking but he did become abusive. After two years Emma McElhaney could take no more. She brought herself and her baby to the house of her mother (at No. 19 Windsor Street in Boston) and was given asylum there. On the above date James McElhaney went looking for his wife. He learned of her whereabouts and hastened there. Upon being admitted to his mother-in-law's house, he went up to the second floor where his wife was staying. Then he asked to have a few minutes alone with her. His request was granted and McElhaney made use of the time to speak with his wife. He asked the young woman to return home with him but she said that she was too ill to do so. Believing this to be a lame excuse, McElhaney began to get angry. He then repeated his request until it became a demand. Each time the woman demurred his temper increased. Finally he became enraged. He then pulled out a pistol and shot his wife dead. Turning the weapon on himself, McElhaney fired two more shots at his own head. He only succeeded in giving himself a nasty flesh wound whereupon he roused himself and jumped out of the second story window. A policeman pounced on him when he hit the ground. McElhaney was patched up and put on trial for capital murder. A conviction resulted as did a sentence of death. McElhaney was subsequently hanged at the Suffolk County jail on March 21, 1873.

Albert Smith, white, age 22. *Murder.* The crime was committed on November 20, 1872, at Westfield, Massachusetts. This young man committed murder because he did not take kindly to being jilted. Smith was born and raised in Maryland. At the age of 19 he came north to seek his fortune. As his luck would have it, he wound up working as a railroad brakeman in Hampden County, Massachusetts. For personal diversion he wooed a young woman named Jenny Bates (white, age 25) and dreamed of marrying her. This went on for several months. Miss Bates allowed Smith to call on her but she remained noncommittal. Then a rival entered the picture. Miss Bates received the addresses of a prosperous bachelor named Charles Sackett (white, age 40) and decided that she preferred him over Albert Smith. The new suitor was more urbane than Smith and far better off financially. Smith knew that he could not compete with Sackett because he was totally outclassed by the man. However, he found it personally insulting that Miss Bates should forsake a young man (himself) for an older one. Anger and jealousy began to rise in Albert Smith. When Jenny Bates told Smith that she had made up her mind once and for all, the rejected suitor decided to retaliate. Smith threatened Sackett's life and he spread obscene rumors about Miss Bates. One night Smith got up the nerve to confront his rival face to face. Sackett noted the volatility of Smith's mood and decided to make a tactical retreat; he told Smith that he would end his relationship with Miss Bates. That pacified Smith for the moment. However, on the above date Smith learned that Sackett had escorted Miss Bates to a Westfield theater. The news was more than he could bear. Arming himself with a revolver, Smith lay in wait for the couple. He figured that Sackett would most likely walk Miss Bates home after the show. And so he did. As the couple walked arm in arm along Poehassic Street they were fired upon by Smith. The young woman was hit three times and painfully wounded. She survived but was left permanently disfigured. Charles Sackett was hit once in the chest. He died two weeks later. Smith fled from the scene but was nabbed within a matter of hours. When he was brought to trial he admitted his guilt but claimed extreme emotional duress as a mitigating factor. The fact that the crime was premeditated, however, earned him a capital conviction. Clemency was rejected by a unanimous vote of the governor-in-council. The end came on June 27, 1873, when Albert Smith was hanged at the Hampden County jail.

1874

Franklin Evans, white, age 61. *Murder.* The crime was committed on October 24, 1872, at Northwood, New Hampshire. This man led the life of a roving mountebank. At alternate times he made a marginal living as a quack doctor, a patent medicine huckster, a fishmonger, an evangelical preacher and a peddler of notions. During the Civil War he did a brisk business with the federal troops stationed around the greater Boston area; he smuggled whiskey into their cantonments and kept them supplied with prostitutes. In the spring of 1872 Evans appeared at Northwood, New Hampshire, where he applied to his brother-in-law, one Sylvester Day by

name. This family connection owned a farm and Evans asked to be taken on there as a laborer. His request was granted and for the next few months Evans earned a legitimate livelihood. Among the members of farmer Day's household was a young girl named Georgiana Lovering (white, age 13). She was a granddaughter of Sylvester Day and a grand-niece of Franklin Evans. On the above date Evans lured this girl into the woods with a request that she come along with him to check some traps that he had set for small game. When they reached a spot that was suitably remote Evans overpowered the girl and strangled her. Then he cut her body open with a knife and used crude surgery to remove each of her internal organs. He carefully examined each organ as he removed it, checking for abnormalities. When he was finally satisfied, Evans concealed the victim's eviscerated remains beneath a rotten tree stump. He also stashed some of the organs in a pile of leaves. Before long the girl was missed. Suspicion of foul play arose and Evans was questioned closely. When the suspect gave evasive answers he was arrested by the sheriff. Taken to the local jail, Evans continued to prevaricate. Then came news that a lynch mob was forming. Evans became terrified and he offered the sheriff a deal: he would divulge the location of the girl's remains plus pay a handsome bribe in return for being allowed to escape. The sheriff feigned agreement with this proposal. In the middle of the night he slipped out of the jail with Evans and made for the deep woods. With only lanterns to guide them, the remains of Georgiana Lovering were located. When asked why he had killed the girl, Evans said that she had caught him in an act of forgery and had threatened to inform on him. When asked why he had cut out her internal organs, he said that he did so in order to improve his understanding of human anatomy. Evans was then brought to a secret location and kept in close confinement.

The question of this man's sanity was hotly debated. In the end he was declared "eccentric" but sane enough to be held accountable for his crime. Ordered for execution, he dictated a pietistic confession in which he owned up to committing a similar child murder at Derry, New Hampshire, in the autumn of 1850. In that incident he abducted a crippled child from its home because he wanted to study its physical defects. He carried the child to a wooded area and strangled it there. However, he forbore his original intention of dissecting the child.

It bears further note that this unbalanced man was also the prime suspect in a double child murder that occurred in the Roxbury section of Boston on June 12, 1865. In that case a young brother and sister named John and Isabella Joyce (whites, aged 12 and 14) were raped and stabbed to death in a wooded area. Evans stubbornly refused to admit the crime but he did divulge certain details about it that had not been published. Another rape-murder in Maine was also attributed to this offender.

Franklin Evans was hanged at the New Hampshire State Prison on February 17, 1874. By court order his body was subjected to a thorough autopsy. All of his internal organs were removed and individually pickled. His skeleton was hung in a frame and put on permanent display at the Dartmouth College anatomical museum.

1875

William Sturtevant, white, age 29. *Murder.* The crime was committed on February 14, 1874, at Halifax, Massachusetts. Thomas Sturtevant (white, age 74) and his brother, Simeon Sturtevant (white, age 70) were thrifty farmers who lived together. Both were lifelong bach-

elors. They employed a female housekeeper named Mary Buckley (white, age 67), who dwelled with them in a roomy farmhouse located about midpoint between the towns of Halifax and Hanson. Neither of the brothers trusted banks and it was generally believed that they had the savings of two lifetimes hidden in their house. Rumors to this effect were heard by a grand-nephew of the brothers named William Sturtevant and the results were lethal for all parties involved. Knowing that his grand-uncles were elderly and lacking offspring of their own, William Sturtevant thought that he might present himself as a prospective heir. He then attempted to ingratiate himself with the wealthy codgers only to be dealt with summarily. He next tried to enter their employment by telling a tale to the effect that he was having trouble making ends meet on his current pay (he worked in a shoe factory) and would be willing to do farm work for some extra money. In this too William Sturtevant was disappointed. Then he decided on murder and robbery. On the evening of the above date this grand-nephew armed himself with a club and went to the home of his relatives. Thomas Sturtevant answered the door and was immediately bludgeoned to death where he stood. The housekeeper, Mary Buckley, saw the attack and tried to flee. She then became the killer's next target. She ran out into the backyard only to be overtaken there and slain in the same manner. After that the killer returned to the house where he found a semi-invalid Simeon Sturtevant in his bed and battered him to death as well. When all three occupants of the house were dead the killer began a search for valuables. He found several hundred dollars in cash but overlooked a far larger amount. Then he fled into the night. On the following day a neighbor happened upon the body of Mary Buckley. An alarm was raised and soon the full extent of the slaughter was revealed.

Suspicion centered on William Sturtevant when he was reported to be suddenly flush with money. Even more significant was the fact that the currency Sturtevant was spending belonged to an outdated issue yet was in an uncirculated condition. It had apparently been part of a long-concealed cache. When the suspect was confronted he removed two rolls of currency from his pockets and attempted to shove them down between the cushions of a sofa unseen. He was caught in the act. When the money was examined it was found to partially consist of $100 bills. Lawmen then demanded to know how it was that a humble shoemaker carried such wealth about him. Sturtevant replied that the cash was bounty money that was paid to him upon his discharge from the Union army in 1865. "Indeed!" said the lawmen. "How could it have been given to you in 1865 when it bears an issue date of 1872?" Sturtevant was caught in a lie. He was then charged with three counts of capital murder. Further investigation turned up additional evidence, yet Sturtevant stubbornly refused to admit his guilt. A jury needed little persuasion to find him guilty as charged. When opponents of capital punishment petitioned the governor-in-council for a commutation of the death sentence, they were dismissed in a contemptuous manner. The end came on May 7, 1875, when William Sturtevant was hanged at the Plymouth County jail.

James Costley, white, age 39. *Murder.* The crime was committed on May 13, 1874, at Braintree, Massachusetts. This man had originally come from Nova Scotia. At the close of the American Civil War his parents and siblings decided to immigrate to California. James Costley declined to go with them. Instead, he drifted southward to Massachusetts and came to a halt at the town of Hanover. There he got a job in the local hotel where over the course of the next few years he worked his way up from the position of hostler to that of general manager. It so happened that Costley's place of business also employed a female housekeeper by the name of Julia Hawkes (white, age 36). Over a course of time she and Costley gravitated to each other. They fell in love and eventually reached a point where marriage was agreed upon. Then a rival entered the picture. Costley met a young woman from a wealthy family who was not only beautiful but possessed of a $30,000 dowry. This other woman (whose name was Sarah Cushing) promptly replaced Julia Hawkes in Costley's personal estimation. The humble hotel maid no longer interested him. Their engagement was accordingly broken. Julia Hawkes did not take kindly to being jilted. Instead of bearing her sorrow in private she became angry and vindictive. She let Costley know what she thought of him in no uncertain terms. Worse, she threatened to tell the Cushings about a former girlfriend of Costley who had died from a botched abortion. Faced with this, Costley decided on murder. On the above date he killed Julia Hawkes with a pistol shot through the head. Then he wrapped her body up in a blanket and dumped it in the Monatiquot River. Eleven days later the woman's remains were found floating in a Braintree estuary. With no other way to identify the body, local authorities ran advertisements asking for public assistance. Finally one person was found who recognized the decedent. James Costley was arrested the same day. He denied all knowledge of the crime and dared prosecutors to convict him. A strong circumstantial case was presented on trial and the jury went for it. James Costley was capitally convicted and ordered for execution. He was hanged at the Norfolk County jail on June 25, 1875.

John Gordon, white, age 29. *Murder.* The crime was committed on June 9,

1873, at Thorndike, Maine. This man conceived a deadly hatred for his younger brother, Almon Gordon (white, age 25), because he felt that he had been passed over for an inheritance that Almon had received. John Gordon also disliked his brother's wife, Emma Gordon (white, age 26), because he thought that she had used gossip to discredit him in the eyes of a certain young woman. Consumed with jealousy and indignation, John Gordon decided to wipe out not only his brother but the man's wife and children as well. At three o'clock in the morning on the above date John Gordon burst into his brother's bedroom with an axe and started swinging. In the slaughter that followed Almon Gordon and his wife were both slain. So was an infant child of theirs which shared the same bed with them that night. The murderer also attacked his five-year-old nephew and left him for dead with severe axe wounds. Then John Gordon splashed kerosene all over the house and set it on fire. Neighbors managed to rescue the five-year-old boy but the other three members of the family were beyond help. When asked what had happened, the five year old said that his "Uncle Johnny" had hit him with an axe. The killer managed to elude a lynch mob at the time but he wound up in the hands of a legal system that was no more lenient with him. A sentence of death was meted out to John Gordon. Shortly before the time set for his execution he nearly succeeded in committing suicide with a concealed knife. Gordon stabbed himself close to the heart and the prison physician said that the wound would almost certainly prove fatal. With no time to waste, prison officials carried the dying man to the gallows even as blood poured from his wound. John Gordon was unconscious when they put the rope around his neck and sent him through the trap. This extraordinary scene took place at the Maine State Prison on June 25, 1875.

Louis Wagner, white, age 29. *Murder.* The crime was committed on March 7, 1873, at Smutty Nose Island, Maine. John and Mary Hontvet, a married couple, were humble seafarers who lived in a weather-beaten cabin on Smutty Nose Island, a barren member of the Isles of Shoals group, located about ten miles off of Portsmouth, New Hampshire. Along with them dwelled two women named Anethe and Karen Christiansen, who were the sister-in-law and sister respectively of Mary Hontvet. Together these four people comprised the entire human population of Smutty Nose Island. On March 6, 1873, John Hontvet went ashore to purchase bait and see to some business in Portsmouth. He was not expected to return until the following day. Late that night one Louis Wagner, a fisherman who had formerly lodged with the Hontvets, secretly set out for Smutty Nose Island. He knew that John Hontvet had gone to the mainland, leaving the three women alone in their isolated cabin. He also suspected the Hontvets of having a hoard of money. With the man of the house away, Wagner reasoned that the three women would make easy prey. At one o'clock in the morning Wagner burst into the Hontvet cabin and attacked the women with an axe. Anethe Christiansen and Karen Christiansen (whites, aged 23 and 38) were both hacked to death. Mary Hontvet recognized the killer. She grappled with him in the darkness and narrowly missed being cut by the wildly flailing axe. Running outdoors dressed only in her nightclothes, she hid among the island's rocky crags for the rest of the cold winter night. When morning finally came, Mary Hontvet was weak from exposure but still alive. She signaled to a fishing boat which came to her rescue. The fishermen found her two companions dead from axe wounds and the cabin ransacked. An all-points bulletin was soon issued for the arrest of Louis Wagner. He was found in Boston later that same day. Within a matter of hours word spread through the fishing villages that the killer was being brought to Portsmouth jail. Without further ado hundreds of angry men converged on the scene. Then for the only time in its history Portsmouth became the scene of a riot. In a determined effort to get its hands on the killer, an irate mob battered its way into the jail. The object of their wrath, however, had been whisked away to a secret location. Wagner lived to face a legal trial for his crime. Convicted and sentenced to death, Wagner made further headlines by escaping from jail. He took to the woods and managed to live off the land for two months. New Hampshire authorities finally caught him when he wandered into the town of Farmington. Wagner was taken to the Maine State Prison and put in solitary confinement. When his appeals failed he was hanged on the gallows there. The date was June 25, 1875.

George Pemberton, white, age 43.

Murder. The crime was committed on March 22, 1875, at Boston, Massachusetts. This man was a down on his luck drunkard who committed a brutal murder simply so he could have money to spend on liquor. On the above date Pemberton was in the midst of a three-day drinking binge. He had visited many saloons and was on his way to yet another one when he felt around in his pockets and found that he had no more money. Not being one to go without his refreshment, Pemberton hit upon a scheme: he went walking down Webster Street and started knocking on doors. When the homeowners there asked him his business he said that he was a Water Company inspector who had come to check the pipes. Receiving no answer at some doors and being denied admittance to others, Pemberton finally came to the house of a Mrs. Margaret Bingham (white, age 30) at No. 97 Webster Street. There he repeated his line of lies and was

allowed to come into the house. Mrs. Bingham led Pemberton to the cellar (where her water pipes were located), only to be attacked by him there. A fierce struggle ensued in which the woman was overpowered. Pemberton crammed coal in her mouth in order to stifle her screams. Then he choked her to death with his bare hands and tore her rings from her fingers. Pausing to wash his hands in the kitchen sink, the killer then fled from the scene without further ado. The victim's badly beaten body was found the same day by members of her immediate family. They had been in another part of the house at the time of the crime but had heard nothing. The killer meanwhile took a train to Salem. Entering the first saloon he saw there, he sold the valuable rings to the bartender for a token amount. Then he drank the proceeds. When Pemberton left the saloon he returned to Boston and went home as if nothing had happened. The Salem saloonkeeper examined his purchases afterward and concluded that he had made an advantageous deal; the rings were worth many times what he had paid for them. A couple of days later, however, a newspaper printed a description of the missing rings and the bartender recognized them as being the ones that he had bought from Pemberton. The man then decided that the rings were too risky to handle and he brought them to the police. The arrest of the killer followed in short order. When Pemberton came to trial he tried to extenuate his guilt by claiming that alcoholism had left him too befuddled to act with deliberate malice. In rebuttal, the prosecution demanded to know why the same thing had not precluded him from attempting to enter private homes under false pretenses. By impersonating a hydraulic company inspector, it was said, Pemberton had evinced a craftiness hardly commensurate with alcoholic disability. The jury agreed and it came back with a capital conviction. Appeals were disallowed and on October 8, 1875, George Pemberton went to his death on the gallows. The scene was the Suffolk County jail.

1876

Samuel Frost, white, age 41. *Murder.* The crime was committed on July 4, 1875, at Petersham, Massachusetts. This man was a shoemaker who decided that he would try his hand at farming. He accordingly selected a suitable piece of property three miles southwest of Petersham on the Hardwick Road. Needing financial assistance in order to pursue his goal, Frost approached his brother-in-law, one Franklin Towne by name (white, age 31), and asked him if he would like to go along as a partner on the farm. A bachelor of independent means, Towne agreed to the proposal. However, he required Frost to sign a series of promissory notes before he would give him any money. Frost signed the notes but soon regretted doing so. He felt himself subjugated by his brother-in-law and grew increasingly resentful. On the above date Towne got up early to milk the cows. Frost followed him stealthily into the barn. There he struck the man down from behind with a sledgehammer. After that the killer buried the decedent in the cellar of the barn and circulated a story about the man going away to California. He also liquidated the brother-in-law's assets and used the proceeds to pay off his bills. However, Frost overplayed his hand when he kept the victim's watch for himself and said that he had received it as a parting gift. A short time later some farmhands noticed a foul smell in the barn. Suspecting the truth, they went to fetch the local authorities. When they returned, however, the source of the stench was gone. Frost had perceived their intentions. During their absence he dug up the decaying body of Franklin Towne

and chopped it to pieces. Then he placed the assorted body parts in burlap bags which he secreted all over the farm. For the next three weeks Frost repeatedly dug up and reburied the reeking bags in order to stay one step ahead of his suspicious employees. He was finally caught in the act one night and charged with murder. When the case came to trial Frost admitted killing his brother-in-law but asked for a verdict of manslaughter on the ground that the crime was not premeditated. He said that he had gotten into a violent argument with Towne and had struck him down in self-defense. The jury saw matters differently and brought in a capital conviction. On May 26, 1876, Samuel Frost was put to death at the Worcester County jail. The sentence called for him to be hanged but the affair was badly bungled. When the gallows mechanism was set in motion the rope tightened around Frost's neck with such force that it literally tore his head off.

Thomas Piper, white, age 22. *Murder.* The crime was committed on May 23, 1875, at Boston, Massachusetts. This troubled young man was a self-admitted serial killer and necrophile. He said that he killed his victims for the express purpose of having sex with them after death.

Piper is first known to have struck in the Dorchester section of Boston on the evening of December 5, 1873. While lurking in the vicinity of Columbia Street he picked up the trail of a female pedestrian and stalked her for several blocks. While he thought that no one was looking he bludgeoned the victim to death with a wagon axle. Then he dragged her body into an alley where he prepared to accomplish his ultimate purpose. The sound of approaching footsteps spooked him, however, and he fled from the scene undetected. The victim was subsequently identified as a young housemaid named Bridget Landergan (white, age 19). Her boyfriend was charged with the crime and even extradited from a foreign country in order to stand trial. However, he was later exonerated by the real killer.

On July 1, 1874, Piper struck again. He approached a prostitute named Mary Tyner and asked her how much she would charge for an all-night assignation. The price was five dollars in gold and Piper agreed to those terms. The two then proceeded to a bagnio on Oxford Street and went about their business. In the morning Piper decided that he would like to indulge his baser craving and get his money back in the same bargain. So he battered the woman about the head with a hammer until she stopped moving. Thinking her dead, Piper raped her repeatedly. Then he took his money and fled. Contrary to expectation, Mary Tyner survived the attack. However, she suffered irreversible brain damage and had to be committed to an insane asylum.

Several weeks later Piper struck a third time. He attacked a female pedestrian named Annie Sullivan and beat her to within an inch of her life. Again he prepared to add rape to his offense but he was frightened off by passersby. Miss Sullivan survived the assault but is said to have never fully recovered.

On May 23, 1875, Piper committed the last and most notorious of his crimes. Having used family influence to obtain the position of sexton at the Warren Avenue Baptist Church, the killer used the cover of that sanctuary to seek another victim. On the above date he enticed a five-year-old girl named Mabel Young (white) into his room and tried to molest her there. When the child said that she would tell her mother, Piper beat her over the head with a cricket bat until brain matter oozed from her wounds. Thinking the victim dead, Piper then carried her body up into the church belfry and stashed it there. It was his intention to keep the corpse as an object

for his sexual gratification. Some time later that same day, however, the child regained consciousness and began to scream loudly. This brought neighborhood residents flocking to the scene. The door to the belfry stairs being locked, the mob sought out the sexton (Piper) and demanded the key thereto. Piper replied that he had no key, whereupon some men broke down the door. Scrambling up the belfry stairs, all were appalled to find the badly injured five year old. She was bleeding profusely and screaming wildly. Piper was arrested a short time later and charged with assaulting the girl with deadly intent. A day later the charge was upgraded to murder. In searching his room, investigators found prima facie evidence of Piper's guilt. They also found a collection of sexual devices and illicit stimulants. The newspapers of the time said that the precise details of Piper's private pastimes were unprintable. More than 120 years later those details are still unprintable.

Piper eventually confessed to his crimes. On May 26, 1876, he was hanged at the Suffolk County jail.

1877

Elwin Major, white, age 27. *Murder.* The crime was committed on December 20, 1874, at Wilton, New Hampshire. A contemporary news account describes this man as a "shiftless, worthless fellow" who did odd jobs for a living. He was also libidinous to a fault. When Major was 22 years old he became involved with a pair of young sisters named Ellen and Ida Lovejoy (whites, ages 15 and 13) and made both of them pregnant. Faced with a difficult problem, Major then killed Ellen Lovejoy with a lethal dose of strychnine. Then he married the other sister and subsequently had three more children by her. At the age of 18 Ida Lovejoy Major was pregnant with a fifth child and in delicate health. Her husband in the meantime had found yet another lust interest and wished himself free of family responsibilities. So he fatally poisoned his pregnant wife just as he had his sister-in-law. When questions were raised about the untimely death, Major said that his wife had been addicted to eating camphor and had thereby brought about her own demise. He also refused to allow an autopsy. This made several people suspicious. A court order was obtained and the body of Ida Lovejoy Major was exhumed three weeks after her death. Chemical analysis of her stomach revealed a lethal quantity of strychnine. As the investigation widened, the remains of Ellen Lovejoy and two of Major's children were likewise exhumed. Tests done on the children were inconclusive but Ellen Lovejoy's viscera was found to be saturated with strychnine. Major was only tried for the death of his wife. During the course of the proceedings he never wavered in declaring his innocence. However, an apothecary told of how Major had purchased strychnine from him for the ostensible purpose of poisoning foxes. Two separate juries decided that Major had used the poison to rid himself of much more than foxes in his henhouse. The verdict was guilty and the sentence was death. A retrial had the same result. On January 5, 1877, still declaring his innocence, Elwin Major was hanged at the New Hampshire State Prison.

1878

Joseph LaPage, white, age 40. *Murder.* The crime was committed on October 4, 1875, at Pembroke, New Hampshire. This man was a Quebecois who earned his living as a thresher and a woodchopper. He was illiterate but still managed to keep himself gainfully employed. He was also a married father of five who diligently provided for his family. Then there was the dark side:

LaPage was prone to sexual violence and was quite probably a psychopath. The details of his crimes admit no other explanation. While still in his native land he raped his sister-in-law and left her for dead. The woman managed to survive contrary to expectation. Whether or not LaPage was ever prosecuted for the crime is uncertain. However, when some of the more perverse details of what he did became known, LaPage deemed it prudent to leave the country. He gathered up his family in the middle of the night and slipped across the border into Vermont. The town of St. Albans became his new abode. For many months thereafter LaPage behaved himself. Then the dark side resurfaced. He began to notice a young schoolteacher who walked by his place of employment each morning. On July 24, 1874, LaPage lay in wait for her. As the woman proceeded along a path which led through a wooded area, she was pounced upon and dragged into the bushes. There LaPage crushed her skull with a rock and raped her repeatedly. Then he cut out her sexual organs with a knife and carried them away as souvenirs. The victim was identified as Miss Marietta Ball (white, age 20), and the discovery of her remains set off a panic in the St. Albans area. Many suspects — including LaPage — were brought in for questioning but all were released for lack of evidence. In the weeks that followed, LaPage again behaved himself. Then in the spring of 1875 he decided to relocate. He packed up his family and moved to Suncook, New Hampshire, where he once again settled into a workaday routine. At harvest time LaPage was called to the nearby village of Pembroke to join some threshers on a job. There the dark side struck again. LaPage could not keep his eyes off some teenage girls as they walked back and forth to school. When he learned that some of them took a shortcut through the woods he lost control of himself. On the above date he lay in wait for the schoolgirls. When one by the name of Josie Langmaid (white, age 17) happened along through the woods LaPage ambushed her. The girl was hit over the head with a stick and dragged into a thicket. There LaPage raped her in every conceivable way. Then he took a knife to the girl and cut off her head. He also used the knife to remove her sexual organs. All of those assorted body parts he carried away with him as personal trophies. Many hours later a search party found the girl's remains. Strong men vomited when they beheld the sight. It took another day of hard searching to locate the victim's head. The more private parts of her person were never found. Meanwhile, back in St. Albans a former acquaintance of LaPage read a newspaper account of the Pembroke murder. That person noted similarities to the unsolved slaying of Marietta Ball. Was it merely a coincidence, that person wondered, that Joseph LaPage had moved to a town nearby? Detectives were informed of the possible connection. LaPage came under further scrutiny when some Pembroke children reported that a "strange Frenchman" had been asking questions about the schoolgirls who lived in the area. Further investigation put LaPage near the scene of the crime at the time in question. A search of his home turned up bloodstained clothing. LaPage claimed innocence through one trial and then a retrial. Eventually, however, he confessed in full. He admitted the murder in Vermont as well as the one in New Hampshire. When asked why he had mutilated the victims he blamed an impulse that he could not control. Not even opponents of capital punishment dared to seek clemency in this case. Such was the feeling against LaPage. On March 15, 1878, he was hanged at the New Hampshire State Prison.

Joseph Ten Eyck, black, age 46. *Murder.* The crime was committed on November 29, 1877, at Sheffield, Massachu-

setts. An illegitimate child, this offender was abandoned at an early age but taken in by a Lenox couple. He was credibly educated for one of his circumstances and had little difficulty finding work on farms throughout Berkshire County. He married at the age of 16 but became separated from his wife. Then he repeated that scenario with two other women. As he grew older, Ten Eyck became a chronic lawbreaker. He served jail time for trespass, assault, public intoxication and for maliciously fouling a well. He also admitted that he was guilty of burglary and barn burning. Early on the evening of the above date Ten Eyck went to the house of an elderly farm couple named Mr. and Mrs. David Stillman (whites, aged 80 and 70) on the pretense of buying homemade butter. Mrs. Stillman admitted the visitor to the house because he was known there from having once done work about the place. Yes, said the woman, she did have butter to sell. So while she busied herself with fetching some, Ten Eyck sat in the parlor where Mr. Stillman (who was in poor health) lay upon a recliner. When the butter was weighed and put in a pail, Ten Eyck asked Mrs. Stillman for a nip of cider. The request was not unusual because it was a holiday. The woman then went down to the cellar to draw cider from a barrel. It was then that Ten Eyck dropped all pretense. He picked up an axe from the woodpile and attacked the invalid Mr. Stillman with it. The elderly man was hacked to death on his recliner. Hearing the commotion above her, Mrs. Stillman came running up the cellar stairs. When she came to the top of them she was struck in the face and tumbled back into the cellar. Ten Eyck then pounced on her and finished her off with the axe. When both of the Stillmans were dead the killer turned his attention to plunder. He ransacked the house and stole a number of undisclosed items. Then he set the place on fire and fled into the night. Within less than an hour Ten

Eyck was in the local saloon squandering his loot on liquor. He was arrested the next day when it was reported that he had more money than usual. He had also been heard to ask whether the Stillmans had butter for sale. It so happened that the killer had left a pail of butter behind at the scene of the crime and investigators traced it to Ten Eyck. When the case came to trial there was little or no dissension among the jury. Ten Eyck was convicted on two counts of capital murder. He was hanged at the Berkshire County jail (in Pittsfield) on August 16, 1878.

1879

William Devlin, white, age 36. *Murder.* The crime was committed on December 8, 1877, at Lowell, Massachusetts. This man was an alcoholic who killed his wife under circumstances of extreme brutality. Born in Ireland, he came to America at the age of 11. His parents settled at Rutland, Vermont, and it was there where Devlin spent his teenage years. When the Civil War broke out Devlin joined the Union army. He served for the duration of the war and participated in some of its bloodiest engagements. Wounds sustained in the battles of Antietam, Malvern Hill and The Wilderness earned Devlin a pension for the rest of his life. He was honorably discharged from the army in July of 1865 and that same month married Miss Hannah Elizabeth Manning at St. Albans, Vermont. The couple spent the next three years at Rutland. In 1868 they moved to Lowell, Massachusetts, where they settled down and started to raise a family. Home for them was a tenement at No. 25 Common Street. For a livelihood Devlin augmented his pension income by working as a fireman, a school janitor and a railroad laborer. At the time of his capital crime he and his wife had five children aged ten years to

one month. Although he was a good provider, Devlin had one overriding vice: he was addicted to liquor. When he had too much to drink he had a tendency to get nasty and belligerent. On paydays his wife and children lived in terror, for it was on such days that "Papa" came home in an ugly mood. On the above date Devlin drew his pay and proceeded, as usual, to get drunk. Then he tottered over to his neighborhood grocer to pay his weekly bill. Devlin found the grocer's bill to be 25 cents higher than he expected. When he asked the reason for the discrepancy he was told that his wife had been there earlier in the day and that she had borrowed 25 cents in order to get a tooth pulled. This sent Devlin into a towering rage. He paid the extra quarter and then went looking for his wife. He found her at home nursing their month-old infant. The look on his face made his family fear the worst. Devlin harangued his wife in a furious tone and demanded to know if it was true that she had borrowed a quarter from the grocer. The woman replied that it was indeed true. Devlin then demanded to know the reason why she had done so. His wife said that she had had a bad tooth that was bothering her and that she had had to go to a dentist to get it pulled. She had no money of her own and so went to the grocer and asked for a loan of 25 cents. At that point Devlin lost his temper. He called his wife a "god damned liar" and began to beat her with great violence. The woman ran from the room with her baby in her arms but Devlin caught up with her in the outside hallway and flung her down a flight of stairs, baby and all. Mrs. Devlin tumbled to a stairway landing where her husband pounced on her. He kicked and stomped her with his heavy work boots while the baby lay screaming beside her. Devlin's other children then came running to the scene and they begged their father not to kill their mother. Devlin paused long enough to pick up the baby and return it to his apartment. When he saw that his wife had regained her feet and had climbed up the stairs, he immediately threw her back down them again and resumed his kicking and stomping. The neighbors called him a brute but did not dare to otherwise interfere. When Devlin had his fill of stomping the woman he dragged her up the stairs by her hair and threw her back into their dwelling. Then he pulled a knife on her and slashed her about her head and face. When the woman begged for mercy, Devlin threw her to the floor and again kicked and stomped her. At that point the neighbors could no longer endure the woman's screams. Some of them got up the courage to enter the Devlin apartment and attempt a rescue. One woman threw a bucket of hot water on Devlin. By then, however, the victim of the assault lay unconscious on the floor. Her husband told the neighbors that she was drunk. Then he tried to rouse her without success. He finally allowed the neighbors to carry his wife (white, age 33) to a bed. Then Devlin declared that he was thirsty and went out to the local saloon. When he returned home later that evening he laid his infant child beside his wife and then went into another room where he passed out drunk. When he awoke the next day he found that both his wife and baby had died. The woman had succumbed to internal injuries and the baby had been overlaid with a heavy blanket. Devlin then crawled back into his bed and he ordered his other children to do the same. There they all remained for the rest of that day. Devlin got up from time to time only to relieve himself and drink more whiskey. The children were too frightened to move. On the day after that Devlin awoke sober. Only then did the full realization of what had happened dawn on him. Then came panic. Devlin left the corpses where they lay and grabbed whatever valuables he could lay his hands on. He sent the other children to their grandparents while he himself hastened to the train station. There he took passage to Vermont. During the hours that followed this precipitous flight word got around Devlin's neighborhood that a murder had been committed. A large crowd gathered outside of his house and police forced an entrance thereto. The bodies of Mrs. Devlin and the baby were found but by then the killer was gone. Detectives were put on his trail and they caught up with him in Vermont. Speedily returned to Massachusetts, Devlin was offered a chance to plead guilty to second degree murder and thereby save his life. He refused the offer whereupon a disgusted jury convicted him of murder with malice, a verdict which meant capital punishment. When his appeals failed, Devlin's lawyer requested clemency from the governor-in-council. After a short deliberation that panel declared that the law must be left to take its course. There was only one dissenting vote. William Devlin was accordingly brought to the gallows at the Middlesex County jail on March 14, 1879. He died in a manner that aroused little comment. A public collection was taken up for the benefit of his orphaned children.

John Pinkham, white, age 38. *Murder.* The crime was committed on January 9, 1878, at New Durham, New Hampshire. Mariam Berry (white, age 65) was a prosperous widow who owned a farm on the valley road between Gilmanton and Farmington. She lived there with a spinster daughter and a teenage foster son. Among her hired laborers was the above-named John Pinkham. He was a seasonal employee whose term of service ended when the autumn harvest was brought in. Since he was unable to find other work following the harvest of 1877 he requested and was granted special permission to stay on with Mrs. Berry through the ensuing winter. It was understood that he would cut firewood in return for his room and board. Pinkham was also granted the right to do any outside jobs that might come his way so long as they did not interfere with his other responsibilities. On January 3, 1878, Pinkham abruptly quit the Berry farm. He felt that he was being overworked and that simple room and board were inadequate compensation. As for Mrs. Berry, she was rather glad to see Pinkham go; he had had a tendency to drink too much. Six days later Pinkham returned. He carried a loaded shotgun which he obligingly left outside when he knocked on the farmhouse door. Upon entering the living room, Pinkham greeted Mrs. Berry and her family in a polite manner and said that he had come for his axe which he had accidentally left there. Mrs. Berry replied that the axe was in the kitchen and that he was free to take it away. Pinkham then fetched the axe and brought it outside where he set it down next to his shotgun. After that he walked back into the house and told Mrs. Berry that he had cut firewood above and beyond the amount that would fairly satisfy his room and board. He then presented the woman with a bill in the amount of seven dollars, saying that he had regarded such a sum as his rightful due. Mrs. Berry replied that by the terms of their prior agreement she was not obligated to pay such a bill. Pinkham did not like that answer. He called the woman "an old cheapskate" or something to that effect and stomped out of the house. Moments later he returned with his shotgun and opened fire. Mrs. Berry was killed instantly by a blast in the face. Her daughter and foster son ran from the scene screaming. They roused the neighbors and soon armed men were looking for the killer. He was found not far away lying wounded in the snow. He had attempted to cut his throat with a pocketknife. A doctor patched up Pinkham and he was made to face the law. A jury convicted him of capital murder and ordered his execution. On March 14, 1879, that order was carried out on the gallows of the New Hampshire State Prison.

Henri Gravelin, white, age 46. *Murder.* The crime was committed on October 6, 1876, at Weathersfield, Vermont. This man was a transplanted Quebecois. He was possessed of a considerable estate but saw his holdings substantially diminished when he came up on the wrong end of a lawsuit. Stung by the reverse to his fortunes, Gravelin vowed to get even with all the parties involved. The plaintiff, one Horace Weston by name, was a close neighbor of Gravelin. On October 10, 1876, the man's assets were nearly wiped out in an arson fire. Weston's house and most of his farm buildings were destroyed. An entire harvest was also lost in the flames. Insurance covered only a fraction of the loss. Suspicion focused on Henri Gravelin because he had a clear motive for revenge. Then an additional factor was thrown into the case: the principal witness in the Gravelin-Weston lawsuit, one Herbert O. White (white, age unknown), had mysteriously disappeared four days earlier. He too was known to be an object of Gravelin's ire. The town fathers decided to conduct a thorough search of Gravelin's property. They were looking for anything that might connect the suspect with either the fire or White's disappearance. Results were not long in coming; in a remote corner of Gravelin's property the searchers found an old well that was carefully concealed. At the bottom of the well was the body of Herbert White. He had been bludgeoned to death. Gravelin was immediately arrested. He was charged with capital murder plus arson in the first degree. A grand jury returned dual indictments and the suspect was put on trial for his life. The prosecution's case was made up entirely of circumstantial evidence. It was shown that Gravelin hated both Weston and White because of the lawsuit they had brought against him. Several witnesses also attested to Gravelin muttering threats against both men. When the defense was called, Gravelin frankly admitted that he had no love for Weston and White. However, he vociferously denied any wrongdoing. He said that he was a victim of circumstance. When questioned about the presence of the dead man's body on his property, Gravelin said that it was a setup job. The jury saw matters differently; as much as it disliked circumstantial evidence it still could not bring itself to believe that the disasters to Gravelin's foes were mere coincidence. The presence of Herbert White's body on Gravelin's land was also thought to be more than a coincidence; the killer had to have prior knowledge of the abandoned well. Who but Gravelin, it was asked, could have known of the well's existence? The verdict was guilty as charged. During the appellate war that followed his conviction, Gravelin gained many allies. Calls for clemency were loud and unrelenting. Many people distrusted a death sentence based on circumstantial evidence and they made their objections known. In addition, Gravelin himself continued to asseverate his innocence. Some people who knew Gravelin said that he had confessed to them in private but Gravelin denied this. When the appellate courts finally upheld the conviction and death sentence, pressure was brought to bear on the governor of Vermont. Requests for executive clemency flooded in from all parts of the country. It was urged that Gravelin should at least be given the benefit of the doubt as far as his life was concerned. In reply, the governor said that he trusted in his innate instincts and that those same instincts told him that Gravelin was guilty. Clemency was therefore denied. On March 14, 1879, Henri Gravelin was hanged at the Vermont State Prison. He insisted on his innocence to the end.

John Phair, white, age 34. *Murder.* The crime was committed on June 9, 1874,
near Rutland, Vermont. This man was an ironworker of poor reputation. He had been born and raised in the town of Vergennes. While in his teens he was convicted of grand larceny and he spent six years in jail. Upon being released he was dogged by a stigma which made his hometown inhospitable to him. Seeking a fresh start, Phair moved to Rutland. There his bad name eventually caught up with him. In at least one respect Phair was his own worst enemy; he struck up a relationship with a known prostitute and then felt ill-used whenever people looked askance at him. This female companion of Phair's was one Ann Elizabeth Frieze (white, age unknown) by name. She presided over a so-called "disorderly house" on the outskirts of Rutland. On the morning of the above date that house was found to be burning. When firefighters entered the devastated structure they found a badly scorched bed on which lay the remains of a woman. It was Ann Elizabeth Frieze. She had been slashed to death. Although her body was severely burned, the marks of violence upon her were unmistakable. Most salient of all was the fact that her throat was cut from ear to ear. It was obvious that whoever killed her had also fired the house in an attempt to cover up the crime. Suspicion at once attached itself to John Phair. He had supposedly been on a train to Rhode Island at the time of the crime but when detectives traced his movements they found a different scenario. It was learned that Phair had checked into a Boston hotel under a false name and that he had used the same alias to pawn various articles belonging to the murdered woman. In addition to that, a Boston jeweler identified Phair as the man who had sold him rings taken from the dead woman's fingers. Phair's handwriting was also found to match that of his alias in both hotel and pawnshop registry books. In his defense, Phair denied any connection with his alias. He also presented alibi witnesses who swore

that they had been with him on the Rhode Island train at the time in question. When a jury considered the evidence it brought in a capital verdict. A lengthy appellate battle then ensued. At one point three jurors even admitted that they had been prejudiced against Phair. The trial judge had allowed them to sit on the jury anyway, their bias notwithstanding. Reversible error was clearly evident yet the State Supreme Court refused to intercede. The governor of Vermont was also hostile to Phair; he declared that he would not allow so-called "technicalities" to thwart the course of justice. Time and again appeals were considered by all three branches of the Vermont state government. Time and again those appeals were rejected. All were bedeviled by an overriding belief that Phair was guilty. On April 10, 1879, the condemned man was hanged at the Vermont State Prison. He claimed innocence to the last.

Joseph Buzzell, white, age 38. *Murder.* The crime was committed on November 2, 1874, at Brookfield, New Hampshire. Shortly after sundown on the above date a young woman named Susan A. Hanson (white, age unknown) was instantly killed by a shotgun blast as she sat with her family at the dinner table. The lethal charge was fired through a closed window by someone outside of the house. The victim's male relatives scrambled to catch the killer but they were unable to find anyone in the darkness. Suspicion was promptly centered on a neighbor named Joseph Buzzell. He was the only one in the rural community who was known to have a motive for such a crime. It so happened that this Joseph Buzzell (who was a farmer and a stonemason by profession) had once been engaged to marry Miss Hanson. He had broken off the commitment, however, when the local authorities forced him to marry another young woman whom he had impregnated.

Susan Hanson was outraged by the revelation of Buzzell's philandering. She then decided to get back at him in a way she knew would hurt him the most: by hitting him in the pocketbook. She filed a lawsuit against Buzzell charging breach of contract and asked for substantial damages. She also had a strong case and Buzzell knew it. In addition to that, the entire community regarded Buzzell as a cad. Therefore indications were that a jury drawn from the local population would find Buzzell liable for a hefty amount. The man ranted and raved over the matter, threatening violence and swearing that he would not pay anything. The case was due to be heard on November 3, 1874, and it seemed too much of a coincidence that the plaintiff was slain on the very eve of that date. Buzzell was arrested on suspicion of murder. He stoutly denied all knowledge of the crime. He also produced his wife and hired man as alibi witnesses for his whereabouts at the time in question. The prosecution based its case solely on circumstantial evidence: the known motive, the threats of violence on Buzzell's part and some footprints near the scene of the crime which matched the suspect's boots. A jury duly considered the matter and asked the judge if it could return a verdict of "Not Proven" instead of "Not Guilty." When the judge replied in the negative the jury came back with a reluctant acquittal. Buzzell walked out of the courthouse a free man but from then on the community despised him. As long as he remained in Brookfield he lived under a cloud of suspicion. In the months that followed this controversial verdict a rash of arson fires plagued Brookfield and vicinity. In desperation the town fathers hired a pair of rather sleazy detectives to solve the matter. Soon a suspect was identified: none other than Joseph Buzzell's hired farmhand, one Charles Cook by name. This individual is described as having been of substandard intelligence. The detectives therefore had little difficulty in getting a so-called "confession" from him. However, Charles Cook went two steps further: he said that he had set the fires at the behest of Joseph Buzzell and that he had also fired the shotgun blast which had killed Susan Hanson — likewise at the behest of Buzzell. This news inflamed popular opinion against Buzzell. Loud demands were made for his rearrest. The State's Attorney then persuaded a grand jury to reindict Buzzell but this time as an accomplice to capital murder rather than as a principal. When the case came to trial Buzzell was convicted and Cook was discharged by order of the court. The appellate battle which followed this verdict was fiercely contested by both sides. The defense claimed double jeopardy while the prosecution stressed the difference between principal and accessory. The situation became even more heated when Cook retracted his testimony. In addition, the detectives who had arrested Cook were themselves arrested for malfeasance. With such a series of developments it was generally anticipated that the State Supreme Court would order a new trial. To the astonishment of all, however, the court did just the opposite. It upheld the conviction and death sentence. Buzzell's lawyers then turned to the governor-in-council. They pleaded their client's case with extreme eloquence but to no avail. A clemency bill was also brought before the state legislature without success. Every effort to save Buzzell was haunted by the fact that the man had had a clear motive for murder. Not even Buzzell's lawyers could deny that. Still, the New Hampshire authorities were clearly troubled by the case. Even in his death row cell the condemned man was badgered and baited for a confession or at least an incriminating remark. Even while standing on the gallows itself Buzzell was pestered with questions. All were disappointed; Buzzell had determined to leave the world guessing. On

July 10, 1879, he was hanged in pursuance of his sentence at the New Hampshire State Prison. He took his knowledge with him to the grave.

Asa Magoon, white, age 58. *Murder.* The crime was committed on October 14, 1875, at Barre, Vermont. Asa Magoon and Rufus Streeter (white, age 70) were aging widowers who lived together. On the above date both men got into Streeter's wagon and rode to Montpelier. There they did a bit of shopping. On the way home they stopped at a bawdyhouse where both were well known. As they got out of the wagon, Magoon checked his purchases and found that a gallon jug of alcohol was missing. He immediately suspected Streeter of making away with it and demanded that the man pay up. Streeter denied the alleged theft and refused to part with any money. Both men then entered the bawdyhouse where, among other things, they had a few drinks. Upon leaving the place, Magoon again demanded that Streeter make good for the missing alcohol. Again Streeter denied knowing anything about its loss. As both men rode away from the scene they were arguing loudly. Then at a point up the road Streeter got down out of the wagon and bade Magoon to join him in checking along the curbs. He said that the jug had probably tumbled out of the wagon and rolled into the roadside bushes. Magoon angrily said that that was ridiculous and he again charged Streeter with theft. In reply, Streeter told Magoon to shut up and join in the search. At that point Magoon lost his temper and was clearly heard threatening Streeter's life. Then a few minutes later some people passing along the road heard a noise like the "smashing of pumpkins," as they later described it. However, they were unable to see anything because of the darkness. A short time afterward Magoon came along driving Streeter's wagon. He was alone. When asked the whereabouts of his companion he contemptuously said that the man had decided to walk home. When the sun came up the next morning Streeter's body was found in a field just off the road. He had been stabbed and slashed to death. His face had also been mashed beyond recognition with a large stone. When lawmen went to the decedent's home they found his wagon awash with blood. Magoon tried to explain away those circumstances by saying that he had been slaughtering sheep. However, the police believed that Magoon had stabbed Streeter as the man had climbed back onto his wagon. They also believed that Magoon had continued slashing at Streeter as he fell into the rear of the wagon and that Magoon had then dragged the man into the adjacent field where he finished him off with a rock. Magoon denied everything to no avail. At his trial he tried to shift the blame onto the madam of the bawdyhouse where he and Streeter had enjoyed themselves on the night of the murder. Magoon said that the madam had a grudge against Streeter because the man had previously reported her to the law. This story failed to create a reasonable doubt in the minds of the jurors and they brought in a capital verdict. Four years later — on November 28, 1879 — Asa Magoon was hanged at the Vermont State Prison. He had to be forcibly dragged to the gallows.

1880

Edward Tatro, white, age 18. *Murder.* The crime was committed on June 2, 1876, at Highgate, Vermont. This young fellow was a farmhand employed by a country squire named Charles Butler. On the above date he put in a full day working the fields. When supper hour came Tatro was somewhat under the influence of liquor. He later said that he had been nipping from a bottle throughout the course of the day. After meal-

time Mr. Butler announced that he was going into town for an hour or two. His wife, Alice Butler (white, age unknown), declined to accompany him, saying that she did not feel well. Mr. Butler then got into his buggy and set out for town by himself while Mrs. Butler remained at home with Tatro. What happened next is uncertain. One account states that Tatro stripped himself naked and attempted to rape Mrs. Butler. Another account is highly suggestive that it was Mrs. Butler who tried to entice her young employee. Whatever the case, something went terribly wrong inside of Squire Butler's house. Tatro had some more to drink and he flew into an alcoholic frenzy. He attacked Mrs. Butler with a chair and battered her with it until she was unrecognizable. Then he ran out of the house all nude and started shouting for the neighbors. He told of being assaulted by burglars. When the neighbors entered the house they found evidence of a violent struggle. Almost every room — upstairs and downstairs — was a shambles. Walls, floors and ceilings were spattered with blood. Tatro was suspected from the start, especially when scratches and blood smears were seen on his person. He denied the crime but no one believed him. A conviction and death sentence followed. When his appeals failed, Tatro made a statement in which he agreed that the evidence pointed to him and that he was — in all probability — the killer. However, he said that he had no memory of the time in question. While standing on the gallows he spotted Charles Butler among the spectators and shouted at him, "Your money caused the commission of the deed!" Exactly what he meant will never be known. The end came for him at the Vermont State Prison on April 2, 1880.

Edwin Hoyt, white, age 38. *Murder.* The crime was committed on June 23, 1878, at Sherman, Connecticut. This man had lived through some of the worst fighting of the Civil War. Among other combat assignments, he served with the Ambulance Corps during the battles of Antietam and Fredericksburg — two of the war's most bloody engagements. He found himself continually exposed to carnage and the experience affected his mind. Hoyt suffered from what would today be known as traumatic stress disorder and he was never quite right mentally for the rest of his life. Hoyt spent long months in military hospitals where he was treated for both physical and psychological ills. Among these were hallucinations and disassociative spells. Upon his discharge (which was an honorable one) he returned to his hometown of Sherman, Connecticut, where he supported himself as a woodcutter and farmhand. He was married in the spring of 1868 and subsequently fathered five children. In the spring of 1872 he bought his father's farm and began raising his own crops. Within two years, however, business reversals and poor health forced him to relinquish the property back to his father. By the spring of 1878 he was brooding over his health and not knowing how to support his family. Hoyt slipped in and out of depression. His father also began to show signs of senility and that matter weighed heavily on Edwin Hoyt because he could barely take care of himself. Then in June of 1878 Edwin's mother died. The loss was more than Edwin could bear and it pushed him to the emotional brink. On the above date Edwin went to his sister's house (where his father was then staying) to talk about settling the distribution of his mother's belongings. He had some harsh words with his brother-in-law on that occasion and went away muttering. He then walked back to his own home about a mile distant where he drank some liquor. Then he took a butcher knife and concealed it on his person. Returning to his sister's house, he found that the inhabitants were eating dinner. He then sat on the porch out-

side and began to act strangely. When asked if he was all right, Hoyt grumbled words to the effect that "he had lived long enough, that he knew that he was soon to die but that he wanted two or three others to die first." When dinner was over, Edwin's father, George Hoyt (white, age 76) came outside and sat down next to him. Edwin Hoyt then went berserk. He pulled out the concealed butcher knife and attacked his father with it. George Hoyt was slashed to death before anyone could help him. Seconds later the men of the house ran outside and disarmed the killer. By then, however, Edwin Hoyt's rage was spent. He later claimed to have no memory of the murder. When the case came to trial Hoyt's defense team tried to make the most of their client's mental instability. The prosecution, however, countered with a convincing show of motive; witnesses said that Hoyt resented his father because the man had passed him over when he designated the primary beneficiary in his will. Edwin Hoyt had read the will and felt that he had been given short shrift. The added fact that Hoyt had deliberately concealed the murder weapon on his person was taken as evidence of premeditation. The verdict was guilty of capital felony. On May 13, 1880, the bustling city of Bridgeport saw its first legal hanging when Edwin Hoyt was executed there for the murder of his father. The scene was the Fairfield County jail, located on North Avenue. Thousands of people queued for a glimpse of the solemn occasion.

Henry Hamlin, white, age 29. *Murder.* The crime was committed on September 1, 1877, at Wethersfield, Connecticut. Henry Hamlin and William Allen were convicts serving time in the Connecticut State Prison for burglary. Although both were scarcely a year away from completing their sentences they formed a daring plan to escape. Having bribed a guard, they were furnished with the following articles of contraband: two loaded pistols, a pair of handcuffs, knives and a key which fit all of the locks in their cellblock. Shortly before midnight on the above date, Hamlin and Allen used the smuggled key to get out of their cells. The lone guard on duty, Wells Shipman (white, age 39), heard the sound of squeaky metal hinges and went to investigate. When he did so he encountered the two escapees moving along the cellblock. Shipman ordered them to halt. He also opened fire on them with his service revolver. Hamlin pretended to be wounded while Allen snuck around the other side of the cellblock. Poor visibility prevented the guard from seeing Allen's movements so he was unprepared for what happened next: while the guard was in the act of subduing Hamlin the other escapee came up behind him and struck him a hard blow on the head. That caused Shipman the guard to lose consciousness. When he awoke minutes later he found himself gagged and handcuffed. Quickly regaining his senses, the guard spat out the gag and began to shout for help. The escapees then warned him to keep his mouth shut or else they would kill him. Shipman disregarded the warning and continued shouting. Hamlin then shot him in the chest. The wound was fatal. Hamlin and Allen next scrambled to the top of the four-tiered cellblock and hacked their way through an overhead ceiling. By so doing they gained access to the prison attic. They then planned to climb through a belfry, make their way across the roof and slide down a drainpipe to freedom. By that time, however, the whole prison had been put on maximum alert. Armed men surrounded the entire prison complex, thus making escape impossible. In the morning Hamlin and Allen were spotted in the belfry. They were fired upon from all sides and ordered to surrender on pain of death. Both men decided to give themselves up. When the

case came to trial Hamlin and Allen were both cast for their lives. Then began a complicated series of appeals. Allen went through no less than five trials before he finally had his sentence reduced to life imprisonment. The guard who had supplied the contraband items was identified and sentenced to a long term in his own prison. Henry Hamlin lost his appeals and was ordered for execution. On May 28, 1880, he was hanged at the Hartford County jail.

1881

Edwin Hayden, white, age 27. *Murder*. The crime was committed on August 31, 1876, at Derby Line, Vermont. This offender was born at Cincinnati, Ohio, on August 25, 1849. When he was six years old his parents moved to Vermont. Young Edwin Hayden went along with them. A year or two later he was sent to live with his maternal grandfather in Montpelier. Although the reason for Edwin's separation from his parents is unclear, his grandfather saw that the boy had every advantage. Edwin was sent to prestigious schools and groomed to be a gentleman. At the age of 15 the lad interrupted his schooling to join the army. He was taken into the paymaster corps and served for a year. In 1865 he was honorably discharged. Returning to Vermont, Edwin took up his scholastic studies once again and completed them to everyone's satisfaction. In 1867 it came time for the young man to enter the business world. Accordingly he moved to Boston where he took a job with an upscale department store. After two years thus spent in retail training, Hayden decided to broaden his horizons. He became a traveling sales representative. Business eventually brought him to the town of Derby, Vermont, and it was there where he found a love interest. Her name was Gertrude Spaulding (white, age unknown), a well-to-do customer of Hayden's employer. She formed a favorable impression of the dapper young salesman and soon a mutual attraction developed. Within a surprisingly short time talk of marriage was heard. At that point Miss Spaulding's family became alarmed. They said that Hayden's urbanity was more semblance than substance. They also worried about $40,000 that the young woman had banked in her own name. One should not rush into marriage hastily, her relatives warned, but Gertrude Spaulding was smitten by love and would heed no counsel. The wedding accordingly took place much to the joy of the bride and much to the chagrin of her family.

No sooner had the couple returned from their honeymoon than Hayden began thinking of ways to spend his wife's money. He finally wheedled her into financing a business venture. Back to Boston went Hayden with enough investment capital to set himself up as a manufacturer of feminine apparel. Two years later a fire wiped out his enterprise. Hayden next went to Stanstead, Quebec, where he opened a hotel. The endeavor did not prosper and for two years Hayden used his wife's money to prop up the flagging business. In 1874 he finally called it quits. Refusing to even consider working for someone else, Hayden moved into his wife's family homestead at Derby, Vermont, where he tried to pass himself off as a gentleman of leisure. In reality, however, he was disillusioned. He also started to drink heavily. By 1875 his wife's money was gone. Hayden slipped into a state of indolence and defeatism. When he refused to stop drinking his wife gave him an ultimatum: either shape up or fend for himself. Then the woman walked out on him and went to live with her sister. He finally settled for a position as a hotel clerk. On the above date he went to Derby Line for the purpose of meeting with his wife. He wanted to effect a reconciliation. When he entered the hotel where the woman was staying, however, he stank of liquor and was noticeably under the influence thereof. Hayden's brother-in-law met him in the lobby and warned him that he was in no condition to see his estranged wife. An argument then broke out. Hayden pulled a gun on his brother-in-law and opened fire. A bullet grazed the man's chest. Then with the furies upon him, Hayden ran into his wife's room and started shooting at her. Gertrude Spaulding Hayden was hit in the abdomen and she died three days later.

Edwin Hayden initially pled guilty to capital murder and said that he would accept his fate. However, he was eventually persuaded to accept a defense team which filed appeals on his behalf. It was argued that temporary insanity had combined with dipsomania to render him not criminally responsible for his actions. Although the appeals were argued by talented attorneys they failed in the end. Edwin Hayden was ordered for execution. He was accordingly hanged at the Vermont State Prison on February 25, 1881.

Royal Carr, white, age 41. *Murder.* The crime was committed on December 11, 1878, at Worcester, Vermont. Royal Carr and Chester Carr were bachelor brothers who bore bad reputations in their community. Both were men of no set occupation. Contemporary accounts describe Royal Carr as a "half wit" who was dominated by his elder sibling. He was also no stranger to the wrong side of the law; in 1863 the untimely death of one Mary E. Loomis had cost him ten years in prison for manslaughter. It so happened that the Carr brothers had a neighbor named William Wallace Murcommack. He was a Native American man whose age is not recorded. He also had a young wife who caught the attention of Royal Carr. Irrespective of the difference in their ages (the woman was only 20 years old), Royal Carr became obsessed with her. He dreamed of supplanting her husband and finally decided that the man had to be eliminated. On the above date Royal Carr induced his rival to join him on a hunting trip. The two men accordingly headed into the woods. When they reached an area that was suitably remote, Royal Carr fired a shotgun blast into Murcommack's back. Then the killer calmly walked over to the injured man and finished him off with four more shots from a pistol. He paused only long enough to stash the victim's body in a thicket. Then he returned home and told his brother everything. When the townspeople began a search for the missing man Chester Carr panicked. He divulged information that resulted in the recovery of Murcommack's body. Royal Carr was promptly arrested and charged with capital murder. During the course of his subsequent legal battle Royal Carr made incriminating statements against his brother. He said that Chester Carr had been the catalyst of the entire affair. His lawyers then pressed the issue by claiming that Royal Carr was a mental submissive who had been dominated by his brother and duped into committing the murder. Chester Carr, it was claimed, had really wanted the decedent's wife for himself. In rebuttal, the prosecution said that this story was nothing more than a spiteful attempt by Royal Carr to get back at his brother for having turned informer. Whatever the truth, Chester Carr was taking no chances; he fled from his home without notice and was never seen again. His ultimate fate is unknown. Royal Carr was sent to the Vermont State Prison under sentence of death. He was hanged there on April 29, 1881.

1882

James Smith, alias "Chip Smith," white, age 22. *Murder.* The crime was committed on December 23, 1880, at Ansonia, Connecticut. This offender came from the lower Naugatuck valley. He was notorious there for rowdy conduct. He liked to run with a gang of ruffians which terrorized the Ansonia-Derby area with muggings, break-ins and acts of vandalism. A pugnacious alcoholic, Smith was at his worst when he was drinking. Even his cronies avoided him then.

During Christmas week in 1880 this "Chip Smith" went on a drunken binge. For three days and three nights he partied around the clock without sleep or decent food. On the fourth day he started the morning off by firing a pistol inside a saloon. Forcibly ejected therefrom, he next decided that it would be a good day to look for a job. So he pulled himself together and called at a local factory only to be told that there were no current openings. Smith walked away from the place only to return a few minutes later. He then began shouting and brandishing his weapon. Chaos erupted in the busy factory as panicked workers ran for the exits. The situation was only brought under control when Smith's sisters (who worked in the same factory) put their arms around him and led him away. After that Smith decided that he wanted more to drink. When he felt around inside his pockets he discovered that he had no money. So he set a course for his mother's house and demanded that the woman give him some money with which to purchase liquor. When Mrs. Smith refused her son's demand the young man got nasty and started smashing things. He also brandished his gun again before stomping out of the house. Mrs. Smith then called the police and asked them to arrest her son. Daniel J. Hayes (white, age 35), the chief of police for the town of Ansonia, decided that he would handle the matter personally. He went out looking for Smith and found him swaggering along Main Street. Hayes confronted the obnoxious drunk and said that he was confiscating his pistol. Smith replied that he had no such weapon on him. At that point Hayes took hold of Smith and placed him under arrest. Smith then said that he would come along quietly if Hayes would unhand him. It was a ruse and Hayes fell for it. No sooner did Hayes release his grip than Smith whipped out his pistol and opened fire. Hayes was hit in the stomach and mortally wounded. He died four days later.

When Smith sobered up he realized the enormity of his crime. He also knew that the prosecution had a strong case against him. His defense team decided to pin its hopes on a plea of extenuating circumstances; it was claimed that Smith was too drunk to be responsible for his actions. The strategy failed and Smith was ordered for execution. In a last-ditch effort to save their client, Smith's lawyers brought a bill before the Connecticut state legislature for the commutation of the death sentence. Their hopes soared when a legislative committee voted unanimously in favor of the bill. However, when the full body of the legislature took up the matter clemency was voted down by a lopsided margin. The end came on September 1, 1882, when James "Chip" Smith was hanged at the New Haven county jail.

1883

Joseph Loomis, white, age 24. *Murder.* The crime was committed on December 1, 1881, at Agawam, Massachusetts. Joseph Loomis and David Levett (white, age 22) were boyhood friends who had grown up in the vicinity of Westfield and Southwick. When Levett came of age he decided that he wanted to be a storekeeper. On his own initiative he applied to lending institutions for the financing to make his dream come true. The result was a successful confectionery at No. 449 Main Street in Springfield. As for Joseph Loomis, he remained an aim-less individual with no set course. On the above date Loomis was roaming around Springfield and decided to pay a call on his pal Levett. The two young men had a cordial meeting which lasted well into the night. Loomis later confessed that evil thoughts entered his mind when he saw some cash which Levett planned to spend with a wholesaler the next day. Quickly forming a scheme, Loomis told Levett that he had unwittingly overstayed his time there and had missed the last train home. Then he asked Levett if he could furnish him with transportation to Southwick. An obliging fellow, Levett hired a livery and offered to personally see Loomis safely home. Both men then climbed into the livery wagon and set out on their journey. Levett drove while Loomis sat next to him. Shortly before midnight they approached a long covered bridge which spanned the Agawam River. Loomis then commented on the chilly air and drew a travel blanket around himself. As he did so, he also drew a loaded handgun from a concealed holster and held it unseen beneath the blanket. When the wagon entered the covered bridge its wheels made a loud clattering noise upon the wooden planking. Loomis then killed Levett with a point-blank shot to the head. The clatter of the wagon wheels upon the bridge boards drowned out the sound of the gunshot so that when the wagon emerged from the bridge no one was the wiser. Loomis brought the wagon to a halt just long enough to tumble Levett's body back into the cargo area and cover it with a canopy. Then he drove the wagon up a deserted country lane where he paused to pick the dead man clean of valuables. Abandoning the wagon there, Loomis spent the rest of the night wandering around on foot. Dawn found him in Westfield where he spent the whole of the ensuing day in one saloon after another. By supper time the police were on his trail. Levett's body had been found and Loomis had been named as the last person seen with him. By that time, however, Loomis had stashed most of his loot. With no incriminating evidence left on his person, he felt emboldened to deny his guilt. However, four months later he was forced to change his tune. David Levett's jewelry (including an engraved gold watch) turned up in some roadside bushes. The items were wrapped in a handkerchief and a glove which were positively determined to belong to Loomis. Faced with a growing amount of evidence, the killer finally admitted the crime. On March 8, 1883, he was hanged at the Hampden County jail.

Emeline Meaker, white, age 43. *Murder.* The crime was committed on April 23, 1880, at Duxbury, Vermont. Published accounts of this woman all agree on one thing: that she was a boorish virago who estranged everyone with whom she came into contact. Even her own husband and children disdained her to a point where they would not accept her body for burial.

About a year or so before the commission of her capital crime, Emeline Meaker's husband was approached by representatives of a child welfare agency. It so happened that an eight-year-old half-sister of Mr. Meaker named Alice Meaker (white) was living in a state-funded orphanage. Conditions being crowded there, the agents asked Mr. Meaker if he would consider taking the child into his home in return for a $400 stipend. The offer was tempting ($400 was a lot of money in those days) and Mr. Meaker accepted it. Accordingly, young Alice Meaker was placed with him.

This did not sit well with Meaker's wife Emeline. The woman took the money fast enough but she regarded the new addition to her family with open hatred. For an entire year the girl was subjected to an unbroken cycle of abuse. She was beaten, starved and otherwise mistreated. In particular, Emeline Meaker used to tie the child to a post and whip her until blood ran from her wounds. Finally the cruel foster mother decided to kill Alice. She ordered her son, Almon Meaker (white, age 19), to fetch a lethal dose of strychnine from an apothecary. Then she had him outfit a wagon and a team of horses in anticipation of a picnic jaunt. On the above date Mrs. Meaker, her son and little Alice set out in the wagon together. When they reached an area that was suitably remote Almon Meaker handed the poison to his mother. She in turn poured it into a bottle of soda pop which she then gave Alice to drink. The girl consumed the poisoned beverage. Twenty minutes later a fatal agony overcame her. While she thrashed about (as strychnine victims do), Mrs. Meaker forcibly held her hand over her mouth to prevent her from crying out. Nor did she release her grip until the child was dead. Passing a boggy area, the killers spotted a hole and threw the girl into it. Almon Meaker later told of how he personally stomped upon the body to force it down into the mud.

During the course of an ensuing investigation into the child's disappearance, Almon Meaker was stricken with pangs of conscience. He told everything to the local sheriff and thereby solved the case. When a court of law considered the matter, both mother and son were sentenced to death. Because of his contrition, cooperation and a belief that he had been dominated by a wicked mother, however, Almon Meaker had his death sentence commuted by the state legislature. Emeline Meaker did not fare as well. Tentative efforts to save her life were begun by opponents of capital punishment only to be aborted following personal interviews with the woman. Such was the bad impression she made on people. Towards the end she tried to feign insanity. She filled the prison atmosphere with demoniacal screams. She also attacked anyone who entered her cell. She only calmed down when she realized that her playacting was futile. Still, she insisted on her innocence right up to the moment of her death.

Emeline Meaker was hanged at the Vermont State Prison on March 30, 1883. Her husband would have nothing to do with her during her imprisonment and he refused to accept her body for burial. Thus did this woman find her last repose among the denizens of Potter's Field.

1884

Although there are known to have been at least 141 legal executions in the United States of America this year, none of them took place in the New England states.

1885

Thomas Samon, white, age 36. *Murder.* His crimes were committed on November 24 and 25, 1883, at Laconia, New Hampshire. This man was a hotel cook by profession. Although he was married to a laundress who worked in the same hotel, he lived apart from his wife. Home for him was a furnished room on Oak Street in Laconia. His landlady, Mrs. Jane Ford (white, age 60), was reputed to have a penchant for younger men. She began a relationship with Thomas Samon soon after he moved in. When the woman's husband found out about the situation he walked out in disgust, leaving the lovers to go their own way. So matters continued until the autumn of 1883. By then the novelty of the romance had worn off for Samon and he wanted to disengage himself from it. Mrs. Ford, however, was loathe to lose her virile partner. She clung to Samon tenaciously and refused to let him go. Finally Samon could take no more. Trapped and disillusioned, he lashed out at Mrs. Ford. The woman was slain with an axe in her own home. After she was dead Samon chopped her legs off.

Then he trussed up the rest of her body with a clothesline, placed it in a storage trunk and threw the severed legs on top of it in the same trunk. That done, Samon set the trunk upon a wheelbarrow and pushed it nearly a mile across town to the house of a Mr. John Ruddy (white, age 45), located on Winter Street. It so happened that Samon had previously made arrangements to lodge there. When he arrived at his destination he was welcomed by the lady of the house, Mrs. Rosa Ruddy (white, age 38). She readily surmised that the trunk contained Samon's personal belongings and therefore did not object when the man asked if he could bring it into the house. Samon then lugged the trunk through the front door of the Ruddy home and set it down in a guest room. A short time later John Ruddy came home and greeted his new boarder. All had supper together without incident. Then they shared a cordial evening and retired at around ten o'clock. Two hours later Samon came into the room where Mr. and Mrs. Ruddy were sleeping and looked nervously out of the window. Mrs. Ruddy asked him if he was all right and he said that he just had a lot of things on his mind. Samon then went back to bed. At four o'clock in the morning he got up again. He looked out the window and then went into the kitchen. This time both of the Ruddys got out of bed. When Mr. Ruddy walked into the kitchen Samon struck him down with a hatchet, killing him instantly. When Mrs. Ruddy came running in response to the sound of the assault she was attacked as well. Samon thought she was dead as she fell across the body of her husband. The next thing the killer did was gather up the straw mattresses and feather pillows from the bedrooms. He brought them into the kitchen where he tore them open and dumped their contents all over the blood-drenched bodies of Mr. and Mrs. Ruddy. Then he sprinkled kerosene all over the place and set the house on fire. By that time an infant child of the Ruddys named Frank Ruddy (white, age 1) began to cry. The noise irked Samon so he took the baby from its crib and chopped its head off. Then he flung the headless baby into the fire and fled into the night. Mrs. Ruddy managed to crawl from the flames despite her terrible wounds. Gathering up what little strength she had, she hurled herself through a picture window and landed on the front lawn. The sound of breaking glass along with her screams roused the neighborhood. Some hearty men ran into the burning house and doused the fire. When the sun came up the full scope of the situation was revealed. Samon was caught near Plymouth a week later. A lynch mob almost got ahold of him but the sheriff succeeded in whisking him away to a secret location. Thus did the killer live to face a court of law. He was hanged at the New Hampshire State Prison on April 17, 1885.

Raphael Capone, white, age 26. **Carmine Santore,** white, age 43. *Murder.* Their crime was committed on September 7, 1883, at Brewer, Maine. These men were criminal vagabonds who refused to seek honest livings. Santore in particular is known to have spent at least 14 years of his life in prison. Both lived in a shack on the outskirts of Bangor. During the summer of 1883 they noticed extensive operations by a railroad track crew not far from where they lived. Observing the laborers closely, they found that they were nearly all Italian immigrants like themselves. They then decided that it would be a good idea to waylay those men one by one and murder them for their valuables. The first man they selected was Charles Pasqui (white, age unknown). Approaching him on payday, the plotters put him off his guard by speaking his native language and feigning camaraderie. They then induced Pasqui to partake of some rather esoteric pleasures with them and

by such a ruse lured him into a wooded area. A contemporary news account says that Capone and Pasqui went walking arm-in-arm together while Santore followed closely behind. It was subsequently revealed that Santore had enticed Pasqui into a homosexual assignation using his younger partner as bait. When the three men reached a spot that was suitably remote, Santore pulled out a handgun and shot Pasqui in the back. When the victim fell face-down on the ground Santore made sure of his demise by blowing off the back of his head with another shot. Then both of the plotters searched the dead man's person. They found $64 in money which they split between them. After that, they rolled the victim over and beat him beyond recognition with a fence stake. The next day Pasqui's workmates became concerned about his absence. They followed the path that he had taken from their camp and soon came upon his battered remains. There followed a hue and cry which encompassed the city of Bangor. Raphael Capone and Carmine Santore were reported as having been seen in the saloons the previous night with more money than usual. It was also reported that Capone had bloodstains on his clothes. Both men were taken in for questioning and they were identified by the surviving railroad workers as those who had walked off with Charles Pasqui. Faced with this, both of the suspects confessed. Capone also divulged where he had hidden a portion of the loot. When the full particulars of the crime became known among the Italian segment of the community, there was a movement to deal summarily with the culprits. However, police were able to keep Capone and Santore beyond public reach. Following their condemnation by a court of law, both men developed an intense hatred for each other. They also repudiated their confessions. Both died on the gallows at the Maine State Prison on April 17, 1885.

Daniel Wilkinson, white, age 37.

Murder. The crime was committed on September 4, 1883, at Bath, Maine. This man was an English-born drifter who wound up becoming a cop killer. After several years spent as a sailor, he came ashore in Maine and there began to wander about the countryside. He worked whatever odd jobs he could find and supplemented that livelihood by committing acts of burglary. At the town of Woolwich he was nabbed in the act and sentenced to a term in the Maine State Prison. However, while awaiting transfer to that place he broke out of the Sagadahoc County jail at Bath and managed to make good his escape. In the course of his flight Wilkinson stopped in Philadelphia. There he made the acquaintance of a kindred spirit named John Elliott. Together the two men decided to form a break-in team. When Philadelphia became too hot for them they took a steamboat to Portland, Maine, and there recommenced their depredations. Wilkinson used his intimate knowledge of Maine geography to further these misadventures. Shortly after midnight on the above date Elliott and Wilkinson attempted to break into a Bath grocery store. An officer of the nightwatch caught them in the act. Ordered to surrender, the two suspects dropped their burglary tools and ran in different directions. The officer then began blowing his whistle and firing his gun. Attracted by the commotion, a second officer named William Lawrence (white, age 60) ran to intercept one of the suspects. While rounding the corner of Broad and Front streets the fleeing Wilkinson literally ran into the oncoming watchman. Having a loaded gun in his hand, Wilkinson opened fire. Officer Lawrence was hit in the face at point-blank range and died instantly. Then both of the robbers escaped into the darkness. In examining the burglary tools that the suspects had dropped, detectives noted a distinctive kind of chisel. It was found to correspond perfectly with some jimmy marks that had been left at the scene of another burglary some days previously. In that earlier case (which occurred at Brunswick) police had suspected a pair of men who resided in a Portland boarding house. Those men were John Elliott and Daniel Wilkinson. When detectives went to the boarding house they found that both suspects had hastily departed therefrom. Elliott had left behind personal effects which confirmed his identity. Wilkinson had left a baggage receipt which enabled detectives to trace his whereabouts. He was found at a logging camp near Bangor and taken into custody. Elliott made good his escape but remained a wanted fugitive. Within a matter of days Wilkinson made a complete confession in which he admitted killing the Bath officer. It was enough to secure him a capital conviction. As the date of his execution drew near, Wilkinson said that he had gone by a false name ever since he came to America. He refused to divulge his true name because he did not want his family to know the disgraceful manner of his death. He was hanged at the Maine State Prison on November 20, 1885.

1886

Allen Adams, white, age 33. *Murder.*

The crime was committed on November 25, 1875, at Amherst, Massachusetts. This man was a Rhode Island drifter who paused at Amherst in the autumn of 1875. There he was taken in by a farmer named Moses Dickinson (white, age 64) and given a job. In return for room, board and a stipend, Adams helped Dickinson bring in his harvest. When the crop was successfully sold, however, the sight of money was too great for Adams to resist. On the above date Adams came upon his employer as the man lay sleeping. He hacked Dickinson to death with an axe and stole every article of value in the farmhouse. Locking the doors behind him, the killer then fled into the night and made a successful escape. The crime was discovered three days later when the farmer's starving livestock attracted attention. By then Adams was long gone. Ten years passed before there were any further developments in the case. Then Adams turned up in Tennessee. He was arrested for forgery there and for some unknown reason he told his interrogators about the murder he had committed in Massachusetts. When he gave details of the crime that only the killer would know, the Tennessee authorities contacted their Massachusetts counterparts and requested verification. The story checked and it was then agreed to extradite the suspect. Adams was brought to Northampton and put on trial for his life. He was convicted and ordered for execution. When his time came Adams did not go quietly. He cursed and swore as he was led from his cell. He also mocked the clergyman who attended him and spat obscenities at the assembled witnesses. The scene was the Hampshire County jail. The date was April 16, 1886.

1887

Samuel Besse, white, age 31. *Murder.* The crime was committed on December 22, 1885, at Wareham, Massachusetts. This man is described as having been the derelict scion of an historic family. Genealogists determined that his forbears had come to Massachusetts in 1635. Samuel Besse himself did nothing to enhance the reputation of his surname. At the age of 15 he was convicted of horse theft and sent to State's prison for seven years. Upon his release he returned to his hometown and launched a wave of burglaries and break-ins thereabouts. Apprehended once again, Besse was locked up for five more years. At the

time of his capital crime he was unemployed and living with his elderly father. On the above date Besse happened to be out gunning in the Wareham woods. Coming to a lonely stretch of road, he saw a lone traveler driving a produce wagon. It was Richard Lawton (white, age 28) of Westport, a man whose business it was to buy eggs from local farmers and resell them in the markets of Fall River and New Bedford. Besse recognized Lawton from having seen him on prior occasions. He readily knew that Lawton was on one of his buying expeditions. Therefore he reasoned that the man must have money on his person. Without further ado, Besse killed Lawton with a gunshot blast and plundered him of every penny he had. Then he loaded the victim's body into the egg wagon and covered it with wooden crates. After that Besse took Lawton's place in the driver's seat and continued along the highway for a considerable distance. All the while he kept nipping from a flask of whiskey. By the time the wagon crossed the Bristol County line Besse was undeniably drunk. Still onward the wagon went with its driver singing bawdy tunes and the lifeless legs of Richard Lawton protruding from the egg crates. By the time the wagon reached the outskirts of New Bedford the driver realized that people he passed along the way were giving him funny looks. Richard Lawton's legs were clearly visible among the egg crates and they did not fail to attract attention. No one challenged Besse, however. It so happened that there was a disreputable roadhouse in that area and all supposed it to simply be a case of one drunken man driving another one home. As the short December day drew to a close, Besse suddenly realized his situation. He then abandoned the wagon by the roadside and fled across the fields on foot. Reaching New Bedford, he went on a shopping spree with the dead man's money. Then he caught a train home to Wareham. On the following morning Lawton's wagon was found where Besse had left it. The horse was in a wretched condition and the body of the murdered man still lay among the egg crates. People on their way to market readily recognized the decedent as Richard Lawton the egg vendor. When his movements were traced the trail stopped at Wareham. It was then that Samuel Besse came under suspicion. Examination of Besse's clothing revealed bloodstains that he could not readily explain. He was also found to have $35 in his possession, a hefty sum in those days for a man who was unemployed. As the investigation continued, witnesses came forward who placed Besse in New Bedford on the day in question. Others told of him driving Lawton's wagon. A jury took 15 minutes to convict Besse of capital murder. Appeals failed and on March 10, 1887, the killer was hanged at the Plymouth County jail.

1888

James Edward Nowlin, white, age 17. *Murder.* The crime was committed on January 4, 1887, at Somerville, Massachusetts. This juvenile offender was motivated by greed. He worked for a milkman named George Codman (white, age 23), who had several delivery routes throughout the Somerville area. On the day previous to the above date Codman made collections from his customers which added up to several hundred dollars. The sight of such money aroused the cupidity of his teenage assistant, Nowlin, who then determined to acquire those funds by any and all means. Long before dawn on the following morning Nowlin met his employer in a Sergeant Avenue barn. The two then proceeded as usual to prepare dairy products for that day's deliveries. Nowlin believed that Codman was carrying the previous day's collection money on his person. He therefore reasoned that the time for

action had come. As soon as he saw his chance, Nowlin plunged a pitchfork into Codman's back. The man fell gravely wounded. Then when Codman attempted to beg for his life Nowlin finished him off by slitting his throat with a butcher knife. When he searched the victim's pockets Nowlin was surprised to find much less money than he had expected. He then concealed the body in some hay and went to Codman's house. There he told a tale to the effect that Codman had gone out of town for a few days and that he, Nowlin, had been entrusted with making the usual deliveries. He also said that he needed Codman's cashbox and account book in order to carry on the business during his employer's absence. Since Nowlin was a familiar figure at Codman's house his story was believed. The cashbox was handed over to him and it was found to contain the balance of the previous day's receipts. Thus being satisfied that he had gotten all the cash there was to get, Nowlin returned to the scene of the crime. He then outfitted Codman's milk wagon and made the day's deliveries single-handed. All the while no one suspected him of any wrongdoing. When he finished making his rounds Nowlin returned to the scene of the crime again. He waited for the sun to go down and then proceeded with the job of disposing of his employer's body. He stripped the decedent naked and bundled up his clothing in a ball. Then he cut the body open with a knife and scooped out all of the internal organs. After that he chopped off the dead man's head with an axe and did the same to his arms and legs. When the job of butchery was done, Nowlin hosed down the barn with water to wash away the blood. Then he loaded the various body parts into the milk wagon and set out with them in the direction of Lexington. All along the way he tossed limbs, guts and organs into roadside bushes. When he finally discarded the head and torso as well,

Nowlin calmly garaged the milk wagon and stabled the horse that had drawn it. Then he went home and ate a hearty supper. On the following day a teamster noticed bloody snow on the Lexington Road. When the man examined the scene further he noticed footsteps in the snow. Following the footsteps a short distance, he was shocked to find a human head staring back at him from atop a snowbank. The hue and cry which followed this discovery brought out hundreds of searchers and before long most of Codman's other remains were located. They were roughly re-assembled at the Lexington Town Hall and put on public display. Soon the authorities had a positive identification. James Edward Nowlin was arrested in short order. A search of his house turned up Codman's cashbox with the contents intact. Any doubts that remained about the suspect's guilt were dispelled when he confessed soon afterward. A capital conviction followed. As Nowlin's execution date drew near his defense team appealed for clemency on the ground that capital punishment for 16 and 17 year olds was without precedent in Massachusetts. It proved to be an ill-advised move; several such cases were cited in rebuttal, thus leaving Nowlin's advocates worse off for credibility. As a result, the executive council of the governor voted seven to two against commuting the death sentence. The end came on January 20, 1888, when James Edward Nowlin was hanged at the Middlesex County jail.

Philip Pallidona, white, age 24. *Murder.*

The crime was committed on June 22, 1887, at Fairfield, Connecticut. This man came to America from his native Italy in 1886. He managed to save up the sum of $40 which he then wired home to his eldest brother, Frank Pallidona (white, age 45), to enable him to also make the trans–Atlantic journey. Philip was on hand to greet Frank when the lat-

ter cleared Ellis Island in the spring of 1887. The brothers then came to the vicinity of Bridgeport, Connecticut, where they found jobs as quarrymen for a stone-crushing company. Frank Pallidona promised to repay his little brother the $40 that he had sent him. Over the course of the next several weeks he accordingly gave him half that amount. He was slow to repay the remainder and Philip became increasingly nettled by what he perceived to be deliberate procrastination. On the above date both brothers were working at the Stratfield Quarries. There they had harsh words. In a rage, Philip Pallidona pulled out a revolver and menaced his brother. As Frank Pallidona turned to flee, he was fatally shot in the back. The killer fled as far as Albany, New York, but was overtaken there. Returned to Connecticut, he was charged with capital murder. On October 5, 1888, the city of Bridgeport became the scene of another legal hanging as Philip Pallidona was brought to the gallows in the North Avenue jail. Alone in a foreign land, the condemned man had no one to claim his body. When that fact became known a special collection was made in the churches which served the Italian community. In such a way was Philip Pallidona accorded a decent burial.

1889

John Swift, white, age 22. *Murder.*

The crime was committed on July 7, 1887, at Hartford, Connecticut. This young man was a machinist by trade. He was unable to hold a job, however, because of his drunken, dissipated habits. A confirmed alcoholic, Swift showed no inclination to reform and he preferred to blame other people for his own shortcomings. After three unhappy years of marriage, his wife, Katie McCann Swift (white, age 23), moved out on him and began divorce proceedings. John Swift had previously sweet-talked his wife out of similar intentions several times before. However, each time he remained as abusive and dissolute as ever. By the summer of 1887 Katie Swift could take no more; she served her husband with divorce papers and let it be known that her decision was final. On the above date John Swift was going about his favorite pastime: playing the piano in a local saloon in return for free drinks. As dinner hour drew nigh Swift was seen to take a handgun from his pocket and place it atop the piano. He then announced to the saloon patrons that he intended to shoot his wife. No one took him seriously. At six o'clock Swift left the saloon and went to a nearby park. There he sat on a bench and waited for his wife, knowing that she would pass that way on her way home from work. When the woman came into sight she was accompanied by two female workmates. As the trio began to walk up Trumbull Street they were accosted by the young husband. Katie Swift then paused to hear what "Jack" had to say. He asked her to give him another chance. In reply, Katie Swift said that it was no use; she had fallen for that line several times before and would not do so again. As she turned to rejoin her companions, John Swift pulled out a handgun and shot her in the back. Katie Swift died shortly after reaching a hospital. Irate passersby chased the killer into an alley and cornered him there. They threw bricks at him until he agreed to surrender. When the case came to trial Swift's prior declaration that he intended to shoot his wife was taken as evidence of premeditation. Therefore a capital conviction was returned. As appeals were argued, however, Swift elicited a considerable amount of sympathy on account of his boyish good looks. A bill to commute his death sentence passed both houses of the state legislature with very few dissenting votes. The governor of Connecticut, however, vetoed the bill. The state senate then voted to override the veto and it was expected that the House of Representatives would do the same. To the surprise of all, the house vote on the override measure fell short of the necessary majority. The veto was thereby sustained and John Swift was doomed. He was hanged at the Hartford County jail on April 18, 1889.

1890

James Palmer, white, age 23. *Murder.* The crime was committed on May 28, 1888, at Portsmouth, New Hampshire. This young man was a machinist who used to work the night shift at the Portsmouth Electric Light Company. He had a bad habit of living beyond his means. When he inevitably fell into debt he sought to remedy the situation by stealing from his employer. Expensive tools were his favorite loot and the electric company was hard pressed to replace them. Eventually the situation became so bad that an internal investigation was begun. When Palmer was named as the prime suspect a warrant was obtained to search his home. The superintendent of the electric company sent his young assistant, Henry T. Whitehouse (white, age 22), to stand by while police executed the search warrant. The search yielded incontrovertible proof of Palmer's guilt: a large cache of pilfered tools which Whitehouse identified as company property. As a result of this, Palmer was fired from his job. He was spared further prosecution, however, when he offered to get out of town. During the days that followed, Palmer brooded over his situation. He was unwilling to accept personal responsibility for his own actions and found it easier to blame Henry Whitehouse for his downfall. From then on all that mattered to Palmer was revenge. He knew that Whitehouse had a fiancée who lived on the other side of the Kittery bridge. He also knew that Whitehouse used to walk over that bridge on Sunday afternoons in order to visit the young woman. In addition, Palmer further knew that Whitehouse was in the habit of returning over the bridge late at night. On the above date then, Palmer lay in ambush for Whitehouse on the New Hampshire side of the Kittery bridge. He sprang upon the unsuspecting man and shattered his skull with a hammer. Then Palmer dragged Whitehouse to the bank of the Piscataqua River. There he continued to batter the corpse until his anger was spent. After that he picked the decedent clean of valuables and cut off his head. The remains of Henry Whitehouse were found the following morning. Low tide revealed a large machinist's hammer lying on some nearby mud flats. The hammer was retrieved and identified as the murder weapon. It also bore a serial number which when checked against electric company records told of its having been issued to James Palmer. In an attempt to explain away the evidence, Palmer told an improbable story of the hammer being stolen from him. A jury refused to believe him. On May 1, 1890, the disgruntled killer was hanged at the New Hampshire State Prison. He was buried next to his mother who had died of grief a short time before.

1891

Jacob Scheele, white, age 63. *Murder.* The crime was committed on January 25, 1888, at New Canaan, Connecticut. This offender had come to the United States as a young man. He was originally from the German city of Stuttgart. For many years he worked as a brewmaster for a bottler of beer and ale. When his employer sold out, Scheele decided to go into business for himself. He started a moonshining operation in the then rural town of New Canaan which supplied a speakeasy which he opened in nearby Norwalk. Four separate arrests did not deter Scheele from selling his homemade beer without a license. In January of 1888 this bootlegger learned that yet another warrant had been issued for his arrest. Irritated by the news, Scheele barricaded himself in his house and bade defiance to any lawman who would dare to come after him. On the above date it became the job of New Canaan town constable Louis Drucker (white, age 44) to bring in Jacob Scheele. As the officer approached Scheele's house he found the place oddly quiet. All the doors and windows were locked and shuttered. Drucker then called out to Scheele saying that he knew he was there and that he had better give himself up. Scheele then took aim at Drucker with a double-barreled shotgun and pulled both triggers. The constable was killed instantly when the lethal charge struck him in the face. Within minutes news of the homicide spread throughout the town. Drucker had been a popular man and there was a call to avenge his death. An angry mob then marched on Scheele's house. Someone fired a shot to get the killer's attention. Then Scheele was told that he had one minute to come out or he would face the consequences. The mob waited for the minute to pass. Then it battered its way into the house with axes and sledgehammers. Scheele was found on the floor bleeding from a self-inflicted gunshot wound. For that reason he was not dealt with summarily. Instead he was patched up and held for the sheriff. Then he was brought to Bridgeport and charged with capital murder. Scheele was convicted when his case came to trial. The penalty was death by hanging. For two years appeals kept the aging killer alive. Then Jacob Scheele ran out of appeals. On June 18, 1891, yet another legal hanging took place at Bridgeport. Thousands of people thronged the vicinity of the North Avenue jail hoping to catch a glimpse of the execution. Jacob Scheele was led to the gallows as a band played a death march. Then a hush fell over the scene. At precisely 10:36 A.M. there was a loud crash as the wooden platform dropped from beneath the condemned man's feet. At that moment all became aware of the fact that Jacob Scheele had paid the death penalty.

1892

Sylvester Bell, white, age 59. *Murder.* The crime was committed on December 26, 1889, at Fairfax, Vermont. This man was 53 years old in 1886 when he married 32-year-old Emma Locke, a respectable white woman. Bell proved to be an abusive spouse and after three years his wife could take no more. She began divorce proceedings and found a separate place to live. On the above date Mrs. Bell went in company with the town constable to her former home (where her estranged husband still resided) in order to remove some of her personal effects. When she had nearly finished her task, the woman decided to go upstairs for a final look around. The constable remained downstairs while Sylvester Bell followed his wife upstairs in a peaceful manner. As Mrs. Bell was in the act of looking in a storage trunk, her husband came up behind her. Without saying a word the man pulled out a revolver and shot her in the back of the head at point-blank range. Hearing the shot, the constable ran up the stairs. Sylvester Bell met him with the smoking gun still in his hand. He told of what he had done and then calmly submitted to arrest. Convicted of capital felony, the killer was sentenced to death. Appeals kept him alive for two years. On January 1, 1892, Sylvester Bell died on the gallows at the Vermont State Prison. When asked if he had a final statement he said that he was innocent of the crime which had brought him to such a fate.

Andrew Borjesson, white, age 32. *Murder.* The crime was committed on August 1, 1890, at New Milford, Connecticut. This man came to America from his native Sweden in 1886. Four years later he briefly returned to his homeland in order to escort a brother of his who had decided that he would also like to seek his fortune in the so-called "land of promise." While making arrangements for the journey, Borjesson was approached by a young woman named Emma Anderson (white, age 21) who asked him if she could come along on the trans–Atlantic voyage. Borjesson found Miss Anderson attractive and for that reason he agreed to let her join his travel party. The trio then packed their belongings and bade farewell to their families. The first leg of their trip was a short cruise across the Baltic Sea to the German port of Hamburg. It was from that place that the immigrant ships sailed for America. Upon reaching Hamburg, Andrew Borjesson sprang a nasty surprise on Emma Anderson. He told her that unless she agreed to marry him when they reached America he would abandon her there in Germany alone and penniless. This made Emma Anderson hate Andrew Borjesson. However, she feigned agreement for the time being because she had already come too far to turn back. The travelers accordingly came to America. They cleared Ellis Island together and then made their way to Connecticut. They decided to settle in the town of New Milford. There Andrew Borjesson and his brother found work on a farm. Emma Anderson was hired by a wealthy squire to serve as his housekeeper. When all were comfortably situated in their new homes, Andrew Borjesson approached Emma Anderson and pressed his marriage suit. She told him to get lost. She also gave the man a piece of her mind, saying that he was no gentleman and a drunkard besides. Andrew Borjesson was disappointed but not totally dissuaded. On the above date he arose between the hours of three and four o'clock in the morning and decided that he would visit Emma Anderson. Making his way to her place of residence, Borjesson placed a ladder against the side of the house and climbed into the servants' quarters. There he found Emma Anderson asleep in her bed. Borjesson woke the woman up and asked her to have sex with him. Emma Anderson could scarcely believe her ears. She slapped the night stalker across his face and told him to get out. Borjesson then attempted to rape Miss Anderson. The woman screamed at that point and roused the entire household. Infuriated by such resistance, Borjesson pulled out a knife and started slashing at Emma Anderson. He did not stop until she was nearly decapitated. Then he jumped out a window and ran off into the darkness. Seconds later the men of the house burst into the servants' quarters. They found Miss Anderson dead. Walls, floor and ceiling were awash with blood. Running outside, the men fired shotguns into the air to wake up the neighborhood. Soon there was a large crowd at the scene of the crime. When daylight came the killer's tracks were clearly visible in the dew. They led to some nearby woods. Dozens of men then armed themselves with whatever they could lay their hands on. All beat a swath through the woods determined to catch the killer. Hunting dogs were also brought into service. Borjesson was finally brought to bay by his pursuers. He was given a simple choice: surrender or die. Borjesson decided to give himself up. He was brought out of the woods by the posse and turned over to the law. Some men wanted to lynch Borjesson but wiser counsels prevailed. When the case came to trial Borjesson confessed his guilt. He was then convicted of capital felony and ordered for execution. On January 29, 1892, thousands of people swarmed around the Litchfield County jail as Andrew Borjesson made his short walk to the gallows. It was the first execution at Litchfield in more than a century and few were willing to forego such an historic occasion. The town green (which faced the jail) was packed with a seething mass of humanity from end to end. There was great fear lest a human stampede erupt. When the black flag of death was hoisted above the jail a great cheer burst forth from the crowd. It was the signal for which all had been waiting. Andrew Borjesson was dead. The hoard of spectators then dispersed without further incident.

Angelo Petrillo, white, age 25. *Murder.* The crime was committed on April 18, 1891, at New Haven, Connecticut. This young man was an Italian immigrant with no set occupation. The proceeds of gambling formed his only source of income. Disgusted with his refusal to find a regular job, Petrillo's wife left him and went to live with her married sister. Petrillo disliked that situation and cast about for a scapegoat. He finally decided to blame his sister-in-law's husband, a saloonkeeper named Michael DeMeo (white, age 33). According to Petrillo's reasoning, DeMeo was responsible for Mrs. Petrillo's estrangement because he had allowed the woman to move into his home. Armed with such logic, Petrillo then approached DeMeo and demanded the payment of $200 as compensation for what he called the alienation of his wife's affections. DeMeo balked at this. On the evening of the above date Petrillo confronted DeMeo at the corner of Minor and Lafayette streets in New Haven. He repeated his demand for $200. When DeMeo replied that he did not have such a sum, Petrillo pulled out a pistol and shot the man dead. Arrested the same evening, Petrillo denied the crime. However, multiple witnesses attested to the contrary. A jury later decided that the crime fit the definition of capital felony when it was told that Petrillo had previously threatened the life of Michael DeMeo. Shortly before the time set for his execution Petrillo became hysterical. Guards had to drag him screaming from his cell to the gallows. The scene was the New Haven County jail. The date was November 14, 1892.

1893

Walter Holmes, white, age 49. *Murder.* The crime was committed on September 1, 1891, at Chicopee, Massachusetts. This man was an alcoholic who repeatedly abused his wife and finally killed her. The woman, Ellen Holmes (white, age 41), had objected to her husband's hard drinking and thereby incurred his wrath. Walter Holmes would tolerate no criticizing of his bad habits. As a result, he took to beating his wife whenever he was drunk and frequently when he was sober as well. Holmes was also deliberately cruel to his wife in other ways. For instance, Holmes used to drive a horsedrawn tram which conveyed many Chicopee residents to their jobs in the mills. Although his wife also held such a job, Holmes would refuse to give her a ride and instead forced her to walk the entire distance. On one occasion when the woman pleaded for a ride on account of bad weather, Holmes attacked her with his horsewhip and severely lashed her with it in the middle of the street. The couple lived in a cottage which was situated in a predominantly French enclave called "Plainville," located about halfway between Chicopee and Chicopee Falls. It was there where on the above date Walter Holmes beat his wife senseless and then buried her alive in the crawlspace beneath his living room. Soon afterward he moved out of the aforesaid cottage and went to Holyoke where he went to work as a stableman for no one other than the chief of police. On November 3, 1891, a man who was walking his dog by the former residence of Holmes had his curiosity

aroused when the animal began to act strangely there. The dog ran beneath the front porch of the vacant cottage and started to frantically dig and scratch at the soft earth. No amount of coaxing would deter the dog from its purpose and soon a crowd gathered to watch. Someone then reasoned that something must be buried there and shovels were brought into action. The diggers soon came upon the body of Ellen Holmes. An autopsy confirmed that she had been buried alive. Walter Holmes, who had said that his wife had run off with another man, was arrested in short order. He stubbornly refused to admit his guilt and was eventually convicted on other evidence. While awaiting execution he forsook the Protestant religion in which he had been raised and converted to Roman Catholicism. That act outraged many people even more than his crime. Walter Holmes was executed at the Hampden County jail on February 3, 1893. He hobbled to the gallows on a pair of crutches and was almost decapitated when the knot of the noose caught him under the chin. His hanging was a very messy one.

William Coy, white, age 33. *Murder.* The crime was committed on August 29, 1891, at Washington, Massachusetts. This man was a lifelong resident of Berkshire County. He lived in a ramshackle house near Washington together with his wife and a male boarder named John Whalen (white, age 35). For his livelihood, Coy did farm work as well as an occasional assignment with a railroad track crew. The boarder, John Whalen, was a full-time employee in that latter capacity. Whalen was also a thrifty sort who managed to amass more money than his landlord. Coy became aware of that fact and seethed with jealousy. He also suspected Whalen of being intimate with Mrs. Coy. The situation became critical shortly before the above date when Coy's wife announced that she was going away for a few days in order to visit some friends. William Coy suspected that the woman was really planning to elope with Whalen. From that time on Coy kept a close watch on Whalen's movements. Soon his suspicions were confirmed by three things: a report that Mrs. Coy had actually gone to Albany instead of the place she had told her husband, the discovery that Whalen had packed his bags and a report that Whalen had suddenly withdrawn all of his money from the local bank. Armed with such information, Coy decided to act. He snuck into Whalen's bedroom as the man was sleeping and attacked him with an axe. Whalen was hacked to death in his own bed. Coy's next move was to drag the decedent out of the house and into the yard. There he chopped off Whalen's legs and also his head. Then the killer tossed the body parts onto a horsedrawn wagon which he drove into the woods via an old logging trail. When he reached a spot that was suitably remote he dug a shallow grave and buried the human remains. After that Coy returned to the scene of the crime and stole all of Whalen's money. Then he caught a train to Albany and went hunting for his wife. When Coy found the woman he did not treat her badly. Instead, he asked her to come home with him and Mrs. Coy complied. In the days that followed townspeople voiced concern about Whalen's disappearance. On October 13, 1891, a man walking through the woods with his dog came upon the dismembered body. The dog had been attracted by the scent of carrion and it led its master to the shallow grave. Coy was arrested the same day and he eventually admitted the crime. He was hanged at the Berkshire County jail on March 3, 1893.

George Abbott, alias "Frank Almy," white, age 34. *Murder.* The crime was committed on July 17, 1891, at Hanover, New Hampshire. This man was the wayward scion of an upper class family. He was born at Salem, Massachusetts, where his forebears had long been prominent. When Abbott was three days old his mother succumbed to complications from childbirth. Abbott's bereaved father was unable to care for a baby single-handedly so it was agreed that young Abbott be taken in by an aunt and uncle. When Abbott was ten years old his foster parents decided to relocate to the vicinity of Thetford, Vermont, where they had substantial holdings. The boy George Abbott went with them and it was soon after that he began to exhibit symptoms of criminal proclivity. The first to suffer were his schoolmates; they endured the theft of many articles. Then came Abbott's playmates, jewelry from their homes being his favorite targets. At the age of 14 this Abbott is reported to have fortified a cave which he used as a repository for stolen goods. When Abbott was aged 17 he graduated from misdemeanors to felonies; he joined with a certain farmhand in his father's employ and committed all kinds of burglaries. Soon the law caught up with him and the result was a four-year term in the Vermont State Prison. So ashamed did Abbott's father become by that circumstance that he committed suicide. The man's estate was then held in trust for the errant son and became payable upon the young man's release from prison. George Abbott squandered his legacy in a year-long spree of gambling and womanizing. Then when his money ran out he was himself reduced to working as a farmhand. He rejoined his former cronies and organized a burglary ring that wrought havoc throughout the greater Thetford area. Once again Abbott was apprehended and this time he was hit with a sentence of 25 years in close confinement. Back to the Vermont State Prison went George Abbott and easier slept the harried residents of Thetford and vicinity. Six years of hard durance followed. Then Abbott escaped from prison. He headed south under an assumed name and is reported to have worked jobs in Delaware, Maryland, Georgia and Texas. Two years later he returned to the northeast. After working a series of odd jobs throughout the Boston area he set a course for his former home at Thetford. He reached the college town of Hanover, New Hampshire, and there decided that it would not be wise to set foot in Vermont. He then applied to a Hanover farmer named Andrew Warden and was taken on by that man as a laborer. It so happened that this farmer had an attractive daughter named Christie Warden (white, age 28). George Abbott, alias "Frank Almy," became infatuated with her and sought to curry her favor. There was something about the new suitor, however, that did not sit well with the young woman or her family; "Almy" gave evasive answers whenever he was questioned about his past. He also seemed out of place as a farmhand, his deportment and general bearing tending to indicate a better than average background. Such factors incited suspicion on the part of the Warden family; they became convinced that "Almy" was hiding something and for that reason he was denied permission to court the young woman. Christie Warden herself concurred in the belief that "Almy" was not to be trusted. She therefore rebuked the man. "Almy" was stung by the rejection and he brooded over it sorely. After a short time, however, he deemed it prudent to leave the area. He quit farmer Warden's employ and drifted back to Boston. Still he could not get Christie Warden out of his mind. He finally decided that he must have her, come what may. On the above date he slipped back into the Hanover area and hid in some roadside bushes. He had previously determined that Christie Warden would pass that way after attending a meeting of the local Grange. Shortly before ten o'clock in the evening Almy's patience was rewarded; Christie Warden came walking along the road with her mother, sister and another woman. Without making any attempt to conceal his identity, Almy jumped out of the bushes and grabbed Christie Warden. Then he forcibly dragged her into a pasture while simultaneously warning off the other women with a handgun. They ran for help while Almy began to forcibly disrobe Christie Warden. He had every intention of raping her. Before he could accomplish his purpose, however, Almy was distracted by the shouts of would-be rescuers. He fired several shots at those persons and thereby forced them to keep their distance. Then he became incensed by the continued struggles of Christie Warden. Almy then brutally pistol-whipped the young woman and shot her dead. Then he fled into the night. Minutes later the great bell of Dartmouth College rang out the general alarm. Every able-bodied man in the vicinity then flocked to the scene. All were armed. Posses were organized to scour the countryside. Many of the college men joined in the manhunt. However, the fugitive outsmarted them all; he headed for the one place where no one thought to look: the Warden family farm. For an entire month Almy hid out in his former employer's barns. He concealed himself in the hay by day and emerged to forage for food by night. One day some mason jars were found on the farm which no one could explain. They contained edibles. After considering every possibility, the property owner became wary. A careful watch was then placed on the farm and late one night Almy was seen emerging from his hiding place. He had to be shot before he could be subdued. When the news of the capture spread through the town there was a movement to mobilize a lynch mob. However, wiser counsels prevailed. The case was allowed to wend its way through the courts but the result was never in doubt. On May 16, 1893, George Abbott, alias "Frank Almy," died on the gallows at the New Hampshire State Prison.

1894

Daniel Robertson, white, age 49.

Murder. The crime was committed on September 9, 1893, at New Bedford, Massachusetts. This man was a Canadian who grew up on Prince Edward Island. He was also a carpenter by trade and a drunkard by habit. So severe was the latter trait that it prevented Robertson from holding a steady job. Alcoholism also inhibited his ability to provide for his family; whenever he drew a pay he would squander the money in saloons. Robertson even pawned his wedding gifts in order to drink the proceeds. His wife, Mary McKenzie Robertson (white, age 43), was forced to fend for herself; she opened a boarding house on Acushnet Avenue in New Bedford and by such means earned the rudiments of a livelihood. She also gave her husband an ultimatum: either stop drinking or get sued for divorce. Robertson scoffed at his spouse and continued in his dissipated ways. Then in the summer of 1893 he passed the point of no return. New Bedford police arrested him for public intoxication (as they had many times before) and brought him before a local magistrate. The penalty was either a ten-dollar fine or 30 days in the House of Corrections. Robertson opted to pay the fine. He had no money of his own, however, so he demanded that his wife dip into her rental income. This the woman was either unable or unwilling to do. Robertson was then locked up for a month. All the while he seethed and several times he was heard to say that he would kill his wife when he got out. On the above date Robertson was released from jail. He immediately went to a saloon and drank himself into a temper — on credit. Then he marched over to his wife's boarding house and clamored for admittance. Mary Robertson was reluctant to let her husband in but she was finally coaxed into doing so by a promise of good conduct. At first Daniel Robertson merely said that he needed a change of clothes. Then he ordered his wife to prepare a meal for him. He also asked the woman whether or not she really intended to divorce him. The answer was enough to send Robertson into a rage. He picked up a butcher knife and attacked his wife with it. The woman was slashed to death in a frenzy of anger. After that the killer helped himself to whatever money he could find about the house. Then he set out on foot for the city limits, calling at every pub along the way. Police eventually found him in one such place and took him into custody. Robertson was too drunk to walk so he had to be carried to a paddy wagon. The fact that this killer had previously been heard to threaten the life of his wife was taken as evidence of premeditation. He was therefore charged with capital murder. A jury saw things the same way and it voted for the death penalty. Such a verdict was upheld on appeal. On December 14, 1894, the historic city of New Bedford saw its first and only legal execution when Daniel Robertson was hanged there.

John Cronin, white, age 37. *Murder.*

The crime was committed on October 6, 1893, at South Windsor, Connecticut. This man was a skilled laborer who worked the tobacco farms of Hartford County. He boarded at the house of a Mr. Albert Skinner (white, age 42), a joiner who lived on the road between Wapping and Ellington. One day during the summer of 1893 Cronin and his landlord decided to go pheasant hunting. They armed themselves with rifles and set out on foot. Along the way they encountered a neighbor who casually said to them, "Gone a'hunting are ye?" to which Skinner replied in the affirmative. "Where is thy dog?" asked the neighbor. Skinner then gestured toward Cronin so as to jokingly reply that he was the dog. Skinner and the neighbor then laughed at Cronin's expense. This incident made Cronin highly indignant. Although he said nothing at the time, Cronin felt himself ill-used. He then resolved to pay back Skinner tenfold. One day shortly afterward Cronin got drunk and marched into Skinner's house. He took a gun off of the wall and began to load it. Skinner's wife saw this and became alarmed. She called to her husband and her son. The two men then confronted Cronin. When they demanded to know his intentions Cronin mocked them by barking like a dog. Then a fight broke out. Skinner and his son overpowered Cronin and disarmed him. However, Cronin threatened Skinner by saying that he would come back one day and shoot him. On the above date Cronin made good his threat. He burst into Skinner's house with a loaded revolver and opened fire on the man. Skinner was taken by surprise and mortally wounded. The fact that Skinner was seated at the breakfast table with his five-year-old daughter did not deter the killer. When the shooting was over Cronin made no attempt to escape. He dallied around the front of the house barking like a dog while Mrs. Skinner ran screaming for help. Some passersby disarmed Cronin and held him for the police. When he was taken into custody Cronin boldly admitted the crime and said he didn't care if he had to hang for it. On December 18, 1894, he did exactly that at the Connecticut State Prison.

1895

Although there are known to have been at least 141 legal executions in the United States of America this year, none of them took place in the New England states.

1896

Angus Gilbert, white, age 28. *Murder.* The crime was committed on April 10, 1895, at Dorchester, Massachusetts. This offender was born and raised in Nova Scotia. It is not clear whether he renounced his Canadian citizenship after coming to the United States. When he attained the age of majority Gilbert set a course for Boston and decided to settle there. He found lodgings in a boarding house at the corner of Savin Hill Avenue and Denny Street; in return for keeping the property neat he was given his meals plus the use of a furnished room which was situated above a stable at that address. Gilbert also earned $20 per month as the evening attendant at the nearby Savin Hill railroad station. For some time previous to the above date Gilbert had become well acquainted with the family of a Mr. George Sterling, a barber who lived at No. 47 Savin Hill Avenue. During the course of his visits to the Sterling home, Gilbert became noticeably fond of a young daughter of his friend, one Alice Sterling by name (white, age 8). He doted on the child and used to playfully say that he would wait for her to grow up so he could marry her. On the above date Gilbert encountered Alice Sterling as she was playing near her home. He lured her away with a contrived promise of some kind and brought her to the stable where he lived. Five witnesses later told of how they had seen Gilbert and the little girl walking through the streets hand in hand. Once inside the stable Gilbert attempted to molest Alice Sterling. When she offered resistance, however, he abandoned his original purpose. Then he killed the girl by splitting her head open with an axe. He carried her body down into the stable's earthen cellar and buried it there. Four days later police managed to trace the victim's movements. The trail led to Gilbert's stable and a careful search of the place yielded evidence of foul play. A further search uncovered the body of Alice Sterling. The killer never admitted the crime outright; he preferred to claim a lapse of memory during the time in question. He was hanged at the Suffolk County jail on February 21, 1896.

Kaspar Hartlein, white, age 39. *Murder.* The crime was committed on February 29, 1896, at Manchester, Connecticut. One and a half miles west of the Manchester Town Hall laid the farm of Frederick Trebbe. The property consisted of a house set on 13 fertile acres, the whole of which fronted on Center Street. Farmer Trebbe was a widower with two adult daughters. The younger daughter, Emma Trebbe Ward, was herself a widow. The elder daughter, Louise Marie Trebbe (white, age 35), was a maiden woman. In the winter of 1895 Frederick Trebbe died of natural causes. Since his daughter Emma had been left financially secure by the estate of her late husband, Frederick Trebbe sought to provide for his other daughter by willing his farm to her. So it was that the farm of Frederick Trebbe was passed along to Louise Marie Trebbe. Soon Emma Trebbe Ward joined her sister there and together the two women carried on the family enterprise.

It so happened that Frederick Trebbe had employed a farmhand named Kaspar Hartlein. Having been raised on a farm in his native Bavaria, this Hartlein was well suited to his occupation. He saw to his duties with expertise and was looked upon favorably by his employer. When Frederick Trebbe died his daughters sought a suitable man to manage the farm. Kaspar Hartlein was the natural choice and he willingly accepted the assignment. Then he began to get grandiose ideas. Knowing that Louise Marie Trebbe was an eligible bachelorette, he conceived the desire to marry her and thereby promote himself from servant to master. Hartlein accordingly did everything he could think of in order to

ingratiate himself to Louise Marie Trebbe. However, when he finally got up the nerve to propose marriage he was told that such a proposal was quite out of the question. Having thus made one mistake, Hartlein then proceeded to make another; he went on a jaunt to Hartford and returned home with the smell of liquor on him. This was more than his employers could bear; the women were fanatic teetotalers and they told Hartlein there and then that his services would no longer be needed. After several days, however, Hartlein managed to sweet-talk his way back into his former position. He apologized for his conduct and solemnly promised to abstain from strong drink. In the weeks that followed, Hartlein kept his word as far as alcohol was concerned. However, he once again began to pester Louise Marie Trebbe with talk of marriage. When his importuning reached a point where it could no longer be tolerated, the Trebbe sisters decided that they had had enough of Hartlein. They wanted to fire him outright but feared that he might turn spiteful and burn down the farm. So the situation dragged on. The final straw came on the above date when Hartlein dared to put his hands on Louise Marie Trebbe. She sternly rebuked him whereupon he became angry and ran her through the heart with a butcher knife. Hartlein fled from the scene but a search party found him hiding in a haystack. He was charged with capital murder based on a remark that he had once made to the decedent: "If you don't marry me you will marry no one." Such was taken as evidence of premeditation. Hartlein pleaded guilty and accepted his fate. He was hanged at the Connecticut State Prison on December 3, 1896.

1897

Thomas Kippie, white, age 41. *Murder.* The crime was committed on January 31, 1896, at New Haven, Connecticut. This man was a Scotch immigrant and a brazier by trade. He lived at No. 24 Silver Street in New Haven with his wife, Mary Zeek Kippe (white, age 35). Both were alcoholics known throughout their neighborhood for nasty quarrels. Thomas Kippe was fined several times for disturbing the peace with drunken tantrums. He had also been arrested for beating his wife. Mary Kippe's conduct was no better. She drank even more than her husband and was once reported to have left the man tied to his bedposts for 24 hours. She also engaged in fistfights with her spouse.

In 1891 Thomas Kippie left New Haven to seek a better life elsewhere. He found a good-paying job in Ohio and made plans to settle there permanently. The situation took a turn for the worse when Kippie sent money to his wife and asked her to join him in Ohio. Instead of using the money to pay for moving expenses, Mary Kippie squandered it all on liquor. She was therefore unable to join her husband. When Thomas Kippie learned of what his wife had done with his money he became extremely angry. Returning to New Haven, he moved back in with his wife amid scenes that were far from harmonious. From that day on the couple's life together was one long argument. On the evening of the above date Thomas Kippie was drunk as usual. Mary Kippie was working in the kitchen with a female lodger when her husband walked in and said that he would like to speak with her in private. Since there was nothing menacing in Kippie's tone the woman agreed to step outside with him. No sooner did she do so, however, than her husband began slashing at her with a knife. Mrs. Kippie ran for her life but her husband chased her down. She was stabbed seven times in the breast and died at the scene. The killer went back into his house and put on warm clothing. Then he calmly walked up the street. By then, however,

a crowd had gathered. Kippie was forcibly detained and held for the police. His only words upon being arrested were, "Well, I've done it this time!" When his case came to trial Kippie was capitally convicted. An appeal failed and so did a bid for clemency. The end came on July 14, 1897, when Thomas Kippie was hanged at the Connecticut State Prison.

Giuseppe Fuda, white, age 31. **Nicodemo Imposino,** white, age 24. *Murder.* Their crime was committed on February 17, 1897, at East Norwalk, Connecticut. These men were Calabrian immigrants who lived in a tenement on West Cedar Street in Stamford. Imposino made advances to Fuda's wife, Maria Carmelia Fuda (white, age 24), without success. Stung by the rejection, Imposino turned vindictive toward the woman and determined to poison the mind of her husband against her. He fabricated stories about the woman sleeping around and this succeeded in alienating the affections of Giuseppe Fuda. The situation deteriorated until it reached a point where the two men agreed to do away with Mrs. Fuda. On the above date they induced the woman to accompany them on a train ride from Stamford to East Norwalk. They said that they wanted her opinion of a certain factory there where they had job opportunities. After getting off the train the trio proceeded to walk along the railroad tracks for a short distance. Darkness had fallen by then and when they reached a stretch of track that was suitably remote the two men turned on the woman. Imposino held her down while Fuda hacked her about the face and head with a hatchet. Then they left her dead upon the railroad tracks. When the killers returned home Fuda declared that the missing woman had absconded with his money. However, this story was soon disproven by witnesses who had seen him, his wife and Imposino at the Stamford train station that afternoon. With Fuda thus caught in a lie, the killers decided to flee. Fuda was later nabbed in the "Little Italy" section of Manhattan by the celebrated Italian detective Joseph Petrosino. The other culprit, Imposino, was caught near Buffalo, New York, as he was about to cross over into Canada. Both men blamed each other for the crime. While in detention they grew to hate each other. After they were cast for their lives they extracted a promise from the authorities that they would not be buried in the same cemetery. Fuda died on the gallows at the Connecticut State Prison on December 3, 1897. His accomplice, Imposino, met the same fate on December 17, 1897.

1898

Jack O'Neil, white, age 26. *Murder.* The crime was committed on January 8, 1897, at Shelburne Falls, Massachusetts. The eldest of 13 children, this offender bore a bad reputation in and around his hometown of Shelburne Falls. He had once worked as a railroad brakeman but he lost that job because of a drinking problem. After sulking for a while he applied to a cutlery mill and was taken on as a machinist. However, he soon drank his way out of that job as well. At the time of his capital crime O'Neil was unemployed and low on money.

Another resident of Shelburne Falls was the widow Hattie Crittenden McCloud (white, age 37). She lived in a cottage on the Buckland Road along with her nine-year-old daughter. Originally from New Haven, she had come to Franklin County in order to be closer to her parents following the death of her husband. On the above date this Hattie McCloud visited the shopping district in Shelburne Falls. Early in the evening she set out for home on foot, carrying her purchases in a bundle. Jack O'Neil caught sight of her as she headed out of town. He noted that the woman was alone and that her route was devoid of street lamps. He decided to follow her at a discreet distance. When Hattie McCloud reached a point on Buckland Road that was a mile out of town, O'Neil made his move. He attacked the woman and overpowered her. Then he dragged her into a thicket where he strangled her with his bare hands. When the woman was dead the killer searched her person for valuables. He found $13 in money. Not satisfied, O'Neil next groped around the private areas of the woman's body hoping to find an additional stash of money. In such a way his hands came into contact with the decedent's breasts, etc. This caused the killer to become sexually aroused. Soon he added rape and necrophilia to his list of crimes.

On the following day Hattie McCloud's parents became worried. They had been baby-sitting their granddaughter and were puzzled as to why the child's mother had not come for her as expected. When the grandparents walked the child home they were further disconcerted to find the place empty. There was no sign of Hattie McCloud. It was then decided to retrace the route which the missing woman would have taken to and from Shelburne Falls. A search party proceeded along the Buckland Road until it came to a spot where there were many footprints in the snow. Hattie McCloud's father noticed a track in the snow which looked as if someone had dragged something into some roadside bushes. Following the track, he soon came upon the frozen body of his daughter. The coroner was notified and he ordered that the fully clothed corpse be brought to the Buckland Town Hall. There a formal inquest was held. Robbery was apparent from the start because the decedent was picked clean of valuables. When the body was undressed, however, the signs of sexual assault were unmistakable. For some reason the killer had taken the time and effort to carefully put the victim's clothes back on her after he had satisfied his baser instincts.

The crime was solved in the following manner: The shopping district of Shelburne Falls was canvassed by detectives. They managed to identify the stores which the dead woman had patronized on the last day of her life. At one store the merchant recalled that Mrs. McCloud had given him a $20 dollar bill for a smaller purchase. Among the change given by the merchant was a five-dollar gold piece which bore a peculiar blemish on one side. Since gold coins were not traded as commonly as other coins, all the storekeepers of Shelburne Falls and vicinity were asked to keep an eye out for any customer who paid with gold. During the next several days reports of such transactions trickled in to the lawmen. All were carefully checked but none of the gold coins thus examined matched the one which detectives had in mind. Then came a lucky break; a saloonkeeper had taken in a five-dollar gold piece from a tippler named Jack O'Neil. When the detectives looked at the coin they knew that they had their man. O'Neil was taken in for questioning. He was unable to satisfactorily explain how he had acquired the blemished coin. Neither could he account for his whereabouts at the time of the murder. The more he tried to talk his way out of the situation the more meshed he became in his own falsehoods. Soon the evidence against him mounted even further. It was enough to convince a jury of his guilt. The end came on January 7, 1898, when Jack O'Neil was hanged at the Franklin County jail.

Lorenzo Barnes, white, age 42. *Murder.* The crime was committed on December 17, 1896, at Maynard, Massachusetts. This offender was an alcoholic farmhand. In the days preceding the above date he found himself without money. He was reduced to borrowing small sums in order to survive. When he reached a point where no one would

extend him further credit he became desperate. Being familiar with most of the farms in the Acton-Maynard area, Barnes reasoned that at least one of them would be vulnerable to robbery. After considering every possibility, he settled on an elderly planter named John Deane (white, age 75), who resided about a mile north of Maynard on the Acton Road. Barnes knew that farmer Deane was usually alone in his house during the afternoon hours. He also knew that Deane had some money about the place. Determined to obtain those funds, Barnes entered the Deane farmhouse and attacked its owner with an axe. John Deane was hacked to death in his kitchen and robbed of whatever monies he had on his person. The crime was discovered several hours later when the victim's grown children came home from their jobs. Lorenzo Barnes became a suspect when he was reported to have been seen near the Deane farm at around the time in question. He was also reported to have suddenly paid off his numerous debts. An attempt to link Barnes with bloody footprints at the crime scene was stymied when he was found in the act of slaughtering swine at yet another nearby farm. However, a search of his person revealed cash and several printed receipts bearing the name of the murdered man. Barnes tried to explain away that evidence by saying that he had found the receipts together with a five-dollar bill not far from the Deane farm. His story was not believed and he was charged with capital murder. Although he protested his innocence throughout a trial and several appeals, Barnes was unsuccessful in attempts to dodge the gallows. When he finally realized that all was lost he broke down and admitted his guilt. He was hanged at the Middlesex County jail on March 4, 1898.

Charles Boinay, white, age 33. *Murder.* The crime was committed on July 22, 1897, at Trumbull, Connecticut.

George Marcus Nichols (white, age 64) was an unabashed miser who lived in a rundown house on Daniels Farm Road with a spinster sister named Mary Nichols (white, age 58). Between the two of them these siblings had amassed a fortune of nearly $100,000 which was rumored to be stashed in their house. Among those who heard such talk were a pair of wastrels named Charles Boinay and David Weeks. They were men of no set occupation who resided in a house not far away from the Nichols homestead. Living primarily on the proceeds of chicanery, this pair used to travel around in search of likely places to rob. When they heard rumors of wealth in an unguarded house in their own locale, however, they found the lure to be irresistible. Boinay and Weeks waited for a night when the weather was especially inclement. Then they armed themselves with revolvers and walked the five miles from their home to that of George and Mary Nichols. At first they hid in a nearby barn and watched the house intently. When they were satisfied as to the layout of the place they proceeded to make their move. They broke down the back door of the house and opened fire on the inhabitants. George Nichols was mortally wounded by a shot through the body. His sister was grazed on the neck and shoulder. Then the intruders began a general search for valuables. They did not find the rumored hoard for which they had come and reasoned that it must be hidden. So they resolved to torture the injured victims into revealing its whereabouts. When they tried to rouse George Nichols they found him already dead. So they turned their attention to his sister and threatened her with death unless she came up with some money. The women then told the killers where gold coins and paper currency lay concealed together with non-negotiable securities. The revelation that the Nichols fortune consisted primarily of stocks and bonds was a disappointment to Boinay and Weeks.

However, they were placated by about $200 in cash which they seized. Then they decided to celebrate there at the scene of the crime. They took food and drink from the farmhouse pantry and sat down to a leisurely meal. They were not disturbed by the presence of a dead man in the dining room. When the killers finished their repast they each gave Mary Nichols a kiss and bid her good night. Then they fled from the scene.

The screams of Mary Nichols and the gunshots of her assailants both went unheard by neighbors because of the torrential rain that was falling at the time. It was not until several hours later — after the sun had come up — that an alarm was raised. Although faint from loss of blood, Mary Nichols managed to make her way to a nearby house and tell what had happened. By then the bandits were long gone. When police finally arrived at the scene they at once noted certain similarities to a string of home invasions that had lately occurred in Dutchess County, New York. Two suspects came to mind: Charles Boinay and David Weeks. Both managed to get out of town before they could be arrested. They remained at large for three months but were finally caught by a stakeout team which watched a place that they were known to frequent.

In order to save his own neck, David Weeks agreed to testify against his accomplice. The fact that Boinay was also his brother-in-law did not deter Weeks. The turncoat swore that Boinay was the one who had fired all of the gunshots in the Nichols house. A jury accepted the testimony and brought in a capital conviction against Charles Boinay. The penalty was death. On April 14, 1898, the gallows was made ready at the Connecticut State Prison. Charles Boinay was allowed to play the clarinet during his final hours. He even had a clarinet solo recorded so that his music would survive him. Then he was brought to the execution chamber and hanged.

Alfred Williams, white, age 21. *Murder.* The crime was committed on July 28, 1897, at Lynnfield, Massachusetts. This offender was a robust Canadian youth who was born and raised on Prince Edward Island. In the spring of 1897 he left his native place and wandered southward. He eventually came to Essex County, Massachusetts, and decided that that was as good a place as any in which to settle down. A Lynnfield farmer gave him a job and so it was that Williams met one John Gullo (white, age 24), a young roustabout like himself. This Gullo was a conspicuous person about the Lynnfield farm; he had a roistering personality and a bad habit of showing off his money. He was known to carry $20 gold pieces on his person plus a thick wad of paper currency. When Williams saw those funds with his own eyes he formed thoughts of murder. Thinking that Gullo's cash would enable him to finance a long-held dream of going to Alaska, he became more determined than ever to turn his thoughts into deeds. It so happened that Gullo lived alone in a wooden shanty on the Lynnfield farm. During the pre-dawn hours of the above date Williams crept into that abode and attacked Gullo. A desperate hand-to-hand battle followed. Gullo was eventually overpowered and knocked unconscious. Then Williams took his money and set fire to his dwelling. When other residents of the farm ran to the scene they were able to clearly see Gullo lying inert upon the floor of the burning shanty. However, they could not get close enough to save him because of the intense heat. When the fire finally burned itself out only Gullo's head remained uncharred and that bore unmistakable signs of violence. When the sun came up a battered looking Alfred Williams wandered into a police station and said that he had been mugged. Hence his beaten-up appearance. He also told an improbable story of finding a cashbox containing $75 by the roadside. This tale was doubted from the moment it was told. Far more likely, police agreed, was another scenario: that the $75 had belonged to John Gullo and that Williams had been bloodied in a fight over it. The clincher came when police searched the room in which Williams lived; two $20 gold pieces were found hidden near his bed. In addition, another $75 in paper money was found upon Williams himself. It was quite a cache for one who had complained only the previous day of not having so much as a dime to pay for a shave. Williams denied the crime and he continued to deny it right to the bitter end. He was hanged at the Essex County jail on October 7, 1898.

Dominique Krathofski, white, age 29. *Murder.* The crime was committed on January 17, 1897, at Springfield, Massachusetts. This man was a Polish immigrant who lived in a crowded tenement at No. 73 Sharon Street in Springfield. A contemporary news account describes the residents of that address as "the worst elements of the city's population." Krathofski himself is described as "a worthless loafer" who was "brutish" and "repulsive looking." He had been accustomed to using his teenaged stepdaughter as a sex slave. His conduct scandalized even his fellow tenement dwellers and they reported him to the police on more than one occasion. Aside from that, little was done to restrain him. On the morning of the above date Krathofski awoke in a randy mood and once again attempted to force himself on his stepdaughter. The girl protested (as she always had done), whereupon Krathofski pulled out a handgun and shot her dead. After that the killer attempted suicide by shooting himself in the head but the wound proved to be more messy than serious. His angry wife attacked him with a stick and he ran out of the house. Police found him staggering down Main Street covered with blood.

The murdered girl was identified as Victoria Pinkos (white, age 16). She was dead by the time police reached the scene of the crime. When the case came to trial Krathofski was capitally convicted and ordered for execution. On December 30, 1898, he was hanged at the Hampden County jail, located in his hometown of Springfield.

Benjamin Willis, white, age 21. *Murder.* The crime was committed on December 17, 1897, at Wilton, Connecticut. In order to understand this complicated case it is necessary to retrace its antecedents.

During the last years of the 19th century Dr. David Samuel Rogers Lambert (white, age 45) was one of the most esteemed citizens of lower Fairfield County. His forebears had been among the first settlers of the town of Wilton where in the year 1715 they built a large homestead. The structure still stands at the intersection of the Norwalk and Westport highways (present-day routes 7 and 33). David Lambert was born there on January 23, 1852. It was also there where he was raised. As a young man he attended Yale University. He also traveled extensively before accepting a teaching position in Washington, D.C. In 1880 he inherited his ancestral home and decided to return to Wilton. There he made improvements to the Lambert property and in the following year announced the opening of Wilton Academy, a select boarding school for privileged young gentlemen. Success attended Lambert's efforts almost from the start. Within a matter of weeks he was operating at full enrollment. By the end of the academy's first year it had gained a favorable reputation far beyond its immediate locale. Upscale New York families were impressed by the high academic standards and attractive country setting. By the academy's fourth year there were even boys from foreign countries among the student body. By the end of the fifth year the headmaster decided that a woman's touch was needed. He therefore sought a suitable consort with whom he could share his personal affection as well as the burden of management. She was Miss Eva L. Ogden (white, age 33) and on September 15, 1886, she became Mrs. Eva Ogden Lambert, wife of Dr. David S.R. Lambert and mistress of Wilton Academy.

Shortly after the Lambert wedding a high-priced New York lawyer came to Wilton Academy. He told the Lamberts that he represented a wealthy banker (in reality a dentist) and that he had been engaged to approach them on a matter of delicacy. Some years earlier, he explained, his client had committed an "indiscretion" with a chorus girl. A child had been born of that "indiscretion"—a boy—for whom the father wished to provide without compromising his good name. If the Lamberts would accept the lad into their school on a year-round boarding basis, said the lawyer, they would be paid well above their usual price of tuition. The Lamberts considered the proposal and were at first inclined to reject it. They disliked the furtiveness of the matter and were further disappointed to learn that the boy was only ten years old—well below the usual age of their students. It was out of politeness more than anything else that they agreed to a second interview at which the boy himself would be present. A few days later the lawyer returned to Wilton Academy with the boy. He introduced him as young Ben Willis and from that moment on the matter was decided. As Mrs. Lambert later said: "He was the most winsome little fellow we had ever met and he was so very pretty besides. We just could not find it in our hearts to turn him away. We decided there and then to make special accommodations for him." So it was that Benjamin Willis enrolled at Wilton Academy. In order to spare him the stigma of bastardy a story was circulated that his parents were missionaries traveling abroad. The other students called him "Baby Benny" and for the next two years all went well. What the Lamberts did not realize at the time was that they had made the worst mistake of their lives.

Baby Benny's expenses were initially paid out of a trust fund set up by his father and managed by the aforementioned lawyer. A generous monthly stipend was also paid to the boy's mother on the condition that she have no contact with him while he attended school. For two years this arrangement continued without incident. Young Ben Willis thrived at Wilton Academy. Then late in the winter of 1888 — during the time of the "Great Snow" — matters took a turn for the worse. Ben's father died of a heart attack and his mother began to involve herself with him contrary to instructions. She began slowly. When the "Great Snow" melted in the spring of 1888 a heavily veiled woman in a handsome carriage was seen near the Wilton Academy campus. As the weather improved she was seen with greater frequency. On several occasions she stopped and spoke with Ben Willis. The Lamberts were aware of this but they chose to benignly look the other way. They knew that the mysterious woman was Ben's mother and they did not have the heart to deny her some private moments with her child. Then one day the boy ran away from the academy. He was absent for more than a week and when he finally returned he was a changed person. He refused to tell where he had gone but it was strongly suspected that his mother was involved.

It so happened that Ben's mother had ended her relationship with his father some years earlier. When age rendered her no longer fit to be a chorus girl she moved to the Tenderloin district of Manhattan where she set herself up as a self-described "clairvoyant." Later accounts allege that that was merely a front for a more sordid calling: that of a brothel manager. Her name was Alice Perkins but she was known to everyone by the sobriquet of Madam Louise.

Such was the person who reentered the life of Ben Willis following the untimely death of his father. Although a corrupt woman, Madam Louise was not a truly *evil* one. She sincerely loved her son. That much must be said in her defense. She wanted what was best for Ben and she personally paid his Wilton Academy expenses when the trust fund terminated. What she failed to realize and even worse, failed to control, was the bad influence of her environment on the boy. Whenever he visited his mother he found himself the pampered darling of a bordello, doted on by prostitutes and others of low caliber. Soon he learned the ways of such people and as he grew older he began to emulate them. This brought his behavior into direct conflict with the prim and proper ways of Wilton Academy. In September of 1888, when he returned to the school from a summer vacation, the change in him was evident. He was cunning and devious. He was also annoyingly precocious. He began to steal from his classmates and cheat at his studies. He organized prize fights among the boys and smuggled contraband to them. He lied, used foul language and was disrespectful of authority. The final straw came in the autumn of 1890 when Ben was nearly 15 years old. Late one night he took Professor Lambert's horse from its stable without permission and raced it all the way to Danbury and back. The animal was found the next day in a wretched condition and the headmaster lost his temper. He gave Ben Willis a severe thrashing and expelled him from the academy.

Willis did not go straight home to his mother. By then a well-developed and handsome fellow, he moved in with a married woman down the street from the school. He had been carrying on with her for some time. When he dared to flaunt the affair openly, however, he was literally run out of town. Several days later he was allowed to return in order to pack up his belongings. He then bilked his benefactress out of a considerable sum of money and caught a train to New York.

Over the course of the next seven years Ben Willis went from bad to worse. He refused to get a job and lived primarily on his mother's largess. Whenever that source of income ran low he would resort to stealing. He also became addicted to his mother's female employees. One day he wandered into Central Park and met a slightly younger fellow, a handsome German youth named Frederick "Max" Brockhaus. It so happened that this Brockhaus was the type who was easily led. When he spoke with the wily Ben Willis he immediately gravitated to him. So it was that a symbiosis was born. Brockhaus and Willis agreed to team up with each other. Willis used more than force of will and persuasive manners to get over on Brockhaus. He would ply his friend with liquor whenever he planned some illegal act. In addition, he used sex as a lure; Brockhaus was introduced to Madam Louise's courtesans and promptly fell in love with one of them. From then on Brockhaus was completely dominated by Willis.

In December of 1897 Willis was staying with Brockhaus in the latter's apartment. Money was short and the two strained their brains trying to think of who they could rob. Willis suggested that they pounce on the landlady there after she collected the rents. They discarded that idea, however, when they deemed it unwise to jeopardize the roof over their heads. Then they toyed with a plan to go over to Brooklyn and break into the house of Willis's paternal grandparents. This they also decided against for various reasons. Finally Willis thought of his old school and the resentment that he still felt for the headmaster of that place. Failing health had forced Professor Lambert to close the place in 1894

but he and his wife still lived on the premises. Willis thought that they were vulnerable. So he and his partner decided to go up to Connecticut and raid the former Wilton Academy.

It is significant to note that the thought of finding honest jobs and legitimate sources of income did not occur to either Brockhaus or Willis.

On the following day — December 17, 1897 — Brockhaus and Willis rose early. After breakfast they sparred with each other in a boxing ring for exercise. Then they went shopping. At different stores they purchased a bottle of whiskey, a bottle of chloroform (by means of a falsified prescription) and two black masks. They also armed themselves with cheap handguns. Both wore winter overcoats and derby hats. One of them carried a black valise. In the afternoon they boarded a shoreline train to Connecticut. They got off the train in Norwalk and went into a saloon where Willis plied Brockhaus with liquor. By the time they finished drinking, the short December day was waning. They then got on a northbound trolley and rode it to the end of the line at a place called Winnipauk Station, the site of the present-day Merritt Seven office park. By then night had fallen. Upon exiting the trolley they walked the remaining two and a half miles across the town line into Wilton. Both of them nipped from their bottle of whiskey along the way.

At the former Wilton Academy meanwhile, Mrs. Lambert had dinner ready and was awaiting the return of her husband from a shopping trip. As she sat in the parlor reading her mail her attention was drawn to the sound of footsteps on the wooden porch outside. Then came a knock at the door. Mrs. Lambert surmised it to be her husband weighed down with parcels so she opened the door without reservation. She was then confronted by two masked men.

"We want something to eat!" demanded one of the men.

"I have nothing to give you!" said the woman.

"Then we want some money!" said the intruder.

"There isn't any money in the house." said Mrs. Lambert.

"We'll see about that!" snapped the man.

Then the one who had done the talking, Willis, bade his accomplice to cover him with his gun while he grabbed ahold of Mrs. Lambert.

"Oh Christ! Have you a mother?" gasped the woman.

"Shut up or we'll kill you!" said the robber. Then he told the other man to pass him the bottle of chloroform. By that time Brockhaus was so drunk that he passed him the bottle of whiskey instead.

"Please don't chloroform me!" begged Mrs. Lambert. "Take the silverware and go!"

Willis then tried to wrap a cord around the woman's wrists.

"You shan't do that!" yelled Mrs. Lambert and she began to struggle. Then she blew out an oil lamp on a nearby table. That plunged the whole room into darkness.

"God damn it!" shouted Willis. "Get the bitch!"

Then both men seized Mrs. Lambert. They overpowered her, tied her up and threw her on the floor. Willis held her down while Brockhaus soaked a rag with chloroform and forced it onto her face. The woman lost consciousness for a moment but then awoke. The bandits then jammed a potato into her mouth, gagged her with a rag and chloroformed her again. Then they sat her groggy form in a chair and tied her ankles and wrists to the arms and legs of the chair. They also gave her another dose of chloroform to make sure she was unconscious. Brockhaus used that opportunity to paw the woman's breasts and do other obscene things to her while Willis ran upstairs and began ransacking the bedrooms.

It was then that Professor Lambert returned from his shopping trip. He was apparently puzzled to see all of the lights on in his house because he pulled his wagon right up to the porch without tethering the horse. When he opened the door and walked inside, the jumpy Brockhaus opened fire on him. Willis then came running to the scene from the second floor and also shot at the injured man. Nine shots were fired in all. Professor Lambert was hit in the side, in a leg, in an arm and in the head. He crashed to the floor mortally wounded. The robbers then pounced on him and rifled his pockets. They took his watch and a small amount of money. Their other booty consisted of two silver watches, two gold pens, a pair of razors, an ivory shoe horn, an ivory button hook and a jewel-handled knife. They did not touch the extensive collection of silverware that had been the pride of Wilton Academy. Mrs. Lambert emerged from her stupor just long enough to hear the gunshots. The robbers saw her stir and they forced more chloroform on her. Then they ran out of the house and jumped onto the professor's wagon. Willis grabbed the reins and frantically lashed the horse. At once they tore out of the schoolyard and onto the highway, breaking off part of a barbed wire fence in the process which they trailed behind them all along their route. Some barrels of coal and turnips which were in the wagon also overturned so that their contents spilled and marked the path of the fleeing vehicle.

More than an hour passed before Mrs. Lambert was able to shake off the effects of the chloroform. She wriggled free of her restraints and stumbled over her husband's body. Feeling the presence of blood about him, she feared the worst. Then she staggered out of the house and made her way to the nearest neighbor. Those people placed Mrs. Lambert in the care of their womenfolk while the men armed themselves and hurried to the scene of the crime. They found Professor Lambert weltering in a pool of blood. Brain matter oozed from his head. The entire house had been looted and the victims' horse and wagon were missing. One man ran for a doctor while another rang the bell of a nearby church to sound the general alarm. Others ran through the streets shouting "Murder! Murder! Horrid Murder!" Soon the entire district was aroused. More than a hundred armed men hastened to the scene. They blocked the roads in an effort to catch the killers who by then had escaped.

The next day investigators were able to trace the route of the fleeing wagon. It had raced toward Westport at a high rate of speed, running two or three other wagons off the road in the process. Then when it reached the Boston Post Road it turned west and headed into Norwalk. A trail of debris marked its route. The wagon was finally found abandoned at the South Norwalk train station. The horse was exhausted and bore the marks of repeated lashing. It soon became apparent that the killers had escaped by train before the alarm had reached South Norwalk.

It was Mrs. Lambert who provided crucial information. When she had finally regained her composure she said that she knew the identity of one of the masked killers. "It was Ben Willis," she said, "a former student of ours. I'd know his voice anywhere. The other one was a stranger."

The next day newspapers from New York to New Haven blared the name of Ben Willis. The town of Wilton even put a price on his head. A couple of days later when it was announced that the killers had in all likelihood fled beyond Connecticut, concerned citizens demanded that the Pinkerton Detective Agency be brought into the case.

The killers, meanwhile, did not stay idle. When they saw the newspapers on the day after the crime they decided to flee. On that same day they crossed over to New Jersey and jumped a southbound freight train. In Philadelphia they pawned Professor Lambert's watch and then continued on to Baltimore. From there they went to Virginia. Then they turned westward and headed for the Appalachian Mountains. They eventually made their way to Chicago where they decided to split up. Brockhaus had a brother there with whom he took refuge. As for Willis, he assumed a false identity and contacted his mother. She in turn wired money to him and gave him instructions to assist him in his flight. He was told to go to a maternal aunt who in turn sent him to another address in Columbus, Ohio. There he was told to wait until his mother sent him the necessary funds with which to leave the country.

Madam Louise also played a shrewd game in order to mislead detectives. It then being a time of anti–Spanish sentiment in the United States, she decided to make use of the same. She sent a private detective to Connecticut with instructions to spread disinformation. A false story was circulated to the effect that the Lambert murder had actually been committed by some Latino laborers who dwelled not far from the scene of the crime. Such then being the mood of the public, anything anti–Spanish was readily believed and the false story proved to be no exception. This was too much for a Cuban gentleman named Joseph Freyre, himself a Latino and alumnus of Wilton Academy. He became annoyed when he heard the aspersions cast upon his countrymen and he decided to act. He went to the sheriff of Fairfield County and told him everything he knew about Ben Willis. The revelations — which were substantial — were in turn passed along to the Pinkertons. Before long detectives had photographs of Ben Willis, the names and addresses of his acquaintances and — above all — the name and address of his crafty mother. She in turn was shadowed by Pinkerton men until she contacted her son. By such means were the assumed name and the whereabouts of Ben Willis ascertained.

Exactly ten weeks after the murder Brockhaus was seized in Chicago. He was eating dinner with his brother when police burst in on him. Two days later Willis was traced to his hiding place in Ohio and taken into custody. Both suspects were roughly handled by the Pinkertons until they each made lengthy confessions. From then on their fates were sealed.

The hangman came for Ben Willis on the frigid morning of December 30, 1898. The scene was the Connecticut State Prison. At precisely 12:20 A.M. the gallows mechanism was set in motion. A 418-pound weight hung suspended from one end of a rope that passed through an overhead beam and fit its other end snugly around the neck of the condemned man. When the weight fell Ben Willis was jerked seven feet into the air and was left there to hang until he was dead. After 11 minutes and 34 seconds he was lowered into a coffin. Then a New York City undertaker claimed his body. Early the next day the remains were brought to Mount Olivet Cemetery in Maspeth, Queens, and there buried without ceremony in an unmarked grave.

And what of Madam Louise? Five weeks later she too was dead. The sight of her son in a death row cell was too much for her to bear. She collapsed from a nervous breakdown and did not recover. Her death certificate gives an ambiguous casus morti. On February 11, 1899, the grave of Ben Willis was opened and the coffin of his mother was placed on top of his. Madam Louise was 52 years old.

1899

Frederick Brockhaus, white, age 20. *Murder.* The crime was committed on December 17, 1897, at Wilton, Connecticut. This offender was the accomplice of the aforementioned Benjamin Willis [1898] in the robbery-murder of Professor David Samuel Rogers Lambert. He was tried separately from Willis for the same crime. Brockhaus himself was a German immigrant. He was born in a village near Dresden and came to the United States as a teenager in 1895. At the time of his capital crime he lived with his parents at No. 105 West 62nd Street in Manhattan. One day in the summer of 1898 he met Ben Willis in Central Park and struck up a friendship with him. It was a fateful encounter. From that time on he and Willis were constant companions. Brockhaus was hanged at the Connecticut State Prison on September 6, 1899. His family being poor and unable to afford the services of an undertaker, the warden of the state prison saw that "Max" received a decent burial. [See Willis — 1898.]

1900

Charles Cross, white, age 17. *Murder.* The crime was committed on November 7, 1899, at Stamford, Connecticut. This juvenile offender came from Brooklyn, New York, where he had been raised amid squalid conditions. His mother was a prostitute who drank herself to death and his father was a mental defective of equally dissipated habits. Charles Cross was orphaned at the age of seven and sent to a home for abandoned children. There he endured a steady regimen of malnutrition, cruelty and sexual abuse. His own grandmother described him as a chronic liar, a thief, a satyr and a chainsmoker. Early in the year 1899 a prosperous New York printer named Freeman King came to the orphanage where Charles Cross resided and told the director thereof that he was looking for a houseboy. He explained that he owned a country home near Stamford, Connecticut, that his wife summered there and that he needed a suitable young man to keep up with the chores thereabouts. He also said that he felt it would be a civil thing to extend such an opportunity to a disadvantaged youth. After examining several prospects Mr. King selected Charles Cross. Accordingly the young man relocated to Stamford. He went about his duties admirably and when the summer ended Mr. King decided to retain him in his position. Cross in the meantime had successfully managed to conceal his vices from his employers. Mr. and Mrs. King allowed him his cigarettes but otherwise had no inkling of his personal history. By November of 1899 young Cross could no longer restrain his well-developed sexual appetite. Tired of manual relief, he began to regard Mrs. King with more than passing glances. On the above date Cross was alone at the Stamford estate with his employer's wife. Although Sarah King (white, age 60) was more than three times his age, the randy youth decided that she would suit his needs. He concealed himself in the woman's bedroom and waited for her to retire for the night. When Mrs. King came upstairs and shut herself up in her chamber, Cross sprang from a closet all nude and attacked her. He knocked the woman to the floor and repeatedly banged her head against the stone sill of the fireplace. In such a way he overpowered her. Then he stripped the woman naked and rolled her onto her bed. What happened next is unprintable. When Cross had had his fill of sexual perversion he battered Mrs. King to death with a coal shovel. Then he ran out of the house and made his way to the nearest neighbor. There he gasped out a story about he and Mrs. King being attacked by burglars. When detectives examined the crime scene they at once suspected that the "burglary" had been contrived. The physical evidence did not support the story told by Cross. The houseboy was

arrested and held on suspicion of murder. Five days later he confessed what he had done. When some of the more depraved details of the crime became known those in favor of clemency shrank to a precious few. Age alone was not enough to save Charles Cross. He was hanged at the Connecticut State Prison on July 20, 1900.

1901

Luigi Storti, white, age 36. *Murder.* The crime was committed on November 7, 1899, at Boston, Massachusetts. Luigi Storti and Michele Calucci (white, age 30) were Italian immigrants who came from the same small village. While still in the old country they were rivals for the hand of a certain young woman. Since both men were poor the woman did not look upon them favorably. Instead, she bade each of them to seek their fortunes in America and she further added that she would be pleased to receive the man who met those terms. Storti and Calucci both accepted the quest and they set out for the New World. They eventually settled at Boston, taking rooms at No. 57 Charter Street. Both got jobs with the Department of Public Works and were assigned to a road repair crew. Long months of hard labor followed. Calucci managed to save up $200 and proudly reported that fact in a letter to his sweetheart. In reply, the young woman declared herself satisfied and she accepted Calucci's proposal of marriage. When Calucci received a letter containing that news he exchanged his money for gold and booked passage on a ship to Italy. However, he could not resist the temptation of bringing the matter to Storti's attention. It was more than Storti could bear. The fact that he was less thrifty than his rival was nettlesome in itself. To that was added jealousy over the woman. The final straw came when Calucci allegedly made obscene remarks about some female members of the Storti family. On the evening of the above date Storti burst into Calucci's room with an axe and hacked his rival to death. So frenzied was the assault that Calucci could not be readily identified by those who found him. Storti fled from the scene but was picked up the following day. He tried to claim self-defense but the fact that Calucci was hacked beyond recognition indicated a baser motive. Luigi Storti was subsequently sent to the Massachusetts State Prison under sentence of death. On December 17, 1901, he died in the electric chair.

Franciszek Umilian, white, age 30. *Murder.* The crime was committed on December 31, 1899, at Granby, Massachusetts. Franciszek Umilian and Casimir Jedrusick (white, age 35) were Polish immigrants who worked for a prosperous farmer named Monroe Keith. Their place of employment was located two miles beyond the center of Granby on the Ludlow Road. Also employed by Mr. Keith was a certain housemaid of whom Umilian was very fond. When Umilian proposed marriage the housemaid accepted and plans were made accordingly. On November 18, 1899, the couple journeyed to a neighboring town to be wed by a priest of their faith. However, a rude surprise awaited them there: the priest told of having received an anonymous letter alleging that Umilian had abandoned a wife and children in the Old Country. Under such circumstances, said the priest, no wedding could be performed. The charge contained in the letter would first have to be satisfactorily disproven. Umilian asseverated his innocence of the allegation and the priest did agree to have an agent check on the matter and report back to him. Inquiries were then made in the Polish community and Casimir Jedrusick was found to be the author of the egregious letter. A motive

was also revealed when it was reported that Jedrusick bore a grudge against Umilian; it so happened that Umilian had previously taken Jedrusick to task for selling pilfered farm produce. The revelation of a grudge on the part of the letter writer satisfied the priest that the charge against Umilian was baseless. Therefore the marriage was performed. Umilian, however, formed a grudge of his own against Jedrusick. On the above date Umilian waited until his employer had gone to church along with the female residents of the farm. Being left alone with Jedrusick, the angry newlywed attacked him with a corn cutter. Jedrusick suffered severe lacerations before he was overpowered. Then Umilian chopped the man's head off with an axe and cut out his heart with a butcher knife. The head and the heart were buried in separate places after which Umilian trussed up the rest of the body in a bean sack and threw it down a well. During the following week little was thought of Jedrusick's absence due to the man's regular habit of going away to visit friends. When weeks turned into months, however, suspicion of foul play was aroused. Umilian was cast as a likely suspect because of his well-known hatred for the missing man. When the ground thawed out in April local officials ordered a thorough examination of the Keith farm. The headless body of Casimir Jedrusick was found in the well. The dead man's clothes were also found beside him neatly folded in a bundle. Umilian was arrested the same day. He insisted upon his innocence but no one believed him. On December 24, 1901, he was electrocuted at the Massachusetts State Prison.

1902

John Cassels, white, age 37. *Murder.* The crime was committed on February 26, 1901, at Longmeadow, Massachusetts. This man was a Scottish immigrant who sold sewing machines for a living.

Although he was married with four children he was not above ogling his female customers. One such person who especially appealed to him was a comely housewife named Mary Lane (white, age 27). She resided in a boarding house on Bliss Road in Longmeadow together with her husband and three children. Cassels professed devotion to Mrs. Lane and seduced her. Then he sought to take the place of her husband on a permanent basis. Cassels accordingly sent his own wife and children to the British Isles on an extended visit. Then he moved into Mrs. Lane's boarding house. When he felt that he had worked his charms on the woman to a sufficient degree, Cassels next proposed an elopement. In response, Mrs. Lane reportedly indicated willingness to leave her husband but she balked at the idea of abandoning her children. This nettled Cassels. He brooded over the matter and then grew impatient. On the above date he confronted Mrs. Lane in her home and demanded that she come to a decision regarding their relationship. The woman then repeated what she had previously said: that she would not run out on her children. Cassels then pulled a gun on Mrs. Lane in the presence of her children. He fired one shot into her which sent her reeling. After that he stood over the wounded woman and deliberately fired two more shots into her. Then he walked out of the house muttering. When he reached the street Cassel took a bottle of carbolic acid from his pocket and attempted suicide by gulping down its contents. Prompt medical attention saved his life but Mary Lane was beyond help. When the case came to trial Cassels pleaded extreme emotional duress in mitigation of his crime. He also said that the victim had encouraged him in order to make use of his money. This last argument was too much for the jury and it promptly brought in a capital conviction. It may well be that Cassels was condemned not so much for being a killer than for being an adulterer and a home-wrecker. Appeals were disallowed in this case and on May 6, 1902, John Cassels was electrocuted at the Massachusetts State Prison.

John Best, white, age 35. *Murder.* The crime was committed on October 8, 1900, at North Saugus, Massachusetts. John Best and George Bailey (white, age 40) were sharecroppers who worked on a farm on Forest Street in North Saugus. Over a course of time their relationship became strained by petty differences. There were quarrels over work methods, quarrels over work apportionment, quarrels over money and rivalry over a woman. On the above date Best settled matters by shooting Bailey dead with a rifle. Then he took an axe to the decedent's body; he hacked off Bailey's arms, legs and head. Together with the torso, he next did up the individual body parts in burlap bags and loaded them into Bailey's farm wagon. Late at night he drove the wagon out onto a pontoon bridge which spanned Wenuchus Pond, a spring-fed body of water that was said to be bottomless. When he reached the midpoint of the bridge he weighted the gory sacks with stones and heaved them into the water. Then he returned to his farm and gave out a story that Bailey had gone away on vacation. A week later the bag containing the victim's torso broke free of its weights and floated to the surface of Wenuchus Pond. It was spotted by two men passing over the pontoon bridge and fished out of the water. Soon an alarm was raised throughout the area and hundreds of people flocked to the scene. A tentative identification of the remains was made on the same day when some of the gawkers claimed to recognize the clothes which clung to the torso as those of the missing George Bailey. Grappling operations subsequently brought up the bags containing the victim's legs. Whether the remaining body parts were ever found is uncertain. John

Best was fingered as a suspect when he gave evasive answers to an inquiry about his fellow sharecropper. A search of his home also turned up evidence of foul play. In addition, Best was found to have concealed Bailey's pocketwatch with a hidden cache of coins. A jury had no difficulty convicting Best of capital murder. Whether the man's aloof demeanor hurt his case as much as the evidence is debatable. An appeal to the State Supreme Court was rejected without dissent. On September 9, 1902, John Best walked to the electric chair at the Massachusetts State Prison. He remained silent to the last.

1903

Although there are known to have been at least 154 legal executions in the United States of America this year, none of them occurred in the New England states.

1904

Paul Misik, white, age 33. *Murder.* The crime was committed on September 22, 1903, at Newington, Connecticut. This man was a Hungarian immigrant who worked in a stone quarry. On the evening previous to his crime he was drinking in a Hartford saloon with several of his co-workers. During that time Misik accidentally dropped some coins on the floor. His drinking buddies then bent down to pick up the coins. When the money was handed back to its owner Misik charged that 30 cents was missing and he angrily accused one Charles O'Brien (white, age 25) of holding back that amount. O'Brien denied the charge but Misik remained adamant. The next morning the two men met at their place of employment. Misik confronted O'Brien and demanded that he give him 30 cents. At that point O'Brien became annoyed and warned Misik off, saying

that he was lucky not to get a punch in the mouth. Misik then shouted, "I'll get even and show you how a Hunky can shoot!" Then he pulled out a handgun and shot O'Brien dead. Fleeing from the scene, Misik took to the woods. He hid out on Cedar Mountain for three days before hunger induced him to come down. Subsequently convicted of capital murder, Misik was hanged at the Connecticut State Prison on February 11, 1904.

Joseph Watson, alias "Nigger Joe," black, age 18. *Murder.* The crime was committed on August 5, 1904, at Hartford, Connecticut. Henry Osborn (white, age 58) was a prominent citizen of Hartford. He had served three terms as that city's police commissioner and he was viewed as a likely mayoral candidate. He lived in a brick rowhouse at No. 23 Capitol Avenue and employed a Negro houseboy named Joseph Watson. In July of 1904 Osborn and his wife made preparations to go to the seashore for the remainder of the summer. They asked the houseboy to accompany them but Watson refused, saying that he was afraid of the water. It was then that Watson began to neglect his duties about the Osborn home. As a result of that he was dismissed from his employer's service. Three weeks later Watson snuck into the Osborn house through a basement window. He then went to sleep in the servants' quarters. In the morning he arose and went upstairs. Then he confronted Mr. Osborn in his bedroom and shot him three times with a handgun. Osborn was fatally wounded. Later that same day Watson was found hiding in a cellar of the same address. He boldly admitted the crime and said that he was glad of having done it even if he had to hang for it. On November 17, 1904, he did exactly that at the Connecticut State Prison. The African-American community of Hartford issued a public statement saying that it was ashamed of Joseph Watson.

1905

Gershom Marx, white, age 73. *Murder.* The crime was committed on March 20, 1904, at Colchester, Connecticut. This offender was a Russian Jew by nationality and a farmer by profession. He owned a hundred acres in the Chestnut Hill district of Colchester where he lived with four small children and a wife who was young enough to be his granddaughter. When advancing age prevented Marx from being the sole upkeep of his property, he began to employ farmhands on a six-month basis. In September of 1903 he hired a Polish immigrant named Paul Rodecki, alias "Joe Pavol" (white, age 35), with the understanding that the man would have room and board plus $53 in cash payable to him at the expiration of his service. Rodecki served his six months faithfully. He also tolerated squalid living conditions. When his term of service was nearly over, however, he opted not to renew it. This set Marx to brooding; he had been having a cash flow problem and could ill afford to pay Rodecki his wages. In an attempt to extricate himself from the dilemma Marx decided on murder.

On the eve of the farmhand's departure Marx gave the man the money which was due him. Then he waited for Rodecki to fall asleep. When he felt that it was safe for him to do so, Marx crept up on the sleeping man and crushed his skull with an axe. Then he took back the $53. After that he chopped off Rodecki's arms and legs and stuffed the assorted body parts into potato sacks. On the following day Marx lugged the reeking sacks to a disused cellar and attempted to conceal them there by piling stones on top of them. Two weeks later a new farmhand had his curiosity aroused when he saw Marx rolling more stones into the cellar. The man waited until Marx went elsewhere and then poked around in the rock-strewn cellar. He found the remains of his predecessor and became badly frightened. Then he fetched a neighbor and confronted Marx. There followed a nasty scene in which Marx attacked his accusers with a scythe. After that he took to the woods and became an elusive target. For the next ten days heavily armed posses scoured the countryside between Lebanon and Old Lyme. However, Marx gave his pursuers the slip and got safely away to New York. There he was seized by law-abiding members of the Jewish community and turned over to authority.

Marx was subsequently identified as the prime suspect in a second murder: that of a farmhand named Paul Parker, whose butchered remains had turned up on another farm which Marx had worked. Even so, Marx was only charged with the slaying of Paul Rodecki. He was capitally convicted and on May 18, 1905, he was hanged at the Connecticut State Prison. He denied his guilt to the last.

Mary Mabel Rogers, white, age 19 at the time of her crime. *Murder.* The capital offense was committed on August 12, 1902, at Bennington, Vermont. This woman murdered her husband, Marcus Rogers (white, age 32), so she could collect his $600 life insurance payout and also be free to marry another man. She was deeply loved by her husband despite her fickle nature. She tired of living a quiet, respectable life with Marcus Rogers and walked out on him after only several months of matrimony. She then led a promiscuous lifestyle and cultivated a reputation that was nothing short of abominable. Among her many lovers was a 17-year-old half-breed Indian named Leon Perham. He was infatuated with Mary Rogers and hoped to marry her. Mary was aware of his devotion and she deliberately strung him along with false hope. In the meantime she set her sights on a respectable citizen of Bennington but knew that he was out of her league. She then reasoned that if she came into possession of $600 — the amount of her husband's life insurance benefit — her social circumstances would be raised to a point where she would no longer be regarded as a common strumpet. She also reasoned that such an elevation would put her on equal footing with the gentleman she hoped to seduce. Marcus Rogers had previously said that he would forgive Mary if she returned to him. She then decided to feign a reconciliation with her husband in order to lure that man to his doom. Leon Perham became her willing accomplice because he thought that Mary would marry him as soon as she became a widow.

Mary's first move was to write a contrite letter to her husband in which she begged his forgiveness for her past errors. She also professed her love and said that she wished to be reunited. Marcus Rogers was completely fooled by the deceitful letter. He agreed to meet Mary in a Bennington picnic grove on the evening of August 12, 1902.

Mary Rogers came to the rendezvous accompanied by Leon Perham. She greeted her husband with a well-acted show of affection and told him that Perham was just a neighborhood boy who had been nice enough to guide her to the spot. This sounded reasonable because night had fallen by then and the grove was a spooky place after dark. Then as Perham stood off to one side, Mary and Marcus Rogers took a private walk together for the purpose of ironing out their differences. About an hour later they returned to the spot where Perham was waiting for them. Both were in a cheerful mood. Mary Rogers then asked Perham to show her and her husband a shortcut home. Perham then acted a part that he had previously rehearsed; he led Mary and Marcus Rogers along a winding path which brought them to a spot that was both scenic and secluded. It overlooked a river which flowed by the picnic grove. Mary Rogers commented

on the beauty of the place and asked her husband to sit down with her there in order to admire the moonlight as it shone upon the river. Perham then spread a picnic blanket upon the ground and all three accordingly took their ease. They chatted for a while together. Finally Mary Rogers said that she had learned a rope trick and that she wanted to demonstrate it. She asked for a volunteer to assist her and Perham, according to plan, offered himself. Mary took a length of cord from her pocketbook and started to loosely tie Perham's wrists. He then easily broke free of the restraint to the pretended disappointment of Mary Rogers. This was repeated several times as Marcus Rogers watched. Perham finally turned to Marcus Rogers and dared him to try his wife's rope trick. The man was in a good mood so he allowed Mary to bind his wrists together. He then broke free of the restraint without difficulty. This was repeated a couple more times. Then Mary bade Perham to try the trick on her husband. Marcus Rogers still did not suspect anything so he allowed Perham to tie his hands behind his back. It was then that Perham made sure to knot the cord securely. When Marcus Rogers was bound and suddenly unable to free himself as before, the plotters dropped all pretense. Mary Rogers took a vial of chloroform and a handkerchief from her purse. She soaked the handkerchief with the anesthetic and thrust it over her husband's face. Marcus Rogers at last perceived his peril. He began to struggle. Perham got ahold of his legs and sat on them as the woman continued to press the chloroform upon her husband. Marcus Rogers came close to breaking free but he was gradually overcome by the cloying stench of the chloroform. When he finally lost consciousness, the conspirators tied his ankles together in addition to his wrists. Then they rolled him into the river that was there. In such a way was Marcus Rogers drowned. A purposed suicide note was left at the scene to mislead those who would later find the body.

Mary Rogers aroused suspicion of foul play when she became unusually aggressive in pursuing her life insurance claim. An investigation began. The more that was learned about Mary Rogers the more convinced detectives became of her guilt. All of her lovers were carefully questioned, including Leon Perham. He took fright and confessed. From then on all went downhill for Mary Rogers. Her teenage accomplice told of the plot to kill Marcus Rogers and the manner in which the crime was committed. There was no doubt of premeditation on the part of the killers. A grand jury needed no prodding when it was asked to indict Mary Rogers and Leon Perham for capital murder. Both were told that they were headed for the gallows. Then Perham got a lucky break: because of his age (17) he was offered a chance to save his life by turning State's Evidence against his lover. The boy jumped at the opportunity. Thus it came to pass that Leon Perham was sentenced to life in prison. In the case of Mary Rogers there was no mercy at all. Prosecutors portrayed her as a shameless harlot who was not only unprincipled but rotten to the core. She was found guilty of willful mariticide and sentenced to death. When her appeals failed it was left to the governor of Vermont to make a final decision as to whether Mary Rogers should live or die. It was a decision not easily made. The governor was deluged with letters and telegrams from every part of the country. Most of them urged clemency on the grounds that executing a woman was not in keeping with chivalry. After carefully reviewing every aspect of the case, the governor decided that the law must take its course. Said he: "I know of no law that is not as much for a woman as for a man." The warden of the Vermont State Prison was then told to proceed with the execution. Mary Rogers walked to the gallows with an air of utter indifference. She neither admitted nor denied her crime. The date was December 8, 1905.

1906

Ephraim Sherouk, alias "Frank Sherry," white, age 25. *Murder.* The crime was committed on January 5, 1905, at Somers, Connecticut. This man was a Polish immigrant who liked to live beyond his means. When he ran short of money he turned to murder. Sherouk had come to America in 1902. Because he did not have a trade he worked a series of low-paying jobs in order to support himself. He found employment in a button mill, in a rag shop and in the tobacco fields. His last assignment was that of an assemblyman for the Somersville Manufacturing Company in Somers. Across the street from that place was a boarding house operated by a Polish couple named Stephen and Ludwica Kulas. They provided accommodations for many of the employees of the Somersville Manufacturing Company. Ephraim Sherouk was one of their boarders. Shortly before Christmas in 1904 Sherouk packed up his belongings and said that he was going to Chicago. Instead, he went to Springfield, Massachusetts, where he took a room and proceeded to live the life of a bon vivant. When his money ran low he cast around for a means by which to get some more. It then occurred to him that the Kulas boarding house offered an opportunity for plunder. On the above date he traveled back to Somers. Then he waited for a time of day when the boarding house residents were away at their jobs. When Sherouk entered the boarding house he found only the landlady there. She was washing dishes at the time. Sherouk snuck up behind the woman and struck her down with a blackjack. Then he strangled her to death with her own dish towel. When Mrs. Kulas (white, age about 45) was dead, the killer searched her person for valuables. After that he turned his attention to other areas of the house. When the factory workers came home that night they found their landlady dead and their rooms looted. Four days later Sherouk was nabbed in Hartford. He had been seen in Somers on the day of the crime. The matter of his guilt was clinched when he was found to have the landlady's jewelry in his possession.

Sherouk was also the prime suspect in a second murder. On November 24, 1903, another Polish landlady named Paraska Shippiler had been found slain in her kitchen at No. 110 Grove Street in Hartford under circumstances nearly identical with the case of Ludwica Kulas. The crime had gone unsolved at the time but the investigation into it was revived when it was reported that Sherouk had once been a tenant of Mrs. Shippiler. Due to lack of conclusive evidence in the Shippiler case, however, Sherouk was tried only for the murder of Ludwica Kulas. A jury had no difficulty convicting him and he was ordered for execution. As the end drew near, Sherouk was granted a 70-day reprieve at the request of the Russian government. Since Sherouk's homeland was then a part of Russia his case was followed with interest by that nation's consulate. However, when favorable evidence failed to materialize, the law was left to take its course. Ephraim Sherouk was hanged at the Connecticut State Prison on January 9, 1906. He denied his guilt to the last.

Charles Tucker, white, age 23. *Murder.* The crime was committed on March 31, 1904, at Weston, Massachusetts. This young man belonged to an otherwise respectable family in the town of Auburndale. He had worked as a railroad baggage handler and as a boathouse attendant but lost both jobs when he was found to be less than honest. In one case he was caught stealing from boathouse lockers and in another instance he was found to

have cashed a stolen check. He avoided prosecution in each case when he made full restitutions. On January 1, 1903, this Tucker married a young Waltham woman named Grace Emily Osborne (white, age 20), only to lose her in a canoeing accident on April 20 of that same year. She had gone to a Charles River boathouse where Tucker was then employed and the young couple set out for a short canoe trip therefrom. Their craft overturned when the water got choppy. Grace Osborne Tucker was drowned. The fact that the water was only four feet deep at the scene of the tragedy gave rise to unflattering talk about Charles Tucker. From that time on he lived under a cloud. At the time of his alleged capital offense he was unemployed and living with his parents.

Through his former job as a baggage handler Tucker was acquainted with another railroad employee named Harold Page. This individual belonged to a socially prominent family in the town of Weston. It is alleged that Tucker used his personal knowledge of the Page family to avail himself of an opportunity to rob their house. On the above date *someone*— alleged to be Tucker — called at the Page residence and there encountered a spinster sister of Harold Page. The caller told a false story to the woman (whose name was Mabel Page, white, age 41) to the effect that her brother had been injured on the job and that she had better hurry along to the hospital to see him. It is alleged that the caller then lingered about until he thought that Miss Page had departed. Then he went upstairs to look for valuables in the bedrooms. While in the act of snooping around, the caller was surprised to find Mabel Page still in her own room. She was in the act of putting on her hat and overcoat. The woman saw the male caller (allegedly Tucker) and challenged him for being in an area of the house that was off limits. The intruder then attacked Mabel Page and stabbed her six times. The woman was left to die at the scene while the assailant hurried away without effecting his original purpose of theft. Charles Tucker was arrested when he admitted to being in Weston at the time in question and when witnesses placed him closer to the Page residence than he claimed.

Although the case against him was based almost entirely on circumstantial evidence, Tucker was capitally convicted. Appeals failed on both the state and federal levels. Doubts about Tucker's guilt caused more than 116,000 people to sign petitions for a commutation of the death sentence. However, the governor's council remained unswayed. The end finally came on July 12, 1906, when Charles Tucker was electrocuted at the Massachusetts State Prison.

John Schidlofski, alias "John Cline," white, age 28. *Murder.* The crime was committed on July 12, 1905, at Belmont, Massachusetts. This man was a Lithuanian immigrant and a barber by trade. According to his own confession, he had married his wife, Marciana Schidlofski (white, age 40), in the belief that she was 12 years younger and bore an $800 dowry. He especially wanted the dowry money in order to finance a move to California. When he learned that his wife was in fact 40 years old and had only $300 he became so angry that he decided to kill her. Shortly before the above date Schidlofski had his wife withdraw her money from the bank. Then he bought two train tickets to California, one of which he soon presented for a refund. He also quit his job in anticipation of what he had in mind. When Schidlofski felt that all was in readiness, he lured his wife onto a remote section of a golf course very close to the Arlington town line. There he turned on the woman with deadly force. Schidlofski is known to have taken some stones from a nearby wall and to have brought them down with such force on his wife's head and

face that she was left unrecognizable. He also decapitated the victim with a carving knife. Then the killer dragged the victim's remains through a barbed wire fence and threw them into a gully where he tumbled more rocks upon them. Some mowers came upon the scene the next morning. The victim was identified by means of a bank withdrawal slip that she had in her purse. All other means of identification had been removed by the killer. When it was learned that the decedent had recently closed her bank account and that her husband was missing, a nationwide alarm was broadcast. Three days later Schidlofski was found on a California-bound passenger train. He had gotten as far as the Rocky Mountains. Returned to Massachusetts, the killer was convicted of capital felony. On July 9, 1906, he was electrocuted at the Massachusetts State Prison.

1907

Henry Bailey, white, age 40. *Murder.* The crime was committed on July 6, 1906, at Middletown, Connecticut. George Goodale (white, age 48) was a seafood dealer who lived alone in a small house in the West Long Hill district of Middletown. He was estranged from his wife and children. For general upkeep about the place he employed a handyman named Henry Bailey. Shortly before the above date, Goodale sold some real estate to the tune of $1000 and kept the cash in his immediate possession. When this became known to Henry Bailey the temptation proved too great. As Goodale reclined in an easy chair on the above date, Bailey snuck up behind him with an axe and split his skull down the middle with it. Then he stole whatever money he could find and rode off with the dead man's horse and wagon. Three days later a neighbor became concerned about Goodale's failure to appear up and about as usual. The neighbor then checked Goodale's house and so discovered the crime. Suspicion pointed to Henry Bailey from the start; the man was unaccountably absent and he had been seen driving Goodale's rig in another town. When that same rig was found abandoned, an all-points bulletin was issued for Henry Bailey. The suspect turned up in Canada a week later. Returned to Connecticut, Bailey admitted killing Goodale but claimed self-defense. He was not believed by a trial jury nor by the State Supreme Court. The Board of Pardons also refused to give credit to the tale of self-defense. Henry Bailey was then left to his fate. He was hanged at the Connecticut State Prison on April 16, 1907.

Alexander Herman, white, age 26. *Murder.* The crime was committed on July 4, 1906, at Bridgeport, Connecticut. This man had been a boarder in the home of a Mr. Martin Korzinsky (white, age 32), located at No. 19 Clinton Avenue in Bridgeport. Having become infatuated with his landlord's wife, Herman determined that the woman's husband had to somehow be eliminated. Preparatory to the actual murder, Herman left Bridgeport in order to make it look like he had moved away permanently. Then on the above date he slipped back into town. When night fell he took up a position outside of the Korzinsky home and waited for Martin Korzinsky to emerge therefrom. At about 11 o'clock in the evening the unsuspecting man decided to go to a nearby saloon in order to fetch beer for his holiday guests. As he was returning from that errand Herman emerged from his hiding place and opened fire with a handgun. Martin Korzinsky was shot dead on his own doorstep. The killer made a successful escape from the scene of the crime. He was later traced through a letter that he sent to a friend in Bridgeport. It was then determined that he was living in New Jersey under an assumed name. Herman was

extradited to Connecticut and charged with capital murder. He was convicted by means of eyewitness testimony. On May 10, 1907, he was hanged at the Connecticut State Prison.

1908

John Washelesky, white, age 28. *Murder.* The crime was committed on December 3, 1903, at New Haven, Connecticut. John Washelesky and Peter Lucasavitch (white, age 29) were Polish immigrants who worked for a vegetable farmer on the outskirts of New Haven. Both lived in a boarding house on Cresent Street in the Westville section of the city. One day Washelesky went to the cellar of his home in order to fetch a bicycle that he had stored there. He became angry when he found that someone had slashed the tires on the bicycle. Blaming Lucasavitch for the damage, Washelesky decided to do the man one better. Both were due to attend a baptism ceremony in the near future and when the day came there was trouble in store. Washelesky, who was supposed to sponsor a baby for baptism according to Polish custom, dramatically refused to do so in front of a whole house filled with guests. When asked his reason, Washelesky charged that the child was illegitimate and that Lucasavitch was the father. This was a horrible insult and it had its desired effect of embarrassing Lucasavitch in front of the other guests. Both men then went outside and began a nasty squabble. It is alleged that while in the course of that dispute, Washelesky tore a board from a nearby picket fence and fatally bludgeoned Lucasavitch with it. Whatever the truth, Lucasavitch vanished that night and was never again seen alive. Three weeks later Washelesky took passage on a ship and returned to Poland. There the matter languished until a year later. On November 24, 1904, some boys hiking through an area known as Beaver Swamp came upon a pair of human feet protruding from the ground. Police were called and soon a decayed corpse was unearthed. Personal items at the scene established the find as the remains of the missing Peter Lucasavitch. A subsequent investigation raised incriminating evidence against John Washelesky; he was the last person seen with the decedent, he was alleged to have had a violent row with that person, he had been seen with bloodstained clothes shortly thereafter and he was reported to have made a number of sidelong remarks about disposal of a body. The fact that he had left the country when he did also looked bad for him. With the suspect safely out of their reach, however, all the local authorities could do was issue a bench warrant for Washelesky's arrest. There the matter might have ended were it not for Washelesky's own stupidity; in the spring of 1907 he returned to New Haven and applied to his former employer for a job. That individual remembered Washelesky and also knew that he was the prime suspect in an unsolved murder. Taken into custody, Washelesky insisted that he was innocent. The state's attorney, however, built up a strong case based on circumstantial evidence. A jury became sufficiently convinced and returned a capital verdict. The State Supreme Court and the Board of Pardons both concurred. On July 1, 1908, John Washelesky was hanged at the Connecticut State Prison. He asseverated his innocence to the last.

Lorenzo Rossi, white, age 33. *Murder.* The crime was committed on January 29, 1908, at Hartford, Connecticut. This case grew out of a barroom brawl. On the above date a billiards enthusiast named Eli Cavanaugh (white, age 33) was displaying his skill in the Syrian Cafe, a seedy resort at No. 161 State Street in Hartford. While there he got into a dispute with two other patrons of the place, one of whom was the above-

named Lorenzo Rossi. The men came to blows and Rossi was worsted. Then Rossi stomped out of the bar with a bad case of injured pride. An hour later he returned and saw that Cavanaugh was still there. Rossi then went across the street to a junk shop and bought a knife. Returning to the Syrian Cafe, he approached Cavanaugh and pretended to be contrite. Rossi also offered to buy Cavanaugh a drink as a gesture of good faith and Cavanaugh accepted the offer. The two men then stepped over to the bar and ordered beer. As they raised their glasses, Rossi dropped his glass to the floor in a feigned act of clumsiness. He then took a bar rag and bent down to sop up the spilled beer. As he did so he carefully watched Cavanaugh. Then when Cavanaugh raised his glass to his lips Rossi pulled out his knife and stabbed the man in the stomach. Cavanaugh collapsed to the floor with a deep wound and Rossi ran out the door. Police found him hiding in an alley soon afterward. When he was arrested, Rossi laughed scornfully at his situation. When he was brought to the local hospital to be identified by the wounded man he laughed in a sardonic manner. When he saw a priest giving the last rites to Cavanaugh he laughed contemptuously and made obscene gestures. Four days later Cavanaugh died. Rossi was then charged with capital murder. He was convicted on his own confession as well as on the testimonies of numerous eyewitnesses. There was no appeal. Nor was there any clemency. Rossi was subsequently hanged at the Connecticut State Prison on July 24, 1908.

John Zett, white, age 48. *Murder.* The crime was committed on August 4, 1908, near Rockville, Connecticut. This man was a Bohemian immigrant who had initially worked in the coal mines of Pennsylvania. At the turn of the century he moved to Connecticut with his wife and children. Settling at Rockville, he got a job in the mills there. By 1906 he had saved enough money to realize his dream of buying a farm. He accordingly found a suitable property four miles outside of Rockville on the Bolton Road. By nature Zett was a foul-tempered man who was prone to fits of rage. In light of subsequent events it is also possible that he was of unsound mind. When Zett acquired his own farm he put the place in his wife's name instead of his own. Why he did so is not known but as time passed he began to worry about it. He feared that if his marriage failed he would be put out of a home and forced to earn his living once again in the mills. Then he reasoned that the only way to avoid such a scenario was to murder his entire family. On the above date Zett attacked his wife, Mary Zett (white, age 47), with a hammer in the bedroom of their home and battered her to death. The woman's skull was broken in six different places. He also killed his little granddaughter, Viola Klotzer (white, age five), in the same manner before slitting her throat with a butcher knife for added measure. When Zett had finished both victims he calmly washed the gore from the murder weapons and put them back in their accustomed places. Then he lay in wait for his son, Andrew Zett (white, age 22), with a sledgehammer. When the young man came home his father attacked him from behind. Andrew Zett managed to dodge a lethal blow and he engaged in a desperate hand-to-hand struggle with his father. Eventually his youthful strength prevailed over that of the older man and he wrested away the sledgehammer. So frenzied was John Zett that his son had to strike him a disabling blow in order to subdue him. Andrew Zett then tied his father up with rope and called the police. Six weeks later John Zett was convicted of capital murder and ordered for execution. There was no appeal. He was hanged at the Connecticut State Prison on December 21, 1908.

1909

Raphael Carfaro, white, age 20. **Giuseppe Campagnolo,** white, age 27. *Murder.* Their crime was committed on August 15, 1908, at North Haven, Connecticut. On the above date a young woman named Bessie Lewis went to visit her fiancé, George Sheehan (white, age 19), in his place of residence at No. 439 Middletown Avenue in the Montowese section of North Haven. When the hour grew late Miss Lewis excused herself and said that it was time for her to go home. George Sheehan then offered to escort her as far as the trolley line on Quinnipiac Avenue. The young couple then set out for the trolley on foot. Their route took them along Barnes Avenue and past the most disreputable place in the neighborhood: the so-called DeLucia property. This was a small farm and farmhouse owned by a father and son who were serving life sentences for murder. In their absence the place remained in operation but was inhabited by Italian immigrants who were looked upon with suspicion and disdain. Raphael Carfaro and Giuseppe Campagnolo were resident farmhands there who did nothing to improve their image in the eyes of the community. Campagnolo in particular was known to be a convicted burglar who had done time in the state prison. The area along Barnes Avenue where these men dwelled was remote in 1908 so Carfaro and Campagnolo allegedly felt that they had little to fear from their neighbors. As they saw George Sheehan and Betsy Lewis walk by their farmhouse they *allegedly* decided that it would be a good idea to rape the young woman. They accordingly took up weapons and hurried after the walking couple. George Sheehan was attacked first. Campagnolo smacked him across the face with a pitchfork and Carfaro killed him with a shotgun blast in the back. Bessie Lewis screamed so loudly that both of the attackers left her unharmed and ran back to their house. Both men were found there by police as were the weapons that they had used. Neither made any attempt to flee and both confessed within a short time. In mitigation of their crime, the men said that they had been having a lot of trouble with thieves in their melon patch. Both men had been drinking at the time in question and they had mistaken the two pedestrians for thieves. George Sheehan had also attempted to defend himself with a blackjack when he was first assaulted and that fact was said to have prompted the shooting. The fact that Sheehan was shot in the back, however, figured heavily against both men. The allegation of intent to commit rape was supported by nothing more than the poor reputations of the suspects. Because of doubts cast upon the motive for the crime, the district attorney offered both men a chance to avoid the death penalty by pleading guilty to murder in the second degree. However, Carfaro and Campagnolo both spurned the offer. They both decided to take their chances with a jury. It was a fatal mistake for both of them. Both were capitally convicted and ordered for execution. On February 24, 1909, they were hanged at the Connecticut State Prison.

Ham Woon, Chinese, age 34. **Min Sing,** Chinese, age 29. **Leon Gong,** Chinese, age 17. *Murder.* Their crime was committed on August 2, 1907, at Boston, Massachusetts. Throughout the summer of 1907 violence flared in Chinese neighborhoods from Boston to Philadelphia as the rival On Leong and Hip Sing Tongs vented their deadly hatred for each other. These secret organizations had long competed for power and influence and they were not adverse to resorting to open warfare whenever they felt the urge. During the months of June and July the On Leongs were on the offensive. As August approached, the Hip Sings planned to retaliate in flamboyant style. What the Hip Sings had in mind was nothing less than a full-scale terrorist attack. The target they chose was the On Leong territory around Harrison Avenue in Boston. From Hip Sing headquarters in New York ten armed men were dispatched. All had orders to shoot to kill. They arrived in Boston on the above date and found conditions there ideal for what they intended. All along the length of Oxford Place (in the Chinatown district) local residents were enjoying a warm summer evening outdoors. Scores of people were lounging around the sidewalks unconcernedly. The cafes and chop suey stands were crowded to capacity. Then shortly before eight o'clock the Hip Sings went walking down Harrison Avenue. All ten of them took up positions at the entrance to Oxford Place and strode boldly along that thoroughfare. In a flash they pulled out large caliber handguns and opened fire indiscriminately on men, women and children. Chaos reigned as panic-stricken people ran for their lives. The gunmen shot at anything that moved; no one was exempt. When it was over, three Chinamen lay dead in the street. Three others lay mortally wounded. At least a dozen more people suffered lesser injuries. The slain were identified as Wong Lee Ching (age 55), Chin Lete (age 45) and Chin Mon Quin (age 48). Critically wounded were Lee Kai (age 29), Shang Gu (age 28) and Goon Jong Gou (age 47), at least two of whom later died of their wounds. In the dragnet that followed this massacre three of the terrorists were caught and positively identified. The others either escaped or could not be tied in to the crime with certainty. In the end, the above-named trio were convicted of capital murder. On October 12, 1909, all three were electrocuted at the Massachusetts State Prison.

1910

John Zawedzianczek, white, age 26. *Murder.* The crime was committed on October 15, 1908, at Glastonbury, Connecticut. On the evening of the above date Michael Wierdack (white, age 30), a Polish immigrant, was chatting with a group of men by a roadside. Along came the daughter of one Peter Rubaka, a Hungarian immigrant, who lived in the same district. The girl was accompanied by a large dog and so was one of the men with whom Wierdack was speaking. When the two dogs saw each other they started to snarl. It was then that a dog fight broke out. Wierdack attempted to separate the animals and wound up getting bitten. Annoyed, Wierdack then went to the house of Peter Rubaka and complained about the dog. Rubaka, who is described as having been argumentative by nature, refused to handle the matter with civility. Instead, he called upon his nephew, John Zawedzianczek, to help him "kill the Polack" as he put it. Zawedzianczek was mashing sauerkraut at the time. He then picked up a butcher knife and attacked Wierdack. Peter Rubaka also joined in with a club. In the melee that followed, Wierdack was slashed along the jugular and bled to death. Both of his assailants were arrested the same night and charged with capital murder. Both were sentenced to death. A retrial resulted in Rubaka's life being spared. He was subsequently sent to the state prison for the remainder of his days. Zawedzianczek was capitally convicted a second time and ordered for execution. He was hanged at the Connecticut State Prison on February 9, 1910.

Napoleon Rivet, white, age 29. *Murder.* The crime was committed on March 1, 1908, at Lowell, Massachusetts. Napoleon Rivet and Joseph Gailloux (white, age 37) were roommates who lived in the Little Canada district of Lowell. The former worked in the mills and the latter was a salesman in a plumbing supply store. At one time Rivet had lent some money to Gailloux on the condition that he secure the loan by making him (Rivet) the beneficiary of a $1000 life insurance policy. Two years later Rivet decided that he wanted to go into the moving picture business but found that he lacked the necessary funds. He then decided to do away with Gailloux for the sake of the insurance proceeds that would become payable to him. On the evening of February 28, 1910, the two men went out drinking together. After midnight they went to the store where Gailloux worked with the intention of continuing their revelry in the back room. When Gailloux was sufficiently primed with liquor, Rivet bludgeoned him with a pipe. Then he poured sulfuric acid in the man's mouth and flooded the room with illuminating gas. The body was discovered a short time later by a policeman making his rounds. The door to the plumbing store was found to be unlocked at an odd hour of the night and the policeman came upon the crime scene when he went inside to investigate. Rivet was arrested the same day and charged with capital murder. On July 29, 1910, he was electrocuted at the Massachusetts State Prison.

1911

Andrei Ipson, white, age 19. **Wasili Ivanowski,** alias "Bill Kovensky," white, age 22. *Murder.* Their crime was committed on June 25, 1910, at Lynn, Massachusetts. These young men were Polish immigrants who lived in New York City. Ipson had no set occupation but Ivanowski worked as a garment presser. They both went to Massachusetts with a deliberate intention of committing a robbery. A week before their capital crime they wandered about the greater Boston area looking for a likely target. They found one at Lynn when they observed a payroll delivery in progress. For the next seven days they hung around Boston. Then on the above date they returned to Lynn with an unidentified accomplice. It was payday there at the Welsh and Landregan shoe factory and the robbers planned to heist the payroll. Shortly after nine o'clock in the morning Mr. Thomas A. Landregan (white, age 46), a managing partner in the shoe factory, emerged from the main office of the Lynn National Bank with a large moneybag. He was accompanied by his regular bodyguard, a Lynn police officer named James H. Carroll (white, age 52). The moneybag contained $4500 — much of it in silver coins — comprising the shoe factory's payroll and it was so heavy that it took both men to carry it. Landregan and Carroll made their way down Market Street and then turned onto Oxford Street. Crossing Central Avenue, they were about to turn onto Willow Street (the site of the shoe factory) when they were attacked from behind by the three armed robbers. No quarter was given as automatic pistol fire rang out. Thomas Landregan was instantly killed by a bullet in the head. The police officer died when he was shot seven times in the back. Then the killers grabbed the moneybag and took off with it up Oxford Street. As they began to run, one of them turned and fired another shot into the body of Mr. Landregan. When the killers crossed Willow Street they ran past a factory there that was filled with working men. Having been alerted by the sound of gunfire, the factory workers flung their tools out of the windows in an attempt to impede the fleeing bandits. Dodging that barrage, one of the robbers paused long enough to shoot out some of the factory windows. Then a riot broke out. Hundreds of angry men poured out of the factory and took up pursuit of the bandits. They brandished makeshift weapons of every kind and were joined by other people from surrounding buildings. Chasing the bandits onto Buffam Street, the mob passed the rear side of Welsh and Landregan shoe works. As it did so, the employees of that place ran out into the street en masse and joined the chase. By then it was estimated that more than 3000 irate men were pursuing the payroll bandits. The chase continued onto Liberty Street, across Highland Square and then left onto Essex Street. In an effort to shake off pursuit, one of the gunmen fired into the crowd while his accomplices continued running with the moneybag. By then the entire Lynn police department had also joined in the chase. However, their horsedrawn vehicles could make no headway through the human stampede and they were forced to borrow automobiles from private citizens in order to circle around and race on ahead of the mob. Meanwhile, the bandits ran to the High Rock Observatory and paused to divide their loot for easier portage. They were also forced to abandon hundreds of silver dollars there because the coins were too heavy. After that they crossed to the other side of High Rock and ran up Valley Avenue. Then they crossed Hollingsworth Street and turned up Bayview Avenue. When they came to the end of Bayview Avenue they crossed over Western Avenue and plunged into a dense thicket which then occupied the ground between Western Avenue and Boston Street. Seconds later the police converged on the scene from one direction and the mob from another. Together the police and the mob surrounded the vast thicket of bushes and other growth and began to beat their way through it in the manner of a tiger hunt. When the vegetation became too dense for further pursuit both the mob and the police rained gunfire into the impenetrable area. This was how one of the bandits met his death. Several minutes later a second bandit (later identified as Andrei Ipson) broke from the thicket and ran as far as Grant Street. There a police wagon spotted him and attempted to run him down. Before Ipson could be trampled by the horses, however, he opened fire on the driver, causing that person to drop the reins and jump for his life. That caused the wagon to run wild and miss the bandit. When the driver regained his bearings he drew his service revolver and brought Ipson down with three well-placed bullets. Badly wounded, Ipson was then captured by the police. The third bandit, Ivanowski, was eventually nabbed deep in the aforesaid thicket. He had three of his fingers severed by gunfire and decided to surrender. When he was brought to police headquarters a lynch mob was waiting. It was only with the greatest of difficulty that Ivanowski was kept from being torn apart.

Ipson and Ivanowski, the two surviving bandits, were subsequently patched up and brought to trial. Both were capitally convicted and ordered for execution. On March 7, 1911, they were electrocuted at the Massachusetts State Prison. Ipson died without incident. Ivanowski died cursing and swearing in his native tongue.

1912

Elroy Kent, white, age 33. *Murder.* The crime was committed on July 24, 1908, at East Wallingford, Vermont. This man was a mental defective who was born less than two miles from the scene of his capital crime. He managed to do farm work on occasion and was regarded more or less as a harmless half-wit. All that changed in 1904 when Kent suddenly attacked one of his uncles with a knife. He was then sent to the state insane asylum at Waterbury from whence he escaped on July 11, 1908. As an escapee, Kent made his way back to the farm where he had been born but found the place abandoned. He then took to sleep-

ing in derelict buildings and survived by raiding vegetable gardens and hen roosts. He eventually wandered onto a small farm at East Wallingford that was owned by a deaf-mute woman named Delia Congdon (white, age 41) and hid out in her barn. From his place of concealment, Kent could see clearly into the woman's bedroom and he became sexually aroused by what he saw there. When Miss Congdon unlocked her door on the morning of the above date, Kent entered the house and attacked her. He throttled the woman with his bare hands, raped her and then battered her to death with a wood-splitter. He made good his escape from the scene of the crime and remained at large for several months. He was eventually found in Pittsfield, Massachusetts, where he was nabbed in the act of stealing a bicycle. Kent was then returned to Vermont where he was tried and condemned for capital murder. The question of his sanity led to a determined effort by some to get his sentence commuted. The matter was passionately debated in the state legislature. When a final vote was taken on a commutation bill, however, it came up short. On the afternoon of January 5, 1912, Elroy Kent was brought to the gallows at the Vermont State Prison. He refused to admit his guilt to the last. An electrical device had been installed which was to spring the gallows trap. It consisted of six separate push-buttons manned by six special deputies. Five of the buttons were dummies and only one actually worked so that no one would know for sure who sent the condemned man to his death. In spite of these rather elaborate precautions, the execution was marred. When the buttons were pushed and the trap gave way Kent shot downward as expected. However, when he did so the rope broke and Kent plunged to the concrete floor below. He writhed about in agony for several minutes ere the hangman could successfully reset the rope and tie another noose. Elroy Kent was then led onto the gallows for a second time and the hanging process was repeated. This time the rope held and the condemned man was soon pronounced dead.

Silas Phelps, white, age 37. *Murder.*

The crime was committed on June 12, 1910, at Monroe Bridge, Massachusetts. This man was a mountaineer who had a fearsome reputation along the Massachusetts-Vermont border. He climaxed a long series of violent incidents by gunning down a sheriff's deputy who had come to arrest him. Phelps initially came to the notice of lawmen at the age of 16 when he was sent to the Concord Reformatory. He subsequently got into trouble for larceny, moonshining, assault, threatening, malicious wounding and for lashing his wife with a horsewhip. He worked as a miner for several years but was fired when he took a shot at his foreman. He lived in a remote cabin about a mile and a half from the village of Monroe Bridge, in the extreme northwestern corner of Franklin County. At the time of his capital crime he was employed as a night watchman for a paper mill just across the border in Readsboro, Vermont. Trouble began on the evening of June 10, 1910, when Phelps reported to his job. He was summoned to the office of the mill superintendent and told that his services would no longer be needed. When Phelps asked the reason, he was cited for drinking on duty among other demerits. Phelps then became enraged. He attacked the paper mill boss with a pocketknife before stomping out of his office. Police were then called. By the time a constable reached the isolated location Phelps had fled back across the border into Massachusetts. Forbidden to enter another jurisdiction in the course of their duties, Vermont authorities contacted their Massachusetts counterparts and requested the arrest of Silas Phelps. A Franklin County deputy named Emmett Haskins (white, age 56) was then detailed to bring in the wanted man. Phelps meanwhile had barricaded himself in his cabin along with his wife and six children. Deputy Haskins knew Phelps from his previous scrapes with the law and he also knew that Phelps was a dangerous man. Moreover, Phelps hated Haskins in particular and had threatened to kill him if he ever again crossed his path. Because of this, Haskins knew better than to go after Phelps alone. He accordingly rounded up some stalwart men and went to Monroe Bridge in their company. The posse reached the Phelps cabin at four o'clock in the morning on June 12. They pounded on the cabin door and demanded that Phelps surrender. After much commotion Mrs. Phelps opened a window and said that her husband was not there. In reply, the deputy said that he knew otherwise and threatened to break down the door. When the occupants of the cabin showed no further sign of yielding the front door was forced. No sooner did Deputy Haskins cross the threshold, however, than he was instantly killed by a shotgun blast. Silas Phelps then emerged from his hiding place and bade defiance to the rest of the posse. He allowed them exactly one minute to remove the deputy's body and then threatened them with death if they dared to linger a second longer. The possemen did as they were told and then hurried back to Monroe Bridge. The sun was coming up by the time sufficient reinforcements were organized but by then Phelps had escaped into the forest. A lot of valuable time was also lost when Phelps emerged from hiding just long enough to sabotage telephone and telegraph wires. Then for three days and three nights he led hundreds of heavily armed manhunters on a merry chase through the Hoosac Mountains. The terrain was extremely difficult but Phelps was a wily woodsman. He lived off the land and gave his pursuers the slip. On the third day a heavy rain set in which soaked both hunters and hunted to the skin. The cold mountain air did the rest and Phelps was left in no condition to flee any further. He was nabbed in a bedraggled condition by possemen who were close to exhaustion themselves.

A Franklin County jury condemned Silas Phelps to the electric chair. A subsequent appeal to the State Supreme Court failed and the execution order was signed. On Christmas Day 1911, the governor of Massachusetts visited Phelps in his death row cell and had a long interview with him. When the governor emerged from the meeting he announced a desire to commute the death sentence. By law this could not be granted without the consent of the executive council. The matter was then appealed to that body and voted down by a lopsided margin. The other members of the council said that the deliberate murder of a law enforcement officer deserved the extreme penalty of the law. Sparing Silas Phelps would set a dangerous precedent. The governor was thereby left powerless to act on his own. Silas Phelps was accordingly left to his fate. On January 26, 1912, he was electrocuted at the Massachusetts State Prison.

Andrea Tanganelli, white, age 25. *Murder.* The crime was committed on September 5, 1911, at New Haven, Connecticut. This man was a bricklayer who lived in the Milldale section of Southington. On the above date he came to New Haven on a bicycle in search of female companionship. Early evening found him in a George Street saloon where he struck up a conversation with a likely looking woman. Unknown to Tanganelli, the object of his attention had already made plans for that night. She let Tanganelli buy her a drink but said that she was waiting for the arrival of another man. When that other man entered the saloon the woman politely disengaged herself from Tanganelli and walked out of the place with the other man. Feeling himself ill used, Tanganelli became angry. He followed the woman and her escort out onto the sidewalk and deliberately bumped into them from behind. The couple then walked across the street in an effort to escape their antagonist. Tanganelli followed them with an intention of making more trouble. However, he backed off when he turned a corner onto Church Street and saw the couple meet up with a brawny friend. The woman and her two male companions then went along their way unmolested because Tanganelli saw himself outnumbered. What Tanganelli did next wound up costing him his life. He went to a nearby pawnshop, purchased a loaded handgun and went looking for the elusive woman. Peering in the window of yet another George Street tavern, Tanganelli spotted the object of his search. He then waited outside until the woman left the place with her male escorts. Then he followed her at a discreet distance. At the corner of Crown and Temple streets the woman's escorts told her to walk on ahead of them while they turned to confront the stalker. It was then that Tanganelli opened fire on the two men. Both dove for cover whereupon Tanganelli ran up to the terrified woman and shot her in the back at point-blank range. Outraged bystanders then tackled Tanganelli and held him for the police. The wounded female was rushed to the hospital but was pronounced dead upon arrival. She was identified as a married woman from Altoona, Pennsylvania, named Mamie Davis (white, age 25), who was also known in the New Haven saloon district as "Norma Clarke." Although there was never any doubt of Tanganelli's guilt, he stubbornly insisted that he was innocent. A jury had no difficulty in finding him guilty. Nor did the jury have any problem with accepting Tanganelli's timely purchase of the murder weapon as evidence of premeditation. The killer was accordingly ordered for execution and on March 29, 1912, he was hanged at the Connecticut State Prison. He denied his guilt to the last.

Clarence Richeson, white, age 34.

Murder. The crime was committed on October 14, 1911, at Boston, Massachusetts. Once a respected clergyman, this offender scandalized the entire country when he fatally poisoned his pregnant paramour. Richeson was born in Virginia. His parents were devout Baptists who carefully groomed their son for a career in the ministry. As a boy Richeson attended prestigious academies in Virginia and Maryland. Then he was sent to a Baptist mission church in Kansas City for an introduction to his future calling. In due course he enrolled at William Jewell College in Liberty, Missouri, and became a member of the class of 1906. During his senior year there occurred an omen of things to come: Richeson was expelled for cheating on his exams. An embarrassing incident with a young woman was also hushed up at the time. Nevertheless, Richeson gained admittance to a Baptist seminary shortly thereafter. He graduated from there in 1909 and was assigned to a pulpit in Hyannis, Massachusetts. While there he became enamored with a teenage choir singer named Avis Linnell and promised to marry her. The couple spent the summer of 1911 together on Cape Cod and they let it be known throughout their social set that they were engaged. When the summer ended, Richeson received an opportunity for advancement: he was offered the ministry of the Immanuel Baptist Church in Cambridge, a much larger, older and more prestigious parish than the one to which he was assigned. The young minister accepted the offer and relocated to Cambridge. He also brought Avis Linnell with him and had her enroll at the New England Conservatory of Music. At around the same time Richeson began to pay his addresses to another young woman, one Violet Edmands, whose

father was a trustee of the Newton Baptist Theological Seminary, the same place where Richeson had trained for the ministry. Richeson realized that Miss Edmands had better social connections than Avis Linnell the choir girl. He then began to regret his earlier engagement. Undeterred by prior commitment, he proposed marriage to Miss Edmands. Then when his proposal was accepted, he even made a formal announcement thereof and began wedding preparations. Avis Linnell (white, age 19) still believed that Richeson would marry her. She also informed her lover that she was pregnant. Richeson then found himself in a ticklish position: he could not break his engagement to Avis Linnell without bringing disgrace upon himself nor could he marry her without doing the same. And what would he say to Violet Edmands? After considering every possibility, Richeson decided that Avis Linnell and her unborn child had to be eliminated. He subsequently sweet-talked Avis Linnell into consenting to an abortion. In such a way, said Richeson, their coming marriage would be free of scandal. Then he took Miss Linnell out to an expensive restaurant and gave her some prescription capsules which he claimed would "solve her problem." Avis Linnell accepted the capsules and swallowed them that night with the intention of ending her pregnancy. What she did not know was that Richeson had spiked the capsules with potassium cyanide, a poison which is deadly in even minute quantities. Two days later Richeson delivered a long sermon to his congregation in which he tearfully dwelled upon the sudden demise of his "dear friend" Avis Linnell. It was a masterpiece of hypocrisy. Meanwhile, the young woman's family refused to accept a medical examiner's finding of suicide. They were also outraged by the post mortem revelation that the decedent was *enceinte.* Soon the newspapers got involved and they came down hard on the

Rev. Richeson. Then the medical examiner conceded that certain aspects of the case did not point to suicide, especially the position of the body when it was found. Suspicions of foul play were sustained shortly afterward when a chemist came forward and told of how he had reluctantly sold some potassium cyanide to Clarence Richeson for the ostensible purpose of euthanizing a dog. Armed with such evidence, detectives swooped down on the murderous minister and placed him under arrest. At first Richeson denied his guilt and hundreds of concerned persons flocked to his defense. His parishioners even refused to accept his resignation pending an acquittal. All were shocked and chagrined by subsequent events: On December 20, 1911, the accused man attempted suicide by emasculating himself with the sharpened lid of a jar. His wounds were severe and he almost died. Two weeks later he crowned all by fully confessing his guilt. He officially withdrew his plea of "not guilty" to an indictment for capital murder and requested immediate adjudication. A judge granted the motion and imposed the mandatory death sentence. There was no appeal. On May 21, 1912, the Rev. Clarence Virgil Thompson Richeson — haggard looking and neutered — was electrocuted at the Massachusetts State Prison. Overcome with shame and self-loathing, this his last attempt at suicide was successful.

Enrico Mascioli, alias "Harry Marshall," white, age 38. *Murder.* The crime was committed on or about September 14, 1910, at Hull, Massachusetts. This man was an Italian immigrant who came to America in 1906. He had no set occupation. In the spring of 1910 he went to Nantasket Beach and took lodgings there with a married couple of his own nationality named Frank and Lena Cusumano. The subsequent events which culminated in the murder of Frank Cusumano (white, age 39) have never been fully explained. What *is* known is that on or about the above date Enrico Mascioli hacked his landlord to death with an axe and buried his body in a sand dune. Three weeks later the killer grew fearful that the burial site was insecure. He then dug up the decomposing remains of the victim and wrapped them in a quilt. When that was done he bound the bundle with wire and drove with it to a point overlooking the sea. Then he tumbled the bundle down a cliff and into an area of deep water. On October 14, 1910, a beachcomber came upon the gory bundle; it had floated to the surface and come in with the tide. Examination of the human remains established them to be those of Frank Cusumano. At that point the decedent's wife and her male boarder were taken into custody. It was charged that the two had had an adulterous affair and had connived to do away with the cuckold. Lena Cusumano was suspected because of her failure to report her husband's disappearance and because the quilt in which the body was wrapped was a product of her handiwork. In addition, a thorough search of the Cusumano home turned up incontrovertible evidence of foul play: bloody clothes, a blood-encrusted axe, a blood-stained wagon and a spool of wire identical to that which had been wrapped around the murdered man. In her defense, Mrs. Cusumano admitted to knowing about the slaying but she blamed the whole thing on Mascioli. She said that he had killed her husband for the sake of some money that he had had in his possession and that he had threatened to kill her as well if she dared to say anything. It was mortal fear, said she, rather than collusion which had caused her not to report the matter. This story was given credence by many people when Mascioli was found to have more money in his possession than might be expected for a man of his circumstances. When the case came to trial Enrico Mascioli and Lena Cusumano were both convicted. Both were sentenced to death. However, the governor's council decided to spare the woman because of lingering doubts about her guilt. The councilors were also squeamish about executing a female. For those reasons the death sentence of Lena Cusumano was commuted to life imprisonment. No mercy was shown to Mascioli. On June 6, 1912, he was electrocuted at the Massachusetts State Prison.

Bertram Spencer, white, age 29.
Murder. The crime was committed on March 31, 1910, at Springfield, Massachusetts. This offender had been born and raised in the town of Lebanon, Connecticut. It was claimed that he suffered a head injury during his childhood there which brought about a change in his personality. He became furtive and devious. He also began to exhibit symptoms of kleptomania. As a teenager, Spencer took pleasure in robbing female pedestrians and sneaking into unlocked houses. As a young naval trainee he would slip ashore during the night and seek likely places to rob. Spencer knew that he had mental trouble and blamed his behavior on an "irresistible impulse" that he was unable to control. He said that he usually went to bed at night without incident but would suddenly awaken with urges that compelled him to go out in search of plunder. Lucid by day, he worked as a railroad brakeman for most of his adult life. At the time of his capital crime he was a receiving clerk in a meat packing plant.

From the autumn of 1908 to the spring of 1910 the city of Springfield was troubled by a series of home invasions that were apparently the work of one man. The culprit would enter upscale homes during the evening hours, confront the occupants with a gun and make off with their valuables. Precautions seemed useless against the bandit be-cause he struck houses that were well-lighted, filled with guests and guarded by watchdogs. He struck nearly two dozen times in Springfield alone and was also known to have been active in other towns as well. His costume was always the same: a black mask, a slouch hat and jet black clothes. Eventually the situation became so bad that public prayers were said in the churches for the capture of the culprit.

Matters took a homicidal turn on the above date when Spencer entered the home of a Miss Harriet Dow on Round Hill in Springfield. The lady of the house was entertaining guests in her parlor when an armed intruder suddenly appeared and demanded that all the persons present surrender their money. One of the guests, Martha Blackstone by name (white, age 39), panicked and ran screaming across the room. The bandit warned her to keep quiet on pain of death. When the terrified woman continued to scream she was shot dead by a bullet through the heart. Another person was also injured before the robber fled from the scene.

Public outrage over this crime was intense and many citizens organized to take action. Large rewards were offered for the capture of the killer. Special detectives were hired and the governor of Massachusetts even issued a special proclamation asking for public assistance. Then a vital clue arose. The victim of one of Spencer's previous heists discovered an engraved locket which the bandit had dropped in a flower garden. The locket bore the initials "B.G.S." and contained cameo portraits of Spencer's mother and sister. Detectives combed the Springfield area for men with the initials "B.G.S." and finally hit paydirt when they came to a shipping and receiving clerk named Bertram Spencer. After being taken into custody, Spencer admitted his crimes but blamed them on his "uncontrollable urges." He also admitted to being an egotist who took pleasure in outwitting police and reading about his exploits in the newspapers. In addition, Spencer said that he was not bothered by any "qualms of conscience." This last admission hardened public opinion against him more than anything else.

Before being brought to trial, Spencer was examined by a special team of mental health experts who unanimously concluded that he was crazy. A judge then ordered Spencer committed to the State Hospital for the Insane in order to undergo further observation. The question of Spencer's sanity subsequently became a hotly debated issue among those who evaluated him. In the end it was determined that Spencer did indeed know the difference between right and wrong. Therefore he was ordered to stand trial. There was never any doubt about Spencer's guilt. The trial was little more than a joust between psychiatrists with conflicting opinions. The jury had few doubts. In less than six hours it returned a capital verdict. Appeals followed which were all based on the issue of Spencer's mental state. When these failed the condemned man's mother sought out the president of the United States and asked him to intervene. The woman was politely told that the president only had jurisdiction in federal matters. On September 17, 1912, time ran out for Bertram Spencer. On that day he was electrocuted at the Massachusetts State Prison.

Chester Jordan, white, age 29. *Murder.* The crime was committed on September 1, 1908, at Somerville, Massachusetts. This man was a vaudeville actor who made away with his wife. He was born and raised in Indianapolis but came east with his parents in 1901. The family settled near Boston and young Jordan made use of his close proximity to seek his fortune in the theater district. He landed a bit part on the stage and gradually developed a repertoire of his own in which he played the role of a hobo in comedy routines. In 1904 the young vaudevillian married a burlesque show actress named Honora O'Reilly and worked the stage with her from Boston to Chicago. The couple's permanent home was at No. 509 Medford Street in Somerville and it was there where Jordan committed his capital crime. On the above date Jordan was puttering in his kitchen when his wife (white, age 30) came in and accused him of sleeping around. Enraged by such a charge, the 6'4", 250-pound Jordan knocked the woman down on the stairs and beat her into unconsciousness. Then he stripped her naked and dragged her into the kitchen where he chopped off her head with a meat cleaver. When that was done, Jordan paused to consider disposal methods. He decided to start with his wife's head. Using a butcher knife, he cut away the scalp and burned it in the kitchen stove. Soon the killer realized that the stove was inadequate so he carried what remained of his wife's head down to his cellar and threw it in the furnace. When he returned to the headless corpse, Jordan used the meat cleaver to chop it into handy-sized chunks. These were then fed into the furnace one by one. Jordan was eventually forced to stop that process when the smoke from his chimney became putrid. So he bundled up the remaining pieces of his wife and put them in a storage trunk. The next day Jordan hired a livery and rode with the trunk to the Boston waterfront where he planned to go aboard an outbound steamer. It was his intention to drop the remaining body parts overboard when the ship was well out at sea. Jordan learned that no ships were sailing that day so he took the trunk and laid over with it in a cheap hotel. The cabdriver who transported him became suspicious of his manner and reported the matter to the police. Jordan was then traced to his hotel room and asked what he had in the trunk. He said that the trunk contained clothing but the police challenged him for transporting stolen goods. Jordan then said that he had no key for the trunk. Police broke it open and were appalled to find the mutilated remains of a woman inside. When Jordan was brought to the police station for further questioning, he admitted that the remains were those of his wife. However, he claimed not to remember anything about how she had come to her death. His main concern, said Jordan, was in discreetly disposing of the body. This killer was subsequently convicted of capital murder but managed to stave off execution for nearly four years. It so happened that one of the jurors who had convicted him went insane and had to be institutionalized. A retrial was then sought based on that circumstance. State and federal courts considered the matter at their leisure before ruling against Jordan. The governor's council also refused to recommend clemency after the courts had had their say. Chester Jordan was accordingly put to death by electrocution at the Massachusetts State Prison on September 24, 1912.

George Redding, white, age 21. *Murder.* The crime was committed on February 24, 1912, at Hamden, Connecticut. Described as "brilliant but erratic," this young man belonged to a respectable family in the Ninth Ward of New Haven. From an early age he felt drawn to the acting profession and he expressed a fervent desire to go on stage. Redding began by becoming the mainstay of his school's drama club. At the age of 17 he got involved with a professional troupe which performed at a New Haven theater. He also busied himself with writing dramatic compositions and was greatly encouraged when a theatrical producer purchased one of his works. In the months that followed, Redding successfully placed more of his literary output

and even had an entire play accepted by a New York theater. When the play debuted, Redding appeared in the lead role himself and achieved "creditable" reviews. He then received some modest offers only to be drawn back to New Haven by the realities of life. Redding became the bookkeeper for a fruit wholesaler and in that capacity came to know most of the farmers and produce dealers in the greater New Haven area. He subsequently took up residence in his employer's spacious home at No. 867 Dixwell Avenue. In his spare time he continued with his creative endeavors. He also became a "solicitor" for the International Correspondence School of New Haven.

It so happened that Redding's boss also employed a live-in nurse to care for his elderly mother. The nurse was seven years older than Redding but the young man fell in love with her. She in turn considered Redding handsome and witty and so consented to his addresses. Both were thereafter seen together with increasing frequency, especially at stage productions and moving picture shows. When talk of marriage began the nurse indicated her willingness. Redding could think of little else but he soon felt the pinch of financial pressure. His literary sales had waned and his meager salary barely covered his expenses. He had no savings because he had spent all of his extra money on dinner dates, theater tickets and gifts for his girlfriend. To use his own words, he "was broke and needed money" to get married. After considering every possibility, Redding decided on robbery and murder. On February 22, 1912, he approached a Jewish produce dealer named Morris Greenberg (white, age 23) and told him that he knew of a Hamden farmer with a fine crop of apples that he was willing to let go for an unbeatable price. Greenberg was already well acquainted with Redding from prior business dealings and so had no cause to suspect danger. He accordingly made a date with Redding to visit the Hamden farm. Two days later the young men rode a trolley up to Hamden. Then they walked to an undeveloped area near West Rock and entered terrain that was densely wooded. Redding led Greenberg up an old wagon path, saying that their destination was just beyond the woods. When they reached a spot that was suitably remote, Redding pulled out a handgun and shot Greenberg twice in the back. Then he rolled him over and shot him two more times in the chest. Redding rifled the dead man's pockets and later said that he had found nothing in them. Two days later some hunters came across the frozen body of Morris Greenberg. When an attempt was made by police to trace the last known movements of the decedent it was reported that he had been seen in the company of George Redding. Police found Redding at his home and brought him in for questioning. At first the suspect denied all knowledge of the crime. By the following day, however, there was a marked change in Redding. He said that Greenberg's ghost had appeared to him in the night and so he dare not deny his guilt any longer. A visibly frightened George Redding was then brought to the scene of the crime where he reenacted his movements for the district attorney and the coroner. When the party of officials was deep in the woods Redding was once again stricken with fear. He said that Greenberg's ghost had risen up out of the ground and beckoned to him.

When the case came to trial a jury found evidence of premeditation sufficiently convincing. For that reason the guilty verdict meant a mandatory sentence of death for the defendant. George Redding was then packed off to the Connecticut State Prison to await his fate. There was no appeal and no clemency. The end came on November 1, 1912, when the budding playwright died on the gallows.

1913

Stefan Borasky, white, age 25. *Murder.* the crime was committed on September 27, 1911, at West Granville, Massachusetts. Stefan Borasky and Anton Koleck were Polish immigrants who worked the farms in and around the town of Granville. Both kept busy at chopping wood and berry picking throughout the summer of 1911 and they stuck together when the time came to find another assignment. On September 25 they called at the farm of one Paul Umansky (a Russian Jew) and offered their services. Negotiations went on until a late hour and in accordance with rural custom the visitors were invited to spend the night there. It is presumed that sometime during their stay at the Umansky farm Borasky and Koleck saw the farmer's mother, Mrs. Rose Umansky (white, age 63), reach for a batch of paper money that she kept pinned to her waistband. On the following morning both of the visitors departed from the farm without incident. Then on the day after that they returned to the vicinity and hid in some nearby woods until they saw Paul Umansky and his wife drive toward town in a loaded wagon. They correctly surmised that the couple would be away for some hours while disposing of their produce and also correctly surmised that Rose Umansky would be alone in the farmhouse, baby-sitting her infant grandchild. Without further ado, Borasky and Koleck forced their way into the farmhouse and attacked Rose Umansky. They beat her up and choked her to death. Then they took her money and dragged her body out into the yard where they threw it down a well. After that they went back into the farmhouse and ransacked every room. When they came upon the baby which the victim had been watching they left it unharmed. However, they did steal every article of value in the house right down to the baby's silverplated rattle. The crime was discovered when the farmer's wife came home. A thorough search of the premises turned up the body in the well and it was at once noted that the decedent's clothing was torn open at precisely the spot where she was known to keep her cash. It was therefore reasoned that the dead woman had been attacked by someone with prior knowledge of her habits. The two recent visitors came to mind and they were quickly hunted down. Borasky denied the crime at first but Koleck named him as the killer. When told of that development in the case, Borasky made a similar charge against Koleck. When the case came to trial, Koleck turned state's evidence in order to save his own life. As a result, Borasky was capitally convicted. On July 15, 1912, Koleck died of a brain tumor and Borasky seized upon that circumstance to claim that the state's evidence was flawed because Koleck's illness had rendered him of unsound mind. An appeal was heard based on that argument but the decision went against Borasky. He was subsequently electrocuted at the Massachusetts State Prison on June 24, 1913.

Louis Saxon, white, age 28. *Murder.* The crime was committed on November 27, 1912, at New Britain, Connecticut. This man was a Russian Jew who had anglicized his surname. He came to America in 1909 and was a tailor by trade. Physically, Saxon was a diminutive man who could have passed for a lad of 15. While still in the old country he was paired with a 14-year-old girl named Annie Spelansky in an arranged union. His parents told him that he would thenceforth be regarded as the girl's husband although no formal marriage ceremony was ever performed. An obedient boy, Saxon accepted the situation as did the girl. When he came of age he decided to seek his fortune in America. Saxon then made the trans–Atlantic crossing and brought Miss Spelansky

with him. The couple settled at Cincinnati and there began to raise a family. Three children followed who all joined their mother in bearing Saxon's surname. This was too much for a certain female busybody who secretly desired to have Saxon for herself. That person accordingly took steps to subvert Saxon's domestic life by spreading gossip in the Jewish community. Saxon's mate was described as a "harlot" and his children were called "bastards." A complaint was also made to the grand rabbi which scandalized Saxon and his family. With her reputation in ruins, Mrs. Saxon, née Spelansky, became distraught and attempted suicide by jumping into the Ohio River with a baby in her arms. Both were rescued whereupon Louis Saxon let it be known that he had had his fill of Cincinnati. He then packed up his household and moved east to Connecticut. There the city of New Britain became his new abode. Alas, Saxon's troubles followed him; the gossip-monger who had hounded him in Ohio actually went to the extreme of seeking him out in Connecticut. Once again Saxon acquired a bad reputation among local Jews but this time with an added touch: the mother of his children was called "unclean" in the eyes of God. From that point on a change became apparent in Louis Saxon. He began to distance himself from his common-law wife. When the woman pleaded with him to formally marry her in order to legitimize their children he became sullen and evasive. Then he parceled out his offspring among relatives and found a separate place to live for himself. Saxon even started to actively persecute his common-law wife; he told unsavory stories about her to her landlords which resulted in her eviction from every place where she found a room. The woman complained to the police saying that her husband was trying to force her to leave town. The police replied that they were powerless to act because no laws had been broken. In desperation, Annie Spelansky attempted to talk Saxon into a reconciliation. She nearly succeeded when she begged the man to reconsider for the sake of their children. Saxon then moved into an apartment with his common-law wife and even agreed to a wedding. Then the gossip resurfaced. Three days later Saxon changed his mind and walked out. Unable to pay the rent by herself, Annie Spelansky was evicted. By mid–November of 1912 she was homeless and destitute. She finally walked into a neighborhood pharmacy and tearfully told the proprietor thereof that she had no place to go. Then she showed the man a bottle of poison and said that she was going to end it all. The pharmacist took pity on the wretched woman. He gave her some money with which to get a room for herself. He also introduced her to the owner of a confectionery who agreed to give her a job. Four days later Louis Saxon met his common-law wife on the street and threatened to shoot her. On the following day he purchased a revolver with which to enforce that threat. He also repeated his nasty trick of slandering the woman to her landlord. Once again Annie Spelansky (white, age 24) complained to the police and once again she was rebuffed by them. On the next day — November 27, 1912, — Louis Saxon started drinking. By evening he was thoroughly drunk. He then walked over to his common-law wife's new place of employment (at No. 13 Lafayette Street) and shot the woman dead. When he sobered up, Saxon was very contrite. When he was made to face the law he feigned insanity. His antics failed to impress a jury and he was convicted of capital murder. On June 27, 1913, he was hanged at the Connecticut State Prison.

1914

Arthur Bosworth, white, age 26. *Murder.* The crime was committed on

June 7, 1911, at Essex Junction, Vermont. This offender was an Englishman by birth and a wanderer by habit. He left Montreal, Canada, in the spring of 1911 and walked to Vermont in search of employment. He finally came to Essex Junction and found work in a hotel there. He lasted on the job six weeks and was then dismissed for improperly importuning a female co-worker named Mae LaBelle (white, age 19). Stung by the loss of his job, Bosworth blamed Miss LaBelle for his misfortune. He also resented her failure to reciprocate his affection. He then determined to take out his frustration on her. On the afternoon of the above date Bosworth got his hands on a .32 caliber revolver and lay in wait for Miss LaBelle at the Essex Junction railroad station. The young woman dutifully arrived there on her way to work and Bosworth — oblivious to bystanders — opened fire on her. Mae LaBelle saw her attacker and ran screaming through the train station with Bosworth in pursuit. He chased her down, firing his weapon as he ran. No less than nine bullets found their mark, mortally wounding Mae LaBelle. When Bosworth ran out of ammunition he was tackled by the stationmaster and held for the police. A judge and jury later decreed that Bosworth was guilty of capital felony. The sentence was death by hanging. On January 2, 1914, that sentence was carried out at the Vermont State Prison.

James Plew, white, age 47. *Murder.* The crime was committed on June 23, 1913, at Cheshire, Connecticut. James Plew and William Wakefield (white, age 45) were farmhands who worked for a wealthy squire in the town of Middlebury. Both were married and lived close to their place of employment together with their wives and children. Plew was described as a "typical countryman" used to physical labor. His only brush with the law had been in 1891 when he went to jail for horse stealing. Wakefield was also a roustabout but is reported to have had a docile temperament. Trouble arose when Plew became infatuated with Wakefield's wife, a rather frumpish woman named Bessie Webster Wakefield (white, age 45). Over a period of time Mrs. Wakefield warmed to Plew's attention and a scandal arose. Her husband became aware of the situation but did little to forestall it; he merely contented himself with making snide remarks. Plew's wife was less indulgent; she walked out in disgust, leaving her spouse with a two-year-old child on his hands. When all of this was reported to the squire for whom Plew and Wakefield worked, that person angrily declared that he ran a respectable farm and would tolerate no adultery among his employees. As a result, Plew and Wakefield were both fired from their jobs. By the spring of 1912 the Plew-Wakefield affair had wrecked one marriage, strained another and cost two men their livelihoods. It would ultimately cost them their lives as well.

The loss of their jobs was a severe blow to both men. Wakefield eventually found other work as a teamster and moved away to Bristol. Plew remained in Middlebury where he used a promise of good conduct to euchre his way back into his former position. He also put his young child to board with the Wakefields and used that circumstance as an excuse to make frequent trips to Bristol. In such a way he kept up his affair with Bessie Wakefield. Finally the two lovers decided to eliminate the cuckold and they formed a shabby scheme to that effect. It was agreed that Plew would bring about the disappearance of William Wakefield after which the woman would report that she had been abandoned by her spouse. Thus the way would be cleared for the lovers to live together as man and wife. On Sunday morning — June 22, 1913 — Plew came to the Wakefield residence for the ostensible purpose of visiting his child. He brought with him a loaded handgun, a bottle of chloroform and a set of handcuffs. After lunch, Bessie Wakefield excused herself and went to Lake Compounce (a nearby amusement park) with her upstairs neighbor. When she returned that evening she was amazed to see her husband and her lover still together in the house. Taking Plew aside, she warned him that he had better cease his dilly-dallying and get on with what they had planned. The hesitant Plew replied that he did not consider the time to be right. It was nearly an hour before midnight when William Wakefield finally told Plew that he had overstayed his welcome. Only then did Plew act; he started arguing with Wakefield and came to blows with him. He throttled Wakefield with his bare hands until the man was faint and gasping. Then he stifled him with the chloroform until he was well under its influence. When Wakefield was no longer in any condition to resist, Plew fettered him with the handcuffs. Then he stood him up and led him out of the house in a groggy, drug-induced state. Proceeding along South Street in Bristol, Plew told several passersby that he was merely helping a drunken friend find his way home. Then he set a course for the Cheshire woods, nine miles away. It being a moonlit night, Plew prodded Wakefield along the entire way on foot. It was not until four o'clock in the morning that they reached a spot that was sufficiently remote for what Plew had in mind. By then Wakefield was emerging from his stupor so Plew shot him six times in the back. Then he rolled the body over and drove a knife into Wakefield's heart. Still not satisfied, Plew removed the laces from the dead man's shoes and fashioned them into a noose with which he then hanged Wakefield from a tree limb. Six days later some deer hunters found the body in an advanced state of decomposition. Bessie Wakefield in the meantime circulated a story that her husband had left her with an intention of committing suicide. She also filed a false police report to that effect. Then she began selling off the contents of her home. Bristol police suspected her story from the start and they had their suspicions heightened when it was reported to them that Mrs. Wakefield had sold all of her husband's clothes to a ragpicker. When the body was found police suspected a link and summoned Mrs. Wakefield to their headquarters. There she was shown the clothing recovered from the crime scene and positively identified them as belonging to her missing husband. An intense interrogation then followed and an hour later the woman made a full confession. Plew was picked up in Middlebury the following day and confessed his guilt as well. When the case came to trial both of the lovers were capitally convicted and sentenced to death. Plew waived an appeal and looked forward to his end. On March 4, 1914, he was hanged at the Connecticut State Prison. In the case of Bessie Wakefield there was a battle. Women suffragists flocked to her defense. They financed an appellate team which secured a retrial for the condemned woman. Again Bessie Wakefield was convicted but she was spared the death penalty. Off to jail she went for the rest of her life while her suffragist friends—finding her without further political value—deserted her.

William Dorr, white, age 31. *Murder.* The crime was committed on April 11, 1912, at Lynn, Massachusetts. This man committed murder for the sake of an inheritance. George E. Marsh (white, age 75) of Lynn was a retired manufacturer who had amassed a considerable fortune during the course of his career. His niece, Orpha Marsh of Stockton, California, was due to inherit a portion of that estate totaling more than $140,000. This Orpha Marsh (who was in failing health) in turn had a live-in nephew named William Dorr who she designated as her sole beneficiary. Dorr was troubled by the increasing possibility that his aunt would predecease George E. Marsh, in which event her bequest would terminate and he, Dorr, would be left with nothing. It therefore became imperative to Dorr that his aunt survive George E. Marsh. In order to ensure such a scenario Dorr decided to eliminate George E. Marsh. He left his home in California and traveled east to Boston. Once there, he purchased an automobile and proceeded to Lynn where he carefully examined the local terrain. Then he visited his relatives— including George E. Marsh—and told them that he was on a cross-country trip and would be in the vicinity for several days before returning to California. On the above date Dorr encountered George E. Marsh walking along a Lynn street and invited him to come along for a ride in his automobile. The unsuspecting Mr. Marsh had never ridden in an automobile before and he was intrigued by the novelty of such an experience. The aging gent then climbed into the passenger seat and allowed his young relative to drive him around. The two men proceeded to a scenic area of the Lynn marshes called "the Point of Pines." There William Dorr turned on his guest, shot him four times in the heart and dumped his body in a bog. A clamdigger found the victim the following day by which time Dorr was already on his way back to California. At first investigators were at a loss for a motive because the decedent was found with his valuables still on his person. Therefore robbery was discounted. Neighbors then reported the presence of a strange automobile in the vicinity at the time when Mr. Marsh disappeared. Further canvassing of the area established that William Dorr had been in town. When Dorr's automobile was found abandoned in Boston it was traced to the dealership where it had been purchased and its ownership established. When Dorr got off a train in California six days after the crime, police were waiting for him. He was then brought back to Massachusetts and charged with capital murder. At his trial Dorr admitted the homicide but told an improbable tale of self-defense. A jury refused to believe him and returned a first degree verdict. Appeals failed when it was shown that Dorr's financial motive offered compelling evidence of premeditation. The final act took place on March 24, 1914, when William Dorr was electrocuted at the Massachusetts State Prison.

Motejius Rikteraites, white, age 26. *Murder.* The crime was committed on May 10, 1913, at Waterbury, Connecticut. This man was a Lithuanian immigrant who lived with his wife and 18-month-old baby at No. 8 Burton Street in Waterbury. He drank too much and was irascible by nature. His mother-in-law later testified that he had begun quarreling with his wife, Mary Rikteraites (white, age 25), within a week of his wedding and that there had been little or no family harmony up until the time of the crime. On the above date Rikteraites was even more crabby then usual. He got into a shouting match with his wife, accusing her of ogling male boarders and failing to prepare his dinner on time. Then he attacked the woman with a razor and slit her throat from ear to ear. When he realized what he had done, Rikteraites was struck with remorse. He then attempted suicide by slashing his own throat with the same razor. He nearly succeeded in ending his life but was patched up and revived. At his trial he stoutly denied all charges and claimed that he and his wife had been attacked by masked intruders. Shortly before the time set for his execution, however, Rikteraites made a full confession. He was hanged at the Connecticut State Prison on May 8, 1914.

Joseph Buonomo, alias "Chicago Joe," white, age 24. *Murder.* The crime was committed on October 22, 1912, at Stratford, Connecticut. This man was a procurer who lived on the illicit earnings of prostitutes. In Chicago he operated a so-called "escort service" for that purpose. Among his young women was one Jenny Cavalieri (white, age 28). Seeking to escape from her lifestyle and from Buonomo in particular, she fled as far as Bridgeport, Connecticut, where she contacted representatives of an anti-vice organization. Bridgeport at that time was a celebrated center of commerce and industry. It was also a retail and entertainment mecca. But there was general corruption there due to the dozens of saloons, gaming dens and bawdy houses which infested the downtown area. Besides that, the city government stank of graft and illegal enterprises flourished there with little or no restraint. Such was the place where Jenny Cavalieri sought refuge. Not surprisingly, word of her whereabouts reached "Chicago Joe" Buonomo. When it was further reported to him that the woman was talking to anti-vice crusaders, Buonomo decided to hunt her down and make an example of her. Arriving in Bridgeport, Buonomo met with members of the local underworld and learned that Jenny Cavalieri had been reduced to earning her money in the only way that she knew. A Water Street grog shop had been her favorite place of assignation and it was there where "Chicago Joe" decided to await her. On the evening of October 22, 1912, the two came face to face with each other in the Water Street dive. Jenny Cavalieri was alarmed to see Buonomo there and probably realized that she was trapped. When the latter greeted her in an affable manner, however, she decided to play along with him in the hope of giving him the slip at an opportune moment. Buonomo then introduced her to four other men with whom he was sharing a table and after a while suggested that they all go for a joyride beyond the city limits. They would find some suitable spot, said he, where they could all make merry. The other men then feigned an amorous desire for the woman but they really had something else in mind. They hired a large chauffeur-driven touring car and set out in the direction of Stratford. They behaved like a party of revelers throughout the course of their ride and they even stopped to buy wine and cigars for added effect. When their vehicle reached Stratford the men ordered the chauffeur to turn north. Passing by Paradise Green, they entered country that was decidedly rural and finally reached the vicinity of Putney chapel. There they had the driver stop the car. The five men got out of the car with the woman and told the chauffeur to turn the vehicle around and wait for them at a point farther up the road. Then they all walked into an old graveyard where it was proposed that the woman have sex with the men. Instead, four of the men surrounded the woman to bar her escape while Buonomo pulled out a large caliber handgun and shot her five times in the head. Hearing the gunshots, the driver of the touring car flashed his headlights on the scene and saw the five men bending over the body of the woman. He realized at once what had happened and he drove off at full speed. The killers were thus left stranded while the chauffeur spread the alarm. Within a short time police officers from three towns converged on the scene. They were joined by a heavily armed posse of Stratford citizens. All roads were blocked by the police while the posse searched a wide area between the Housatonic River and the Trumbull town line. By morning three suspects had been caught. One of them was "Chicago Joe" Buonomo. He still had the murder weapon on his person. Although he admitted his guilt almost immediately, Buonomo still underwent two trials. He was finally hanged at the Connecticut State Prison on June 30, 1914.

Joseph Bergeron, white, age 40. *Murder.* The crime was committed on June 4, 1913, at New Haven, Connecticut. This man was a tinsmith who abandoned his wife and five children in order to pursue a comely widow. When the woman remained steadfast in a refusal to marry him, Bergeron drank himself into a temper and killed her. The woman in question — Mrs. Elizabeth Dowsette (white, age 41) — lived at No. 53 Locke Street in New Haven. On June 3, 1913, Bergeron left his home in New Britain and headed for New Haven with the intention of calling on Mrs. Dowsette. He brought his younger brother along with him. When the two men reached their destination the woman refused to receive them. She told Joseph Bergeron that she had neither the desire to marry him nor the temperament to further tolerate his repeated importunings. She also advised him to return to his wife and children. Bergeron left her doorstep disappointed. After spending the night in a New Haven hotel he rose early and told his brother to expect some "fun" that day. He then went to a pawnshop and bought a loaded handgun. After that both men went to a saloon and drank heavily. When they felt themselves to be sufficiently primed they set a course for the Dowsette residence. When they arrived there Joseph Bergeron told his brother to wait at a point down the street. Then he pounded on the woman's door and demanded admittance. When Mrs. Dowcette came to the door Bergeron forced his way into her house and said that he was going to give her one final chance to accept his proposal of marriage. In reply, the woman scolded Bergeron for being drunk and ordered him to get off the property. It was then that Bergeron drew his weapon and opened fire. Mrs. Dowsette was hit four times and fatally wounded. The killer paused long enough to place the victim's two-year-old child in the care of a neighbor. Then he rejoined his brother and calmly walked away. Police found him strolling along a sidewalk unconcernedly when they searched the immediate area. Bergeron unabashedly admitted the crime and pleaded guilty when he was brought to trial. It then remained for a jury to determine the degree of guilt. The fact that he had bought the murder weapon less than an hour before the crime was proof of premeditation. Bergeron was therefore capitally convicted and ordered for execution. He was hanged at the Connecticut State Prison on August 11, 1914.

1915

Biagio Falzone, white, age 33. *Murder.* The crime was committed on December 20, 1914, at Wakefield, Massachusetts. Maurice Albertson (white, age 44) ran a jewelry store in the city of Lawrence. He not only sold his wares over the counter but also from door to door. Some of his most profitable sales routes were in the Italian immigrant communities north of Boston. On December 17, 1914, two well-dressed Italian men came to Albertson's store and examined some of his better items. After some time spent in knowledgeable conversation it was proposed that the jeweler come to Wakefield on the following Sunday. The two customers explained that they were relatives of a young couple who were soon to be married and that they wanted to purchase a suitable gift of jewelry for them. They liked the merchandise they saw but were concerned lest their wives not share their taste. Therefore they requested that Albertson make a housecall and bring with him the selections they had made together with some similar patterns so that the womenfolk might see them before a final decision was made. This did not sound unreasonable to the jeweler because he had made many housecalls before. He was also familiar with the Italian section of Wakefield, having made

numerous sales there in the past. On the above date then, Albertson placed items to the value of $2000 (a significant sum in those days) in his traveling case and journeyed to Wakefield. He first made some collections from existing customers there and then called at No. 34 Columbia Road, the address given him by his visitors of three days before. When told that no such persons were at that address, Albertson next surmised that the visitors must have really meant a cottage to the rear of that place. He then went to the cottage and was never after seen alive. In retracing his movements several days later, detectives came to the cottage and found it empty. In examining the premises, however, they found evidence of fresh digging in an underground crawlspace. They were also astonished to find the entire place rigged for combustion and booby-trapped with dynamite. After successfully clearing the hazards which had been deliberately placed in their way, investigators started digging in the crawlspace. At a depth of six feet they found what they were looking for: the body of Maurice Albertson wrapped in a bloody sheet. He had been garroted with a rope (which was still around his neck) and stabbed 11 times in the throat, chest and stomach. His person was also picked clean of valuables. The last inhabitant of the cottage was identified as one Biagio Falzone, a young Italian. He in turn was known to be chummy with two others named Ignazio Morrella and Luigi Grassadonia, both of whom were subsequently identified as the men who had called at the jewelry store and made the fatal date with the murdered man. Within a short time all three suspects were rounded up. Grassadonia saved his own skin by turning state's evidence against his two companions. As a result, Morrella was sentenced to life imprisonment and Falzone was sentenced to death. On May 11, 1915, Biagio Falzone was electrocuted at the Massachusetts State Prison.

Bernard Montvid, white, age 23.

Murder. The crime was committed on February 8, 1915, at New Britain, Connecticut. Bernard Montvid and Peter Krakus (white, age 25) were Lithuanian immigrants who came to the United States shortly before the outbreak of World War I. Both were itinerant barbers by trade. They were also habitual criminals who specialized in the theft of jewelry and fine watches. When their travels brought them to Connecticut they sought out a municipality with a sizable enclave of their fellow countrymen. New Britain met their specification and so it was there where they took up lodgings. Going about their haircutting trade in order to give themselves a visible means of support, they all the while kept alert for any sign of illicit pickings. Within a matter of days they noticed that the church which served the local Lithuanian community was very well attended. From that circumstance they surmised that the parish must be a prosperous one. So they telephoned the resident priest, the Rev. Joseph Zebris (white, age 54), and used threats of violence in an attempt to extort money from him. Father Zebris did not yield to the shakedown but he did notify the New Britain police. He also became noticeably guarded in his movements. Undeterred, Montvid and Krakus decided to take the matter a step further: they went to the rectory where Father Zebris lived (St. Andrew's Roman Catholic Rectory at No. 396 Church Street) and forced their way in. They attacked Father Zebris in his sitting room and beat him without mercy. Then they garroted him with a nylon cord and shot him four times in the chest. When the slain priest's housekeeper, Iva Gilmanaitis (white, age 36), came downstairs to check the source of the commotion she was pursued by the killers from room to room until they finally cornered her in the attic. There a desperate struggle took place in which the housekeeper was overpowered and strangled with a clothesline. When both of the rectory's occupants were dead the killers began a frenzied search for valuables. They ransacked every single room with the utmost thoroughness, stealing among other things, the priest's watch, his silver rosary beads and even his hat.

The crime was discovered the following morning. News of it spread rapidly through the Roman Catholic neighborhoods. Within a short time thousands of angry people took to the streets. They marched on the city hall to demand apprehension of the killers. Montvid and Krakus circulated among the crowd unrecognized by all. Three days later they packed up and left town. Montvid went a few miles west to Waterbury where he took a room. Krakus set a course for Massachusetts. Both planned to eventually meet up with each other in Philadelphia.

A few days later Montvid overplayed his hand; he sent a minacious letter to a second New Britain priest: the Rev. Lucian Bojnowski, pastor of the Most Sacred Heart of Jesus Roman Catholic Church which served the city's Polish community. The letter demanded $10,000 and warned that Father Bojnowski risked the same fate as Father Zebris.

A badly frightened Father Bojnowski turned the letter over to detectives who at once came to the conclusion that they were dealing with criminals from beyond New Britain. Experience with the local underworld convinced them that no hometown criminal — not even the worst of them — was of such a temperament that he would dare to kill a priest. What was also known for certain was that Father Bojnowski's extortion letter had been written in fluent Polish. In addition, it was known that the person who had threatened Father Zebris by telephone had spoken fluent Lithuanian. The police therefore began a thorough canvassing of all lodging establishments which catered to customers of those nationalities. Careful attention was paid to those tenants who had either arrived or departed recently. It was in such a way that detectives picked up Montvid's trail. By the time they traced him to Waterbury he had moved on. However, his landlord there told of how Montvid had allowed him to use a portable typewriter that he had in order to type an important letter. This letter was successfully recovered and compared with Father Bojnowski's extortion letter. The typeface was found to be an exact match. An expert in such matters also confirmed that both letters had been typed on the same typewriter. A warrant was accordingly issued for the arrest of Bernard Montvid on a charge of criminal extortion. Krakus was also named in the warrant when he was identified as Montvid's erstwhile roommate. A link to the murder of Father Zebris, however, remained to be found.

A month later Montvid and Krakus made their Philadelphia rendezvous. There they pawned Father Zebris's pocket watch. Then they moved on to Wilmington, Delaware. Once again they attempted to pawn some items of personal adornment. This time the pawnbroker's suspicions were aroused and police were called when Montvid and Krakus went on their way. A running gun battle ensued as police officers chased the suspects through the streets of Wilmington. Krakus managed to kill one of his pursuers before being disabled by gunfire. Montvid was also pounced upon when he threw his gun away. When Delaware authorities searched the prisoners they found a cache of expensive jewelry. They also found pawn tickets and train tickets bearing Massachusetts and Connecticut place names. It was not long before both suspects were found to match an all-points bulletin that had originated in Connecticut. New Britain detectives were then invited to come to Delaware and examine both men. Then arose the evidence which tied them in with the murder of Father Zebris: the

keys to the New Britain rectory were found in Montvid's possession. The priest's pocket watch was also recovered by means of a pawn ticket found on Krakus. In addition, Krakus was found still to be wearing Father Zebris's hat. When the evidence finally became overwhelming Montvid broke down and admitted that he had been present when Father Zebris was killed. He denied, however, taking an actual part in the murder.

The Connecticut and Delaware authorities finally came to a mutual agreement: Montvid would be returned north to answer for killing the priest while Krakus would remain in Delaware to answer for killing the Wilmington policeman. Two speedy trials followed and appeals were disallowed. On May 14, 1915, Peter Krakus swung to his doom from a Delaware gallows. On August 13, 1915, Bernard Montvid met a similar fate at the Connecticut State Prison. It is significant to note that the Roman Catholic Church did not seek clemency in either case.

Frank Grela, white, age 41. *Murder.*

The crime was committed on June 6, 1915, at Hartford, Connecticut. This man was a Galician immigrant who lived in a crowded tenement at No. 450½ Main Street in Hartford. The lack of privacy there created friction between Grela and his wife, Nellie Grela (white, age 27), when the former came to suspect that the latter was not behaving with proper modesty in the presence of male boarders. In order to escape the situation, Grela took a job in a New Jersey foundry and temporarily moved away. During his absence he was kept informed by letter of his wife's conduct. After three months he returned to Hartford unannounced and was met with more gossip. Grela readily believed every word he heard and he became visibly upset. Without bothering to verify the rumors or confront his wife about them,

Grela went to a hardware store and purchased a handgun. Then he deliberately waited until a late hour when all were asleep in his tenement. Letting himself in with a passkey, he furtively approached the door to his apartment, expecting to find his wife with another man. When he peeked in the keyhole he saw the woman sleeping on a cot with a baby in her arms. Grela then opened the door and silently slipped into his apartment. He fired two shots into his wife's face, killing her instantly. In the uproar that followed Grela fled from the scene. He was nabbed within a matter of minutes, however, when a policeman saw him running past the Hartford Public Library with a gun in his hand. Once in custody, Grela frankly admitted the crime and said that he could care less about the consequences. Brought to trial within a matter of days, he was convicted of premeditated murder and ordered for execution. There was no appeal. Frank Grela was subsequently hanged at the Connecticut State Prison on August 13, 1915.

1916

Oscar Comery, white, age 31. *Murder.* The crime was committed on November 29, 1914, at Manchester, New Hampshire. This man was a Quebecois by birth. His father died when he was very young, leaving his mother destitute with five children on her hands. Not being one to apply for charity, Mother Comery packed up her brood and moved to southern New Hampshire where workers were needed in the mills. She finally settled at Manchester and found employment there along with her two eldest children. When young Oscar reached sufficient age he was apprenticed to a dairyman. He served his time faithfully and drove a milkwagon for most of his teenage years. Then as the 20th century dawned Oscar began to notice a gradual change on the roads: newfangled gadgets called "automobiles" were beginning to compete with horsedrawn vehicles. While the older generation looked askance at the "horseless carriages" young Oscar Comery was quick to recognize them as the wave of the future. He reasoned that they were going to need constant upkeep so in his spare time he studied every aspect of automobiles and maintenance thereof. When Oscar reached the age of majority he went to work as one of Manchester's first full-time auto mechanics and chauffeurs. In 1909 the young auto buff married a lady from Clinton, Massachusetts, named Bertha Catharine Schaller. One child was subsequently born to them.

While Oscar Comery was generally recognized as an excellent driver and garageman he was also known as a rake. Women were his weakness and he provided much grist for local gossip. He is also said to have kept himself in a perpetual state of "financial difficulty" because of his many dalliances. He finally overplayed his hand at the age of 31 when he impregnated an underage girl. So smitten was he that he sought to supplant his own wife and child with the expectant young mother. Then his legitimate child died suddenly—whether from natural causes or not remains open in light of subsequent events. Shortly afterward—on November 29, 1914—Comery's wife also succumbed at the age of 26. The woman died in agony but a death certificate was issued giving "acute indigestion" as the casus morti. Unknown to Comery, his wife had confided certain misgivings in the minister who conducted her funeral. That individual had also buried Comery's child some weeks before and now began to get suspicious. He was also piqued by the unseemly haste with which Comery applied for the payout on the dead woman's life insurance policy. The clergyman approached police and he was listened to attentively because of his status in the community. Based on what he said, an investigation was begun. The body of Bertha Comery was exhumed and her viscera was found to be saturated with strychnine, a deadly poison. It was subsequently determined that Comery had purchased a lethal amount of that substance from a chemist for the ostensible purpose of putting down a dog. When confronted with the evidence, Comery confessed that he had put the poison in some cold capsules which his wife was then taking by prescription.

When Comery came to trial he pleaded guilty in anticipation of a prison sentence. The presiding judge, however, remanded to a jury the question of what penalty to impose. In such a way were several unsavory details brought out in addition to the admission of poisoning. It was revealed that Comery had been sleeping with his paramour ever since she was 12 years old — a revelation which so disgusted the jury that it took less than an hour to order the death penalty. An appeal was subsequently taken to the State Supreme Court and it was rejected by a unanimous vote. The Governor's Privy Council was also unanimous in denying clemency. The end came on February 18, 1916, when Oscar Comery was hanged at the New Hampshire State Prison.

Harry Rowe, white, age 22. **Isaac Williams,** white, age 27. *Murder.* Their crime was committed on November 28, 1914, at Barkhamsted, Connecticut. These men came from Poughkeepsie, New York, and Bridgeport, Connecticut, respectively. They had gotten to know each other while employed as ice cutters in the tiny town of Colebrook. Rowe is described as a mental submissive who was dominated by Williams. On the above date both men went to Barkhamsted. There they entered a country store operated by one Hubert B. Case (white, age 58), a postmaster and member of the Litchfield County Board of Commissioners. This Hubert Case had closed his place of business for the day and was making entries in his ledgers when Rowe and Williams burst in on him. The intruders attacked the storekeeper with metal wagon axles and beat him so severely that he died the following day. They also rifled the man's pockets before fleeing from the scene. Eight weeks later Williams was arrested in Bridgeport. Rowe was found in the Dutchess County jail where he had been detained on an unrelated charge. Police were initially put on the right path by a witness who claimed to have seen both Rowe and Williams near the scene of the Barkhamsted murder. Further investigation revealed that the witness had actually acted as a lookout during the assault and robbery of Mr. Case. An examination of the lengthy police record amassed by Williams also turned up several incriminating facts. This led to a deal in which the "witness" agreed to turn state's evidence against his two partners. The result was capital conviction for both Rowe and Williams. Neither man admitted his guilt. They preferred to go to the gallows in silence. On March 3, 1916, they did exactly that at the Connecticut State Prison.

Pasquale Zuppa, white, age 27. *Murder.* The crime was committed on September 6, 1915, at Guilford, Connecticut. Pasquale Zuppa and Antonio Corsi (white, age 23) were railroad laborers who lived in the same New Haven boarding house. The above date being a holiday, neither man had to report to his job. They therefore decided to go fishing together. Being told that the bluefish were running off the coast of Guilford, both men set out early for that town. They went to the shoreline area known as Sachem's Head and spent the entire day there. In the evening they gathered up their catch and began to walk to a nearby trolley line. While proceeding along Leete's Island Road a plan which Zuppa had previously formed was put into effect; he struck Corsi down from behind with a rock and drove a dagger into his back. Then he pulled the man into some roadside bushes where he stripped him naked. Zuppa stole Corsi's pocket money along with his basket of fish. The body was found the next morning. Zuppa was arrested within a matter of hours and charged with capital murder. He admitted the crime and was sentenced to death. On March 10, 1916, he was hanged at the Connecticut State Prison.

Anton Retkovitz, white, age 35. *Murder.* The crime was committed on March 14, 1914, at Fall River, Massachusetts. Anton Retkovitz and Donkna Peremjbida (white, age 27) were an immigrant couple who came from the same village in Russia. After clearing Ellis Island they made their way to Pittsburgh, Pennsylvania, where both found jobs and settled down. Retkovitz became a railroad laborer while the woman took up housekeeping. Initially they boarded in the same rooming house and looked to each other for moral support. Their relationship became strained, however, when Retkovitz sought to make it more than platonic. Donkna knew that Retkovitz had a wife and children in the Old Country and it was for that reason that she refused to become intimate with him. Retkovitz was loath to be scorned. He began stalking Donkna and otherwise pestering her. When the situation became intolerable Donkna packed her bags and headed east. She had only enough money to make train fare as far as Fall River, Massachusetts, so it was thus that her destination was determined. On the train she made the acquaintance of a kind-hearted couple who were themselves returning to Fall River. Donkna told them her story and cried from despair. Her listeners were touched by her plight and they offered to see her safely resettled. So they found the young woman a room in Fall River

and secured a job for her in a respectable residence at No. 182 Spring Street.

Several weeks later Retkovitz learned of Donkna's whereabouts. He immediately quit his job with the railroad and set a course for Fall River. When he got there he inquired for a recently arrived Russian woman and said that he was her husband. He soon found out where Donkna was staying and he took a room for himself in the same lodging house. Then he resumed his unwanted attentions. One day an argument broke out and Retkovitz assaulted Donkna. She reported the matter to the police and Retkovitz was arrested. He wound up serving 30 days in the House of Correction. By the time of his release he was seething with resentment. He then declared that if he could not have Donkna then neither would any other man. On the above date Retkovitz arose before dawn and went to Donkna's place of employment. Making use of an unlocked window, he snuck into the first floor kitchen and waited there with a razor. He knew that Donkna began each day by going there to prepare breakfast. When the woman entered the rear door of the house Retkovitz attacked her. He slashed her about the face and neck — fatally — and then fled from the scene. Nine days later he was captured in Boston. Two trials followed in which Retkovitz swore that he was innocent. Right up to the time of his execution he continued to deny his guilt in the face of overwhelming evidence. On March 14, 1916 — the second anniversary of his crime — Retkovitz was electrocuted at the Massachusetts State Prison.

1917

Francis Ducharme, white, age 26. *Murder.* The crime was committed on October 21, 1916, at Chicopee, Massachusetts. This man was a sexual degenerate who outraged the greater Springfield area. He was born at Salem and raised as a ward of the state. When he reached the age of majority he migrated to the Connecticut River valley area where he worked a series of jobs on farms and in the mills. He was never able to hold a steady position and drifted from one short assignment to another. His personal reputation was abominable; there were numerous complaints made against him for lewdness and public intoxication. On the above date he lured a three-year-old toddler named Leona Kaczar (white) into a crawlspace at No. 16 Depot Street in Chicopee. There he raped the child and left her to die of vaginal trauma. When Ducharme was arrested two days later he nonchalantly admitted the crime. When he was brought to the local police court for arraignment a lynch mob was waiting. More than 1000 irate citizens prepared to storm the building. Ducharme got safely away only when he was smuggled out of a rear door dressed as a police officer. He subsequently pled guilty to a charge of capital felony. Then he was ordered for execution. On September 11, 1917, this offender was electrocuted at the Massachusetts State Prison. Note: Ducharme was also the prime suspect in the fatal rape of a five-year-old Holyoke girl which occurred 11 months prior to the Chicopee crime.

Joseph Castelli, white, age 23. **Francisco Vetere,** white, age 24. *Murder.* Their crime was committed on April 23, 1916, at New Haven, Connecticut. These men were deaf-mutes who lived in New York City. Castelli had marital problems with his wife, Annie Fortia Castelli (white, age 31), and became greatly incensed when the woman (who was herself a deaf-mute) complained of the matter to fellow parishioners at their church. In fact, so incensed did Castelli become that he made plans to do away with his wife. He approached a life-long friend of his — Francisco Vetere — and

proposed a sordid scheme: Vetere would sexually seduce Castelli's wife (with her husband's secret consent) and then elope with her to Connecticut. Castelli would then follow closely behind them and strike the woman down at an opportune time. According to Vetere's subsequent confession, he agreed to go along with the plan partly out of desire to please Castelli and partly in return for an undisclosed sum of money. Over a course of time the seduction of Mrs. Castelli by Francisco Vetere did indeed occur. Then after that guilty move had been achieved, Vetere talked the woman into running away with him. On the morning of the above date the two lovers boarded a train to New Haven. Unknown to Mrs. Castelli, her husband rode along in a different passenger car. When the train reached its destination the supposed elopers went to a rooming house at No. 260 Crown Street and took a lodging. Then after freshening up a bit they went out to dinner. As soon as they left the rooming house, Joseph Castelli slipped into the place unseen. He found the room his wife had taken and gained entry to it by the door which his accomplice Vetere had left unlocked. Then he hid in a closet and awaited his wife's return. Two hours later Vetere and the woman came back to the room. As Mrs. Castelli sat in a chair with her back to the closet her husband leapt from his place of concealment and bludgeoned her with a crowbar. Then the two conspirators dragged the woman into a bathroom where they poured poison down her throat and faked a scene to make it look as if she had slipped on soap and struck her head. After that both men hurried back to New York. On the following day the landlady of the rooming house sensed that something was wrong. She let herself into the room with her passkey and discovered the body of Annie Castelli. The woman was still alive but she died soon after reaching a hospital. She was successfully identified through a missing persons report which her husband filed soon after reaching New York. When investigators first questioned Joseph Castelli (in sign language), he showed them a postcard which he claimed to have received from his wife which told of her supposed elopement. When the postcard was shown to the dead woman's mother, the handwriting on it was found not to match that of Annie Castelli. Her husband was then subjected to an intense interrogation and he eventually confessed. Vetere also admitted his part in the crime. Both men were returned to Connecticut and charged with capital murder. At a subsequent trial that was conducted entirely in sign language for the benefit of the defendants, the written confessions of both men were entered as evidence. Premeditation was also proven by the prosecution. A dual conviction followed and both men were sent to the Connecticut State Prison under sentence of death. They were hanged there on October 5, 1917.

Stephen Buglione, white, age 21. **Giovanni Don Vanso,** white, age 21. *Murder.* Their crime was committed on September 25, 1917, at New Britain, Connecticut. These young men lived together at No. 631 East 37th Street in Manhattan. Both were meat cutters by profession. It so happened that Don Vanso had originally come from the central Italian town of Nola. There he had had a maternal uncle murdered in 1902. The killer had fled to America because he dreaded a vendetta by the family of the slain man. Giovanni Don Vanso was only six years old at the time but as he grew he was carefully groomed to be the instrument of his family's revenge. Fifteen years passed before Don Vanso's family felt that the time was right. They had succeeded in tracing the killer, Raphael Simonelli (white, age 35), to New Britain, Connecticut, and young Giovanni Don Vanso was given his instructions based on that information.

Accordingly, Don Vanso journeyed to New Britain accompanied by his friend and roommate, Stephen Buglione. Both men carried firearms. When they arrived at their destination they proceeded to the vicinity of Chestnut Street. There they lay in wait near the address of Raphael Simonelli. When they spotted a pedestrian who they believed to be Simonelli they approached the man in a friendly way and struck up a conversation with him. Not perceiving his danger, Simonelli chatted amicably with Don Vanso and Buglione. When he was asked by way of conversation from what part of the "Old Country" he came, he confirmed that he was a Nolan. Then when he was asked how he came to be in America he matter-of-factly admitted that he was a fugitive. When asked the nature of his offense he confirmed that it was a homicide of 15 years' standing. Then when asked the name of the person he had killed, he replied with the name of Don Vanso's uncle. With Simonelli's identity thus established beyond any doubt, Don Vanso pulled out his handgun and shot the man in the neck. Then Buglione shot him as well. Both of the killers fled from the scene on foot and were chased through the streets by angry residents of the neighborhood. They outran their pursuers and then made their way to New Haven by trolley, taxicab and jitney bus. Police pounced on them at the New Haven railroad station. Both were placed on trial within a week. Both pleaded guilty to a charge of murder but they still had to endure a trial in order to have the degree of their guilt assessed. Sentenced to death, they waived appeals to higher courts. Their lawyers did plead for them before the Board of Pardons, however. When clemency was refused they took the news gamely. Both died on the gallows at the Connecticut State Prison on November 16, 1917.

William Wise, white, age 23. *Murder.* The crime was committed on September 19, 1917, at New Britain, Connecticut. This offender was a Jewish man originally from New York. He came to Connecticut in 1915 and settled at New Britain where he took a waiter's job in an upscale restaurant. Among the customers he served was a married woman named Anna Bacon Tobin (white, age 25). She became attracted to Wise and began an illicit relationship with him. Soon their affair was an open scandal which neither attempted to conceal. Mrs. Tobin's husband knew of the situation but did nothing about it. Indeed, his wife threatened to leave him if he intervened. Mr. Tobin, being of an obsequious nature, let the woman have her way. As for Wise, he gradually grew to regret his indiscretion. Mrs. Tobin doted on him to a point of excess and he became weary of her cloying attentions. Seeking an escape, Wise joined the army and was taken into the Quartermaster Corps. He was then posted to Fort Slocum in New York and there learned how to be a cook. Mrs. Tobin continued to pester him from afar with maudlin letters and daily telephone calls. In September of 1917 Wise was granted a furlough for the duration of the Jewish holy days. He returned to New Britain only to be clung to by Mrs. Tobin. On the evening of September 18 he attended a banquet given in honor of the Jewish men of New Britain who were then serving in the armed forces. While eating his dinner he was called away by a telephone call from his paramour. By that time Wise had had enough. He went for a long nocturnal walk with Anna Tobin in Walnut Hill Park. There he is presumed to have made an attempt to dissuade her. When the woman objected the situation grew tense. By the time the couple turned onto Pearl Street Wise was exasperated. He took a razor from his pocket and slashed Mrs. Tobin across the throat, killing her. Then he turned the weapon on himself and made some nasty gashes around his own neck and throat.

Shortly before two o'clock in the morning a passerby found both Wise and Mrs. Tobin sprawled out on a sidewalk. Both were awash in blood. The woman was dead but Wise was still alive. Carried to a hospital, he gasped out an improbable story about being attacked by a male assassin. When investigators cleared Mrs. Tobin's husband of involvement in the crime Wise himself became the prime suspect. He was put on trial as soon as his wounds were reasonably healed. Convicted of capital murder, he protested his innocence but did not pursue any appeals. William Wise was hanged at the Connecticut State Prison on December 14, 1917.

1918

Frederick Small, white, age 47. *Murder.* The crime was committed on September 28, 1916, at Ossipee Lake, New Hampshire. This man killed his third wife for the sake of her life insurance. His story began at Portland, Maine, where he was born in the year 1869. There he grew up while attending local schools. At the age of 20 he married a young woman named Nettie Davis (who came from the town of Minot) and set himself up as a grocer. Within three years both his private and professional lives met with misfortune: his wife died in childbirth and his business foundered. Feeling that Portland held no further opportunities for him, Small relocated to Boston where he took a job as a hotel clerk. In 1893 he began to dabble in real estate. When he made some lucrative brokerage commissions he felt confident enough to open an office. He also played the stock market with moderate success. By 1899 he felt that he was prosperous enough to seek another mate and on July 31 of that year Small married an Everett woman named Laura Patterson. Together the couple made a home at West Somerville. During the course of the next decade Small settled down and concentrated on increasing his holdings. In addition to his home in West Somerville he acquired and maintained a fashionable apartment in Boston. He also purchased residential properties in the Massachusetts towns of Salem and Southborough. Then in 1909 his life entered a period of decline. Small's level of debt caught up with him and he found it increasingly difficult to maintain his standard of living. Instead of reducing his overhead he sought to augment his income by filing a scandalous lawsuit. The defendant was one Arthur Soden, the president of the Boston National Baseball League. The charges were "adultery and alienation of affection." Small alleged that Soden had carried on an illicit affair with Mrs. Small that had ruined his marriage and caused him extreme anguish. The litigation dragged on for three years, at the end of which time Small was granted a divorce from his second wife and a monetary award of $10,000. The judge who heard the case did not mince words when he let Mr. and Mrs. Small know what he thought of them. The judge called Mrs. Small "a character who needed no great persuasion or inducement to be led astray" and whose "conduct was an inducement to Soden to pursue the course toward her that he did." As for Frederick Small, the judge said that he was "an indifferent husband who after he knew that his wife was doing wrong, was willing that she should and was ready to take advantage of any error she might make either by way of obtaining a divorce or of making a profit." As a result of this judicial tongue-lashing Frederick Small bore a tarnished reputation for the rest of his life.

On December 3, 1913, Small married his third and final wife: Florence Curry of Southbridge. Then in June of 1914 occurred the "Great Fire" at Salem, Massachusetts. The house of Frederick Small was one of hundreds that were lost in that disaster. When an insurance company adjuster notified Small that he would be receiving a handsome settlement for his loss, the latter was inspired with dreams of easy money. He is alleged to have formed plans to defraud the insurer of his Southborough property. The following month Small and his wife left Southborough and went to a summer cottage of theirs on the shore of New Hampshire's Lake Ossipee. On the day after their departure for that place, the Southborough residence was destroyed in a suspicious fire. Rumors swirled to the effect that Small had left a delayed-action incendiary device in the house but when hard evidence of such was not found, Small collected another $10,000.

It was on September 28, 1916, that Small finally overplayed his hand. He murdered his wife, Florence Curry Small (white, age 35), in their Lake Ossipee residence and hurried back to Boston to establish an alibi. While he was on his way to Massachusetts, the Lake Ossipee cottage caught fire and burned to the ground with the body of Mrs. Small inside. Unexpectedly for the killer, the woman's body landed in a puddle of swill water when it fell through a burning floor to the cellar below. In such a way was the upper portion of the body preserved despite the roaring flames. When police arrived to examine the scene they found the nearly intact remains of Mrs. Small. The woman had been repeatedly bludgeoned and she also had a clothesline tightly knotted about her throat. The evidence of foul play was unmistakable. When Small was notified of the tragedy by telephone he rushed back to the scene. He pretended to be distraught and offered a sizable reward for the apprehension of the killer/arsonist. Within a very short time Small found himself under arrest. It was charged that he had committed the murder and left a delayed-action incendiary device in the cottage. On January 15,

1918, Frederick Small was brought to the gallows in the New Hampshire State Prison. When asked if he had any last words he remained silent. One minute later he was dead.

Francisco Dusso, white, age 25. **Carmine Lanzillo,** white, age 24. **Carmine Pisaniello,** white, age 21. *Murder.* Their crime was committed on November 27, 1916, at West Haven, Connecticut. A Jewish man named Morris Goldstein (white, age 42) operated a tailor shop on Chapel Street in New Haven. Among his customers were the brothers Carmine and Luigi Lanzillo, men of no set occupation. On the afternoon of the above date one of the Lanzillos went to Goldstein's shop to discuss a tailoring job. During the course of the conversation Lanzillo offered to sell the tailor a watch. Goldstein replied that he already had a watch and showed his visitor a very handsome gold one that he carried on his person. He did, however, agree to buy Lanzillo's proffered watch at a reduced price. Lanzillo agreed and Goldstein doled out payment to him from a fat roll of currency. The sight of the tailor's valuables aroused Lanzillo's cupidity and he formed a plan to acquire those valuables by force. When Lanzillo left the tailor shop he hastened to an Italian clubhouse where he had many friends. Then he told a select few of those friends that he needed their help. He outlined a plan to mug Morris Goldstein as he came home from work that night. His listeners liked the proposal and they agreed to go along with it. Accordingly, a five-man gang consisting of Carmine and Luigi Lanzillo, another man named Carmine Battiata and the above-named Francisco Dusso and Carmine Pisaniello rode a trolley out to the Savin Rock section of West Haven. They knew that the tailor rode the same trolley home each evening and got off of it at the intersection of Campbell Avenue and Blohm Street. There all five

men lay in wait with guns, knives, black-jacks and brass knuckles. When Goldstein failed to appear after two hours of waiting several of the gang proposed to abort the scheme. Carmine Lanzillo, however, would not hear of it and he prevailed upon his cronies to wait a little while longer. The cold November night was draining their stamina but they all agreed to stay. Then at precisely 9:30 P.M. Goldstein was seen at the trolley stop. As he walked up Blohm Street he was attacked by the five muggers. When he attempted to resist he was shot dead. The sound of gunfire roused the neighborhood and people poured out of the nearby houses. The muggers were then forced to flee empty-handed. They ran all the way to the railroad tracks where some of them hopped onto a slow-moving freight train. Soon a hue and cry was raised through all the surrounding towns. The alarm reached into the Naugatuck valley where Pisaniello and Carmine Lanzillo were caught by railroad men. When the suspects were returned to West Haven they were subjected to a grueling ordeal. Soon police had a full confession and the names of all those who were involved. The other three muggers were then quickly rounded up. When the case came to trial mitigating factors were found regarding Carmine Battiata; he was accordingly sentenced to a term of from 3 to 15 years in prison. Luigi Lanzillo was sentenced to life behind bars. Carmine Lanzillo, Francisco Dusso and Carmine Pisaniello were all capitally convicted and ordered for execution. On June 17, 1918, all three were hanged at the Connecticut State Prison. It is said that Lanzillo had to be carried to the gallows.

1919

Erasmo Perretta, white, age 27. **Joseph Perretta,** white, age 32. *Murder.* Their crime was committed on June 3,

1918, at New Britain, Connecticut. These men were siblings who had come from Italy. They settled at New Britain where they opened a cobblery at No. 76 Cherry Street. Both of the brothers lived together in an apartment above their place of business. On the evening of June 2, 1918, the Perrettas gave a party at their residence which was attended by many neighborhood *paisani*. Among those present was a hod carrier named Frank Palmese (white, age 45), much to the displeasure of the hosts. There had been ill feelings between the Perrettas and Palmese stemming from an incident two years earlier when Joseph Perretta had disciplined a nephew of Palmese. Whether some cross words were exchanged at the party was never determined but for some reason the Perrettas became annoyed with Palmese. When the party broke up shortly after midnight the Perrettas armed themselves and furtively followed Palmese. Six doors away, in front of No. 70 Cherry Street, they attacked the man. Joseph Perretta slashed Palmese about the head and neck with a knife while Erasmo Perretta shot him in the stomach. When police were called to the scene they followed a trail of blood into the yard of the Perretta house where they found Palmese in a dying condition. Carried to the hospital, the wounded man held on just long enough for the Perretta brothers to be brought before him. There the dying man identified both brothers as his assailants in an ante-mortem statement. Weapons alleged to have been used in the assault were also found in the Perretta home. Both brothers protested their innocence to no avail. Convicted of capital murder, they were hanged at the Connecticut State Prison on June 27, 1919.

George Warner, white, age 48. *Murder.* The crime was committed on November 4, 1914, at Andover, Vermont. This man was the blacksmith in the lit-

tle town of Andover. He was also an alcoholic wife abuser. By the autumn of 1914 his spouse had had her fill of him and she began divorce proceedings. Warner resented this intensely and he came to the conclusion that his wife's parents had put her up to it. On the above date Warner drank himself into a temper and decided to have his revenge. He then stomped over to the Simonsville General Store (where his wife was the postmaster) and started trouble. Warner beat up his wife and then ran amok in the general store, knocking merchandise from the shelves and smashing display cases. Then he went home and armed himself with a rifle. His next step after that was to go looking for his in-laws. Arriving at their house, Warner found only his mother-in-law there. He shot the woman dead. Then he hid her body in a woodshed and lay in wait for his father-in-law. That man had previously been called to the general store by his injured daughter. He was in the act of comforting the woman while his wife was being murdered. When he returned home in his horse-drawn wagon his waiting son-in-law shot him dead in the driver's seat. The slain were identified as Henry Filmore Wiggins (white, age 66) and Georgia Anne Wiggins (white, age 61). George Warner took to the woods when he learned that lawmen were on his trail. A posse caught up with him the next day. His anger spent, Warner offered no resistance. He was brought to the Windsor County jail and charged with two counts of capital murder. When the case came to trial a jury refused to recommend mercy. George Warner was accordingly sentenced to death. Appeals kept him alive for more than four years but the end was never in doubt. On July 12, 1919, an electric chair snuffed out the life of George Warner at the Vermont State Prison.

Nikifor Nechesnook, white, age 28. *Murder.* The crime was committed on

March 12, 1919, at Waterbury, Connecticut. In the closely knit Russian immigrant community at Waterbury it was widely known that Fedor Torrant (white, age 42) was a miser who distrusted banks. It was said that the man carried a large sum of money on his person, sewed into the linings of his clothes. Nikifor Nechesnook was a member of that same ethnic enclave who heard the rumors about Torrant and he decided that they were too tempting to leave unexploited. It was during the evening hours of the above date that Nechesnook lured Torrant to a secluded area along Rumford Street. There he struck the man down from behind with a hatchet. Nechesnook continued to hack at the fallen man until he was unrecognizable. Then he used a razor-sharp knife to cut every single bit of clothing from Torrant's body and methodically rip them apart in a search for hidden valuables. All he found were a few coins and a bus token. Nechesnook was arrested the following day when he was reported to have been seen in company with the murdered man. In his pocket was a laundry check which when traced led to a bloodstained shirt. A search of Nechesnook's residence also turned up bloody garments. Lastly, when a blood-smeared hatchet was found near the scene of the crime a hardware dealer identified it as one that he had sold to Nechesnook. In spite of the evidence, Nechesnook denied his guilt right up to the day of his execution. Only then did he confess to his attorney. He was hanged at the Connecticut State Prison on December 3, 1919.

1920

Daniel Cerrone, white, age 33. *Murder.* The crime was committed on June 8, 1919, at Hamden, Connecticut. This offender was an Italian quarryman who lived at No. 14 Dudley Street in Hamden. With him dwelled his wife and a 14-year-old stepdaughter named Raphaela Comaoda (white). The relationship between Cerrone and his stepchild was said to have "reached a compromising stage" and to have caused trouble between the man and his wife. Matters worsened when Cerrone forbade the girl to receive the addresses of a certain young man. Shortly after midnight on the above date Cerrone came home drunk and put his fist through a window. The sound of breaking glass awoke his wife and some other tenants of the house. Mrs. Cerrone then put on her robe and went to see what had happened. By then her husband had opened the front door and stumbled into the vestibule. When the man caught sight of the woman he said, "Don't worry, I'm not going to touch you." Then he climbed the stairs to his second floor abode and went to the door of his stepdaughter's bedroom. The door was locked and Cerrone pounded on it loudly, demanding admittance. When he received no answer he broke down the door. As the terrified girl cowered in her bed Cerrone began beating her. When his wife tried to restrain him he became even further enraged. He then pulled a revolver from one of his pockets and shot the girl point-blank in the head. Raphaela Comaoda died instantly. Cerrone then pulled her body out of the bed and dumped it on the floor. When he finally realized what he had done, he ran out of the house in search of a doctor. When he returned police were waiting for him. Subsequently convicted of capital murder, Daniel Cerrone was hanged at the Connecticut State Prison on March 5, 1920.

Francisco Feci, white, age 29. *Murder.* The crime was committed on October 28, 1918, at North Billerica, Massachusetts. Louis Fred Soulia (white, age 40) was an unmarried Quebecois employed by the Boston & Maine railroad. He lived alone in a little house on Oak Street in North Billerica, then a remote district. When he failed to report to his job for several successive days his co-workers became concerned and went to his house. When no one answered their repeated knockings they forced their way in. Louis Soulia was nowhere to be found but the searchers did notice droplets of dried blood which led out the back door and across the yard. Following this trail, the search party entered a wooded area where they came upon a shallow grave. There they found the remains of their friend. An autopsy revealed that the decedent had been badly beaten. In addition to that, he had been shot three times and stabbed 15 times. It soon became apparent that Soulia had been attacked by more than one assailant. Detectives concentrated their scrutiny on a former co-worker of the murdered man named Joseph Cordio. This man in turn was linked to a pair of cousins named Luigi and Francisco Feci, the latter of whom lived in the city of Lawrence. Bloody shoes and a bloody knife were found in Cordio's home. An analysis of Francisco Feci's shoes also revealed traces of blood. In addition, a pistol with three spent shots was found among Feci's effects. Luigi Feci was never located. In the end, Francisco Feci confessed to being present when the murder was committed. He denied striking any blows, however. Joseph Cordio was subsequently tried and acquitted. Francisco Feci was capitally convicted. On August 16, 1920, he was electrocuted at the Massachusetts State Prison. The motive for the crime was never determined for certain.

1921

Elwood Wade, white, age 23. *Murder.* The crime was committed on August 29, 1920, at Bridgeport, Connecticut. This offender was employed as a milkman in Bridgeport. His father owned a dairy there. Although married with two children, Elwood Wade was an adulterer who carried on rather openly with a married woman named Ethel Hutchins Nott. The woman's husband, George B. Nott (white, age 42), was aware of the situation. As a result, he and his rival were antagonistic towards each other. By the summer of 1920 Elwood Wade had decided that George Nott had to be eliminated. Early on the morning of the above date he went to the Nott residence at No. 265 Judson Place in Bridgeport. Mrs. Nott then entertained Wade in a second floor kitchen while her husband slept in an attic room above them. After about 30 minutes Wade tiptoed up the attic stairs to the room where George Nott was sleeping. He then attacked the man with a pipe and bludgeoned him in his bed. George Nott awoke with a start and a desperate struggle ensued between him and his assailant. Eventually Nott lost his footing and tumbled down the attic stairs. He fell to a second floor landing in a dazed condition. Wade then pounced on Nott and continued beating him with the pipe. Then he flung the injured man head-first down the stairs to the first floor where he finished him off with a butcher knife. Nott was stabbed more than 20 times. After that, Mrs. Nott busied herself with wiping up the many bloodstains thereabouts. Wade stuffed the body of the murdered man into a storage trunk. Later the same day he got together with a trusted lackey and borrowed a small truck. Placing the storage trunk in the back of the truck, the two men then drove to an isolated swamp in Easton where they weighted the trunk with stones and sank it in some quicksand. Wade eventually confessed what he had done. He was hanged at the Connecticut State Prison on May 20, 1921. Ethel Nott drew a long prison term.

John Kausarauskas, white, age 36. *Murder.* The crime was committed on

February 1, 1921, at Milford, Connecticut. This offender was an ex-convict who worked at the Bridgeport plant of the Columbia Graphophone Company. He had served four years in the Connecticut State Prison for robbery and attempted murder. Among his workmates was a Milford man named John Cernock. A friendly rapport developed between Kausarauskas and Cernock. On their days off they would sometimes go fishing together. Kausarauskas was also a frequent guest in the Cernock home. Somehow Kausarauskas became aware of the fact that Cernock and his wife, Anna Cernock (white, age 35), had saved up the sum of $110 with the intention of applying that money against the principal of their mortgage. That knowledge aroused the cupidity of a false friend. On the above date Kausarauskas called in sick at his job. He then went to the vicinity of the Cernock home on Old Gate Lane in Milford. Hiding out in the woods, Kausarauskas waited until John Cernock left his house to go to work. From prior knowledge of the family, Kausarauskas reasoned that the man's wife would then be alone with her four small children, aged five weeks to six years. When the man of the house was gone, Kausarauskas smeared himself with blackface and donned a mask. He wanted to make himself look like a Negro in order to mislead anyone who might see him. When he felt that the time was right, Kausarauskas barged into the Cernock house and demanded money. Anna Cernock screamed at the intrusion and ran out the front door. Kausarauskas pursued the woman and caught up with her in the front yard. He then picked up a stone and battered Mrs. Cernock with it. She managed to break free and ran back into the house. Kausarauskas followed her and chased her from room to room with a hatchet. He finally caught her in the upstairs nursery and there hacked her to death as some of her children watched in horror. Then he tumbled the woman's body down the stairs and ransacked the house. An 11-year-old daughter of the victim heard screams as she was coming home from school so she ran to the house of a neighbor. That person took a shotgun off his wall and went to investigate. As he neared the Cernock house the neighbor saw the killer jump out a window and run off into the woods. He fired on the fleeing culprit repeatedly but missed. The noise of the gunfire brought other neighborhood residents flocking to the scene. Soon more than 200 men were organized into a posse which scoured the countryside thereabouts. Kausarauskas gave his pursuers the slip but he did shed an overcoat which the posse found. In the pockets of that overcoat was tissue paper of an unusual kind. When it was shown to the husband of the murdered woman he identified it as being the kind used to wrap record albums at the Bridgeport plant of the Columbia Graphophone Company. The overcoat was then brought to the Bridgeport factory and was there recognized as the property of an employee named John Kausarauskas. When police were told that the suspect had called in sick that day they hurried to his home. There they found Kausarauskas and arrested him. Charged with capital murder, Kausarauskas was soon tried and convicted. Cast for his life, he chose not to appeal. On May 27, 1921, he was hanged at the Connecticut State Prison.

1922

Emil Schutte, white, age 49. *Murder.* The crime was committed on December 10, 1915, at Haddam, Connecticut. This lethal man had come from Germany at an early age and settled in the rural town of Killingworth. He eventually moved to nearby Haddam and there became a citizen of substance. He owned and operated a well-patronized general store in the Shailerville section of the town. He also served two terms as Haddam's town constable and tax collector. In addition, Schutte was a noted landowner and the master of a prosperous farm. He was married to a faithful spouse and had eight children consisting of seven sons and one daughter.

A stern disciplinarian, Schutte ruled his household with an iron hand. He sometimes quarreled violently with his wife and he was not adverse to thrashing his sons when he felt that they deserved it. Sometimes he was rough on his family to a point of excess. As a result, his teenage boys lived in fear of him. It was that fear combined with a growing sense of loathing that would induce Schutte's children to turn on him with fatal results.

Schutte owned a parcel of woodland on the Bethel Camp Road. He employed lumberjacks to work the property and built a bungalow there to accommodate them. Whenever he was called upon to deliver provisions to this work site or otherwise visit it in person, Schutte was obliged to pass by the dwelling of a neighbor named Joseph Ball (white, age 50), with whom he did not get along. For more than a decade hard feelings had festered between Ball and Schutte stemming from a pair of incidents in which Schutte, as town constable, had arrested Ball. Feeling himself ill-used, Ball nursed a grudge against Schutte and the animus was shared by his wife, Grace Rose Ball (white, age 50), and his son, Jacob Ball (white, age 16). For the most part, the Ball family contented itself with making obscene gestures whenever Schutte passed by their house. By the autumn of 1915, however, the situation had escalated to shouted insults. Then came an incident in which Joseph Ball was alleged to have menaced a potential buyer of the Schutte woodlot with a shotgun. On December 9, 1915, Ball aimed a gun at Schutte himself as the latter was driving a wagon along the Bethel Camp Road. Schutte could take

no more. He decided that the entire Ball family had to be eliminated.

That evening after supper, Schutte took his second son aside and said that they had better go down to the woodlot bungalow in order to protect it. He explained that the lumberjacks had departed, leaving the bungalow empty, and he feared that Joseph Ball might seize upon the opportunity to vandalize the place. Not daring to disobey his father, Schutte's second son, Julius Schutte (white, age 16), agreed to come along. Father and son then armed themselves with a shotgun and rifle respectively and set out for the bungalow on foot. They also carried with them a can of kerosene, ostensibly for the lamps that were there. When they reached the bungalow, Emil Schutte announced his true intentions to his son: They were to sneak over to the Ball residence, splash around the kerosene and burn the people out of their home.

At two o'clock in the morning Schutte and his son left the bungalow and furtively approached their target. Passing through a cornfield, they scooped up two sacks of tinder-dry husks to bring with them. When they reached the Ball home (which was merely a wooden shanty) they placed one sack of husks against the front door and another against the back door. Then they splashed the kerosene all over the building's exterior. Emil Schutte took up a concealed position near the front door with his shotgun and he ordered his son to do likewise with his rifle near the back door. He also told the boy to shoot down any members of the Ball family that might cross his line of fire.

Emil Schutte flicked a lighted match onto the kerosene-soaked husks. At once the shanty became enveloped in flames. Within seconds a woman screamed and the rush was on to escape the blaze. First Joseph Ball, then Mrs. Ball and finally Jacob Ball came running out of the front door. All were gunned down by Emil Schutte as they did so.

Julius Schutte also shot Jacob Ball. When all three members of the Ball family lay mortally wounded on the ground Emil Schutte went among them and finished off each of them with point-blank shotgun blasts. Then he ordered his son to help him drag the bodies by their ankles and throw them back into the burning building. Father and son then left the scene and headed for their home. Along the way they paused in a cemetery and watched as the flames devoured the last of the Ball family residence. Emil Schutte remarked on the "beauty" of the sight. Then he swore his son to secrecy on pain of death.

A milkman discovered the tragedy when the sun came up. The charred remains of the Ball family were found among the ruins of their home. Local authorities examined the scene and announced that an overheated stove was to blame. Without further ado the remains of Joseph Ball, his wife and son were put into pauper's coffins and buried at public expense.

Five years passed. Julius Schutte grew to manhood in constant dread of his father. He did not dare to tell what had happened on that December night in 1915 but the matter weighed heavily on his conscience. Finally in an effort to put it all behind him he went and joined the navy.

Emil Schutte continued as he always had: as a prosperous businessman and a stern patriarch. His other sons continued to live in fear of him but they were still too young to escape. In 1921 Julius Schutte came home from the navy and found his domestic situation unchanged. His father was still as brutal and overbearing as ever. Then to make matters worse, Emil Schutte displayed his ferocity once again: He butchered one of his farmhands, an aging drunkard named Dennis LeDuc (white) and cremated his body in a raging bonfire. The final crisis came on May 13, 1921, when Schutte chased his wife across the fields with a loaded gun. His children were

appalled and they finally got up the nerve to take action. Fearing that their mother or any one of them might become the next victim of their father's malice, they went to the state's attorney for Middlesex County and told him enough to literally hang Emil Schutte.

Soon after this a grisly scene took place in Potter's Field. The remains of the Ball family were exhumed. At first the gravediggers could not remember exactly where they had buried the three decedents. Many other coffins were disinterred and opened by mistake before the right ones were found. A careful sifting of the charred corpses revealed them to be riddled with buckshot and wadding. A rifle bullet was also found among the remains of Jacob Ball.

At the subsequent trial of Emil Schutte those same remains were entered as evidence. The skulls of Joseph, Grace and Jacob Ball grinned at the defendant from a display table. Most damning of all was the testimony of Julius Schutte; the young man — then aged 22 — told in graphic detail how his father had induced him to participate in the Ball family slaughter. In return for his revelations and because he was a minor at the time of the crime, Julius Schutte was granted immunity from prosecution. His father went to the Connecticut State Prison under sentence of death. On October 24, 1922, the hangman dispatched the former tax collector and town constable of Haddam. Only then did his survivors feel safe from him.

1923

Paul Dascalakis, alias "Pappas," white, age 27. *Murder.* The crime was committed on December 26, 1919, at Boston. A Greek immigrant, this man worked alternately as a waiter and a baker in the Chelsea section of Boston. In September of 1919 he came to reside in a rooming house at No. 517 Columbus Avenue. The landlady there, Alice Arsenault (white, age 30), initially made arrangements with her new lodger for him to tend the furnace in exchange for a discount on his rent. Soon Dascalakis was servicing the landlady in a more intimate way. He moved in with her and announced to the other tenants that he was the woman's legal spouse. The landlady, who had previously abandoned her true husband in Lynn, allowed Dascalakis to carry on this charade. On the evening of Christmas Day, 1919, the landlady and Dascalakis stayed up late entertaining the residents of their rooming house. On the following day it was noticed that Mrs. Arsenault was missing. When she failed to appear during the ensuing days, Dascalakis gave out a story to the effect that she had run off with a rich boyfriend. Then he started selling off her possessions. Three weeks after the woman's disappearance Dascalakis fraudulently sold her interest in the rooming house for $800 and disappeared himself. Nothing further was thought of him until after the spring thaw. During the second week in May, 1920, the owner of a produce market which occupied the first floor of the rooming house noticed a foul odor in the cellar. Furnace ashes had been allowed to accumulate there throughout the course of the previous winter and it was surmised that some stray cats had died amid them, thereby accounting for the bad smell. A cleaning crew was brought in to clear away the ashes. In the course of the removal operation the diggers uncovered a mattress that had been covered over by several feet of ashes. Beneath the mattress was found a female corpse in a good state of preservation. An examination of the remains identified them as those of Alice Arsenault. She had been repeatedly stabbed in the throat. An alarm was immediately broadcast for the missing Paul Dascalakis but he was long gone. As was subsequently revealed, he had gone to

Montreal. There he married in December of 1920 and had taken up an otherwise routine existence. During the summer of 1921 his wife became displeased with him for reasons that were never made clear. She knew what he had done in Boston and she informed lawmen about it. On September 10, 1921, Dascalakis was arrested. Six days later he was back in Boston to face charges of capital murder. He asseverated his innocence but the evidence against him was compelling. Among those who testified for the prosecution was his Canadian wife. On June 15, 1922, a jury brought in a guilty verdict against Paul Dascalakis. He was then ordered for execution. Subsequent appeals stressed that the evidence against him was circumstantial but the conviction held up. On July 14, 1923, this offender was electrocuted at the Massachusetts State Prison.

1924

Cyrille Van den Hecke, white, age 47. *Murder.* The crime was committed on August 9, 1918, at Lawrence, Massachusetts. Cyrille Van den Hecke and Geldine Shureman (white, age 25) were Flemish immigrants who worked in the Lawrence textile mills. Both were married with children. Van den Hecke seduced Shureman's wife (who was much younger than he) and ran away with her. An incensed Geldine Shureman then tracked the lovers down, tracing them first to Connecticut and then to Pennsylvania. It was in the latter place that Shureman confronted his wife and offered to forgive her if she would return home with him. The woman complied and so was reunited with her husband. This enraged Van den Hecke. He then went to Shureman's home at No. 287 Water Street in Lawrence and demanded to speak with Mrs. Shureman. A nasty scene ensued between the two men. Shureman ordered Van den Hecke to get off the property. At that point Van den Hecke pulled out a gun and fatally shot Shureman in the head. Shots were also fired at Mrs. Shureman. The killer paused to fire two more shots into the dead man's body. Then he fled from the scene and got over the Canadian border. From there he took a ship to Europe. Van den Hecke wandered throughout Belgium and France for some time and he even went to Egypt for a while. From the latter place he sent a taunting postcard to Massachusetts authorities. After four years spent on the run Van den Hecke decided to return to Canada. He settled at Renfrew, Ontario, and secured a respectable job there as the general manager of a woolen mill. He also bigamously married a local woman there and had a child by her. This bigamous wife had formerly lived in Lawrence, Massachusetts, and when the identity of her new husband became known to her friends there it did not go unreported. Both Van den Hecke and his bigamous wife were unaware of each other's ties with the city of Lawrence and it came as a great surprise to both when detectives knocked on their door in February of 1923. Canadian authorities sent Van den Hecke to Massachusetts. There he was tried and convicted of capital murder. Although there was never any doubt about his guilt, Van den Hecke insisted on his innocence to the last. He was electrocuted at the Massachusetts State Prison on July 30, 1924.

1925

Although there are known to have been at least 144 legal executions in the United States of America this year, none of them took place in the New England states.

1926

Gerald Chapman, white, age 34. *Murder.* The crime was committed on October 12, 1924, at New Britain, Con-

necticut. This man attained celebrity status during his lifetime as a bandit, bon vivant and escape artist. Newspapers called him "The Prince of Thieves" and "The Count of Gramercy Park," among other sobriquets. To say that he was a jailbird, a fraud and a murderer would be closer to the truth.

Chapman's story began inauspiciously in an Irish ghetto on the lower east side of Manhattan. There he was born in the year 1890 and there he was raised among ruffians, drunkards and thieves. In 1907 he dropped out of school and promptly got into trouble for stealing jewelry. Sent to the Elmira Reformatory, he was paroled in the following year when a job opportunity arose for him. The Standard Oil Company put young Chapman to work as a $14 per week office trainee. Within a month, however, he embezzled some money from his new employer and got into trouble again. He was not only fired from his job but sentenced to a term in Auburn prison. Paroled after three and a half years, he got a job with a trolley company in the Bronx. Four months later he was fired when it was discovered that he had not divulged his prison record on his job application. Thereafter Chapman never made any effort to seek an honest livelihood. He resolved instead to live by his wits. In 1912 he was nabbed once again for stealing money and sent back to Auburn.

It was during his second stint in Auburn that Chapman had a life-altering experience. He was placed in the same cell with a foppish con artist named George "Dutch" Anderson and soon fell under that man's influence. Anderson (whose real name was Ivan Dahl von Teller) had expensive taste and a pronounced appetite for the finer things in life. He knew how to dress and act like a gentleman of substance, being erudite and cultured, quite unlike the common variety of jailhouse inhabitants. Chapman was deeply impressed by Anderson's ways and the two men gravitated toward each other. Anderson for his own part became fond of Chapman and resolved to make him his protégé. So was born a symbiosis that would achieve national notoriety.

Chapman and Anderson were both released in 1919. They then decided to join forces. Buying themselves some stylish clothes and stealing themselves a fancy car, they set out for Indiana. There they posed as investment bankers and swindled their way into a considerable fortune. When things got too hot for them, they moved on to New York City. There they set themselves up in a posh apartment in Gramercy Park, one of the most prestigious residential areas of Manhattan, and settled down to enjoy life. What followed for them was a long round of high living. They attended gala social functions, gave lavish parties and mingled with the elite. They dined at the finest restaurants, attended the theater regularly and held court in chic nightspots. They shopped at the finest stores, gave generous tips and showered high-priced courtesans with expensive gifts.

When their cash ran short — as it inevitably did — Chapman and Anderson did not become greatly alarmed. They simply put their heads together and planned another coup. It had come to their attention that unguarded mail trucks made daily runs from the Manhattan financial district to the main post office. Inside those trucks were sacks of registered mail containing all kinds of money and negotiable securities. The "gentlemen bandits" (as they were called) accordingly made plans to heist one of those mail trucks. They enlisted the aid of a jailhouse crony named Charles Loerber (who incidentally worked as their butler and chauffeur) and rehearsed their plan twice a week for several months. Then on October 24, 1921, they struck for real. As a mail truck departed from Wall Street, Chapman and Anderson followed it in a car driven

by Loerber. They forced the driver of the truck to pull over at gunpoint and unlock his vehicle. Then they rummaged through the numerous bags of mail until they found those which bore security seals. The specially marked bags they tossed into their getaway car. Leaving the rest, they tied up the truck driver and took off over the Brooklyn Bridge. They did not stop until they reached Lake Ronkonkoma, far out on Long Island. Then they brought their booty into a barn and examined it. They were astounded to find that the registered mail bags contained cash and securities in excess of two million dollars — an unheard of sum in those days. The entire country was also astonished as newspapers blared the story of what was up till then the greatest mail robbery in American history.

For several months thereafter Chapman continued to live in a flamboyant style. Then he made a mistake: He paid his landlord with a bearer bond that had been part of the mail robbery loot. When the landlord attempted to redeem the bond it was linked to those which had been stolen. Federal investigators then got involved and soon Chapman, Anderson and Loerber were identified as ex-convicts. All three were arrested on July 3, 1922.

While in the custody of the U.S. postal inspectors, Chapman attempted to escape. He snuck out a third floor window of the main post office in Manhattan and inched his way along the ornamental frieze on the building's exterior. Then he reentered the building by another window and hid in a lavatory. He was caught when officers made a systematic search of the premises.

When their case came up in U.S. District Court, Chapman and Anderson were betrayed by their pal Loerber. The latter turned government witness and testified for the prosecution. As a result, Chapman and Anderson were each convicted and sentenced to 25-year terms in the Atlanta Federal Penitentiary.

Eight months later — on March 26, 1923 — Chapman made a sensational escape from the federal prison. He had bluffed his way into the prison infirmary by feigning a sore throat. Once inside the infirmary, he overpowered a guard and then waited for an accomplice to trip up a circuit breaker that plunged the entire prison into darkness. No one knew what had caused the power failure and confusion reigned. Chapman used this time to go out a window on a rope made of bedsheets and then successfully climb over the prison wall to freedom. He managed to get as far as Athens, Georgia, where he was caught two days later. Bloodhounds ran him down in a cotton field but he had to be shot before he gave up. He was taken to the local hospital in Athens because of his wounds. Then on April 4, 1923, he made yet another attempt to escape. Chapman somehow made his way to the hospital basement where he hid for two days. Then when the alarm had subsided he slipped out of the building by night and disappeared. He made his way to Indiana where he holed up in a former hideout. There he was soon after joined by his pal Anderson who had himself escaped from Atlanta by means of a tunnel.

The authorities of the Atlanta Federal Penitentiary became the laughing-stocks of the entire country.

Together once again, the "Gentleman Bandits" ranged far and wide in their illegal activities. They committed many burglaries throughout the midwestern states and got away with them all. When they felt themselves coming under pressure they decided to split up for a while. Anderson went to Michigan where he was killed in a shoot-out with lawmen. Chapman headed east to New England where he hoped to develop fresh hunting grounds. The latter finally settled at Springfield, Massachusetts, where he had an underworld connection. That party turned out to be one Walter E. Shean (white, age 33), a high-

born wastrel who lived in a swanky hotel at his father's expense. Together Chapman and Shean planned to go into counterfeiting. They purchased a stylish home at South Hadley to use as their headquarters. It was while thus involved that Chapman yielded to his new partner's desire to pull off a safecracking job. Accordingly, the two men slipped across the border into Connecticut where they sized up a New Britain department store. This was the establishment of Davidson & Leventhal, Inc., located at No. 21 Main Street. In the offices of this rather large store were two massive iron safes. Shean correctly surmised there to be a hefty sum of money therein and Chapman concurred in that belief. During the predawn hours of October 12, 1924, the two robbers broke into the department store and went to work on the safes. Chapman successfully cracked one of the safes by using nitroglycerin on it. His presence in the store, however, had not gone unreported. A passerby did not trust the looks of Chapman and Shean despite their being dressed as repairmen. A call was then placed to one of the store owners who confirmed that no repairmen were expected on the property. This in turn brought a call to the local police and three officers were sent to investigate. Shean was nabbed in the street as he was stashing the contents of the first safe into a getaway car. As the officers entered the department store itself Chapman saw them coming and opened fire on them with a handgun. A policeman named James Skelly (white, age 56) was mortally wounded. In the confusion that followed, Chapman ran out of the front door of the store and got away — much to the chagrin of the New Britain police.

Walter Shean could not conceal his sense of self-importance due to his having been on the job with the "great" and "infamous" Gerald Chapman. He bragged about that fact openly to the police and from that time on the hunt for the federal prison escapee turned cop killer was unrelenting. Chapman was finally caught in Indiana on January 13, 1925, when a luggage ticket that he had left behind in Springfield put detectives on his trail. Because the federal government had a prior claim on him, Chapman could not be immediately returned to Connecticut to face state murder charges. That problem was solved, however, when the president of the United States issued a special commutation of Chapman's federal prison sentence. Chapman tried to fend off the state prosecution by refusing to accept the federal commutation and a complicated court battle followed. In the end, the state of Connecticut was granted custody of the prisoner. A sensational trial for capital murder followed in Hartford Superior Court but the end was never in doubt. On April 6, 1926, the celebrated Gerald Chapman walked unassisted to the gallows in the Connecticut State Prison. There he died without flinching.

Richard Stewart, alias "Frank Johnson," black, age 31. *Murder.* The crime was committed on August 24, 1925, at Wilmington, Massachusetts. This man was an idler who had abandoned his wife and children in Pennsylvania and come east to the Roxbury section of Boston. When he wore out his welcome in Roxbury he pitched a sob story to an acquaintance named William James (black, age 28) and induced that man to give him shelter. James brought Stewart home with him and gave him a place to stay. Stewart then repaid his benefactor by ogling his wife. He even tried to talk Mrs. James into abandoning her six children and running away with him. The woman not only declined Stewart's proposals but told him to get a job. Stewart then became irritated and reasoned that the woman would be more amenable if she was a widow. Late on the evening of the above date Stewart took a pistol and fatally shot William James as the man

lay sleeping in his own bed. Then Stewart dragged the slain man's body from the house and threw it down a well. He also dumped an entire ton of rubble down the well in an attempt to conceal the crime. Searchers discovered the body 17 days later when Mrs. James finally overcame her fright and told of what had happened. In his defense, Stewart said that he was too drunk on moonshine liquor at the time to have realized what he was doing. He also tried to claim self-defense. Experts testified that Stewart had the mental age of a 12 year old. In rebuttal, the prosecution said that the crime was clearly premeditated since Stewart had previously told Mrs. James that he intended to kill her husband. He also warned her on the night of the murder not to let any of her children sleep in the same bed as their father. Richard Stewart was electrocuted at the Massachusetts State Prison on May 5, 1926.

1927

John Devereaux, white, age 24. **Edward Heinlein,** white, age 25. **John McLaughlin,** white, age 30. *Murder.* The crime was committed on October 4, 1925, at Waltham, Massachusetts. These men became notorious as the so-called "Car Barn Bandits." Devereaux and McLaughlin lived in Allston while Heinlein was a Brighton resident. All were known to the police as petty criminals. Shortly after midnight on the above date they ganged up with two others of their ilk named Joseph Bennett (white, age 26) and Peter King (white, age 24) for the purpose of pulling an armed raid on the headquarters of the Middlesex & Boston trolley car company. They all proceeded to the target premises on Upper Main Street in Waltham shortly after the last trolley car had been garaged for the night. One robber remained behind the wheel of a getaway car while two others took up lookout positions in the front yard of the trolley barn and at the base of a stairway leading to the second floor office. The remaining two then ran up the stairs and confronted the office personnel at gunpoint. They then scooped up nearly $1600 in silver coins and fled with the same. When they reached the bottom of the stairway they encountered an accomplice which they had left on guard there (Devereaux) and saw that he had forced two other trolley company employees to lay face-down on the ground. Devereaux then prodded the two hostages with his gun and demanded to know if there was anyone else around. In reply he was told that there was a watchman on the property. Devereaux then sought out the watchman, James Ferneau (white, age 67), and shot him down with a bullet to the leg. As the watchman fell wounded he was pounced upon by the gunman and literally pistol-whipped to death. Then all of the bandits got into their getaway car and took off with the heavy moneybags. When the trolley company employees tried to call the police they found that the telephone lines had been cut. The resultant delay in raising an alarm enabled the robbers to make a successful escape. Despite the fact that all of the gang wore masks and gloves, police were quick in identifying them. Exactly how they did so has never been divulged. Three days after the crime early morning police raids nabbed four of the culprits asleep in their beds. The fifth member of the gang was caught as he was getting out of a taxi. Guns and ammunition were found along with each of the arrested men together with many rolls of coins which bore the name of the trolley company on their wrappers. When the case came to trial Peter King turned state's evidence in return for having his indictment nolled. Joseph Bennett was tried as an accessory by order of the presiding judge. They were dealt with leniently because they had not participated directly in either the holdup or the

murder. Devereaux, Heinlein and Mc-Laughlin were not so lucky. The first was condemned because he had killed the watchman. The other two—the ones who had stolen the money—were also condemned because they were willful accessories to a homicide committed in the course of another felony, namely armed robbery. Great efforts were made to save Heinlein and McLaughlin based on the contention that Devereaux had committed the murder on his own initiative and without the prompting of the other two. All appeals failed. On January 6, 1927, the "Car Barn Bandits" were electrocuted at the Massachusetts State Prison.

Celestino Madeiros, white, age 22.

Murder. The crime was committed on November 1, 1924, at Wrentham, Massachusetts. This young man came from the Bristol County town of Seekonk. His heritage was Portuguese. He joined up with a four-man robbery team for the purpose of raiding the National Bank of Wrentham. On the morning of the above date the robbers proceeded to the bank in a stolen car. Three of them (including Madeiros) went inside while the fourth remained behind the wheel of the getaway vehicle. Customers and bank employees were first ordered to raise their hands by the bandits. Then the elderly cashier of the bank, James Carpenter (white, age 79), was ordered to open the vault. Instead of doing as he was told, Carpenter tripped an alarm. This caused the robbers to abort their mission. Before fleeing from the scene, however, Madeiros made it a point to shoot the disobedient cashier. Carpenter was hit by two bullets. He died a week later. On the same day that Carpenter died detectives traced the robbers to a Rhode Island rooming house. There the entire gang was captured at gunpoint. The Rhode Island authorities agreed to relinquish custody of the bandits even though they were wanted for holdups there. Madeiros was subsequently singled out as the slayer of the Wrentham bank cashier. Therefore he alone was ordered for execution. He was electrocuted at the Massachusetts State Prison on August 23, 1927.

Nicola Sacco, white, age 29. **Bartolomeo Vanzetti,** white, age 32. *Murder.* Their alleged crime was allegedly committed on April 15, 1920, at South Braintree, Massachusetts. There is a distinct possibility that either one or both of these men were innocent of the crime for which they were executed. The evidence which convicted them must be regarded as flimsy at best. On the afternoon of the above date a paymaster named Frederick Parmenter (white, age 34) and a bodyguard named Alessandro Berardelli (white, age 44) were walking along Pearl Street in South Braintree, headed toward the Slater & Morrell shoe factory. It was payday there and Mr. Parmenter was carrying cashboxes containing close to $16,000. As the paymaster and his guard approached the factory, three young men (who had been loitering about) opened fire on them with handguns and a rifle. No quarter was given. The bodyguard was killed instantly by multiple gunshots fired at point-blank range. The paymaster was shot in the back and dropped the cashboxes. As he staggered from the scene clutching at his wound he was deliberately shot again. Then the gunmen picked up the cashboxes and jumped into a waiting automobile that was in the command of two other accomplices. As the getaway vehicle raced from the scene, the bandit with the rifle stood up in the back seat and opened fire on a crowd that had begun to gather. He also fired on the gatekeeper of a nearby railroad crossing when that man tried to lower his crossing gates. Then the getaway car dashed through the crossing just before a freight train rumbled by. When order was restored the only casualties were

found to be the paymaster and his bodyguard. Both were fatalities.

Two days later the getaway car was found abandoned in a wooded area. Tracks of another car were seen leading away from it. Among the many lawmen who examined the site of this discovery was the police chief of the town of Bridgewater. He concluded that the tracks leading away from the abandoned getaway car belonged to a vehicle owned by an Italian man named Michael Boda — a suspicious character in the police chief's opinion. Boda's car was subsequently traced to a West Bridgewater repair shop where it was having some work done on it. The police chief then left instructions with the owner of the repair shop to notify him when anyone came to get the car. On the evening of May 5, 1920, Michael Boda came for his car. Accompanying him were three other men of his own nationality. Two of those other men were identified as Nicola Sacco, a shoemaker who worked in the town of Stoughton, and Bartolomeo Vanzetti, a fishmonger from Plymouth. Both of these men were arrested on a trolley car later that same night and found to be carrying concealed handguns. Both were reported to have attempted to draw their weapons on arresting officers. (This last allegation almost certainly a face-saving lie on the part of the police.) What really caught the eyes of lawmen, however, was an inflammatory political leaflet — with Bolshevik overtones — found on Sacco's person which advertised an upcoming speech to be given by Vanzetti. It being a time of high anti–Bolshevik tension in the United States, the possession of such literature and involvement in such politics put Sacco and Vanzetti in a very bad light. Both men were also unable to produce immediate alibis for the time of the South Braintree murders. Vanzetti was furthermore unable to account for his whereabouts at the time of an earlier attempted holdup which took place at Bridgewater on Christmas Eve, 1919.

Police attempts to link Sacco and Vanzetti with the Bridgewater and South Braintree crimes through means of witness identification were handled in a most dubious manner. Instead of being placed in lineups, the two men were merely shown to witnesses who were then asked to confirm whether or not they were seen at the crime scenes. Some witnesses said that they did see a resemblance while others did not.

During the early summer of 1920 Vanzetti was put on trial for the attempted holdup that had occurred at Bridgewater in December of 1919. He was convicted principally on the testimonies of witnesses who claimed to have seen him there. He was sentenced to a prison term of from 12 to 15 years in maximum security.

The joint trial of Sacco and Vanzetti for the South Braintree crime opened on May 31, 1921, and lasted until July 14, 1921. The judge — a noticeably hostile one — was the same one that had presided over Vanzetti's earlier trial. The jury was allowed to hear references to the leftist political views of the defendants even though such things were completely irrelevant to the charge at hand. Even worse, both defendants were revealed to have deliberately dodged the draft during World War I. Their lawyer also made a bad impression on both judge and jury with his imperious demeanor and unfavorable reputation.

The trial evidence which dealt specifically with the crime itself should have — at the very least — raised a reasonable doubt in the minds of the jury. Of the numerous eyewitnesses to the South Braintree murders, 31 testified that Vanzetti was *not* among the five bandits they had seen. Many others who did testify to the visual identification of Sacco and Vanzetti admitted on the witness stand that they might be mistaken. Very few were positive in their identifi-

cations. In addition, there were other witnesses who testified that Vanzetti was in Plymouth on the day of the crime while an attaché to the Italian consulate in Boston confirmed that Sacco had been there applying for a visa at the time in question. Ballistics evidence was inconclusive.

The fact that most of the defense witnesses were Italian and Roman Catholic did not play well with the Protestant-dominated jury. Nor did the revelations about draft dodging and pro–Bolshevism appeal to the jury's sense of patriotism. Such defendants, the jury concluded, could not possibly be innocent. And even if they *were* innocent, according to the jury's rationale, they were scoundrels who deserved the death penalty anyway.

The conviction of Sacco and Vanzetti aroused indignation all over the world. Massachusetts justice was excoriated in hundreds of sermons, speeches and editorials. Demands for a new trial and pleas for clemency were unrelenting. What ultimately proved fatal to the defendants, however, was the same thing that has doomed many others in their position: xenophobia. The fact that nearly all of the protests came from *outside* Massachusetts wound up doing Sacco and Vanzetti more harm than good. Despite an unprecedented series of appeals and numerous delays, both men died in the electric chair at the Massachusetts State Prison on August 23, 1927.

Chin Lung, Chinese, age 32. **Soo Hoo Wing,** Chinese, age 22. *Murder.* Their crime was committed on March 24, 1927, at Manchester, Connecticut. In the year 1927 the month of March was a time of high anxiety in Chinese neighborhoods across the country. On the 24th day of that month was set to expire a two-year truce between the arch-rival On Leong and Hip Sing tongs, secret Chinese organizations which hated each other with deadly enmity. For many years the tongs had battled for control of gambling and prostitution rackets. They also levied "dues" from Chinese businesses and competed with each other in the opium trade. Open warfare periodically raged between the tongs and the fatalities associated with those conflicts were many. By March of 1927 hostilities were set to resume unless a soon-to-expire truce was renewed. Western observers were at a loss for answers as the deadline drew near. The Chinese tongmen would themselves reveal nothing. Was it to be peace or war? No one seemed to know. Then a week before the expiration of the truce was seen an omen of things to come: Tongmen from Boston to San Francisco were suddenly going about attired in their finest clothing. They remained dressed that way throughout the final days of the truce. Those familiar with Chinese ways knew this to be an omen of the worst kind. When the sun came up on the 24th of March all uncertainty was removed as tong assassins struck in six different places. A reign of terror followed. The dreaded "hatchetmen" of the Hip Sings and the fearsome "highbinders" of the On Leongs were at it again. Chinese businesses closed as their panic-stricken employees went into hiding. Chinese men and women barricaded themselves in their homes. Chinese children were plucked from the schools lest they too become targets. In the Chinatown districts of Boston and New York the alarm was so great that police were stationed every 20 paces — and still the killings continued. In the "Little China" district of Hartford, Connecticut, the On Leongs met in emergency session. All were heavily armed. In nearby Manchester a member of their tong had been slain in his place of business by Hip Sing gunmen. Seldom had the New York–based Hip Sings dared to strike so deep in enemy territory. The victim of the Manchester rubout was identified as one Ong King

(Chinese, age 36), a laundryman who practiced his trade at No. 25 Oak Street there. When a police dragnet caught up with the killers at New Haven later that same day the state's attorney for Hartford County announced drastic action: A special grand jury would be convened within four days to bring capital indictments against the Hip Sing assassins. Trial would follow shortly thereafter. It was the stated purpose of the state's attorney to send a clear message that tong violence would not be tolerated in Connecticut. Chin Lung and Soo Hoo Wing, the two Hip Sing assassins, were accordingly indicted and put on trial. Both were convicted and sentenced to death. Both were hanged at the Connecticut State Prison on November 8, 1927.

1928

Jeremiah Gedzium, alias "Jerry the Pole," white, age 22. *Murder.* The crime was committed on September 29, 1925, at Cambridge, Massachusetts. This young man ganged up with three unidentified confederates for the purpose of heisting a payroll. Early on the morning of the above date the robbery team took up positions outside of the Ward Baking Company, a large producer of baked goods on Albany Street in Cambridge. It was payday there and the robbers knew that a delivery car bearing money was due to arrive from a local bank. One robber waited behind the wheel of a getaway car while three others took up positions in a nearby alley. When the bank vehicle pulled up in front of the baking company the three waiting gunmen ran up to it and opened fire on the driver and payroll guards. No quarter was given. One of the robbers — later identified as Gedzium — fired through the vehicle's windshield, instantly killing the driver. Slain was Edward C. Ross (white, age 20), a messenger for the Central Trust Company of Cambridge. After that the bandits disabled the payroll guards. Then Gedzium snatched a moneybag containing more than $10,000 in small bills and silver coins. Within seconds he and his cronies made good their escape. It took 11 months for detectives to hunt down Jeremiah Gedzium. His identity had become known within days of the holdup but he could not be found. He was finally located on the Upper West Side of Manhattan where he had assumed a new identity and moved in with a young woman. His accomplices were never positively identified. Returned to Massachusetts, Gedzium was placed on trial for his life. Witnesses identified him as the gunman who had shot the payroll driver and grabbed the moneybag from the bank car. In spite of that, Gedzium claimed that he was innocent right to the end. He was electrocuted at the Massachusetts State Prison on February 28, 1928.

Herbert Gleason, white, age 19. *Murder.* The crime was committed on November 27, 1926, at Medford, Massachusetts. Crime reporters dubbed this felon the "Babyface Bandit." His parents being separated, Gleason lived with an aunt at Jamaica Plain. His father was a disabled veteran who lived at the Chelsea Soldiers Home and his mother resided at a summer camp in Maine. It was at the latter place where young Gleason found his only legitimate employment. On the evening of the above date Gleason got together with an accomplice and decided to pull a stickup. The site selected was a little provisions store at No. 557A Main Street in Medford. When the robbers walked into the store they pulled out handguns and ordered everyone to raise their hands. At first the store employees complied but when one of them suddenly ducked behind a counter gunfire rang out. It was then that the store owner, James Monagle (white, age 48), flung a meat cleaver at

Herbert Gleason. The weapon cut Gleason and caused him to bleed, whereupon Gleason opened fire on the store owner. Bullets struck Monagle in the arms and in the stomach. Instead of falling to the floor, Monagle, who was a big burly man, came after Gleason with a knife in each hand. Gleason then came to grips with the wounded man and severely pistol-whipped him. Then the two bandits ran out of the store empty-handed with Monagle in pursuit. They managed to outrun the furious store owner and get away. Monagle walked back to his place of business oblivious to the fact that he was dangerously wounded. He finally allowed a neighbor to drive him to the hospital where he dropped dead moments after walking in unassisted. Gleason managed to get his wound dressed and flee the area before police caught up with him. A cabdriver later tipped detectives to a Jamaica Plain address where he had taken a young man matching the bandit's description. There was found a broken down car with a Maine registration which was traced to the address of the summer camp where Gleason had previously been employed. There he was found to be in hiding. He was arrested on his 20th birthday. When Gleason was returned to Massachusetts he confessed what he had done. He tried to claim self-defense through the fact that the victim had attacked him but it was to no avail. Herbert Gleason was convicted of capital murder and ordered for execution. He was electrocuted at the Massachusetts State Prison on March 13, 1928.

Nathan Desatnick, white, age 25. *Murder.* The crime was committed on June 5, 1927, at Shrewsbury, Massachusetts. This man was an orthodox Jew who peddled fruit for a living. When he sired a daughter out of wedlock he found himself in a difficult position. He dared not marry the child's mother under such circumstances nor openly acknowledge his own paternity. So he boarded the child with a wet nurse at a rate of $10 per week and awaited further developments. Four months later he did proceed to marry the mother of the child. He did not, however, take the baby into his new home. He wanted to start a family afresh without the stigma of bastardy. So he reimpregnated his wife — this time legitimately — and told his hired wet nurse that he had made arrangements to place the existing baby with a Jewish family in New York. On the evening of the above date Desatnick left his home in Dorchester and went to the wet nurse's residence in Arlington Heights. He paid the wet nurse for her services and took the baby away with him. Instead of sending the baby to New York as he had said, however, he drove with it to Shrewsbury and threw it alive into Lake Quinsigamond. On the following day the infant was found floating in the lake. Desatnick was traced through the wet nurse and charged with capital murder. In his defense he insisted that he had given the baby to a man named Harry Balkin and that individual was supposed to transport the baby to New York. However, Balkin was never located and was subsequently revealed to be Desatnick's alter ego. Faced with this set of circumstances, a grand jury indicted Desatnick on two counts: being a principal to capital murder and being an accessory thereto with the imaginary Harry Balkin. A trial jury then acquitted Desatnick on the first indictment but convicted him on the second. The defendant was then ordered for execution as a willing accessory to capital murder. He was electrocuted at the Massachusetts State Prison on July 17, 1928.

1929

George Taylor, white, age 46. *Murder.* The crime was committed on June 5, 1927, at Salisbury, Massachusetts. A week before her untimely death, Stella Pomikala (white, age 21) of Lawrence came to Salisbury Beach to take a summer job in a seaside photography studio. Shortly after dark on the above date she told her employer that she was going to take a solitary stroll along the shore. She did not return. Early the next morning a beachcomber found Miss Pomikala lying dead in the sand. Her clothing had been torn from her body and lay strewn about. The area around her also gave evidence of a fierce struggle, the sand being marked by many disconcerted footprints. In addition, the decedent's throat and face were discolored and bruised, indicating that she had been manually strangled. Another detail that was not immediately made public was that evidence of rape was also found. As a first step, police checked Miss Pomikala's former suitors and ruled them out as suspects. Then four days after the crime came a substantial clue when the victim's wristwatch turned up in New Hampshire. It was sold by a slovenly looking man for three dollars. Armed with this information, detectives issued an all-points bulletin for an itinerant barber named George Taylor. He was known to have been at nearby Hampton Beach on the day before the murder. He had moved on to Salisbury Beach the following day and was known to have purchased a pair of tortoiseshell sunglasses similar to ones which were found at the scene of the murder. In addition, the New Hampshire man who had bought Miss Pomikala's watch identified Taylor as the seller. Six weeks after the crime Taylor was picked up for vagrancy in Vermont. It was also learned that he had served five years in the West Virginia State Penitentiary for assault and robbery. Returned to Massachusetts, he denied any knowledge of the murder but admitted selling the dead woman's wristwatch. When asked how he had come by the watch he said that he had found it. A jury refused to believe Taylor's story and he was capitally convicted. On March 6, 1929, he was electrocuted at the Massachusetts State Prison. He died protesting his innocence.

Frederick Hinman Knowlton, Jr., white, age 36. *Murder.* The crime was committed on March 29, 1928, at Concord, Massachusetts. This offender was a respected businessman in the town of Framingham. He operated an establishment there called the Knowlton Electric Company, a retailer of electrical apparatus, batteries and related merchandise. His father was a Framingham selectman who also operated a small business college. Although married and a father, the younger Knowlton was a philanderer who carried on an illicit affair with one Marguerite Isabelle Stewart (white, age 27), an instructor at the Beverly School for the Deaf in nearby Beverly. The trysters were accustomed to meet on Thursday nights and on the evening of March 29, 1928, they met as usual. Something apparently went wrong on this particular occasion because Miss Stewart was seen to be crying in an automobile on the Concord-to-Cambridge turnpike. On the following morning she was found dead on the roadside with her skull crushed. At first she was thought to be the victim of a hit and run mishap but evidence of foul play was soon discerned. For instance, there was little blood around the area where she was found despite a gaping wound on her head. This led detectives to suspect that she had been slain inside a vehicle and dumped at the scene. Several days later it was learned that the decedent had been in the company of Frederick Hinman Knowlton, Jr., on more than one occasion. When investigators went to check Knowlton out they learned that he had just redone the interior of his car and had scrubbed the same with a strong cleansing solution. Thinking that he might have really been washing away bloodstains, detectives impounded the car and soon had their suspicions confirmed. After a marathon interrogation Knowlton admitted that he had been with Miss Stewart on the night in question. He also admitted to being romantically involved with her. His wife gave him an alibi for the time of the murder but a jury disbelieved her. Knowlton was capitally convicted. He was subsequently put to death by electrocution at the Massachusetts State Prison on May 14, 1929. He never admitted his guilt.

Charles Trippi, white, age 21. *Murder.* The crime was committed on November 11, 1928, at Charlestown, Massachusetts. At the time of his capital crime this young man was a convict in the Massachusetts State Prison. He had previously served time at the Shirley and Concord reformatories. Originally from Fitchburg, he was nabbed for an armed robbery there plus the attempted shooting of the police officers who arrested him. In the spring of 1927 he drew a term of 15 to 18 years in state's prison and was subsequently hit with additional time for car theft and illegal weapons possession. By the autumn of 1928 Trippi had somehow gotten his hands on the ultimate in jailhouse contraband: a fully loaded revolver and additional ammunition to go with it. He stashed those items in a balcony overlooking the prison chapel. On the morning of the above date he attended services in the chapel and snuck up a set of stairs to the balcony. There he armed himself with his hidden weapon and waited with the intention of later shooting his way out of prison. When he was missed shortly afterwards a search was begun for him. As two guards named Frederick Pfluger (white, age 41) and George Connolly (white) advanced up the stairway to the chapel balcony Trippi opened fire on them. Pfluger died instantly of a shot through the heart. Other bullets missed Connolly but he was knocked out cold when Trippi pistol-whipped him. The

sound of gunfire soon brought other guards running to the scene. When Trippi paused to reload his weapon the other guards rushed him and successfully overpowered him. He was subsequently convicted of capital murder and transferred from the general prison population to that area reserved for the condemned. On December 3, 1929, he died in the electric chair.

John Feltovic, white, age 19. *Murder.* The crime was committed on March 23, 1929, at Bridgeport, Connecticut. This teenage offender was described by newspapers as "a product of the Bridgeport slums." At the time of his capital crime he already had a record of five arrests for burglary and breach of the peace. On the above date Feltovic ganged up with two of his cronies and decided to rob a grocery store located at the corner of Berkshire and Noble avenues. It was ten o'clock at night when a car carrying the holdup men came to the neighborhood where the store was located. As one man stayed behind the wheel of the idling vehicle, Feltovic and another man entered the unlocked door of the grocery store. The store manager, Lester Jacobs (white, age 39), was still there. He had dismissed his clerks for the night and was in the act of making some final entries in his ledger books. Feltovic pointed a loaded revolver at Jacobs and demanded money. Instead of complying with the bandit's orders, Jacobs picked up a pair of scales and flung them at Feltovic's head. Then when Feltovic ducked to avoid the scales, Jacobs rushed at him. Feltovic immediately opened fire on the store manager and killed him with a bullet through the heart. Both of the bandits fled empty-handed. However, they were seen by a 14-year-old stockboy who was hiding in the shadows. When police were given a description of the gunman by the stockboy they immediately thought of John Feltovic. He had shown off a shiny nickel-plated revolver some

days earlier and it was such a weapon that had been used to kill Lester Jacobs. The suspect was nabbed within a short time. He was subsequently convicted of capital murder and ordered for execution. On December 10, 1929, he was hanged at the Connecticut State Prison.

1930

Frank DiBattista, alias "The Cowboy," white, age 25. *Murder.* The crime was committed on April 1, 1929, at Hartford, Connecticut. This offender was the eldest of eight children. His parents were poor but honest. His father, Domenico DiBattista, was an Italian shoemaker who worked long hours to support his family. When the elder DiBattista fell ill with tuberculosis he became permanently disabled. His family, left destitute, had to go on public assistance. Young Frank DiBattista despised these circumstances and opted to go off on his own. Instead of working to support his parents and siblings he headed for New York City. There he took a room and got a job as an elevator boy. He also got into trouble for petty theft. Then he secured a job as a maintenance man in a respectable apartment building. When he robbed one of the tenants there of some jewelry, however, he was fired. Frank DiBattista also wound up serving two years of hard time on Blackwell's Island. At the expiration of his jail sentence he returned to Hartford. Not daring to impose himself on the family that he had abandoned, he shared a rent with some other young men. During the course of his travels he had acquired a gun — a .38 caliber revolver — and when he found himself without money in the early spring of 1929 he decided to pull a stickup. While walking around Hartford late on the evening of the above date, DiBattista had his attention drawn to a small grocery store at No. 116 Jefferson

Street. Looking in the store window, DiBattista noticed that the cash register was unattended. He then went into the store with an intention of grabbing some money from the till. No sooner did DiBattista reach the cash register than he was challenged by the grocer, Samuel Kamaroff (white, age 37). He then pulled out his revolver and ordered the grocer to raise his hands. Instead of doing as he was told, Kamaroff went on the attack. DiBattista then shot the man in the head — killing him instantly — and ran out of the store empty-handed. In his flight, the killer dropped four .38 caliber bullets on the floor of the store. Several days later DiBattista's landlady reported finding the same kind of bullets in her rooming house. At first the bullets were thought to belong to the killer's roommate but when that person was questioned he implicated DiBattista. Confronted with the evidence, DiBattista confessed what he had done. He was subsequently tried and condemned on a charge of capital murder. On February 21, 1930, Frank "The Cowboy" DiBattista was hanged at the Connecticut State Prison.

Henry Oswald Lorenz, white, age 25. *Murder.* The crime was committed on March 31, 1930, at Wethersfield, Connecticut. This young man had been born in Germany to a Hungarian father and a Mexican mother. During World War I his parents sent him to Sweden for safekeeping. There he was adopted by a compassionate aunt. When he was 20 years old Lorenz joined with a friend of his own age who planned to go to Mexico. Being already fluent in Spanish (thanks to his mother), the youthful Lorenz saw a chance to broaden his horizons. He accordingly went to Vera Cruz and became an oiljack there. By 1927 he had tired of that line of work. His next move was to illegally enter the United States. Lorenz made his way to Connecticut where he found work with a

Hartford picture framer. His ability to speak five languages made him a special asset to his employer because that person had many customers among the immigrant population. Lorenz was also noted for his personal deportment; he was always polite and impeccably dressed. His only apparent fault was that he had a tendency to live beyond his means.

One day Lorenz attended a church social and there met a young lady named Elizabeth Benson (white, age 18). Both were drawn to each other and soon Lorenz became Miss Benson's steady suitor. He also became an accepted friend of the Benson family. Such was the way in which Lorenz got to know one Nils Einor Anderson (white, age 28), an uncle of his girlfriend. When it was found that Lorenz spoke excellent Swedish (the native tongue of Nils Anderson) the two men became fast friends.

The onset of the Great Depression boded ill for the parents of Elizabeth Benson. They fell behind on their mortgage and faced foreclosure. Nils Anderson wanted to help them out financially because Mrs. Benson was his sister. The man accordingly dipped into his savings. Then to raise additional cash, Anderson called in a loan that he had previously made to Henry Lorenz. This put Lorenz in a difficult position. He was unable to repay the loan in a lump sum but feared to openly default on it because he did not want to queer his relationship with the Benson family. Lorenz then made a disastrous decision to do away with Nils Anderson.

According to his subsequent confession, Lorenz got in touch with Anderson on the evening of the above date and made arrangements to pick the man up in his car. The two then motored over to Wethersfield on the pretext of fetching the loan money from a third party. Lorenz eventually brought his car to a halt in front of a certain house and pretended to go inside the place while Anderson waited in the car. When Lorenz returned to the car he told Anderson that he had the money and that he would give it to him when they got back to Hartford. Then while driving along Garden Street in Wethersfield, Lorenz claimed to hear an "annoying rattle" beneath his car. He and Anderson then got out of the car to check the cause of the supposed trouble. As Anderson looked over the back end of the car Lorenz took a revolver and shot the man in the head at point-blank range. The fatal bullet passed clear through Anderson's head and shattered the rear window of the car. The killer then crammed the dead man into the car's rumbleseat and drove to a marshy area along River Road. There he dumped the body among the reeds.

The murdered man was found the following day and quickly identified as Nils Anderson. Robbery was ruled out as a motive because the decedent's wallet and money were still in his pockets. Detectives then began to check into Anderson's known acquaintances. Henry Lorenz aroused suspicion when he was reported to have replaced a rear window in his car and to have sent bloodstained clothes to a cleaner. A car wash also reported that the interior of the Lorenz vehicle had been stained with blood. When Elizabeth Benson received a note from Lorenz saying that he had gone to Central America in order to escape the immigration authorities, the hunt was on. All border crossings were notified to be on the watch. Lorenz was nearly caught at Niagara Falls but he managed to get into Canada. He was finally picked up in Windsor, Ontario, by the Royal Canadian Mounted Police. When detectives from Connecticut arrived to take charge of him, Lorenz made a full confession.

The trial of Henry Lorenz was not long in coming. A conviction for capital murder was followed up with an order for the execution of the defendant. No appeals were filed. On August 12, 1930, the condemned man was hanged at the Connecticut State Prison. On the following day he was buried next to his victim.

1931

Paul Hurley, white, age 19. *Murder.* The crime was committed on August 3, 1930, at Brookline, Massachusetts. Paul Hurley and Thomas Healey (white, age 19) were clean-cut preppy boys who had gotten to know each other at a private academy. Neither of them had a criminal record. On August 1, 1930, Healey left his home in Pittsburgh, Pennsylvania, and journeyed east to Boston. It was his intention to visit his pal Hurley there for a few days. When Healey arrived in Boston he was told the bad news that Hurley had lost his job. Money was accordingly tight and Hurley felt bad about not being able to show his visitor around the town in style. Hurley then got an idea; he proposed that he and Healey join forces and pull a stickup. Then they would have enough money to suit their needs. Healey hesitated but finally allowed himself to be coaxed. The two young fellows then stole a car and drove out to Carleton Street in Brookline. There they spotted a likely looking store (a pharmacy) and decided that it would suit their purpose. They parked their vehicle and were in the act of walking toward the store when they were challenged by a police officer named Joseph O'Brien (white, age 32). The cop did not like the furtive manner of the two young men and he demanded that they identify themselves. He also required Healey and Hurley to submit to a search for weapons. Healey allowed himself to be frisked but Hurley resisted. He told the cop to keep his hands to himself and he put up a fight. Officer O'Brien then pulled his service revolver on Hurley and fired two shots which actually pierced Hurley's clothing. In an instant Hurley pulled out a concealed firearm that he was carrying and shot the policeman. O'Brien was hit in the head and stomach. He died the following day. Healey and Hurley escaped from the scene in their stolen car. Then they split up. On the following day Hurley's roommate informed on him. Police were also told of Healey's involvement. Word was flashed along the eastern seaboard to check all trains and buses coming in from Boston. It was through such means that Healey was caught in a New York bus terminal. He meekly agreed to cooperate with the authorities but by then Hurley had fled. It was not until several months later that the fugitive was found. He turned up in Baltimore with dyed hair and a false mustache. Returned to Massachusetts, Hurley was convicted of capital murder. Then he was sent to the state prison under sentence of death. On September 15, 1931, he died in the electric chair.

Joseph Belenski, white, age 38. *Murder.* The crime was committed on May 21, 1930, at Stow, Massachusetts. This man worked for a farm couple named William and Stacia Stefanowicz (whites, aged 57 and 60) on their 170-acre property near the Hudson town line. He dreamed of becoming master of the farm and he decided on murder in order to achieve that aim. On the above date Belenski lured Mr. Stefanowicz to a wooded area where he hacked him to death with an axe. When Mrs. Stefanowicz came running to the scene in response to her husband's screams, she too was slain in the same manner. Belenski then buried the couple in a shallow grave and took over their farm. He circulated a story that the missing pair had sold out to him and went to Chicago. In the days that followed this announcement Belenski began to sell off the assets of the victims. He sent most of their livestock to market and pocketed the proceeds. He also hired and fired farm workers at will. Suspicion mounted because Belenski was slow to pay his workmen. When one of them filed a legal attachment against the farm it was discovered that the property had never been transferred into Belenski's name. Relatives of William and Stacia Stefanowicz also doubted the story about them going to Chicago. Suspicions were heightened when those relatives poked around the farmhouse and found the couple's wardrobes undisturbed. Eleven weeks after the murders police search teams descended on the Stefanowicz farm. So did hundreds of concerned citizens. Extensive digging operations were carried out on the property with negative results. Then after five days of fruitless searching some boys stumbled over the protruding arms of the victims as they played in nearby woods. Belenski was caught in Boston shortly afterward when a sales clerk recognized him from a wanted poster. He was electrocuted at the Massachusetts State Prison on October 20, 1931.

1932

Bert Stacey, white, age 52. *Murder.* The crime was committed on April 18, 1931, at Berlin, Vermont. This offender was a jealous husband who murdered his estranged wife. Bert and Ruth Stacey (white, age 31) lived at Barre. Trouble began one day when a male caller came to their house and asked to speak with Mrs. Stacey. From that time on Bert Stacey never treated his wife in a civil manner. He accused the woman of infidelity and took to beating her whenever he felt like it. By the spring of 1931 Ruth Stacey had had enough of her husband's abuse. She took her six-year-old daughter by a previous marriage and went to the town of Berlin. There she went to work as a housekeeper for a prosperous farmer named Louis Sweeney. When Bert Stacey learned of his wife's whereabouts he decided to go after her. On the above date he arose early and went to a hardware store. There he purchased a .32 caliber handgun and plenty of bullets. Several hours later Bert Stacey went to the Sweeney farm in order to confront his wife. The farmer himself was not there at the time. Instead, Stacey came upon his young stepdaughter playing in the barnyard. He asked the child if she knew the whereabouts of her mother. When told that the woman was in one of the barns, Stacey went thereto and started an argument. When Ruth Stacey turned to flee, her husband pulled out his gun and shot her twice in the back. Not satisfied with that, the angry man then turned his wrath upon his six-year-old stepdaughter. He fired on her before fleeing from the scene. A bullet went clear through the little girl's chest without mortally wounding her. Even though both of her lungs were pierced, the child managed to seek out her mother unassisted. When the slain woman failed to stir, the child laid next to her for a while. Then she went into the farmhouse and fell asleep on a sofa. There she was found by Louis Sweeney when he came home. The little girl (whose name was Alta Slack) made a complete recovery from her bullet wound and later became a star witness against her stepfather. He was found walking along the Montpelier Road shortly after the crime. When the case came to trial a disgusted jury refused to append a mercy recommendation to its verdict of guilty. That meant capital punishment for the defendant. Bert Stacey was sent to the Vermont State Prison under sentence of death. He was electrocuted there on July 7, 1932.

Sylvester Fernandes, white, age 25. *Murder.* The crime was committed on December 23, 1931, at Barnstable, Massachusetts. This young man belonged to a Portuguese clan which used to work the cranberry crop on Cape Cod. His marriage became strained when his wife announced that she could no longer endure their low standard of living. She had already left Fernandes more than once and she threatened to leave him permanently unless he did something to improve their circumstances. Fernandes then thought of his cousin, John Alves (white, age 44), a recluse of sorts who was rumored to have a lot of money. On the above date Fernandes and Alves both attended a family gathering at the house of the former's father. Fernandes and his wife left early but when they got home Fernandes said that he had to go back in order to borrow his father's car. He did just that and drove to the vicinity of Parker Road in Barnstable, the place where John Alves lived in a rundown cabin. Then he hid near the cabin with a shotgun and waited for Alves to return home from the family gathering. When Alves did return Fernandes shot him in the back. Then he dragged the victim into the cabin still alive and finished him off there by cracking his skull with the stock of the shotgun. When Alves was dead the killer began a methodical search of the premises. He took up the carpets and floorboards in the belief that money might be hidden beneath them. He ransacked the cabinets and drawers, dug up all around the outside of the cabin and even dismantled a clock looking for the rumored stash of cash. He found $110 in the dead man's pockets which he used the next day to buy a fur coat for his wife. The crime was discovered two days later when Alves failed to show up for a Christmas dinner. Fernandes came under suspicion when it was reported that he had purchased an expensive coat which was beyond his usual means. When Fernandes was confronted with the evidence he confessed what he had done. He was electrocuted at the Massachusetts State Prison on August 12, 1932.

1933

Although there are known to have been at least 162 legal executions in the United States of America this year, none of them occurred in the New England states.

1934

Ahmed Osman, white, age 38. *Murder.* The crime was committed on December 25, 1932, at Norwood, Massachusetts. This man was a Turkish peddler who lived on the top floor of a three-family house at No. 29 Oolah Avenue in Norwood. On the second floor of the same house resided a Mr. and Mrs. Joseph Keras with their four daughters, aged 6, 9, 13 and 14. The Keras family regarded Osman as a good neighbor. He had been widowed for about a year previous to the time of his crime and in the absence of his wife, he used to have the two elder Keras girls assist him with his housework. Their usual rewards for such tasks were candy and coins. The Keras family became alarmed when its third daughter, Nellie Keras (white, age nine), failed to return home from a neighborhood store. No one could account for her strange disappearance. It was the neighbor, Ahmed Osman, who finally notified police. An intensive two-day search was then conducted in which hundreds of people took part. All wooded areas in the vicinity of Oolah Avenue were carefully examined as were all bodies of water. Police finally decided to conduct a systematic search of the Keras family house. They found the little girl's body in the cellar carefully hidden in a woodbin which was kept locked by Ahmed Osman. As the police later explained, Osman had lured the child into his apartment as she was returning from the store. He then strangled her with a cord and raped her dead body. After that he bound her limbs with the cord and stuffed her into a burlap bag along with her bloodied clothes. Then he stashed everything beneath the kindling in his woodbin. The details of the crime combined with the fact that it happened on Christmas Day caused outrage in the Norwood community. When police brought the suspect to the scene of the crime a lynch mob quickly formed. It was only with extreme difficulty that Osman was safely taken away. A court later sentenced him to death. On January 23, 1934, a Moslem holy man was brought to the Massachusetts State Prison. There he guided Ahmed Osman through the ritual ablutions of his faith. Then the condemned man was brought to the electric chair and put to death.

Henry Clay Bull, white, age 22. *Murder.* The crime was committed on August 7, 1933, at Greenfield, Massachusetts. This young man came from Brooklyn, New York. He was suspected of pulling a number of stickups prior to the one which cost him his life. Shortly before dawn on the above date Bull drove a stolen car into a Greenfield filling station and rather matter-of-factly told the attendant that he needed some money. Then he pulled out a handgun and announced a holdup. The attendant, one Arthur Mannix by name, balked at Bull's demand and wound up engaging him in a verbal altercation. The two men stood there arguing for several minutes. Finally the attendant shouted to a passerby to go and fetch a policeman. When an officer arrived at the scene he found Bull still standing there bickering with Mannix. As the officer tried to place the gunman under arrest Bull started shooting. The policeman was hit in the stomach and mortally wounded. The filling station attendant was also injured but he still had strength to tackle the gunman. In the struggle that followed, the attendant wrested a blackjack from Bull and disabled him with a hard blow on the head. Thus was the culprit disarmed and captured. The wounded policeman, whose name was Albert Jordan (white, age 49), succumbed after 12 hours of agony. Henry Clay Bull — the inept holdup man — was then charged with capital murder. He was electrocuted at the Massachusetts State Prison on February 22, 1934.

John Donnellon, white, age 22. **Herman Snyder,** white, age 20. *Murder.* Their crime was committed on April 9, 1931, at Somerville, Massachusetts. At precisely 7:30 on the evening of the above date these young men drove into a filling station at No. 13 Somerville Avenue (at the Cambridge town line) with robbery on their minds. One accomplice remained behind the wheel of the car while Donnellon and Snyder approached the station's office. Donnellon then stood watch by the door while Snyder confronted the station manager with a handgun and demanded money. When the manager hesitated to do as he was told, the skittish bandit killed him with a shot through the heart. Donnellon and Snyder both ran from the scene empty-handed. They jumped into their getaway car and took off at a high rate of speed. The dead man was identified as one James M. Kiley (white, age 39), then in his second day on the job. Homicide detectives eventually succeeded in hunting down those who were in on the crime. In the end Herman Snyder was convicted as a principal and John Donnellon as a willful accessory to capital felony. Both were sentenced to death. They were electrocuted at the Massachusetts State Prison on February 22, 1934.

1935

Alexander Kaminski, white, age 23. *Murder.* The crime was committed on October 22, 1933, at Springfield, Massachusetts. This offender had originally come from New Britain, Connecticut. A job search brought him to Springfield where he was caught carrying a concealed weapon. Kaminski wound up getting sentenced to a six-month term in the Hampden County jail. While there he met another young inmate named Paul Wargo (white, age 21) and conspired with him in a plan to escape. On the above date the two prisoners lay in wait for a guard named Merritt W. Hayden (white, age 50) in the prison workshop. When the guard came down from his watch tower he was set upon by Kaminski and Wargo. They beat him about the head with a blunt instrument. They also took the guard's keys and used them to effect their escape. Wargo was caught the same day not far from the prison. Kaminski managed to elude capture for several weeks. He was eventually nabbed in Lynchburg, Virginia. In the meantime Officer Hayden died of his injuries. Wargo wound up drawing a life sentence for his part in the crime. Kaminski was brought to trial in February of 1934 but had the proceedings disrupted by another escape attempt. A sibling of his named John Kaminski set off a bomb in the courtroom where the case was being heard. John Kaminski also shot at the court officers with a handgun before he was subdued. The sheriff of Hampden County was wounded in the melee. Seven months later while he was awaiting sentencing for capital murder, Alexander Kaminski broke out of the Springfield jail once again. He eluded a dragnet by Massachusetts and Connecticut state police and got across the border into New York. Two months later he was caught by a fluke circumstance. It so happened that Kaminski accidentally left a travel bag containing weapons in the waiting room of an Albany bus station. The bag was found by a cleaning woman who called police. When Kaminski came back for the bag he was arrested. Returned to Massachusetts, the fugitive Kaminski was speedily sentenced to die. On February 19, 1935, he was executed in the electric chair.

Abraham Faber, white, age 25. **Irving Millen,** white, age 20. **Morton Millen,** white, age 25. *Murder.* Their crimes were committed over a period of time from December of 1932 to February of 1934. These young men formed a holdup team which became progressively more violent as time went on. Abraham Faber was the mastermind. A 1931 graduate of the Massachusetts Institute of Technology, he was considered a genius in the field of electronics. He owned and operated a successful radio supply store on Columbus Avenue in Boston where he legitimately employed the brothers Irving and Morton Millen. Neither Faber nor the Millens had any criminal record and the reason why they turned to crime has never been explained. They started out during the winter of 1932-1933 by robbing small merchants and theater box offices. On March 10, 1933, the Millen brothers attempted to hold up the Oriental Theater in Mattapan Square and fired shots at a female cashier. Failing to gain admittance to the locked box office, they waited for 23 days and then abducted the manager of the theater from the driveway of his home. The man was forced to go to the theater with the Millens and open the box office safe. The bandits then stole $89 and fled. On October 9, 1933, they got an impressive haul from the Palace Theater in Worcester. Monies totaling $4500 were seized on that occasion — a considerable sum for what was then the bleakest period of the Great Depression. Emboldened by their success, the Faber-Millen gang next decided that it needed to improve its arsenal. So the gang set its sights on a Fitchburg sporting goods store which was well-stocked with guns and ammunition. On the evening of December 11, 1933, they attempted to abduct the store manager, Ernest W. Clark (white, age 37), as he walked home from work. When the man resisted he was shot dead. Nine bullets were later taken from his body. Three weeks later, on January 2, 1934, the gang struck the Paramount Theater in Lynn. They stole $200 from the box office there and fatally gunned down a bill poster named Frederick Sumner (white, age 56) when he got in the way. Disappointed with the size of their haul, the gang decided that it was tired of theater robberies in general. Their solution was to move up to bank robberies. They still needed to upgrade their arsenal, however, so they carefully examined a public display of state police armaments at the Mechanics Building in downtown Boston. Late on the night of January 27, 1934, they broke into that place, tied up the watchman and cleaned out the state police exhibit. A fully loaded machine gun was among their loot. Six days later — on February 2, 1934 — they burst into the main office of the Needham Trust Company and announced a holdup. They were armed with the stolen machine gun, automatic pistols and a sawed-off shotgun. One of the gang members shot his way into the bank's vault — wounding the vaultkeeper in the process — and helped himself to what monies he found there. When a police officer named Forbes McLeod (white, age 34) came running towards the bank in response to the vault alarm he was cut down by machine-gun fire and killed. After that the bandits paused only long enough to clean out the teller drawers. Then they herded two bank employees out the door with them and made them stand on the running board of the getaway car to act as human shields. The car took off down Great Plain Street at a high rate of speed, turned onto Maple Street and passed right in front of the Needham Police Department. Then the car spun onto Oak Street, then Chestnut Street and back onto Great Plain Road. Somehow the two bank employees managed to hang on for dear life. At Highland Avenue the vehicle spun around the corner on two wheels and then raced towards Needham Heights at speeds nearing 100 mph. At Needham Heights a policeman named Frank Haddock (white, age 41) waved his gun at the speeding car in an effort to halt it. He too was killed by a burst of machine-gun fire. Another man shoveling snow nearby was badly hurt. At a point about three miles from the bank both of the human shields were thrown to the pavement. Then the car made good its escape. The hue and cry which followed this incident was unprecedented in the history of Massachusetts. So great was the alarm that for the first time the Faber-Millen gang decided to flee the area. They burned their getaway car, divided up their loot and headed west. As things turned out, the burning of the getaway car proved to be the one mistake that led to the gang's undoing. Arson investigators discovered that the car's battery had been *rented* from an auto supply store. The renter was thereby traced and identified as one of the Millen brothers. Then when the car itself was linked to the Needham bank robbery the solution of the police killings came swiftly. The Millens were traced to a hotel in New York where they were captured at gunpoint. They were also beaten up in the process. Faber was caught the same day in Boston as he was preparing to get out of town. Soon he made a full confession detailing every crime in which he and the Millens had been involved. This was followed a short time later by disclosures from Irving Millen in which he admitted being the machine-gunner at the Needham bank job. When the full details of the crimes and the identities of the culprits became known, the Jewish community of Greater Boston was scandalized to learn that three of its sons were at fault. Several prominent rabbis made a public statement expressing their shock and dismay. On June 7, 1935, more than 5000 people gathered in the street outside of the Massachusetts State Prison as Abraham Faber and the two Millen brothers were put to death in the electric chair.

1936

Miller Frank Clark, white, age 44. *Murder.* The crime was committed on December 20, 1933, at Boston, Massachusetts. This offender was described as a "middle-aged eccentric" who had a hard time fitting into society. He became infatuated with a young bakery clerk named Ethel Zuckerman (white, age 18) and made a nuisance of himself by pressing his attentions on her. At first Miss Zuckerman tried tactful ways to discourage Clark. When those failed she told the man in plain language that his importunings were in vain. When Clark asked for reasons, Miss Zuckerman told him that there was a substantial difference in their ages. She also explained that she belonged to an orthodox Jewish sect which had a rigid set of principles. Clark did not like those answers. He brooded over the rejection until his mind snapped. Then he declared that no other man would succeed where he had failed. On the above date Clark worked himself into a rage and stomped over to Miss Zuckerman's place of employment, a kosher bakery at No. 314 Harrison Avenue. Finding the young woman alone behind the counter, Clark went berserk and attacked her. First he beat her with his fists. Then he battered her with a rolling pin until every bone in her head was broken. Still not satisfied, Clark next took a long bread knife and used it to carve a cross into the victim's forehead. In such a way he sought to mock her Jewish heritage. Then the killer ran the blade of the knife through Miss Zuckerman's throat with such force that it pinned her body to the wooden floor of the bakery. So was the victim found with the bread knife protruding from her gullet. Before fleeing from the scene of the crime, Clark helped himself to the contents of the bakery's cash drawer. He took eight dollars and escaped into the night. An old Jewish lady came upon the scene about five minutes later. Several months passed before detectives cracked this case. By then Clark had convinced himself that he would never be caught. He was electrocuted at the Massachusetts State Prison on January 14, 1936.

John Simborski, white, age 28. *Murder.* The crime was committed on March 5, 1935, at New Haven, Connecticut. This man was an habitual criminal who went to the gallows for killing a police officer. Simborski first ran afoul of the law when he was ten years old. He was sent to a reform school then for shooting another boy of the same age. During his teenage years he was arrested numerous times for burglary, robbery and other acts of theft. In 1930 he drew a term in state's prison of from three to seven years. Paroled after four years, Simborski rented a room in West Haven. There he supported himself with the proceeds of many illegal acts. On the above date Simborski awoke early and decided that it would be a good day to go on a robbery spree. He accordingly went to New Haven and looked around for vulnerable sites. At around 8:30 A.M. he broke into the house of a police officer at No. 460 Dixwell Avenue. While searching the place for valuables he came across a fully loaded .38 caliber revolver and added that weapon to his loot. Then he went to No. 669 Elm Street and there entered another house. Simborski swiped eight handkerchiefs from a linen closet while the homeowner chatted with a caller at the front door. Hearing footsteps above her, the homeowner realized that there was an intruder in her house. She then screamed for the neighborhood beat cop but Simborski was gone by the time the officer arrived. Policemen throughout that ward of the city were then put on alert. Then as an officer was in the act of writing down the Elm Street homeowner's statement there came a radio report of a burglary in progress at No. 12 Harding Place. Simborski had broken into his third house within a two-hour period. As officers raced to the scene they saw the culprit running therefrom. They then commandeered an automobile from a private citizen and set off in pursuit. Simborski ducked into an alley at No. 963 Sherman Avenue. A policeman named Walter Koella (white, age 53) then jumped from the running board of the pursuing automobile and chased the suspect on foot. As the officer ran around the rear corner of the house at the Sherman Avenue address, Simborski opened fire on him with the gun he had stolen that same morning. Officer Koella was fatally wounded by two bullets in the chest. The slain patrolman's partner then engaged Simborski in a running gun battle which shattered the calm of the Sherman Avenue neighborhood. The fleeing bandit finally caught a bullet in the leg and fell to the ground wounded. He was then pounced upon by other policemen and taken into custody. When Simborski was brought to trial he was condemned to be hanged. He met that fate accordingly at the Connecticut State Prison on April 7, 1936.

Newell Sherman, white, age 26. *Murder.* The crime was committed on July 20, 1935, at Worcester, Massachusetts. This man lived in the town of Sutton. He was a portly fellow who weighed 242 pounds. His wife, Alice Sherman (white, age 23), was a petite 118-pound mother of two. Newell Sherman worked in a Whitinsville factory. In his spare time he was a choir singer and a scoutmaster. Becoming infatuated with a 17-year-old girl, Sherman asked her if she would marry him. The girl scoffed at Sherman, saying that he was already married. Sherman then said that he would be single once again. The girl told him not to talk like that and so thought the matter ended. Sherman, however, resolved to do away with his wife. After forming a plan in his mind, he chose the above date as the time for action. On his way to work that morning Sherman stopped by the boat concession at Lake Singletary. He then reserved a canoe for that evening. When Sherman returned home from work he put his young children to bed and then proposed a romantic outing with his wife. It was a warm summer evening and Alice Sherman agreed to go for a canoe ride with her husband. It was a fatal mistake. After hiring a baby-sitter, the couple went to Lake Singletary. The water being placid, they had no difficulty paddling to a point far out on the lake. Then Newell Sherman deliberately upset the canoe. He and his wife both fell into the deep water. Unable to swim, Alice Sherman tried to grasp ahold of her husband, only to be pushed away by him. She then tried to grab onto the overturned canoe but Newell Sherman pushed it beyond her reach. When the drowning woman sank from sight her husband swam safely to shore and reported her death as an accident. Sherman had the nerve to tell his 17-year-old love interest what he had done. When the girl heard the story she was appalled. She promptly went to the police and informed them that a murder had been committed. When the truth about the alleged drowning mishap became known, Newell Sherman was charged with capital felony. He was convicted when he was shown to be a strong swimmer who made no effort to save his wife even though he was fully capable of doing so. The electric chair claimed this man at the Massachusetts State Prison on August 4, 1936.

1937

Joseph James McElroy, white, age 47. *Murder.* The crime was committed on August 10, 1936, at New Haven, Con-necticut. A diminutive man, this offender came to America from Ireland in 1909. Although he became a naturalized citizen of the United States, the outbreak of World War I brought him to Montreal. There he enlisted with a combat battalion of the Royal Canadian Army. Sent to the battlefields of France, McElroy served for 18 months and took part in some of the worst fighting of the war. He was honorably discharged when a poison gas attack left him unfit for further military service. When he recovered his strength, McElroy returned to the United States. He settled at New Haven and found employment there as a hospital porter. Over the course of the next several years McElroy became acquainted with a somewhat younger woman named Anna Mae Johnson (white, age 32), a nurse's aide who worked in the same hospital. This Anna Mae Johnson had been deserted by her husband. When she learned that McElroy had a divorce pending she indicated her willingness to have a personal relationship with him. Thus began a six-year association between the hospital porter and the nurse's aide. The couple lived together for most of that time. It so happened that McElroy had a violent temper. Although he is not known to have physically abused Anna Mae Johnson, the woman was not pleased with the bellicose aspect of McElroy's character. After six years her romantic feelings cooled. She told her lover that she wanted to end her involvement with him. McElroy would not hear of it. He adopted a choleric mood from that time on and said that he would rather see Anna Mae Johnson dead than involved with another man. This frightened Anna Mae Johnson. One day when McElroy was out of town she packed up her belongings. Then she moved into a dormitory for hospital workers at the corner of Congress Avenue and Cedar Street in New Haven. When McElroy came home and found his lover gone he was furious. He immediately inquired about the woman's new habitation and made plans for an ambush. On the above date Anna Mae Johnson joined some fellow hospital employees for an outing at the Savin Rock amusement park. While she was gone McElroy snuck into her place of residence. He hid in a janitor's closet and drank a whole pint of whiskey in order to keep up his courage. Shortly after 11 o'clock that night Anna Mae Johnson came home from the amusement park. She bade farewell to her friends on the sidewalk and then let herself into the dormitory with her passkey. She began to climb the stairs to her apartment and was last seen waving from the window of a second story landing. All at once there was heard a loud scream. McElroy had leapt from his hiding place and attacked Anna Mae Johnson. The woman was slashed across the throat with a razor and kicked down two flights of stairs. McElroy then ran out of the dormitory and right past the woman's erstwhile companions. They recognized him. Anna Mae Johnson was brought to her own hospital but pronounced dead on arrival. For the rest of that night the killer hid in the swamps on the outskirts of New Haven. The next morning he was found wandering in a peach orchard dazed and confused. The state's attorney for New Haven County called McElroy's crime "the most perfect case of first degree murder I have ever seen." The element of premeditation was clearly evident. For that reason there was no plea bargain. There was also no doubt about the defendant's guilt. Sentence of death was mandatory following conviction in a court of law. On February 10, 1937, an electric chair ended the life of Joseph James McElroy at the Connecticut State Prison.

1938

Anthony DiStassio, white, age 22. **Frank DiStassio,** white, age 51. *Mur-*

der. The crime was committed on May 6, 1935, at the town of Hudson, Massachusetts. These offenders were a father and son. Both were residents of Revere. The elder DiStassio was a candymaker by profession. Six weeks prior to their crime Frank DiStassio's wife succumbed to a lengthy illness. Her widower was left deep in debt. He wished to remarry but lacked the necessary funds to do so. He then got together with his son and hatched a deadly scheme. It was decided to fake the death of the elder DiStassio so that his son, as his beneficiary, would collect a $20,000 life insurance payout. According to plan, the elder DiStassio drove his car into the slums of Boston while his son followed closely behind him in another vehicle. On Union Park Street he spotted an obviously disadvantaged man named Daniel Crowley (white, age 52) and invited him to go for a ride. Crowley went along and was soon drinking heavily as Frank DiStassio plied him with liquor. They then drove merrily about the Boston suburbs as the younger DiStassio followed them. Eventually Frank DiStassio reached the town of Hudson and parked in a lonely spot near Lake Boone. The site had previously been selected for what DiStassio had planned. By then Daniel Crowley was too drunk to care. Frank DiStassio then feigned a desire to get out of the car and he bade Crowley to do the same. When Crowley did so he was struck down from behind with a crowbar and beaten to within an inch of his life. Both of his arms and legs were broken and his skull was fractured in numerous places. Then he was stuffed back into the car *still alive and conscious.* Frank DiStassio next took a can of gasoline from the trunk of the car. He splashed its contents all over the inside of the vehicle and all over Daniel Crowley. Then he tossed a lighted match into the car. It was assumed by the killers that the discovery of a charred body in Frank DiStassio's car would be all that was needed to dupe the insurance company. Frank DiStassio even tossed his signet ring into the blazing car for added effect. Then he got into the second car which was driven by his son and hurried from the scene. At first it was believed that the remains found in the burnt car were indeed those of Frank DiStassio. However, suspicions of foul play were soon aroused. Physical differences were noted between DiStassio and the remains of the victim. It was also determined from the position of the body that the signet ring had been planted as a false clue. Two days later Frank DiStassio was spotted in a Boston auto showroom by an alert police officer and placed under arrest. He soon confessed the crime as also did his son. The elder DiStassio was convicted as principal on an indictment for premeditated murder. His son was convicted as a willing accessory. Both drew mandatory death sentences. They were electrocuted at the Massachusetts State Prison on January 18, 1938.

Frank Palka, white, age 25. *Murder.* The crime was committed on September 30, 1935, at Bridgeport, Connecticut. This notorious offender came from Buffalo, New York. There he was convicted of forcible rape and sentenced to ten years in the Elmira Reformatory. Paroled after serving barely half of that sentence, Palka came to Connecticut in search of employment. He took a room at Bridgeport and went to work as a riveter for the nearby Sikorsky Aircraft Corporation. On the evening of September 29, 1935, Palka went out drinking with a workmate. He carried a loaded revolver on his person. Shortly after midnight Palka and his companion exited a saloon in the downtown section of Bridgeport. They then went walking along Fairfield Avenue toward yet another such resort. As they passed a row of stores their attention was drawn to the display window of an electronics retailer. There they saw a selection of handsome

radios. Palka and his pal then decided that they must each have one of those radios. So they smashed the display window and helped themselves to the merchandise. A rooming house matron saw this illegal act and called police. By the time officers arrived at the scene the two thieves had split up and run in different directions. Patrol cars then spread out to check the nearby streets for any suspicious persons. One car overtook Palka on Golden Hill Street near the Fairfield County courthouse. A police sergeant named Thomas Kearney (white, age 49) and a uniformed patrolman named Wilfred Walker (white, age 44) then got out of their squad car to challenge Palka. As they did so, Palka opened fire on them with his revolver. Both of the policemen were fatally wounded. Palka managed to elude the dragnet which gripped Bridgeport for the remainder of that night. The next day he reported to his job as usual and he continued in that manner for two more weeks. Then he suddenly took fright and fled the area. That was a fatal mistake. When Palka failed to report to his parole officer shortly thereafter, suspicion was aroused. A search of the missing man's room turned up a brand new radio which was identified as one taken during the smash and grab incident linked to the double police killing. When it was learned from the parole bureau that Palka came from Buffalo, New York, police in that city were asked to be on the watch for him. Palka almost predictably made the mistake of returning to Buffalo, a city where he was known to the police. There he was caught. A confession which he made at that time may or may not have been beaten out of him. Palka was sent back to Bridgeport where he underwent two trials. When the juries asked to view the crime scene they merely had to look out the courthouse windows. Frank Palka was sent to the Connecticut State Prison under sentence of death. He was electrocuted there on April 12, 1938.

Edward Simpson, white, age 39. *Murder.* The crime was committed on August 21, 1937, at Newton, Massachusetts. This man was an habitual criminal who had been arrested more than 20 times. On April 25, 1937, he broke out of the Charles Street jail (where he was serving a term for larceny) and remained at large until four months later when he committed a capital crime. On the above date he was riding around in a stolen car with a 17-year-old girl. When the vehicle ran a red light on Watertown Street in Newton it was pursued and pulled over by two policemen named Henry Bell (white, age 27) and William Whalen. Simpson tried to talk his way out of the situation by saying that he was teaching the girl how to drive. The two policemen, however, decided to run a check on the car. Officer Bell then stood by while Officer Whalen went to a nearby callbox. At that point Simpson knew the game was up. He pulled out a handgun and ordered Officer Bell to disarm himself. Then he had the girl get out of the car and further ordered Officer Bell to take her place in the driver's eat. The car then took off up the street with the captive policeman driving. Officer Whalen saw what happened and called for reinforcements. Within seconds a motorcycle patrolman named Lawrence Murphy (white, age 31) pulled alongside the suspect vehicle and ordered it to pull over. Murphy was astonished to see a fellow officer driving the fleeing vehicle. At that point Simpson opened fire on the motorcycle officer and hit him twice in the stomach. Murphy then fell to the pavement but managed to get off some shots of his own. One bullet struck Simpson in the shoulder. When Officer Bell attempted to stop the speeding car which contained him and Simpson, the gunman lost his temper and shot him (Bell) twice in the side. Then Simpson jumped out of the car and ran to Watertown Square. There he carjacked a woman and made his escape.

Officer Bell died of his wounds the following day. Officer Murphy managed to hang on for three weeks. Then he too succumbed. Simpson was hunted down to a Dorchester tenement by police officers determined to find the killer. He was caught six days after the crime. He was electrocuted at the Massachusetts State Prison on May 13, 1938.

1939

Howard Long, white, age 32. *Murder.* The crime was committed on September 10, 1937, at Gilford, New Hampshire. This man had been born at Hartford, Connecticut, but came to the greater Boston area as a teenager. As he grew to adulthood he became a compulsive pederast and as such served a sentence at the Bridgewater State Farm. In 1935 he was paroled and relocated to Alton, New Hampshire, where he opened a filling station. His craving for boys remained undiminished throughout that time. According to his subsequent confession, Long's first violent encounter occurred on November 12, 1936. It was then that he enticed a young Dover boy into his car. After riding around with the lad for more than ten hours he made an attempt at molestation. The victim, whose name was Armand Nadeau (white, age nine), became frightened and jumped from Long's moving vehicle. In doing so, he struck his head on the hard pavement and sustained a fatal injury. Long retrieved the boy's body and brought it to the town of Rollinsford. There he stashed it in the cellar of an abandoned house. The corpse was found a month later when the house burned down. On September 10, 1937, Long was driving around Laconia when he spotted a likely looking lad near the post office. He enticed the boy into his vehicle and drove with him to a secluded spot in Gilford. There he raped the boy, whose name was Mark Neville Jensen (white, age ten), and beat him to death with an automobile jack. Long was arrested four days later when he was questioned in connection with a check of known sex offenders. The tires of his car were found to match tracks left at the murder scene. In addition, Long admitted what he had done after a marathon interrogation. He was hanged at the New Hampshire State Prison on July 14, 1939.

Wallace Green, white, age 20. **Walter St. Saveur,** white, age 19. *Murder.* Their crime was committed on May 31, 1938, at Somerville, Massachusetts. These young men were residents of the town where they committed their capital crime. Needing some quick cash, they decided to rob a small grocery store on Perkins Street. Walking into the place with guns drawn, they demanded money from employees and customers alike. The feisty grocer, William Phillips (white, age 53), answered the bandits with a barrage of bottles. Both gunmen opened fire. Phillips suffered multiple gunshots and died at the scene. Before running out of the store, the culprits scooped up some coins from the cash register. Their total take amounted to $3.50 in silver. Three weeks later the robbers were found in Utah riding in a stolen car. St. Saveur was armed with a handgun which was determined to have been used in the Somerville slaying. A third member of the holdup team, Henry Richards (white, age 21), of Malden was also apprehended. When the case came to trial Richards got off lightly because he was a non-triggerman. He had also cooperated with authorities. Green and St. Saveur were capitally convicted. Both were then ordered for execution. They were electrocuted at the Massachusetts State Prison on August 2, 1939.

1940

Vincent Cotts, white, age 32. **Ira Allen Weaver,** white, age 35. *Murder.*

Their crime was committed on January 21, 1939, at Middletown, Connecticut. These men were employed with a traveling carnival which had its winter quarters at Middletown. Cotts came from nearby Shelton. Weaver came from King's Mountain, North Carolina. The latter had a lengthy criminal record which included a dishonorable discharge from the army. When their employer settled into its winter quarters in November of 1938 both men were given furloughs until the following spring. They then settled into temporary lodgings and made a marginal living selling Christmas trees and firewood. By mid-January of 1939 they were nearly destitute and behind on their rent. Not knowing what else to do, they decided to pull a stickup. They chose a butcher shop at No. 261 Ridge Road in Middletown. On the evening of the above date Cotts and Weaver drove to the target premises. Cotts remained behind the wheel of the car while Weaver entered the butcher shop via an unlocked rear door. The owner of the store, Joseph G. Dripps (white, age 51), was doing his books in a back room at the time. Weaver pointed a handgun at him and demanded money. When the store owner hesitated he was shot once in the stomach. He then tossed a money pouch to the gunman which was later found to have contained six dollars in silver. Weaver ran from the store with that paltry loot and escaped in the waiting car. Dripps died of his wound three days later. On the same day that Dripps died Cotts was picked up by police for writing a bad check. His car was found to match one which a bystander had seen drive away from the scene of the fatal holdup three days earlier. After some questioning, Cotts broke down and admitted the part he had played in the homicide. He also implicated Weaver who in turn confessed to being the gunman. When the case came to trial Weaver tried to repudiate his confession and shift all of the blame onto Cotts. In the end both defendants were capitally convicted, Weaver as the principal and Cotts as an accessory. Both were electrocuted at the Connecticut State Prison on April 30, 1940.

1941

Joseph Leo Rousseau, alias "Joe Brooks," white, age 23. *Murder*. The crime was committed on May 16, 1940, at Milton, Massachusetts. This man was a New Yorker by nativity. He had drawn a 20-year term for armed robbery there and had served nearly seven years of that time in Sing Sing prison before being paroled. When he learned soon afterward that he was wanted for parole violation he made his way to Boston. There he took up company with some minor hoodlums. Late on the evening of May 15, 1940, this Joseph Rousseau, alias Brooks, teamed up with a crony and robbed a man in a garage at no. 20 Chardon Street, Boston. The victim was left tied up at the scene but otherwise unharmed. Then Rousseau, alias Brooks, and his pal stole a car. They picked up some more acquaintances and went for a joy ride. As the stolen vehicle passed through the town of Milton during the early morning hours of May 16 it was observed by two police officers named Edward Lee (white, age 57) and Stephen Slack. The policemen recognized the car as stolen and they gave chase. They soon overtook the suspects and placed them under arrest. Shortly before two o'clock in the morning the squad car containing the joyriders and the arresting officers pulled up in front of the Central Avenue police station in Milton. As the occupants of the vehicle prepared to go inside the station, Rousseau (Brooks) suddenly pulled out a handgun and shot Patrolman Lee point-blank in the stomach. He was then restrained by the wounded officer's partner. Patrolman Lee was rushed to a hos-

pital but was pronounced dead on arrival. Rousseau survived a gunshot wound that he received in the same altercation. He was charged with capital murder and duly convicted. On April 22, 1941, he was electrocuted at the Massachusetts State Prison.

1942

Paul Giacomazza, white, age 17. **James Nickerson,** white, age 21. *Murder*. Their crime was committed on September 9, 1940, at Melrose, Massachusetts. These young men were residents of Everett and Malden respectively. Together with a second Maldenite named William Lenehan (white, age 19) they formed a stickup team which specialized in robbing gas stations. Late on the night of the above date this trio set its sights on one such place at the corner of Lynn Fells Parkway and Main Street in Melrose. The night attendant there was a 72-year-old white man named Oscar Thomas. He was a spry man for his age. He had also been robbed several times in the past. As this Oscar Thomas was sitting alone in his filling station Giacomazza walked in and went into the lavatory. A few seconds later Nickerson came in brandishing a handgun. Thomas reached for his own weapon but Nickerson shot him in the wrist as he did so. Then Giacomazza came out of the lavatory armed and shot Mr. Thomas in the back. Both bandits fled empty-handed and escaped in a getaway car driven by William Lenehan. At first the wounds suffered by the elderly gas station attendant were not thought to be dangerous. Seven weeks later, however, the man took a sudden turn for the worse and died. A lengthy investigation by Massachusetts state police finally solved the case. In March of 1941 Giacomazza was nabbed for another Middlesex County holdup. He then implicated Nickerson who in turn implicated Lenehan. Because the latter was a non-triggerman he was offered a chance to turn state's evidence and thereby save his own life. Thus were the other two defendants convicted. On June 30, 1942, both of them were electrocuted at the Massachusetts State Prison.

1943

Peter Gurski, white, age 26. *Murder.*

The crime was committed on July 1, 1942, at Terryville, Connecticut. A machinist by trade, Gurski bore an unsavory reputation in his hometown of Plymouth. He had been arrested five times on charges of public intoxication, breach of peace and disorderly conduct. Shortly after midnight on the above date Gurski was wandering the streets when he spotted an unescorted woman near the Terryville library. She was later identified as one Nellie Bourke (white, age 66), a retired schoolmarm. Miss Bourke had visited relatives in Terryville earlier that evening. Having missed the last bus of the night, she proceeded to walk the four miles to her home. As the woman made her way along a shoulder of Route 6 she realized that she was being followed. She then hastened to a nearby filling station in search of help but found the place closed for the night. A nearby house became her next destination. It was then that the stalker made his move. Gurski tackled Miss Bourke and dragged her screaming into the woods. There he beat her with his fists and raped her. Then he strangled her to death with his bare hands. In the meantime the woman's screams had not gone unheard. Police were called but they failed to arrive in time to forestall the crime. A search of the area soon produced the battered victim. Bloodhounds were called in and they led police to the house of Peter Gurski, half a mile away. He was not home at the time but was traced to the abode of a nearby relative and placed

under arrest. Several hours later he confessed to what he had done. This was followed by a conviction for capital felony in the Superior Court of Litchfield County. Sentenced to death, Gurski was sent to the Connecticut State Prison to await his fate. He was electrocuted there on February 23, 1943.

Wilson Funderburk, black, age 28.

Murder. The crime was committed on April 7, 1942, at Hartford, Connecticut. This offender came from Sumter, South Carolina. There he had a wife and two children. Abandoning his family, Funderburk drifted north after the outbreak of World War II and went from city to city in the capacity of an itinerant barber. Negro neighborhoods were his destinations of choice because such places made ready use of his services. On April 2, 1943, Funderburk closed up shop at Springfield, Massachusetts. He then moved on to Hartford, Connecticut, the next city on his route. There he plied his trade for four days. On Portland Street a young girl named Christine Paramore (black, age 11) attracted Funderburk's attention. On the afternoon of the above date business was slow for Funderburk. He then made use of his time to strike up a conversation with Christine Paramore. The girl accepted Funderburk's invitation to go for a walk with him in Riverside Park. Arriving at the park, Funderburk paused to smoke some marijuana. Then he brought the girl to a gravel pit not far away. Finding the place to be suitably remote, Funderburk turned on the girl and overpowered her. He stripped her naked and raped her. When he had his fill of nonconsensual sex, Funderburk grew fearful that the girl might report him. So he stabbed her 37 times with his barber's scissors and left her dead in the gravel pit. He also carried off all of her clothes and hid them someplace. Funderburk escaped from the scene and set a southward course. A month later he was in Washington, D.C.

In the meantime the body of Christine Paramore had been found. Hartford detectives learned that she had been seen in the company of a traveling barber of such and such a description. An all-points bulletin was flashed to police in all cities of the northeast to be on the watch for such a person. On May 6, 1942, the culprit was arrested by Washington police for carrying a dangerous weapon. It was then determined that he matched the description of the Hartford sex slayer. As police dug deeper into Funderburk's paper trail, they learned more and more about him. For instance, he had a criminal record dating back to when he was 14 years old. His offenses included burglary, larceny, trespassing and illegal weapons possession. A recent arrest in Springfield, Massachusetts, placed Funderburk near Hartford at the time of the Christine Paramore murder. It was also learned that Funderburk spoke Spanish and Arabic in addition to English — a fact which enabled him to move freely among West Indian and Moorish peoples. When the suspect was returned to Connecticut he was linked to the murder by more than just circumstantial evidence. The crime scene itself yielded important clues which pointed to Funderburk. A jury brought in a capital verdict and declined to recommend mercy. There was no appeal. Funderburk was accordingly put to death at the Connecticut State Prison on April 20, 1943. It took five massive charges of electricity to kill him.

Robert Howard Gray, black, age 34.

Murder. The crime was committed on July 7, 1942, at Roxbury, Massachusetts. This man was an habitual criminal who had been arrested 31 times in an 11-year period. He was a handyman by profession but had spent most of his adult life in jail. He had been paroled from the Bridgewater State Farm barely a week prior to committing his capital crime. On the above date Gray was without money and cast around for a means by which to get some. He snuck into an apartment building at No. 65 Westminster Avenue and lay in wait for the occupants. When a housewife named Mrs. Zelda Karchmer (white, age 26) emerged from her apartment with a basket of laundry and headed for the rooftop clotheslines, Gray decided to jimmy her door and snatch whatever valuables he could find. Unexpectedly, Mrs. Karchmer came back to her apartment and caught Gray in the act of robbing the place. A fierce struggle then ensued between the tenant and the intruder. Gray finally overpowered Mrs. Karchmer and slashed her to death with a razor. Then he tore the rings from the woman's fingers and helped himself to the contents of her jewelry box. The law caught up with Gray that very same day. Within an hour of the crime he was in a pawnshop attempting to dispose of the stolen jewelry. He pawned a ring for $75 and promptly squandered the money on a horse race. Needing more, he then returned to the same pawnshop and was arrested on the spot. It so happened that Gray's demeanor had aroused the suspicion of the seasoned pawnbroker. Police were called and the ring which Gray had pawned was identified as the property of the slain woman. Police then staked out the pawnshop in a correct belief that the killer would return. Robert Gray subsequently confessed to the murder of Zelda Karchmer. On June 25, 1943, he was electrocuted at the Massachusetts State Prison.

Donald Millard, white, age 18.
Joseph Sheppard, white, age 24.

Murder. Their crime was committed on January 1, 1942, at West Bridgewater, Massachusetts. These young men were natives of Nashua and Worcester respectively. Both had been declared incorrigible by the Massachusetts courts. At the time of their capital crime they were serving so-called "indeterminate life sentences" at the Bridgewater State Prison Farm. Together with some other prisoners they formed a desperate plan to escape. Millard and Sheppard wound up going at it alone, however, when their co-conspirators backed out. Trouble began on the above date when a guard named Franklin Weston (white, age 62) called upon inmates Millard and Sheppard to carry a ladder into a latrine area so he could use it to change a high overhead lightbulb. The two prisoners did as they were bidden. When the guard was in the act of changing the lightbulb, however, one of the convicts snuck back into the area from whence they had gotten the ladder and armed himself with a heavy iron bootjack. Then the armed inmate struck Officer Weston down from behind with the bootjack, killing him instantly. Millard and Sheppard next broke into a tool chest and armed themselves with hammers, chisels and crowbars. They then returned to where the dead guard lay and proceeded to mutilate his body. Taking the keys from the victim's utility belt, the killers used them to gain entry to the cellblock area of the prison. Then they proceeded along the first tier of cells until they encountered two other guards named George Landry (white, age 63) and Howard Murphy (white, age 47). The guards ordered the inmates to surrender and chased them up the cellblock stairs. Officer Murphy caught up with them on the third level but was fatally bludgeoned there with a crowbar. As Officer Landry ran to his assistance he was overpowered and stabbed to death. Both of the slain guards also had their bodies mutilated by their desperate assailants. Another guard named Frederick Marshall then came running to the scene but he was forced back when Millard and Sheppard opened up on him with a high-pressure firehose. By that time three guards had been slain. Then the general alarm rang out. At once the entire prison was placed on maximum alert. Every

guard took up riot gear and braced for action. They were soon joined by special contingents of heavily armed police. In the meantime Millard and Sheppard set mattress fires all over the cellblock section of the prison. Within seconds the entire prison complex was filled with toxic smoke. Hundreds of inmates trapped in their cells screamed for air and banged against the metal bars which hemmed them in. To make matters worse, tear gas was fired into the cellblock by lawmen who overestimated the size of their opposition. Firemen hacked holes in the roof and sprayed torrents of water into the building in an effort to douse the mattress fires. When state police burst into the cellblock they fired machine guns and automatic rifles into the swirling smoke and tear gas so that bullets ricocheted everywhere. One hearty veteran of World War I later said that the scene in the cellblock was just like a battlefield during a poison gas attack. Rioting inmates flung metal tools into the maelstrom of smoke and tear gas but the toxic clouds were so dense that neither side could see the other. Shock troops finally groped their way through the inferno and forced the unruly prisoners back. Millard and Sheppard retreated from the first tier to the fourth tier where they took refuge in an unlocked cell. Their pursuers then ordered them to surrender on pain of death. Both men ran out swinging hammers in a banzai attack. Terrible was the hand-to-hand combat which followed. It finally ended when Millard and Sheppard were bludgeoned with riot guns. Then both were pounced upon and beaten so badly that the prison chaplain was called in to administer the last rites. Unexpectedly, both of the rioters survived to face three counts of capital murder. On June 25, 1943, both were electrocuted at the Massachusetts State Prison. Both said that they preferred death to a life behind bars at the Bridgewater State Farm.

1944

Carlo James DeCaro, white, age 19. *Murder.* The crime was committed on September 25, 1943, at Thompsonville, Connecticut. This offender was a portly youth who weighed more than 300 pounds. He worked as a machinist at the Somersville Manufacturing Company. Weekday mornings usually saw DeCaro carpooling with one Salvatore Bonnelli (white, age 61), a fellow employee who had helped him get his job. This Salvatore Bonnelli was a well-known gambler. Card games were his specialty and he usually won more than he lost. It was said that Bonnelli always carried cash on his person lest he not be ready to try his luck at a moment's notice. Carlo DeCaro heard the rumor that Bonnelli was a walking bank. He wondered if the rumor was true. One day his doubts were dispelled when Bonnelli gave him some money to pay for gasoline. The man reached into his pocket and pulled out a wad of currency the size of a baseball. It was then that DeCaro turned his mind to thoughts of robbery and murder.

September 24, 1943, was payday at the Somersville Manufacturing Company. After work that day DeCaro drove Bonnelli home as usual. Then he went to a sporting goods store and used his pay to buy a handgun and a box of bullets to go with it. Early the next morning DeCaro drove to Bonnelli's house and picked the man up. It then being wartime, every worker was expected to report for duty on Saturdays. September 25, 1943, was no exception. While heading toward their place of employment, DeCaro stopped at a roadside coffee truck. He purchased some snacks there. Then he drove down Elm Street in Thompsonville and pulled off onto a dirt road. There he parked the car for the ostensible purpose of pausing to eat the snacks which he had bought. As Bonnelli rummaged in a paper bag for his snack,

DeCaro took out his newly purchased handgun and shot the man six times in the head. Then he calmly reloaded the weapon and fired another bullet through Bonnelli's heart. It was a very messy killing. When DeCaro was sure that Bonnelli was dead he searched the victim's pockets. He found more than $1500 — all of it soaked with blood. Then the killer dragged the dead man into a deserted gravel pit that was there and buried him in a shallow grave. DeCaro went home from there and changed out of his blood-spattered clothes. Then he called in sick to his job. Later he drove to Springfield where he visited his ailing mother in a hospital. There DeCaro was overcome with remorse. When he left the hospital he walked to a bridge which spanned the Connecticut River. There he discarded all of the bloodstained money. Some of it was later found floating in the river.

When DeCaro returned home police were waiting for him. The body of Salvatore Bonnelli had been found and successfully identified. The dead man's daily movements being known, DeCaro was named as a likely suspect. A search of his home turned up the bloody clothes he had worn that morning. A search of his car turned up an abundance of fresh bloodstains. DeCaro meekly confessed his crime. He then led lawmen to the spot where he had dumped the murder weapon. Clear evidence of premeditation precluded plea bargaining in this case. DeCaro was capitally convicted and sentenced to death. There was no appeal. On May 3, 1944, the young killer was executed at the Connecticut State Prison. His obesity almost disabled the electric chair.

1945

Nicholas Rossi, black, age 32. *Murder.* The crime was committed on September 22, 1943, at Plainville, Connecticut. Nicholas Rossi and his half-brother Robert Rossi (black, age 27) were both born in Montreal. Their mother was a white woman of poor reputation. Nicholas and Robert were the results of her relations with different black men. When the half-brothers came of age they decided to leave Canada. They set a course for the United States and chose to remain together. Eventually they made their way to Connecticut. Physically, the Rossi brothers were a mismatched pair; Nicholas was a hulking, heavyset man whereas Robert was an effeminate sissy type who liked to dress and act the part of a woman. So it was that Nicholas and Robert Rossi passed themselves off as a husband and wife. When they reached Connecticut both of the Rossis looked for employment. Nicholas Rossi found a job in a New Britain hotel. Robert Rossi, posing as a woman, went a few miles away to Plainville. There he went to work as a maid for one Hedwig Wegner (white, age 60), a moderately wealthy widow. This Hedwig Wegner lived in a large farmhouse located on New Britain Avenue. She was well known in the community for a roadside produce stand that she owned. Oddly, she never caught on to the fact that Robert Rossi was really a man. His cooing voice and transvestite costumes completely fooled her. The woman even gave the Rossis rent-free accommodations in her servant quarters because she believed them to be a married couple. Then came a time when the Rossis decided that they had had enough of Connecticut and enough of Mrs. Wegner in particular. They formed a plan to rob the woman and leave the area. On the above date Robert Rossi used some pretext to lure Mrs. Wegner down into her cellar. There Nicholas Rossi lay in wait. When the unsuspecting woman came down the cellar stairs she was hit over the head so hard that her dentures flew out of her mouth. Nicholas Rossi then beat Mrs. Wegner to death with a crowbar. Robert Rossi

picked her person clean of valuables. He took her earrings, necklace and bracelets and he pulled all of the rings from her fingers. Then the killers wrapped the dead woman in a quilt and stashed the bundle in a detached garage. Returning to the victim's house, the killers went from room to room and stole every article of value that they could find. After that they packed their bags and took off in Mrs. Wegner's car. A nationwide alarm was issued for the Rossis following discovery of the crime. Three days later the killers were caught in Missouri. A policeman pulled their car over for a routine traffic check. He became suspicious when he looked at Nicholas Rossi's draft card and found it to be a forgery. Police reinforcements were then called to the scene. The next thing the officer did was to go around to the passenger side of the car to have a closer look at the person purported to be the driver's wife. Something seemed odd about the passenger's coy smile and elaborately coifed hair. Suspecting the truth, the officer plucked the wig from Robert Rossi's head. So was the alleged woman revealed to be a man in drag. Returned to Connecticut, both of the Rossis confessed their crime. Both were convicted of capital murder in Hartford Superior Court. The sentence for each was death in the electric chair. Nicholas Rossi suffered that fate at the Connecticut State Prison on June 18, 1945. The sentence of Robert Rossi was commuted to life behind bars.

1946

Raphael Skopp, white, age 35. *Murder.* The crime was committed on December 30, 1944, at Boston, Massachusetts. This man was a Brooklyn Jew who had spent most of his adult life in prison. At the age of 19 he was convicted of armed robbery. The penalty was 15 years in the Elmira Reformatory. While there he was ordered to serve an additional ten years for participating in a fatal brawl. Skopp was paroled in September of 1944. He soon broke his parole by leaving the state of New York without permission. Declared a fugitive, he found New York too hot for him. Then he caught a train to Boston. On the morning of the above date Skopp walked into a liquor store at No. 10 Federal Street and placed an order for six bottles of wine. He left a cash deposit and said that he would return later in the day. At about six o'clock P.M. he did return and said that he wanted eight additional bottles of wine. As the merchandise was being packaged, Skopp suddenly pulled out a handgun and ordered the three male employees of the store to line up against the wall. The employees did as they were told. Skopp then cleaned out the cash register. After that Skopp ordered the three men to take off their pants. When one of them balked at that order Skopp opened fire on all three. A clerk named Bronislaw Petruswicz (white, age 57) was killed by two bullets in the chest. The store manager was shot in both arms. The third employee was uninjured. Skopp fled from the scene and remained unidentified for more than seven months. He got as far as Reno, Nevada, where he pulled another holdup. On January 28, 1945, he was arrested for that crime and subsequently wound up in the Nevada State Prison. He was linked to the Boston homicide by chance. The survivors of that affair had told of the killer having a scar on his upper lip. That meager information was picked up on by federal agents in Utah who suspected such a man of transporting stolen cars across state lines. They then checked on that person's whereabouts and learned that he was a newly arrived inmate at the Nevada State Prison. Boston detectives were informed of the possible connection and the inmate's signature was found to match that on a pawn ticket signed by a man answering to the same description. Then the bullets from the Boston crime scene were found to have been fired from the same gun that had been confiscated from the Nevada robber. When he was confronted with such evidence Skopp admitted that he had killed the Boston sales clerk. He was then returned to Massachusetts and made to answer a charge of capital murder. On August 16, 1946, he was electrocuted at the Massachusetts State Prison.

Raymond Lewie, white, age 17. **James McCarthy,** white, age 21. **Arthur Tomaselli,** white, age 24. *Murder.* Their capital crime was committed on March 9, 1945, at Wethersfield, Connecticut. These young men were state prison inmates who killed a guard during an attempted escape. In order to understand them more fully they must first be described on an individual basis.

According to surviving accounts, James McCarthy was the worst of the trio. The son of a Danbury fireman, he was vicious by nature and had absolutely no sense of decency. While still a young teenager he was declared a menace to society and sent to the notorious Connecticut School for Boys at Meriden. There he went from bad to worse. Paroled at the age of 17, he returned to Danbury where he soon added robbery and murder to his resumé. On December 30, 1942, this tousle-haired delinquent went to a small variety store at No. 19 West Wooster Street armed with a large hunting knife. Locking the door behind him, McCarthy sprang upon the storekeeper, one Gottfried Seegelken (white, age 35) by name and slashed him to death. Of the ten stab wounds which the coroner later found on the victim's body, all of them were of a deep and rending type — each one individually sufficient to cause death. After killing the storekeeper, McCarthy stole $50 from the cash register. Then he dumped the victim down the cellar stairs and put a "closed" sign in the window. He also locked up the store as he left. Detectives were initially puzzled to find the murdered merchant locked inside his own store. A check of known criminals indicated that James McCarthy lived nearby. Danbury police accordingly went to his home at No. 56 Lincoln Avenue. Armed with a search warrant, they found the stolen money and the murder weapon in the suspect's bedroom. McCarthy was sardonic when police questioned him. He spat in a detective's face and proudly admitted the crime. Because he was only 17 years old the state's attorney for Danbury did not demand the death penalty for McCarthy. He settled for a sentence of life imprisonment. Within a very short time that public official had cause to regret his leniency. McCarthy quickly became one of the worst disciplinary cases in the state prison system. He wound up spending most of his time in solitary confinement. He was also destined to become a recidivist killer.

Raymond Lewie was a close second to McCarthy in terms of his criminal record. The only noticeable difference between the two was that Lewie lacked McCarthy's innate malevolence. The product of a severely dysfunctional family, Lewie was born at Manchester on May 16, 1927. His parents split up when he was very young, abandoning their son in the process. Raymond Lewie was then placed in an orphanage where he was subjected to an unbroken regimen of brutality, malnutrition and sexual abuse. When the boy reached the age of understanding he blamed his parents for all that had befallen him. Bitter and resentful, he carried a burden of anger for the rest of his life. When Lewie outgrew the orphanage he was transferred to the Connecticut School for Boys. There he was repeatedly raped and beaten. In June of 1943 the then 16-year-old Lewie was released from state custody. He was no longer regarded as a threat to society so the state simply turned him loose with no job, no money and no place to go. Alone and homeless, Lewie sought out

his father only to have the door slammed in his face. Then he went to Rhode Island where his mother took him in. All did not go well for him there because his emotional scars were too deep. By November of 1943 the young fellow set out on his own. He made his way to New Britain where he got himself a room and went to work as a dishwasher. It was during this time that Lewie sought to soothe his inner wretchedness by cultivating a "tough guy" image. He began smoking cigars and hanging around pool halls. He spoke with a gangster brogue and carried a gun. He even scarred his otherwise handsome face. It then being wartime, Lewie lied about his age in an effort to join the army. He was bitterly disappointed when he was only put on a waiting list. In the meantime he found it almost impossible to live on dishwasher's pay. So on April 2, 1944, this troubled young man teamed up with a chum named Edward Barrows (white, age 16) and decided to rob a grocery store. The place they chose was located at No. 172 North Street in New Britain. Entering the store, Lewie approached the elderly grocer, Melkan Shahanian (white, age 77), and pointed a gun in his face. Instead of raising his hands as he was ordered, Shahanian reached for a weapon of his own. Lewie then killed him instantly with a bullet through the left eye. Both of the robbers fled from the scene but were eventually caught. Lewie hitchhiked all the way to Virginia. Three days later he was nabbed in Norfolk. Unsuccessful in his attempt to join the army, he there intended to apply to the navy. He wound up coming back to Connecticut in chains. Lewie was spared the death penalty because of his age. On June 16, 1944, he entered the Connecticut State Prison as a lifetime convict. As things turned out, the placing of a 17-year-old boy among the ranks of adult inmates had its usual result. Lewie became the target for every pervert in the prison. Determined not to be victimized as he had been in the reform school, Lewie fought savagely to defend himself. For that reason he was declared a "disruptive element" and thrown into solitary confinement. When he rejoined the general prison population he was a seething personality ready to dare anything.

Arthur Tommaselli was not in the same league as Lewie and McCarthy. He was merely a thief—and not a very adroit one at that. Convicted of burglary at New Haven, he was sent to the Connecticut State Prison in the spring of 1942 under a sentence of from 2 to 14 years. On October 23, 1942, he escaped from the prison only to be recaptured and punished with an additional 2 to 10 years behind bars.

Such was the trio that conspired to break out of the Connecticut State Prison on March 9, 1945. After breakfast that morning all three reported in sick to the officer of the day. Instead of going to the infirmary as ordered, they turned off a passageway leading in that direction and joined a line of other inmates who were on their way to assignments in the prison workshops. All three then slipped into the maintenance shop where they encountered a lone guard named Herbert O. Parsell (white, age 53), a tenured veteran of the corrections department. As Lewie stood watch by the door, Mc-Carthy and Tommaselli picked up a heavy wrench and a pipe respectively. Then the armed pair attacked the guard. Parsell managed to set off an alarm before he was overpowered. McCarthy and Tommaselli beat him into a coma. The former was especially aggressive when it came to bludgeoning the guard. When they thought that the guard was dead, McCarthy and Tommaselli chased all of the other inmates out of the maintenance shop. Only Lewie was allowed to join them as they barricaded the door. In the meantime the entire prison complex went on maximum alert. Riot gear was distributed to the guards. Then came the inevitable confrontation. Heavily armed guards tried to force their way into the maintenance shop. The three killers replied with a well-aimed barrage of metal tools. Hammers, wrenches and heavy files all went flying through the air. It took tear gas to finally overcome the rampaging inmates. All three were beaten without mercy.

When the case came to trial all three defendants were charged with capital felony. It was then that Lewie lost his will to live. He refused to cooperate with his defense counsel. He also deliberately changed his testimony and swore that he had taken an active part in assaulting the slain prison guard. Later he forbade his attorney to approach the Board of Pardons on his behalf. When asked why he did such things, Lewie said, "Because I want to burn!" The three young killers were all sentenced to death in Hartford Superior Court. There was no clemency. On October 1, 1946, they were electrocuted at the Connecticut State Prison. Although Lewie got his death wish as he desired, yet another indignity awaited him: His apathetic father signed his body over to a medical school because he was too cheap to pay for a funeral.

1947

Ronald Watson, white, age 20. *Murder.* The crime was committed on December 24, 1945, at Chittenden, Vermont. This offender was a Newfoundland native who came to Vermont during World War II. He worked long hours as a farmhand. He also earned some extra money by entertaining at social clubs with his guitar and creditable singing voice. It so happened that Watson had promised to buy his girlfriend a diamond ring for Christmas. As the festive season approached he was chagrined by a realization that he could not afford to keep his pledge. Two days before Christmas found Watson still short of the required amount for a down payment on a diamond ring. Try as he might, he could not get up the nerve to go back on his word. He then became desperate. After visiting with his sweetheart on December 23, Watson went to a Rutland speakeasy and tried to drink away his anxiety. Well after midnight he called for a cab and asked the driver to bring him home to Pittsford. Along the way Watson got the idea to rob and kill the cabby. He had the taxi turn up the Chittendon Road and stop in front of an old schoolhouse that was there. Watson then took a quart-sized bottle of whiskey from his coat pocket and smashed it over the driver's head. Then he took a hunting knife and repeatedly stabbed the injured man until he died. When Watson was satisfied that the driver was dead he dragged his body from the cab and draped it over a barbed wire fence. He took the victim's wallet containing $106 but oddly spurned an additional $40 in silver that he found. The dead man was later identified as one Henry Teelon (white, age 45), a familiar figure in and around Rutland. The next day Watson went to a jewelry store and made a down payment on a diamond ring. The small-town jeweler was amazed to see the hitherto impecunious Watson suddenly flush with money. Later that day came news of the murder. The jeweler then became suspicious and called the police. Watson was questioned about his movements during the previous 24 hours. When witnesses said that they had seen him getting into Teelon's cab, Watson broke down and confessed. A Rutland County jury decided that Watson should die for his crime. He was accordingly electrocuted at the Vermont State Prison on January 2, 1947.

Phillip Bellino, white, age 29. **Edward Gertsen,** white, age 33. *Murder.* Their crime was committed on August 8, 1945, at Lynn, Massachusetts. These offenders were residents of Boston

and Everett respectively. Both were members of a five-man holdup team which planned to raid a New Hampshire dice game. The youngest member of the gang, Robert "Tex" Williams (white, age 18), of Haverhill had indicated personal knowledge of the dice game and had proposed it as a target, saying that there would be at least $10,000 in cash there. Accordingly the gang set out for the site of the dice game, a summer camp in Newton, New Hampshire. When they arrived at the clubhouse where the game was in progress Robert "Tex" Williams took up a lookout position in order to avoid being recognized. The other four members of the gang then burst in upon the gamesters with guns drawn. A nasty scene followed in which the intruders roughed up everyone in the clubhouse and picked them clean of valuables. In all, 13 men were robbed. One was shot when he did not move fast enough to suit the bandits. Robert "Tex" Williams acted his part by cutting telephone wires and slashing the tires of every car there but his own. In such a way the alarm would be delayed. When the gang later met to divide its loot there was fury all around. The total did not amount to even $200, let alone $10,000. Because of this the other gang members turned against "Tex" Williams. Four days later two of them — identified as Bellino and Gertsen — abducted Williams and drove with him to a lonely spot in the Lynn marshes. There they severely beat Williams before finishing him off with a shot through the neck. The body was found three days later. When detectives finally hunted down the other gang members, one of them, Charles Mantia (white, age 29) of Boston, turned state's evidence against his fellows. In such a way was Phillip Bellino identified as the trigger-man and Edward Gertsen as an active accessory. Both of those defendants were capitally convicted. Both were electrocuted at the Massachusetts State Prison on May 9, 1947.

1948

Robert Bradley, black, age 37. *Murder.* His crimes were committed in September of 1946 at East Haven, Connecticut. This African-American serial killer victimized three other men of his own race. With the help of an accomplice named William Lisenby (black, age 34), Bradley lured the victims to a wooded area in East Haven on the pretext of arranging trysts with white women. He even tricked the victims into digging their own graves, saying that barbecue pits were needed in order to cook the edibles that were said to be part of the arrangements. When the "barbecue pits" were completed, Bradley struck down each victim from behind with an axe. Then he robbed their persons and tumbled their bodies into the "barbecue pits" where they were hastily buried. In each case Bradley also stole the automobiles which the slain men had driven to the supposed assignations. He would then drive the vehicles to New York and dispose of them on the black market. The victims of this deadly ruse were later identified as Oscar Mathen (black, age 38), Henry Edwards (black, age 43) and Benjamin Carter (black, age 35). As part of a plea bargain, Lisenby was allowed to plead guilty to a reduced charge of second degree murder. He then testified against Bradley and drew a term of life imprisonment. Bradley was capitally convicted and ordered for execution. He died in the electric chair at the Connecticut State Prison on April 12, 1948.

1948–1953

Although there are known to have been at least 451 legal executions in the United States of America during this time period, none of them took place in the New England states.

1954

Francis Blair, white, age 32. **Donald Demag,** white, age 31. *Murder.* Their capital crime was committed on August 1, 1952, at Springfield, Vermont. These men attained national notoriety during their lifetimes. Demag in particular is remembered not only as a recidivist killer but as a major embarrassment to opponents of capital punishment. Their story begins on March 11, 1948, at Burlington, Vermont. It was then that Donald Demag committed his first murder. He was 26 years old, married with one child and another on the way. He was also unemployed and desperate for money. Not knowing where else to turn, he went to the shop of an elderly harness maker named Francis Racicot (white, age 81) at No. 24 Center Street and asked the man for a loan. Racicot refused the request whereupon Demag battered him to death with an iron stove shaker. Then he took his wallet. Captured three days later, Demag was charged with capital murder. He subsequently drew a term of life imprisonment when he agreed to plead guilty to a reduced charge of second degree murder.

On August 27, 1950, this Donald Demag made a successful break from the Vermont State Prison. He managed to get across the Canadian border without incident. Days later, however, he was caught in an attempt to get back into the United States. Returned to prison, Demag began plotting his next move. On July 30, 1952, he made that move. He teamed up with Francis Blair, a fellow convict from Fitchburg, Massachusetts, who was serving time for larceny, and staged a second successful break from the maximum security prison. The two men seized an unguarded moment to slip into the driver's compartment of a ten-ton work truck that was idling in the prison driveway. Then they crashed the vehicle through the massive front gates of the prison and escaped to freedom. The manhunt which followed was unprecedented in Vermont history. Hundreds of law enforcement officers joined with heavily armed posses of citizens to scour the densely wooded countryside. So great was the alarm that one traveler reported passing through 12 roadblocks in a ten-mile stretch. The fugitives spent two days and two nights in the deep woods. Then they made their way to the vicinity of Springfield and sought a source of food and clothing there. Late at night they broke into the house of a middle-aged couple named Donald and Elizabeth Weatherup (whites, aged 56 and 54) and attacked the occupants with metal pipes. Both of the Weatherups were severely beaten. The woman died of her injuries. When the details of this crime became known public anger ran so high that nearly every able-bodied man in the Springfield area joined in the hunt for the killers. Bloodhounds and airplanes were also pressed into service. Finally some of the possemen made contact with Blair and Demag in the woods about three miles from the Weatherup house. They let loose with a massive shotgun barrage and threatened the fugitives with death unless they surrendered immediately. At that point Blair and Demag gave up.

Proponents of capital punishment seized upon this case to bolster their cause. They argued that life imprisonment was a proven failure for killers like Donald Demag. If he had been executed for his first murder, said they, his second murder would have been precluded. Death penalty opponents remained silent. This time there was no plea bargaining. Two separate juries also refused to recommend mercy. The penalty was death for both defendants. Both were returned to the Vermont State Prison to await their fates. On February 8, 1954, Francis Blair was electrocuted pursuant to his sentence. Donald Demag met the same fate on December 8, 1954.

1955

William Lorain, white, age 34. *Murder.* The crime was committed on August 12, 1952, at Wethersfield, Connecticut. William Lorain and John Petetabella (white, age 38) were habitual criminals with long police records. Both served time in the Rhode Island State Prison for armed robbery and aggravated assault. There they got to know each other. On March 10, 1952, Lorain was released on parole. He then went to Providence where he bided his time waiting for his pal to join him. Then on August 2, 1952, Petetabella was also paroled. He and Lorain were reunited the same day. Both disdained the thought of finding honest jobs. Instead they wandered around Providence looking for likely places to rob. On the morning of August 12, 1952, the Lorain-Petetabella symbiosis went into action. The two men burst into a Providence funeral parlor and tied up the mortician. Then they looked for valuables but came up empty-handed. When it dawned on Lorain and Petetabella that there was nothing in the funeral parlor worth stealing they turned spiteful and proceeded to vandalize the place. Floral tributes were flung down and thrown all over the viewing rooms. Closets and cabinets had their contents strewn about. Office files were scattered in every direction. Furniture was smashed and broken. Toxic formaldehyde and other embalming fluids were dumped from their containers. An hour later the culprits caught the bus to Hartford. Afternoon found them in a Park Street diner. There they struck up a conversation with a customer named George Zgierski (white, age 47) and asked if he would give them a ride to a supposed job site. When the unsuspecting man nodded his assent Lorain and Petetabella followed him to the parking lot. No sooner did they get into Zgierski's car than they pulled guns on the man. They first forced him to surrender all of his valuables. Then they ordered Zgierski to get into the back seat. There Lorain held him at gunpoint while Petetabella started up the car and drove off. Thus did George Zgierski become an unwilling passenger in his own vehicle. From the diner Petetabella headed south. Entering the town of Wethersfield, the carjacked sedan came within sight of the Connecticut State Prison. Zgierski pointed out the brooding edifice and told his captors that they were headed for that place sure enough. This caused Lorain to momentarily avert his eyes in the direction of the prison. It was then that Zgierski made a grab for his gun. At once Lorain began shooting. Zgierski was hit with five bullets at point-blank range. He died almost instantly. Petetabella then changed course and made his way to Deming Road in Berlin. There he and Lorain heaved the dead man into a brook. Then they resumed their joyride. Five days later the car was found abandoned in New Haven. A break in the case came when a gas station manager called police after reading about the murder in a newspaper. Two men had stopped at his place of business in the same kind of car as that of the murdered man. They needed a tank of gas but said that they had no money. It was then agreed that they should have some gas in return for a secured I.O.U. The collateral they left with their note was a man's wristwatch bearing the initials "G.Z." The watch was positively identified as the property of George Zgierski. When detectives examined the I.O.U. they recognized the signature as that of an alias used by a Rhode Island convict named John Petetabella. Police then knew for whom they were looking. Eight days after the murder both of the culprits were arrested in Rhode Island. Both were returned to Connecticut to face charges of capital murder. Lorain confessed his part in the crime but later retracted his confession. He was convicted and sentenced to death. On July 11, 1955, he died in the electric chair at the Connecticut State Prison. John Petetabella got off with a lighter sentence.

John Donahue, white, age 22. *Murder.* The crime was committed on February 13, 1953, at Trumbull, Connecticut. This offender came from the town of Arlington, Massachusetts. In 1950 he was sent to the Concord Reformatory under a five-year term for kidnapping. Donahue was paroled after serving barely half of his sentence. Then he committed a capital offense. Desiring to visit a girl in New York, the young man found himself at a loss for transportation. He then decided to steal a car. In Brookline he found a vehicle idling in a private driveway. Donahue jumped into the driver's seat and took off for New York. He got as far as Milford, Connecticut, without any untoward incidents. There a state trooper observed him speeding along the Wilbur Cross Parkway. A pursuit then began. Donahue crossed over onto the Merritt Parkway via the Housatonic River bridge. In Trumbull a state trooper caught up with him and ordered him to pull over. Donahue then brought his vehicle to a halt on a grassy shoulder of the parkway. Patrolman Ernest Morse (white, age 33) of the Connecticut State Police pulled up behind Donahue and got out of his squad car. He walked over to the driver's side window of Donahue's car in order to ask the speeder for his operator's license. When the officer came abreast of the window Donahue shoved the muzzle of a handgun into his abdomen and pulled the trigger. Patrolman Morse died at the scene. Donahue then took off down the parkway at a high rate of speed. At the next exit he ditched his vehicle. Then he stole a second car and continued on toward New York. In Greenwich he crashed through a roadblock. Then began a wild chase. Police pursued Donahue through residential streets. When the speeding vehicles spilled onto the Boston Post Road the suspect smashed through a second road-block. Police fired on the fleeing car with a machine gun. At that point a rear tire blew and Donahue was forced to abandon his car. He then fled on foot through private yards and was finally found hiding in a barn. Brought to trial soon afterward, Donahue was capitally convicted by the Superior Court of Fairfield County. The sentence was death. On July 18, 1955, this young cop killer was executed at the Connecticut State Prison. The shock of the lethal current made Donahue's fingernails dig into the wooden arms of the electric chair. The marks are clearly visible to this day.

Robert Malm, white, age 31. *Murder.* The crime was committed on December 9, 1953, at Hartford, Connecticut. This man was a decorated veteran of World War II. He saw hard action as a naval gunner and was awarded 11 battle stars plus a presidential citation. On the down side he was a pervert with an insatiable appetite for little girls. His police record (which was a lengthy one) dated all the way back to when he was 12 years old. Most of the entries on that record involved sexual offenses with underage females. While attending submarine school in New London, this troubled man took to drink. He wound up in jail following a conviction for aggravated robbery. Paroled in due course, Malm was unable to find a good job because of his police record. He wound up washing dishes at a state-run sanitarium. On the above date Malm left his home in Newington and went to Hartford. There his urges came upon him once again. While walking along Coolidge Street he saw a young girl named Irene Fiederowicz (white, age 11) playing on the sidewalk. Malm lured the girl into the backyard of a nearby house. There he forced her to remove all of her clothes irrespective of the cold weather. What happened next is unprintable. When Malm had his fill

of sexual perversion he told the girl to put her clothes back on. As she placed a scarf around her neck Malm suddenly grabbed the ends of it and pulled them tightly. He did not let go until the girl was fatally strangled. The next day news of this murder was heard by another young girl who Malm had molested. She then went to police and told them her tale. Certain similarities between her bad experience and the Fiederowicz murder were noted. Police were especially interested in those details because they were not public knowledge. The girl was then shown mug shots of known sex offenders. She positively identified a picture of Robert Malm. He broke down under questioning and admitted his guilt. The Superior Court of Hartford County sentenced him to death. The end came on July 18, 1955, at the Connecticut State Prison. Malm walked to the electric chair with his head bowed and his eyes closed. The warden later told reporters that Malm acted that way in his final moments because he was deeply ashamed of himself.

1956–1958

Although there are known to have been at least 180 legal executions in the United States of America during this time period, none of them occurred in the New England states.

1959

George Davies, white, age 40. *Murder.* The crime was committed on May 13, 1957, at Wolcott, Connecticut. This offender was born on a Bridgeport coal barge. He never knew his real parents because they dumped him in an orphanage within days of his birth. Davies was subsequently adopted by a Thomaston couple who raised him as their own. When he reached the age of majority he remained in Thomaston but moved into a home of his own. He earned honest pay as a self-employed handyman. By the time of his death he was a twice-married father of four. Although few people initially knew it, Davies had a dark side. In 1952 he was convicted of molesting young girls and sentenced to state's prison for three years. He was paroled after serving barely one year. Following his release from jail Davies tried to control his pedophile urges. He was not entirely successful. Then in the spring of 1957 he abandoned all restraint. On May 10 he was riding around in his car when he spotted a good looking girl named Gaetane Boivin (white, age 16) walking along a Waterbury street. Davies abducted her in broad daylight and forced her into his vehicle. Then he drove to an undeveloped area on Greystone Road where he attempted to rape his captive. He wound up choking her to death with his bare hands. Then to make sure that the victim was dead, he stabbed her numerous times with a screwdriver. Three days later Davies struck again. In nearby Bristol he spotted a little girl named Brenda Jane Doucette (white, age nine) and enticed her into his car. Then he drove her to a secluded area in Wolcott. Once there, Davies forced the child to submit to acts of perversion. He wound up killing her in the same manner as he had the other victim three days earlier. The discovery of these crimes resulted in a roundup of all known sex offenders in the Waterbury-Bristol area. Among those asked to account for their movements was George Davies. When detectives found inconsistencies in his answers they questioned Davies further. Eventually he confessed both murders. A sentence of death was passed on Davies in Waterbury Superior Court. Appeals were heard and rejected. The end came on October 20, 1959, when George Davies was electrocuted at the Connecticut State Prison.

Frank Wojculewicz, white, age 34. *Murder.* The crime was committed on November 5, 1951, at New Britain, Connecticut. This man was a habitual criminal who occasionally earned honest pay as a truck driver. He had a record of 15 arrests dating back to when he was ten years old. Wojculewicz counted burglary, car theft, post office robbery and attempted rape among his demerits. He did jail time in Ohio, Pennsylvania, Missouri and Connecticut. On December 18, 1950, he took part in a bank heist which netted $19,000 in cash. Wojculewicz was never apprehended for that latter crime but he admitted to it while awaiting execution.

On November 5, 1951, this unscrupulous man single-handedly attempted to rob the payroll of the AYO Meat Packing Company, a sizable employer of skilled laborers located at No. 332 Washington Street in New Britain. Shortly after five o'clock in the afternoon Wojculewicz entered the front door of the company holding a newspaper over his face. He made his way to the office where he pulled out a pistol and demanded money. Seeing a bag of cash on the paymaster's desk, Wojculewicz told that person that he would save him the trouble of counting it. He then grabbed the money bag and ran out of the office. Less than a minute later, Wojculewicz returned to the company office and declared that he was not satisfied. He then ordered the paymaster to open the office safe on pain of death. While this was happening, another employee of the plant saw the robbery in progress and backed away from the door unseen. That person then hastened to a pay phone and called police. Quickly dispatched to the scene were Sergeant William Grabeck (white, age 54) and Patrolman Theodore Wojtusik of the New Britain police department. When they arrived at the AYO Company they deftly made their way down a corridor and peeked into the office. There they saw Wojculewicz rummaging in the safe. Sergeant Grabeck snuck up behind the robber and poked him in the back with the muzzle of his gun. Then he ordered Wojculewicz to surrender. Instead of doing as he was told, Wojculewicz quickly spun around and opened fire with his pistol. All six bullets found their marks. Grabeck was hit five times and killed. The sixth bullet fatally wounded a bystander named William Otipka (white, age 33). As the dying officer fell to the floor he managed to squeeze off some shots of his own. One bullet struck Wojculewicz in the spine. He survived the wound but was left paralyzed from the waist down. It was in such a physical condition that he spent the rest of his life. Unable to walk or even bend his legs, Wojculewicz had to be borne to court face-down on a cot. On his good days he was able to sit in a wheelchair with a special support beneath his legs. When a jury convicted him on two counts of capital murder, Wojculewicz had a mandatory death sentence passed upon him. Then began more than seven long years of appeals. Opponents of capital punishment poured their utmost into this case. Central to their defense strategy was a claim that it was "cruel and unusual punishment" to execute a paralytic. The state of Connecticut countered with arguments of its own: There was no doubt of the defendant's guilt nor of his mental capacity. It was also asserted that handicapped persons were entitled to equal justice under the law; to spare Wojculewicz because of his physical condition would be creating a double standard amounting to reverse discrimination against the physically fit. The appellate courts agreed with the state of Connecticut. They found no error in the record of the condemned man's trial. As for the executing of a paralytic, the courts said that while such a thing might be considered distasteful that did not necessarily make it illegal. The State Board of Pardons concurred

in that opinion and added one of its own: The killer of a police officer could not be spared for any reason short of incurable insanity. To make an exception for Wojculewicz would set a dangerous precedent. The warden of the Connecticut State Prison was accordingly told to make ready for an atypical execution.

Time ran out for Frank Wojculewicz on the frosty night of October 26, 1959. Death row guards found him lying face-down as usual. They gently lifted the helpless man from his mattress and placed him in a wheelchair. Then began a slow procession. One by one the other condemned men called their farewells to Wojculewicz as he was wheeled past their cells. The scene was extremely affecting. When the procession entered the execution chamber it was greeted by the warden. He then asked Wojculewicz if he had a last request. Bitter to the end, the doomed man asked that the prison chaplain not be allowed near him. He said that he neither wanted nor needed any pious prepping for what he was about to face. The warden was displeased but he granted the request. Guards then wheeled Wojculewicz to the middle of the chamber. There they carefully lifted him from the wheelchair and put him in the electric chair. A wooden box was used as a stool to support his paralyzed legs. When the guards completed the task of affixing the electrodes and adjusting the straps they signaled that all was ready. Then the executioner turned on the current and Frank Wojculewicz was no more.

1960

Joseph Taborsky, alias "The Chin," alias "Death Row Joe," alias "Mad Dog Taborsky," white, age 33. *Murder.* The crimes for which he was put to death were committed over a period of time from December 15, 1956, to January 26,

1957, throughout the state of Connecticut. Opponents of capital punishment don't like to talk about this man. He has been frequently cited as anathema to their cause. For decades leftist thinkers have struggled to explain Taborsky. Efforts have been made to explain him on a pragmatic basis and on a psychological basis. There have also been efforts to explain him away. What follows is an unbiased account of this most controversial of cases.

Taborsky was an erstwhile choirboy who never amounted to much. He worked odd jobs and occasionally tagged along as a truck driver's assistant. When times were lean he turned to crime. Taborsky was 27 years old when he committed his first known murder. On March 23, 1950, he got together with his younger brother, Albert Taborsky, for the purpose of pulling an armed stickup. The two men drove to a liquor store located at No. 407 New Park Avenue in West Hartford. There Albert Taborsky remained behind the wheel of the car while Joseph Taborsky entered the store. Once inside, Joseph Taborsky pulled a gun on the shopkeeper, Louis Wolfson (white, age 40), and demanded money. When Wolfson was slow to comply he was shot in the face. The gunman then fled from the scene empty-handed and made a successful getaway. Three days later the wounded merchant died. For ten months the crime remained unsolved. Then something unexpected happened: Albert Taborsky was questioned by police about an unrelated matter and suddenly divulged details of the Wolfson murder. Soon detectives had the full story of that crime. Joseph Taborsky was arrested and charged with capital murder. When the case came to trial the testimony of Albert Taborsky was pivotal to the prosecution. On June 7, 1951, a jury returned guilty verdicts against both Taborskys in Hartford Superior Court. Joseph Taborsky stood convicted as a principal to first degree murder. He

was sentenced to death. Albert Taborsky was convicted as an accessory to his brother's offense. He drew a sentence of life imprisonment. Both defendants were then brought to the Connecticut State Prison at Wethersfield. There Albert Taborsky joined the ranks of ordinary inmates. Joseph Taborsky was put on death row.

Two months after his admittance to state's prison Albert Taborsky began to show signs of insanity. His symptoms grew progressively worse until he had to be sent to a lunatic asylum. There the man was certified by mental health experts to be suffering from incurable dementia. When this news became public knowledge it brought opponents of capital punishment flocking to the defense of Joseph Taborsky. They portrayed the condemned man as a guiltless victim of circumstance. The mental collapse of Albert Taborsky was eagerly seized upon in order to impeach his testimony. Appeals were filed claiming that Joseph Taborsky was an innocent man who had been falsely convicted by means of unreliable evidence. On February 10, 1953, the Connecticut State Supreme Court upheld the conviction and sentence of Joseph Taborsky in a split decision. Anti-death penalty activists then redoubled their efforts until they eventually persuaded that same court to grant Taborsky another hearing. On July 29, 1955, the Connecticut State Supreme Court reversed itself and ordered a retrial in the case of Joseph Taborsky. This put the State's Attorney for Hartford County in a difficult position. Bereft of his principal witness (due to the insanity of Albert Taborsky), that official had no choice but to enter a *nolle presequi* when the time came for the retrial. Death penalty opponents were jubilant in their victory. On October 6, 1955, the hitherto condemned Joseph Taborsky was released from prison. He literally walked out of death row a free man.

Returned to society, Joseph Taborsky vowed to go straight. He swore that from then on he would never incur even so much as a parking ticket. Deeming it prudent to leave Connecticut for a while, Taborsky then went to New York where he got married and found a job. By the autumn of 1956, however, Taborsky was back in Hartford. There he got together with a pal named Arthur Colombe (white, age 33), himself an ex-convict suspected of numerous armed robberies. Together both men embarked upon a series of holdups and murders which not only terrorized the state of Connecticut but earned them the sobriquet of the "Mad Dog Killers."

Their rampage began at Hartford on November 27, 1956. It was then that Colombe and Taborsky walked into a hotel and beat the desk clerk with blackjacks. Then they cleaned out the hotel's cash drawer and fled. On December 15, 1956, the bandits struck again. This time they entered a tailor shop at No. 517 Zion Street in Hartford where they beat up the proprietor and demanded money. Injured was Mr. Nicola Leone (white, age 67), a hard-working master at his craft. Taborsky shot the man in the face when he tried to defend himself. Dissatisfied with the contents of the tailor's till, Colombe and Taborsky decided to pull a second heist that night. They then went to New Britain. There they chose as their target a filling station at No. 1707 Stanley Street. Both of the robbers burst into the filling station office with guns drawn. They ordered the station manager and a male customer to lie face-down on the floor. Colombe took their wallets. Then Taborsky killed both men by shooting them execution style. Each died from two bullets fired into the backs of their heads at close range. Slain were Edward Kurpewski (white, age 30) and Daniel Janowski (white, age 31), the station manager and customer respectively. On December 21, 1956, the killers went to the rural town of Coventry. There they invaded a general store and severely beat the elderly proprietors. On December 26, 1956, they went to East Hartford. There they attacked a liquor store at No. 72 Pleasant Street. The storekeeper, Samuel Cohn (white, age 65), was shot dead behind his counter. Colombe and Taborsky then fled with the slain man's pocket money and the contents of his till. On January 5, 1957, the killers struck again. They turned up at North Haven where they burst into a shoe store at No. 449 Washington Avenue. There they attacked the store manager, Frank Adinolfi (white, age 44), and beat him to within an inch of his life. They also forced two customers who were present at the time to lie face-down on the floor. Colombe then proceeded to clean out the cash register. When that was done, Taborsky killed both of the store customers by shooting them in the backs of their heads execution style. Slain were a married couple named Bernard and Ruth Speyer (whites, ages 50 and 43). The only reason why the battered storekeeper was not also shot was because Taborsky thought that he was already dead. As the killers were leaving the scene of this latest crime they took the dead woman's pocketbook and the wallets of both men. On January 26, 1957, the Colombe-Taborsky duo attacked a drugstore at No. 4 Maple Avenue in Hartford. This time Taborsky did not even order the storekeeper to hand over his money first before killing him. Slain was John Rosenthal (white, age 69), a registered pharmacist. He was killed behind his prescription counter by two bullets in the chest. Then his cash register was plundered.

By this time the so-called "Mad Dog Killers" were the terror of Connecticut. Their toll was six people murdered and several others severely injured. They might have gone on indefinitely were it not for an astute detective and his keen sense of detail. When the wounded manager of the North Haven shoe store had recovered to a point where he was able to answer questions, he furnished investigators with a vital clue to the identities of the culprits. As a trained purveyor of footwear, Frank Adinolfi had noticed that one of his assailants had been wearing shoes of an unusually large size. This made one detective search his memory for known criminals with big feet. Joseph Taborsky then came to mind. A check of Taborsky's movements confirmed that he was back in Connecticut. He was also reported to be hanging around with an unsavory character named Arthur Colombe. Both men matched the general descriptions given by the other survivors of their attacks. They were also known to be unemployed but adequately supplied with money. It was decided to bring them in for questioning. Neither man was able to satisfactorily account for his whereabouts when the killings took place. Interrogations continued until Colombe finally cracked. The man made a series of confessions in which he admitted to being present at all of the crime scenes. Yes, said Colombe, he had robbed most of the victims but it was Taborsky who had done all the killing. Eventually Taborsky himself admitted that the allegations against him were true.

The revelation that "Death Row Joe" Taborsky was in on the "Mad Dog Murders" caused a scandal which has never been forgotten. Critics of capital punishment were excoriated in the press and scolded from the pulpit. The crowning blow came when Taborsky acknowledged that he was indeed guilty of the 1950 murder for which he had been condemned but freed.

This time Taborsky did not receive an outpouring of support by anti–death penalty activists. He was eschewed by nearly all of them. Those who had been conspicuous on his behalf in 1953 this time made themselves even more conspicuous by their silence. Indeed, to this day opponents of capital punishment keep a low profile whenever the name "Taborsky" is mentioned.

On May 17, 1960, the electric chair finally claimed this recidivist killer at the Connecticut State Prison. His partner Arthur Colombe died of natural causes before his appeals ran out. Although few imagined it at the time, there would be no other legal executions in New England during the 20th century.

Sources

1623

On the Unidentified man at Weymouth: Proceedings of the 250th Anniversary of the Permanent Settlement of Weymouth. Wright & Potter, State Printers, Boston, 1874, pp. 12–13.

1630

On John Billington: *Plymouth Colony, Its History & People* by Eugene Stratton. Ancestry Publishing Company, Salt Lake City, 1986, p. 52.

1637

On William Schooler: Winthrop's Journal. James Savage Edition. Little Brown & Company, Boston, 1853, vol. 1, pp. 288–290.
On John Williams: *Ibid.*, page 288.

1638

On Arthur Peach: Thomas Jackson & Richard Stinnings: *Bradford's History of Plymouth Plantation.* Random House Edition. 1981. pp. 335–337.
On Dorothy Talbye: Winthrop's Journal. Charles Scribner & Sons Edition, New York, 1908. vol. 1, pp. 282–283. See also Records of the Quarterly Courts of Essex County, Massachusetts, [Salem, Mass., 1911] vol. 1. See also Historical Collections of the Essex Institute, [Salem, Mass., 1865] vol. VII.

1639

On Nepaupauck: New *Haven Colony Records.* Hoadly Edition. Case, Tiffany & Company, Hartford, 1857, vol. 1, pp. 22–24.

1641

On William Hackett: Winthrop's Journal. James Savage edition. Little Brown & Company, Boston, 1853. vol. 1, pp. 58–60. See also Records of the Governor & Company of Massachusetts. William White, Boston, 1853. vol. 1, p. 344, entry dated December 10, 1941.

1642

On George Spencer: *New Haven Colony Records.* Charles Hoadly Edition. Case, Tiffany & Company, Hartford, 1857, vol. 1, pp. 62–73.
On Thomas Graunger: *Bradford's History of Plymouth Plantation.* Random House Edition, 1981, pp. 355–356.

1644

On Mary Latham & James Britton: Winthrop's Journal. Harvard University Press edition, 1996, pp. 246–247.

On William Franklin: Winthrop's Journal. James Savage edition. Little Brown & Company, Boston, 1853, pp. 225–227.

On Busheage: *New Haven Colony Records*. Hoadly Edition. Case, Tiffany & Company, Hartford, 1857, vol. 1, pp. 135 & 146. See also Winthrop's Journal, entry dated August 1644.

On Goodwife Cornish: *History of York, Maine*, by Charles Edward Brooks. Baltimore, 1967. See also Winthrop's Journal, vol. 2, p. 157.

1646

On William Plaine: Winthrop's Journal, entries for May–June 1646. See also *A History of the Plantation of Menunkatuck and the Original town of Guilford, Connecticut*, by Bernard Steiner. Published by the Author, Baltimore, 1897.

1647

On Mary Martin: Winthrop's Journal, entries for March, 1647. See also *Pillars of Salt: An History of some Criminals Executed in this Land for Capital Crimes* by Cotton Mather. Boston, 1699.

On Alse Youngs: *Entertaining Satan: Witchcraft and the Culture of Early New England* by John Putnam Demos. Oxford University Press, 1982, p. 505 and chapter 11, footnote #29.

1648

On Margaret Jones: Winthrop's Journal, entries for June, 1648. See also Records of the Middlesex County General Court, Session Papers for 1648. See also *A Modest Inquiry into the Nature of Witchcraft* by Rev. John Hale. Boston, 1702.

On Alice Bishop: *Records of the Colony of New Plymouth in New England*. Nathaniel Shurtleff edition, vol. 2. White & Company, Boston, 1855.

On Mary Johnson: *Records of the Particular Court of Connecticut, 1639–1663*.

vol. 1, p. 43. Entry dated August 21, 1646: "Mary Johnson for 'theuery' to be presently whipped and to be brought forth a month hence at Wethersfield and there whipped." Historians have hitherto been unanimous in interpreting the word "theuery" (as it appears in the original manuscript) as "thievery." They might be unanimously wrong in their interpretation. All have overlooked the possibility that "theuery" might actually be either the garbled or misread word "theurgy" which is a noun connoting the casting of spells and/or working of popular folk magic. Such "folk magic" or so-called "White Magic" usually involved innocuous practices like chiromancy, geomancy, the use of good luck charms, etc. In his book *Witchcraft at Salem*, Chadwick Hansen argues convincingly that such practices were widely (though clandestinely) used in 17th century New England. The fact that such practices were officially regarded as sinful by the Puritan establishment cannot be disputed. However, there was a distinct difference between what was considered "White Magic" and what was considered "Black Magic." Therefore it is not at all surprising that one of them might merely bring a person to the whipping post while the other might bring a person to the gallows. As for Mary Johnson, if the word "theuery" indeed meant "theurgy" we may regard the 1646 court record as a critical clue revealing that she bore the reputation of a witch for some years previous to her final indictment. See also *Particular Court*, vol. 1, p. 56. See also *Memorable Providences Relating to Witchcrafts and Possessions* by Cotton Mather. Boston, 1689.

1650

On Alice Lake and Elizabeth Kendall: While it is certain that both of these women were in fact hanged, the dating of their executions must be at least partially based on conjecture. Writing in the year 1697, Rev. John Hale in his *Modest Inquiry into the Nature of Witchcraft* mentions both cases. He places the Lake case antecedent to the Kendall case. Moreover, Governor John Winthrop's famous *Journal* runs until the year 1649 yet makes no mention of these cases. It is highly unlikely that Winthrop would have neglected to mention them if they had occurred in 1649 or earlier. According to Demos, four children survived Alice Lake. If the shred of evidence about her alleged witchcraft is accurate, she then had at least one more child which did not survive her.

On Thomas Newton: For personal information about Peter and Elizabeth Johnson, see *History and Genealogy of the Families of Old Fairfield* by Donald Lines Jacobus (1930). The illegitimate child of Thomas Newton and Elizabeth Johnson (named Benoni Newton) was born in prison early in the year 1650. He was apprenticed from birth to the jailer's son, Nathaniel Ruscoe of Stratford. The legal problems of Thomas Newton and Elizabeth Johnson may be traced through entries in the *Connecticut Colonial Records* and *Particular Court Records* bearing the following dates: March 28, 1650, May 15, 1650, May 21, 1650, July 8, 1650, May 15, 1651, May 20, 1652, March 1, 1655. See also Franklin B. Dexter edition, *New Haven Town Records*, vol. 1, p. 32, in which a convictive reference is made to Newton's execution and Johnson's condemnation. The circumstances of the Newton-Johnson affair have been badly bungled by both Connecticut and Fairfield historians. First of all, Joseph M. Taylor in his *The Witchcraft Delusion in Colonial Connecticut* [1908] made the rather inept mistake of confusing Elizabeth Johnson of Fairfield with Mary Johnson, the witch of Wethersfield who was executed in 1648. Secondly, Donald Lines Jacobus in his *History and Genealogy of the Families of Old Fairfield* made *three* errors in his profile of Thomas Newton. First, he recorded as Newton's wife a woman who was actually his daughter-in-law. Newton never had a second wife! Secondly, he confused Newton himself with his son and namesake. Third, he misinterpreted an entry dated July 8, 1650, in the *Record of the Particular Court* to mean that several Fairfield men contrived Newton's escape when that entry in the record actually meant no such thing. It is easy to see why Jacobus erred in the

way that he did. The source materials are worded in a tricky manner. A Thomas Newton appears with regularity in the *Records of New Amsterdam* at this time and when considering the words *"for neglecting their charge of Thomas Newton, prisoner"* (Particular Court, July 8, 1650) it is easy to surmise that such means that the men under censure in the court record contrived Newton's escape and that he absconded to New Amsterdam — beyond the reach of Connecticut authorities. The error sounds even more plausible when one considers the rarity of the English name "Thomas Newton" in a Dutch domain. The actual fact of the matter is that the Thomas Newton of New Amsterdam was not the Fairfield Newton at all. It was the Fairfield Newton's son. Thomas Newton Junior, who had previously grown up and moved away to New Amsterdam. As for *"the neglect of their charge of Thomas Newton, prisoner,"* the word "escape" is never mentioned. The negligent Fairfield men were almost certainly penalized for merely sleeping on guard duty or something similar. The pettiness of their fines indicates this.

I must now explain how I dare to state that Thomas Newton Senior was executed for adultery at Fairfield on May 27, 1650. I base my findings principally upon an entry in the *New Haven Town Records* dated June 11, 1650 (Franklin B. Dexter edition, vol. 1, p. 32), in which a Fairfield man named Nathaniel Seeley complains against one Mark Meggs for indecently fondling his wife. In its address to the defendant, the New Haven court said *"within these last 14 days he hath seen one executed for adultery and another under ye sentence of death for unnatural filthiness."* Although the names of the condemned persons are not mentioned, they can be none other than Thomas Newton and Elizabeth Johnson. First of all, the dates fit exactly with the Newton-Johnson case. Secondly the specified transgression of adultery is known to have been the charge in the Newton-Johnson case. Thirdly, plaintiff Nathaniel Seeley was a resident of Fairfield and since his wife was fondled by Mark Meggs at her home, it means that the offense occurred at

Fairfield. By counting back 14 days from the date of the June 11 court session we arrive at May 27 in Fairfield when Mark Meggs was a witness to an execution for adultery. Since time, date and offense all point to the Newton-Johnson affair and since Elizabeth Johnson is definitely known to have been reprieved on ground of pregnancy, it is virtually impossible that the executed person referred to by the New Haven court could have been anyone other than Thomas Newton.

1651

On Joan and John Carrington: See Particular Court Records, vol. 1, p. 93. See also *The Diary of Matthew Grant*. Connecticut State Library. See also Demos, citing passenger list for the *Susan & Ellen* voyage of May 1635 in Charles E. Banks, *The Planters of the Commonwealth*. Boston, 1930. See also Charles W. Manwaring's *A Digest of the Early Connecticut Probate Records*. Hartford, 1904. vol. 1, pp. 103–104 John Carrington's estate aggregated to the paltry total of £23-11-00 when an inventory was taken of it following his execution. Outstanding debts further eroded his net worth. Moreover, according to the Records of the Particular Court, Carrington was hit with a severe fine for bartering a gun with an Indian. Such a fine (£10) undoubtedly left him destitute.

On Mary Parsons: *Wonders of the Invisible World* by Cotton Mather [London, 1693]. While Mather does not identify by name his "malefactor accused of witchcraft as well as murder executed in this place more than 40 years ago," he is certainly referring to Mary Parsons. She is the only known person who fits Mather's description. Mary Parsons was indeed tried for *both* witchcraft and murder. Her case took place exactly 41 years previous to Mather's writing and her execution took place at Boston — the "this place" where Mather was stationed.

See *History of Ancient Windsor* by Henry R. Stiles Lockwood & Brainard Company, Hartford, 1892, and Particular Court, vol. 1, concerning the estate of Thomas Marshfield.

See *Massachusetts Historical Society Proceedings*, October 1930–June 1932, vol. LXIV, quoting manuscript of the original court records of this case dated May 29–30, 1649.

The testimony of the Widow Marshfield against Hugh Parsons was taken before Magistrate William Pynchon on March 22, 1651, and is cited in *Annals of Witchcraft* by Drake Benjamin Blom & Company edition, New York, 1967.

The Parsons children were Hannah, born on August 7, 1646, and died shortly afterward; Samuel, born on June 8, 1648, and died in September 1649; and Joshua, born on October 26, 1650, and died on March 4, 1651.

See *Records of the Massachusetts General Court*, entry dated March 8, 1651. See also a London newspaper called the *Mercurius Publicus*, dated September 25, 1651.

Another account of the Parsons case may be found in *The First Century of Springfield, Massachusetts*, by Henry M. Burt. Springfield, 1898, vol. 1, pp. 73–79.

On Goodwife Bassett: The principal source for what happened at Stratford in 1651 is a second-hand reference to the case that was made during a 1654 libel suit: *Staples vs. Ludlow*. New Haven Colonial Records, vol. 1. See also Connecticut Colonial Records, vol. 1, p. 220. The case is also mentioned by Jacobus in his *History and Genealogy of the Families of Old Fairfield*.

1653

On Goodwife Knapp: Records of the New Haven Colony Court, entry dated October 2, 1644. Also see the principal source for this case which is the record of the lawsuit *Staples vs. Ludlow* printed in *New Haven Colonial Records*, vol. 1. Another reference may be found in Connecticut Colonial Records, entry dated October 29, 1653.

1654

On Lydia Gilbert: See Stiles, *Genealogies and Biographies of Ancient Windsor* Lockwood & Brainard Company, Hartford, 1892. See also: *Witch Hunting in 17th Century New England* by David D. Hall. Northeastern University Press, 1991, pp. 88–89.

1655

On Walter Robinson: *New Haven Colony Records*. Hoadly Edition. Case, Tiffany & Company, Hartford, 1857, vol. 2, pp. 132–133. Also see the unpublished and extremely obscene portion of the record in this case in the original manuscript at the New Haven Colony Historical Society.

On John Knight: *Ibid.*, pp. 137–139. Due to the obscene nature of this case most of the testimonies have never been published. They may be found in the original manuscript of the trial record which is housed along with that of Walter Robinson at the New Haven Colony Historical Society.

1656

On Anne Hibbins: *Witchcraft in Boston* by William F. Poole. Published in Winsor's *Memorial History of Boston*, 1881. Demos, Drake and Hall also make mention of this case in their respective books.

1659–1661

On William Robinson, Marmaduke Stevenson, Mary Dyer and William Leddra: See *Quakers and Their Damnable Heresies*, published as chapter 10 in Edwin Powers's *Crime and Punishment in Early Massachusetts, 1620–1692*. Beacon Press, Boston, 1966.

1662–1663

On William Potter: *New Haven Colony Records*, vol. 2, pp. 440–443. See also Mather's *Pillars of Salt*, cited above.

On the Hartford Witch Hunt: The legal problems of William and Judith Ayres can be followed through entries in the records of the *Particular Court of the Colony of Connecticut* under the following dates: March 7, 1651, June 1652, December 7, 1654, June 7, 1655, December 1655, December 4, 1656, March 4, 1657, May 18, 1658, March 3, 1659, March 6, 1662, and May 13, 1662. See also *Public Records of the Colony of Connecticut*, vol. 2, p. 531. The trials and tribulations of Andrew Sanford can be traced through a *Particular Court* entry dated September 1, 1659, and his indictment by that court dated June 13, 1662. Another source for this affair is the Samuel Wyllys Collection at the Connecticut State Archives which contains many original trial documents. See also *The Mather Papers* published in Massachusetts Historical Society Collections, 4th Series, vol. 8, pp. 466–469. The Hartford affair of 1662-1663 is also described by Increase Mather in his *Remarkable Providences* (London, 1684), which has numerous reprint editions. As for the ultimate fate of William and Judith Ayres, see *Records of the Court of Trials of the Colony of Providence Plantations, 1662–1670*, vol. 2, pp. 6–7, session dated October 14, 1662 (Rhode Island Historical Society, 1922). As for the earthquake of 1663 see J.W. Barber's *Interesting Events in the History of the United States*. Published by the author, New Haven, 1832. Most of the original documents dealing with this case are reprinted in David D. Hall's *Witch Hunting in 17th Century New England*. Northeastern University Press, 1991.

1667

On Peter Abbott: Bradstreet's Journal, published in the New England Historical and Genealogical Record, vol. 9 (1855), p. 43. See also Minutes of the Connecticut Court of Assistants, 1665–1711, Record Group 3, Box 648, pp. 7–8, located at the Connecticut State Archives. See also *History and Genealogy of the Families of Old Fairfield* by Donald Lines Jacobus. Genealogical Publishing Company, Inc., Baltimore, 1976, pp. 5–6.

1668

On Ruth Briggs: Records of the Quarterly Courts of Essex County, Massachusetts, entries dated December 29, 1647, January 1, 1648, January 2, 1648, July 11, 1649, April 27, 1650, July 24, 1650, April 30, 1952, September 30, 1952, September 3, 1955, September 29, 1955, April 24, 1956, September 30, 1956, March 27, 1960, and April 30, 1663.

See also Lewis and Marshall's *History of Lynn*. John L. Shorey, Publisher, Boston, 1865. See also *New Haven Town Records*, entry dated December 14, 1665. See also *Crimes & Misdemeanors*, Series One, Connecticut State Archives. The case is also mentioned in Bradstreet's Journal. N.E.H.G.R., vol. 9, 1855, p. 44.

On the Unidentified Woman at Boston: Bradstreet's Journal. N.E.H.G.R., vol. 9, 1855, p. 44.

1670

On the two Unidentified men: *Ibid.*, p. 45.

On Thomas Flounders: Records of the Colony of Rhode Island, vol. 2, pp. 341–344 & 363. See also Records of the Court of Trials of the Colony of Providence Plantations, 1662–1670, vol. 2, pp. 97–98. Rhode Island Historical Society 1922.

1671

On Young Matoonas: *A Rhode Islander Reports on King Philip's War*. Rhode Island Historical Society 1963, pp. 81–83. See also Bradstreet's Journal, p. 46.

On the Unidentified Man: Bradstreet, *ibid.*, p. 46.

On William Thomas: Record Book of the General Court of Trials (1671–1724), vol. A, pp. 2–3 & 7. Judicial Records Center, Pawtucket, Rhode Island See also *Records of the Colony of Rhode Island*, vol. 2, p. 393.

1672

On the Unidentified Man: Bradstreet, *ibid.*, p. 46.

On Thomas Rood: Minutes of the Connecticut Court of Assistants, 1665–1711, Record Group 3, Box 648, pp. 35–37, Connecticut State Archives.

1673

On William Forest, John Smith and Alexander Wilson: Records of the Court of Assistants of the Colony of Massachusetts, 1673–1692. Published by the County of Suffolk, 1901, pp. 12–13. See also Mather's *Pillars of Salt*.

On Thomas Cornell: Record Book of the General Court of Trials, vol. A, pp. 10–17, Judicial Records Center, Pawtucket, Rhode Island.

On Indian John, alias Punneau: *Ibid.*, vol. A., p. 11.

On Jankssick: *Ibid.*, vol. A., p. 19.

1674

On Benjamin Goad: Records of the Court of Assistants of the Colony of Massachusetts, 1673–1692. Published by the County of Suffolk, 1901, pp. 10–11. See also the Diary of Samuel Sewell, entry dated April 2, 1674. Massachusetts Historical Society.

On Quaognait: Rhode Island Court of Trials, vol. A., p. 20.

On Indian Tom: Court of Assistants, 1673–1692. *Ibid.*, pp. 21–22.

1675

On Robert Driver and Nicholas Feavour: Court of Assistants, pp. 30–32. Also Sewall's Diary, entries dated February and March 1675. See also Mather's *Pillars of Salt*. B. Green, Boston, 1699.

On Henry Green and Negro Cloyes: Connecticut Court of Assistants, 1665–1711, pp. 58–59. Record Group 3, Box 648, Connecticut State Archives.

On Tobias, Mattashunnamo and Wampapaquan: *The Name of War* by Jill Lepore. Alfred Knopf, New York, 1998, pp. 21–26.

On the Unidentified Indian at Plymouth: *London Gazette*, no. 1017.

On Little John: Court of Assistants, 1673–1692, p. 53.

On Samuel Guile: *Ibid.*, p. 50.

1676

On the Two Men at Taunton: *A Narrative of the Indian Wars in New England* by the Rev. William Hubbard. Worcester, Mass., 1801, pp. 161–163.

On Joshua Tift: *The Name of War* by Jill Lepore. Alfred Knopf, Inc., 1998, pp. 131–136.

On Canonchet: *An Historical Memoir of the Colony of New Plymouth* by Francis Baylies. Wiggin & Lunt, Boston, 1866, vol. 2, pp. 116–117.

On Capt. Tom and One Unidentified Man: Sewall's Diary, entry dated June 22, 1676.

On the Man at Northampton: *Bradstreet's Journal*, entry dated July 1676.

On Wotuchpo: *The History of King Philip's War* by Increase Mather. Samuel Drake edition, Boston, 1862, pp. 175–176 & 251.

On Woodcock, Quanapowhan, John Num and Keeweenam: Increase Mather, pp. 251–253. See also Plymouth Colony Records, Press of William White, Boston, 1856, vol. 5, pp. 204–206.

On Old Matoonas: *A Rhode Islander Reports on King Philip's War*. Rhode Island Historical Society, 1963, pp. 81–83.

On Sam Barrow: *Diary of King Philip's War* by Col. Benjamin Church. Published by the Little Compton, Rhode Island Historical Society, 1975, p. 148.

On Potock: Increase Mather, pp. 192–193.

On Quanopan, Sunkoorunasuck, Wonanquabin and John Woropoak: Rhode Island Court of Trials, vol. A, pp. 34–37.

On Choos: William Hubbard, *ibid.*, pp. 268–269.

On the Eight Unidentified Men: Sewall's Diary, entry dated September 13, 1676.

On the Three Unidentified Men: *Ibid.*, entry dated September 21, 1676.

On Stephen Goble and Daniel Goble: Court of Assistants, pp. 71–73. See also Sewall's Diary, entries dated September 21, 1676, and September 26, 1676.

On Sagamore Sam, Netaump, Maliompe and Old Jethro: William Hubbard, p. 117. See also Sewall's Diary, entry dated September 26, 1676.

On Caleb and Columbine: Court of Assistants, p. 76. See also Sewall's Diary, entry dated October 12, 1676.

On Annawon and Tispaquin: Benjamin Church, *ibid.*, p. 173. See also Francis Baylies, *ibid.*, pp. 173–184.

1677

On Cornelius: William Hubbard, *ibid.*, p. 272.

On Benjamin Tuttle: Crimes & Misdemeanors, 1st Series, vol. 1, pp. 80–84, Connecticut State Archives. See also History of Stamford, Connecticut, by the Rev. E.B. Huntington. Published by the author, Stamford, 1868, p. 43.

1678

On John Stoddard: Crimes & Misdemeanors, 1st Series, vol. 1, pp. 104–114, Connecticut State Archives. See also *History of New London* by Frances Caulkins. H.D. Utley Co., New London, 1895, pp. 369–370. See also *Bradstreet's Journal*. N.E.H.G.R., vol. 9, 1855, p. 49.

1679

On Peter Pylatt: Rhode Island Court of Trials, vol. A, p. 51.

1681

On William Cheney: Court of Assistants, pp. 199–200. See also Cotton Mather's *Pillars of Salt*. B. Green, 1699.

On Negro Jack: Proceedings of the Colonial Society of Massachusetts, vol. 6, pp. 323–336.

On Negress Maria: *Ibid.*

1682

On Allumchoyse: Collections of the Connecticut Historical Society, vol. XXI, pp. 277–281.

1686

On Squampum: Connecticut Court of Assistants, vol. 1, pp. 146–148.

On James Morgan: Court of Assistants (Massachusetts), pp. 294–295. See also Mather's *Pillars of Salt.*

On Jonathan Neponet: Record Book of the Superior Court of Judicature, 1686–1700, p. 13. Massachusetts State Archives. See also Sewall's Diary, entry dated November 18, 1686.

1687

On the Unidentified Woman: Sewall's Diary, entry dated November 3, 1687.

1688

On Ann Glover: *Memorable Providences Relating to Witchcrafts and Possessions* by Cotton Mather. Boston, 1689. See also *Narratives of the Witchcraft Cases.* Charles Scribner & Sons, New York, 1914. Also Sewall's Diary, entry November 16, 1688.

1689

On Pammatoock: *History of Martha's Vineyard* by Charles Edward Brooks. Press of George H. Dean, Boston, 1911, vol. 1, p. 270. See also *Magnalia Christi Americana* by Cotton Mather. New Haven edition, 1820, vol. 2, pp. 386–387.

1690

On Hugh Stone: Court of Assistants, pp. 303–304. See also Cotton Mather's *Pillars of Salt.*

On Thomas Johnson: Court of Assistants, pp. 309–310. Also Sewall's Diary, entry dated January 27, 1690.

On John de la Forest: *Records of Plymouth Colony* (Judicial Acts), 1636–1692, Press of William White, Boston, 1857. vol. 7, pp. 305–307.

1692

My sources for the Salem witch trials were the following:

Burr, George Lincoln, ed. *Narratives of the Witchcraft Cases, 1648–1706.* Charles Scribner & Sons, New York, 1914.

Hall, David D. *Witch Hunting in 17th Century New England, a Documentary History, 1638–1692.* Northeastern University Press, 1991.

Hansen, Chadwick. *Witchcraft at Salem.* George Braziller, Inc., New York, 1969.

Robinson, Enders A. *The Devil Discovered: Salem Witchcraft 1692.* Hippocrene Books, New York, 1991.

Starkey, Marion L. *The Devil in Massachusetts: A Modern Enquiry into the Salem Witch Trials.* Alfred A. Knopf, New York, 1949.

Woodward, ed. *Records of Salem Witchcraft* (1864). Also a reprint known as the Burt Franklin edition (New York, 1972). This is the single most important source for the Salem Witch Trials, being a reprint of all the surviving court records of that affair as taken from the original manuscripts.

1693

On Elizabeth Emerson: Supreme Judicial Court, Case nos. 2549, 2636 & 2668. Massachusetts State Archives. See also Court of Assistants, p. 357, entry dated September 26, 1691. See also Record Book of the Supreme Court of Judicature, 1692–1695, pp. 50–51. See also Cotton Mather's

Pillars of Salt. See also Sewall's Diary, entry dated June 8, 1693.

On Negress Grace: SCJ, 1692–1695, pp. 51–53. Massachusetts State Archives.

1694

On Jacob: Record Book of the Superior Court of Judicature, 1692–1695, pp. 94–95. Massachusetts State Archives.

On Zachalenaco: *Ibid.*, pp. 100–102. See also Mather's *Pillars of Salt.*

On Daniel Matthews: Connecticut Court of Assistants, 1665–1711, pp. 200–201. See also Crimes & Misdemeanors, Series One, pp. 199–201. Connecticut State Library. See also Public Records of the Colony of Connecticut, vol. 4, pp. 132–133.

1695

On Joseph Hyde: SCJ, vol. 1 (1692–1695), pp. 150–151. Massachusetts State Archives.

1696

On John, Esther and Susannah Andrews: Supreme Judicial Court Case no. 3279. Massachusetts State Archives. See also SCJ, vol. 2 (1695–1700), pp. 49–50. See also *Records of the Colony of New Plymouth in New England.* Nathaniel B. Shurtleff edition, Boston, 1856, vol. 4, pp. 77–79, 139; vol. 5, p. 118; vol. 6, p. 82. See also *The Mayflower Descendent*, vol. 24, p. 137. See also *Records of the Town of Plymouth.* Avery & Doten Book & Job Printers, Plymouth, 1889, vol. 1, p. 103. See also the minutes of a town meeting held on October 19, 1699, in which the prison fees for John Andrews were ordered paid.

On Mowenas and Moquolas: History of Greenfield, Massachusetts, by Francis Thompson. Privately published, 1904, vol. 1, p. 66.

1698

On Sarah Smith: SJC, Case no. 3718. Massachusetts State Archives. See also SJC, vol. 2, pp. 193–194. See also Cotton Mather's *Pillars of Salt.*

On Sarah Threeneedles: SJC, vol. 2, pp. 199–200. Massachusetts State Archives. See also Sewall's Diary, entries dated October 29, 1698, and November 17, 1698. See also Cotton Mather's *Pillars of Salt: An History of Some Criminals Executed in This Land for Capital Crimes.* B. Green, Boston, 1699. Harvard College Library Rare Books Dept.

1700

On the Three Unidentified Men: *A Statistical Account of the City of New Haven* by Timothy Dwight. Connecticut Academy of Arts & Sciences, New Haven, 1811, pp. 35–36.

1701

On Esther Rogers: *Death the Certain Wages of Sin, etc.*, a contemporary pamphlet which deals with the case of Esther Rodgers, located at the American Antiquarian Society, Worcester, Mass. Note: In his book *Hang by the Neck* (CC Thomas & Co., Springfield, IL, 1967), p. 80, the late Professor Negley K. Teeters erroneously states that the dead body of Esther Rodgers was "gibbeted" in irons after her execution. This error is based upon an earlier error in Joseph Felt's *The History of Ipswich, Essex and Hamilton, Massachusetts* (Boston, 1834), in which it is stated (erroneously) that a "gibbet" was erected for Esther Rodgers. So eager was Teeters to take Felt at his *literal* word that he failed to recognize the true context in which the word "gibbet" was used. It simply meant an upright post with a crosspiece projecting at a right angle from its upper end from which a condemned criminal would be hanged, hence any common gallows of the period. Teeters also made another error when he stated that Esther Rodgers was the only female to have been gibbeted in the history of the United States. Not only was Esther Rodgers not gibbeted at all (i.e., her dead body exposed in an iron cage), but there were indeed instances elsewhere in the history of the United States in which female offenders did suffer such a fate. For instance, in May of 1723 a slave woman named Hannah was hung in irons near Annapolis, Maryland, for murdering a white man. Likewise, on July 4, 1755, a slave woman named Jenny suffered the same fate at Port Tobacco, Maryland, for poisoning her master.

1704

On the Six Pirates: *Pirates of the New England Coast, 1630–1730* by George Francis Dow and John Henry Edmonds. Marine Research Society, Salem, MA, 1923. See also *Boston Newsletter*, 7/3/04 (2:1).

On Finch: *Boston Newsletter*, 6/5/04 (2:2). See also *The History of Nantucket* by Obed Macy. Hilliard, Gray & Co., Boston, 1835, p. 65.

1705

On Negro Rochester: SCJ (1700–1714), p. 170. Massachusetts State Archives.

1708

On Abigail Thompson: Connecticut Court of Assistants, May Session, 1706. Original court minutes located at the Connecticut State Archives]. See also Public Records of the Colony of Connecticut, entries dated October 10, 1706, May 8, 1707, May 13, 1708, May 26, 1708, and May 28, 1708. See also original depositions of witnesses in this case located at Connecticut State Archives.

1709

On Josias: SCJ (1700–1714), p. 242. Massachusetts State Archives. See also

Sewall's Diary entry dated October 3, 1709. See also *The Woeful Effects of Drunkeness: A Sermon Preached at the Execution of Two Indians, Josias and Joseph, for Murder.* B. Green, Boston, 1710.

On Joseph Tanqua: SCJ (1700–1714), p. 242. Massachusetts State Archives.

1710

On Hannah Degoe: SJC, Case no. 8148. Massachusetts State Archives.

1711

On Waisoiusksquaw: Connecticut Court of Assistants, 1665–1711, pp. 796–802.

On Young Squamp: *Ibid.* Connecticut State Archives.

1712

On Negro Mingo: SCJ (1700–1714), p. 269. Massachusetts State Archives. See also Sewall's Diary entries dated January 29, 1712, January 30, 1712, and February 15, 1712.

On Negress Betty: SJC, Case no. 8600. Massachusetts State Archives. See also Sewall's Diary, entries dated March 26, 27, and 28, 1712.

On Job the Indian: Rhode Island Court of Trials, vol. A, pp. 198–199. See also *Boston Newsletter*, 6/30/12 (2:2) and 9/15/12 (2:2).

1713

On David Wallis: SJC, Case no. 9174. Massachusetts State Archives. See also *Boston Newsletter*, 8/31/13 (2:2) and 9/28/13 (2:2).

1715

On Jeremiah Meachum: Rhode Island Court of Trials, vol. A, p. 225. See also *Boston Newsletter*, 3/28/15 (2:1) and 4/18/15 (2:1).

On Margaret Callogharne: SJC, Case no. 10355. See also *Boston Newsletter*, 6/13/15 (2:2).

1716

On Negro Welcome: SJC, Case no. 10151. See also SCJ (1715–1721), p. 132. Massachusetts State Archives.

1717

On Jeremiah Phoenix: SCJ (1715–1721), p. 182. See also *Boston Newsletter*, 6/17/17 (2:1).

On the Six Pirates: *Boston Newsletter*, 10/28/17 (2:2) and 11/18/17 (2:2). See also *Pirates of the New England Coast 1630–1730* by Dow and Edmonds, pp. 116–131.

1719

On William Dyer: Rhode Island Court of Trials, vol. A, p. 301. See also *Boston Newsletter*, 4/27/19 (2:2).

1720

On Negro Coffee: Fairfield County Superior Court Files, 1720–1729. Record Group 3, Box 616. Connecticut State Archives.

On Joseph Pease: SJC, Case nos. 14762 and 14763 [Massachusetts State Archives].

On Reuben Hull: Rhode Island Court of Trials, vol. A., p. 312. See also *Boston Newsletter*, 6/27/20 (4:1).

On Elizabeth Atwood: SJC, Case no. 14363. See also History of Ipswich, Essex and Hamilton, Massachusetts, by Joseph Felt. Boston, 1834, p. 117.

1721

On Joseph Hanno: SJC, Case nos. 14687 and 15186. See also *Boston Newsletter*, 5/29/21 (2:1).

1723

On Joseph Ewitt: SJC, Case nos. 16124, 16957 and 17698. Massachusetts State Archives.

On Negro Diego: SJC, Case no. 16899. See also *New England Courant*, 4/8/23 (2:2).

On the 26 pirates: *Boston Newsletter*: 6/20/23 (1:2), 7/4/23 (2:1), 7/18/23 (2:2), 7/25/23 (2:1) and 8/1/23 (2:1).

1724

On John Archer and William White: *Boston Newsletter*, 4/7/24 (2:1), 5/14/24 (2:2) and 6/4/24 (2:2). See also *Pirates of the New England Coast 1630–1730* by Dow and Edmonds, pp. 310–327.

1725

On Peter Westcott: Rhode Island Court of Trials, vol. B, p. 20. See also *Boston Newsletter*, 4/29/25 (2:1).

On Josiah Challenge: SJC, Case no. 18457. Massachusetts State Archives.

1726

On Joseph Quasson: SJC, Case no. 19323. Massachusetts State Archives. Note: Until the year 1820 Massachusetts had jurisdiction over what is now the state of Maine.

On Samuel Cole, William Flye and Henry Greenville: *Boston Newsletter*, 7/14/26 (2:2). See also *Pirates of the New England Coast* by Dow and Edmonds, pp. 328–337.

On the Five French and Indian Pirates: *Boston Newsletter*, 9/8/26 (2:2), 10/6/26 (2:2), 11/3/26 (2:2) and 11/17/26 (2:2).

1727

On Elizabeth Colson: SJC, Case no. 20195. Massachusetts State Archives.

1730

On Joseph Fuller: SJC, Case no. 29483. See also *New England Weekly Journal*, 12/8/29 (2:2) and 6/1/30 (2:2). This case is also reported by the *Pennsylvania Gazette*, 6/11/30.

1731

On Negro Tom: SJC, Case no. 31054. See also *New England Weekly Journal*, 8/11/30 (2:2) and 2/15/31 (2:2).
On Negress Hannah: New Haven County Superior Court Files, September Session, 1731. Record Group 3, Connecticut State Archives.

1732

On Richard Wilson: The *Weekly Rehearsal* (Boston), 8/21/32 (2:2) and 10/23/32 (2:1). Also see *Boston Newsletter*, 10/27/32 (2:1). Also see *New England Weekly Journal*, 10/23/32 (2:2).
On Negro Jack: SJC, Case no. 34082.

1733

On Julian: SJC, Case nos. 30449, 31330, 34703, 34773. See also *Boston Newsletter*, 9/14/32 (2:1) and 3/30/33 (2:2).
On Rebeckah Chamblitt: SJC, Case no. 35693. See also *Boston Gazette*, 4/14/33. See also *Boston Newsletter*, 5/17/33. See also *The Declaration, Dying Warning and Advice of Rebeckah Chamblitt, etc.* (a broadside at the American Antiquarian Society).

1734

On John Stoicks: SJC, Case no. 36822. See also *Boston Newsletter*, 2/14/34 (2:2) and 3/28/34 (2:1).
On Amaziah Harding: SJC, Case nos. 37237 and 37376.
On John Ormsby: SCJ (1733–1736),

pp. 117–118. See also *Boston Newsletter*, 12/27/33 (2:1) and 8/22/34 (2:1).
On Matthew Cushing: SJC, Case no. 165983. See also SCJ (1733–1736), p. 118. See also *Boston Newsletter*, 8/22/34 (2:1).
On Negro London: SJC, Case nos. 37890 and 38267. See also *Boston Newsletter*, 11/14/34 (2:2).

1735

On Patience Boston: SJC, Case no. 39912. See also *A Faithful Narrative of the Wicked Life and Remarkable Conversion of Patience Boston* (a pamphlet at the American Antiquarian Society).

1736

On Robin Nasson: SJC, Case nos. 41429, 41568, and 42140.

1737

On Abiah Comfort: SJC, Case no. 44575.
On Ann, alias Mulatto Nanny: Original Case File (*Dom Rex vs. Ann*) located at the Supreme Court Judicial Records Center, Pawtucket, Rhode Island.
On Hugh Henderson: SJC, Case nos. 44640 and 44647. See also *Boston Evening Post*, 12/5/37 (2:1).

1738

On Katharine Garrett: New London County Superior Court Records, November Session, 1737. Connecticut State Archives. See also *History of New London* by Frances Caulkins. Privately printed, 1852, p. 410.
On Philip Kennison: SJC, Case nos. 40162, 46909, 47292 and 47502. See also *Boston Evening Post*, 9/18/38 (2:1).
On the Four Rhode Island Pirates: Original trial papers located at the Supreme Court Judicial Records Center, Pawtucket,

Rhode Island. See also *Boston Evening Post*, 11/6/38 (2:1).

1739

On John Comfort: SJC, Case nos. 49547, 49602 and 49943.

On Sarah Simpson and Penelope Kenny: Colonial Records Series, Case no. 20062. New Hampshire State Archives. See also *Boston Newsletter*, 8/23/39.

1740

On George Necho: SJC, Case no. 137029.

On Edmund Brown: SJC, Case no. 52396. See also *Boston Evening Post*, 9/3/39 (2:1).

1742

On Harry Jude: *Boston Gazette*, 7/13/42 (3:1). See also *History of Nantucket* by Obed Macy. Hilliard, Gray & Company, Boston, 1835, p. 65.

On Jabez Green: SJC, Case no. 56063. See also *Boston Newsletter*, 11/4/42 (2:1).

1743

On Margaret Fennison: SJC, Case no. 56937.

On Simon Hew: SJC, Case no. 33710. See also Minutes of the Governor's Council dated June 23, 1743. Massachusetts State Archives. See also Obed Macy, p. 65.

On Negro Jack: Connecticut Superior Court Records, vol. 11, p. 204. See also Hartford County Superior Court Case Files, 1742–1744, Record Group 3, Box 86. Connecticut State Archives. See also *Boston Gazette*, 6/28/43 (3:2).

On Negress Kate: Connecticut Superior Court Records, vol. 11, p. 201. See also Hartford County Superior Court Case Files, Record Group 3, Box 86. Connecticut State Archives.

On Negro Barney: Connecticut Superior Court Records, vol. 11, pp. 205 & 236–237. See also Hartford County Superior Court Case Files, 1742–1744, Record Group 3, Box 86. Connecticut State Archives.

1744

On Negro Barney: *Ibid.*

On Edward Fitzpatrick: SJC, Case nos. 58364, 59403, 59587. See also *Boston Newsletter*, 3/22/44 (2:2). See also *The Examination & Confession of Edward Fitzpatrick* (a broadside at the Rare Books & Manuscripts Division of the Harvard College Library).

1745

On Negro Jeffrey: *Boston Newsletter*, 9/20/45 (2:2). See also *Boston Post Boy*, 10/28/45 (2:2).

On Elizabeth Shaw: Windham County Superior Court Records, October Term, 1745. Connecticut State Archives. See also *History of Windham County, Connecticut*, by Ellen Larned. Published by the author, Worcester MA, 1874, vol. 1, pp. 288–289.

1746

On James Cattee, Peter Ferry and Thomas Rigby: *Boston Gazette*, 7/1/46 (2:2) and 7/29/46 (3:1). See also *Boston Post Boy*, 7/28/46 (2:2).

1747

On Elizabeth Wakefield: SJC, Case no. 63539.

On Mulatto William: *Boston Newsletter*, 3/26/47 (1:2); *Boston Post Boy*, 10/19/47 (2:1); *Boston Gazette*, 3/24/47 (3:1) and 10/20/47 (3:2).

1749

On Negro Cuff: New Haven County Superior Court Files, Record Group 3, Drawer No. 327. Connecticut State

Archives. See also Crimes & Misdemeanors, First Series, vol. 4, pp. 118–119. Connecticut State Archives.

1751

On Thomas Carter: Washington County Supreme Court Minutes, Book A (1747–1763), pp. 72–73. Also original trial papers. Supreme Court Records Center, Pawtucket, Rhode Island. See also *Boston Newsletter*, 3/7/51 (2:1), 4/18/51 (2:1) and 5/20/51 (2:1).

On Negress Phillis: SJC, Case no. 67676. See also *Boston Newsletter*, 4/18/51 (2:1) and 5/23/51 (2:1).

1753

On Sarah Bramble: New London County Superior Court Records, September Term, 1753. Connecticut State Archives. See also *History of New London* by Frances Caulkins. Privately printed, 1852, p. 468.

1754

On William Welch: *The Last Speech & Dying Words of William Welch* (a broadside at the Massachusetts Historical Society). See also *Boston Evening Post*, 11/26/53 (4:2). See also *Boston Gazette*, 11/27/53 (3:1) and 4/16/54 (3:1).

On William Wier: SJC, Case nos. 73040 and 73187. See also *Boston Gazette*, 4/9/54 (3:1) and 11/26/54 (3:1). See also *Boston Post Boy*, 11/25/54 (2:2).

1755

On Eliphaz Dow: Provincial Court Records, Case no. 27132. New Hampshire State Archives.

On John Seymour: SJC, Case nos. 73005, 74301 and 74388. See also *Boston Gazette*, 7/16/54 (2:2) and 9/1/55 (3:3).

On Mark and Phillis: Proceedings of the

Massachusetts Historical Society. March 1883, pp. 122–146.

1756

On Negro Toney: SJC, Case no. 137014. See also *Boston Newsletter*, 7/1/56 (2:2) and 8/5/56 (3:2).

On Joseph Hughes: *Boston Evening Post*, 10/25/56 (4:2).

1757

On John Harrington: SJC, Case nos. 76175, 76602 and 76769. See also *Boston Evening Post*, 9/6/56 (2:1) and 3/21/57 (1:2).

Oh John Absalom: Providence County Superior Court Record Book (1757–1769), no. 1, p. 196, plus original trial papers. Supreme Court Records Center, Pawtucket, Rhode Island. See also *Boston Newsletter*, 10/20/57 (2:1) and 11/24/57 (2:2).

1760

On Samuel Parks and Benjamin Hawkins: *Boston Evening Post*, 4/14/60 (2:3), 7/28/60 (3:2) and 8/25/60 (3:2).

1762

On Fortune Price: Newport County Superior Court Minutes Book, vol. E (1754–1772), pp. 183–184. Supreme Court Records Center, Pawtucket, Rhode Island. See also *Boston Evening Post*, 3/1/62 (3:1), 3/8/62 (3:1) and 5/17/62 (3:1).

1763

On Negro Bristol: SJC, Case no. 145054. See also *Boston Evening Post*, 6/13/63 (2:3) and 12/5/63 (3:1).

1764

On John Shearman: Newport County Superior Court Minutes Book, vol. E

(1754–1772), pp. 182–183, plus original trial papers. Supreme Court Records Center, Pawtucket, Rhode Island. See also *Newport Mercury*, 11/19/64 (3:2).

1765

On Joseph Lightly: SJC, Case no. 147371. See also *Boston Gazette*, 11/25/65 (3:3) and *Boston Evening Post*, 11/25/65 (3:1).

1768

On Nathan Quibby: SJC, Case no. 101221. See also *Boston Gazette Supplement*, 10/19/67 (1:1).

On Isaac Frasier: *A Brief Account of the Life and Abominable Thefts of the Notorious Isaac Frasier* (a pamphlet at the American Antiquarian Society).

On Negro Arthur: SJC, Case no. 152339. See also *Boston Newsletter*, 10/27/68 (1:3). See also *The Life and Dying Speech of Arthur* (a broadside at the American Antiquarian Society).

On Richard Ames: *Boston Weekly Newsletter* (Supplement), 11/3/68 (1:3).

On John Jacob: *Connecticut Courant*, 2/29/68 (3:2) and 11/7/68 (2:2).

On Ruth Blay: Original Case File (*The King vs. Blay*), Case no. 4262. New Hampshire State Archives. See also *New Hampshire Gazette*, 9/23/68 (3:2), 9/30/68 (3:3), 11/25/68 (3:2), 12/8/68 (3:2) and 1/6/69 (3:1). Most of the misinformation about this case comes from an old book entitled *Rambles About Portsmouth* by Charles W. Brewster (*Portsmouth Journal* office, 1859), pp. 287–289. The author of that book was long on tall tales and short on historical accuracy. For instance, he couldn't even get the names of the sheriffs right when he wrote about the New Hampshire executions of 1739, 1755 and 1768. He incorrectly stated that the sheriff who presided at the Ruth Blay execution was the same sheriff who presided at the 1739 executions of Simpson and Kenny. However, according to the endorsements on the back of the original death warrants of Simpson and Kenny (also located in the N.H. State

Archives), the sheriff of 1739 was a man named Eleazer Russell; he was *not* the Thomas Packer of 1768. The same error is repeated in an even older book entitled *Annals of Portsmouth* by Nathaniel Adams (published by the author, 1825), p. 172. Later writers have been overly eager to take Brewster and Adams at their word. Thus did a false legend grow up around Ruth Blay. Feature articles on her which appeared in the *Boston Herald* (3/8/1931), the *Manchester Guardian* (1/6/1877) and the *Laconia Citizen* (12/20/1961) are all based on erroneous information.

1770

On William Lindsay: SJC, Case nos. 152407 and 152512. See also *Boston Gazette*, 10/29/70 (3:1).

On William Shaw: SJC, Case no. 157636. See also *Boston Newsletter*, 12/20/70 (3:1).

1771

On Caesar Hazard: Minutes of the Washington County Court of Judicature, Assize and General Gaol Delivery, vol. B (1763–1782), pp. 303–304. Also original trial papers. Supreme Court Records Center, Pawtucket, Rhode Island. See also *Providence Gazette*, 7/6/71 (3:3), 10/19/71 (3:1), 11/16/71 (3:1) and 11/30/71 (3:2).

1772

On Bryan Sheehan: SJC, Case no. 132119. See also *Essex Gazette*, 9/24/71 (3:3) and 1/21/72 (3:2). See also *An Account of the Life of Bryan Sheehan* (a broadside at the Historical Society of Pennsylvania).

On Moses Paul: *Connecticut Courant*, 12/17/71 (3:2) and 9/8/72 (3:3).

On Solomon Goodwin: SJC, Case no. 139479. See also *Boston Gazette*, 6/8/72 (3:1) and 11/23/72 (3:1).

1773

On Levi Aimes: SJC, Case no. 102314. See also *Boston Gazette*, 8/30/73 (2:2) and 10/25/73 (3:1). See also *The Last Words and Dying Speech of Levi Ames* (sic) (a broadside at the American Antiquarian Society).

1774

On Daniel Wilson: Providence County Superior Court Record Book (1769–1790), vol. 2, pp. 297–298. Also original trial papers (*Rex. vs. Wilson*). Located at the Supreme Court Records Center, Pawtucket, Rhode Island. See also *Providence Gazette*, 4/30/74 (3:2). See also *The Life and Confession of Daniel Wilson* (a broadside at the American Antiquarian Society).

On Valentine Duckett: *Boston Gazette*, 9/12/74 (2:3).

On William Ferguson: *Boston Gazette*, 12/26/74 (3:1).

1777

On Moses Dunbar: *Connecticut Courant*, 1/27/77 (3:1) and 3/24/77 (3:1). See also *Norwich Packet*, 3/24/77 (3:3).

On Daniel Griswold: *Connecticut Journal* (New Haven), 4/7/77 (2:2).

On John Hart: *Providence Gazette*, 5/17/77 (3:2) and 5/24/77 (3:2).

On William Stone: *Connecticut Courant*, 6/2/77 (3:2).

On Robert Thompson: *History of Fairfield County* by Lynn Winfield Wilson. S.J. Clark Publishing Co., Chicago and Hartford, 1929, pp. 162–164.

On John Dennis: *Connecticut Gazette* (New London), 1/10/77 (3:2), 1/24/77 (3:2) and 8/8/77 (3:2). See also *Norwich Packet*, 8/11/77 (3:3).

On Thomas Lake: *Independent Chronicle* (Boston), 10/9/77 (3:1). See also *Continental Journal* (Boston), 10/9/77 (3:3).

1778

On John Fretter: *Providence Gazette*, 5/30/78 (3:2).

On David Redding: *Memorials of a Century: The Early History of Bennington, Vermont*, by Isaac Jennings. Gould & Lincoln Publishers, Boston, 1869, p. 356. See also *Vermont Historical Magazine*, p. 159.

On William Brooks, James Buchanan, Ezra Ross and Bathsheba Spooner: *American Criminal Trials* by Peleg Chandler. Little, Brown & Carter, Boston, 1844, vol. 2, pp. 1–58 and 375–383. See also *American State Trials*. 1914 edition, vol. 2, pp. 175–201. See also *Independent Chronicle* (Boston), 7/9/78 (3:2).

On Thomas Steele: *Independent Chronicle* (Boston), 7/9/78 (3:2). See also *Boston Gazette*, 7/13/78 (3:2).

On Elisha Smith: *Norwich Packet* (Connecticut), 11/9/78 (2:1).

On John Blair and David Farnsworth: *Connecticut Courant*, 11/10/78 (3:2). See also *Boston Gazette*, 11/16/78 (3:1).

On John Bushby: *Providence Gazette*, 11/28/78 (3:3).

1779

On Edward Jones and John Smith: *History of Fairfield County* by Lynn Winfield Wilson. S.J. Clarke Publishing Co., Chicago and Hartford, 1929, pp. 160–161.

On Robert Young: SJC, Case no. 153011. See also *Massachusetts Spy* (Worcester), 9/9/79 (3:3), 10/14/79 (3:2) and 11/11/79 (3:3). See also *The Last Words and Dying Speech of Robert Young* (a broadside at the American Antiquarian Society).

1780

On Barnett Davenport: Litchfield County Superior Court Records, 1780–1789, Box 190, File D. Connecticut State Archives. See also *Connecticut Courant*, 2/15/ 80 (3:2) and 5/9/80 (3:1). See also *A Brief Narrative of the Life and Confession of*

Barnett Davenport (a pamphlet at the American Antiquarian Society].
On Jeremiah Braun: *History of Thomaston, Rockland and South Thomaston, Maine*, by Cyrus Eaton. Masters Smith & Co., Hallowell ME, 1865, pp. 139–140.
On James Duncan: *Providence Gazette*, 9/23/80 (3:2).

1781

On Alexander McDowell: *Connecticut Courant*, 3/27/81 (3:1).
On the Unidentified Man: *Newport Mercury*, 6/2/81 (3:2).
On Michael Lobidal: SJC, Case no. 158265. This case has also been pieced together from three other sources. First, the *Springfield Republican* issue of April 16, 1886, ran an article on the history of executions in Hampden and Hampshire counties in which it reported the legal hanging of an unidentified man there on November 8, 1781. The same newspaper ran a similar article in its issue of June 28, 1873 (5:3), in which it recounted the details of the crime from oral traditional thereabouts. The names of the killer and victim turned up in the *Massachusetts Spy* (Worcester) issue of October 11, 1781 (3:2), which reported that the Supreme Judicial Court of Massachusetts then sitting at Springfield had passed sentence of death on one Michael Lobidal for the murder of James McMullen — thus confirming the 1873 and 1886 newspaper accounts in the upshot.

1783

On William Huggins and John Mansfield: SJC, Case no. 153329. See also *Massachusetts Spy* (Worcester), 6/26/83 (3:4). See also *The Last Words of William Huggins and John Mansfield* (a broadside at the American Antiquarian Society).

1784

On Cassumo Garcelli: *Boston Gazette*, 11/10/83 (3:2) and 1/19/84 (3:2). See also

The Life, Last Words and Dying Speech of Cassumo Garcelli (a broadside at the American Antiquarian Society).
On Francis Coven and Derek Grout: SJC, Case nos. 103472 and 103477. See also *Life, Last Words and Dying Speech of Derek Grout and Francis Coven* (a broadside at the New York Historical Society).
On John Dixon: SJC, Case no. 1461332. See also *Massachusetts Spy* (Worcester), 11/11/84 (3:3). See also *Independent Chronicle* (Boston), 11/18/84 (3:2).
On Richard Barrick and John Sullivan: SJC, Case nos. 149055 and 103510. See also *The Lives and Dying Confessions of Richard Barrick and John Sullivan* (a broadside at the American Antiquarian Society).
On Alexander White: SJC, Case no. 149051. See also *Independent Chronicle* (Boston), 11/26/84 (3:2). Also see *The American Bloody Register: Containing the Dying Confession of Alexander White* (a pamphlet at the American Antiquarian Society).

1785

On William Scott and Thomas Archibald: *Independent Chronicle* (Boston), 11/26/84 (3:2) and 3/10/85 (3:2). See also *Boston Gazette*, 5/9/85 (3:1).
On Hannah Peggin: SJC, Case no. 158644. See also *Connecticut Courant*, 8/1/85 (3:2).
On Thomas Goss: *Connecticut Courant*, 3/1/85 (3:2) and 8/29/85 (2:2). See also *Litchfield Weekly Monitor*, 11/15/85 (3:3). See also *Barkhamsted Heritage*, edited by Richard Wheeler and George Hilton. Barkhamsted Historical Society, 1975, pp. 85 & 141. See also *The Last Words and Dying Speech of Thomas Goss* (a broadside at the New York Public Library).

1786

On Johnson Green: SJC, Case nos. 154711 and 154717. See also *Worcester Magazine* for the year 1786, pp. 50, 62, 206 & 242.

On Hannah Occuish: *Connecticut Gazette* (New London), 7/28/86 (3:2) and 12/22/86 (3:2). See also *History of New London* by Frances Caulkins. Privately printed, 1852, pp. 576–577.

On Isaac Combs: *Massachusetts Gazette*, 5/29/86 (3:4), 11/18/86 (3:2) and 12/23/86 (3:3).

1787

On John Sheehan: *Massachusetts Sentinel*, 9/8/87 (3:2) and 11/24/87 (3:2). See also *Life, Last Words and Dying Speech of John Sheehan* (a broadside at the American Antiquarian Society).

On William Clark: SJC, Case no. 160286. See also *Hampshire Gazette*, 12/12/87 (3:2).

On John Bly and Charles Rose: SJC, Case no. 160576. See also *Hampshire Gazette*, 10/17/87 (3:1) and 12/19/87 (3:3).

1788

On Archibald Taylor and Joseph Taylor: *Independent Chronicle* (Boston), 11/8/87 (3:2). See also *Massachusetts Sentinel*, 5/10/88 (3:1).

On Elisha Thomas: *Boston Gazette*, 2/18/88 (3:3). See also *Massachusetts Spy*, 6/19/88 (3:1). See also *The Last Words and Dying Speech of Elisha Thomas* (a broadside at the American Antiquarian Society).

On Abiah Converse: SJC, Case no. 159022. See also *Hampshire Gazette*, 4/16/88 (3:2) and 7/23/88 (3:1).

On John O'Neil: *Hampshire Gazette*, 4/2/88 (3:2). See also *Massachusetts Spy*, 9/18/88 (3:3).

1789

On Rachel Wall, William Smith and William Donogan: *Life, Last Words and Dying Confession of Rachel Wall* (a broadside at the American Antiquarian Society). See also SJC, Case nos. 105405 and 105406. See also *Boston Gazette*, 9/9/85 (3:2). Also

Massachusetts Sentinel, 9/20/88 (3:3). Also *Hampshire Gazette*, 4/15/89 (3:1).

1790

On Thomas Bird: *Cumberland Gazette*, 7/24/89 (3:3), 7/31/89 (3:2) and 6/7/90 (3:2). Also *Boston Gazette*, 7/5/90 (3:1).

On John Bailey: SJC, Case no. 105699. See also *Life, Last Words and Dying Confession of John Bailey* (a broadside at the Massachusetts Historical Society).

On Edward Vail Brown: SJC Case no. 105680 and 105739. See also *Boston Gazette*, 10/18/90 (3:3).

On Joseph Mountain: *Sketches of the Life of Joseph Mountain* (a pamphlet at the Connecticut Historical Society). See also *Connecticut Journal* (New Haven), 6/2/90 (3:2) and 10/27/90 (3:2).

On Samuel Hadlock: SJC, Case no. 140729. See also *Columbian Sentinel* (Boston), 10/16/90 (3:2). Also *Boston Gazette*, 11/15/90 (3:3).

1791

On David Comstock: Providence County Superior Court Record Book, vol. 3 (1790–1797), pp. 40–43. Supreme Court Records Center, Pawtucket, Rhode Island. See also *Providence Gazette*, 1/1/91 (3:1) and 5/28/91 (3:2).

On Thomas Mount: Washington County Superior Court Minutes Book, April Term 1791, pp. 4–5. Also original trial papers. Supreme Court Records Center, Pawtucket, Rhode Island. See also *The Confession of Thomas Mount* (a pamphlet at the Connecticut Historical Society). See also *Newport Mercury*, 6/2/91 (2:3).

1793

On Samuel Frost: *Massachusetts Spy* (Worcester), 10/2/83 (3:4), 4/29/84 (3:3), 7/18/93 (3:2), 9/26/93 (3:3) and 11/6/93 (3:3).

1794

On John Baptist Collins, Emanuel Furtado and Augustus Palacha: *Hampshire Gazette*, 4/23/94 (3:1). Also *Columbia Sentinel*, 8/2/94 (3:2). Also *Independent Chronicle* (Boston), 4/7/94 (3:4) and 7/31/94 (3:2).

On Edmund Fortis: *The Last Words and Dying Speech of Edmund Fortis* (a pamphlet at the American Antiquarian Society).

1795

On Negro Pomp: *Dying Confession of Pomp* (a broadside at the Essex Institute). See also *Salem Gazette*, 2/17/95 (3:2) and 8/11/95 (3:3).

1796

On Henry Blackburn: *Annals of Salem* by Joseph B. Felt. James Munroe & Company, Boston, 1849, vol. 2, pp. 464–465. See also *Salem Gazette*, 8/18/95 (3:1) and 1/19/96 (3:2).

On Thomas Powers: *The Narrative and Confession of Thomas Powers* (a pamphlet at the Library of Congress). Also *State vs. Powers*. Original trial papers in the office of the Clerk of the Grafton County Superior Court, Haverhill, New Hampshire. Also *History of the Town of Haverhill, New Hampshire*, by William Whitcher. Privately printed, 1919, pp. 361–362.

1797

On John Stewart: *Columbian Sentinel* (Boston), 3/11/97 (2:3) and 4/8/97 (3:1). See also *The Confession, Last Words and Dying Speech of John Stewart* (a broadside at the American Antiquarian Society).

On Richard Doane: Hartford County Superior Court Files, September Term, 1796. Record Group 3, Drawer 24. Connecticut State Archives. See also *American Weekly Mercury* (Hartford), 6/12/97 (3:3).

On Thomas Starr: Middlesex County Superior Court Records (original trial papers), 1790–1797, File S, Connecticut State Archives. See also *Middlesex Gazette*, 8/5/ 96 (3:2), 8/19/96 (3:2) and 6/16/97 (3:3).

On Stephen Smith: *Life, Last Words and Dying Speech of Stephen Smith* (a broadside in the Rare Books Division of the Boston Public Library). See also *Columbian Sentinel* (Boston), 9/6/97 (2:4) and 10/14/97 (2:4). Also *Independent Chronicle* (Boston), 10/16/97 (2:5).

1798

On Hopkins Hudson: Providence County Superior Court Record Book, vol. 4, pp. 34–35. Also original trial papers. Supreme Court Records Center, Pawtucket, Rhode Island. See also *Newport Mercury*, 9/18/98 (3:1) and 10/30/98 (3:2).

On Negro Anthony: *History of Fairfield County* by Lynn Winfield Wilson. S.J. Clarke Publishing Co., Chicago, 1929, p. 404. See also *History of Danbury, Connecticut 1684–1896*, by James Montgomery Bailey. Burr Printing House, New York, 1896, pp. 116–117. See also *Crimes & Misdemeanors*, First Series, Connecticut State Archives. See also *Connecticut Journal* (New Haven), 11/15/98 (3:3).

1799

On Samuel Smith: *The Last Words and Dying Speech of Samuel Smith* (a broadside at the American Antiquarian Society).

1801

On Jason Fairbanks: *Biography of Mr. Jason Fairbanks and Miss Eliza Fales* (a broadside at the American Antiquarian Society). See also *Columbian Minerva* (Dedham), 5/19/01 (3:3) and 9/15/01 (3:2).

1802

On Ebenezer Mason: *Columbian Minerva* (Dedham), 5/25/02 (3:3). Also *Columbian Sentinel* (Boston), 10/9/02 (2:2).

1803

On Caleb Adams: *Windham Herald*, 9/29/03 (3:3) and 12/1/03 (3:3).

1804

On John Battus: *Columbian Minerva* (Dedham), 7/3/04 (3:4) and 7/10/04 (3:2). See also *The Confession of John Battus, etc.* (a pamphlet at the American Antiquarian Society).

1805

On Samuel Freeman: *New York Spectator*, 10/2/05 (2:1). Also *Hampshire Gazette*, 11/27/05 (2:4).

1806

On Ephraim Wheeler: *New York Spectator*, 10/2/05 (2:1). Also *Pittsfield Sun*, 2/24/06 (3:2).

On Dominic Dailey and James Halligan: *Hampshire Gazette*, 11/13/05 (3:2), 11/20/05 (3:3) and 6/11/06 (3:3). See also *A Brief Account of the Murder of Marcus Lyon, etc.* (a pamphlet at the American Antiquarian Society).

On Josiah Burnham: *An Analysis or Outline of the Life and Character of Josiah Burnham, etc.* (a pamphlet at the American Antiquarian Society). Also *History of the Town of Haverhill, New Hampshire*, by William Whitcher. Privately published, 1919, pp. 362–364.

1807

On Harry Niles: New London County Superior Court Records. Original case files. Summer Session, 1807. Connecticut State Archives. See also *Connecticut Gazette* (New London), 11/11/07 (3:2).

1808

On Joseph Drew: *Eastern Argus* (Portland ME), 1/14/08 (3:1) and 6/2/08 (3:2). Also *Portland Gazette*, 7/25/08 (3:1). Also *The Life and Confession of Joseph Drew, etc.* (a pamphlet at the American Antiquarian Society).

On Cyrus Dean: *The Vermont Historical Gazetteer*, edited by A.M. Hemenway. Published by the editor, Burlington VT, 1867, vol. 1, pp. 467–468.

1811

On Ebenezer Ball: *The Trial of Ebenezer Ball, etc.* (a booklet at the American Antiquarian Society). See also *The Eagle* (Castine ME), 11/7/11 (3:2).

1812

On Samuel Tully: *A Report of the Trial of Samuel Tully and John Dalton, etc.* (a pamphlet at the American Antiquarian Society). Also *Columbian Sentinel* (Boston), 12/12/12 (2:5).

1813

On John Cummings & David Lord: *Albany Herald*, 8/12/13 (3:4).

On Henry Pyner: Hampshire County Supreme Court Docket Book, entries dated April 25, 1809, and September 24, 1813. Massachusetts State Archives. Also *Hampshire Gazette*, 9/29/13 (3:2) and 11/10/13 (3:3).

On Ezra Hutchinson: *Pittsfield Sun*, 11/11/13 (3:3). Also *A History of the County* of *Berkshire* by David Dudley Field. Printed by Samuel W. Bush, Pittsfield MA, 1829, pp. 110–111.

1814

On James Anthony: *Hampshire Gazette*, 3/16/14 (3:3), 4/20/14 (3:2) and 5/4/14 (2:2). Also *The History of Rutland County Vermont* by Associated Writers. White River Paper Company, White River Junction VT, 1882, pp. 1070–1071. Also *Trial of James Anthony, etc.* (a booklet at the American Antiquarian Society).

On Adam Wilson and John Goodenough: War Department Records (Court Martial Case Files), Box #6, File D-12. National Archives, Washington DC.

1816

On Miner Babcock: *The Life and Confession of Miner Babcock, etc.* (a pamphlet at the American Antiquarian Society). Also *Connecticut Courant*, 2/13/16 (3:4) and 6/18/16 (3:4).

On Peter Lung: *A Brief Account of the Life of Peter Lung, etc.* (a pamphlet at the American Antiquarian Society). Also *Middlesex Gazette*, 6/27/16 (3:1). Also *Connecticut Courant*, 6/25/16 (3:4).

1817

On Henry Phillips: *Report of the Trial of Henry Phillips, etc.* (a booklet at the American Antiquarian Society). Also *Columbian Sentinel* (Boston), 3/15/17 (2:2).

On Amos Adams: *Connecticut Courant*, 9/9/17 (3:4) and 11/25/17 (2:6). Also see *History of Fairfield County* by Lynn Winfield Wilson. S.J. Clarke Publishing Co., Chicago, 1929, p. 404. Also see *History of Danbury, Connecticut 1684–1896* by James Montgomery Bailey. Burr Printing House, New York, 1896, pp. 117–118.

1818

On Samuel Godfrey: *A Sketch of the Life of Samuel E. Godfrey, etc.* (a pamphlet at the American Antiquarian Society).

1819

On Francis Frederick, John Rogg, Peter Peterson and John Williams: *Lives and Confessions of John Williams, Francis Frederick, John P. Rogg and Peter Peterson, etc.* (a pamphlet at the American Antiquarian Society). See also *Columbian Sentinel* (Boston), 2/20/19 (2:6). See also *Narrative of the Mutiny Aboard the Schooner PLATTSBURG, etc.* (a pamphlet at the American Antiquarian Society).

On Peter Johnson: *Berkshire Star* (Stockbridge MA), 5/27/19 (3:2), 9/23/19 (3:1) and 12/2/19 (3:3). See also *Pittsfield Sun*, 12/8/19 (2:4).

1820

On Luther Virginia: *The History of St. Albans, Vermont,* by L.L. Dutcher. Published by Stephen E. Royce, St. Albans, 1872, p. 298.

On Michael Powers: *The Life of Michael Powers, etc.* (a pamphlet at the New York Historical Society). Also *Columbian Sentinel* (Boston), 5/27/20 (2:2).

On Edward Roswaine, William Holmes and Thomas Warrington: *The Trial of William Holmes, Thomas Warrington and Edward Roswaine, etc.* (a pamphlet at the New York Historical Society). See also *Execution of the Pirates, etc.* (a broadside at the New York Historical Society). See also *Columbian Sentinel* (Boston), 6/17/20 (2:5).

1821

On Stephen Merrill Clark: *An Account of the Short Life and Ignominious Death of Stephen Merrill Clark, etc.* (a pamphlet at the New York Historical Society). See also

Newburyport Herald, 8/22/20 (3:3), 5/11/21 (2:4) and 5/11/21 (3:2). See also *Essex Register*, 2/17/21 (3:1) and 5/12/21 (3:2). See also *Salem Gazette*, 2/20/21 (3:2).

On Michael Martin: *The Life of Michael Martin, etc.* (a booklet at the American Antiquarian Society). See also *The Trial of Michael Martin, etc.* (a pamphlet at the American Antiquarian Society). See also *Newburyport Herald*, 12/25/21 (2:1). See also *Essex Register*, 12/22/21 (2:3) and 1/9/22 (2:5).

On Daniel Davis Farmer: *The Life and Confessions of Daniel Davis Farmer, etc.* (a pamphlet at the American Antiquarian Society). See also *The Farmer's Cabinet* (Amherst NH), 4/14/21 (3:2) and 1/3/22 (3:3).

1822

On Gilbert Close and Samuel Clisby: *Essex Register*, 1/5/22 (2:3), 1/9/22 (2:1) and 3/9/22 (2:4).

On Samuel Greene: *Life of Samuel Greene, etc.* (a pamphlet at the New York Historical Society). Also see *Essex Register*, 4/27/22 (2:2).

1824

On George Henry Washington: Tolland County Superior Court Records (1818–1830), original case files (W–Z). Connecticut State Archives. See also *Connecticut Courant*, 6/8/24 (3:4).

On Perez Anthony: *Essex Register*, 5/31/24 (2:5) and 12/23/24 (2:4).

1825

On Seth Elliott: *Eastern Argus* (Portland ME), 8/10/24 (3:1), 11/9/24 (2:6), 12/7/24 (2:5) and 2/15/25 (2:2). See also *The Trial of Seth Elliott for the Murder of His Son, etc.* (a pamphlet at the Harvard Law Library).

On Horace Carter: *A Brief Sketch of the Life of Horace Carter, etc.* (a pamphlet at the American Antiquarian Society). See

also: *Massachusetts Spy* (Worcester), 10/12/25 (3:1), 12/14/25 (3:3) and 12/21/25 (3:2). See also *National Aegis* (Worcester), 12/14/25 (3:2). See also *Salem Gazette*, 12/13/25 (3:1).

1826

On John O'Halloran: Supreme Judicial Court Case Files (Suffolk County), November 1825 through March 1826, Box #50. Massachusetts State Archives. See also *Essex Register*, 12/22/25 (3:1) and 3/6/26 (2:4). See also *Haverhill Gazette*, 3/11/26 (2:5).

On Samuel Charles: *Berkshire Star* (Stockbridge MA), 10/27/25 (3:3), 9/26/26 (3:3) and 11/30/26 (2:1).

1827

On John Duncan White and Winslow Curtis: *The Trials of John Duncan White alias Charles Marchant and Winslow Curtis alias Sylvester Colson, etc.* (a booklet at the American Antiquarian Society). Also see *The Confession of Winslow Curtis, etc.* (a pamphlet at the New York Historical Society). Also see *Haverhill Gazette* and *Essex Register*, 2/3/27 (2:1).

1829

On John Boies: *Report of the Trial of John Boies, etc.* (a pamphlet at the American Antiquarian Society). Also see *The Village Register* and *Norfolk County Advertiser*, 7/9/29 (2:2).

1830

On John Francis Knapp and Joseph Jenkins Knapp, Jr.: *Appendix to the Report of the Trial of John Francis Knapp, etc.* (a booklet at the American Antiquarian Society). Also see *Essex Gazette*, 4/10/30 (2:3), 10/2/30 (3:2) and 1/8/31 (3:3).

1831

On Joseph Gadett and Thomas Collinett: *Daily Evening Transcript* (Boston), 4/25/31 (3:1), 5/25/ 31 (2:3) and 7/1/31 (2:1).

On Oliver Watkins: *The Trial and a Sketch of the Life of Oliver Watkins, etc.* (a pamphlet at the American Antiquarian Society).

1832

On Amasa Walmsley: *Life and Confession of Amasa E. Walmsley, etc.* (a pamphlet at the New York Historical Society). See also *Providence Daily Journal*, 6/2/32 (2:1).

1833

On William Teller and Caesar Reynolds: *Confessions of Two Malefactors, Teller & Reynolds, etc.* (a pamphlet at the New York Historical Society). Also see *Connecticut Courant*, 5/7/33 (3:1) and 9/9/33 (3:1).

On Amos Miner: *Trial, Life and Confession of Amos Miner, etc.* (a pamphlet at the New York Historical Society). Also see: *Providence Daily Journal*, 6/23/32 (2:2) and 12/28/33 (2:1).

On Charles Brown: Supreme Court Record Book, vol. 11, pp. 289–290. Judicial Records Center, Pawtucket, Rhode Island. See also *Providence Journal*, 12/28/33 (2:1).

1834

On David Sherman: New London County Superior Court Records, September Term, 1833. Original case files. Connecticut State Archives. See also *Norwich Courier*, 6/12/33 (3:3). Also see *New London Gazette*, 6/18/34 (3:2).

On Henry Joseph: *The Trial of Henry Joseph, etc.* (a pamphlet at the New York Historical Society). See also *Daily Evening Transcript* (Boston), 12/2/34 (2:1).

1835

On Joseph Sager: *Trial of Sager for the Murder of his Wife, etc.* (a pamphlet in the Special Collections Dept. of the Harvard Law Library). Also see *The History of Augusta, Maine*, by James W. North. Clapp & North, Augusta ME, 1870, pp. 558–560. Also see *Eastern Argus* (Portland ME), 1/6/35 (3:1).

On Pedro Gilbert & Crew: *Essex Gazette*, 9/6/34 (3:1). Also see *Daily Evening Transcript* (Boston), 6/11/35 (2:1) and 9/12/35 (2:1).

1836

On Abraham Prescott: *Report of the Trial of Abraham Prescott, etc.* (a pamphlet at the American Antiquarian Society). Also see *History of Pembroke, New Hampshire 1730–1895*, by N.F. Carter. Republican Press Assoc., Concord NY, 1895, vol. 2, p. 43. See also *Life and Times in Hopkinton, New Hampshire*, by C.C. Lord. Republican Press Assoc., Concord NH, 1890, pp. 131– 133.

On Simeon Crockett and Stephen Russell: *A Voice from Leverett Street Prison or the Life, Trial and Confession of Simeon L. Crockett, etc.* (a pamphlet at the New York Historical Society). Also see *Boston Evening Transcript*, 10/23/35 (2:1) and 3/16/36 (2:1).

1839

On Archibald Bates: The *Pittsfield Sun*, 10/11/38 (2:1) and 2/21/39 (3:3). See also *History of Bennington County, Vermont*, by Lewis Cass Aldrich. D. Mason & Co. Publishers, Syracuse, NY, 1889, pp. 274–275.

On Benjamin Cummings: *Massachusetts Spy* (Worcester), 11/7/38 (2:4) and 8/14/39 (2:4).

1844

On Lucian Hall: *An Account of the Life and Crimes of Lucian Hall, etc.* (a pamphlet at the New York Historical Society). See also *Hartford Daily Courant*, 6/22/44 (2:4).

1845

On Thomas Barrett: *Trial and Execution of Thomas Barrett, etc.* (a pamphlet at the New York Historical Society).

On John Gordon: *Last Days of Gordon: Being the Trial of John & William Gordon, etc.* (a pamphlet at the New York Historical Society). See also Supreme Court Record Book, vol. 15, pp. 456–460. Judicial Records Center, Pawtucket, Rhode Island.

1846

On Andrew Howard: *Notable Events in the History of Dover, New Hampshire*, by George Wadleigh. Privately printed, Dover NH, 1913, pp. 247 & 251. See also *History of the Town of Rochester, New Hampshire*, by Franklin McDuffie. John B. Clarke & Co., Manchester NH, 1892, pp. 309–313.

On Andrew Potter: *Trial and Confession of Andrew P. Potter, etc.* (a pamphlet at the New York Historical Society). See also *New Haven Daily Register*, 7/20/46 (2:3) and 7/21/46 (2:3). See also *New Haven Daily Morning Courier*, 7/21/46 (2:1).

1849

On Enos Dudley: *Independent Democrat & Freeman* (Concord NH), 4/6/48 (2:1) and 4/13/48 (2:2). See also *The Execution of Enos Dudley, etc.* (a pamphlet at the American Antiquarian Society). See also original trial papers (*State vs. Dudley*). Clerk's office, Grafton County Superior Court, Haverhill, New Hamp.

On Washington Goode: *Trial and Execution of Washington Goode, etc.* (a pamphlet at the Harvard Law Library). See also *Boston Daily Evening Transcript*, 5/25/49 (2:3).

1850

On Daniel Pearson: *Boston Daily Evening Transcript*, 4/13/49 (2:1) and 7/26/59 (2:3). See also *Boston Daily Journal*, 7/26/50 (2:4).

On John Webster: *Report of the Case of John W. Webster, etc.* (a booklet at the Yale University Law Library). See also *Boston Daily Journal*, 8/30/50 (2:4); also *Boston Evening Transcript*, 8/30/50 (2:1).

On Henry Foote: *A Sketch of the Life and Adventures of Henry Leander Foote, etc.* (a pamphlet at the American Antiquarian Society). Also *Death Cell Scenes or Notes, Sketches & Memorandums of the Last 16 Days and Last Night of Henry Leander Foote* (a pamphlet at the American Antiquarian Society). See also *New Haven Register*, 9/15/49 (2:4) and 10/2/50 (2:3). Also *New Haven Morning Journal & Courier*, 10/2/50 (2:3) and 10/3/50 (2:3). Also *New Haven Palladium*, 9/15/49 (2:5). 9/16/49 (2:3), 9/27/49 (2:4) and 10/2/50 (2:2).

On James McCaffrey: *New Haven Palladium*, 11/1/49 (2:3), 11/2/49 (2:3) and 10/2/50 (2:2).

1854

On James Clough: *New Bedford Evening Standard*, 12/14/1894 (10:7), retrospective account. See also *Boston Daily Journal*, 4/29/54 (1:5).

On Michael Jennings: *New Haven Morning Journal & Courier*, 7/25/53 (2:1) and 7/26/53 (2:3), 7/28/53 (2:6, 7/11/54 (2:4) and 7/12/54 (2:4). See also *New Haven Daily Register*, 7/22/54 (2:4). See also *New Haven Daily Palladium*, 7/25/53 (2:1) and 7/11/54 (2:3).

On Thomas Casey: *Boston Daily Journal*, 9/18/52 (2:2) and 9/29/54 (2:3).

1858

On James McGee: *Boston Daily Journal*, 12/15/56 (2:4), 12/16/56 (2:4) and 6/25/58 (2:4).

On Abraham Cox and Peter Williams: *The Case of the ALBION COOPER Murderers* (a pamphlet at the Library of Congress). See also the *Eastern Argus* (Portland ME), 1/13/58 (2:3), 1/15/58 (2:3) and 8/28/58 (2:4).

1861

On Alexander Desmarteau: *Springfield Republican* (evening edition), 4/26/61 (1:2) and 6/28/73 (5:3), retrospective account.

1862

On George Hersey: *Report of the Case of George C. Hersey, etc.*, by James Yerrinton. A. Williams & Co., Boston, 1862.
On Gerald Toole: *Hartford Daily Courant*, 3/28/62 (2:4), 3/29/62 (2:2) and 9/20/62 (2:3).

1863

On William Lynch: *Boston Morning Journal*, 6/17/63 (2:6). See also *Civil War Justice*, by Robert Alotta. White Mane Publishing Co., Shippensburg PA, 1989, p. 69.
On William Laird: *Ibid.*, Alotta, pp. 70–73.
On James Callender: *Berkshire County Eagle*, 9/18/62 and 11/12/63.

1864

On William Barnet: *Burlington Daily Free Press*, 1/23/64 (2:3). See also *Burlington Free Press*, 9/5/62 (1:6).
On Sandy Kavanaugh: *Burlington Daily Free Press*, 1/9/62 (2:2), 1/10/62 (2:3) and 1/23/64 (2:3).
On Charles Carpenter and Matthew Riley: *Boston Morning Journal*, 4/23/64 (2:1).
On Francis Spencer: The *Eastern Argus* (Portland ME), 5/16/63 (2:3). See also Annual Report of the Maine State Prison (1864).

1866

On Edward Green: *New York Herald*, 12/17/63 (1:5) and 4/14/66 (1:3). See also *The Life, Character and Career of Edward*

W. Green, etc. (a pamphlet at the Harvard Law Library).
On Albert Starkweather: *The Manchester Homicide: A Sketch of the Life of Albert L. Starkweather, etc.* (a booklet at the Connecticut Historical Society). See also *Hartford Daily Courant*, 8/2/65 (2:3) and 8/18/66 (1:4). See also *New York Herald*, 8/18/66 (8:3).

1868

On John Ward: *John Ward or the Victimized Assassin: A Narrative of Facts Connected with the Crime, Arrest, Trial and Imprisonment and Execution of the Williston Murderer, etc.* (a booklet at the Harvard Law Library). See also *New York Herald*, 3/21/68 (4:5).
On Samuel Mills: *Burlington Free Press* (Vermont), 12/20/66 (2:2). See also *New York Herald*, 5/7/68 (4:1).
On Charles and Silas James: *New York Herald*, 2/29/68 (5:2) and 9/26/68 (5:1).

1869

On Josiah Pike: *New York Herald*, 11/10/69 (3:1). See also *New York Tribune*, 11/10/69 (1:6).
On Clifton Harris: *New York Herald*, 3/13/69 (4:5).
On Hiram Miller: *New York Herald*, 6/26/69 (4:1).

1871

On Henry Welcome: *New York Times*, 1/21/71 (1:3). See also *New York Tribune*, 1/21/71 (1:4).
On James Wilson: *Hartford Daily Times*, 8/15/70 (3:1) and 10/13/71 (2:2).

1873

On James McElhaney: *Boston Daily Globe*, 8/19/72 (8:3) and 3/22/73 (8:1).
On Albert Smith: *Springfield Daily Re-*

publican, 11/21/72 (4:4), 6/27/73 (4:4) and 6/28/73 (5:1).

1874

On Franklin Evans: *Boston Globe*, 11/4/72 (5:4) and 2/18/74 (1:7). See also *New York Herald*, 2/17/74 (4:5) and 2/18/74 (3:4). See also *Boston Evening Transcript*, 6/19/65 (4:1).

1875

On William Sturtevant: *Boston Daily Globe*, 2/17/74 (1:5), 2/18/74 (5:1), 2/19/74 (1:6), 2/20/74 (1:7), 5/7/75 (1:3) and 5/8/75 (1:4). See also *New York Herald*, 5/8/75 (4:5) and 2/18/74 (3:7).

On James Costley: *Boston Daily Globe*, 6/22/75 (1:2) and 6/26/75 (1:6). See also *New York Herald*, 6/26/75 (5:1).

On John Gordon and Louis Wagner: *Boston Daily Globe*, 6/25/75 (1:6) and 6/26/75 (1:6). See also *New York Herald*, 6/26/75 (5:1).

On George Pemberton: *Boston Daily Globe*, 3/23/75 (1:4), 3/24/75 (8:2), 3/25/75 (1:4), 3/26/75 (1:3), 10/8/75 (8:1) and 10/9/75 (2:1).

1876

On Samuel Frost: *Worcester Daily Press*, 5/27/76 (1:2). See also *Worcester Daily Spy*, 5/27/76 (1:2).

On Thomas Piper: *New York Herald*, 5/25/76 (9:1) and 5/27/76 (3:4). See also *Boston Daily Globe*, 5/24/75 (1:4), 5/25/75 (1:4), 5/26/75 (1:4), 5/27/76 (1:6) and 5/27/76 (2:1).

1877

On Elwin Major: *Boston Morning Globe*, 1/5/77 (4:6) and 1/6/77 (5:1).

1878

On Joseph LaPage: *Boston Daily Globe*, 3/15/78 (1:1). See also *New York Herald*, 3/16/78 (5:3).

On Joseph Ten Eyck: *Berkshire County Eagle*, 12/6/77 and 8/15/78.

1879

On William Devlin: *Boston Morning Globe*, 12/11/77 (5:3), 3/14/79 (4:1) and 3/15/79 (6:2).

On John Pinkham: *Boston Daily Globe*, 1/11/78 (3:1), 3/14/79 (4:4), 3/15/79 (6:3). See also *New York Herald*, 3/15/79 (5:2).

On Henri Gravelin: *New York Herald*, 3/15/79 (5:2). See also *Boston Daily Globe*, 3/14/79 (4:4) and 3/15/79 (6:2).

On John Phair: *New York Herald*, 4/11/79 (3:5).

On Joseph Buzzell: *New York Herald*, 7/11/79 (4:1).

On Asa Magoon: *New York Herald*, 11/29/79 (6:1).

1880

On Edward Tatro: *New York Herald*, 6/4/76 (9:4) and 4/3/80 (3:2). See also *Boston Daily Globe*, 6/5/76 (5:2).

On Edwin Hoyt: *Bridgeport Daily Standard*, 6/24/78, p. 2, 5/13/80, p. 2, and 5/14/80, p. 2.

On Henry Hamlin: *Hartford Weekly Times*, 9/6/77. See also *Hartford Daily Times*, 5/28/80.

1881

On Edwin Hayden: *New York Herald*, 2/26/81 (5:1).

On Royal Carr: *New York Herald*, 4/30/81 (3:4).

1882

On James Smith: *New Haven Journal-Courier*, 12/25/80 (2:3) and 12/29/80 (2:4).

See also *New Haven Evening Register*, 9/1/82 (1:1).

1883

On Joseph Loomis: *Springfield Daily Republican*, 12/3/81 (4:5) and 3/8/83 (4:5).

On Emeline Meaker: *New York Herald*, 3/30/83 and 3/31/83. See also *New York Times*, 3/31/83.

1885

On Thomas Samon: *Boston Daily Globe*, 11/26/83 (1:1). See also *New York Herald*, 4/17/85 (5:6) and 4/18/85 (10:1).

On Raphael Capone and Carmine Santore: *Daily Eastern Argus* (Portland ME), 9/10/83 (1:2). See also *New York Herald*, 4/18/85 (10:1).

On Daniel Wilkinson: *Daily Eastern Argus* (Portland ME), 9/5/83 (1:1) and 9/17/83 (1:2). See also *New York Times*, 11/21/85 (1:5).

1886

On Allen Adams: *Hampshire Gazette*, 11/30/75 (2:4) and 4/20/86 (2:1). See also *Springfield Daily Republican*, 4/17/86 (4:4).

1887

On Samuel Besse: *Boston Morning Globe*, 12/24/85 (1:4) and 3/10/87 (1:5). Also *Boston Evening Globe*, 3/10/87 (1:6). Also *Boston Herald*, 3/11/87 (8:6).

1888

On James Edward Nowlin: *Boston Morning Globe*, 1/6/87 (1:7) and 1/20/88 (1:5). Also *Boston Evening Globe*, 1/20/88 (1:5).

On Philip Pallidona: *Bridgeport Morning News*, 6/23/87, p. 2, and 10/6/88, p. 2. Also *Bridgeport Daily Standard*, 10/5/88, p. 2.

1889

On John Swift: *Hartford Weekly Times*, 7/14/87 (2:1) and 4/18/89 (1:1).

1890

On James Palmer: *Boston Morning Globe*, 5/29/88 (1:5) and 5/1/90 (1:5). See also *Boston Evening Globe*, 5/1/90 (8:6).

1891

On Jacob Scheele: *Bridgeport Evening Standard*, 1/26/88, p. 1, 6/18/91, p. 1. See also *Bridgeport Morning News*, 6/18/91, p. 2, 6/19/91, p. 2.

1892

On Sylvester Bell: *Burlington Daily Free Press*, 1/2/92 (1:4).

On Andrew Borjesson: *New Milford Gazette*, 8/8/90 and 1/29/92. See also *Litchfield Enquirer*, 2/4/92, p. 3, 8/7/90, p. 2.

On Angelo Petrillo: *New Haven Journal-Courier*, 4/20/91 (2:2), 4/21/91 (2:5), 11/14/92 92:3) and 11/15/92 (4:3). Also *New Haven Evening Register*, 11/14/92 (1:5).

1893

On Walter Holmes: *Springfield Daily Republican*, 11/4/91 (6:6), 11/5/91 (5:5), 2/3/93 (5:3) and 2/4/93 (8:1).

On William Coy: *Berkshire County Eagle*, 10/15/91 (1:4), 10/22/91 (1:5) and 3/3/93 (1:1).

On George Abbott, alias Frank Almy: *Boston Sunday Herald*, 7/19/91 (1:6). Also *Boston Herald*, 5/16/93 (1:6) and 5/17/93 (1:4).

1894

On Daniel Roberton: *New Bedford Evening Standard*, 9/9/93 (1:2), 9/11/93 (1:4) and (8:2) and 12/14/94 (9:1).

On John Cronin: *Hartford Courant*, 12/18/94 (1:5).

1896

On Angus Gilbert: *Boston Sunday Globe*, 4/14/95 (1:5). Also *Boston Morning Globe*, 2/21/96 (1:6). Also *Boston Evening Globe*, 2/21/96 (1:6).

On Kaspar Hartlein: *Hartford Daily Courant*, 3/2/96 (3:1) and 12/3/96 (1:1).

1897

On Thomas Kippie: *New Haven Journal-Courier*, 2/1/96 (1:1) and 7/14/97 (1:1). Also *Hartford Courant*, 7/14/97 (1:7).

On Giuseppe Fuda and Nicodemo Imposino: *Stamford Daily Advocate*, 2/19/97, p. 1, 2/20/97, p. 1, 2/23/97, p. 1, 2/24/97, p. 1, 12/3/97, p. 1, 12/17/97, p. 1.

1898

On Jack O'Neil: *Greenfield Gazette & Courier*, 1/16/97, p. 3, 1/8/98, p. 1.

On Lorenzo Barnes: *Boston Morning Globe*, 12/19/96 (12:4). Also *Boston Evening Globe*, 3/4/98 (1:4).

On Charles Boinay: *Bridgeport Evening Post*, 7/22/97, p. 1, 4/14/98, p. 6. Also *Bridgeport Morning Union*, 7/23/97, p. 1, 7/28/97, p. 1, 10/27/97, p. 1, 12/8/97, p. 1.

On Alfred Williams: *Boston Evening Globe*, 10/7/98 (1:4).

On Dominique Krathofski: *Springfield Daily Republican*, 1/18/97 (3:3) and 12/31/98 (4:1).

1898–1899

On Benjamin Willis and Frederick Brockhaus: *Norwalk Evening Gazette*, 12/18/97, p. 1, 12/20/97, p. 1, 12/21/97, p. 1, 12/22/97, p. 1, 12/23/97, p. 1, 12/27/97, p. 1, 1/25/98, p. 1, 3/10/98, p. 1, 3/12/98, p. 1, 3/14/98, p. 1, 3/15/98, p. 1, 3/17/98, p. 1. See also *Bridgeport Sunday Herald*, 12/19/97, p. 1, 2/20/98, p. 2, 3/13/98, p. 1, 4/17/98, p. 1, 5/29/98, p. 5. Also see *Bridgeport Evening Post*, 5/25/98, p. 3, 5/26/98, pp. 2–6, 5/27/98, p. 2. Also see *Bridgeport Morning Union*, 12/18/97, p. 1, 12/20/97, p. 1, 12/22/97, p. 1, 12/23/97, p. 1, 12/24/97, p. 1, 3/10/98, p. 1, 3/12/98, p. 1, 3/14/98, p. 1, 3/15/98, p. 2, 3/17/98, p. 2, 3/18/98, p. 2, 5/25/98, p. 2, 5/26/98, p. 5, 5/27/98, p. 1, 5/31/98, p. 3, 6/1/98, p. 1, 12/30/98, p. 1, 3/1/99, p. 1, 302/99, p. 1, 3/4/99, p. 1, 9/6/99, p. 1.

1900

On Charles Cross: *Stamford Daily Advocate*, 11/10/99, p. 1, 11/11/99, p. 1, 11/13/99, p. 1, 11/14/99, p. 1, 7/20/00, p. 2.

1901

On Luigi Storti: *Boston Evening Globe*, 11/7/99 (1:5) and 12/17/01 (5:5). See also *Northeastern Reporter*, vol. 58, pp. 1021–1023.

On Franciszek Umilian: *Boston Evening Globe*, 4/11/00 (14:6). Also: *Boston Morning Globe*, 4/12/00 (14:8) and 12/24/01 (1:8). Also *Daily Hampshire Gazette* (Northampton MA), 4/11/00 (1:1), 4/12/00 (1:2), 12/24/01 (8:3).

1902

On John Cassels: *Boston Daily Globe*, 5/6/02 (1:1).

On John Best: *Boston Evening Globe*, 10/17/00 (1:6), 10/18/00 (1:6). Also *Boston Morning Globe*, 10/18/00 (1:5), 9/9/02 (1:3). Also *Northeastern Reporter*, vol. 62, pp. 748–750.

1904

On Paul Misik: *Hartford Daily Courant*, 9/23/03 (8:1) and 2/11/04 (9:1).

On Joseph Watson: *Hartford Courant*, 8/6/04 (1:1) and (10:1) and 11/17/04 (2:2).

1905

On Gershom Marx: *Hartford Courant*, 4/9/04 (1:1), 4/11/04 (1:7), 5/18/05 (1:5). See also *Northeastern Reporter*, vol. 78, pp. 25–29.

On Mary Rogers: *Burlington Free Press*, 12/9/05 (2:1). Also *Bennington Evening Banner*, 12/8/05 (1:6).

1906

On Ephraim Sherouk: *Hartford Courant*, 1/6/05 (1:0), 1/10/05 (1:7), 1/9/06 (1:7).

On Charles Tucker: *Boston Daily Globe*, 4/1/04 (1:5), 4/10/04 (1:1), 6/12/06 (1:1).

On John Schidlofski: *Boston Daily Globe*, 7/14/05 (1:7), 7/9/06 (1:7).

1907

On Henry Bailey: *New Haven Journal-Courier*, 7/10/06 (2:3), 4/16/07 (1:3).

On Alexander Herman: *Bridgeport Telegram*, 7/5/06, p. 1, 7/6/06, p. 1, 5/10/07, p. 1. Also *Bridgeport Post*, 7/5/06, p. 1.

1908

On John Washelesky: *New Haven Evening Register*, 11/6/07 (1:7). Also *New Haven Journal-Courier*, 10/23/07 (10:4), 10/24/07 (16:1), 11/7/707 (3:4). Also *Hartford Courant*, 7/1/08 (1:2).

On Lorenzo Rossi: *Hartford Courant*, 1/30/08 (1:6), 1/31/08 (6:5), 2/3/08 (1:3), 7/24/08 (12:5).

On John Zett: *Hartford Courant*, 8/5/08 (1:1), 12/21/08 (1:4).

1909

On Raphael Carfaro and Giuseppe Campagnolo: *New Haven Journal-Courier*, 8/17/08 (1:7). Also *New Haven Evening Register*, 8/17/08 (1:7), 8/21/08 (1:3). Also *Hartford Courant*, 2/24/09 (1:7).

On Ham Woon, Min Sing and Leon Gong: *Boston Herald*, 8/3/07 (1:8), 10/12/09 (1:2).

1910

On John Zawedzianczek: *Hartford Courant*, 10/16/08 (1:5), 2/9/10 (1:2).

On Napoleon Rivet: *Boston Morning Globe*, 3/2/08 (1:4). Also *Boston Herald*, 7/29/10 (1:6).

1911

On Andrei Ipson and Wasili Ivanowski: *Boston Morning Globe*, 6/26/10 (1:7). Also *Boston Herald*, 3/7/11 (1:2).

1912

On Elroy Kent: *Bennington Evening Banner*, 7/25/08 (1:5), 7/27/08 (1:5) and 1/5/12 (1:6).

On Silas Phelps: *Boston Morning Globe*, 6/13/10 (1:8). Also *Boston Herald*, 6/13/10 (1:7), 1/26/12 (1:7).

On Andrea Tanganelli: *New Haven Journal-Courier*, 9/6/11 (1:7). Also *Hartford Courant*, 3/29/12 (1:4).

On Clarence Richeson: *Boston Evening Transcript*, 10/20/11 (5:3). Also *Boston Herald*, 5/21/12 (1:7).

On Enrico Mascioli: *Boston Evening Globe*, 10/14/10 (5:8), 10/15/10 (1:1). Also *Boston Morning Globe*, 10/17/10 (1:1), 10/18/10 (2:1), 10/19/10 (15:1), 6/6/12 (1:8). Also *Boston Herald*, 10/15/10 (1:7), 10/17/10 (1:6), 6/6/12 (1:2).

On Bertram Spencer: *Springfield Republican*, 4/1/10 (9:1). Also *Boston Herald*, 9/17/12 (1:4) and (2:2).

On Chester Jordan: *Boston Herald*, 9/4/08 (1:7), 9/24/12 (1:5).

On George Redding: *New Haven Journal-Courier*, 2/27/12 (1:7), 2/28/12 (1:5), 2/29/12 (1:7). Also *Hartford Courant*, 11/1/12 (1:5)

1913

On Stefan Borasky: *Springfield Daily Republican*, 9/29/11 (11:1). Also: *Boston Herald*, 9/29/11 (10:7), 6/24/13 (4:4).

On Louis Saxon: *Hartford Courant*, 11/28/12/ (1:8), 11/29/12 (13:1), 11/30/12 (13:1), 6/27/13 (1:1).

1914

On Arthur Bosworth: *Burlington Free Press*, 6/8/11 (1:3). Also *Barre Daily Times*, 6/9/11 (1:5), 1/2/14 (1:5).

On James Plew: *Hartford Courant*, 7/2/13 (1:6), 3/4/14 (1:8). Also *New Haven Journal-Courier*, 7/2/13 (1:7).

On William Dorr: *Boston Evening Globe*, 4/12/12 (1:7). Also *Boston Morning Globe*, 7/13/12 (1:6), 3/24/14 (1:4).

On Motejius Rikteraites: *Waterbury Republican*, 5/11/13, p. 1, 5/12/13, p. 1, 5/8/14, p. 1.

On Joseph Buonomo: *Bridgeport Post*, 1/23/12, p. 1, 10/24/12, p. 1, 10/25/12, p. 1, 10/26/12, p. 1. Also *Bridgeport Telegram*, 6/30/14, p. 1.

On Joseph Bergeron: *New Haven Evening Register*, 6/4/13 (1:7). Also *New Haven Journal-Courier*, 6/5/13 (3:1). Also *Hartford Courant*, 8/11/14 (8:4).

1915

On Biagio Falzone: *Lawrence Sun-American*, 12/24/14 (8:5). Also *Boston Herald*, 12/23/14 (14:3), 12/24/14 (1:1), 12/25/14 (1:1). Also *Boston Morning Globe*, 5/11/15 (1:3).

On Bernard Montvid: *Hartford Courant*, 2/10/15 (1:7), 3/10/15 (1:1), 3/11/15 (1:6), 3/12/15 (1:1), 3/13/15 (1:6), 3/14/15 (1:7), 8/6/15 (1:1).

On Frank Grela: *Hartford Courant*, 6/6/15 (1:1), 6/7/15 (11:1), 8/13/15 (11:5).

1916

On Oscar Comery: *Manchester Leader & Evening Union*, 11/30/14 (7:3), 2/18/16 (1:6).

On Harry Rowe and Isaac Williams: *Hartford Daily Courant*, 3/3/16 (1:4). Also *Waterbury Republican*, 11/29/14, p. 1, 11/30/14, p. 1, 3/3/16, p. 1. Also *Bridgeport Telegram*, 1/16/15, p. 6, 3/3/16, p. 1. Also *Bridgeport Post*, 1/15/15, p. 1, 3/3/16, p. 2.

On Pasquale Zuppa: *New Haven Journal-Courier*, 9/7/15 (1:2). Also *New Haven Register*, 9/7/15 (4:1). Also *Hartford Daily Courant*, 3/10/16 (17:4).

On Anton Retkovitz: *Fall River Evening News*, 3/14/14 (1:6), 3/16/14 (1:6), 3/24/14 (1:7), 3/14/16 (1:5).

1917

On Francis Ducharme: *Springfield Union*, 10/23/16 (1:7), 10/24/16 (1:7), 10/25/16 (1:7), 10/26/16 (1:6), 9/11/17 (1:5).

On Joseph Castelli and Francisco Vetere: *New Haven Journal-Courier*, 4/24/16 (1:3), 4/27/16 (1:1). Also *Hartford Daily Courant*, 10/5/17 (1:2).

On Stephen Buglione and Giovanni Don Vanso: *Hartford Daily Courant*, 9/26/17 (1:1), 11/16/17 (1:7).

On William Wise: *Hartford Daily Courant*, 9/20/17 (2:1), 9/21/17 (4:4), 12/14/17 (1:2).

1918

On Frederick Small: *Boston Herald*, 9/29/16 (1:3), 9/30/16 (1:1), 1/15/18 (1:4).

On Francesco Dusso, Carmine Lanzillo and Carmine Pisaniello: *New Haven Journal-Courier*, 11/28/16 (1:7), 6/17/18 (1:2). Also *New Haven Evening Register*, 11/28/16 (2:7). Also *Hartford Courant*, 6/17/18 (1:4).

1919

On Erasmo and Joseph Perretta: *New Britain Herald*, 6/3/18 (1:5), 6/4/18 (9:5). Also *Hartford Daily Times*, 6/3/18 (14:1). Also *Hartford Courant*, 10/2/18 (6:1), 10/3/18 (5:1), 10/4/418 (6:1), 10/5/18 (6:3), 6/27/19 (1:3).

On George Warner: *Springfield* (VT)

Reporter, 11/13/14 (1:4). Also *Burlington Free Press*, 7/14/19 (9:3). Also *Rutland Daily Herald*, 11/6/14 (1:1), 11/5/14 (1:4).

On Nikifor Nechesnook: *Waterbury Republican*, 3/14/19, p. 1, 3/15/19, p. 1, 3/16/19, p. 1, 12/3/19, p. 1.

1920

On Daniel Cerrone: *New Haven Journal-Courier*, 6/9/19 (1:2), 3/5/20 (1:2). Also *Hartford Daily Courant*, 3/5/20 (1:7).

On Francisco Feci: *Boston Herald*, 11/5/18 (14:3), 11/6/18 (8:3), 8/16/20 (4:6). Also *Boston Globe*, 8/16/20 (1:5).

1921

On Elwood Wade: *Bridgeport Telegram*, 8/31/20, p. 1, 5/20/21, p. 1. Also *Bridgeport Post*, 5/20/21, p. 1.

On John Kausarauskas: *Bridgeport Telegram*, 2/21/21, p. 1, 5/27/21, p. 1. Also *Bridgeport Post*, 2/21/21, p. 1, 5/27/21, p. 1.

1922

On Emil Schutte: *Hartford Courant*, 12/11/15 (12:6), 10/7/21 (1:3), 10/11/21 (9:3), 10/12/21 (1:4), 10/13/21 (1:2), 10/14/21 (1:2), 10/15/21 (1:4), 10/18/21 (10:1), 10/19/21 (1:6), 10/20/21 (4:1), 10/21/21/ (1:1), 10/24/22 (1:8).

1923

On Paul Dascalakis: *Boston Morning Globe*, 5/12/20 (1:1), 5/13/20 (5:4), 7/14/23 (1:7). Also *Boston Evening Globe*, 5/12/20 (1:2). Also *Boston Herald*, 5/12/20 (1:1), 5/13/20 (13:3), 5/14/20 (11:5), 7/14/23 (1:2).

1924

On Cyrille Van den Hecke: *Boston Globe*, 8/9/18 (5:8), 7/30/24 (1:8). Also *Boston Herald*, 6/19/23 (12:5), 6/21/23 (14:3), 7/30/24 (1:4).

1926

On Gerald Chapman: *Hartford Courant*, 10/13/24 (1:7), 4/6/26 (1:7).

On Richard Stewart: *Boston Globe*, 9/11/25 (1:6), 5/5/26 (1:3).

1927

On John Devereaux, Edward Heinlein and John McLaughlin: *Boston Globe*, 10/5/25 (1:7), 10/7/25 (1:1), 1/6/27 (1:7).

On Celestino Madeiros: *Boston Evening Transcript*, 11/1/24 (1:4), 11/7/24 (1:5), 11/8/24 (13:4). Also *Boston Globe*, 8/23/27.

On Nicola Sacco and Bartolomeo Vanzetti: *Boston Morning Globe*, 4/16/20 (1:7). Also *Boston Evening Globe*, 4/16/20 (1:4). See also *The Sacco-Vanzetti Case* by Osmond K. Fraenkel [Alfred A. Knopf, New York, 1931].

On Chin Lung and Soo Hoo Wing: *Hartford Courant*, 3/25/27 (1:1), 11/8/27 (1:1).

1928

On Jeremiah Gedzium: *Boston Evening Transcript*: 9/29/25 (1:7), 9/30/25 (1:2), 8/25/26 (5:3), 11/15/26 (9:7), 11/16/26 (5:3), 11/18/26 (5:1), 2/28/28 (5:1).

On Herbert Gleason: *Boston Globe* 11/28/26 (1:3), 3/13/28 (1:5). Also *Boston Herald*, 3/13/28 (1:5)

On Nathan Desatnick: *Boston Globe*, 11/3/27 (3:5), 11/4/27 (1:6), 7/17/28 (1:7). Also *Boston Herald*, 7/17/28 (1:6).

1929

On George Taylor: *Boston Globe*, 6/6/27 (1:1), 6/7/27 (1:3), 7/12/27 (1:8), 3/6/29 (1:1).

On Frederick Hinman Knowlton: *Boston Evening Transcript*, 3/31/28 (II, 6:6), 4/25/28 (8:1), 5/14/29 (25:6). Also *Boston Herald*, 5/14/29 (1:5). Also *Boston Globe*, 5/14/29 (1:4).

On Charles Trippi: *Boston Evening Transcript*, 11/12/28 (3:7), 12/3/29 (5:2).

On John Feltovic: *Bridgeport Post*, 3/24/29, p. 1, 3/25/29, p. 1, 3/26/29, p. 1, 12/10/29, p. 1. Also *Bridgeport Telegram*, 3/25/29, p. 1, 3/26/29, p. 1, 12/10/29, p. 1.

1930

On Frank DiBattista: *Hartford Courant*, 4/2/29 (1:8), 4/3/29 (1:6), 4/6/29 (1:7), 4/7/29 (12:3), 4/8/29 (13:7), 4/9/29 (1:8), 4/10/29 (1:4), 2/21/30 (1:5).

On Henry Lorenz: *Hartford Courant*, 4/2/30 (1:8), 4/3/30 (1:8), 4/4/30 (1:8), 4/5/30 (1:8), 4/6/30 (1:7), 4/7/30 (1:7), 4/12/30 (1:4).

1931

On Paul Hurley: *Boston Globe*, 8/4/30 (1:1), 8/5/30 (1:7), 8/6/30 (1:5), 9/15/31 (1:5). Also *Boston Herald*, 9/15/31 (1:7).

On Joseph Belenski: *Boston Globe*, 8/8/30 (1:8), 8/9/30 (1:8), 8/11/30 (1:8), 10/20/31 (1:6). Also *Boston Herald*, 10/20/31 (10:2).

1932

On Bert Stacey: *Bennington Evening Banner*, 4/21/31 (1:6), 5/20/31 (1:6), 5/23/31 (1:6), 7/8/32 (1:1).

On Sylvester Fernandes: *Boston Herald*, 12/26/31 (4:3), 8/12/32 (1:2).

1934

On Ahmed Osman: *Boston Herald*, 12/27/32 (1:5), 12/28/32 (1:1), 12/29/32 (1:5), 1/23/34 (1:4). Also *Boston Globe*, 1/23/34 (1:6).

On Henry Clay Bull: *Boston Globe*, 8/8/33 (4:6), 2/22/34 (1:6). Also *Boston Herald*, 8/8/33 (24:3), 2/22/34 (1:4).

On John Donnellon and Herman Snyder: *Boston Herald*, 4/10/31 (1:2), 2/22/34 (1:4). Also *Boston Globe*, 2/22/34 (1:6).

1935

On Alexander Kaminski: *Boston Globe* 10/23/33 (1:1), 2/19/35 (1:1).

On Abraham Faber, Irving Millen and Morton Millen: *Boston Herald*, 2/3/34 (1:8), 2/4/34 (1:8), 2/5/34 (1:8), 2/6/34 (1:8), 2/7/34 (1:1), 2/8/34 (1:1), 2/14/34 (1:3), 2/27/34 (1:7), 2/28/34 (1:7), 3/1/34 (1:8), 3/2/34 (1:7), 3/3/34 (1:8), 6/7/35 (1:7).

1936

On Miller Clark: *Boston Herald*, 1/14/36 (1:2). Also *Boston Evening Transcript*, 12/21/33 (1:4), 12/22/33 (1:2), 12/23/33 (1:6), 1/14/36 (10:6).

On John Simborski: *New Haven Journal-Courier*, 3/6/35 (1:1), 3/7/35 (1:5), 4/7/36 (1:1).

On Newell Sherman: *Boston Evening Transcript*, 7/22/35 (1:5), 8/4/36 (3:4). Also *Bridgeport (CT) Post*, 10/1/35 (1:3).

1937

On Joseph McElroy: *New Haven Journal-Courier*, 8/11/36 (1:8), 3/12/36 (1:8). Also *Hartford Courant*, 2/11/37 (1:1).

1938

On Anthony and Frank DiStassio: *Boston Evening Transcript*, 5/7/35 (1:1), 5/8/35 (1:7), 5/9/35 (1:7). Also *New Haven Evening Register*, 1/18/38 (26:3).

On Frank Palka: *Bridgeport Post*, 10/1/35, p. 1, 4/13/38, p. 1.

On Edward Simpson: *Boston Evening Transcript*, 8/23/37 (1:2), 8/24/37 (1:3), 8/25/37 (1:4), 8/26/37 (1:1), 8/28/37 (1:4), 8/30/37 (1:2), 9/14/37 (3:8), 9/16/37 (21:1), 11/1/37 (1:5), 11/3/37 (1:6), 5/13/38 (3:5).

1939

On Howard Long: *Boston Evening Transcript*, 9/11/37 (1:7), 9/15/37 (1:7), 9/16/37

(24:7). Also *New Haven Evening Register*, 7/14/39 (3:6).

On Wallace Green and Walter St. Saveur: *Boston Evening Transcript*, 6/1/38 (8:3), 6/28/38 (2:7), 8/2/39 (2:3).

1940

On Vincent Cotts and Ira Weaver: *Hartford Courant*, 1/33/39 (1:6), 1/25/39 (1:1), 5/1/40 (1:2).

1941

On Joseph Rousseau: *Boston Daily Globe*, 5/16/40 (1:3), 5/17/40 (24:7), 4/22/41 (1:6).

1942

On Paul Giacomazza and James Nickerson: *Boston Daily Globe*, 9/10/40 (1:3) and 6/30/42 (1:4).

1943

On Peter Gurski: *Waterbury Republican*, 7/2/42, p. 1, 7/3/42, p. 2, 2/24/43, p. 1.

On Wilson Funderburk: *Hartford Courant*, 4/9/42 (6:1), 4/10/42 (6:4), 11/18/42 (16:3), 11/19/42 (9:6), 4/21/43 (1:2).

On Robert Gray: *Boston Globe*, 7/8/42 (1:5), 6/25/43 (1:4). Also *Boston Herald*, 6/25/43 (1:6).

On Donald Millard and Joseph Sheppard: *Boston Globe*, 1/2/42 (1:1), 1/3/42 (5:1), 6/24/43 (1:4). Also *Boston Herald*, 6/25/43 (1:6).

1944

On Carlo DeCaro: *Hartford Courant*, 9/26/43 (1:1), 9/27/43 (8:4), 5/4/44 (6:1).

1945

On Nicholas Rossi: *Hartford Courant*, 9/24/43 (1:6), 9/25/43 (2:6), 9/26/43 (1:1), 9/27/43 (1:1), 6/19/45 (1:2).

1946

On Raphael Skopp: *Boston Globe*, 12/31/44 (1:3), 1/1/45 (23:8), 8/18/45 (1:6), 8/16/46 (1:4).

On James McCarthy, Raymond Lewie and Arthur Tommaselli: *Hartford Courant*, 1/3/43 (1:5), 1/4/43 (1:5), 1/5/43 (8:6), 4/3/44 (1:2), 4/4/44 (1:4), 4/5/44 (6:8), 4/6/44 (2:3), 3/10/45 (1:2), 10/2/46 (1:1).

1947

On Ronald Watson: *Bennington Evening Banner*, 12/26/45 (1:5), 12/27/45 (1:1), 1/3/47 (1:6).

On Philip Bellino and Edward Gertsen: *Boston Globe*, 8/12/45 (18:4), 8/19/45 (11:3), 6/18/46 (12:5), 6/19/46 (8:6), 5/9/47 (1:2).

1948

On Robert Bradley: *New Haven Register*, 4/13/48, p. 1.

1954

On Francis Blair and Donald Demag: *Burlington Free Press*, 3/12/48 (1:1), 3/15/48 (1:1), 2/9/54 (1:1), 12/9/54 (1:1). Also *Bennington Evening Banner*, 7/31/52 (1:1), 8/2/52 (1:6).

1955

On William Lorrain: *Bridgeport Post*, 8/13/52, p. 1, 8/21/52, p. 1. Also *Bridgeport Telegram*, 8/21/52, p. 1. Also *Hartford Courant*, 7/12/55, p. 1. Also *Connecticut Reports*, vol. 141, pp. 694–701.

On John Donahue: *Bridgeport Telegram*, 2/14/53, p. 1. Also *Bridgeport Post*, 2/14/53, p. 1. Also *Hartford Courant*, 7/19/55, p. 1.

On Robert Malm: *Hartford Times*, 7/19/55, p. 1. Also *Hartford Courant*, 7/12/55, p. 2, 7/19/55, p. 1.

1959

On George Davies: *Waterbury Republican*, 10/21/59, p. 1. Also *New Britain Herald*, 10/21/59, p. 1.

On Frank Wojculewicz: *New Britain Herald*, 11/6/51, p. 1, 10/27/59, p. 1.

1960

On Joseph Taborsky: *Hartford Times*, 3/24/50, p. 1, 2/25/57, p. 1, 2/28/57, p. 1, 5/18/60, p. 6. Also *Hartford Courant*, 1/19/51, p. 1. Also *New Haven Sunday Register*, 1/6/57, p. 1. Also *New Britain Herald*, 1/28/56, p. 1, 12/17/56, p. 1, 12/27/56, p. 1. Also *Connecticut Reports*, vol. 39, pp. 475–490. Also *Atlantic Reporter*, vol. 116, pp. 433–439.

Index